Research Directions in Concurrent Object-Oriented Programming

Research Directions in Concurrent Object-Oriented Programming

edited by
Gul Agha, Peter Wegner, and Akinori Yonezawa

The MIT Press
Cambridge, Massachusetts
London, England

This book was printed and bound in the United States of America.

Library of Congress Cataloging-in-Publication Data

Research directions in concurrent object-oriented programming / edited by Gul Agha,
 Peter Wegner, and Akinori Yonezawa.
    p.   cm.
 Includes bibliographical references and indexes.
 ISBN 0-262-01139-5
 1. Object-oriented programming (Computer science) 2. Parallel processing (Electronic computers) I. Agha, Gul A. II. Wegner, Peter. III. Yonezawa, Akinori.
 QA76.64.R47   1993
 005.2--dc20

 93-11303
 CIP

Contents

Preface

The problem of designing systems for concurrent programming is an important area of research in computer science. In sequential computers, software engineering considerations, such as the need for abstraction and program modularity, have led to a recent surge in the popularity of object-oriented programming. Because parallelism is a natural consequence of the use of objects, the development of systems for concurrent object-oriented programming is providing important software support for a new generation of concurrent computers.

This book represents a timely collection of papers covering significant research efforts on a broad range of topics. They are written at a tutorial level and will be accessible to a wide audience, including researchers, programmers, and advanced students. The book will be particularly important to the object-oriented, parallel and distributed programming communities.

The papers discuss general concepts as well as provide descriptions of specific languages, systems, and applications. Although the contributions were invited, they were subsequently refereed to ensure both the quality of content and the accessibility of the presentation.

We would like to acknowledge the support of the National Science Foundation in supporting the first Workshop on Object-Based Concurrent Programming (NSF CCR-881-4055). The workshop was helpful in identifying much of the ongoing research projects in the area. We would also like to thank Rajendra Panwar for his editorial and typesetting assistance.

Summary of Papers

Part I: Language Issues

Abstraction and Modularity Mechanisms for Concurrent Computing

This paper describes a paradigm to support abstraction and modularity in concurrent systems. The constructs proposed allow generic and reusable specification of coordination patterns, temporal ordering, resource management, and dependability protocols. The developement is in the framework of the Actor model.

Tradeoffs between Reasoning and Modeling

Object-oriented and logic-programming paradigms are shown to be incompatible as component-based models of computation. This "impossibility result," based on a new notion of observability of interactions among components, suggests that combining object-oriented with logic programming is not merely hard but impossible. It implies the more general incompatibility of reasoning and modeling and the impossibility of reducing modeling to reasoning as in automatic program verification. The paper proposes practical research that will contribute to the development of component-based software technology.

A Survey of Logic Programming-Based Object-Oriented Languages

Languages which augment logic programming with object-oriented programming features are surveyed by considering how they deal with the representation of objects and classes, message passing, state, inheritance, and their relationship with other paradigms. The ideas behind concurrent logic programming are also described in some detail. The paper concludes with speculation on future directions for the field.

Analysis of Inheritance Anomaly in Object-Oriented Concurrent Programming Languages

Inheritance is a key feature in many object-oriented languages. It has been pointed out that *inheritance* and *synchronization constraints* in concurrent object systems often conflict with each other, resulting in an *inheritance anomaly* which requires re-definitions of inherited methods in order to maintain the integrity of concurrent objects. The paper proposes a scheme whereby high degree of superclass encapsulation can be achieved for code re-use while retaining utmost efficiency on conventional massively parallel architectures.

Composing Active Objects

Many of the shortcomings of present-day object-oriented programming languages can be traced to two phenomena: the lack of general support for software composition, and the semantic interference between language features addressing operational and compositional aspects of object-oriented programming. To remedy this situation, the paper proposes the development of a "pattern language" for active objects in which objects are constructed by composing software patterns. The relevant semantic issues are also discussed.

Part II: Programming Constructs

Supporting Modularity in Highly-Parallel Programs

The Actor model is extended to allow the construction of multi-access data abstractions. This extended actor model, called the *Aggregate Model*, introduces the notion of collections of actors (aggregates) – accessible by a single group name. Messages sent to the group are directed to one of the members of the collection. Because each of the actors can receive messages concurrently, the abstraction implemented by the group need not be serializable. The paper describes four different usage paradigms for aggregates. In addition, two detailed program examples are given; these examples show how the introduction of aggregates decreases serialization and increases program concurrency.

Multiple Concurrency Control Policies in an Object-Oriented Programming System

Different parallel and distributed applications have different consistency models, so *multiple concurrency control policies* are needed. When objects are shared among applications with different policies, multiple policies must operate simultaneously and compatibly. The paper shows how the distributed object-oriented programming language MELD is used to support concurrency models. The relevant language constructs, programming problems, and implementation issues are described.

Ports for Objects in Concurrent Logic Programs

Ports are introduced to provide communication support for object-oriented programming in concurrent constraint logic programming languages. From a pragmatic point of view ports provide efficient many-to-one communication, object identity, mechanisms for garbage collection of objects, and opportunities for optimised compilation techniques for concurrent objects. From a semantic point of view, ports preserve the monotonicity of the constraint store which is a crucial property of all concurrent constraint languages. Ports are available in AKL, the Andorra Kernel language, a concurrent logic programming language that provides general combinations of don't know and don't care nondeterministic computations.

Part III: Language Design

Specifying Concurrent Languages and Systems with Δ-Grammars

The use of graph grammars for specifying concurrent systems and languages is described. The model used in this paper, Δ-GRAMMARS, is rooted in existing graph grammar theory and provides a convenient framework in which to specify both static and dynamic concurrent systems.

Interaction Abstract Machines

Linear Objects is an abstract linguistic model for concurrent computation whose theoretical background is given by Linear Logic, a logic recently introduced by Jean-Yves Girard to provide a theoretical account for the notion of *action*. This paper characterizes

Linear Object computations in terms of *Interaction Abstract Machines* (IAMs), in the same vein of such metaphors as the Chemical Abstract Machine. IAMs allow interactions among independent, locally defined subsystems — a crucial requirement for capturing the global behavior of open systems.

CC++: A Declarative Concurrent Object-Oriented Programming Notation

Compositional C++ is a parallel object-oriented notation which extends C++. The goals of CC++ include developing a theory, notation, and tools for reliable scalable concurrent program libraries. CC++ also aims to unify declarative programs and object-oriented imperative programming. This paper is a brief description of CC++, and its extensions. Included are some example programs together with reasoning about their correctness.

A Logical Theory of Concurrent Objects and Its Realization in the Maude Language

A new theory of concurrent objects is presented. The theory has the important advantage of being based directly on a simple logic called *rewriting logic* in which concurrent object-oriented computation exactly corresponds to logical deduction. An axiomatization of objects, classes, and concurrent object-oriented computations in terms of rewriting logic is proposed as a general semantic framework for object-oriented programming. The theory is used to develop a new language, called Maude. Maude provides a simple and semantically rigorous unification of functional programming and concurrent object-oriented programming. The relationship with Actors and with other models of concurrent computation is discussed. The model theory of rewriting logic and an initial model semantics for Maude modules are also presented.

Part IV: Operating Systems

CHOICES: A Parallel Object-Oriented Operating System

The *Choices* parallel object-oriented operating system design is a collection of interconnected frameworks. Each subframework's design specifies the possible concurrent messages, control flow, and synchronization between a dynamic number of component objects. In addition, objects within a subframework have other dependency relationships that vary dynamically. *Choices* has a number of implementations on different hardware platforms and with different resource allocation and management algorithms. The paper describes the problem-oriented models of concurrency and communication implemented in *Choices* as attributes that are defined for an abstract subframework and inherited by more concrete subframeworks.

COSMOS: An Operating System for a Fine-Grain Concurrent Computer

COSMOS is an operating system for the J-Machine, a fine-grain message-passing concurrent computer. COSMOS provides a global virtual namespace, object-based memory management, support for distributed objects, and low-overhead context switching. Its memory management system provides fast, transparent access to storage distributed across the machine. COSMOS is designed to efficiently support fine-grain concurrent computation and is tailored for an environment where local computation is inexpensive. COSMOS provides a shared global name space across the nodes of a message-passing concurrent computer. In COSMOS, all data and code are stored in objects. Objects are free to migrate between nodes to balance load or to exploit locality. The system also supports distributed objects.

Part V: Performance Monitoring

Monitoring Concurrent Object-Based Programs

The paper develops a simulation of multiprocessor architectures executing concurrent applications. The simulation has focussed on the communication and scheduling support facilities of architectures. The monitoring facilities of the simulator have then aided in identifying bottlenecks—both in the application and in the underlying multiprocessor system—leading to refined implementations with better performance. The applications are programmed in a concurrent, object-oriented extension of Lisp called Lamina. The instrumentation facility directly exploits the programming model. The facility provides a comprehensive, customizable library of modules for aggregating this information, for organizing it along various dimensions, and for presenting it visually.

I Language Issues

1 Abstraction and Modularity Mechanisms for Concurrent Computing*

Gul Agha, Svend Frølund, WooYoung Kim, Rajendra Panwar, Anna Patterson, and Daniel Sturman

1.1 Introduction

The transition from sequential to parallel and distributed computing has been widely accepted as a major paradigm shift occurring in Computer Science. It has been observed that the sequential programming model is inadequate for parallel and distributed computing. At a conceptual level, one can compare the fundamental intuition between sequential and concurrent computing as follows:

- The sequential programming model defines a computation as a sequence of instructions which manipulate a global store. The standard abstraction mechanism for sequential programs is procedures. Procedures glue a sequence of instructions; they allow genericity by parameterization and reuse by substitution. While this provides a good building block for much of sequential programming, it is an unsatisfactory model for parallel and distributed computing because it does not provide a communication model and it is not a meaningful abstraction of coordination between concurrent components.

- In a *parallel computation* some actions overlap in time; by implication these events must be *distributed* in space. *Concurrency* refers to the *potentially* parallel execution of programs. In a concurrent computation, the execution of some parts of a program may be sequential, or it may be parallel. Since concurrent programs specify a partial order of actions, it provides us with the flexibility to interleave the execution of commands in a program, or to run them in parallel. Therefore, some of the details of the order of execution are left unspecified. We can instead concentrate on conceptual issues without necessarily being concerned with the particular order of execution that may be the result of the quirks of a given system.

Part of the complexity of reasoning about concurrent programs results from the fact that partial orders allow considerable indeterminacy in execution. In other words, there are many potential execution paths. Furthermore, concurrent programs are complicated by the fact that there are a number of different kinds of design concerns, such as locality and synchronization, that are transparent in sequential execution environments. To simplify the construction of concurrent systems, concurrent abstractions must support a separation of design concerns by providing *modularity*.

The complexity of concurrent systems requires new *abstraction* methods to be developed. There are four important requirements for concurrency abstractions. First, the abstraction must allow specification of the complex organizational and coordination structures that are common in concurrent computing. Second, they must provide genericity and reuse of the coordination patterns, much as procedures do for sequential

---

*Based on "Abstraction and Modularity Mechanisms for Concurrent Computing" by Gul Agha, Svend Frølund, WooYoung Kim, Rajendra Panwar, Anna Patterson, and Daniel Sturman in *IEEE Parallel and Distributed Technology: Systems and Applications*, May '93, © 1993 IEEE.

programming. Third, concurrency abstractions must simplify the task of programming by separating design concerns. Finally, the abstractions must allow efficient execution on concurrent architectures.

This paper describes a number of radical programming language concepts that support abstraction and provide modularity in concurrent systems. Specifically, the constructs we propose allow abstract and modular specification of coordination patterns, temporal ordering, resource management, and dependability protocols. In particular, specifications using these constructs are generic and reusable. The next four sections develop our methodology and apply it to a number of problems as follows:

Actors: we describe the Actor model of concurrent computation. The Actor model provides the basic building blocks for concurrent programming which may be used to build a wide variety of computational structures.

Communication abstractions: three communication abstractions are discussed. These are call/return communication, pattern-directed message passing, and constraints on reception. To provide a concrete representation, we show how call/return communication is transformed to primitive actor message-passing.

Modular decomposition: we describe a set of abstractions and discuss how they may be used to factor out multi-actor coordination patterns, resource management strategies, and protocols for dependability.

1.2   Actors

The universe we live in is inherently parallel and distributed. This suggests that the natural language constructs we use to describe the world may also be useful for modeling computational systems. It can be reasonably asserted that the most important concept we use to model the world is categorizing it in terms of objects. In fact, the first elements of natural language children learn are names of objects.

Computational objects encapsulate a state and an expected behavior. Furthermore, objects provide an interface defined in terms of the names of procedures that are visible. These procedures, called *methods*, manipulate the local state of the object when invoked. In particular, this implies that representations which support the same functionality may be interchanged transparently. This is an important advantage of object-based programming which has proved its utility in software engineering of sequential systems.

Traditional object-oriented programming is limited by a mind set which views programming as a sequence of actions. In particular, this mode confounds the natural autonomy and concurrency of objects: sequential object-oriented languages allow only one object to be active at a time. An object's behavior is viewed as a sequence of actions, and this sequence is blocked by invoking a method in another object. This is a rather contrived view: it is more natural to view objects as computational agents which may compute *concurrently*.

The *Actor* model unifies objects and concurrency. The model's building blocks can be described and justified in fairly intuitive terms. Actors are autonomous and concurrently executing objects which execute asynchronously (i.e., at their own rate). Actors may send each other messages. Since actors are conceptually distributed in space, communication between them is asynchronous. Asynchronous communication preserves the available potential for parallel activity: an actor sending a message asynchronously need not block until the recipient is ready to receive (or process) a message. If a model requires a sender to block, it reduces the concurrency which may be available.

In response to receiving a message, an actor may take the following sorts of actions:

send: asynchronously send a message to a specified actor.

create: create an actor with the specified behavior.

become: specify a new behavior (local state) to be used by the actor to respond to the next message it processes.

The *message send* primitive is the asynchronous analog of procedure invocation. It is the basic communication primitive, causing a message to be put in an actor's mailbox (*mail queue*). To send a message, the identity (*mail address*) of the target of a communication needs to be specified. Finally, note that although the arrival order of messages is nondeterministic, every message sent to an actor is guaranteed to be eventually delivered.

The *become* primitive gives actors a history-sensitive behavior necessary for shared, mutable data objects. This is in contrast to a purely functional programming model. The *create* primitive is to concurrent programming what procedure abstraction is to sequential programming. Newly created actors are autonomous and have a unique mail address. Furthermore, create dynamically extends computational space, it thus subsumes the functionality of `new` in Pascal or `malloc` in C.

Actor primitives form a simple but powerful set upon which to build a wide range of higher-level abstractions and concurrent programming paradigms. The Actor model was originally proposed by Hewitt [13] and later developed by Agha [1]. A formal theory of actors, including proof techniques for establishing the equivalence of actor systems, appears in [3]. A high level actor programming language is described in [14]. Techniques for garbage collecting actors are described in [21].

1.3   Communication Abstractions

Although point-to-point asynchronous message sending is the most efficient form of communication in a distributed system, concurrent languages must provide a number of communication abstractions to simplify the task of programming. Programmers using parallel or distributed computing need to understand the advantages and limitations of different communication abstractions. We describe three basic communication abstractions, namely call/return communication, pattern-directed communication, and constrained reception.

1.3.1   Call/Return Communication

In call/return communication, an object invokes a number of other objects and waits for them to return a value before continuing execution. A standard mechanism for call/return communication in concurrent programming is *remote procedure call*: a procedure calls another procedure at a remote node and waits for the result. The result is returned to the point where the call is made. RPC extends the sequential procedure call model where procedure calls follow a stack discipline which can be efficiently implemented on sequential processors. In case of high-level actor languages, concurrent RPC-style calls allow a simple expression of functional parallelism. In actor languages, whether two actors are on the same node or on different nodes is transparent to the application code.

Blocking a sender in a call/return communication is generally not desirable: if the actor invoked is on a different node, available concurrency may be unnecessarily lost. If the sender "holds" the processor while *busy waiting* for results, processor time is wasted. Otherwise, extra context switching is needed to change the executing actor from the sender to another actor.

Whenever feasible, we allow the calling actor to continue computation as soon as it has asynchronously *sent* a request. In order to support ease of programming without incurring an unnecessary performance penalty, we transform a program containing a call/return communication to a semantically equivalent one containing asynchronous message sends only. The transformations used preserve the maximal concurrency in a program. Optimizing this form of communication by using a concurrent analog of continuation passing style program transformation avoids incurring unnecessary costs.

Example: *Program Transformations for Call/Return Communication*

We use one of two transformations on call/return communication [16]. First, if the response of a sending actor to the next message is not dependent on the results from a call/return communication, the program is transformed by changing the calls to asynchronous sends and creating a *join continuation* actor [2]. The join continuation actor performs a part of computation of the original sender actor that is dependent on the results. Consider the following expression:

```
send B (v, C.request1(), D.request2())
```

send represents an asynchronous send. When executed, actor C and D receive messages request1 and request2, respectively. Then, actor B is sent a message with results from actor C and D along with v. Figure 1.1 pictorially represent the execution of the program before and after the transformation, respectively.

Second, if the response of an actor to the next message is partly determined by the results of the calls to other actors, we separate out the continuation as a method within the original actor. Note that no purpose would be served by creating a join continuation actor: the original sender cannot process other messages until a result is received. The continuation method is triggered by the results of the remote actor invocations. In order to guarantee consistency between state changes, the transformation creates a synchronization constraint (see next section) for the continuation method. This new constraint prevents other messages from being processed until the continuation method has been invoked.

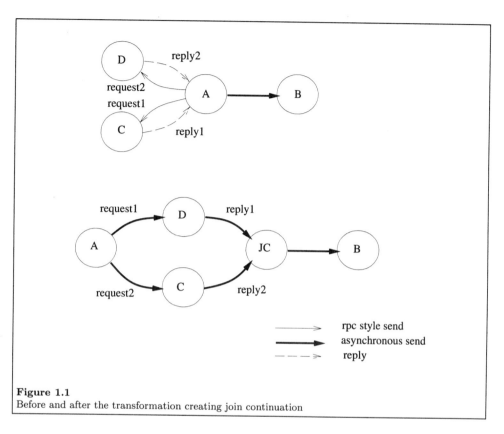

Figure 1.1
Before and after the transformation creating join continuation

1.3.2 Pattern-directed Communication

An advantage of point-to-point asynchronous communication mechanism is that it allows locality to be directly expressed and optimized. However, in some cases, it is sufficient to communicate with an arbitrary member of a group. If the recipient must name all potential receivers, the book-keeping involved can be cumbersome. Furthermore, a level of abstraction is lost. The use of pattern-directed communication allows an abstract specification of a group of potential recipients. Thus, the actual recipients may be transparently changed: none of clients needs to know the exact identities of potential receivers or to poll them to determine if they satisfy some pattern.

In the ActorSpace model, a communication model based on destination patterns is defined [4]. An *actorSpace* is a computationally passive container of actors which acts as a context for matching patterns. Note that actorSpaces may overlap; in particular, an actorSpace may be wholly contained in another. Patterns are matched against listed attributes of actors and actorSpaces that are *visible* in the actorSpace. Both visibility and attributes are dynamic. Messages may be sent to one or all members of a group defined by a pattern. An actor may send a message to a single (arbitrary) member of a group, or broadcast it to the entire group. In particular, broadcasting can be used to disseminate common protocols to an entire group.

ActorSpace provides a useful model for many distributed applications. For example, if an actorSpace of servers is defined, none of the clients need to know the exact identities of the potential servers or explicitly poll them to determine if particular ones are suitable. This provides an abstraction that allows replication of services, for example to enhance reliability or increase performance.

Linda [8] defines a communication abstraction similar to that of actorSpace; however, the semantics of Linda, unlike ActorSpace, require explicit read operations by recipients. This results in at least two significant differences. First, race conditions may occur as a result of concurrent access by different processes to a common space. Second, communication cannot be made secure against arbitrary readers – for example, there is no way for a sender to specify that a process with certain attributes may not consume a message (called a tuple in Linda). By contrast, in ActorSpace, the attributes of a message's potential recipient are determined by the sender.

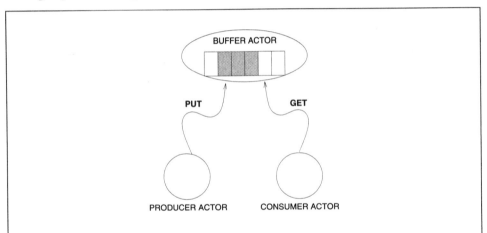

Figure 1.2
Producers and Consumers. The producer actor deposits a data item into the buffer by invoking put method defined in the buffer actor. The consumer actor retrieves a data item from the buffer by invoking **get** method of the buffer actor. The producer actor may not invoke put method on a full buffer. And the consumer actor may not invoke **get** method on a empty buffer.

1.3.3   Synchronization Constraints

In sequential programs, there is a single thread of control and the programmer must explicitly fix a calling sequence for all objects – essentially by calling them one at a time and passing the control to them. Generally a stack discipline is used and control returns to the calling object once the called object has finished executing. In fact, this calling discipline corresponds quite poorly to the nature of many computations. In concurrent systems, more distributed forms of synchronization supporting partial orders are needed.

Consider producer actors and consumer actors which communicate through a buffer actor. Since actors are autonomous and asynchronous, they do not know if a particular message they send may be meaningfully processed in the current state of a receiving actor. Therefore, it is possible for a producer actor to send a `put` request to a full buffer, or, for a consumer actor to send a `get` request to an empty buffer (Figure 1.2). Thus, it is necessary to specify *when* different computational objects may be invoked. Rather than *reject* messages which may not be processed in the current state we *defer* the request.

Our view is that constraints which limit invocations of a concurrent object – i.e., its *synchronization constraints* – should be a part of the actor's interface. A programmer may associate such constraints with each method. The separation of synchronization constraints from the representation of the methods frees the programmer from explicitly specifying code to manage messages received by an actor which it is not in a state to process. A message not satisfying the constraint is buffered until such time when the actor's state satisfies the constraint. Essentially, synchronization constraints provide an abstract representation of the reactive behavior of an actor. Using synchronization constraints, it is possible to reason about the effect of composing actors.

Actor programs, unlike iteration in sequential programming languages, do not use *global* loops for sequencing actions; the usual semantics of such loops implies that an iteration should be completed before the next one may be initiated. Instead, actors support message driven programming. Synchronization constraints may be used to *locally* ensure consistent sequencing of iterations. By not creating unnecessary data dependencies, message driven programming maintains the maximal concurrency available in an algorithm (see example). The use of actors for message driven programming of multicomputers is described in [11].

Example: *Overlapping Communication and Computation*

Actor programming naturally leads to efficient parallel execution in a number cases. We illustrate this by an iterative matrix algorithm for the Cholesky Decomposition (CD) of a dense matrix ([6]). Specifically, the matrix is represented by a collection of actors which execute different iterations in response to messages they receive. Since the arrival order of messages is indeterminate, local synchronization constraints are used to ensure that the iterations are executed in the correct order.

Table 1.1 compares the results of an implementation of CD algorithm which pipelines the execution of iterations with an implementation which completes the execution of one iteration before starting the next. Note that the pipelining naturally follows from the fact that control is distributed between actors.

1.4   Separating Design Concerns

We describe three mechanisms to develop modular and reusable components for concurrent systems. These mechanisms allow:

- The use of abstractions to specify multi-actor coordination patterns. The coordination patterns include atomicity and temporal ordering.

Matrix	32×32		64×64		128×128		256×256	
Nodes	Seq	Pipe	Seq	Pipe	Seq	Pipe	Seq	Pipe
1	.13	.12	.87	.85	6.45	6.41	49.6	49.6
2	.12	.11	.78	.76	5.75	5.68	44.1	43.9
4	.10	.08	.58	.51	3.93	3.76	29.8	29.3
8	.10	.04	.44	.30	2.53	2.18	17.5	16.6
16	.13	.02	.45	.17	1.88	1.20	10.7	8.9
32	.22	.01	.64	.09	1.98	.93	8.0	5.6

Table 1.1
Results from an implementation of the CD algorithm on an Intel iPSC/2. The columns *Seq* represent
the implementation which completes the execution of one iteration before starting the execution of the
next iteration. The columns *Pipe* show the values obtained by pipelining the execution of iterations.
The times shown are in seconds.

- Separation of functionality and resource management strategies. For example, policies for actor placement may be specified in terms of an actor group abstraction
  independent of the representation and invocations of a particular group satisfying the
  abstraction.

- The ability to develop generic, application independent code for protocols which increase dependability. In particular, the architecture we propose allows the dynamic
  installation or removal of protocols to change the fault-tolerance and security characteristics of a running system.

1.4.1 Synchronizers

Synchronization constraints provide modular expression of constraints which need to be
satisfied by a *single* actor before it may process a communication it has received. Although synchronization constraints are often promoted as a way to describe coordination
of concurrent objects (e.g., [11]), they are unsatisfactory when describing multi-actor coordination: synchronization constraints depend only on the local state of a single actor.

    In distributed computing, a group of object invocations often must satisfy certain
temporal ordering or atomicity constraints. Conventional programming languages do
not allow multi-object constraints to be specified in a modular and reusable manner.
This creates a number of problems. Considerable programming effort is required to express multi-object constraints in terms of low level message passing. Moreover, expressing
these constraints by explicit message passing "hard wires" both the constraints and their
implementation into the application software. Thus, the same abstract multi-object constraints must be re-programmed for use with different objects. Finally, the implementation of the multi-object constraints may not be transparently changed. These difficulties
suggest that new high-level coordination language constructs are needed to simplify the
task of programming.

    We have developed high level language constructs which allow *multi-actor constraints*
to be directly expressed [12]. We define two types of multi-actor constraints: temporal

orderings on, and atomicity of, invocations of shared distributed actors. Multi-actor constraints are described in terms of conditions that must be satisfied for a group of method invocations to be accepted: if the conditions are not met, the invocations are delayed. Thus multi-actor constraints coordinate concurrent objects by restricting their activation. As the following examples suggest, a large class of coordination schemes can be efficiently expressed using invocation constraints:

- Consider a group of cooperating resource administrators who must share a limited resource. The administrators must therefore adhere to a collective policy limiting the total number of resources allocated at a given point in time. Enforcement of a collective policy can be expressed as a multi-actor constraint on invocations that request resources: an allocation request can only be serviced if there are resources available.

- A group of dining philosophers is organized so that each philosopher shares her two chopsticks with two others. The number of philosophers is equal to the number of chopsticks and a philosopher needs the two chopsticks next to her in order to eat. Deadlocks may be avoided by enforcing a multi-actor constraint that requires atomic invocation of the pick method in two chopstick actors by a single philosopher.

We build on the observation that multi-actor constraints can be specified independent of the representation of the actors being coordinated. Specifying multi-actor constraints in terms of the interfaces enables better description, reasoning and modification of multi-actor constraints. Specifically, utilizing only knowledge about interfaces to describe multi-actor constraints allows code for coordination to be separated from that for the actor's functionality. This separation enables system design with a larger potential for reuse. Actors may be reused independent of how they are coordinated; conversely, multi-actor coordination patterns may be reused on different groups of actors. In particular, it is possible to abstract over coordination patterns and factor out generic coordination structures.

We describe multi-actor constraints using *synchronizers*. Conceptually, a synchronizer is a special kind of actor that observes and limits the invocations accepted by a group of actors. The functionality of synchronizers is illustrated in Figure 1.3. In that figure, pattern matching is depicted as matching shapes between patterns and messages. Synchronizers may disable certain patterns: disabled patterns are black and enabled patterns are white. Arrows illustrate the status of messages: an arrow that ends at an object starts at an enabled message and an arrow that ends at a pattern starts at a disabled message. Objects that are not pointed to by an arrow have no messages to process in the current system state. The messages at B are disabled whereas the message at C is enabled. The E message is unconstrained since it does not match any pattern. Patterns may be grouped together into atomicity constraints that ensure that multiple invocations are scheduled as an atomic action. Grouping of patterns into atomicity constraints is depicted by boxes around the groups. The messages at A satisfy the atomicity constraint whereas the message at D is blocked waiting for another message before both can be scheduled atomically.

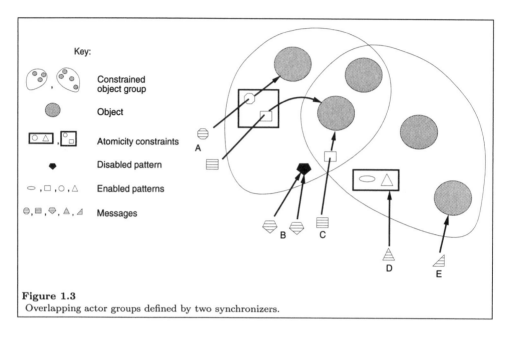

Figure 1.3
Overlapping actor groups defined by two synchronizers.

Operationally, synchronizers are implemented using primitive actor communication. The advantage of synchronizers is that the involved message-passing is transparent to the programmer who specifies multi-actor constraints in a high-level and abstract way. The implementation of synchronizers may either involve direct communication between the constrained actors, indirect communication with a central "coordinator," or a hybrid. Thus, by using a high-level specification of multi-actor constraints, we provide the flexibility to map the same multi-actor constraint to different implementations.

A synchronizer can be defined and instantiated by a client actor when accessing shared servers. Thus clients can use constraints to enforce customized access schemes. Alternately, a synchronizer can be permanently associated with a group of servers when the servers are first put into operation. In this case, the constraints can express the default interdependence between servers. A more detailed discussion of multi-actor constraints including an account of related work is available in [12].

Example: *Cooperating Resource Administrators*
Consider two cooperating resource administrators (spoolers) which manage a common printer pool. Suppose the pool has n printers. When an administrator receives a print request, it performs some bookkeeping computations and then sends the request through a common bus so that one of the free printers can grab the request and start printing. The use of two spoolers allows greater concurrency and increases availability. We use a coordination constraint to ensure that requests are not relayed when there are no free printers. The constraint also ensures that the two spoolers cooperate to maintain the correct count of available printers.

Maintenance of common information about the number of free printers can be described

```
AllocationPolicy(spooler1,spooler2,numPrinters) =
{ numUsed := 0;

   numUsed = numPrinters  disables (spooler1.print  and spooler2.print),
   (spooler1.print  or spooler2.print)  updates increment(numUsed)
   (spooler1.done  or spooler2.done)  updates decrement(numUsed)
}
```

Figure 1.4
A synchronizer which coordinates two print spoolers. A synchronizer has an encapsulated state that
is updated through an **updates** operator. The state of the above synchronizer is held by the variable
numUsed. The **disables** operator delays invocation of the constrained actors. Delays of invocations are
expressed as conditions over the state of the synchronizer.

external to the spoolers as a synchronizer. Figure 1.4 contains a synchronizer which
enforces the global allocation policy. The names spooler1 and spooler2 are references
to the two constrained spoolers. The synchronizer prevents the processing of a request
when there is no free printer in the pool.

Synchronizers are general tools for describing interdependence between servers performing a service. Using synchronizers, interdependence is expressed independent of the
representation of the servers. The resulting modularity makes it possible to modify the
coordination scheme without changing the servers and vice versa. In particular, it is
possible to dynamically add new printers to the printer pool or add new administrators
to the system without changing codes for already existing printers or administrators; new
synchronizers may simply be instantiated.

1.4.2   Modular Specification of Resource Management Policies

Expressing a parallel algorithm in terms of primitive actors provides a logical specification of the algorithm. Such a specification may be called an *ideal algorithm* [15]. The
time taken by the ideal algorithm, in the presence of unbounded resources and zero
communication cost, is determined by the sequential depth of the longest path in the
partial order defined by the actor computation. However, neither of these assumptions
is realistic.

In particular, communication costs for an algorithm are a function of the latency and
bandwidth of an architecture. Latency is the time taken to send a message from one node
to another and bandwidth is the rate at which information may be transmitted between
two halves of an architecture (see the glossary in [20]). For example, if a problem, such as
sorting, requires half the data on a distributed computer to be moved, the performance
of an algorithm solving the problem will be bound by the bandwidth. In any physically
realizable architecture, the bandwidth may grow by at most $P^{2/3}$, where P is the number
of processors. This follows from the fact that space is three dimensional, therefore a given
technology yields a constant bandwidth per unit area, and a bisecting plane may grow
by at most $P^{2/3}$. There is a similar theoretical bound on I/O. In case of sorting, this
means that the speed up is bound by $P^{2/3}$ in general (and $\sqrt{P}$ on a two dimensional

network) [19].

Since the performance of an algorithm is dependent on how many messages have to be sent and to which nodes, the efficiency of execution depends in part on the placement and scheduling of objects. In general, the problem of finding an optimal placement policy is intractable. However, for a given algorithm, a user may be able to determine the most efficient placement policy.

Specifications of resource management policies, such as placement, introduce a new layer of complexity to programming concurrent architectures. In particular, the same ideal algorithm executed on the same architecture may yield a different efficiency depending on the resource management policy used. Specifically, the efficiency obtained may depend on a number of factors such as:

- the problem or input size,

- characteristics of the concurrent computer including its latency, bandwidth, size, and processor speeds,

- the placement policy used to map objects to physical resources,

- scheduling strategies used to manage the concurrency.

Current programming methods for concurrent computers intermix specification of resource management policies with the code specifying the ideal algorithm. The resulting conflation of design goals complicates the code and reduces its reusability. We propose to separate the specification of an ideal algorithm from the strategies used to map it to a concurrent architecture. Specifically, we describe a mapping policy in terms of actorSpace types. An actorSpace type may defined as a group of actors together with both the abstract operations and the concurrent access constraints on them. actorSpace types generalize and abstract over Concurrent Aggregates[9]; the latter captures the operational notion of a distributed data structure [10].

For example, consider an $n \times n$ array. The array can be mapped on a two-dimensional mesh of $p \times p$ processors in a number of ways including:

- *Block placement policy:* the $(i,j)^{th}$ element is assigned to the $(i$ div k, j div $k)^{th}$ processor, where $k = n/p$.

- *Shuffle placement policy:* the $(i,j)^{th}$ element is assigned to the $(i$ mod p, j mod $p)^{th}$ processor.

Although the abstract operations and concurrent access constraints of an array are the same, different ideal algorithms may be executed more efficiently using different mapping policies. Linear equation solution techniques, such as Gaussian Elimination or Cholesky Decomposition, are generally efficient when the matrix is mapped using a shuffle placement policy. On the other hand, algorithms for low-level image processing applications, domain decomposition techniques for solving Partial Differential Equations, perform efficiently when their matrix representation is mapped using the block placement policy.

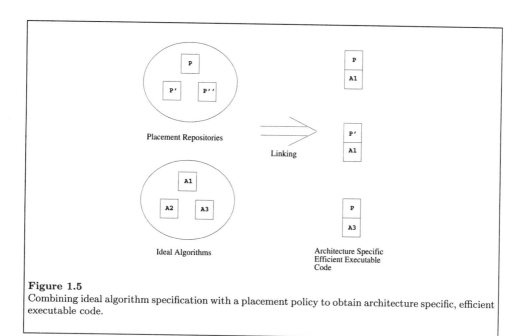

Figure 1.5
Combining ideal algorithm specification with a placement policy to obtain architecture specific, efficient executable code.

Note that the correspondence between an algorithm and the optimal placement of its actorSpace type is not one to one. Different placement policies may be more efficient for the same ideal algorithm on different architectures, and, sometimes for the same algorithm and architecture but a different input size. Organizing a computation in terms of its actorSpace type's provides modularity and promotes reuse. The task of programming can be simplified by composing and reusing modules from a repository of placement policies for a given actorSpace type.

Example: *Reuse of Resource Management Strategies*
Although we are developing better language support for resource management functions in terms of ActorSpace types, the same functionality could be mimicked in some cases using current tools. Consider a dense matrix ActorSpace type. We represent each matrix element by an actor in the space. The behavior of the actors is specified separately; for example, the actors might implement Gaussian Elimination or matrix multiplication. A simple set of functions can specify a placement of the actors. Changing the definitions of these functions changes the placement policy and can affect performance drastically.

Consider the problem of mapping a matrix M of size $n \times n$ to a $p \times p$ array of processors. We can divide M into submatrices of uniform size $k \times k$ where $k = n/p$ and place each submatrix on a separate processor. The placement is specified using two functions: ElemToProc which gives the processor coordinates for a given element, and LocalIndex, which specifies the coordinates within the sumbatrix.

The following C-like code specifies the block placement policy:

```
ElemToProc(i,j) Return(i/k,j/k)
```

```
LocalIndex(i,j) Return(i%k,j%k)
```

These functions can be easily redefined to implement a different placement policy, such as the shuffle placement policy, without changing the code for an ideal algorithm.

```
ElemToProc(i,j) Return(i%p,j%p)
LocalIndex(i,j) Return(i/p,j/p)
```

1.4.3   Customizing Dependability

Currently, a protocol for dependability must either be built into the system architecture or be re-implemented for each application. Moreover, development of dependable software is expensive: the increased complexity caused by mixing the code for a set of dependability protocols with that of the application code is itself a source of bugs. A significant savings in software development and maintenance costs may be realized if abstract, application-independent specifications of dependability protocols are possible.

We have developed a methodology which allows the code for a dependability protocol to be specified independently of the application specific code [5]. The methodology has been implemented in an experimental kernel called *Broadway*. Our reflective model allows *compositionality* of dependability protocols. Compositionality means that we can specify and reason about a complex dependability scheme in terms of its constituents. Thus, logically distinct aspects of a dependability scheme may be described separately resulting in a methodology which allows dependability protocols to be implemented as generic, composable components.

We employ *reflection* as the enabling technology to allow modular specification and dynamic installation of dependability protocols. Reflection means that an application can access and manipulate a description of its own behavior and execution environment. The actors representing such a description are called *meta-level* actors. For our purposes, the meta-level contains a description sufficient to model the dependability characteristics of an executing application; reflection thus allows dynamic changes in the execution of an application with respect to dependability.

The most general form of reflection leads to interpretation and is costly. For our purposes, we use a limited reflective model in which each actor has three meta-actors: its *dispatcher*, its *mail queue* and its *acquaintance list*. The acquaintances meta-actor represents the current state (behavior) of the actor. The dispatcher and mail queue meta-actors implement the communication primitives of the runtime system so that the interaction between actors can be modified to change the dependability characteristics of an application.

Specifically, a dispatcher meta-actor is a representation of the implementation of an actor's transmission behavior. When customized, messages sent by the corresponding base actor are rerouted to the customized dispatcher. An actor's mail queue meta-actor represents the mail buffer holding messages received by the actor. If a customized mail queue meta-actor is installed, all messages to the base actor are rerouted through it. A customized mail queue may alter the order of messages to the base actor, e.g., to enforce local synchronization constraints.

A number of protocols which increase dependability of a system can be expressed in terms of a customized mail queue, dispatcher and acquaintance list. These protocols include two phase commit, three phase commit, primary back-up, full replication, check-pointing, and encryption. Composition of dependability protocols is achieved by transparently manipulating the meta-actors of the meta-actors. The resulting system allows not only dynamic installation of generically specified protocols but their dynamic removal. The limited form of reflection we use supports incremental compilation and increases execution time by only a very small constant.

Example: *A Replicated Server*

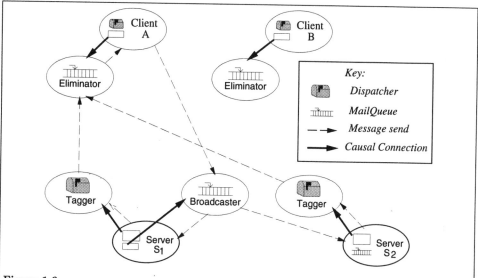

Figure 1.6
A replicated service protocol. `Client` *A* initially sends a message to `Server` S_1. The message is routed to the mail queue `Broadcaster`. Broadcaster passes a copy of the message off to S_1 and sends a copy to S_2. Both servers eventually reply and their replies are tagged by the two `Tagger` dispatchers. The `Eliminator` mail queue then passes only one copy of the two messages onto *A*.

To illustrate how *Broadway's* reflective architecture may be used to support dependability protocols, we describe the meta-level implementation of a replication protocol. The protocol involves replicating a server to resist crash failures.

Our original system is a service with two clients. Figure 1.6 shows the result of installing the meta-actors for this protocol in the system. A clone is made of the service and the appropriate meta-actors are installed at the service and at the clients. The meta-actors are designed to manipulate generic messages. As a result, in combination with the system's ability to clone actors, this protocol is implemented transparently of the base actors. Furthermore, since the protocol is generic, it may be reused with any application.

For each client, a meta-actor — a customized mail queue (Eliminator) — is installed at its node. This mail queue will eliminate duplicate messages from the copies of the server. For the server and its replicated copy, customized meta-actors are installed to handle the transmission and reception of messages. The dispatcher Tagger tags all outgoing messages so that the clients (using the mail queue Eliminator) may eliminate duplicate responses. The mail queue Broadcaster copies to server S_2 all messages sent to server S_1. The repetition of messages is necessary to keep the state of the two servers consistent. When a message is sent to the service, the get method of the customized meta-mail queue is invoked instead. When the service requires a new message to process, the Broadcaster mail queue is sent a put message. The code for the Broadcaster actor class is shown below. Notice that the transparency of the protocol is preserved by the methods get and put. These methods manipulate entire messages, never needing to inspect the message contents:

```
class Broadcaster
  var S2, Base;
  /* Setup this actor */
  init(copy,orig)
    S2 := copy;
    Base := orig;
  end
  /* A new message is received */
  method get(msg)
    send S2 msg;
    myqueue.enqueue(msg);
    end
  end
  /* The base actor requests a message */
  restrict put() with (!myqueue.empty());
  method put()
    send Base myqueue.dequeue();
  end
end
```

In Figure 1.6, the results of a sample message transaction are shown. Note that additional dispatcher meta-actors are required to correctly handle messages that may be sent by the client after the server crashed, but before that crash was detected. To keep this example simple, these additional actors were not shown.

1.5 Conclusions

Because of the costs of learning new programming languages and rewriting old code, the conversion to new programming paradigms has been slow. This has led some observers to downplay the importance of research in programming languages. At the same time, there is a perception of a software crises as the cost of maintaining programs has escalated. In fact, what exasperates the software maintenance problem is the use of old languages and methodologies which are insufficiently expressive and provide little support for software maintenance.

The acceptance of new programming paradigms is now likely to come more rapidly. There are two reasons for this. First, the cost of developing code in newer languages often outstrips the cost of maintaining old code. For example, consider the increasingly deployed object-oriented software technology. The technology enables programmers to reduce development time by providing support for design and to reduce software maintenance costs by allowing them to incrementally modify their code. Second, the increasing computational power available and, the ever lowering cost, of concurrent computers implies that at least portions of the code need be rewritten to take advantage of concurrent computers.

The need for new programming paradigms is by no means the dominant force in parallel or distributed computing research. For example, considerable effort has gone into the development of parallelizing compilers which attempt to extract parallelism from existing sequential code and then automatically determine the mapping to concurrent computer architectures. Although the approach provides useful results in the short term, it suffers from two limitations. First, code based on sequential algorithms cannot be generally translated to the best parallel algorithms. Second, no general techniques can allow efficient placement and scheduling strategies for arbitrary algorithms on a concurrent computer.

The development of new programming paradigms should allow more complex programs to be written with less effort. Furthermore, it should make the expression of potential parallelism simpler. However, to be practical, new paradigms must not place unrealistic restrictions on expressiveness. For example, although purely functional, or state-less programming, has some nice concurrency properties, shared mutable state is an essential requirement of distributed computing.

Gains in programmer productivity can only be realized by the greater use of new abstractions and modularity mechanisms. Modularity is gained by separating design concerns: code for different purposes should be independently specified and composed. Abstraction allows increased genericity and reuse. Furthermore, it raises the granularity of programming by allowing code to be expressed in terms of more intuitive structures.

We have discussed a number of ways in which modular construction of multi-component concurrent systems can be supported. These include the use of constraints for expressing coordination patterns over distributed objects; actorSpace types for abstracting over resource management strategies for groups of actors; and meta-programming for dependability protocols. Although the resulting modularity allows concurrent programming to be simplified, this is only a small part of the gain. More importantly, the application independence provides a basis for constructing software repositories:. for example, code stored in repositories can include specifications and implementations of constraints, placement and scheduling policies, and dependability protocols. The executable specifications may then be dynamically linked with different application code without the need for reimplementing any of them. The average application developer need not understand the details of the representation – rather she needs to know only the relevant properties of the abstraction (including properties such as the performance characteristics of certain access patterns).

The concurrent programming language abstractions and modularity mechanisms we propose are certainly not a complete set. They do, however, suggest ways of drastically reducing software development and maintenance costs, scaling up software systems, and making it feasible to use the power of parallel and distributed computing. We believe that the successful application of these methods will further stimulate research in the development of a new generation of realistic high-level programming languages.

Acknowledgments

The authors' work is supported by the Office of Naval Research (ONR contract numbers N00014-90-J-1899 and N00014-93-1-0273), by the Digital Equipment Corporation, and by joint support from the Defense Advanced Research Projects Agency and the National Science Foundation (NSF CCR 90-07195). The authors would like to thank other members and former members of the Open Systems Laboratory including Christian Callsen, Shingo Fukui, Chris Houck, Shakuntala Miriyala, Shangpin Ren, R.K. Shyamasundar, Nalini Venkatasubramanian and Takuo Watanabe. The research described in here has strongly benefited from the first author's discussions with Carl Hewitt and Carolyn Talcott, among others.

References

[1]   G. Agha. *Actors: A Model of Concurrent Computation in Distributed Systems.* MIT Press, 1986.

[2]   G. Agha. Concurrent Object-Oriented Programming. *Communications of the ACM*, 33(9):125–141, September 1990.

[3]   G. Agha, I. Mason, S. Smith, and C. Talcott. Towards a Theory of Actor Computation. In *Third International Conference on Concurrency Theory (CONCUR '92)*, pages 565–579. Springer-Verlag, August 1992. LNCS.

[4]   G. Agha and C.J. Callsen. ActorSpace: An Open Distributed Programming Paradigm. In *Principles and Practice of Parallel Programming '93*, 1993. Sigplan Notices (To be published).

[5]   G. Agha, S. Frølund, R. Panwar, and D. Sturman. A Linguistic Framework for Dynamic Composition of Dependability Protocols. In *Dependable Computing for Critical Applications III, IFIP Transactions*. Elsevier Science Publisher, 1993. (to be published).

[6]   G. Agha, C. Houck, and R. Panwar. Distributed Execution of Actor Systems. In D. Gelernter, T. Gross, A. Nicolau, and D. Padua, editors, *Languages and Compilers for Parallel Computing*, pages 1–17. Springer-Verlag, 1992. Lecture Notes in Computer Science 589.

[7]   W. Athas and C. Seitz. Multicomputers: Message-Passing Concurrent Computers. *IEEE Computer*, pages 9–23, August 1988.

[8]   N. Carriero and D. Gelernter. How to Write Parallel Programs: A Guide to the Perplexed. *ACM Computing Surveys*, 21(3):323–357, September 1989.

[9]   A. A. Chien. *Concurrent Aggregates: Supporting Modularity in Massively Parallel Programs.* MIT Press, 1993.

[10]   W. Dally. *A VLSI Architecture for Concurrent Data Structures.* Kluwer Academic Press, 1986.

[11]   Bjorn N. Freeman-Benson and Alan Borning. Integrating Constraints with an Object-Oriented Language. In O. Lehrmann Madsen, editor, *Proceedings ECOOP '92*, LNCS 615, pages 268–286, Utrecht, The Netherlands, July 1992. Springer-Verlag.

[12]   S. Frølund and G. Agha. A Language Framework for Multi-Object Coordination. In *Proceedings of ECOOP 1993*. Springer Verlag, 1993. To appear in LNCS.

[13]   C. Hewitt. Viewing Control Structures as Patterns of Passing Messages. *Journal of Artificial Intelligence*, 8(3):323–364, 1977.

[14]   C. Houck and G. Agha. HAL: A high-level actor language and its distributed implementation. In *Proceedings of th 21st International Conference on Parallel Processing (ICPP '92)*, volume II, pages 158–165, St. Charles, IL, August 1992.

[15]   L. H. Jamieson. Characterizing Parallel Algorithms. In R. J. Douglass L.H. Jamieson, D.B. Gannon, editor, *The Characteristics of Parallel Algorithms*, pages 65–100. MIT Press, 1987.

[16]   W. Kim and G. Agha. Compilation of a Highly Parallel Actor-Based Language. In U. Banerjee, D. Gelernter, A. Nicolau, and D. Padua, editors, *Proceedings of the Workshop on Languages and Compilers for Parallel Computing*. Yale University TR DCS RR-915, 1992. to appear in LNCS, Springer-Verlag.

[17]   S. Matsuoka and A. Yonezawa. Analysis of Inheritance Anomaly in Object-Oriented Concurrent Programming Languages. In G. Agha, P. Wegner, and A. Yonezawa, editors, *Research Directions in Object-Oriented Programming*. MIT Press, 1993. (to be published).

[18]   B. Shriver and P. Wegner (Eds.), editors. *Research Directions in Object-Oriented Programming*. MIT Press, Cambridge, Mass., 1987.

[19]   V. Singh, V. Kumar, G. Agha, and C. Tomlinson. Scalability of Parallel Sorting on Mesh Multicomputers. *International Journal of Parallel Programming*, 20(2), April 1991.

[20]   G. V. Wilson. A Glossary of Parallel Computing Terminology. *IEEE Parallel and Distributed Technology: Systems and Applications*, pages 52–67, 1(1), February 1993.

[21]   N. Venkatasubramaniam, G. Agha, and C. Talcott. Scalable distributed garbage collection for systems of active objects. In *Proceedings International Workshop on Memory Management*, pages 441–451, St. Malo, France, September 1992. ACM SIGPLAN and INRIA, Springer-Verlag. Lecture Notes in Computer Science.

2 Tradeoffs between Reasoning and Modeling*

Peter Wegner

Object-oriented and logic-programming paradigms are shown to be incompatible as component-based models of computation. This "impossibility result," based on a new notion of observability of interactions among components, suggests that combining object-oriented with logic programming is not merely hard but impossible. It implies the more general incompatibility of reasoning and modeling and the impossibility reducing modeling to reasoning as in automatic program verification. While paradigmatic incompatibility is the most startling result of this paper, its novel use of models and metrics is of independently interest. We introduce a notion of software complexity that parallels computational complexity and a notion of "LP-completeness" that parallels NP-completeness. In a final section we propose practical research that will contribute to the development of component-based software technology.

2.1 Components, Reactiveness, and Encapsulation

Deductive reasoning constrains problem solving so severely that it precludes flexible computational (or conceptual) modeling. This incompatibility, which depends on precise definitions of deductive reasoning and modeling, supports the intuition that logical people (and computers) are unadaptable and inflexible. The deductive reasoning paradigm (exemplified by logic programming) computes by proving theorems from axioms by rules of inference, while the modeling paradigm (exemplified by object-oriented programming) represents application domains (modeled worlds) so that their behavior can be described, predicted, and computed.

Though reasoning and modeling paradigms are equivalent in "what" they can compute, they differ in "how" they organize computation. Reasoning paradigms view computation as "action-oriented" transformation (by instruction execution), while modeling paradigms view computation as "object-oriented" communication (among persistent software components). Differences between reasoning and modeling can also be expressed in terms of *centralized* versus *distributed* models of computation, or in terms of *reduction* (to subgoals) versus *reaction* (to stimuli).

reasoning → action-oriented transformation → centralized → reductive

modeling → object-oriented communication → distributed → reactive

Incompatibility can be demonstrated by identifying any property possessed by one paradigm but not by the other. We demonstrate incompatibility in terms of a *component-based* model of computation:

DEFINITION A model of computation is *component-based* if software components are the basic program unit and messages are the atomic unit of execution. Messages may in general have two kinds of effects: internal effects (side-effects) that change a component's state, and external effects on the environment.

---

*A shorter version of this paper appears in the Proceedings of the Twenty-Sixth Annual Hawaii International Conference on Systems Sciences, 1993.

Though component-based models provide a framework for both modeling and reasoning paradigms, they clearly favor modeling at the expense of reasoning. We nevertheless choose component-based models as a basis for paradigm comparison because they are the preferred program structure for programming in the large, and because communication among components dominates computation within components for large, complex programs.

Since modeling dominates reasoning for component-based models, logic (and mathematics) is a second-class form of component-based computation. This result balances the view, widely held by mathematicians, that computation is a second-class form of mathematics. The second-class status of logic (and mathematics) as a computational technique, taken together with the second-class status of computation as a mathematical technique, indicates that neither discipline dominates the other.

The fundamental feature of modeling languages not possessed by reasoning languages is incremental adaptability. We focus on two forms of incremental adaptability, *reactiveness* and *encapsulation*, that respectively capture temporal and spatial incrementality:

DEFINITION A component is said to be *reactive* if its lifetime is longer than that of the messages (atomic interactions) which it executes. Component-based programs are said to be *reactive* if they have persistent components that incrementally execute messages.

DEFINITION Components are *encapsulated* if they have an interface that hides their implementation from clients. Encapsulation supports localized incremental modification so that the propagation of change is carefully controlled.

Encapsulation supports localized incremental extension of components by external agents, while reactiveness facilitates incremental evolution of components in response to stimuli. Systems are said to be *open* if they are both encapsulated and reactive, *weakly open* if they are one but not both, and *closed* if they are neither.

open system = encapsulated + reactive
            = spatial extensibility + temporal evolution

Object-oriented programs are quintessential open systems, while logic programs are at best weakly open. Incremental adaptability, the key property of open systems, distinguishes modeling from reasoning. Reasoning is incompatible with modeling because problem solving by rigorous deductive computation is incompatible with problem solving by adaptive incremental interaction. We demonstrate this for component-based models of computation but conjecture that this result is asymptotically true in general as problems become so large that communication complexity dominates transformation complexity.

2.2 The Logic Programming Paradigm

The polarization between reasoning and modeling dates back to the Greeks, being a computer-age continuation of the 2000-year philosophical debate between rationalism and empiricism (see appendix). Rationalism asserts that physical phenomena are *necessarily* deducible from (a-priori) logical principles, while empiricism insists that laws of nature can be derived only *contingently* by observation. Logic programming takes no epistemological position on whether the "real world" is inherently logical or contingent, but makes the weaker claim that acquired knowledge can and should be logically represented and manipulated. Logic programming is rationalist in its goal of attempting to reduce problem solving to deductive logic, while object-oriented programming is empiricist in its goal of describing applications by computational objects that simulate the behavior of objects in the problem domain.

The logic programming language Prolog has inference rules called clauses that infer goals from facts specified by database predicates:

> Prolog clause: *mortal(x) :- human(x)*.
> Prolog fact: *human(Socrates)*.
> Prolog goal: *mortal(Socrates)*.

The Prolog clause *mortal(x) :- human(x)* specifies that "x is mortal if x is human." It allows the goal *mortal(Socrates)* to be inferred from the fact *human(Socrates)*.

The clause *P(x) :- Q(x)* asserts that the set of facts or objects satisfying Q is a subset of those satisfying P, or equivalently that "*Q(x)* implies *P(x)* for all *x*". A Prolog goal *G(x)* is true if there are facts in the database that can be inferred from *G* by virtue of the clauses of the Prolog program.

Inferences of the form *set(x) if subset(x)* are surprisingly powerful, permitting all of mathematics to be expressed in terms of set theory. But the exclusive use of *set if subset* inference for computation and/or thinking is unduly constraining. Thinking includes heuristic mechanisms like generalization, inductive inference, and free association that go beyond set/subset inference.

The *procedural reading* of Prolog programs views a clause $P :- Q_1, Q_2, ..., Q_n$ as a procedure for computing (proving) the goal P by reduction to the subgoals $Q_1, Q_2, ..., Q_n$. Reasoning in Prolog proceeds by a sequence of problem reductions of goals P to subgoals $Q_1, Q_2, ..., Q_n$ until all goals are unconditionally true (occur as facts of the database).

The fact that Prolog predicates may be interpreted as procedures and Prolog clauses as computation rules (reduction rules) allows logic to be reduced to computation. However, logic is a particular, stylized form of computation, and the converse reduction of computation to logic is not generally possible. Hobbes was correct in his observation that *reasoning is but reckoning,* but the converse statement that *reckoning is but reasoning* is not true. Reasoning is reducible to reckoning, while reckoning (computing) is essentially richer than reasoning. The greater richness of reckoning over reasoning cannot be measured in terms of computing power, but can be measured in terms of reactiveness and extensibility.

2.3 Component-Based Logic Programming

Sets of clauses with the same predicate P in their clause head are *components* of a Prolog program. Semantically, the clauses of a component P constitute alternative ways of proving the goal P by reducing it to predicate sequences $B_i = Q_{i1}, Q_{i2}, ..., Q_{ik}$:

$P(E_1)$:- B_1 - each B_i is a clause body
$P(E_2)$:- B_2 - consisting of a sequence of predicates Q_{ij}
...
$P(E_n)$:- B_n - if Bi is empty the clause is a fact

Clauses of a component P can be viewed as its methods, while goals of the form $P(E)$ can be viewed as messages for P. When P receives the message to reduce $P(E)$, it tries all clauses (methods) for which E unifies with E_i and returns failure only if the goal cannot be reduced by any of the component's clauses. Each successful reduction determines a substitution for (constraint on) values of variables. Solutions must satisfy the set of all unification constraints.

DEFINITION Component-based programs are said to be *reductive* if the primary computational step causes reduction of a goal to a set of subgoals.

Prolog programs are reductive, since execution of a Prolog clause of the form:

P :- $Q_1, Q_2, ... , Q_k$ reduces the goal P to the subgoals $Q_1, Q_2, ... , Q_k$.

2.4 Don't-Know Nondeterminism

To prove the goal $P(E)$ we can choose any clause in the component for P such that E unifies with E_i. In pure Prolog, all clauses for which E unifies with E_i may in principle be executed in parallel. This may be simulated sequentially by choosing one clause and making provision to try each of the others if the chosen clause should fail or if all solutions are desired. This form of nondeterminism is called *don't-know nondeterminism* because the selection mechanism need not know which of the clauses leads to a correct solution, since all of the solution paths will eventually be chosen. Don't-know nondeterminism can be expressed by a *choice* control structure:

choice $(E_1|B_1, E_2|B_2, ..., E_N|B_N)$
nondeterministically execute the bodies B_i of all clauses whose clause head $P(E_i)$ unifies with the goal $P(E)$.

Bodies B_i are guarded by patterns E_i that must unify with E for B_i to qualify for execution. Prolog programs explore all alternatives until a successful inference path is found and report failure only if no inference path allows the goal to be inferred. The order in which nondeterministic alternatives are explored is determined by the system rather than by the user, though in actual (impure) Prolog systems the user can influence execution order by the order of listing alternatives. Depth-first search may cause unnecessary nonterminating computation, while breadth-first search avoids this problem but is usually less efficient. Impure Prolog provides mechanisms like the cut which allows search mechanisms to be tampered with. This extra flexibility undermines the logical purity of Prolog programs.

Because all alternatives of the choice statement must be explored to determine if the goal P is satisfied, we cannot commit to any particular choice until its consequences have been fully explored. Since a chosen alternative may have to be aborted, we cannot commit to irrevocable consequences of a choice. The execution of predicates for a given choice cannot involve sending messages that the sender cannot cancel.

In the procedural interpretation of logic programs predicates are viewed as procedures and the clause P :- $Q_1, Q_2, ..., Q_k$ is viewed as a problem reduction of the procedure P to the procedures $Q_1, Q_2, ..., Q_k$. Don't-know nondeterminism prohibits procedures from sending messages to each other.

2.5   Retractiveness

Because failure to reduce a goal requires the process of reduction to have a null effect, components cannot have side-effects on other components during reduction. Thus components of a logic program cannot interact during their execution; they can return only the answers "yes with associated substitution" or "no". The answer "yes with substitution" is provisional, since it may have to be retracted on failure of a higher-level subgoal.

DEFINITION   Components whose effects may have to be revoked on failure are said to be *retractive*. A component-based program whose components are retractive is said to be retractive.

Retractive-reductive paradigms prohibit incremental reactive responses because their effects must be retractable on failure. In contrast, object-oriented programs are quintessentially reactive.

Principal Result: The object-oriented and logic paradigms are incompatible as component-based models of computation. Moreover, the object-oriented paradigm dominates the logic-programming paradigm as an interactive component-based paradigm of computation.

2.6   Paradigmatic Incompatibility

The idea that paradigmatic incompatibility is something that can be proved is novel. But once the question is posed, the choices of a component-based model and of the metric of reactiveness are fairly obvious. The idea that paradigms can be incompatible rather than merely different needs justification. Apples and oranges are proverbially different, but we can make a fruit salad containing them both. Multiparadigm logic/object environments (computational fruit salads) cannot be realized because logic is an incompatible ingredient, like hot pepper in a fruit salad.

Logic programming is a "difficult" paradigm not easy to live with under the same paradigmatic roof. Logic programs cannot be "a little bit logical", or "almost completely logical" they are either logical or they are not. Logical properties like backtracking (or lazy evaluation) are completely undermined when the paradigm is even a little impure. Small logical impurities have large (disastrous) effects on logicality, and conversely conformance to logic places onerous constraints on potential paradigmatic partners. The intolerance of impurity combined with the heavy price of logical conformance escalate paradigmatic differences into incompatibilities.

The fundamental reason for paradigmatic incompatibility can be expressed as follows:
Fundamental Incompatibility: Retractiveness is incompatible with reactiveness.

Other incompatibility results can be derived from this fundamental incompatibility by the following rule:
Rule of inference: (x is retractive) and (y is reactive) $\rightarrow$ incompatible(x,y)

If we accept that reasoning is necessarily retractive and modeling is necessarily reactive it follows that reasoning is incompatible with modeling:

(reasoning is retractive) and (modeling is reactive) $\rightarrow$ incompatible (reasoning, modeling)

The distinction between reasoning and modeling can be extended to rationalism versus empiricism. Rationalism, like logic, is both reductive and retractive. It is reductive in that it tries to reduce mathematics and natural science to reasoning. It is retractive because failure of a reduction in a chain of reductions requires retraction of all assumptions. Empiricism is reactive in that phenomena are modeled by their reactive, observable, interactive behavior. Thus, rationalism is incompatible with empiricism a view implicitly accepted by both rationalist and empiricist philosophers:

(rationalism is retractive) and (empiricism is reactive) $\rightarrow$ incompatible (rationalism, empiricism)

Identifying retractiveness and reactiveness as the source of the incompatibility between reasoning and modeling provides a precise computational basis for the intuition that being logical conflicts with interactive adaptation. By expressing mathematical and philosophical dichotomies in computational terms, abstract distinctions such as that between reasoning and modeling are reduced to precise computational distinctions.

2.7   Observability of Component Interactions

The incompatibility of reasoning and modeling is based on a novel criterion of observability of interactions among components. Observability criteria for computability such as the Turing test [4], which can observe just functional (input/output) behavior, cannot distinguish between logic-based and object-oriented styles of programming. The component-based model of computation uses a more sensitive observation mechanism than input/output behavior to make paradigmatic distinctions more sensitive than computability.

The requirement that component interactions be observable is not unreasonable for distributed programs or neural nets. Once modes of interaction are accepted as a criterion for distinguishing paradigms, many other distinctions among models of computation become possible. The binary dichotomy between reactiveness and retractiveness effectively demonstrates the incompatibility of object-oriented and logic programming.

Since interaction is an integral part of component-based program design, input/output behavior is an insufficiently sensitive observability criterion for programming in the large. Functional correctness alone does not determine the quality of program design, or the grade of students in a software engineering course. Modes of interaction are legitimate observable properties of component-based computational models.

Paradigmatic incompatibility based on the observability of interactions does not directly challenge Turing's claim that intelligence is reducible to computation. But it does challenge the claim that intelligence is reducible to deductive reasoning viewed as a retractive subgoal reduction paradigm. When viewed as a component-based paradigm, logic programming is strictly less reactively powerful than object-oriented programming.

The incompatibility of object-oriented and logic programming paradigms is a new kind of impossibility result. Like other such results, it implies that certain research goals, such as the development of multiparadigm object-oriented logic-programming systems, are unattainable. Some of the implications of this result for logic programming, program verification, and program synthesis are quite controversial.

2.8   Committed-Choice Nondeterminism

Objects compute by executing messages that may cause a change of local state and a response. The fundamental control structure for message execution is a "select" statement for selecting among messages to execute an object's operations:

$select\ (op_1, op_2, ..., op_n)$

The select mechanism is essentially a read-eval-print loop. It waits for arrival of a message to execute one of its operations, performs the operation, and is then ready to accept another message. The select statement is a high-level control structure governing computation among components that complements low-level control structures governing algorithm execution within components.

Though implicit in sequential objects, select statements are explicit in concurrent languages. For example, Ada has an explicit select statement to select among alternative operations at entry points to a task:

$select\ (G_1||B_1, G_2||B_2, ..., G_N||B_N)$

Each of the alternatives is guarded by a guard Gi that must be true for the associated body Bi to be a candidate for execution. For example, concurrent access to a buffer with an APPEND operation executable when the buffer is not full and a REMOVE operation executable when the buffer is not empty can be specified as follows:

select (notfull∥APPEND, notempty∥REMOVE)

When the buffer is neither full nor empty and there are both $APPEND$ and $REMOVE$ operations waiting to be executed, then the system must choose nondeterministically between executing an $APPEND$ and a $REMOVE$ operation. However, if the buffer is either empty or full, or if only $APPEND$ or $REMOVE$ operations are waiting to be executed, then the operation of the buffer is deterministic in the sense that at most one operation is eligible for execution.

It is useful to distinguish between *indeterminism* (when an object does not know which action it will next execute) and *nondeterminism* (when an object must choose among several next actions) [7]. Sequential objects are indeterministic; the select statement waits for an incoming message to determine the next action. Concurrent objects may be busy when a message arrives and may need to make a nondeterministic choice among several waiting messages.

Select statements resolve indeterminism by selecting messages in order of their arrival, and resolve nondeterminism by making an irrevocable committed choice to the selected alternative. *Committed-choice nondeterminism* is also called *don't-care nondeterminism*, since agents faced with multiple choices behave as though they do not care which alternative is chosen.

DEFINITION Nondeterministic choice among several next actions that is resolved by irrevocable commitment to one alternative is called *committed-choice nondeterminism (don't-care nondeterminism)*.

2.9   Concurrent Logic Languages

Concurrent logic languages specify the alternative actions for a goal predicate P by a set of guarded clauses:

$P(E_1)$:- $G_1|B_1$ - head $P(E_i)$, guard G_i, body B_i
$P(E_2)$:- $G_2|B_2$ - reducible if unifies(E, E_i) and G_i
...
$P(E_n)$:- $G_n|B_n$ - irrevocable committed choice

Unlike sequential Prolog, which resolves choices among candidates for execution by don't-know nondeterminism, concurrent logic languages use committed-choice nondeterminism [3]. The syntax of concurrent logic languages is similar to that of Prolog, but the committed-choice control structure is a variant of the Ada-style concurrent select statement:

select $((E_1; G_1)∥B_1, (E_2; G_2)∥B_2, ..., (E_N; G_N)∥B_N)$ *commit to* B_i *if E unifies with* E_i *and* G_i *is satisfied*

The decision to use committed-choice rather than don't-know nondeterminism as the fundamental control structure for concurrent logic languages was motivated in part by considerations of combinatorial tractability. An even more important reason for committed-choice nondeterminism is to permit reactive computation in concurrent logic programs. Because they commit, subgoals need not worry about retracting their effects and may interact freely during computation. Pruning the subgoal tree to a single branch at each reduction step both reduces the number of execution paths to manageable proportions and allows reactive communication among subgoals.

Concurrent logic programs have a *process reading* analogous to the object-oriented (procedural) reading for Prolog. Goals play the role of processes and clauses play the role of operations of a process. Because subgoals commit when they reduce, the analogy between reducing a goal to a set of subgoals and executing a method of a process is much closer for concurrent logic languages than for Prolog. Concurrently executing subgoals can communicate reactively because they can have irrevocable effects just like objects in object-oriented programming languages.

Though pure (reductive) logic programs cannot be reactive, they can be highly concurrent. The lack of reactiveness increases potential concurrency because subgoals are unconstrained by interaction. Reactiveness is orthogonal to concurrency and facilitates concurrency by guaranteeing noninteraction. Committed-choice nondeterminism reduces potential concurrency by eliminating concurrent exploration of alternative subgoals and by permitting reactive interaction.

2.10   Reactiveness Versus Completeness

A logic is sound if every provable theorem is true and complete if every true theorem is provable. A logic programming language is said to be complete if all theorems true in the logic can be proved by computation in the programming language. Pure Prolog is sound and complete in the sense that complete (breadth-first) search of subgoal trees generated by nondeterministic subgoal reduction "proves" any true goal in a finite number of steps. Don't-know nondeterminism in Prolog, which compactly specifies complete search of the subgoal tree, realizes logical completeness.

The incompatibility between object-oriented and logic programming, expressed operationally by don't-know versus don't-care nondeterminism, is essentially an incompatibility between reactiveness and completeness. By pruning the subgoal tree to a single alternative at each reduction step, concurrent logic programs discard branches that may contain solutions. Complete search of the subgoal tree interferes with reactiveness, since goals cannot interact until they determine whether they succeed or fail. The price paid by concurrent logic programming languages for reactiveness and combinatorial tractability is a loss of logical completeness. Both sequential and concurrent languages must choose between completeness and reactiveness. In choosing reactiveness over complete search of the subgoal tree, concurrent logic programming languages sacrifice their logical integrity.

Incompatibility between reactiveness and completeness exemplifies the intuitive incompatibility between complete and careful performance of a task and reactive responsiveness to interruptions or to changes of plan. The incompatibility between single-minded dedication to a task and reactive interruptibility is formulated precisely in terms of computational incompatibility between the quest for logical completeness and reactive responsiveness.

Nonreactiveness is acceptable for small programs and short time intervals in computer systems, just as in real life, but reactiveness is essential for large programs and large time intervals. Concurrent logic programs choose reactiveness over completeness because the program size and temporal longevity of concurrent programs are generally so large that reactiveness is indispensible.

2.11 Declarativeness

A computational specification is *declarative* if it defines *what* is to be computed independently of *how* it is computed.

This definition of *declarativeness* is broader than current usage of this term in the functional and logic programming communities. There are many different ways of specifying what is to be computed independently of how and therefore many ways of being declarative. We distinguish between application-independent declarative specifications that specify what is to be computed for a logic or a programming language and application-dependent declarative specifications that specify what is to be computed for specific objects of an application domain.

Both mathematical and object-oriented notations strive to be declarative, but in very different ways. The functional and pure logic paradigms specify what is to be computed in terms of a mathematical model, while the object-oriented paradigm has a descriptive *what* specification defined in terms of all possible interactions of the object with its clients. We call the logic-programming kind of declarativeness *mathematical* and the object-oriented kind of declarativeness *component-based*. Mathematical declarativeness specifies what is to be computed in terms of a mathematical domain of functions and predicates, while component-based declarativeness specifies what is to be computed in terms of a correspondence with properties of an application domain.

It is no coincidence that both logic and object-oriented programming appeal to the notion of a model to define the meaning (semantics) of a declarative specification. Both logic and object-oriented programs are syntactic specifications whose semantics is specified in a domain of interpretation. Both view the syntactic specification as a model of an independently given but inaccessible semantics. The difference between mathematical and component-based models is that mathematical models are conceptual abstractions while component-based models are rooted in a preexisting application domain. Component-based models start from the application domain and validate their syntactic specification by its correspondence with the application domain, while mathematical models start from a general-purpose syntactic notation and develop the abstract model to satisfy the formal syntactic properties of the general-purpose formalism. The goal of component-based modeling is effective simulation of a preexisting situation, while the goal of mathematical modeling is consistency between a formalism and an abstract domain. The correspondence between a mathematical formalism and its abstract domain need not be constructive provided it preserves consistency, while the component-based systems must constructively simulate the modeled behavior.

The relation between mathematical and component-based modeling is a fundamental question whose interest extends beyond component-based systems. Since component-based modeling is intimately related to scientific modeling (see section 2.3 above), this discussion effectively concerns the relation between scientific and mathematical modeling a question which lies at the intellectual core of scientific scholarship. Computing has the potential of clarifying such issues by expressing abstract arguments in computational terms. By expressing the question of mathematical versus component-based reasoning in terms of the computational paradigms of logic versus object-oriented programming, we frame abstract distinctions in terms of concrete computational consequences and bring them down to earth.

Objects "declare" what is being modeled in terms of the responses of the modeled entity to all potential stimuli:

   entity = forall potential stimuli. response

This modeling philosophy, which is the basis for operationalism in physics and behaviorism in psychology, is also the basis for object modeling and simulation. Objects are in fact defined by a two-level quantification scheme: First operations (procedures) are defined in terms of their response for all possible arguments and then objects are defined in terms of their behavior for all possible operations. Messages first select an operation and then supply arguments to that operation:

   operation = forall arguments. response
   object   = forall messages. response
             = forall operations. (forall arguments. response)

Whereas reasoning specifies *what* in terms of a predefined mathematical model, modeling specifies *what* in terms of responses to all potential stimuli, just like empirical scientific models. The empirical *what* specification of modeling is at least as respectable and declarative as the mathematical *what* specification of reasoning and mathematics.

Consider the following popular divide-and-conquer aphorisms of the 1970s:

   programs = algorithms + data structures [8]
   algorithm = logic + control [2]

Separation of algorithms and data structures is inappropriate for components that combine algorithms with their local data, while separation of logic and control for algorithms is not as central to communication-oriented as to action-oriented models. These divide-and-conquer slogans, though enthusiastically embraced by procedure-oriented and logic programmers, are inappropriate for component-based models. A better dichotomy is the following:

   program = what + how = declarative + imperative = components + messages

Mathematical declarativeness is based on partitioning what is to be computed into algorithms and data, so that it can focus on the declarative specification of algorithms. Component-based models develop a notion of declarativeness for components that combine algorithms with their data and in this way capture empirical properties of objects of the application domain by their notion of declarativeness.

2.12   Reasoning Versus Modeling Revisited

The design space for component-based modeling can be characterized by *what* and a *how* specifications, where *what* is specified by rules (transitions) or components, and *how* is specified by retractiveness or reactiveness (see Figure 1):

> *what* dimension: reasoning by rules versus modeling by components
> *how* dimension: retractiveness (backtracking) versus reactiveness (commitment)

The pure logic paradigm computes by retractive rules while the object-oriented paradigm computes by reactive components:

> pure logic programming (LP)   → retractive + rules
> object-oriented programming (OOP) → reactive + components

Since *what* and *how* specifications determine a two-by-two grid, two other possibilities must be considered:

> concurrent logic programming (CLP)→ reactive + rules
> distributed logic components (DLC) → retractive + components

The combination "reactive + rules" corresponds to concurrent logic programming. The combination "retractive + components" does not currently correspond to any well-established language, but is being investigated [1] in terms of distributed logic components that are retractive because of local don't-know nondeterminism but are distributed in having only a local and not a global state. In particular, unification within a distributed logic component affects only the local state and not the state beyond the component boundary.

The combinations of retractive rules and reactive components appear more stable than the other two combinations. For example, they each have a well-defined declarative semantics. Reactive rule and retractive component systems are hybrid design alternatives having no well-defined declarative semantics.

Concurrent logic programmers claim that reactive rules capture the best of both worlds, while researchers in other language paradigms feel that this approach falls between two stools, being neither logical nor reactive. Distributed logic systems are even less well explored than reactive rule systems. Here again it could be claimed that combining distributed locality and completeness is an advantage, but it is more likely that local completeness will be found to be an inadequate hybrid because it is neither reactive nor a reasoning system.

The notion of declarativeness provides an alternative yardstick for classifying these four alternatives. Reactive modeling is associated with application-dependent (fine-grained) declarative semantics at the per-component level. Retractive reasoning is associated with application independent (coarse-grained) declarative semantics at the level of language constructs. Reactive reasoning and retractive modeling have an operational semantics but no well-defined declarative semantics.

The argument that logic programming is weaker than object-oriented programming as a computational paradigm is inconsistent with Turing's result that both paradigms are equivalent in their computing power. We make the weaker argument that LP is weaker than OOP as a component-based paradigm for programming in the large because it cannot handle reactive communication among components. If this argument is accepted, then it can still be argued that component-based paradigms are not the right model for programming in the large and that the right model will be one in which reasoning and modeling are equivalent in their computational power (for example Turing machines). However, the argument that logic programming (or functional programming) paradigms for programming in the large have not yet succeeded but will succeed becomes inadmissible when communication power is substituted for computation power as the basis for paradigm evaluation.

2.13   From Computational to Software Complexity

We postulate a communication-based notion of software complexity for component-based software technology and make some assertions about the kinds of properties it should have. Computational complexity is a deep subdiscipline of computer science with a precise notion of complexity: the number of instructions executed as a function of problem size. We have no precise metric for software complexity, but show that simple assumptions about the properties of the metric yield a notion of software complexity classes that has remarkable parallels with computational complexity.

Instead of starting with a metric and defining its properties, we define the properties we would like our metric to have. We would problem size for our notion of software complexity to be determined by the number of software components, and to examine the properties of programs for large numbers of components. Software complexity should be defined in terms of a relation between the number of components and the complexity of communication patterns. Metrics based on communication complexity should have asymptotic propeties as the number of components becomes very large, and should accurately reflect limitations of software designers in developing large component-based systems. Like computational complexity, communication complexity models should come into their own for very large values of the size parameter. The idea of measuring complexity in terms of a measure of communication complexity that increases with the number of components is quite concrete, and has interesting consequences that hold for all specific metrics with the given assumed properties.

The assumption that software complexity is dependent only on communication complexity and not on component complexity encourages specifications to have large-granularity components. This accords with the view that very complex situations can be more simply described by large than by small abstractions. Moreover, it suggests that software complexity is not an inherent property of problems but depends on the granularity at which the problem is viewed. Communication complexity automatically has the above *nice* properties that accord with our intuitive notions of complexity. The intuitive nature of the notion of software complexity in turn reinforces the feeling that component-based models with a communication-oriented notion of observability are natural and right.

We wish to consider a class of *nice* software complexity classes, where *nice* may, as a first approximation, be thought of as the software-complexity analog of polynomial time. Though the notion *nice* cannot be precisely defined, this is not a fatal flaw since the theory holds for a broad spectrum of different notions of *nice*. In fact, our theory may be viewed as a "generic theory" parameterized by the notion *nice*.

Let LP be the class of problems that can be formulated as "nice logic programs" and let OO be the problem class expressible as "nice object-oriented programs." We conjecture that OO contains significant problem classes not in LP (those naturally formulated as encapsulated, reactive component-based systems).

Let LO be the union of LP and OO: the class of problems that can be formulated as nice logic or object-oriented programs. The question "Is logic programming practical?" can be reformulated as "LP = LO?". We conjecture that LP is strictly smaller than LO and possibly that LP is included in OO (or equivalently that OO = LO).

Precise definition of the intuitive notion of *nice programs* is probably impossible, just as is defining classes like *table* by finite sets of attributes. The intuitive notion of *nice*, like the class *table*, is a *natural kind* not definable in terms of other kinds of things. However, just as the class of tables can be adequately approximated by a finite set of properties, so we conjecture that sets of properties can approximate the component-based notion of niceness sufficiently to *prove* relations like OO ≠ LP).

Since *nice* is a parameter, we have the freedom to choose a notion of *nice* with "nice" properties. Relations between software complexity classes could be viewed as defining properties of a chosen notion of *nice* rather than as potential properties of a preexisting notion of niceness. The property OO ≠ LP can be viewed as a defining property of niceness rather than a provable property of a specific notion of niceness. A class FP of *nice functional programs* could be introduced with the requirement that LP = FP be a defining property (every nice functional program has a nice logic program and vice versa).

The fact that "niceness" can be approximated makes this theory tractable and interesting. Though intuitive niceness may be an inherently unrepresentable Platonic ideal, approximate niceness, like approximate real numbers, is sufficient for practical purposes. Component-based models provide a basis for practical discrimination among methodologies for "nice" programming.

2.14 LP-Completeness

We do not need a specific notion of niceness to explore the properties of our family of notions of niceness. To illustrate this we explore the hypothesis that LP ≠ OO by introducing a notion of LP-completeness that parallels NP-completeness and identifying a family of LP-complete problems that provide evidence for LP $\neq$ OO.

The problem "P = NP?" has given rise to a class of NP-complete problems such that solving any one of these problems by an algorithm in P implies that P = NP. The fact that no NP-complete problem has yet been solved provides evidence for the belief that P is not equal to NP. We will define a class of LP-complete problems such that solving any one of them implies LP = LO and suggest that failure to solve any one of these problems provides evidence for their inherent intractability and for the hypothesis that LP $\neq$ LO. Since LO is the union of LP and OO, this in turn implies that LP $\neq$ LO.

It turns out (fortuitously) that there is a class of LP-complete problems such that solving any problem in the class implies that LP = LO. This class can be intuitively defined as problems that imply the reduction of computation or empirical modeling to logic. They include the problem of automatic program verification, the problem of developing a universal logic programming language, and possibly the reduction to logic of problems in natural language comprehension and robotics.

The question "LP = LO?", like "P = NP?," is concerned with the equivalence of problem classes associated with paradigms of computation. Moreover, the evidence that LP is not equal to OO is of precisely the same nature as the evidence that P is not equal to NP. The fact that no problem in LP has yet been solved provides evidence for LP $\neq$ LO just as the fact that no problem in NP has yet been reduced to P provides evidence that P $\neq$ NP.

A formal proof that the problems of automatic verification and developing a universal logic language are reducible to each other would require a more precise definition of these problems and is beyond the scope of this paper, but an informal demonstration runs as follows. Solving the automatic verification problem provides a method of translating computational formalisms to logic and thereby into a logic programming lanmguage. Conversely, developing a practical, universal logic programming language would provide a means of direct logical specification for large interactive computations. Solving either problem would provide an effective means reducing computational to logical specifications, and a practical solution of one of them would provide a basis for a practical solution of the other.

The relation of the above problems to natural language comprehension and robotics problems is more distant because these problems are not in LO unless natural language comprehension is computable. They are representative of a more ambitious class of *Turing-Test-Complete* problems whose solution would demonstrate practicality of the Turing test and of the reducibility of intelligence to computation. Automatic program verification and universal logic programming languages definitely appear to be in the class of LP-complete problems, while natural language comprehension and robotics are only LP-complete if intelligence is reducible to computation.

Because of our evidence that the problem of reducing computation to logic is intractable, it is very unlikely that LP = LO for any reasonable notion of niceness. The fact that problems like program verification and natural language understanding resist reduction to logic provides evidence against LP = LO. If, as seems likely, LP is not equal to LO, then LP-complete problems like program verification are not merely hard but inherently unsolvable.

Software complexity, like computational complexity, refines the notion of Turing com-

putability. But the refinement classes for software complexity differ from those for computational complexity, being related to communication criteria rather than to computation
time. Notions of niceness for different problem-solving paradigms can in principle lead to
different refinements of the class of computable functions. We are particularly interested
in LP, OO, and other component-based notions of niceness.

Since an NP-complete problem is defined as one whose solution would imply P = NP,
P is an effective parameter and a more complete characterization of NP-completeness
should really be (P, NP)-completeness. The corresponding notion for software complexity likewise requires two parameters. A problem will be called (X, Y)-complete for
complexity classes (X, Y) if its solution implies that X = Y. The term "(X, Y)-complete"
can be abbreviated to X-complete or Y-complete if the omitted class is implied by the
context. Thus, (P, NP)-complete is usually abbreviated by NP-complete and (LP, LO)-
complete has been abbreviated by LP-complete in our discussions of software complexity
above. Though LO-complete is more directly analogous to NP-complete, LP-complete is
acceptable since LO is implied by the context.

These definitions suggest a deep analogy between "computational complexity" and
"software complexity". The weakness of the analogy lies in its imprecise notion of "nice"
and imprecise "software complexity classes" like OO, LP, and LO. However, the remarkable resilience of these definitions for unspecified notions of "nice" indicates that the
theory has a robust structure. Computational complexity may be viewed as one instance
of a parameterized class of theories that includes theories of software complexity as well
as theories of computational complexity. The problem "P = NP?" is isomorphic to a
family of problems "LP = LO?" for different notions of "nice."

There is a relationship between computational complexity classes defined by "time of
execution" and software complexity measures defined by "niceness":

computational complexity → time of execution software complexity → niceness

The classes NP and LP are related because both are defined in terms of don't-know
nondeterminism. The computational complexity of proofs in nice logic programs is in
NP, though generally not in P.

The deterministic computational complexity class P is probably smaller than NP, while
the deterministic software complexity class LO is probably larger than LP. Computational
complexity views nondeterminism as a mechanism for increasing computational power,
while software complexity views nondeterminism as a mechanism that restricts reactiveness. Further exploration of this contravariance between computational and software
complexity is an interesting research question.

Another relation between NP-completeness and our study of component-based software
systems arises from the fact that reasoning systems are classic examples of NP-complete
systems. The tradeoff between reactiveness and logical completeness for nondeterministic
reasoning systems can be reinterpreted as a warning that the implementation of nondeterminism by retractiveness in NP-complete systems restricts communication flexibility.
The loss of communication power associated with the transition from P to NP deserves
further study.

2.15   Towards Practical Component-Based Technology

The primitive building blocks of component-based systems are more complex than primitive units of state transition systems. Software components have more degrees of freedom than instructions or statements of a programming language for several reasons:

semantic complexity: instructions represent state transitions while components are semantically more complex, representing a variety of different potential procedural effects paramaterized by an internal state

interface complexity: the interface specification of components can be more complex and varied than an instruction specification

modeling complexity: the entities being modeled by components can be more complex and varied than individual programming language instructions

Relations among components are likewise more complex than relations among state transition primitives; component composition is not as well defined as sequential statement composition. Because of the greater complexity of component-based systems their analysis is not as neat as that of state transition systems. There is no analog of automata theory or algorithm analysis for component-based systems. Component-based software technology is a vast research area whose surface has hardly been scratched. Research on component-based systems requires a phase of empirical data gathering to provide a basis for the development of models that account for the data. We identify four broad areas of work that can contribute to the practical development of component-based software technology:

Exploring and mapping the component-based design space.

The component-based design space can be explored by assembling a database of component-based systems that are representative of distinct regions of the design space. We have started this task by choosing eight initial representative systems: objects, Ada, actors, megaprogramming, Hermes, Linda, Hypertext, and Prolog (see section 2.4 and the appendix). A more complete database would include multidatabases, module interconnection formalisms and a total of between 30 and 50 representative systems. In developing such a database some standard ways of describing systems will emerge. The system description should not be too stereotypical, leaving some room for capturing the individuality of each system, but should include a standard format that allows systematic comparisons. We have developed descriptions for the eight initial representative systems and hope to refine our descriptions of the existing systems as well as add new ones.

Developing component-based models of computation.

Component-based models of computation should borrow from existing formal models such as CCS and the π-calculus as well as from system descriptions in the database and standardization attempts like OMG. A balance between precision and practicality is needed to describe real systems in a way that is precise, useful, and conceptually uniform. Formal techniques such as those of the π-calculus will not take us very far and we will have to rely on operational semantics and other techniques of systematic description.

Reflective models will be useful in capturing the structure of many different models and examining tradeoffs between them.

Developing requirements for component-based systems.

Requirements for components can be developed by choosing a set of categories and then considering alternative specific requirements in each category. Both the categories and the specific requirements will be suggested in large measure by attributes of representative systems in the database. This approach is similar to that taken during the development of Ada requirements, where categories like types, control structures, subprograms, parallelism, and libraries were chosen by abstraction from current languages, and specific requirements for each category were chosen to correct perceived deficiencies in existing languages like Pascal.

Requirements for software components will have a different flavor from Ada requirements because of the focus on communication rather than computation. Interfaces may well prove to be the dominant category, but internal component structure, communication and composition, debugging, and user interfaces will also be included. Here is a provisional list of categories for requirements:

- interfaces: protocols, system interfaces, user interfaces
- module interconnection: static versus dynamic, point-to-point versus patterns
- heterogeneity: mediated communication, transduction
- module composition: interface composition, program composition
- constraints: for synchronization, integrity, coordination
- encapsulation, ontologies, local knowledge
- databases, multidatabases, transactions, atomicity
- debugging, tracing, monitoring, reproducibility, recovery
- nondeterminism, logic components, backtracking

Developing a testbed for experimenting with component-based designs.

It is unlikely that we will converge in the short term on a specific set of component-based requirements, so that a testbed for experimenting with tradeoffs among requirements might be a more important tool than developing a specific component-based language. Such a testbed would contain tools for rapid prototyping of component-based design requirements and could teach us much about the underlying operational semantics of component-based design alternatives. A reflective architecture for the testbed could be useful in providing a causally connected model for experimenting with design alternatives.

The first of these areas of work is empirical, the second abstracts from empirical data to develop a model, the third uses the data and model to develop practical requirements and designs, and the fourth provides for empirical testing of designs. These four tasks should help us to understand the component-based design space, tradeoffs among alternatives in the design space, and requirements for good design.

We have indicated some of the issues that must be addressed in developing a component-based software technology, recognizing that this subject is complex. Whereas the complexity of state transitions derives from the world of mathematics and computing, the complexity of components derives from the world that is being modeled and cannot be captured by notions of logic or mathematics that are independent of the modeled world. Component-based software technology provides systematic mechanisms for directly relating computational models to the application domain that is being modeled.

References

[1]   Seif Haridi and Sverker Janson. "Kernel Andora Prolog and its Computation Model," *ICLP '91 Proceedings*.

[2]   Robert Kowalski. "Algorithms = Logic + Control," *CACM*, July 1979.

[3]   Ehud Shapiro. "The Family of Concurrent Programming Languages," *Computing Surveys*, September, 1989.

[4]   Alan Turing. *Computing Machinary and Intelligence, Mind*, 1950.

[5]   Peter Wegner. Object-Oriented Versus Logic Programming, *Proc International Conference on Fifth-Generation Computing*, Tokyo, June 1992.

[6]   Peter Wegner. Dimensions of Object-Oriented Modeling, *IEEE Computer*, October 1992.

[7]   Peter Wegner. Design Issues for Object-Based Concurrency, in *Object-Based Concurrent Programming*, Eds Tokoro, Nierstrasz, Wegner, Springer Verlag Lecture Notes in Computer Science #612, 1992.

[8]   Niklaus Wirth. Algorithms + Data Structures = Programs, Prentice-Hall, 1976.

Appendix: Rationalism Versus Empiricism

Plato, in ascribing greater reality to abstract ideas than to real objects, was a rationalist, while Aristotle's empiricist belief in the reality of objects motivated him to engage in empirical investigations, even though he was the father of the syllogism.

Descartes' *cogito ergo sum* succinctly asserts the rationalist credo that thinking is the basis of existence. Descartes' success in reducing geometry to arithmetic spurred more ambitious rationalist efforts to reduce empirical sciences and mathematics to logic. Logic programming is Cartesian in its attempt to reduce computation to logic.

Hume was called an empiricist because he showed that inductive inference and causality could not be proved deductively, thereby demonstrating the limitations of rationalism. Kant, "roused from his dogmatic slumbers" by Hume, wrote the *Critique of Pure Reason* to show the limitations of pure reason as a tool of thought. The emergence of modern science in the eighteenth and nineteenth centuries was motivated by empiricism, but rationalist revivals continued to have great appeal. Hegel, whose "dialectical logic" extended the reach of "pure reason" beyond its legitimate domain, profoundly influenced both social philosophers like Marx and mathematical philosophers like Russell. George Boole, in calling his logic treatise *The Laws of Thought*, demonstrated that rationalism was very much alive in the mid-19th century.

The influence of Frege, Russell, and Hilbert led to rationalist (formalist) domination of mathematics in the early 20th century. However, Godel incompleteness, Turing noncomputability, and quantum-theoretic uncertainty demonstrated theoretical limitations of mathematics, computation, and physics. Godel's incompleteness result (that arithmetic cannot be expressed by logic) demonstrates the impossibility of Hilbert's formalist mathematics program. Turing noncomputability shows that certain functions cannot be computed, while quantum-theoretic uncertainty shows that the "real world" cannot be mechanically modeled. The reaction against formalism is exemplified by Von Neumann, who was a disciple of Hilbert in his early years but devoted his later years to computing.

The evolution of artificial intelligence has been dominated by the conflict between rationalism and empiricism. The early rationalist optimism that intelligence could be realized by a *general problem solver* gave way in the 1970s to an empiricist emphasis on domain-dependent knowledge representation. Logic-based AI is rationalist, while low-level vision and expert systems are empiricist.

The debate during the early 1970s concerning declarative versus procedural knowledge representation was resolved in a rationalist manner in favor of the predicate calculus. Turing's rationalist hypothesis that intelligence is reducible to (and achievable by) computation dominated the 1960s and 1970s, while distributed and connectionist models staged a comeback in the 1980s. The distributed artificial intelligence view that problem solving is a cooperative activity among distributed agents (as in Minsky's *The Society of Mind*) is empiricist rather than rationalist.

In the programming languages field the debate between rationalism and empiricism has focused on logic versus object-oriented languages. Early optimism that programming languages can describe applications according to rationalist principles is giving way to the realization that reasoning is a restricted form of modeling that cannot easily handle changes in modeling requirements. There is no golden rule, silver bullet, or logical inference system that can impose rationalist order on empirical chaos, even after the knowledge has been acquired. Though some problems have an inherently inferential structure, modeling and simulation of application domains and especially the evolution and management of such models, can be better handled by object-oriented than by logic programming. Object-oriented programming imposes a scalable, decentralized, divide-and-conquer structure on computations that becomes a dominant factor in managing program complexity as programs become very large.

3 A Survey of Logic Programming-Based Object-Oriented Languages

Andrew Davison

Languages which augment logic programming (LP) with object-oriented programming (OOP) features are surveyed by considering how they deal with the representation of objects and classes, message passing, state, inheritance, and their relationship with other paradigms. To further clarify the structure of the survey, the languages are subdivided into four groups based on different implementation approaches. These are called the clauses view, the committed choice process view, the backtracking process view, and the meta-interpretation view. After the language issues have been discussed, the advantages and disadvantages of these four views are summarised, and the paper concludes with some speculation on future directions for the field. Many of the concepts of OOP and LP are explained during the discussion, although some knowledge of the paradigms is assumed. However, the ideas behind concurrent LP are described in some detail.

Introduction

In the last few years, a large number of languages have been proposed which combine logic programming (LP) and object-oriented programming (OOP). The intention of this paper is to survey these languages by looking at the design and implementation issues behind those which might be termed *LP-based OOP languages*.

In the majority of cases, the LP component of these languages is Prolog, but other kinds of LP languages are considered. The usual meaning of OOP is relaxed so that languages such as T-Prolog [73], and Delta Prolog [160] can be discussed, although normally they are not considered to be object-oriented. Essentially, any LP language which offers some form of encapsulated entity that communicates via message passing is considered to be object-oriented in this paper. However, most emphasis will be placed on languages which contain other OOP features, such as inheritance and self communication.

One group of languages excluded from this discussion are the OOP and LP interface languages, where the two paradigms are kept separate and a more or less sophisticated interface is defined between them [17, 183, 93]. An interesting example of such an approach is an OOP system for window environments called PCE, which is linked to Prolog via a small set of predefined commands [7]. High level user interfaces can be built using these commands, which represent the various entities on the screen as objects. A commercial version of PCE, called ProWindows, has been developed which supports abstraction, inheritance, polymorphism and message passing [163].

The other group not described are the object-based LP languages, which extend OOP languages to support LP features. To this author's knowledge, only two languages of this type exist; one is called ALF [132], and the other is Prolog/V [59]. They both encorporate aspects from Prolog by programming them in Smalltalk. For example, predicates are defined as subclasses of a `Predicate` class, and unification is a method in the class `Object`. An important design goal for ALF was to ensure that any object in Smalltalk could be a term, and vice versa. ALF is strongly influenced by LOGIN [4], an LP language augmented with inheritance.

In this paper, LP-based object-oriented languages will be discussed by examining five issues related to their design and implementation:

- Object and Class Representation
- Message Passing
- State
- Inheritance
- Relationship with Other Paradigms

The representation of objects and classes, message passing, state, and inheritance are examined because of their central roles in OOP. All LP-based object-oriented languages combine the LP and OOP paradigms, but a few also subscribe to other paradigms which affect the language. For this reason, the fifth design issue is included.

As a further structuring device, each issue will be analyzed with respect to four implementation approaches:

- the clauses view
- the committed choice process view
- the backtracking process view
- the meta-interpretation view

These four categories were motivated by similar ones proposed in various papers [117, 89, 120], and will be described briefly in section 2. Each view will be more closely examined in the design issue sections, and their advantages and disadvantages summarised in section 8. Initially, however, section 1 will consider the reasons for combining OOP and LP.

It is assumed that the reader is familiar with LP concepts and Prolog, and has some knowledge of OOP, although certain aspects of these will be discussed in the text. An excellent introduction to LP has been written by Sterling and Shapiro, while Stefik, Bobrow and Thomas have produced overviews of OOP [180, 179, 188]. A paper by Wegner, which classifies features of OOP, is also recommended [198].

When references are cited in the text to support a statement, not all the relevant languages will necessarily be included, only those which highlight the point in a clear manner.

3.1 Reasons for Combining OOP and LP

Listed below are a number of reasons for combining the two paradigms. Sections 1.1 and 1.2 describe the benefits to LP of adding object-oriented features. Sections 1.3, 1.4, 1.5 and 1.6 outline benefits of LP to OOP. Section 1.7 describes some of the novel applications of LP-based OOP languages.

3.1.1   The OOP Paradigm

The main advantage of OOP for LP is the introduction of the OOP paradigm as a guiding principle for writing programs. This offers a simple but powerful model for encoding applications as computational entities, or objects, which communicate with each other via message passing. The presence of clearly defined entities is probably the reason why object-oriented systems are so easy to visualise.

An object is usually an instance of a template, or class, with the behaviour of the class but its own data (state). The class encapsulation mechanism means that its internal workings can be ignored when considering its function, and instead it can be characterised by the set of messages which it will accept. This allows each class to have a well defined interface, and polymorphism means that an interface can be shared by many classes. Ease of class reuse, via inheritance, is also a valuable property. These features encourage programming by experimentation, and fast prototyping.

3.1.2   Programming in the Large

The class construct removes one of the weaknesses of LP: its lack of structure for programming in the large, due to its reliance on the predicate as its main structuring mechanism.

Typically, the alternative to the class has been a module mechanism, which exists in two main forms: those based on a partitioned name space [182, 41], and those based on a partitioned predicate space [36].

In the name space approach, modules import and export constant symbols, including predicate names. This can lead to lengthy import and export lists, and increases the possibility of name clashes when different modules export the same name. It can also be argued that the predicate is the basic computational unit, implying that a name space partition is at too low a level.

A partitioned predicate space also has some problems, mainly when metalogical predicates such as `assert`, `retract` or `call` are used. A well known example is:

```
X =.. [foo, a, b], call(X)
```

The problem with this is that the definition of the `foo` predicate may reside either in the module containing `call`, or in the module which exports the `foo` symbol.

At the very least, a module system must specify how communication is to take place between modules, and how modules can be reused in different applications. These problems are solved easily by using the OOP paradigm.

A current area of research is concerned with the use of intuitionistic logic for the development of languages with modularity *and* a clean semantics. Miller's work typifies this approach, where ordinary logic programs can include implication goals in the bodies of Horn clauses and in queries. An implication goal has the form $D \supset G$ (G is a goal, D a set of clauses called a module). In order to solve G, the module D is loaded prior to the derivation of G and unloaded after [137]. In recent work, universal quantification is permitted on clauses and goals, which allows predicate hiding and variable inheritance [138, 150]. Related work can be found in [76, 146]. The Moscowitz and Shapiro paper contains a good introduction to this area.

Perhaps the main difference between a module and a class is that the latter is a collection of operations and *state*, and so allows a programmer to deal with state changes within the object-oriented formalism. However, it has been shown that state can be supported in an intuitionistic LP language (see section 5.1) [88].

3.1.3   Expressive Relationships

LP is especially suited for defining relationships between entities by utilising predicates [154]. Examples include master/servant, lender/borrower, spatial, temporal, grammar-based, family hierarchies and constraints. Conventional OOP language have few ways of specifying relationships between classes, except by inheritance.

3.1.4   Flexible Data Access

The don't know non-determinism found in many LP languages is useful for dealing with search problems. Don't care non-determinism, present in concurrent LP languages, also offers powerful search capabilities but is arguably less versatile because of the absence of backtracking.

The logical variable can be utilised for such things as assignment, testing, data construction, and various forms of parameter passing.

3.1.5   Formal Semantics

Most OOP languages do not have a formal semantics, although semantics have been developed for simpler languages, such as those based on actors which can be viewed as object-oriented [1]. Nevertheless, valid semantic insights can be gained by representing an OOP language as a form of LP language [78, 129].

3.1.6   Power for specifying Concurrency

The key advantage of concurrent LP for OOP is the availability of simple ways to specify concurrency, synchronisation, and state change. Concurrent LP also offers committed choice non-determinism which may, in certain situations, be more suited for coding simulations and systems software than don't know non-determinism. This is because such programs should only be able to undo actions explicitly, which is not the case when backtracking is available.

3.1.7   Usefulness for applications

A measure of the utility of a language, and indeed of a programming paradigm, is whether worthwhile programs can be written using it. Using such a measure, LP-based object-oriented languages have proved very successful.

McCabe has investigated object-oriented graphics by representing simple forms, such as lines and circles, using objects [130]. These can be grouped together to create more complex pictures, and operations applied to them via messages.

ESP has been used to implement the SIMPOS operating system for the PSI Machine [36]. Other interesting applications written in this language, including a task modelling package for office support [171] and a parser [141]. In fact, several languages have been utilised for parsing programs [209, 93].

A number of applications have been built using Polka [54], including a blackboard problem solver [50], simulation tools [51], a budget management system [52], and several programming environment utilities [47].

Some other interesting OOP applications include a system configuration language, and a query-the-user expert system [134], while Coscia discusses debuggers and programming with uncertainty [46]. Simulation examples are popular [73, 11]. Fukunaga and Hirose describe a colour graphics oriented user interface, and also an expert system for annotating assembler programs [71]. A diagnostic system for glaucoma is encoded with LOOKS [142]. The contextual Prolog features of units (modules) and contexts (linear hierarchies of units) are employed as software engineering tools to develop a programming environment for the language in [135].

See section 9.6 for a discussion of possible future application areas.

3.2   Four Implementation Views

The important attributes of each implementation view for representing classes, objects, message passing, state, and inheritance will be described. Further information on these issues will be supplied in later sections, which will allow their strengths and weaknesses to be assessed.

3.2.1   The Clauses View

Languages which subscribe to the clauses view combine OOP and LP by equating a class with a set of clauses which represent its methods.

An instance of a class is created by asserting new clauses as a means of recording its state. As the state of the instance changes, these clauses are retracted and new clauses asserted in their place. The state clauses for different instances are distinguished by a unique *instance name* argument in each clause.

A message sent to an instance is translated into a goal which is applied to the clauses representing the class. The goal will contain the instance name so that the relevant state clauses can be manipulated.

Inheritance is implemented by a clause (or clauses) which redirects an unanswered message to the inherited class (or classes). Inheritance, in this context, is more accurately described as delegation, or message forwarding.

It is possible to treat a class as an abstract data type (ADT). In the OOP context, an ADT is a behaviour specification that can be used to generate object instances having that behaviour. This allows a large body of work on the semantics of types to be applied to OOP [78]. It may also help to guide equivalence preserving program transformations for optimisations, and aid debugging and verification. However, the ADT metaphor breaks down when the `assert` and `retract` encoding of state is utilised.

3.2.2 The Process View

The process view is predominately used by concurrent LP-based OOP languages, but languages based on AND-parallel versions of Prolog also utilise a version of it. The two types will be distinguished by being called the committed choice and backtracking process views respectively. The names highlight the distinction between how the two kinds of process search their solution space.

3.2.2.1 The Committed Choice Process View

A program in a concurrent LP language is a collection of clauses written using Horn clause logic, but the computation involves the parallel evaluation of a goal with respect to these clauses. It is this parallel evaluation, and in particular the AND- and OR-parallelism exhibited, that differentiates a concurrent logic program from one written in a sequential logic programming language such as Prolog.

Another way of distinguishing concurrent and sequential logic programming languages is by their underlying interpretation. Both paradigms allow programs to have a declarative and procedural interpretation. In concurrent logic programming, a third interpretation is possible where a conjunction of goals can be regarded as a system of concurrent processes. Each process is an executing recursive predicate, and the processes communicate by partially instantiating shared variables. This process interpretation is the basis of all the languages which combine OOP and concurrent LP.

A paper by Shapiro and Takeuchi was the first to investigate the connections between concurrent LP and OOP [176]. Their model can be summarised by the following points:

1. An object can be represented as a process which calls itself recursively and holds its internal state in unshared arguments.

2. Objects communicate with each other by instantiating shared variables.

3. An object becomes active when it receives a message, otherwise it is suspended.

4. An object instance is created by process reduction.

5. A response to a message can be achieved by binding a shared variable in the message.

6. Inheritance is implemented by forwarding unrecognised messages to another object. As with the clauses view, it would be more correct to call this mechanism delegation.

3.2.2.2 The Backtracking Process View

A network of objects is represented by a conjunction of goals executing in AND-parallel, one goal for each object. An object is represented by a recursive predicate, in a similar way to in the Shapiro and Takeuchi model. However, a predicate is a set of sequential clauses and so an object will not exhibit the multi-threaded properties of a concurrent LP-based object. Shared logical variables are sometimes used to implement message passing (and inheritance), but generally a much wider variety of message passing techniques are utilised. This is a reflection on the number of approaches which the underlying LP languages use for communication.

One important problem with AND-parallel objects based on sequential LP is what to do when backtracking occurs. Backtracking in OOP is related to three kinds of actions: state changes, object creation and message sends, and problems arise out of how to undo these things, if at all, when backtracking causes the computation to roll back over them.

3.2.3   The Meta-interpretation View

The views described above allow OOP features to be translated into LP constructs at compile time. At run time, this means that objects, message passing, and other OOP functionality are supported by the LP run time environment.

Greater flexibility is possible if the execution of objects, message passing, and so on, can be defined and controlled inside the language. This is possible if classes can be manipulated as first order citizens, and meta-interpreters can be written for the language.

An advantage of this type of view is the ability to support multiple representations, because different meta-interpreters can be developed to support different formalisms. Other advantages include the ease of encoding protection mechanisms for classes, various forms of communication protocols, inheritance, and exception mechanisms [16, 122, 133].

The power of the meta-interpretation view is only limited by the expressibility of the meta-interpreter, and is general enough so that both the clauses and process views can be simulated.

Generally, classes and objects are represented by terms, message passing corresponds to goal reduction, and inheritance is dealt with by clauses which specify that *class* terms are related.

3.3   Object and Class Representation

A class is usually mapped to a set of Horn clauses in the underlying LP language. However, there are more varied mappings possible for instances of classes (objects), including sets of clauses, processes, or terms.

3.3.1   The Clauses View Representation

At the language level, the clauses (methods) of a class are grouped together and labelled with a Prolog term which includes its name and any parameters used by the clauses. Syntax for this might be:

```
class_name(Parameters) [Clauses].
```

e.g.

```
square(Length) [ area(Area) if Area is Length * Length. ].
```

Note that the clause in the class is represented by a Horn clause – a common design decision. The class can be read as representing a `square` which has one clause for calculating its area.

An instance is simply an invocation of a class with some (or all) of the parameters of the label bound. For example, instances of `square` can be assigned different lengths through the `Length` parameter.

A common practice is to use the instantiated label as the name of the instance, which means that the instance can be manipulated inside predicates and classes. For example, an instance of the `square` class, whose length is 10, can be referred to by the label:

```
square(10)
```

An obvious problem with such a label is that it precludes the creation of another `square` instance with a length of 10. The normal solution is to include a parameter which is instantiated to a unique value:

```
square(square1, 10)
```

The instance's name is `square1`, and has a length of 10.

Since classes and instances can both be alluded to by labels, the distinction between them can be blurred, and several language do not distinguish between them at all; instead preferring to call everything an object [154, 148].

The simplest compilation strategy for the clauses view is to convert a label into a predicate, and transform the class clauses into arguments of the clauses of that predicate [129]. Thus:

```
square(Length) [ r if s.
                 s if t. ].
```

becomes:

```
square(Length, r) if square(Length, s).
square(Length, s) if square(Length, t).
```

This will be known as the *label/predicate* translation technique in later sections. The transformation of the right hand side of a class clause is sometimes simpler if any of the body goals is a built-in operation, as illustrated below:

```
square(Length) [ area(Area) if Area is Length * Length. ].
```

becomes:

```
square(Length, area(Area)) if Area is Length * Length.
```

An alternative to the label/predicate transformation is to map the label of a class onto a new argument in each of its clauses, which then become Horn clauses [209, 11]. Thus:

```
square(Length) [ r if s.
                 s if t. ].
```

becomes:

```
r(square(Length)) if s(square(Length)).
s(square(Length)) if t(square(Length)).
```

This will be known as the *label/argument* translation technique in later sections. As with the label/predicate approach, if the right hand side of a clause contains a call to a built-in, then the translation can be less complicated:

```
square(Length) [ area(Area) if Area is Length * Length ].
```

becomes:

```
area(square(Length), Area) if Area is Length * Length.
```

There is not much to choose between the two translation techniques, although the label/predicate translation preserves the class name as the predicate name, which can make predicate generation slightly easier. Label/argument translation may require the rearrangement of clauses so that similarly named ones are grouped together. However, the main difference between the two translation strategies becomes apparent when considering inheritance (see section 6.1).

Another way of representing a class is by using the module constructs of the LP language [64, 190]. This requires that module names can be passed as arguments of predicates, and it is also useful if a module can be parameterised, although import lists can be used instead.

As might be expected, these translation techniques lend themselves to implementation by compilation, although there are benefits to be gained by extending the underlying Prolog system to directly support classes and objects [129, 44]. These benefits include better compilation because local and global variables can be distinguished, and because most computation is local to a class. Also, method indexing can be optimised.

Several companies have developed graphical environments for representing classes, objects and the relationships between them. For instance, Prolog++ has MacObject [125], and users of Quintec-Prolog can utilise a graphical object hierarchy browser [162].

The above discussion suggests that the clauses view is based solely on the translation of object-oriented features into LP constructs, allowing the translated program to be run in a 'vanilla' LP environment. However, many systems do not completely compile away the OOP notation, augmenting the run time system instead [209, 71, 115]. A common example of this is the direct manipulation of the inheritance information for an object at run time, which is discussed further in section 6.1.

3.3.2 The Committed Choice Process View Representation

A discussion of this approach will require some knowledge of a concurrent LP language. This paper will utilise Parlog, since it has been used as the basis of an OOP language [54]. For information on other concurrent LP languages, the survey by Shapiro can be consulted [175].

3.3.2.1 An Overview of Parlog Parlog differs from Prolog in three important respects: concurrent evaluation, don't care non-determinism and its (optional) use of mode declarations to specify communication constraints on shared variables.

A Parlog clause is a Horn clause optionally augmented with a commit operator, ':', which is used to separate the right hand side of the clause into a conjunction of guard conditions and a conjunction of body conditions:

```
r(t1, ..., tk) <- <guard conditions> : <body conditions>
```

where t1, ..., tk are argument terms. A clause without any <guard conditions> does not need to include a commit operator ':' between the '<-' and its <body conditions>. Both the <guard conditions> and the <body conditions> are conjunctions of predicate calls. There are two types of conjunction: the parallel ',' (c1 , c2) in which the conjuncts c1 and c2 are evaluated concurrently and the sequential '&' (c1 & c2) where c2 will only be evaluated when c1 has successfully terminated. The use of the parallel conjunction allows Parlog to display AND-parallelism in the execution of its goals.

During the evaluation of a call r(t1',..., tk'), all of the clauses for the predicate r can be searched in parallel for a candidate clause. The above clause is a candidate clause if the head r(t1,...,tk) matches the call r(t1',..., tk') *and* the guard succeeds. It is a non-candidate if the match or the guard fails. If all clauses are non-candidates the call fails, otherwise one of the candidate clauses is selected and the call is reduced to the substitution instance of the body of that clause. There is no backtracking on the choice of candidate clause since we *don't care* which candidate clause is selected.

The absence of backtracking in Parlog is partially compensated for by guard tests which should be used as a means of ensuring that the correct clause is chosen.

The search for a candidate clause can be controlled by using either the parallel clause search operator '.' or the sequential clause search operator ';' between clauses. For instance, if a predicate is defined by the clauses:

```
clause1.
clause2;
clause3.
```

Then, clause3 will not be tried for candidacy until both clause1 and clause2 have been found to be non-candidate clauses. The presence of the parallel search operator allows Parlog to display OR-parallelism during the search for a candidate clause.

A Parlog predicate definition may have a mode declaration associated with it, which states whether each argument is input (?) or output (^). For example, the predicate merge has the mode (?, ?, ^) to merge lists X and Y to create list Z:

```
mode merge(?, ?, ^).
merge([Element|X], Y, [Element|Z]) <-    % X element output on Z
    merge(X, Y, Z).
merge(X, [Element|Y], [Element|Z]) <-    % Y element output on Z
    merge(X, Y, Z).
merge([], Y, Y).                          % X finished, output Y
merge(X, [], X).                          % Y finished, output X
```

Syntax similar to that of Edinburgh Prolog is used for program examples throughout [42].

The first clause places an element from the X list onto the Z list, while the second does a similar task for an element from the Y list. The parallel search operator between these two clauses means that a non-deterministic choice will be made between them if there is a `merge` call with elements on both X and Y. The third clause allows Y to become the remaining part of the Z list by unification since the X list has terminated. Similarly, X becomes the rest of the Z list when the Y list is exhausted.

A query for `merge` might be:

```
<- merge([1, 2, 3|X], [a, b, c|Y], Z).
```

which may produce the binding:

```
Z = [1, a, b, 2, 3, c|_]
```

The '_' as the tail of the list is actually an uninstantiated variable which indicates that the list is only partially instantiated because the X and Y lists are not fully bound.

Non-variable terms that appear in input argument positions in the head of a clause can only be used for input matching. If an argument of the call is not sufficiently instantiated for an input match to succeed, the attempt to use the clause suspends until some other process further instantiates the input argument of the call. For example, the first clause for `merge` has `[Element|X]` in its first input argument position. Until the call has a list or partial list structure of the form `[Element|X]` in the first argument position the first clause is suspended. If all clauses for a call are suspended, the call suspends but a candidate clause can be selected even if there are other, suspended, clauses.

More details on Parlog can be found in [39, 81, 45].

3.3.2.2   Concurrent LP and OOP   Shapiro and Takeuchi's model (discussed in section 2.2.1) allows a Parlog predicate to be viewed as a template, or class. This will be illustrated by looking at a small predicate called `filestore`. It can store file information indexed by a key, and retrieve it when prompted with the key. The predicate can also ignore incorrect requests and report errors.

```
mode filestore(?, ?, ^).
filestore([], Files, []).        % terminate the program
filestore([add(Key, File)|Input], Files, Errors) <-
  % add a file with a key to the store
  filestore(Input, [ file(Key, File)|Files], Errors).
filestore([extract(Key, File, Ok)|Input], Files, Errors) <-
  % extract a file successfully
  extract_file(Key, F, Files, NewFiles) :
  Ok = done, File = F,
  filestore(Input, NewFiles, Errors);
filestore([extract(Key, File, Ok)|Input], Files, Errors) <-
  % file extraction error
  Ok = no_entry_for(Key),
  filestore( Input, Files, Errors);
filestore([Msg|Input], Files, [not_understood(Msg)|Errors]) <-
  % ignore any other messages
  filestore(Input, Files, Errors).
```

```
mode extract_file(?, ^, ?, ^).
% only mode given for brevity
```

When `filestore` is invoked, a process is created by virtue of the recursive nature of the clauses. In OOP terminology, this process can be viewed as an object. This object has two input arguments and one output argument.

At run time, the first argument is treated as a list and partially instantiated with terms which act as input messages. Thus, the list under construction is being treated like an input message stream.

The second argument is used to store the key-file terms sent to the object, and so can be thought of as a state variable.

The last `filestore` clause partially instantiates the third argument with terms which are output from the object. This suggests that the argument can be viewed as an output stream.

The object will terminate when its input stream is closed (the first argument is bound to []). Termination occurs because the relevant `filestore` clause (the first) does not recursively call `filestore` in its body.

By looking at the permitted instantiations of the first argument of the predicate in the various clauses, it is possible to state what types of message the class can recognise:

```
add(Key, File)
extract(Key, File, Ok)
```

An `add` message is dealt with by the second clause which changes the `Files` state, not by destructive assignment, but by argument replacement when `filestore` recursively calls itself.

The third and fourth clauses deal with an `extract` message; the third clause uses a guard to do a test before the message is accepted or rejected. The call to `extract_file` attempts to remove a file term with a `Key` argument from `Files`. It will either succeed and return a value for `File` and bind `NewFiles` to the new file list, or will fail and so reject the `extract` message. If rejected, the message is handled by the fourth clause which is a simple error handling clause for `extract` messages. In either case, the `Ok` variable is bound to a term which indicates the outcome of the computation and illustrates the way that a response can be communicated back to the sender of the message. In fact, `Ok` need not be bound to a term, but could be used as a message stream or more complicated communication structure.

The fifth clause is a general purpose error handling clause and outputs an error message when the input message is not understood. This is more general than the error reporting technique used for an `extract` message where `Ok` is bound. This clause can handle any message but cannot simply bind a variable in the message in order to report an error since the message format is unknown. An obvious alternative to outputting the message on a stream is to print an error report, but the stream approach allows the message to be forwarded to another object which can handle the message.

A crucial attribute of such objects is their fine grained parallelism, which means that an object may be able to process several messages simultaneously, and also carry out more than one action at a time.

A call to `filestore`, with `Files` originally empty, would be:

```
<- filestore(Input, [], Errors),
Input = [add(1, a1), add(2, a2), extract(1, File1, Ok1),
          extract(3, File2, Ok2), hello|_]
```

The five messages sent along `Input` would produce the following results:

```
File1 = a1       Ok1 = done
File2 unbound    Ok2 = no_entry_for(3)
Errors = [not_understood(hello)|_]
```

Note that `File2` is unbound.

This example shows how an object can be equated with a process, but it also illustrates that the process is typically generated from simple recursive clauses – most have the form:

```
filestore(<arguments>) :-
  <goals>,
  filestore(<modified arguments>).
```

Processes can be generated in more varied ways than this, which can be equated with objects exhibiting different behaviours [54, 102]. For example, consider the clause:

```
filestore([spawn(NewInput)|Input], Files, Errors) :-
  filestore(NewInput, [], Errors1),        % new filestore object
  merge(Errors1, Errors2, Errors),
  filestore(Input, Files, Errors2).
```

This doubly recursive clause can be thought of as a method for dynamically spawning a new `filestore` object. The new object's input stream is supplied as the argument of the `spawn` message. An interesting aspect is the use of `merge` to combine the two error streams so that both objects can report errors through `Errors`. The AND-parallel conjunctions are essential in the body so that the objects (and `merge`) can execute concurrently.

A `filestore` object can be graphically represented as figure 1. The circle is an object, while the arrows are message streams.

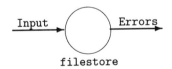

Figure 3.1
A filestore Object

The graphical representation of concurrent LP programs is an on-going research topic. Several authors have looked at the pictorial description of programs and processes [49, 168, 105, 24], and Kahn is working on an object-oriented notation for message passing, object creation, and change [102]. Fellous is also designing a visual formalism, but is more concerned with inheritance and other relationships between classes [68]. Some of the unresolved questions are how to represent recursion, state change and communication. An object-oriented notation simplifies the first two since recursion is hidden and state change looks simpler. However communication can still be very complex if partially instantiated terms are used as messages. One way of handling the specification of complex communication protocols is to appropriate graphical design methodologies from software engineering which can specify entities whose interaction is via message passing [178].

Shapiro and Takeuchi's work did not deal with some of the fundamental issues involved in OOP, such as encapsulation, multiple inheritance, self communication, the accessing of inherited state variables and clauses, and the dynamic manipulation of objects and classes. Also, no syntactic support for OOP was proposed. As a consequence, the concurrent LP-based OOP languages developed since have tended to investigate different solutions to these problems.

The user level syntax for these languages has been quite varied but two distinct approaches seem possible. Either the language can allow a mixture of objects and predicates [156, 54, 186], or only objects are allowed [106, 208]. This is something like the distinction between the conventional OOP languages Simula67 [15] and Smalltalk [79].

The languages which permit both objects and predicates allow predicates such as extract_file to be used inside an object, and for state to be manipulated as terms. This is more expressive but also means that two paradigms are visible at the user level.

An attempt was made to address this criticism by the designer of Polka, with the introduction of a simpler language called Parlog++ [56]. Parlog++ has the basic object-oriented features of encapsulation, data hiding and message passing, but is a subset of Polka since it does not support multiple inheritance or self communication.

The 'objects only' approach does without predicates which simplifies the semantics of the language but does not necessarily simplify understandability. This is because programs which would normally be written as relations need to be recoded in an object and message passing style.

A well developed example of this type of language is Vulcan, which offers a uniform way of dealing with functions, objects and terms [106]. This has lead to the treatment of terms as immutable objects which means that terms can be sent messages. This is implemented with the predicate:

```
sendToTerm(Term, Message)
```

sendToTerm defines the action that a message has on a term.

Since terms are immutable objects, they are accessed via messages like so:

```
1 : add(2, Z)
```

This example shows an `add` message being sent to the immutable object 1, which will cause Z to be bound to the immutable object 3. To help with programming in this style, several immutable classes have been defined including vector, associative table, string, and integer.

3.3.3   The Backtracking Process View Representation

Languages of this type encode classes using recursive Prolog predicates, in an analogous way to in the Shapiro and Takeuchi model. A set of AND-parallel goals for these predicates is equated with a system of concurrently executing objects. However, an object executes in a sequential manner internally, unlike the committed choice process view [152, 90, 64].

DLP [62] stands for Distributed LP, although the emphasis of the work is on creating AND-parallel objects. The allocation of objects can be achieved through a number of means: the object can be invoked on a specified node, it can be allocated to a branch in a node tree, or to a node in a matrix topology. DLP is intended to run on a coarse grained parallel topology consisting of at most 100 nodes.

3.3.4   The Meta-interpretation View Representation

The other implementation views are generally based on the idea that the object-oriented features of a language can be compiled away, and the translated program run in a (fairly) standard LP environment. The meta-interpretation view takes quite a different line, by assuming the presence of an interpreter which can directly execute programs written in the LP-based OOP language [20, 90, 16, 135]. Typically, classes are invoked by a meta-interpreter, like the `demo` predicate found in LP [116, 21]. This relies on a class being encoded as a first order citizen of the language, such as a term or a collection of terms.

This approach enables languages to be developed which follow the Smalltalk philosophy of letting classes be objects. In other words, meta classes can be defined which contain methods for defining, creating, manipulating and destroying classes. For example, ObjVProlog contains classes called `class` and `object` which play a similar role to their counterparts in Smalltalk [127]. SP-Object [165], an object-oriented extension to SP-Prolog, is closely modelled on the Smalltalk philosophy – every class is an object, and its inheritance mechanism is derived from that used in Smalltalk/V.

A commonly used technique is *reflection*, whereby a goal at the object level of the language is passed to the meta level to be solved. In OOP terms, this means passing a message sent to an instance to its class object.

Coscia observed that the inefficiency of interpretation is removed by partially evaluating the class with respect to its interpreter, which can easily produce an order of magnitude increase in speed [46]. A problem with this is that the flexibility of manipulating classes is lost, and so only selective partial evaluation should be utilised.

One of the potential drawbacks of this implementation view is the introduction of higher-order facilities which have a complex semantics. However, it is possible to develop first order semantics for a meta-interpretation view language, as long as some restrictions are made to its functionality [139, 33].

The meta-interpreter view has been used to implement languages which have features of both the clauses and the process view, as illustrated below.

EPSILON is an extension of Prolog which allows *theories* to be manipulated by their own inference engines [46]. It is possible for new inference engines to be defined, which require operations to be specified for querying and updating theories. Theories tend to be sets of Prolog-like clauses, but other formalisms are permitted because of the flexibility of meta-interpretation.

The meta-interpreter view was used in Mandala, an object-oriented knowledge representation language built on top of Concurrent Prolog [72]. Each class has a meta class, called a manager, which includes a meta-interpreter for creating instances. Concurrent Prolog allows each instances to exhibit fine grain parallelism and for processes to be implemented.

Polka includes a meta-interpreter for invoking special *term* classes. Term classes are terms at the base LP level, and so can be manipulated much more easily than standard classes [54]. Polka differs from Mandala in that meta-interpretation is used solely for term classes while the rest of the language is based on the committed choice process view. This means that meta-interpretation is only utilised when absolutely necessary, so limiting its overheads.

3.4   Message Passing

Message passing allows a looser connection between the object and its user since it does not specify how a message will be realised (a subroutine jump, system trap, or an interprocess communication in a multitasking or distributed system). The only burden on the programmer is to define a suitable operation for handling a message when it does arrive.

A useful feature is the run time interpretation of message passing (also called late or dynamic binding). This allows a message to be matched with the right object at run time, which improves rapid prototyping. Early binding is also possible, but only when variables are strongly typed so that messages can be matched to objects at compile time.

Wegner argues that although message passing is obviously required for communication, the precise nature of communication is not central to the definition of OOP [198].

Message passing in the clauses view is predominately synchronous, since a message is represented as a goal which must be solved before the main computation can continue. The concurrency inherent in the process view permits asynchronous communication since a sender can continue its execution while the transmitted message is being dealt with by the receiver. Both synchronous and asynchronous communication can be found in meta-interpretation view-based languages.

3.4.1   Message Passing in the Clauses View

Section 3.1 explained how an instance name is an instantiated class label. In order to send a message to an instance, the message and this label must be combined in some way, like so:

```
instantiated-label :: message
```

e.g.

```
square(10) :: area(Area)
```

The example shows an **area** message being sent to the **square** instance whose length is
10. Conceptually, the message is treated as a goal to be applied to the clauses of the
class. This allows the usual call/return semantics of message passing to be replaced by
one based on success and failure [75]. With respect to the example **square** class at the
start of section 3.1, this means that the goal:

```
area(Area)
```

will be applied to the clause:

```
area(Area) if Area is 10 * 10.
```

Note that **Length** has been replaced by 10.

In the implementation, if the label/predicate translation is used, the above message
send will become the goal:

```
<- square(10, area (Area)).
```

In comparison, the label/argument translation of the message is:

```
<- area(square(10), Area).
```

The label/argument approach would seem to require the use of a meta call in the cases
when a message is unbound, but axiom schema can be utilised instead [195]. A simple
example is:

```
$call(area(Area)) if area(Area).
$call(perimeter(Peri)) if perimeter(Peri).
```

The message form will be:

```
<- $call(Message).
```

$call is used instead of a meta call, and can execute either the method for **area**
or **perimeter** when the message is a variable. The same technique can be applied in
the label/predicate translation method when a class label is unbound at execution time.
Thus, in either translation it is relatively straightforward to send an unbound message
to an object, or an ordinary message to an unspecified object. Combined with Prolog's
non-determinism, this enables all methods of an object to be accessed, and for a message
to be broadcast to all objects. This has been seen as one of the most powerful features
of using LP with OOP [82, 75, 44].

The message/goal equivalence enables message passing to be carried out by calling
goals in predicates, which means that many forms of message transmission can be encoded, including different kinds of broadcasting [129]. For instance, the delivery of a
message to a list of objects might be represented using the following predicate:

```
and_cast([], Msg).                    % no more instances
and_cast([Label|List], Msg) if
  Label :: Msg,                       % send Msg to Label instance
  and_cast(List, Msg).
```

A call might be:

```
<- and_cast([square(10), circle(2)], draw).
```

This sends a **draw** message to two instances: **square(10)** and **circle(2)**.

In general, message passing is synchronous, but variables in messages need not be used until required and can be shared between objects. This can be seen as a bug because it allows any object that has a copy of such a variable to affect another object.

A new inference rule, called the *object clause*, has been proposed to help communication between predicates and objects [43]. A typical object clause looks like:

```
g1, g2 if c1, c2.
```

During execution, two goals are selected from the goal list and simultaneously unified with the head of the object clause. A new resolvent is created from the remaining input literals and the literals in the body of the object clause. Backtracking can occur in the normal way.

An object clause allows predicates and objects to communicate because one of the goals in the head can be a message supplied by a predicate (or an object), while the other goal is the object. For example:

```
push(Element), stack(Id, Stack) if stack(Id, [Element|Stack]).
```

This clause defines how a **push** message is dealt with by a **stack** object. The **stack** list is extended with the new element when **stack** is recursively called.

The benefits of this approach can be seen in an example which compares a expression evaluator written in conventional Prolog with one which uses a stack object [44]. In the object-oriented version, messages to a stack replace parameter passing in the Prolog version. The object-oriented version is clearer since fewer parameters are present, and it is safer because the stack data structure is accessible only by message passing.

One of the problems with message passing is how it interacts with backtracking. The issue is one of semantics: what should the meaning be of a message send that can cause a chain of actions in another object which can later be undone by a failure in the object? This question is made more difficult by the possibility that the actions can include message sends to other objects.

Perhaps the most intuitive solution is to have a message 'returned' to its sender when backtracking goes over the message acceptance. Since message passing is synonymous with goal reduction in the clauses view it is easy to implement this as goal failure, which will cause the sender to backtrack [131].

Other language designers have taken the view that a message send should not fail. In [37], an attempt is made to avoid failure by transmitting a message from a clause only when the rest of the clause has succeeded. This is not satisfactory since the receiver may still fail, so rejecting the message.

Another possibility is to have a different form of message passing which can report errors instead of failing [71]. This is done by binding a variable which is part of the transmitted message. The sender can monitor this variable and can then respond to a error report.

3.4.2 Message Passing in the Committed Choice Process View

Message passing in these languages is based on the idea of partially instantiating lists, as illustrated by the `filestore` program in section 3.2.2. At the user level, this mechanism may be hidden although it is sometimes useful to directly manipulate a message stream as a list [54]. A common example of this is when messages must be removed from the stream in an unusual order. This is easily achieved by allowing a predicate to search through the stream as if it was a list.

If several objects wish to communicate with the same object, usually each must have its own output stream which is merged with the other output streams to form a single input stream for the receiver object. This requires the programmer to be adept at the use of predicates such as `merge`, described in section 3.2.1. Of course, the advantage of stream visibility is that streams can be merged together in esoteric ways.

It is not normally possible for multiple senders to share the same stream to a receiver since this would make it possible for two objects to attempt to partially instantiate the same variable with different values. One would succeed, the other fail because the variable would be bound. This would probably cause the object to fail since backtracking is not available in the committed choice process view.

The *stream hiding* philosophy is found in the work of Ohki [156]. The language supports a `send` primitive which an object can use to send a message to another object:

```
send(<name of the object>, <message>)
```

The advantage of such a construct is that there is no need to manipulate streams between objects, but the disadvantage is that a global data structure is required, which maps names of objects to their streams. In addition, there must be a process which accepts all the messages generated and puts them onto the right streams. This process may become a bottleneck in the system.

Stream communication need not be the only form of message passing because the underlying use of shared logical variables for communication is much more flexible. One possible alternative is to use channels, which enables two independent objects to send messages along the same channel without specifying an order of transmission [191].

The discussion so far has assumed that an object has one input stream, but multiple inputs are quite possible. An interesting interpretation of multiple input streams is as *capabilities* offered by the object. For example, one stream could permit priority access, while messages on the slow stream would have to wait.

Since streams are first order entities, they can be sent to other objects as messages, which means that dynamic reconfiguration of the links between objects is feasible.

Languages in the Concurrent Prolog (CP) family can use the read-only (RO) variable which is more powerful than synchronisation primitives tied to predicate definitions, such as modes in Parlog [172]. A RO variable is an occurrence of a variable marked by a '?' annotation, and if unification attempts to bind a RO occurrence of a variable, then the offending call suspends. It is reactivated when the variable is instantiated via some non-RO occurrence. One important application of a RO variable is as a form of dynamic constraint because it can unify with an ordinary variable at run time and make it read-only. Little work has been done on the use of RO variables in OOP, but they are useful for the protection of input streams, and the generation of unique and unforgeable tokens [140]. Such tokens could be used to protect and identify messages sent between objects. More recently, further synchronisation constructs based on variable annotations have been proposed for versions of CP [175]. These include atomic test-and-set and atomic output primitives which are likely to be useful for OOP. For instance, atomic primitives can permit multiple senders to share the same output stream to a receiver.

A'UM introduces a notation for streams which differentiates between variables being used as input and output streams [208]. This annotation permits better compilation of the A'UM code since the compiler knows more about streams. In Polka, this kind of information is present for variables declared in a class but does not extend to variables in messages [54].

Polka allows an object to execute a method without waiting for a message to arrive. This is useful when encoding clocks, producers, or other types of generator, but means that point no.3 of the Shapiro and Takeuchi model is not always true:

> An object becomes active when it receives a message, otherwise it is suspended.

Polka also has a special type of message called a *suspendable* message. In essence, this is an ordinary message tagged with a list of logical variables. The semantics of such a message are that it will not be delivered to its destination until all the variables on its associated list become bound. This sort of message is extremely useful for explicitly constraining the processing order of messages, which can be difficult in fine grain parallel objects, where several actions can be executing at once and several messages may be processed simultaneously. A similar technique has also been proposed by Cutcher [49].

3.4.3 Message Passing in the Backtracking Process View

One important issue is what to do when backtracking passes back over a message send, or the reception of a message. The simplest answer is to leave this up to the programmer who must encode some kind of undo message protocol. However, T-Prolog automatically backtracks an object which is in communication with a failed object [73]. This may cause others to backtrack and so, because efficiency is crucial, a form of intelligent backtracking is used.

Several asynchronous communication protocols have been developed in the backtracking process view, which can be separated into two categories: shared logical variables and mailboxes. There are also two main forms of synchronous communication: event goals and d-clauses. Each of these communication techniques is described below.

3.4.3.1   Shared Logical Variables   Many languages use shared logical variables to enable objects to communicate [152, 90, 103, 64]. The sender partially instantiates the variable with a message which eventually appears as the input of the receiver, in a similar way to in the committed choice process view. The important difference is that both objects are written in Prolog and so the receiver will require a suspension mechanism to allow it to wait for input.

The following example is based on a generator object passing a stream of elements to a buffer object. To simplify matters, no object-oriented syntax is shown, and instead an object is shown as its underlying process. Termination clauses and other important features are also not presented because they are not central to the problem of communication.

At the top level, the generator object, called gen, and buffer are linked via a shared Stream variable when they are invoked in AND-parallel using the '//' operator:

```
<- gen([1, 2, 3, 4], Stream) // buffer(Stream, []).
```

Messages will be passed from gen to buffer by partially instantiating Stream. The first argument of gen is a list of elements, while the second argument of buffer acts as a store for the elements which it receives.

gen will send messages along Stream by using a clause like:

```
gen([El|List], [put(El)|Out]) if gen(List, Out).
```

It shows how gen transmits the elements of its list as put messages.

buffer receives the put messages using a clause such as:

```
buffer([put(El)|Input], Store) if
   in(El, Store, Store1) : buffer(Input, Store1).
```

The first argument of the head is the input stream, while the second stores the buffer contents. in adds the element to the buffer, which is then committed to via the use of a cut. The cut is not necessary for the communication but ensures that backtracking cannot undo the message passing.

In addition to its clauses, buffer will also require a wait declaration which states what arguments it should suspend upon. For example, the declaration might be:

```
wait buffer(?, ?).
```

This ensures that buffer cannot start binding Stream with put messages.

Using logical variables for communication allows a great deal of scope for different communication protocols; back communication is possible, for example.

Shared variables can be expensive to implement when the objects are physically distributed among processors which use message passing hardware to communicate rather than shared memory. This is the situation with PMS-Prolog [202] which is implemented on a Transputer architecture. Communication overheads are reduced by making shared variables unidirectional, which means that a receiver only obtains a copy of a sender's message. Consequently, messages cannot use variables to set up new communication links between objects. Simple communication also aids the implementation of backtracking algorithms for message passing.

3.4.3.2   Mailboxes   Objects communicate via mailboxes in a similar way to in the shared logical variable approach, but the two mechanisms are differentiated here because mailbox functionality must be added to the basic LP language while shared variables are already part of it.

In CPU [122], the mailbox is a queue object. When created, its name is passed to the participants in the intended communication so that they can store and read messages. Only ground messages are allowed and communication is non-backtrackable. However, the object does offer inspection and manipulation facilities.

Several languages enable objects to communicate by means of a common global database (or blackboard) [73, 61, 192]. The sender can add terms to the blackboard, and the receiver uses a `wait`-like predicate to suspend until a suitable term appears. Back communication is not possible since the variables in a term are renamed as it is removed from the board. However, a sender name can be included as part of the term and is then available to the receiver as a means of labelling its return message so that the sender can find it on the board. See section 9.3 for more discussion of blackboard-type communication.

3.4.3.3   Event Goals   Event Goals are a rendezvous mechanism which allows a message to be transferred between two objects safely by ensuring that both objects are 'locked together' before the message transfer can take place. It therefore provides object synchronisation, and mutual exclusion because a sender can only rendezvous with one receiver at a time.

Event Goals are utilised in Delta Prolog [143, 160, 48], and have the form:

```
X ? E : C
```

and

```
X ! E : C
```

X is a term (the message), ? and ! are complimentary communication modes, E is a Prolog atom (the event name), and C is an optional goal expression (the event condition). Two objects which wish to communicate will use event goals with complimentary modes and a common event name. The communication will be successful if the two messages unify and their associated conditions evaluate to true. After a successful rendezvous, the messages should contain no unbound variables. Partly, this is due to implementation concerns, but it also ensures that the event mechanism does not affect the semantics of unification [159]. Model-theoretic, fixpoint and operational semantics for a version of Delta Prolog have been developed [26].

Using event goals, the top level of the generator-buffer example will become:

```
<- gen([1, 2, 3, 4]) // buffer([]).
```

Thus, a shared variable does not need to be specified, but **gen** and **buffer** must use event goals with complimentary modes and the same event name.

The **gen** clause for sending a **put** message will be:

```
gen([El|List]) if put(El)!store, gen(List).
```

`store` is the event name. The relevant `buffer` clause is:

```
buffer(Store) if
  put(El)?store, in(El, Store, Store1), buffer(Store1).
```

As before, `in` adds the element to the buffer, but the clause does not contain a cut after the call to `in` since Delta Prolog allows distributed backtracking across event goals. In this example, it would mean that the failure of this `buffer` clause would cause `gen` to backtrack.

Delta Prolog allows event names to be generated at run time, and to be sent to other objects as messages since they are Prolog atoms. This permits dynamic linking of objects, although an event name should not be used by more than two objects since it may affect the completeness of the computation.

Delta Prolog's communication mechanism is symmetric because both participants must use a common event name. In Multilog [107], communication is asymmetric since the sender knows where to send its message, but the receiver is unaware of its origin. The receiver utilises the predicate:

```
wait_to_accept(Message)
```

This suspends execution until a suitable message arrives. A variant of this is:

```
accept(Message)
```

This fails immediately if no suitable message is present. Unification is used by the predicates to select a message from the queue at the object. Unlike Delta Prolog, backtracking is not possible across a rendezvous. Also, backtracking over `wait_to_accept` and `accept` does not cause a further search of the relevant queue; the predicate simply fails.

In DLP [62], the rendezvous of two objects is also based on `accept` statements. An object has two types of clauses – constructor and method clauses. The constructor clauses are invoked when the object is initiated, and define what method clauses can be utilised at any given time. When an object receives a method call, a process is created for handling the rendezvous, for evaluating the goal and for returning any answer substitutions. The process also records information required for backtracking (which can pass between objects). An `accept` can include a guard, and a goal which is evaluated if the guard succeeds:

```
accept( method-name : guard -> goal )
```

3.4.3.4 D-clauses Monteiro's paper on Distributed Logic [143] which first formulated the ideas behind Delta Prolog, also briefly described another form of rendezvous mechanism called the *distributed clause* (the d-clause). Its general form is:

```
g1, g2 if c1, c2.
```

Goals are matched against the head, and substitutions applied simultaneously; the body goals then join the on-going evaluation. The object clause, proposed by Conery, bears a close resemblance to a d-clause (see section 4.1).

The main difference between the d-clause and the event goal approach is that d-clauses are part of the language, rather than special communication primitives.

The two methods used in the generator-buffer example can be rewritten as a single d-clause:

```
gen([El|List]), buffer(Store) if
  in(El, Store, Store1) : gen(List), buffer(Store1).
```

Neither of the two goals in the head of a d-clause need be for objects, and could just as easily be messages. This is true in Mello and Natali's language [134] where the relevant buffer clause might be:

```
buffer(Store) if modify(Store, Store1), buffer(Store1).
```

The gen clause might be:

```
gen([El|List]) if put(El), gen(List).
```

and the two objects communicate using the d-clause:

```
modify(Store, Store1), put(El) if in(El, Store, Store1).
```

The modify goal is supplied by buffer, the put goal by gen. The call to in modifies Store, returning Store1 which is passed back to buffer. Thus, modify and put can be seen as messages sent by objects.

Since d-clauses make no distinction between objects, messages, and goals, they can be used for more unusual transformations. An operation to combine two messages might be expressed as:

```
put(El1), put(El2) if put2(El1, El2).
```

put2 can be thought of a message packet, which can be processed by buffer with the following clause:

```
buffer(Store), put2(El1, El2) if
  in(El1, Store, Store1), in(El2, Store1, Store2),
  buffer(Store2).
```

buffer stores El1 and El2 by calling in twice.

A d-clause could also be used to combine two objects:

```
free_taxi(TaxiInput), customer(CustInput) if
  busy_taxi(TaxiInput, CustInput).
```

This can be seen as creating a new busy_taxi object from the free_taxi and customer objects.

The d-clause has hidden overheads for the Prolog inference mechanism since two goals must be chosen from the executable goal list, which means that the computationally efficient left-to-right selection strategy must be sacrificed. Also, if backtracking rolls over a d-clause, the two clauses which supplied its head goals should fail, which may be expensive to implement.

At the end of the communication between the `gen` and `buffer` objects, the final goals will be:

```
<- gen([]) // buffer([1, 2, 3, 4]).
```

In order for the goals to terminate successfully, the clauses:

```
gen([]).
buffer(Store).
```

should be added to the respective objects. However, if the new `buffer` clause is placed incorrectly, then it may be chosen too soon and cause the object to terminate prematurely. This problem can be dealt with by syntactically differentiating between these termination clauses and others. The inference engine can then delay their use until it can determine that all communication has finished. This is possible if it knows what predicates represent objects, and so which communication-related goals in the executable goal list still need to be processed. When all these communication goals have been solved, termination clauses can finish the computation.

A further complication is that the user may wish to include clauses for `gen` and `buffer` which should be executed in the absence of communication. When these should be selected is another problem.

These problems also occur with event goals.

3.4.4   Message Passing in the Meta-interpretation View

In languages which use the meta-interpretation view, an object can pass a message to the meta level to be processed. It is then possible to redirect the message to another object, or to process the message at the meta level. The message may be synchronous if only one object can execute at once, but if AND-parallel execution is possible then message passing between objects can be asynchronous.

Usually, the message destination is encoded in the message itself, but a more flexible alternative is to store the information in a clause which the meta level can access. This allows the information to be readily changed by simply altering the clause, which makes it possible to dynamically reconfigure the communication links between objects at run time.

Another approach to communication is taken by Honiden, who uses temporal logic and petri net information at the meta level to define how objects can communicate [90].

3.5   State

There are four basic approaches to representing state in LP-based object-oriented languages:

- there is no permanent state
- `assert` / `retract` type primitives
- new inference rules
- arguments in processes

Generally, the first three mechanisms are used by languages based on the clauses view, while the last appears in process-based languages (not unsurprisingly). In the meta-interpretation view, all of the approaches have been utilised.

3.5.1   State in the Clauses View

State is only generated as a byproduct of the evaluation of a message in some languages and is not retained between messages [100, 11]. For example, the message:

`square(10) :: area(Area)`

will return a 'state' value of 100 for **Area**. This is not recorded anywhere in the **square** object. McCabe has discussed a partial solution to this, which relies on the instance's label being returned at the end of message processing [129]. The label will contain new state values as its parameters, and these can be used as the initial state for the instance when it is next invoked. However, all other instances must be sent this label in order for them to use the changed instance. The main advantage of this approach is that the semantics of instances become much simpler. McCabe has given such a language both a proof theoretic and model theoretic semantics. The proof theoretic approach introduces two new proof rules to deal with classes and the use of inheritance. The model theoretic approach shows how classes and inheritance can be mapped to Prolog clauses. In [83], the semantics of McCabe's Class Templates were investigated further – another model theory was presented and a fixpoint semantics was examined. Stable models were also discussed as a way of describing certain types of program.

In most of the other languages which treat classes as sets of clauses, the most popular way of dealing with state information is to store it as extra clauses, which are asserted or retracted when the state of an instance needs to be changed. The state clauses for different instances can be distinguished by including the instance's label as one of the arguments of each clause. The main problem is that the semantics of these operations are not well defined, and are also non-monotonic. An additional feature, or bug depending on the situation, is that backtracking over asserts and retracts does not normally undo them. However, this technique does have the benefit of being relatively simple to implement.

Aside from state clauses for instances, it is also possible to utilise them in classes. This allows classes to be treated as objects, so blurring the class - instance distinction.

In some languages, the assertion and retraction of state clauses are hidden by using a slot mechanism, which supplies predefined operations for storing, retrieving and changing state information [36, 71, 92]. Usually, slots are divided into those for classes and those for instances, but this is not always the case [82].

The storage of state as clauses means that any predicate can access the state information. It also makes it possible to write predicates which collect information about the state of all objects. Another useful feature is the ability to define constraint relationships between state clauses. For example, the update of one instance can be linked to the value of another instance.

In SPOOL, the compiler attempts to reduce the number of asserts and retracts by analysing message passing and collecting together sets of state accesses and changes [206].

To try to deal with the semantic problems with assertion and retraction, Porto has suggested new rules of inference which accommodate them, although the semantic basis of these rules still needs to be fully explored [161].

Chen and Warren have utilised an *intensional* semantics to describe Horn clause logic, which allows intension variables to be used in programs [34]. Such a variable is actually a function from a state to a set of values, and also contains a sequence of states which represents the partial history of the object. A frame assumption is used to make the history complete.

In [88], the underlying LP language is based on intuitionistic logic [18, 138]. Syntactically, this means that an atomic formula Bi in a clause can be replaced by formulae of the form:

```
H1 /\ . . . /\ Hm => Bi    ( m >= 0 )
```

H1, ... Hm are Horn clauses and '=>' is the converse of ':-'. To prove such a goal the clauses H1, ... Hm are first loaded into the program and only then is the atom Bi attempted. After Bi succeeds or fails, these clauses are removed.

State changes can be encoded by using an implicational goal such as:

```
?- object(new_state) => goal.
```

This adds the object literal to the program before attempting the goal. Thus, it is similar to using assert in Prolog like so:

```
?- assert(object(new_state)).
?- goal.
```

A program typically progresses by adding new clauses via implicational goals, which represent new states.

3.5.2 State in the Committed Choice Process View

In section 2.2.1, point no.1 of the Shapiro and Takeuchi model states:

> An object can be represented as a process which calls itself recursively and holds its internal state in unshared arguments.

This can be seen in action in the `filestore` example of section 3.2.2 where `Files` is the state of the object. The main advantage of this approach is that state changes are implemented without resorting to metalogical primitives or to new inference rules.

The committed choice process view makes it possible for many messages to be processed at once. However, there is a proviso: the potential concurrency is constrained by the need to carry out state changes in a specified order. This can be understood by realising that each message is processed by a clause which manipulates state by changing the argument of a recursive call to the process. An example in `filestore` is the clause for `extract` messages which replaces `Files` with `NewFiles`. A message sent after an `extract` will start to be processed at about the same time but if the clause uses `Files` then the execution will suspend until the clause processing the `extract` gets round to binding `NewFiles`.

At the language level, state variables are normally treated either as ordinary logical variables [54], or as objects that must be sent messages to access or alter their values [106]. Mapping state to logical variables enables the language to use predicates to manipulate it, but implies that both objects and predicates are in the language. This can be compared to the mix of paradigms in a language like SIMULA or C++. Equating data with objects is comparable with the Smalltalk view of OOP where everything is an object.

The committed choice nature of these languages means that earlier states cannot be retrieved by backtracking. However, if this kind of functionality is required then it can be encoded [54].

Trehan proposes three object models for committed choice languages [189]. Each is based on the Shapiro and Takeuchi model, but also describes how information is shared between objects. The *closed* object model defines the traditional object, which only permits its data to be accessed via message passing. The *open* object model allows an object to share data with other objects, but care must be taken about updating it. The *filofax* object model describes an object which stores data about other objects. It achieves this by regularly polling all objects in order to keep its information up to date. A more satisfactory approach is to make the objects send information to the filofax object when they change.

Sharing state between objects is difficult in the committed choice process view because of the issue of concurrent updates; since objects are executing concurrently, they may attempt to update the shared state at the same time. The eventual outcome is uncertain and so to preserve consistency some notion of atomicity is required. Naturally, this problem arises in concurrent LP, and some languages have atomic test-and-set primitives for manipulating variables [175]. These can be used to implement object-oriented shared state constructs.

In Sandra [65], atomicity is achieved by using the notion of *transaction*, a concept borrowed from the distributed database field.

A variation of the Shapiro and Takeuchi model is to encode state as a separate process whose message stream is held as the unshared argument in the process for the object. This has the advantage that if state is represented as an object at the language level then the mapping is simpler. However, the major benefit is for state sharing, since this can be represented as multiple output streams (one for each object sharing the state) which are merged together into one stream entering the 'state' process. This allows issues of mutual exclusion and atomicity to be controlled very easily, as demonstrated in [57] where shared 'state' processes are represented at the language level as shared blackboards offering atomic actions for manipulating data.

3.5.3 State in the Backtracking Process View

Objects in these languages are processes and so state has an explanation as the arguments of a recursive predicate in the same way as in the committed choice process view. In the subset of these which use `wait` annotations [152, 64], Kahn and Miller have shown that state change can be efficiently implemented [103].

Some languages allow data to be asserted and retracted, which is harder to do safely in a concurrent language because of the problem of mutual exclusion [73, 134].

In addition to state being represented by process arguments in DLP, destructive assignment can be used on non-logical variables, which can be inherited [62].

3.5.4 State in the Meta-interpretation View

In this view, an instance is invoked by using a meta-interpreter to execute a class. Therefore, the state associated with an instance depends on the meta-interpreter's representation of the instance. This means that any of the approaches discussed in the previous sections can be employed.

Sometimes state change is viewed as the generation of a new object [20]. This leads to practical problems since other objects will need to be informed that they should now communicate with the new object.

ObjVProlog asserts and retracts state information but the meta-interpreter also stores an update history which permits the changes to be undone [127].

The process argument technique can be utilised if the meta-interpreter represents an object as a process. Even if the object is not a process, the meta-interpreter can itself be a process and store the object's state as one of its own arguments.

3.6   Inheritance

Inheritance increases code sharing by allowing the language rather than the programmer to reuse code from one class in another class.

A more stringent notion is *subtyping* which guarantees that an instance of a subtype can always be used in place of a supertype. This can be taken to mean that the subtype has the same behaviour as the supertype, but can also mean that the subtype has the same operations as the supertype. A related notion is *strictness*: if inheritance is strict then there is behavioural compatibility between a class and its inherited class. If non-strict inheritance is employed then a class can arbitrarily redefine an inherited method.

A useful distinction, that is sometimes made, is between inheritance of behaviour and inheritance of code. The former is implementation dependent while the latter is not.

Another design decision is whether to permit multiple or single inheritance. Multiple inheritance increases sharing because it makes it possible for one class to combine the behaviour of several other classes. This can be illustrated by using an inheritance graph shown in figure 2. The circles represent the classes, while the arrows indicate the inheritance links.

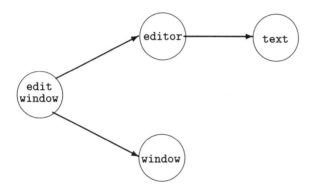

Figure 3.2
An Inheritance Graph

The graph shows that the edit_window class uses multiple inheritance in order to call upon the methods in editor and window, while editor utilises only single inheritance. In the following discussion, classes on the left of an inheritance graph will be described as being 'lower down' the class hierarchy than classes on the right.

In general, LP-based OOP languages offer non-strict, multiple inheritance, which is implemented by forwarding messages from the object to one or more of its designated 'ancestors' objects. This is called *delegation* in the OOP field. Wegner considers inheritance to be a specialization of delegation, in which the entities that inherit are classes [198]. Lieberman differs, believing delegation and inheritance to be different mechanisms [124]. In the literature, ancestor objects are normally called prototypes, and it is noted that they serve both as instances and as templates for descendents.

Built into most OOP languages are ways for a class to refer directly to its inherited classes (cf. *super* in Smalltalk), and to carry out self communication (cf. *self* in Smalltalk) [79].

Of these two, self communication is most important since it allows the meaning of the self application of a method from a class to depend on method definitions in classes below it in the inheritance graph. Typically, this is achieved through late binding, which identifies the object on whose behalf an operation is being executed rather than the textual module in which the self reference occurs. This means that a **self** message is always initially tried against methods in the class at the bottom of the inheritance graph *for a particular invocation.*

For example, an invocation of `edit_window` causes all the `self` messages transmitted by its inherited methods to be applied to the `edit_window` methods. If no method is suitable, methods from `editor` and `window` are tried. An important issue is the order in which these methods are examined.

To show the importance of the actual class invoked, consider the situation when an instance of `editor` is created. `self` messages will be applied to methods in `editor` first, since the invocation only involves the fragment of the inheritance graph containing `editor` and `text`.

An excellent discussion of different inheritance models are described in [199].

3.6.1   Inheritance in the Clauses View

Consider two classes called `square` and `rectangle`:

```
square(Length) [ area(Area) if Area is Length * Length. ].
```

and

```
rectangle(Height, Width)
   [ perimeter(P) if P is 2 * Height + Width. ].
```

Inheritance rules refer to classes by their labels. For example, a rule which states that `square` inherits `rectangle` might be:

```
square(Length) inherits rectangle(Length, Length).
```

Note the use of the `Length` variable in the `rectangle` label to ensure that its height and width are equal, and the same as `square`.

Occasionally, the inheritance rule is written inside the class, and then the inheritor is not named.

Since instances can be referred to by instantiated class labels, they can be created using an inheritance rule:

```
squ1 inherits square(10)
```

`squ1` is an instance of `square` with sides of length 10. This approach is normally utilised when the language does not distinguish between classes and instances [154].

The LP representation of an inherits rule depends on the class translation method. In the label/predicate approach, the rule:

```
square(Length) inherits rectangle(Length, Length).
```

becomes something like:

```
square(Length, Message) if rectangle(Length, Length, Message).
```

This clause enables any unrecognised `square` messages (goals) to be rewritten as `rectangle` messages.

Using the label/argument translation, a single `inherits` rule will generate one new clause for every clause in the original class. For example, a `square` class with methods for the `x1` and `x2` messages:

```
square(Length) [ x1 if y1.
                 x2 if y2. ].
```

will be translated into two clauses:

```
x1(square(Length)) if y1(square(Length)).
x2(square(Length)) if y2(square(Length)).
```

In addition, the `inherits` rule will generate two extra clauses:

```
x1(square(Length)) if x1(rectangle(Length, Length)).
x2(square(Length)) if x2(rectangle(Length, Length)).
```

The meaning of these two new clauses is that if a method in `square` cannot handle a `x1` or `x2` message then the corresponding method is tried in `rectangle`.

The above example illustrates that the label/argument translation generates many more clauses than the label/predicate approach when used to encode inheritance.

Both implementation strategies ensure that a message can reach all the relevant inherited clauses through the use of backtracking. However, this can be restricted by specifying clauses which are not to be inherited, or by listing particular clause instantiations which should be ignored [108, 129]. A possible syntax for this is:

```
edit_window inherits editor - cursor_pos/1
```

This states that the `edit_window` class inherits everything from the `editor` class, apart from the clauses for `cursor_pos` of arity 1. This can be implemented at the Prolog level by the use of `not` [129], but normally restrictions on inheritance are achieved by using cuts [115]. The difference should be transparent to the user, but the underlying Prolog cannot be totally ignored because its search strategy affects the order in which inherited clauses are tried.

When classes have a meaning in terms of types, inheritance can be thought of as a type hierarchy, which places extra constraints on how classes can be specialised [11, 78]. In Bancilhon's approach for example, multiple inheritance and method overriding are not possible, but more compile time checks can be applied.

In Phocus, exceptions to inheritance are dealt with by adding tests to clauses which check the class of the instance. This is based on a typing system for variables [32].

Many languages based on the clauses view do not permit either `super` messages or self communication, although they are not difficult to implement [11, 129, 190]. A `super` message can be translated into an immediate call to the inherited class, while self communication requires an extra argument in every message. This extra term will contain the name of the initially invoked class, and then if a `self` message is necessary, the corresponding Prolog goal will use this name to invoke that class. A more complex approach is used in BiggerTalk, which uses a stack to keep account of the self references [82]. This allows the destination to be left out of a message, and instead it is popped off a `self` stack.

In Prolog++, there is a `myself` message which is applied to the method in the class in which the `myself` occurs [148].

An important problem occurs when multiple inheritance is used, and a class is inherited twice, as `cursor` is in the inheritance graph shown in figure 3.

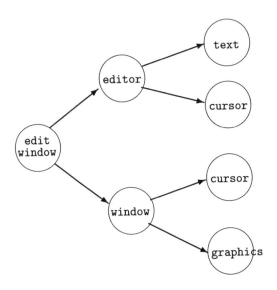

Figure 3.3
One form of Multiple Inheritance

In the graph, a message that can be dealt with by `cursor` may be answered twice. Sometimes such a behaviour is not desirable, but it is not a simple matter to override Prolog's backtracking mechanism. Aside from the use of `not` and cuts to restrict backtracking, information can be stored during the search to indicate that certain clauses have already been tried. Another method is to use a metalogical predicate like `set_of` to return all the answers to a given message and then choose between them [99]. In the object-oriented version of SISCtus Prolog, the problem is dealt with by not allowing multiple inherited instances of the same class [64], making the graph look like figure 4.

This may be suitable if `cursor` is meant to represent the same thing in both `editor` and `window`. However, special provision must be made to deal with broadcast messages, which will result in two messages going to a single `cursor` method, and so perhaps incorrectly altering the state.

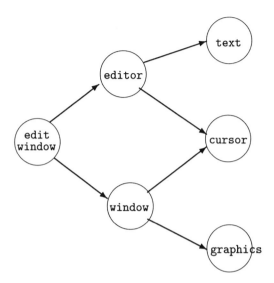

Figure 3.4
Another form of Multiple Inheritance

Although the use of backtracking for implementing multiple inheritance presents some problems, it is, in many ways, an elegant mechanism. This will become clearer in section 6.2 when the complicated approachs used in the committed choice process view are examined.

Another technique for searching the inheritance graph is by employing an interpreter rather than leaving it to Prolog [209, 98]. This enables more flexible types of search to be carried out, such as breadth-first search.

Just as interpreters can deal with inheritance information in special ways, they can also recognise other types of relationships [115]. One example is the **sub** relation, which returns the name of the class below the current one in the inheritance graph, and through backtracking can return them all. **sub** can be thought of as the inverse of the inheritance relation [209].

Since an inheritance rule is usually represented as a Prolog clause, the matching of a message with an inherited clause is carried out at run time. This means that the choice of inherited clause can be dynamically altered, and also allows inherited classes to be changed, although it is difficult to encode such ideas without using metalogical predicates [36, 82].

Another implementation approach for inheritance, is to copy all the clauses of the inherited classes over to their inheritor at compile time [37, 78]. This reduces the run time costs, but increases the size of classes and makes it harder to incrementally recompile them. A possible advantage is that a change to an inherited clause will not affect the same clause inherited by other classes.

A major problem with copying is that the stratification of clauses into different classes is lost. For example, if the `editor`, `text`, and `cursor` classes were:

```
editor [ p. ].                  % one 'p' clause
editor inherits text, cursor.   % multiple inheritance

text [ p if r.                  % a 'p' and 'r' clause
      r. ].

cursor [ r. ].                  % one 'r' clause
```

With copying, `editor` will become:

```
editor [ p.
        p if r.     % from 'text'
        r.          % from 'text'
        r. ].       % from 'cursor'
```

This shows that the order in which clauses are copied will affect the execution order of the new class. Also, the second `p` clause can be proved twice because of the `r` clause from `cursor`. This is incorrect because `text` is unrelated to `cursor`. One answer is to rename the copied clauses but this makes it harder to set up the inheritance links.

The problems with copying are not unique to this approach, but are most commonly seen in the clauses view; since a class is equated with a set of clauses, clause copying is an easy way to encode inheritance.

An approach to inheritance similar to that used in McCabe's Class Templates was explored in [144] where derivation rules and a fixed-point semantics were developed for a LP language containing modules (units). Proofs are context-dependent on the units and it is possible to move from one context to another during a derivation. A particularly useful feature is the ability to combine units dynamically as well as in a static manner. Dynamic combination of units enables hypothetical reasoning to be carried out, and the associated semantics have been investigated [27]. Also related is the possible world semantics of Miller's module theory [137].

In [145], the semantics of multiple inheritance with overriding was investigated in three different ways by transforming inheritance into pure Horn clauses, a meta-level logic language and into a contextual LP language. Inheritance with predicate extensions was also briefly examined.

An extension to the Warren Abstract Machine to support contextual LP was developed in [121]. At the language level, the concepts of binding time (eager or lazy) for predicates, dynamic unit creation, and lexical or dynamic scope for units were introduced. Subsequently, partial evaluation was used to enhance this compilation mechanism by concentrating on units with a fixed associated context where context handling overheads can be largely eliminated [28].

A powerful form of inheritance is based on augmenting unification [114, 101]. For example, to state that a `square` class inherits the functionality of `rectangle`, would require the clause:

`square(Length) = rectangle(Length, Length)`

A message to `square` might be:

`square(10) :: area(Area)`

This should return the area of a square of sides of length 10, but if such a method is not defined in `square` then the message can be transferred to `rectangle`, becoming:

`rectangle(10, 10) :: area(Area)`

The elegance and power of this approach is that it also works in the opposite direction: if `rectangle` does not understand a message then it can be passed to `square`. This inheritance mechanism is supported by extending unification, and also requires extra control safeguards to stop looping [114].

An influential object model is employed by the LOGIN language [4]. LOGIN is essentially Prolog, with a built-in type inference mechanism which uses a lattice theoretic approach to computation based on a calculus of partially-ordered type structures. Terms can be thought of as objects which are in an inheritance hierarchy denoted by the lattice. This enables unification to be replaced by a greatest lower bound operation on the terms. Following LOGIN, Maier developed O-logic [126] which generalises the approach to include formulae. This has some semantic problems and so was revised in [111] to utilise a set-based semantics. F-logic [110] further extends O-logic by incorporating inheritance into its semantic framework. In addition, Chen and Warren have developed C-logic [35], which is also based on O-logic. It treats objects as binary predicates, so permitting formulae to be translated into first-order logic.

All of these proposals concentrate on the structural aspects of objects, although F-logic does include certain behavioral capabilities (methods). An excellent survey of this family of languages can be found in [109].

The use of constraints will become increasingly important, as they are a natural means of denoting the relationships between objects. This idea was used in the FREEDOM language [207] which is implemented using ESP [36] and the constraint LP language CAL [2]. Constraint satisfaction is used in FREEDOM to calculate state values but more unusually is also utilised to search for a clause in a class hierarchy. For instance, if a state value is modified so that constraint satisfaction fails in that class, then the class can be replaced by another which satisfies the constraint. They call this constraint-based taxonomic reasoning.

3.6.2   Inheritance in the Committed Choice Process View

An inheritance link between a class and its ancestor is usually implemented by a shared logical variable which acts as a stream for forwarding messages from the class. In addition, an extra clause is added to the inheritor, which places a message onto the stream when it cannot be processed by any of the other clauses. Such a clause is added to every class which inherits another class.

For instance, if a `database` class inherits the `filestore` class (see section 3.2.2), the extra clause in `database` might be:

```
database([Message|Input], [Message|Out]) <-
  database(Input, Out).
```

`database` clauses have two arguments: the first is its input stream, the second an output stream. This clause will only be tried when all the other clauses in `database` have been rejected as candidates, and it simply places the input message onto the `Out` output stream. Note, that the destination of the stream is not specified; this is handled by the top level Parlog conjunction which links `database` and `filestore`:

```
?- database(Input, Out), filestore(Out, [], Errors).
```

In the object-oriented language version of this query, the `Out` stream would be invisible, but would still allow unrecognised messages to be sent from `database` to `filestore`. When an instance of the `database` class is created, a `database` object *and* a `filestore` object will be invoked, and linked with such a stream. This may be graphically represented as figure 5.

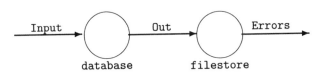

Figure 3.5
A database Object

More generally, whenever an instance of a class is created, a set of objects are invoked which represent each class in the part of the inheritance graph above the invoked class. The objects are linked by hidden message streams which allow an object to forward messages to its inherited objects.

Kahn has argued that a metaphor closer to message forwarding should be adopted, rather than one based on inheritance [102].

Multiple inheritance presents a problem since languages based on concurrent LP cannot use backtracking to search through the inherited objects for the right clause, and once a message has been forwarded to a particular object, the choice is fixed. One answer is to broadcast the same message to all the inherited objects, but this makes it possible for a variable in the message to be bound more than once, causing one or more of the objects to fail. In Polka, broadcasting primitives exist which automatically make unique copies of a message for each inherited object [54]. Even so, problems still remain about what to do if more than one copy of the message is successfully processed, or if all the copies fail to be dealt with.

Self communication is normally implemented by adding an extra output message stream to every object. All of these streams are merged into a single stream which enters the object at the bottom of the inheritance graph *for the particular invocation*. This mechanism permits self communication to be converted into a message send along the `self` output stream of the particular object [54]. So, in the example above, `self` streams will leave the `database` and `filestore` objects and be merged back into `Input`. However, if an instance of `filestore` is invoked then its `self` stream will go back to `filestore` since the invocation does not involve `database`.

`self` streams can exist throughout the lifetime of the objects, but an alternative is to only set them up for the duration of the computation of a forwarded message, as in Vulcan [106].

Some of the important problems with self communication include making sure that `self` messages are given priority over external communication, and that state changes caused by self communication do not interfere with calculations using the old state.

Although inheritance as message forwarding is the norm, Vulcan also permits copying, so that the `database` class could be expanded to include the clauses from `filestore` [106]. This makes self communication simpler to implement, but the copying technique leads to similar problems to those outlined in section 6.1.

Inheritance is dealt with in a totally different way by Ohki: inherited objects do not have a separate existence, but are invoked inside a meta call when required [156]. This means that inheritance is implemented as a procedure call, so enabling messages to be sent to inherited objects from guards. This is not possible in most other languages because a guard does not allow the manipulation of output streams because the clause may be rejected as a candidate. If this occurs, any bindings transmitted from the object would be invalidated. The main drawback of Ohki's approach is that an inherited object cannot retain its state between the processing of messages. This is solved by making the bottom object in the graph of inherited objects carry all of the state variables around itself. These are passed to an inherited object when it is called, which means that there is no encapsulation of data in the inherited object and the bottom object must initialise all of the state variables.

Many committed choice process view languages do not permit state to be inherited. This is due to the implementation of state as unshared arguments of a process, which makes it difficult to share with other processes. The normal solution is to force the state in an inherited object to be explicitly manipulated by clauses which are activated by messages sent by the inheritor. The use of such messages may interact unfavourably with messages from other parts of the object network which manipulate the same state. Also, the presence of clauses for manipulating state means that the user is able to alter the state, which may be undesirable. In most languages, it is left to the programmer to enforce the correct use of inherited state, although Polka allows explicit constraints to be placed on state manipulation operations [54]. More recently, an extension to Polka, called

Polka-B has been proposed which permits state to be inherited [57]. This is achieved via a blackboard mechanism which allows a subclass to inherit and specialise the boards defined by its superclass. As an extra benefit, state searching and updating is simplified when state is encoded as a board.

In [El], McCabe's class templates language was implemented on top of the committed choice LP language FGDC [167]. This meant that the implementation of multiple inheritance was able to take advantage of FGDC's atomic test-and-set primitive for variables. This enables the choice of which inherited class to use to be indeterministic and also be carried out in parallel. Essentially, when a clause in an inherited class commits, it binds a shared variable which causes the searchs in the other inherited classes to terminate when the shared variable is tested.

3.6.3   Inheritance in the Backtracking Process View

In these kinds of languages, inheritance is encoded by passing an unrecognised message to some other object which is specified as its inherited object. The actual form of communication mechanism varies but depends on the mechanism used for ordinary message passing. An important factor is the presence of backtracking, which means that the search of multiple inherited objects is much more straightforward than in the committed choice process view. However, self communication is still complicated and some languages avoid the problem by disallowing self communication [160]. Others treat `self` messages as internal predicate calls, which avoids the `self` message priority problem but requires a global name space for predicates [93].

Inheritance in DLP [62] is based on copying, so that an object obtains a copy of all the clauses and state variables of its ancestors.

An interesting extension of LP based on linear logic [77] has been proposed in [6]. Their Linear Objects (LO) language utilises the usual idea of equating an object with a process, and state with process arguments, but this is encoded using clauses containing multiple literals in their heads:

```
(H1 @ ... @ Hn) <- Body.
```

The @ acts as a disjunction. Each clause can be thought of as a method, while the head literals correspond to object states. A method is selected if its head matches the goal corresponding to the object in its current state. A crucial aspect of the matching is that it is done in terms of multiset inclusion – the object must contain at least all of the states in the head. This permits an object to contain more state values than the method it is using, and so the object can be thought of as a more specialised instance of the class whose methods it is utilising. This is a very elegant way of encoding inheritance since an object will only consist of one structured process. This is in contrast to an approach which uses delegation as its inheritance mechanism, where there will be as many processes as there are classes, and a complex communication protocol is required.

Although LO is called an OOP language, it could be more accurately described as an attribute/value rewrite rule language.

3.6.4   Inheritance in the Meta-interpretation View

Inheritance in the meta-interpretation view is seen as just one way in which different classes can be linked at the meta level [46]. Thus, when a message cannot be answered by a method, it is passed to the meta level and then to its inherited class. Usually, Horn clause definitions specify the search strategy for the classes.

A related method is utilised in the PPS (Parlog Programming System), a multiprocessing programming environment which supports Parlog [38]. Users interact with the PPS by querying and updating collections of clauses, termed databases. The PPS understands certain clauses, called meta clauses, as describing meta level information such as system configuration details, the status of user deductions, and relationships between databases. Meta clauses are stored in the meta database for a database. Inheritance is coded by routing a failed query to an inherited database which is specified in the meta database.

One area in which many meta-interpretation view languages are weak is in their treatment of forwarded goals. These are goals which could not be answered in one class and so were forwarded to an inherited class. If a rule is present in this class it will be applied to the goal, so creating new subgoals. Usually these are solved with respect to the current class, but it would be better if they were solved in the class which originally forwarded their parent goal.

3.7   Other Paradigms

All of the languages in this survey are based on LP and OOP, and so are multi-paradigm languages. Some designers have encorporated additional paradigms into their languages, and these are discussed here.

3.7.1   Other Paradigms in the Clauses View

The most common extra paradigm in languages of this type is functional programming, which has been studied in detail by McCabe [131]. The aim of that work was not only to add first order functional ability to the language, but also to include lambda expressions and function variables for higher-order programming. However, this is constrained by his desire to map these extensions to first order logic, so it is not possible to compare arbitrary relations in the language, which would require higher order unification. Of the functional additions, lambda expressions are particularly useful since they can be used to directly describe a function. The nearest Prolog equivalent is the meta call which is really a mapping from a constant symbol to a relation. The extensions are based on condition equalities of the form:

```
f(Args) = Answer if Conditions.
```

where **Answer** is returned if the call unifies with **f(Args)**, and all the conditions evaluate to true. Related extensions have been proposed which extend unification rather than compile equalities down to first order logic [114, 101]. However, the results are the same since functional, logic and object-oriented programming can be carried out. Kornfeld also notes that constraint LP is possible.

LIFE [5] integrates functions, relations and types and is, partially, an extension of LOGIN [4]. A generalisation of the CLP scheme [95] is used to define a class of interpretations of approximation structures to represent objects.

Several languages contain the notion of data-oriented programming, which allows demons to be fired when certain events occur, such as state updates [36, 115, 13]. Some also use forward chaining, although this is easily simulated using backward chaining [115, 13].

3.7.2   Other Paradigms in the Process View

Meseguer has developed a logic for concurrent object-oriented computation, where deduction is performed by concurrent rewriting [136]. The Maude language, which uses this logic, can be viewed as an extension of the order-sorted functional language OBJ3, with additional notation for applying equations concurrently. In the paper, the rewriting logic is axiomatised, its relationship to actors discussed, and a model theoretic semantics based on categories developed. However, similarities to concurrent LP languages are not examined.

Vulcan subscribes to the committed choice process view of objects but the language is also important as one part of the Vulcan system which will contain many forms of abstractions and tools [106]. Although the system is still at an early stage, these abstractions and tools may include a functional language [123], an OR-parallel Prolog [174], channels [191], types [205], a keyword notation [87], a constraints language [169], lexical FCP [164], public key encryption [140] and a hardware description language [200]. Consequently, the Vulcan language does not possess a complete set of OOP tools, but can call upon the facilities in the rest of the Vulcan system when necessary.

3.7.3   Other Paradigms in the Meta-interpretation View

Since a class is executed by a meta interpreter, its actual contents can be almost anything as long as a suitable interpreter can be found, and its objects can communicate through message passing. For instance, classes in Mandala can consist of Prolog clauses, first order logic, or equations [72].

3.8   Summary

The discussion has illustrated the wide range of languages which combine OOP and LP. Different languages tend to emphasis different issues; some concentrate on semantics, some on functionality, and some on investigating particular extensions, such as augmented unification. However, the preceding sections have highlighted most of the strengths and weaknesses of the four main approaches to extending LP with OOP features, and this section will summarise them.

3.8.1   Summary of the Clauses View

The clauses view is probably the best for explaining the semantics of OOP, either as a syntactic extension to Horn clause logic, or as types. The conservative extensions to LP required for supporting OOP also mean that other paradigms, such as functional programming, can be easily added. The clauses approach also offers a straightforward means of dealing with inheritance (multiple inheritance in particular), and self communication.

On the negative side, clauses view languages are not particularly good at dealing with state, except at the expense of semantic clarity. Also, backtracking causes some problems with respect to the undoing of object creation, message passing, and state changes. On a more general level, backtracking may not be a suitable mechanism for typical OOP applications such as systems software and simulations.

3.8.2   Summary of the Process View

The process view was subdivided into the committed choice and backtracking approaches, but they share a number of qualities. They both deal with the representation of state in a simple manner, and both allow concurrency at the inter-object level. However, their semantics are quite complex because of the interaction between concurrency and Horn clause logic.

3.8.2.1   Summary of the Committed Choice Process View   Its message passing mechanism, based on shared logical variables, enables many unusual communication strategies to be encoded. The requirement to explicitly link objects with shared variables may seem to be a disadvantage, but this is probably outweighed by the usefulness of being able to manipulate such variables as first order entities. The inherent fine grain parallelism allows an object to carry out many actions simultaneously and to process many messages at once. This internal concurrency is also something of a hindrance when dealing with self communication and inherited state variables, and the language level resolution of these problems is an important issue. The don't care non-determinism of objects makes their execution simpler to understand, and perhaps closer to what is required by an OOP language. Unfortunately, it makes the treatment of multiple inheritance more difficult.

3.8.2.2   Summary of the Backtracking Process View   This has produced some interesting forms of communication, which often have uses outside of the message passing domain. The utilisation of sequential LP inside objects means that multiple inheritance is as simple as in the clauses view, but the presence of backtracking also produces the problems found in the clauses view, which are compounded by the availability of inter-object concurrency.

3.8.3   Summary of the Meta-interpretation View

The meta-interpretation view is the most flexible and powerful approach for combining OOP and LP. In particular, inheritance can be viewed as just one of many possible relationships between classes which can be simply expressed in Horn clause logic at the meta level. Also, the 'class as object' approach, as typified by Smalltalk, follows directly from treating a class as a first order entity.

The main drawback of the meta-interpretation view is that it is hard to implement efficiently.

3.9   Current Trends and Future Directions

In this section, some predictions are made about future research into the augmentation of LP with OOP functionality. Some of this will be extrapolated from work described earlier, but an attempt is also made to suggest new avenues of research by indicating how work in other areas may be utilised. By its very nature, much of this section is pure speculation.

3.9.1   Non-standard Logics

Just as sequential LP languages, AND-parallel LP languages and concurrent LP languages have distinctive object-oriented extensions, so do languages based on non-standard logics. OOP languages based on intuitionistic logic [88], and linear logic [6] already exist (see sections 5.1 and 6.3 for details).

A strange omission is the lack of any object-oriented extensions to a modal logic [91]. In the context of OOP, a modal logic would supply a basis for state representation and for transformations between states. Traditionally, such logics have also been found useful for formalising imperative programming languages, and for real-time and embedded systems [97].

Extensions to temporal logic would be a profitable research area [166]. It has a long history of being used for reasoning about updates to databases, and more recently for reasoning about concurrent programs and distributed systems. Two key advantages over the predicate calculus are the explicit representation of time, and the ability to clearly separate temporal information from the application data [147, 74]. Communication strategies for a meta-interpretation language were expressed using temporal logic in [90].

Intensional logics [67] are concerned with assertions and expressions whose meanings depend on an implicit context. The first imperative language based on this formalism was Lucid [193], which evaluated its expressions and variables depending on an implicit natural number time parameter. Time indices were manipulated explicitly with intensional operators such as **next** and **fby** (followed by). THLP [194] exploited these ideas in a LP context, and illustrated how it was possible to encode processes without using infinite terms (the method used in concurrent LP). More recently, an intensional semantics was employed in [34] to deal with state change in a clauses view language, but more work needs to be carried out, especially with respect to OOP and concurrent intensional LP.

Logics concerned with knowledge and belief [66] would be a good basis for a meta-interpretation view language. Knowledge and belief are distinguished by the way that an agent cannot *know* false facts, but can *believe* them. Much work has been done on developing semantics which reflect how agents cannot be logically omniscient, either because of lack of awareness of others, resource bounds on computation, or missing/inconsistent rules. These logics also allow an agent to believe invalid formulae, and be self critical. A first order formalism with these features have been developed for multi-agent systems [113].

Within the LP community, it is inevitable that further extensions to first order logics will generate new object-oriented formalisms. For instance, extending Prolog with abduction capabilities [118] permits a novel form of default reasoning and exception handling – both of which are useful for inheritance. Also of interest is the event calculus [119], a Prolog-based temporal reasoning notation which can talk about the history of states of a computation.

The backtracking process view and the committed choice process view are based on AND-parallel Prologs and committed choice LP languages respectively. However, an increasing number of LP languages have been developed which combine AND- and OR-parallelism, and none of them have yet been utilised as the basis for an object-oriented language.

For instance, Andorra [204] is a computational model designed to transparently extract stream AND-parallelism and OR-parallelism from Prolog programs. Andorra Prolog [84] uses the Andorra model as the basis of an extension to Prolog with features for delaying computation.

The Extended Andorra Model (EAM) is a set of rewrite rules on AND-OR trees that combines features of sequential and concurrent LP [197]. Kernel Andorra Prolog is a 'language framework' based on the EAM with additional constraint notions [85]. An instance of this framework is the Andorra Kernel Language (AKL) [94].

Related work includes Parallel NU-Prolog [153] which has recently been modified to support the model [157]. Pandora [10] can be viewed as a generalisation of the Andorra model. It permits both don't know and don't care relations in a program, combining features of Prolog and Parlog. P-Prolog [203] and ANDOR-II [184] are similar to Pandora in their wish to combine committed choice LP with don't know non-determinism. Pandora's main difference is the utilisation of lazy non-determinism.

Other proposals for combining Prolog and Parlog are explored in [40, 55].

3.9.2   Constraint-based Languages

Constraint LP is an exciting research area, which is rapidly being investigated.

In the clauses view category, FREEDOM [207] and LIFE [5] have already explored how taxonomies can be expressed as constraints.

Work on concurrent constraint LP [169] has recently borne fruit in the form of a simple language called Lucy [104], designed to mimic the actor model of computation [1]. Objects (agents) can communicate only by posting and checking constraints upon bags (unordered collections possibly with duplicate elements). Lucy is a syntactic subset of Janus [170], a concurrent constraint language closely akin to concurrent LP languages.

In the backtracking process view, the POOL language allows computations to be represented as a collection of parallel objects which communicate via asynchronous message passing [112]. The unusual feature of this work is that each object is encoded as a CLP(R) program [96]. In addition, the programs are distributed over a network of workstations, each containing a CLP(R) machine.

Inevitably, meta level constraints will be used in an object-oriented language. An interesting paper on these types of constraints in CLP(R) is [86].

A relevant sub-area of research is the definition of preferential constraints, in addition to the usual required constraints [19]. By allocating strengths to different constraints, a constraint hierarchy is created which can express different forms of non-monotonicity, default reasoning and state.

3.9.3   Linda

Linda is a coordination language which can be added to a programming language to facilitate process creation, and communication between the processes [30, 31]. The authors argue that programming languages should only define computing elements, while Linda should supply I/O and the mechanism for storing and retrieving state. This is an extreme separation for imperative programming languages, where I/O and state are central to their programming paradigm. However, these features are not part of the LP (or functional programming) paradigm and, consequently, combining Linda with Prolog would seem to be an easier task than combining it with a language like C. In fact, two Prolog+Linda languages are being developed: Shared Prolog and Prolog-D-Linda.

Shared Prolog [25] allows the creation of AND-parallel Prolog processes which communicate by posting terms to a globally accessible area known as a tuple space.

Prolog-D-Linda [181] is similar but extends the notion of tuple space to allow the storage of Prolog facts and rules – they call this a deductive tuple space.

There are interesting parallels between the Prolog+Linda idea and the computational model employed by Janus and Lucy, where operations can be applied to a pool of constraints accessible by many processes.

Linda's potential utility in the area of object-oriented and LP is that it allows AND-parallel objects to be easily encoded, and to communicate in a very expressive manner. Other relevant features include its control over the amount of parallelism exploited, and the ability to link in agents written in other languages.

The possibilities available by using the Linda model in the committed choice process view are illustrated in Polka-B [57] which uses it to inherit and share state.

Some areas of research include: developing hierarchical tuple spaces, exploring the connections between tuple spaces, blackboards and constraint stores, and integrating unification with Linda's communication mechanism.

3.9.4   Distributed Programming Languages

The notions of object and concurrency have been found useful in distributed programming where the unit of distribution and the amount of concurrent activity are important issues. This motivated the extension of committed choice LP languages with distributed programming features [173, 187]. Strand is a commercial language based on some of these ideas [70]. A similar approach has been used to augment the committed choice process view [53] and the backtracking process view [62].

Sandra [65] has perhaps the most fully developed support for distributed programming. The basic unit of distribution is called a guardian agent, which is reminiscent of an object because of its message passing interface, hidden state and inheritance. Sandra also offers support for real-time control through timing constraint expressions, and can survive logical and hardware failure.

The semantics of distributed concurrent constraint LP have been addressed in Janus [170]. Both Janus (and the related language Lucy) avoid logical failure and inconsistent constraint stores. However, they do not address issues such as processor allocation or recovery from hardware failure.

An important research topic concerns the trade-off between inheritance (encouraging code sharing) and distribution (encouraging code separation). The two seem incompatible, and probably inheritance should be replaced by delegation, which also interacts more favourably with the fine grain concurrency present in committed choice LP. Since most inheritance mechanisms in LP-based OOP languages are implemented using different forms of delegation, this should not be too hard.

A difficult topic is the language support necessary for recovering from failure. Logical failure can be handled by guards, exception mechanisms or backtracking within a LP framework. However, hardware failure (node failure, communication breakdown) is less easily dealt with, especially if a semantic basis for the constructs is desired.

3.9.5   Process Semantics

The backtracking process view and committed choice process view both characterise programs as networks of processes, which in turn can be identified with objects communicating by message passing. Increasingly, these analogies are being utilised to assign semantics to AND-parallel and committed choice LP languages.

The Actor formalism has attracted increasing interest as a means of linking concurrent LP with OOP. It is claimed that Lucy [104] is the 'missing link' between concurrent LP and actors, while Maude [136] can be viewed as a generalised form of actor language. Of most interest in this context is the use of actor semantics to give a meaning to committed choice process view languages.

[149] developed a process semantics for Parlog, by denoting a process as a set of input/output histories.

In [14], a sequential LP language was parallelised by mapping each clause in the program onto one CCS process.

Much of the work on the semantics of conventional process languages tends to be based on temporal constructs [128, 155] which can be seen as another reason for exploring object-oriented extensions to temporal LP languages.

3.9.6   Applications

Two major application areas which need to be investigated further are natural language processing and object-oriented databases.

3.9.6.1   Natural Language Processing   It is increasingly clear that the representation of natural language requires a *richer* system of terms for dealing with issues such as disjunction, scoping, subtyping and attribute slots than Prolog can offer [158]. Many of these concerns are also central to OOP, as can be seen in DL, a conventional OOP language for encoding natural language [201]. DL contains classes for representing linguistic entities such as words, sentences and grammar rules. It also has a simple object relation mechanism, and procedures for operating upon objects.

In this context, a useful object-oriented LP language is LOGIN [4], which offers both subtyping and more expressive term descriptors. LOGIN was influenced by a non-LP language KRYPTON [22], which utilises two sub-languages – the TBOX and ABOX. The TBOX is used for defining descriptive terms which are linked within a taxonomy. A TBOX term contains concepts (cf. frames) and roles (cf. slots). The ABOX is a first order predicate calculus whose logical symbols are TBOX entities. In a natural language setting, TBOX terms are like noun phrases, while ABOX formulae are like sentences.

The precursor of KRYPTON was KL-ONE [23], and in the last decade many systems have been built using its notion of knowledge separation.

The TBOX formalism is sometimes called a concept language or term subsumption language, and recently, the connections between such concept languages and constraint domains have been investigated [9].

3.9.6.2 Object-Oriented Databases Increasingly, object-oriented databases are being seen as an advance over the usual hierarchical, network or relational database models [60, 12, 8, 80]. They enable reuse of database structures, code sharing, encapsulation, and a way of clustering similar properties. Languages for coding object-oriented databases need a sophisticated query interface to deal with complex objects, dynamic object creation, distinct notions of class and object, and self-describing functionality. Clearly, many of these properties are already present in object-oriented LP languages.

3.9.7 Odds and Ends

This section contains a few predictions which do not fit under any general heading, but seem worthwhile to mention.

In the clauses view, research on the semantics of inheritance looks set to restrict it to a form of type specialisation, so that a simple denotation can be achieved [5, 109]. Inheritance is also likely to disappear in the committed choice process view, because of its unfavourable interaction with distributed programming concerns and with fine grain concurrency. However, in the latter case, the problems may be solved by constraining the concurrent evaluation of messages. A high level notation for message protocols which can specify these forms of restrictions is Open Path Expressions (OPEs) [29, 185].

Within the backtracking process view, the wish for a clearer explanation of the role of backtracking between objects will motivate languages designed with novel communication primitives. An alternative is to replace backtracking with OR-parallelism. The Extended Andorra Model offers an interesting way of transparently exploiting both OR-parallelism and stream AND-parallelism [197].

3.9.8 Inheritance in the Backtracking Process View

In these kinds of languages, inheritance is encoded by passing an unrecognised message to some other object which is specified as its inherited object. The actual form of communication mechanism varies but depends on the mechanism used for ordinary message passing. An important factor is the presence of backtracking, which means that the search of multiple inherited objects is much more straightforward than in the committed choice process view. However, self communication is still complicated and some languages avoid the problem by disallowing self communication [160]. Others treat `self` messages as internal predicate calls, which avoids the `self` message priority problem but requires a global name space for predicates [93].

Inheritance in DLP [62] is based on copying, so that an object obtains a copy of all the clauses and state variables of its ancestors.

An interesting extension of LP based on linear logic [77] has been proposed in [6]. Their Linear Objects (LO) language utilises the usual idea of equating an object with a process, and state with process arguments, but this is encoded using clauses containing multiple literals in their heads:

```
(H1 @ ... @ Hn) <- Body.
```

The @ acts as a disjunction. Each clause can be thought of as a method, while the head literals correspond to object states. A method is selected if its head matches the goal corresponding to the object in its current state. A crucial aspect of the matching is that it is done in terms of multiset inclusion – the object must contain at least all of the states in the head. This permits an object to contain more state values than the method it is using, and so the object can be thought of as a more specialised instance of the class whose methods it is utilising. This is a very elegant way of encoding inheritance since an object will only consist of one structured process. This is in contrast to an approach which uses delegation as its inheritance mechanism, where there will be as many processes as there are classes, and a complex communication protocol is required.

Although LO is called an OOP language, it could be more accurately described as an attribute/value rewrite rule language.

3.9.9 Inheritance in the Meta-interpretation View

Inheritance in the meta-interpretation view is seen as just one way in which different classes can be linked at the meta level [46]. Thus, when a message cannot be answered by a method, it is passed to the meta level and then to its inherited class. Usually, Horn clause definitions specify the search strategy for the classes.

A related method is utilised in the PPS (Parlog Programming System), a multiprocessing programming environment which supports Parlog [38]. Users interact with the PPS by querying and updating collections of clauses, termed databases. The PPS understands certain clauses, called meta clauses, as describing meta level information such as system configuration details, the status of user deductions, and relationships between databases. Meta clauses are stored in the meta database for a database. Inheritance is coded by routing a failed query to an inherited database which is specified in the meta database.

One area in which many meta-interpretation view languages are weak is in their treatment of forwarded goals. These are goals which could not be answered in one class and so were forwarded to an inherited class. If a rule is present in this class it will be applied to the goal, so creating new subgoals. Usually these are solved with respect to the current class, but it would be better if they were solved in the class which originally forwarded their parent goal.

3.10   Other Paradigms

All of the languages in this survey are based on LP and OOP, and so are multi-paradigm languages. Some designers have encorporated additional paradigms into their languages, and these are discussed here.

3.10.1   Other Paradigms in the Clauses View

The most common extra paradigm in languages of this type is functional programming, which has been studied in detail by McCabe [131]. The aim of that work was not only to add first order functional ability to the language, but also to include lambda expressions and function variables for higher-order programming. However, this is constrained by his desire to map these extensions to first order logic, so it is not possible to compare arbitrary relations in the language, which would require higher order unification. Of the functional additions, lambda expressions are particularly useful since they can be used to directly describe a function. The nearest Prolog equivalent is the meta call which is really a mapping from a constant symbol to a relation. The extensions are based on condition equalities of the form:

```
f(Args) = Answer if Conditions.
```

where `Answer` is returned if the call unifies with `f(Args)`, and all the conditions evaluate to true. Related extensions have been proposed which extend unification rather than compile equalities down to first order logic [114, 101]. However, the results are the same since functional, logic and object-oriented programming can be carried out. Kornfeld also notes that constraint LP is possible.

LIFE [5] integrates functions, relations and types and is, partially, an extension of LOGIN [4]. A generalisation of the CLP scheme [95] is used to define a class of interpretations of approximation structures to represent objects.

Several languages contain the notion of data-oriented programming, which allows demons to be fired when certain events occur, such as state updates [36, 115, 13]. Some also use forward chaining, although this is easily simulated using backward chaining [115, 13].

3.10.2   Other Paradigms in the Process View

Meseguer has developed a logic for concurrent object-oriented computation, where deduction is performed by concurrent rewriting [136]. The Maude language, which uses this logic, can be viewed as an extension of the order-sorted functional language OBJ3, with additional notation for applying equations concurrently. In the paper, the rewriting logic is axiomatised, its relationship to actors discussed, and a model theoretic semantics based on categories developed. However, similarities to concurrent LP languages are not examined.

Vulcan subscribes to the committed choice process view of objects but the language is also important as one part of the Vulcan system which will contain many forms of abstractions and tools [106]. Although the system is still at an early stage, these abstractions and tools may include a functional language [123], an OR-parallel Prolog [174], channels [191], types [205], a keyword notation [87], a constraints language [169], lexical FCP [164], public key encryption [140] and a hardware description language [200]. Consequently, the Vulcan language does not possess a complete set of OOP tools, but can call upon the facilities in the rest of the Vulcan system when necessary.

3.10.3   Other Paradigms in the Meta-interpretation View

Since a class is executed by a meta interpreter, its actual contents can be almost anything as long as a suitable interpreter can be found, and its objects can communicate through message passing. For instance, classes in Mandala can consist of Prolog clauses, first order logic, or equations [72].

3.11   Summary

The discussion has illustrated the wide range of languages which combine OOP and LP. Different languages tend to emphasis different issues; some concentrate on semantics, some on functionality, and some on investigating particular extensions, such as augmented unification. However, the preceding sections have highlighted most of the strengths and weaknesses of the four main approaches to extending LP with OOP features, and this section will summarise them.

3.11.1   Summary of the Clauses View

The clauses view is probably the best for explaining the semantics of OOP, either as a syntactic extension to Horn clause logic, or as types. The conservative extensions to LP required for supporting OOP also mean that other paradigms, such as functional programming, can be easily added. The clauses approach also offers a straightforward means of dealing with inheritance (multiple inheritance in particular), and self communication.

On the negative side, clauses view languages are not particularly good at dealing with state, except at the expense of semantic clarity. Also, backtracking causes some problems with respect to the undoing of object creation, message passing, and state changes. On a more general level, backtracking may not be a suitable mechanism for typical OOP applications such as systems software and simulations.

3.11.2   Summary of the Process View

The process view was subdivided into the committed choice and backtracking approaches, but they share a number of qualities. They both deal with the representation of state in a simple manner, and both allow concurrency at the inter-object level. However, their semantics are quite complex because of the interaction between concurrency and Horn clause logic.

3.11.2.1 Summary of the Committed Choice Process View

Its message passing mechanism, based on shared logical variables, enables many unusual communication strategies to be encoded. The requirement to explicitly link objects with shared variables may seem to be a disadvantage, but this is probably outweighed by the usefulness of being able to manipulate such variables as first order entities. The inherent fine grain parallelism allows an object to carry out many actions simultaneously and to process many messages at once. This internal concurrency is also something of a hindrance when dealing with self communication and inherited state variables, and the language level resolution of these problems is an important issue. The don't care non-determinism of objects makes their execution simpler to understand, and perhaps closer to what is required by an OOP language. Unfortunately, it makes the treatment of multiple inheritance more difficult.

3.11.2.2 Summary of the Backtracking Process View

This has produced some interesting forms of communication, which often have uses outside of the message passing domain. The utilisation of sequential LP inside objects means that multiple inheritance is as simple as in the clauses view, but the presence of backtracking also produces the problems found in the clauses view, which are compounded by the availability of inter-object concurrency.

3.11.3 Summary of the Meta-interpretation View

The meta-interpretation view is the most flexible and powerful approach for combining OOP and LP. In particular, inheritance can be viewed as just one of many possible relationships between classes which can be simply expressed in Horn clause logic at the meta level. Also, the 'class as object' approach, as typified by Smalltalk, follows directly from treating a class as a first order entity.

The main drawback of the meta-interpretation view is that it is hard to implement efficiently.

3.12   Current Trends and Future Directions

In this section, some predictions are made about future research into the augmentation of LP with OOP functionality. Some of this will be extrapolated from work described earlier, but an attempt is also made to suggest new avenues of research by indicating how work in other areas may be utilised. By its very nature, much of this section is pure speculation.

3.12.1   Non-standard Logics

Just as sequential LP languages, AND-parallel LP languages and concurrent LP languages have distinctive object-oriented extensions, so do languages based on non-standard logics. OOP languages based on intuitionistic logic [88], and linear logic [6] already exist (see sections 5.1 and 6.3 for details).

A strange omission is the lack of any object-oriented extensions to a modal logic [91]. In the context of OOP, a modal logic would supply a basis for state representation and for transformations between states. Traditionally, such logics have also been found useful for formalising imperative programming languages, and for real-time and embedded systems [97].

Extensions to temporal logic would be a profitable research area [166]. It has a long history of being used for reasoning about updates to databases, and more recently for reasoning about concurrent programs and distributed systems. Two key advantages over the predicate calculus are the explicit representation of time, and the ability to clearly separate temporal information from the application data [147, 74]. Communication strategies for a meta-interpretation language were expressed using temporal logic in [90].

Intensional logics [67] are concerned with assertions and expressions whose meanings depend on an implicit context. The first imperative language based on this formalism was Lucid [193], which evaluated its expressions and variables depending on an implicit natural number time parameter. Time indices were manipulated explicitly with intensional operators such as next and fby (followed by). THLP [194] exploited these ideas in a LP context, and illustrated how it was possible to encode processes without using infinite terms (the method used in concurrent LP). More recently, an intensional semantics was employed in [34] to deal with state change in a clauses view language, but more work needs to be carried out, especially with respect to OOP and concurrent intensional LP.

Logics concerned with knowledge and belief [66] would be a good basis for a meta-interpretation view language. Knowledge and belief are distinguished by the way that an agent cannot *know* false facts, but can *believe* them. Much work has been done on developing semantics which reflect how agents cannot be logically omniscient, either because of lack of awareness of others, resource bounds on computation, or missing/inconsistent rules. These logics also allow an agent to believe invalid formulae, and be self critical. A first order formalism with these features have been developed for multi-agent systems [113].

Within the LP community, it is inevitable that further extensions to first order logics will generate new object-oriented formalisms. For instance, extending Prolog with abduction capabilities [118] permits a novel form of default reasoning and exception handling – both of which are useful for inheritance. Also of interest is the event calculus [119], a Prolog-based temporal reasoning notation which can talk about the history of states of a computation.

The backtracking process view and the committed choice process view are based on AND-parallel Prologs and committed choice LP languages respectively. However, an increasing number of LP languages have been developed which combine AND- and OR-parallelism, and none of them have yet been utilised as the basis for an object-oriented language.

For instance, Andorra [204] is a computational model designed to transparently extract stream AND-parallelism and OR-parallelism from Prolog programs. Andorra Prolog [84] uses the Andorra model as the basis of an extension to Prolog with features for delaying computation.

The Extended Andorra Model (EAM) is a set of rewrite rules on AND-OR trees that combines features of sequential and concurrent LP [197]. Kernel Andorra Prolog is a 'language framework' based on the EAM with additional constraint notions [85]. An instance of this framework is the Andorra Kernel Language (AKL) [94].

Related work includes Parallel NU-Prolog [153] which has recently been modified to support the model [157]. Pandora [10] can be viewed as a generalisation of the Andorra model. It permits both don't know and don't care relations in a program, combining features of Prolog and Parlog. P-Prolog [203] and ANDOR-II [184] are similar to Pandora in their wish to combine committed choice LP with don't know non-determinism. Pandora's main difference is the utilisation of lazy non-determinism.

Other proposals for combining Prolog and Parlog are explored in [40, 55].

3.12.2 Constraint-based Languages

Constraint LP is an exciting research area, which is rapidly being investigated.

In the clauses view category, FREEDOM [207] and LIFE [5] have already explored how taxonomies can be expressed as constraints.

Work on concurrent constraint LP [169] has recently borne fruit in the form of a simple language called Lucy [104], designed to mimic the actor model of computation [1]. Objects (agents) can communicate only by posting and checking constraints upon bags (unordered collections possibly with duplicate elements). Lucy is a syntactic subset of Janus [170], a concurrent constraint language closely akin to concurrent LP languages.

In the backtracking process view, the POOL language allows computations to be represented as a collection of parallel objects which communicate via asynchronous message passing [112]. The unusual feature of this work is that each object is encoded as a CLP(R) program [96]. In addition, the programs are distributed over a network of workstations, each containing a CLP(R) machine.

Inevitably, meta level constraints will be used in an object-oriented language. An interesting paper on these types of constraints in CLP(R) is [86].

A relevant sub-area of research is the definition of preferential constraints, in addition to the usual required constraints [19]. By allocating strengths to different constraints, a constraint hierarchy is created which can express different forms of non-monotonicity, default reasoning and state.

3.12.3 Linda

Linda is a coordination language which can be added to a programming language to facilitate process creation, and communication between the processes [30, 31]. The authors argue that programming languages should only define computing elements, while Linda should supply I/O and the mechanism for storing and retrieving state. This is an extreme separation for imperative programming languages, where I/O and state are central to their programming paradigm. However, these features are not part of the LP (or functional programming) paradigm and, consequently, combining Linda with Prolog would seem to be an easier task than combining it with a language like C. In fact, two Prolog+Linda languages are being developed: Shared Prolog and Prolog-D-Linda.

Shared Prolog [25] allows the creation of AND-parallel Prolog processes which communicate by posting terms to a globally accessible area known as a tuple space.

Prolog-D-Linda [181] is similar but extends the notion of tuple space to allow the storage of Prolog facts and rules – they call this a deductive tuple space.

There are interesting parallels between the Prolog+Linda idea and the computational model employed by Janus and Lucy, where operations can be applied to a pool of constraints accessible by many processes.

Linda's potential utility in the area of object-oriented and LP is that it allows AND-parallel objects to be easily encoded, and to communicate in a very expressive manner. Other relevant features include its control over the amount of parallelism exploited, and the ability to link in agents written in other languages.

The possibilities available by using the Linda model in the committed choice process view are illustrated in Polka-B [57] which uses it to inherit and share state.

Some areas of research include: developing hierarchical tuple spaces, exploring the connections between tuple spaces, blackboards and constraint stores, and integrating unification with Linda's communication mechanism.

3.12.4   Distributed Programming Languages

The notions of object and concurrency have been found useful in distributed programming where the unit of distribution and the amount of concurrent activity are important issues. This motivated the extension of committed choice LP languages with distributed programming features [173, 187]. Strand is a commercial language based on some of these ideas [70]. A similar approach has been used to augment the committed choice process view [53] and the backtracking process view [62].

Sandra [65] has perhaps the most fully developed support for distributed programming. The basic unit of distribution is called a guardian agent, which is reminiscent of an object because of its message passing interface, hidden state and inheritance. Sandra also offers support for real-time control through timing constraint expressions, and can survive logical and hardware failure.

The semantics of distributed concurrent constraint LP have been addressed in Janus [170]. Both Janus (and the related language Lucy) avoid logical failure and inconsistent constraint stores. However, they do not address issues such as processor allocation or recovery from hardware failure.

An important research topic concerns the trade-off between inheritance (encouraging code sharing) and distribution (encouraging code separation). The two seem incompatible, and probably inheritance should be replaced by delegation, which also interacts more favourably with the fine grain concurrency present in committed choice LP. Since most inheritance mechanisms in LP-based OOP languages are implemented using different forms of delegation, this should not be too hard.

A difficult topic is the language support necessary for recovering from failure. Logical failure can be handled by guards, exception mechanisms or backtracking within a LP framework. However, hardware failure (node failure, communication breakdown) is less easily dealt with, especially if a semantic basis for the constructs is desired.

3.12.5   Process Semantics

The backtracking process view and committed choice process view both characterise programs as networks of processes, which in turn can be identified with objects communicating by message passing. Increasingly, these analogies are being utilised to assign semantics to AND-parallel and committed choice LP languages.

The Actor formalism has attracted increasing interest as a means of linking concurrent LP with OOP. It is claimed that Lucy [104] is the 'missing link' between concurrent LP and actors, while Maude [136] can be viewed as a generalised form of actor language. Of most interest in this context is the use of actor semantics to give a meaning to committed choice process view languages.

[149] developed a process semantics for Parlog, by denoting a process as a set of input/output histories.

In [14], a sequential LP language was parallelised by mapping each clause in the program onto one CCS process.

Much of the work on the semantics of conventional process languages tends to be based on temporal constructs [128, 155] which can be seen as another reason for exploring object-oriented extensions to temporal LP languages.

3.12.6   Applications

Two major application areas which need to be investigated further are natural language processing and object-oriented databases.

3.12.6.1   Natural Language Processing   It is increasingly clear that the representation of natural language requires a *richer* system of terms for dealing with issues such as disjunction, scoping, subtyping and attribute slots than Prolog can offer [158]. Many of these concerns are also central to OOP, as can be seen in DL, a conventional OOP language for encoding natural language [201]. DL contains classes for representing linguistic entities such as words, sentences and grammar rules. It also has a simple object relation mechanism, and procedures for operating upon objects.

In this context, a useful object-oriented LP language is LOGIN [4], which offers both subtyping and more expressive term descriptors. LOGIN was influenced by a non-LP language KRYPTON [22], which utilises two sub-languages – the TBOX and ABOX. The TBOX is used for defining descriptive terms which are linked within a taxonomy. A TBOX term contains concepts (cf. frames) and roles (cf. slots). The ABOX is a first order predicate calculus whose logical symbols are TBOX entities. In a natural language setting, TBOX terms are like noun phrases, while ABOX formulae are like sentences.

The precursor of KRYPTON was KL-ONE [23], and in the last decade many systems have been built using its notion of knowledge separation.

The TBOX formalism is sometimes called a concept language or term subsumption language, and recently, the connections between such concept languages and constraint domains have been investigated [9].

3.12.6.2   Object-Oriented Databases   Increasingly, object-oriented databases are being seen as an advance over the usual hierarchical, network or relational database models [60, 12, 8, 80]. They enable reuse of database structures, code sharing, encapsulation, and a way of clustering similar properties. Languages for coding object-oriented databases need a sophisticated query interface to deal with complex objects, dynamic object creation, distinct notions of class and object, and self-describing functionality. Clearly, many of these properties are already present in object-oriented LP languages.

3.12.7   Odds and Ends

This section contains a few predictions which do not fit under any general heading, but seem worthwhile to mention.

In the clauses view, research on the semantics of inheritance looks set to restrict it to a form of type specialisation, so that a simple denotation can be achieved [5, 109]. Inheritance is also likely to disappear in the committed choice process view, because of its unfavourable interaction with distributed programming concerns and with fine grain concurrency. However, in the latter case, the problems may be solved by constraining the concurrent evaluation of messages. A high level notation for message protocols which can specify these forms of restrictions is Open Path Expressions (OPEs) [29, 185].

Within the backtracking process view, the wish for a clearer explanation of the role of backtracking between objects will motivate languages designed with novel communication primitives. An alternative is to replace backtracking with OR-parallelism. The Extended Andorra Model offers an interesting way of transparently exploiting both OR-parallelism and stream AND-parallelism [197].

References

[1]   Agha, G. 1986. *Actors: A model of Concurrent Computation in distributed systems*, MIT Press, Cambridge, MA.

[2]   Aiba, A., et al. 1988. "Constraint Logic Programming Language CAL", In *Proc. of Int. Conf. of 5th generation Computer Systems 1988*, pp. 263-276.

[3]   Akama, K. 1986. "Inheritance Hierarchy Mechanism in Prolog", In *Proc. of the 5th Int. Conf on Logic Programming*, E. Wada (ed.), LNCS 264, Springer-Verlag, Tokyo, Japan, June, pp. 12-21.

[4]   Ait-kaci, H., and Nasr, R. 1986. "LOGIN: A Logic Programming Language with built-in Inheritance", Journal of Logic Programming, vol. 3, no. 3, pp. 185-215, October.

[5]   Ait-kaci, H., and Podelski, A. 1991. "Is there a Meaning to LIFE?", Invited paper in *PLILP'91 : 3rd Int. Symp. on Programming Language Implementation and LP*, Springer LNCS 528, Passau, Germany, August, pp.255-286.

[6]   Andreoli, J-M., and Pareschi, R. 1991. "Linear Objects: Logical Processes with Built-in Inheritance", In *New Generation Computing*, 9, Nos 3 and 4, Springer Verlag, pp.445-473. Also in *Proc. of OOPSLA'91, SIGPLAN Notices*, Vol. 26, No. 11, November, pp.212-229.

[7]   Anjewierden, A. 1986. "How about a Prolog Object?", Draft Paper, Dept. of Computing, Universit d'Amsterdam, Holland.

[8]   Atkinson, M., Bancilhon, F., DeWitt, D., Dittrich, K., Maier, D., and Zdonik, S. 1989. "The Object-Oriented Database System Manifesto", In *DOOD'89: 1st Int. Conf. on Deductive and Object-Oriented Databases*, W. Kim, J-M. Nicholas, S. Nishio (eds.), Kyoyo, Japan, December, pp.40-57.

[9]   Baader, F., Burckert, H. J., Hollunder, B., Nutt, W., and Siekmann, J.H. 1990. "Concept Logics", In *Proc. of the Symp. on Computational Logics*, Brssel, November.

[10]   Bahgat, R., and Gregory, S. 1988. "PANDORA: Non-deterministic Parallel Logic Programming",
In *Proc. of the 6th. Int. Conf. on Logic Programming*, K. Bowen and R.A. Kowalski (eds.), MIT Press,
pp.1277-1297.

[11]   Bancilhon, F. 1986. "A Logic-Programming /Object-Oriented Cocktail", *SIGMOD RECORD*, Vol.
15, No. 3, September, pp. 11-21.

[12]   Bancilhon, F. 1988. "Object-Oriented Database Systems", In *Proc. 7th ACM SIGART-SIGMOD-
SIGACT Symp. on Principles of Database Systems*, ACM Press.

[13]   Bartual, R. 1989. "LPA Prolog and Flex Expert", *Program Now*, Vol. 3, No. 2, February, pp.43-47.

[14]   Beckman, L., Gustavsson, R., and Wrn, A. 1986. "An Algebraic Model of Parallel Execution of
Logic Programs", In *Logic in Computer Science*, Cambridge, Mass.

[15]   Birtwistle, G.M., Dahl, O-J., Myhrhaug, B., and Nygaard, K. 1973., *SIMULA BEGIN*, Petrocelli
/ Charter, New York.

[16]   Black, D., and Manley, J. 1987. "A Logic-based Architecture for Knowledge Management", In
Proc. of 10th IJCAI, Vol. 1, Milan, Italy, pp. 87-90.

[17]   Bobrow, D.G., and Stefik, S. 1983. "The LOOPS Manual", Xerox PARC, Palo Alto, CA, December.

[18]   Bonner, A.J., McCarthy, L.T., and Vadaparty, K. 1989. "Expressing Database Queries with Intuitionistic Logic", In *Logic Programming: Proc. of the North American Conf.*, pp. 831-850.

[19]   Borning, A., Maher, M., Martindale, A., and Wilson, M. 1988. "Constraint Hierarchies and Logic
Programming", Tech. Report 88-11-10, Computer Science Dept., Univ. of Washington, November.

[20]   Bowen, K.A. 1985. "Metalevel Programming and Knowledge Representation", *New Generation
Computing*, 3 (1985), pp. 359-383.

[21]   Bowen, K.A., and Kowalski, R.A. 1982. "Amalgamating language and metalanguage in logic programming", In *Logic Programming*, K.L.Clark, and S.A. Tarnlund (eds.), Academic Press, New York,
pp. 153-172.

[22]   Brachman, R.J., Pigman Gilbert, V. and Levesque, H.J. 1985. "An Essential Hybrid Reasoning
System: Knowledge and Symbol Level Accounts of KRYPTON", In *9th IJCAI*, Vol.1, August, pp.532-
539.

[23]   Brachman, R.J. and Schmolze, J.G. 1985. "An Overview of the KL-ONE Knowledge Representation System", *Cognitive Science*, 9(2), April, pp.171-216.

[24]   Brayshaw, M. 1991. "An Architecture for Visualizing the Execution of Parallel Logic Programs",
In *12th IJCAI*, J. Mylopoulous and R.Reiter (eds.), August, Sydney, Australia, Morgan Kaufmann Pub.
Inc., Vol. 2, pp.870-876.

[25]   Brogi, A., and Ciancarini, P. 1991. "The Concurrent Language Shared Prolog", In *ACM Trans.
on Prog. Langs. and Systems*, Vol. 13, No. 1, January, pp.99-123.

[26]   Brogi, A., and Gorrieri, R. 1989. "Model-theoretic, Fixpoint and Operational Semantics for a
Distributed Logic Language", In *Proc. of the 6th Int. Conf. on LP*, G. Levi and M. Martelli (eds.),
Lisboa, Portugal, MIT Press, pp.637-652.

[27]   Brogi, A., Lamma, E., and Mello, P. 1990. "Inheritance and Hypothetical Reasoning in Logic Programming", In *ECAI 90: Proc. of 9th European Conf. on AI*, L.C. Aiello (ed.), August 6-10, Stockholm,
Sweden, Pitman Publishing, pp. 105-110.

[28]   Bugliesi, M., Lamma, E., and Mello, P. 1990. "Partial Evaluation for Hierarchies of Logic Theories",
In *Proc. of the 1990 North American Conference on Logic Programming*, S. Debray and M. Hermenegildo
(eds.), Austin, Texas, MIT Press, October, pp.359-376.

[29]   Campbell, R.H., and Habermann, A.N. 1974. "The Specification of Process Synchronization by
Path Expressions", In *Lecture Notes in Computer Science 16*, Springer-Verlag, pp. 89-102.

[30]   Carriero, N., and Gelernter, D. 1989a. "Linda in Context", *Comm. ACM*, April (32, 4), pp.444-458.

[31]   Carriero, N., and Gelernter, D. 1989b. "How to Write Parallel Programs: A Guide to the Perplexed", In *ACM Computing Surveys*, Vol. 21, No. 3, September, pp.323-357.

[32]   Chan, D., Dufresne, P., and Enders, R. 1987. "PHOCUS: Production Rules, Horn Clauses, Objects

and Contexts in a Unification-based System", Actes du Sm. Prog. en Logique, Trgastel, May, pp.77-108.

[33] Chen, W., Kifer, M. and Warren, D.S. 1989. "HiLog: A First-Order Semantics for Higher-Order Logic Programming Constructs", In *Logic Programming: Proc. of the North American Conf.*, E.L. Lusk. and R.A. Overbeek (eds.), MIT Press, pp.1090-1114.

[34] Chen, W., and Warren, D.S. 1988. "Objects as Intensions", In *Logic Programming: Proc. 5th Int. Conf. and Symposium*, R.A. Kowalski, and K.A. Bowen (eds.), Seattle, Washington, Sponsored by ALP and IEEE, pp. 404-419.

[35] Chen, W., and Warren, D.S. 1989. "C-Logic of Complex Objects", In *Proc. of the 8th ACM SIGACT-SIGMOD-SIGART Symp. on the Principles of Database Systems*.

[36] Chikayama, T. 1984. "ESP Reference Manual", ICOT Technical Report: TR-044, Tokyo, Japan.

[37] Chusho, T., and Haga, H. 1986. "A multilingual modular programming system for describing knowledge information processing systems", In *Information Processing 86*, H. J. Kugler (ed.), Elsevier, North Holland, New York, NY.

[38] Clark, K.L., and Foster, I.T. 1986. "A Declarative Environment for Concurrent Logic Programming", Tech. Report PAR 86/4, Dept. of Computing, Imperial College, London.

[39] Clark, K.L., and Gregory, S. 1986. "PARLOG: Parallel Programming in Logic", *ACM Trans. on Programming Languages and Systems*, 8 (1), pp. 1-49.

[40] Clark, K.L., and Gregory, S. 1987. "Parlog and Prolog United", Presented at the *4th Int. Logic Programming Conf.*, Melbourne, Australia, May.

[41] Clark, K.L., and McCabe, F.G. 1984. *micro-PROLOG: Programming in Logic*, Prentice Hall, Englewood Cliffs, NJ.

[42] Clocksin, W.F., and Mellish, C.S. 1990. *Programming in Prolog*, 3rd Ed., Springer-Verlag, New York.

[43] Conery, J.S. 1987. "Object-Oriented Programming with First Order Logic", CIS-TR-87-09, Univ. of Oregon.

[44] Conery, J.S. 1988. "Logical Objects", In *Logic Programming: Proc. 5th Int. Conf. and Symposium*, R.A. Kowalski, and K.A. Bowen (eds.), Seattle, Washington, Sponsored by ALP and IEEE, pp. 420-434.

[45] Conlon, T. 1989. *Programming in Parlog*, Addison Wesley, Reading, Mass.

[46] Coscia, P., Franceschi, P., Levi, G., Sardu, G., and Torre, L. 1988. "Meta-level Definition and Compilation of Inference Engines in the Epsilon Logic Programming Environment", In *Logic Programming : Proc. 5th Int. Conf. and Symposium*, R.A. Kowalski and K.A. Bowen (eds.), Seattle, Washington, Sponsored by ALP and IEEE, pp. 359-373.

[47] Cowan, W.R. 1988. "Polka Programming Environment Tools", Thesis for PGDip in Computing and Artificial Intelligence, South Bank Polytechnic, London.

[48] Cunha, J.C., Ferreira, M.C., and Pereira, L.M. 1989. "Programming in Delta Prolog", In *Proc. of the 6th Int. Conf. of Logic Programming*, G. Levi and M. Martelli (eds.), The MIT Press. pp. 487-502.

[49] Cutcher, M.G. 1986. "Techniques of Parallel Logic Programming", Systems and Architectures Dept. Report, ICL, Reading, England, July.

[50] Davison, A. 1987. "Blackboard systems in Polka", *Int. Journal of Parallel Processing*, Vol. 16, No. 5, October, pp.401-424.

[51] Davison, A. 1988. "Simulation techniques in Polka", Tech. Report PAR 88/5, Dept. of Computing, Imperial College, London, June.

[52] Davison, A. 1989a. "BMS and Polka", Tech. Report PAR 89/2, Dept. of Computing, Imperial College, London, January.

[53] Davison, A. 1989b. "Distribution Issues in Polka", Tech. Report, Dept. of Computing, Imperial College, London, August.

[54] Davison, A. 1989c. "Polka: A Parlog Object-Oriented Language", PhD Thesis, Dept. of Computing, Imperial College, London, September.

[55] Davison, A. 1990a. "Hermes: A Combination of Parlog and Prolog", Tech. Report, Dept. of

Computing, Imperial College, London, August.

[56]   Davison, A. 1991. "From Parlog to Polka in Two Easy Steps", In
PLILP'91 : 3rd Int. Symp. on Programming Language Implementation and LP, Springer LNCS 528,
pp.171-182, Passau, Germany, August.

[57]   Davison, A. 1992. "Polka-B: Polka with Blackboards", In *ACSC-15: the Australian Computer
Science Conf.*, Hobart, Tasmania, Australia, January.

[58]   Dieng, R., Fornarino, M., and Pinna, A-M. 1988. "OTHELO: Objects, Typing, Inheritance and
Logic Programming", Tech. Report, INRIA, Valbonne, France, March.

[59]   DIGITALK INC. 1988 "Prolog/V documentation with Smalltalk/V Mac".

[60]   Dittrich, K.R. 1986. "Object-Oriented Database Systems: the Notion and the Issues (extended
abstract)", In *Proc. of 1986 Int. Workshop on Object-Oriented Database Systems*, K. Dittrich and U.
Dayal (eds.), Sept. 23-26, pp. 2-4.

[61]   Doman, A. 1986. "Object-PROLOG: Dynamic Object-Oriented Representation of Knowledge",
Tech. Report, SzKI Comp Research and Innovation. Center.

[62]   Eliens, A. 1991. "DLP – A Language for Distributed Logic Programming", PhD Thesis, University
of Amsterdam, February. Also see *AI Communications*, vol. 4, no. 1, March, pp. 11-21.

[63]   El-Kholy, A. 1990. "Object Modules in FGDC", MEng IV Final Year Project Report, Dept. of
Computing, Imperial College, London, June.

[64]   Elshiewy, N.A. 1988. "Modular and Communicating Objects in SICStus Prolog", In *Proc. Int.
Conf. on Fifth Generation Computer Systems 1988*, ICOT, Tokyo.

[65]   Elshiewy, N.A. 1990. "Robust Coordinated Reactive Computing in SANDRA", PhD Thesis, The
Royal Institute of Technology KTH, Sweden.

[66]   Fagin, R., and HALPERN, J.Y. 1985. "Belief, Awareness, and Limited Reasoning", In *Proc. of
the 9th Int. Conf. on AI*, Los Angeles, Morgan-Kaufmann, pp.491-501.

[67]   Faustini, A.A., and Wadge, W.W. 1986. "Intensional Programming", In *2nd Conf. on Languages
and Problem Solving*, Applied Physics Laboratory, John Hopkins Univ., June.

[68]   Fellous, J-M., Rizk, A., and Tueni, M. 1988. "An Object-Oriented Formalism in the Concurrent
Logic Programming Language Parlog", BULL and INRIA Tech. Report, Massy, France, August.

[69]   Finin, T., and McGuire, J. 1990. "Inheritance Hierarchies in Logic Programming Languages", In
Inheritance Hierarchies in Knowledge Representation, M. Lenzerini, D. Nardi and M. Simi (eds.), Wiley.

[70]   Foster, I., and Taylor, S. 1989. *Strand: New Concepts in Parallel Programming*, Prentice Hall,
Englewood Cliffs, N.J.

[71]   Fukunaga, K., and Hirose, S. 1986. "An Experience with a Prolog-based Object-Oriented Language", *OOPSLA '86 Proceedings*, *SIGPLAN Notices*, Vol. 21, No. 11, September, pp.224-231.

[72]   Furukawa, K., Takeuchi, A., Kunifuji, S., Yasukawa, H., Ohki, M., and Ueda, K. 1984. "MAN-
DALA: A Logic Based Knowledge Programming System", In *Proc. Int. Conf. 5th Gen. Computer Systems*, ICOT, Tokyo, Japan, pp. 613-622.

[73]   Futo, I., and Szeredi, J. 1984. "System Simulation and Co-Operation Problem-Solving on a Prolog
Basis", In *Implementations of Prolog*, J.A. Campbell (ed.), Ellis Horwood, Chicester, pp 163-174.

[74]   Gabbay, D.M. 1987. "Modal and Temporal Logic Programming", In *Temporal Logics and their
Applications*, A. Galton (ed.), Academic Press.

[75]   Gallaire, H. 1986. "Merging Objects and Logic Programming: Relational Semantics", In *Proc.
AAA1 86*, Philadelphia, PA, pp. 754-758.

[76]   Giordano, L., Martelli, A., and Rossi, G.F. 1988. "Local Definitions with Static Scope Rules in
LP", In *Proc. of the Int. Conf. on 5th Gen. Computer Systems*, ICOT, Tokyo, Japan, pp.389-396.

[77]   Girard, J.Y. 1987. "Linear Logic", *Theoretical Computer Science*, 50:1, pp. 1 -102.

[78]   Goguen, J.A., and Meseguer, J. 1986. "Extensions and Foundations of Object-oriented Programming", *SIGPLAN Notices*, Vol. 21, No. 10, October, pp.153-162.

[79]   Goldberg, A. 1983. *Smalltalk-80: The Language and its Implementation*, Addison Wesley, Reading,

MA.

[80]   Gray, P.M.D., 1989. "Expert Systems and Object-Oriented Databases: Evolving a new Software Architecture", In *Research and Development in Expert Systems V*, Kelly and Rector (eds.), Cambridge Univ. Press, pp. 284-295.

[81]   Gregory, S. 1987. *Parallel logic programming in PARLOG*, Addison Wesley, Reading, Mass.

[82]   Gullichsen, E. 1985. "BiggerTalk: Object-Oriented Prolog", MCC Technical Report, No. STP-125-85, 9430 Research Blvd., Austin, Texas.

[83]   Gurr, C.A. 1990. "A Declarative Semantics for Class Template Programming", Tech. Report, Dept. of Computer Science, Univ. of Bristol, UK.

[84]   Haridi, S. and Brand, P. 1988. "Andorra-Prolog: An Integration of Prolog and Committed Choice Languages", In *Proc. of the Int. Conf. on 5th Generation Computer Systems*, Tokyo, November.

[85]   Haridi, S., and Janson, S. 1990. "Kernel Andorra Prolog and its Computational Model", In *Proc. of the 7th Int. Conf. on LP*, Jerusalem, MIT Press.

[86]   Heintze, N., Michaylov, S., Stuckey, P., and Yap, R. 1989. "On Meta Programming in CLP(R)", In *Logic Programming: Proc. of the North American Conf.*, Vol. 1., E.L. Lusk, and R.A. Overbeek, (eds.), MIT Press, pp. 52-66.

[87]   Hirsh, S., Kahn, K. M., and Miller, M.S. 1987. , "Interming: Unifying Keyword and Positional notations", Tech. Report, Xerox PARC, Palo Alto, CA.

[88]   Hodas, J.S., and Miller, D. 1990. "Representing Objects in a Logic Programming Language with Scoping Constructs", In *Logic Programming: Proc. of the 7th Int. Conf.*, D.H.D. Warren and P. Szeridi (eds.), Jerusalem, June 18-20, MIT Press, Cambridge, MA, pp. 511-526.

[89]   Hogger, C.J., and Kowalski, R.A. 1987. "Logic Programming", In *Encyclopaedia of Artificial Intelligence*, S.C. Shapiro (ed.), John Wiley & Sons, New York, NY, pp.544-558.

[90]   Honiden, S., Uchihira, N., and Kasuya, T. 1985. "MENDEL: Prolog Based Concurrent Object Oriented Language", ICOT Technical Memorandum: TM-0144, Tokyo, Japan.

[91]   Hugher, G.E., and Cresswell, M.J. 1972. *An Introduction to Modal Logic*, Methuen, London.

[92]   Iline, H., and Kanoui, H. 1987. "Extending Logic Programming to Object Programming: The System LAP", In *Proc. 10th IJCAI*, Vol. 1, August, Milan, Italy, pp. 34-39.

[93]   Ishikawa, Y., and Tokoro, M. 1986. "Orient84/K: An Object Oriented Concurrent Programming Language for Knowledge Representation", In *Object-Oriented Concurrent Programming*, A. Yonezawa, and M. Tokoro (eds.), MIT Press, Cambridge, MA.

[94]   Janson, S., and Haridi, S. 1991. "Programming Paradigms of the Andorra Kernel Language", In *Proc. of the 1991 Int. Symp. of LP*, V. Saraswat, K. Ueda (eds.), MIT Press, pp.167-183.

[95]   Jaffar, J., and Lassez, J-L. 1987. "Constraint Logic Programming", In *Proc. 14th ACM Symp. on Principles of Programming Languages*, Munich, West Germany, January.

[96]   Jaffar, J., and Michaylov, S. 1987. "Methodology and Implementation of a CLP System", In *Proc. of the 4th Int. Logic Programming Conf.*, J.-L. Lassez (ed.), The MIT Press, Vol. 1, pp. 196-218.

[97]   Jeremaes, P., Khosla, S., and Maibaum, T.S.E. 1986. "A modal (action) logic for requirements specification", Tech. Report, Dept. of Computing, Imperial College, London.

[98]   Johnson, M. 1988a. Email message to 'comp.lang.prolog' news group, johnson@csli.UUCP, 2nd June.

[99]   Johnson, M. 1988b. Email message to 'comp.lang.prolog' news group, johnson@csli.UUCP, 13th June.

[100]   Kahn, K.M. 1982. "Intermission – Actors in Prolog", In *Logic Programming*, K.L. Clark, and S.A.Tarnlund (eds.), Academic Press, New York, pp. 213-228.

[101]   Kahn, K.M. 1986. "Uniform – A language based upon Unification which unifies (much of) Lisp, Prolog and Act 1, In *Logic Programming: Relations, Functions and Equations*, D. DeGroot, and G. Lindstrom (eds.), Prentice Hall, Englewood Cliffs, NJ, pp. 411-438.

[102]   Kahn, K.M. 1989. "Objects – A Fresh Look", In *Proc. of the 3rd European Conf. on OOP*,

Cambridge Univ. Press, July, pp.207-224.

[103]   Kahn, K.M., and Miller, M.S. 1988. "Objects with State in Prologs with Freeze", Tech. Report, Xerox PARC, Palo Alto, CA.

[104]   Kahn, K.M., and Saraswat, V.A. 1990a. "Actors as a Special Case of Concurrent Constraint Programming", Tech. Report SSL-90-13, Xerox PARC, Palo Alto, CA.

[105]   Kahn, K.M., and Saraswat, V.A. 1990b. "Complete Visualizations of Concurrent Programs and their Executions", In *Proc. of the IEEE Visual language Workshop*, October.

[106]   Kahn, K.M., Tribble, D., Miller, M.S., and Bobrow, D.G. 1987. "Vulcan: Logical Concurrent Objects", In *Concurrent Prolog: Collected Papers*, E.Y. Shapiro (ed.), MIT Press, Cambridge, MA, Vol. 2, Chapter 30, pp.274-303. Also in *Research Directions in Object-Oriented Programming*, B. Shriver, P. Wegner (eds.), MIT Press, 1987.

[107]   Karam, G.M. 1988. "Prototyping Concurrent Systems with Multilog", Tech. Report, Dept. of Systems and Computer Eng., Carleton Univ., Canada, January.

[108]   Kauffman, H., and Grumbach, A. 1986. "MULTILOG: MULTiple worlds in LOGic programming", In *ECAI '86*, Vol. 1, Brighton, England, pp. 291-305.

[109]   Kesim, F.N. 1990. "A Brief Survey of Object Logics for Object-Oriented Databases", Research Report, Dept. of Computing, Imperial College, London, June.

[110]   Kifer, M., and Lausen, G. 1989. "F-Logic: A Higher-Order Language for Reasoning about Objects, Inheritance, and Schema", In *Proc. of the ACM-SIGMOD Symp. on the Management of Data*, pp. 134-146.

[111]   Kifer, M., and Wu, J. 1989. "A Logic for Object-Oriented Logic Programming (Maier's O-Logic Revisited)", In *Proc. of the 8th ACM SIGACT-SIGMOD-SIGART Symp. on the Principles of Database Systems*.

[112]   Koegel, J.F. 1989. "Parallel Objects on Distributed Constraint Logic Programming Machines", In *Proc. of the ACM SIGPLAN Workshop on Object-based Concurrent Programming*, G. Agha, P. Wegner and A. Yonezawa (eds.), *SIGPLAN Notices*, Vol.24, No.4, April, pp. 123-125.

[113]   Konolige, K. 1982. "A First Order Formalization of Knowledge and Action for a MUlti-agent Planning System", In *Machine Intelligence 10*, J.E. Hayes, D. Michie, and Y.H. Pao (eds.), Ellis Horwood, pp.41-72.

[114]   Kornfeld, W.A. 1983. "Equality for Prolog", In *Proc. 8th IJCAI*, Vol. 1, Karlsruhe, Germany, August, pp. 514-519.

[115]   Koseki, Y. 1987. "Amalgamating Multiple Programming Paradigms in Prolog", In *Proc. 10th IJCAI*, Vol. 1, August, Milan, Italy, pp. 76-82.

[116]   Kowalski, R.A. 1979. *Logic for problem solving*, Elsevier, North Holland, New York, NY.

[117]   Kowalski, R.A. 1986. "Report on S-LONLI", Tech. Report, Dept. of Computing, Imperial College, London, June.

[118]   Kowalski, R.A., 1990. "Problems and Promises of Computational Logic", In *Computational Logic Symp. Proc.*, J.W. Lloyd (ed.), Brussels, Springer-Verlag, November 13-14, pp.1-36.

[119]   Kowalski, R.A., and Sergot, M.J. 1986. "A Logic-based Calculus of Events", *New Generation Computing*, Vol. 4, No.1, pp. 67-95.

[120]   Kwok, C.S. 1988. "A Survey of Structuring Mechanisms for Logic Programs", Tech. Report, Dept. of Computing, Imperial College, London, November.

[121]   Lamma, E., Mello, P., and Natali, A. 1989. "The Design of an Abstract Machine for Efficient Implementation of Contexts in Logic Programming", In *Proc. of the 6th Int. Conf. on LP*, G. Levi and M. Martelli (eds.), Lisboa, Portugal, MIT Press, pp.303-317.

[122]   Leonardi, L. and Mello, P. 1988. "Combining Logic- and Object-Oriented Programming Language Paradigms", In *Proc. of the 21st Annual Hawaii Int. Conf. on Systems Sciences*, B.D. Shriver (ed.), Vol II, IEEE, pp. 376-385.

[123]   Levy, J. 1986. "CFL: A Concurrent Functional Language, Embedded in a concurrent logic programming environment", CS86-26, Weizmann Institute, Rehovot, October.

[124]   Lieberman, H. 1986. "Using Prototypical Objects to Implement Shared Behaviour in Object Oriented Languages", In *Proc. of OOPSLA'86, SIGPLAN Notices*, Vol. 21, No. 11, November, pp.214-223.

[125]   Logic Programming Associates Ltd. 1989. "Prolog++" and "MacObject" Reference Manuals, November.

[126]   Maier, D. 1986. "A Logic for Objects", In *Proc. of the Workshop on Foundations of Deductive Databases and Logic Programming*, Washington, D.C., August, pp. 6-26.

[127]   Malenfant, J., Lapalme, G. and Vaucher, J. 1989. "ObjVProlog: Metaclasses in Logic", In *Proc. of ECOOP '89*, S. Cook (ed.), The BCS Workshop Series, Cambridge University Press, Cambridge, pp. 257-269.

[128]   Manna, Z., and Wolper, P. 1984. "Synthesis of Communicating Processes from Temporal Logic Specifications", *TOPLAS*, Vol. 6, NO. 1, January, pp.68-93.

[129]   McCabe, F.G. 1987a. "Logic and Objects", Research Report DOC 86/9, Dept. of Computing, Imperial College, London, May.

[130]   McCabe, F.G. 1987b. "Denotational Graphics", Tech. Report, Dept. of Computing, Imperial College, London, July.

[131]   McCabe, F.G. 1988. "Logic and Objects", PhD Thesis, Dept. of Computing, Imperial College, London.

[132]   Mellender, F. 1988. "An Integration of Logic and Object-Oriented Programming", *SIGPLAN Notices*, Vol. 23, No. 10, October, pp.181-185.

[133]   Mello, P. 1989. "Concurrent Objects in a Logic Programming Framework", In *Proc. of the ACM SIGPLAN Workshop on Object-based Concurrent Programming*, G. Agha, P. Wegner and A. Yonezawa (eds.), SIGPLAN Notices, Vol.24, No.4, April, pp. 37-39.

[134]   Mello, P., and Natali, A. 1986. "Programs as Collections of Communicating Prolog Units", *ESOP 86*, In *LNCS 213*, B. Robinet, and R. Wilhelm (eds.), Springer-Verlag, pp. 274-288.

[135]   Mello, P., and Natali, A. 1989. "Logic Programming in a Software Engineering Perspective", In *Logic Programming: Proc. of the North American Conf.*, E.L. Lusk. and R.A. Overbeek (eds.), MIT Press, pp.441-458.

[136]   Meseguer, J. 1990. "A Logical Theory of Concurrent Objects", In *Proc. of ECOOP – OOPSLA '90*, N. Meyrowitz (ed.), Also in *SIGPLAN Notices*, Vol. 25, No. 10, October 21-25, pp.101-115.

[137]   Miller, D.A. 1986. "A Theory of Modules for Logic Programming", In *Proc. of the 1986 Symp. on Logic Programming*, IEEE Computer Society Press, Washington, D.C, September, pp. 106-114.

[138]   Miller, D.A. 1989. "Lexical Scoping as Universal Quantification", In *Proc. of the 6th Int. Conf. on LP*, G. Levi and M. Martelli (eds.), Lisboa, Portugal, MIT Press, pp.268-283.

[139]   Miller, D.A. and Nadathur, G. 1986. "Higher-Order Logic Programming", In *Proc. of the 3rd Int. Conf. on Logic Programming*, London, LNCS 225, E. Shapiro (ed.), Springer-Verlag, July, pp.448-462.

[140]   Miller, M., Bobrow, D., Tribble, E.D., and Levy, J. 1987. "Logical Secrets", In *Concurrent Prolog: Collected Papers*, E.Y. Shapiro (ed.), MIT Press, Cambridge, MA, Vol. 2, Chapter 24, pp.140-161.

[141]   Miyoshi, H., and Furukawa, K. 1987. "Object-Oriented Parser in the Logic Programming Language ESP", ICOT Tech. Report, Tokyo, Japan.

[142]   Mizoguchi, F., Ohwada, H., and Katayama, Y. 1984. "LOOKS: Knowledge Representation System for Designing Expert Systems in a Logic Programming Framework", In *Proc. of the Int. Conf. on 5th Generation Computer Systems*, ICOT, Japan, pp. 606-612.

[143]   Monteiro, L. 1984. "A Proposal for Distributed Programming in Logic", In *Implementations of Prolog*, J.A. Campbell (ed.), Ellis Horwood, Chicester, pp.329-340.

[144]   Monteiro, L. and Porto, A. 1989, "Contextual Logic Programming", In *Proc. of the 6th Int. Conf. on Logic Programming*, G. Levi and M. Martelli (eds.), Lisboa, Portugal, The MIT Press, pp. 284-299.

[145]   Monteiro, L., and Porto, A. 1990. "A Transformational View of Inheritance in Logic Programming", In *Logic Programming: Proc. 7th Int. Conf.*, D.H.D. Warren and P. Szeridi (eds.), MIT Press, Jerusalem, June 18-20, pp.481-494.

[146]   Moscowitz, Y., and Shapiro, E. 1991. "Lexical Logic Programs", In *Proc. of the 8th Int. Conf. of LP*, K. Furukawa (ed.), Paris, France, MIT Press, pp.349-363.

[147]   Moszkowski, B. 1986. *Executing Temporal Logic Programs*, Cambridge Univ. Press.

[148]   Moss, C. 1990. "An Introduction to Prolog++", Tech. Report, Dept. Of Computing, Imperial College, London, June.

[149]   Murakami, M. 1988. "A Declarative Semantics of Parallel Logic Programs with Perpetual Processes", In *Proc. of the Int. Conf on 5th Generation Computer Systems*, ICOT, Tokyo, pp.374-381.

[150]   Nadathur, G., and Miller, D.A. 1989. "An Overview of λProlog", In *Proc. of the 5th Int. Conf. and Symp. on LP*, K. Bowen and R. Kowalski (eds.), MIT Press, pp.1180-1198.

[151]   Nakashima, H. 1984. "Knowledge Representation in Prolog/KR", In *Proc. IEEE 1984 Symp. on Logic Programming*, Boston, MA, pp. 126-130.

[152]   Naish, L. 1985. "Negation and Control in Prolog", Tech. Report 85/12, DoCS, Univ. of Melbourne, Australia.

[153]   Naish, L. 1988. "Parallelizing NU-Prolog", In *Logic Programming: Proc. 5th Int. Conf. and Symposium*, R.A. Kowalski, and K.A. Bowen (eds.), Seattle, Washington, Sponsored by ALP and IEEE, pp. 1546-1564.

[154]   Newton, M., and Watkins, J. 1988. "The Combination of Logic and Objects for Knowledge Representation", *Journal of Object Oriented Programming*, November/December, pp. 7-10.

[155]   Nguyen, V., Demers, A., Gries, D., and Owicki, S. 1986. "A Model and Temporal Proof System for Networks of Processes", *Distributed Computing*, No. 1, pp.7-25.

[156]   Ohki, M., Takeuchi, A., and Furukawa, K. 1988. "An Object-Oriented Programming Language based on the Parallel Logic Programming Language KL1", In *Logic Programming: Proc. of the 4th Int. Conf.*, J.L. Lassez (ed.), MIT Press, Cambridge, MA, Vol. 2, pp. 894-909.

[157]   Palmer, D., and Naish, L. 1991. "NUA-Prolog: An Extension to the WAM for Parallel Andorra", In *ICLP'91: 8th Int. Conf on LP*, Paris, June.

[158]   Pereira, F.C.N. 1990. "Prolog and Natural-Language Analysis: Into the Third Decade", Invited Lecture, In *Proc. of the 1990 North American Conference on Logic Programming*, S. Debray and M. Hermenegildo (eds.), Austin, Texas, MIT Press, October, pp.813-832.

[159]   Pereira, L.M., Monteiro, L., Cunha, J.C., and Aparicio, J.N. 1988. "Concurrency and Communication in Delta Prolog", Conf. Proc. IEE Int. Specialist Seminar on "The Design and Application of Parallel Digital Processors", Lisbon, pp. 99-104.

[160]   Pereira, L.M., and Nasr, R. 1984. "Delta Prolog: A Distributed Logic Programming Language", In *Int. Conf. on 5th Generation Systems*, ICOT, Tokyo, Japan, November, pp.283-291.

[161]   Porto, A. 1983. "Logical Action Systems", In *Proc. Int. Workshop on Logic Programming*, Praia da Falsia, Portugal, pp. 192-203.

[162]   Quintec Systems Ltd. 1991. "Quintec-Objects Overview", February.

[163]   Quintus Computer Systems Inc. 1988. ProWINDOWS Reference Manual", Evaluation Version, CA, August.

[164]   Rauen, J. 1987. "Lexically scoped FCP", Presented at the Concurrent LP workshop , Xerox PARC, Palo Alto, CA, September.

[165]   Reix, T. 1989. "SP-Object: Object Extensions in the SP-Prolog v2.1 System", In *TOOLS 89*.

[166]   Rescher, N., and Urchart, A. 1971. *Temporal Logic*, Springer-Verlag, New York.

[167]   Ringwood, G.A. 1989a. "A Comparative Exploration of Concurrent Logic Languages", In *The Knowledge Engineering Review*, Vol. 4 : 4, pp.305-332.

[168]   Ringwood, G.A. 1989b. "Predicates and Pixels", In *New Generation Computing*, 7, pp.59-80.

[169]   Saraswat, V.J. 1989. "Concurrent Constraint Programming Languages", PhD Thesis, Carnegie-Mellon University, January. Also 1989 ACM Dissertation Award, MIT Press.

[170]   Saraswat, V.J., Kahn, K.M., and Levy, J. 1990. "Janus – A Step towards Distributed Constraint Programming", In *Proc. of the North American LP Conf.*, MIT Press, October.

[171] Sato, H., and Matsumoto, H. 1986. "Intelligent support for office work with a Prolog-based Object-Oriented Programming Language ESP", ICOT Technical Report: TR-172, Tokyo, Japan.

[172] Shapiro, E.Y. 1983. "A subset of Concurrent Prolog and its interpreter", ICOT technical report, TR-003, Tokyo, Japan.

[173] Shapiro, E.Y. 1985. "Systolic Programming: A Paradigm of Parallel Processing", Tech. Report CS84-16, Dept. of Applied Mathematics, The Weizmann Institute of Science, Israel, January.

[174] Shapiro, E.Y. 1987. "Or-Parallel Prolog in FCP", In *Concurrent Prolog: Collected Papers*, E.Y. Shapiro (ed.), MIT Press, Cambridge, MA, Vol. 2, Chapter 34, pp.415-441.

[175] Shapiro, E.Y. 1989. "The Family Of Concurrent Logic Programming Languages", *ACM Computing Surveys*, Vol. 21, No.3, September, pp.413-510.

[176] Shapiro, E., and Takeuchi, A. 1983. "Object Oriented Programming in Concurrent Prolog", *New Generation Computing* 1 (1983), pp.25-48.

[177] Stabler, E.P. 1986. "Object-Oriented Programming in Prolog", *AI Expert*, Vol. 1, No. 3, October, pp. 46-57.

[178] Steer, K. 1990. "Methodologies and Tools for Parallel Processing", In *BCS CASE on Trial*, September.

[179] Stefik, M., and Bobrow, D.G. 1986. "Object Oriented Programming: Themes and Variations", *The A.I Magazine*, Vol. 6, No. 4, January, pp. 40-62.

[180] Sterling, L., and Shapiro, E.Y. 1987. *The Art of Prolog: Advanced Programming Techniques*, MIT Press Series in Logic Programming, Reading, MA.

[181] Sutcliffe, G., and Pinakis, J. 1991. "Prolog-D-Linda: An Embedding of Linda in SICStus Prolog", Tech Report 91/7, Dept. of Computer Science, Univ. of Western Australia, Nedlands, 6009, Australia.

[182] Szeredi, P. 1982. "Module Concepts for PROLOG", SZKI Collection of Logic Programming Papers, Budapest, Hungary.

[183] Takeuchi, I., Okuno, H., and Ohsato, N. 1986. "A List Processing Language TAO with Multiple Programming Paradigms", *New Generation Computing* 4 (1986), pp. 401-444.

[184] Takeuchi, I., Takahashi, K. and Shimizu, H. 1987. "A Parallel Problem Solving Language for Concurrent Systems", In *Proc. of IFIP Workshop on the Concepts and Characteristics of Knowledge-based Systems*, M.Tokoro (ed.), Mt. Fuji, Japan, November.

[185] Tam, C.C. 1988. "On Evaluating and Improving Open Path Languages", Tech. Report, Dept. of Computing, Imperial College, London, May.

[186] Tanaka, H. 1989. "A Parallel Object Oriented Language FLENG++ and Its Control System on the Parallel Machine PIE64", In *UK-Japan Joint Workshop*, Oxford University

[187] Taylor, S., Av-Ron, E., and Shapiro, E.Y. 1988. "A Layered Method for Process and Code Mapping", In Concurrent Prolog: Collected Papers, (ed.) Shapiro, E.Y., MIT Press, Cambridge, MA, Vol. 2, Chapter 22.

[188] Thomas, D. 1989. "What's in an Object", *BYTE*, March, pp.231-240.

[189] Trehan, R., Wilks, P., and Buckley, M. 1988. "Object Models in the Committed Choice Non-deterministic Logic Languages", DAI Research Paper No. 368, Univ. of Edinburgh.

[190] Trenouth, J. 1988. Email message to 'comp.lang.prolog' news group, jtr@expya.UUCP, 15 April.

[191] Tribble, E.D., Miller, M.S., Kahn, K., Bobrow D.G. and Abbott, C. 1987. "Channels: A generalization of streams", In *Proc 4th International Conference of Logic Programming*, J. L. Lassez (ed.), Melbourne, Vol.2, pp. 839-857.

[192] Vaucher, J., Lapalme, G., and Malenfant, J. 1988. "SCOOP: Structured Concurrent Object-Oriented Prolog", In *Proc. of ECOOP '88*, LNCS 322, Springer-Verlag, pp. 191-211.

[193] Wadge, W.W., and Ashcroft, E.A. 1985. *Lucid, the Dataflow Programming Language*, Academic Press, UK.

[194] Wadge, W.W. 1987. "Tense Logic Programming: a Respectable Alternative (Extended Abstract)", Tech. Report, Computer Science Dept., Univ. of Victoria, Victoria BC, Canada.

[195]   Warren, D.H.D. 1982a. "Higher-order extensions to Prolog: are they needed?", In *Machine Intelligence 10*, J. Hayes, D. Michie, and Y.-H. Pao (eds.), Ellis Horwood, Chicester, pp. 441-453.

[196]   Warren, D.H.D. 1982b. "Perpetual Processes – An Unexploited Prolog Technique", Short Communication, *Logic Programming Newsletter* (3), Summer.

[197]   Warren, D.H.D. 1990. "The Extended Andorra Model with Implicit Control", In *ICLP'90 Workshop on Parallel LP*, Israel, June.

[198]   Wegner, P. 1987. "The Object-Oriented Classification Paradigm", In *Research Directions in Object Oriented Programming*, P. Shriver, P. Wegner (eds.), MIT Press, pp.479-560. Also see *Proc of OOPSLA'87, SIGPLAN Notices*, Vol. 22, No. 12, pp.168-181.

[199]   Wegner, P., and Zdonik, S.B. 1989. "Models of Inheritance", In *Proc. of the 2nd Int. Workshop on Database Programming Languages*, R. Hull, R. Morrison and D. Stemple (eds.), June, pp.248-255.

[200]   Weinbaum, D., and Shapiro, E.Y. 1986. "Hardware Description and Simulation using Concurrent Prolog", In *Concurrent Prolog: Collected Papers*, E.Y. Shapiro (ed.), MIT Press, Cambridge, MA, Vol. 2, Chapter 36, pp.470-490.

[201]   Winograd, T. 1983. *Language as a Cognitive Process*, Addison-Wesley, Reading, MA.

[202]   Wise, M.J. 1988. "PMS-Prolog: A Parallel Prolog with Processes, Modules and Streams", Tech. Report, Dept. of Computer Science, Univ. of Sydney, Australia.

[203]   Yang, R. 1987. *P-Prolog: A Parallel Logic Programming Language*, World Scientific, Singapore.

[204]   Yang, R. 1988. "Programming in Andorra-I", Tech. Report, Dept. of Computer Science, Univ. of Bristol.

[205]   Yardeni, E., and Shapiro, E.Y. 1987. "A Type System for logic Programs", In *Concurrent Prolog: Collected Papers*, E.Y. Shapiro (ed.), MIT Press, Cambridge, MA, Vol. 2, Chapter 28, pp.211-244.

[206]   Yokoi, S. 1986. "A Prolog Based Object Oriented Language SPOOL and its Compiler", In *Proc. of the 5th Int. Conf on Logic Programming*, E. Wada (ed.), LNCS 264, Springer-Verlag, Tokyo, Japan, June, pp. 116-125.

[207]   Yokoyama, T. 1989. "An Object-Oriented and Constraint-Based Knowledge Representation System for Design Object Modeling", ICOT Technical Memorandum: TM-0809, ICOT, Japan, October.

[208]   Yoshida, K., and Chikayama, T. 1988. "A'UM – A Stream-Based Concurrent Object-Oriented Language", In *Proc. of FGCS'88*, ICOT, Tokyo, Japan, 1988, Also in *New Generation Computing 7–2, 3* (1990), pp.127-157.

[209]   Zaniolo, C. 1984. "Object-Oriented Programming in Prolog", In *Proc. IEEE 1984 Symposium on Logic Programming*, Atlantic City, NJ, February, pp. 265-270.

4 Analysis of Inheritance Anomaly in Object-Oriented Concurrent Programming Languages

Satoshi Matsuoka and Akinori Yonezawa

It has been pointed out that *inheritance* and *synchronization constraints* in concurrent object systems often conflict with each other, resulting in *inheritance anomaly* where re-definitions of inherited methods are necessary in order to maintain the integrity of concurrent objects. The anomaly is serious, as it could nullify the benefits of inheritance altogether. Several proposals have been made for resolving the anomaly; however, we argue that those proposals suffer from the incompleteness which allows room for counterexamples. We give an overview and the analysis of inheritance anomaly, and review several proposals for minimizing the unwanted effect of this phenomenon as well as investigate their limitations. We also propose a scheme whereby high degree of superclass encapsulation can be achieved for code re-use while retaining utmost efficiency on conventional massively-parallel architectures.

4.1 Introduction

Inheritance is the prime language feature in *sequential* OO (*Object-Oriented*) languages, and is especially important for code re-use. Another important feature is concurrency; although many OO languages in use today (such as C++ and Smalltalk) are sequential, it is natural to consider objects as being a unit of concurrency. A recent breed of OOCP (*Object-Oriented Concurrent Programming*) languages attempt to provide maximum computational and modeling power through concurrency of objects; in particular, our current prototype ABCL/onEM-4 language exhibits a real-life message passing latency less than 10 μseconds for two concurrent objects located on a separate physical node of a multicomputer[49, 42].

Several researchers, however, have pointed out (albeit fragmentarily) the conflicts between inheritance and concurrency in OO languages[3, 22, 37, 43, 10]. More specifically, concurrent objects and inheritance seemingly have conflicting characteristics, thereby inhibiting their simultaneous use without heavy breakage of encapsulation. We have coined such a phenomenon as *inheritance anomaly* in OOCP. Its 'inauspicious' presence has persuaded OOCP languages *not* to support inheritance as a fundamental language feature. Some of the examples are families of Actor languages[23], POOL/T[3], Procol[45], and also, ABCL/1[51, 50]. There are other OOCP languages that do provide inheritance, yet are not concerned with the problems of conflicts — for those languages, we believe that the difficulties presented in this paper are unavoidable in practice.

Inheritance anomaly entails a severe drawback for the development of large-scale and complex systems in OOCP languages, because there, the greatest benefits of using the OO framework are inheritance and encapsulation. It is therefore essential that clean amalgamation of inheritance and concurrency be achieved in order for large-scale systems to be constructed with OOCP languages. Unfortunately, previous work have largely neglected the proper analysis of the problem, and merely proposed ad-hoc solutions that are applicable for certain types of problems, but as we will see, are inapplicable for others. Instead, we argue that we must first analyze and categorize the conflicts, and based on the analysis, explore if an ideal solution is in fact possible.

The remainder of the paper is organized as follows: First, we give an overview of inheritance anomaly. We will then present non-trivial examples where the (rather simplistic) previous proposals for solutions are limited in their applicability. Next we will analyze and categorize the cause inheritance anomaly more generally. We then examine some latest proposals by others for reusing synchronization code by controlling the inheritance anomaly problem. Finally, we make a proposal in which not only the code for the synchronization but also the *synchronization scheme*—the basic language features such as guards for *programming* synchronization—could be encapsulated in the superclass. Our proposal allows efficient implementation by almost-lossless incorporation into our proposed highly-efficient implementation scheme for our language ABCL[50] on massively parallel architectures such as Fujitsu's AP1000 and Thinking Machine Co.'s CM-5[42].

4.2   Inheritance Anomaly in OOCP

One of the prime concerns in OOCP is *synchronization* of concurrent objects: when a concurrent object is in a certain state, it can accept only a subset of its entire set of messages in order to maintain its internal integrity. We call such a restriction on acceptable messages the *synchronization constraint* of a concurrent object. For example, consider a bounded buffer with methods `put()` and `get()`, where `put()` stores an item in the buffer and `get()` removes the oldest one; then, the synchronization constraint is that one cannot `get()` from a buffer whose state is *empty* and cannot `put()` into a buffer whose state *full* is likewise prohibited.

In most OOCP languages, the programmer explicitly programs the methods to control the set of acceptable messages for each object, in order to *implement* the object *behavior* that satisfy the synchronization constraint. *Synchronization code* is the term we use to refer to the portion of the method code where object behavior with respect to synchronization is controlled. The synchronization code must always be *consistent with* the synchronization constraint of an object; otherwise the object might accept a message that it really should not accept, resulting in a semantical error during program execution[1]. Here, in order to program the synchronization code, the programming language must provide some primitives for object-wise synchronization, such as semaphores, guards, etc.; we refer to the scheme for achieving object-wise synchronization using those primitives in the language as the *synchronization scheme* of the language.

Unfortunately, it has been pointed out that *synchronization code cannot be effectively inherited without non-trivial class re-definitions*. This conflict, which we have coined as *inheritance anomaly* in OOCP, has been identified by several researchers[22, 37, 43], although a comprehensive analysis has not been given yet to our knowledge. Inheritance anomaly is more severe than the violation of class encapsulation in sequential OO-languages that has been pointed out by Snyder[41], because in some of the schemes it is possible to create a general counterexample where NONE of the parent methods can be inherited. We will defer the more detailed analysis of inheritance anomaly until the latter sections; here, we identify the following situations where the benefits of inheritance

---

[1]Such a distinction between the synchronization constraints as a specification versus the behavior of the actual code that implements it, have not been clearly addressed in the previous literatures to our knowledge; in fact, the term 'synchronization constraints' has been confusingly used to mean both in various contexts.

is lost:

1. Definition of a new subclass K' of class K necessitates re-definitions of methods in K as well as those in its ancestor classes.

2. Modification of a new method m of class K within the inheritance hierarchy incur modification of the (seemingly unrelated) methods in both parent and descendent classes of K.

3. Definition of a method m might force the other methods (including those to be defined at the subclasses in the future) to follow a specific protocol which would not have been required had that method not existed. Encapsulated definition of *mix-in classes* would thus be very difficult.

One notable fact is that the occurrence of inheritance anomaly *depends on* the synchronization scheme of the language; in other words, re-definitions would be required for classes in an OOCP language that adopted a certain synchronization scheme, while the (semantically identical) classes could be safely inherited in another language that provids an entirely different synchronization scheme. This implies that the heart of the problem is the semantical conflicts between the descriptions of object-wise synchronization and inheritance within the language, and not on how the language features are implemented underneath. Moreover, it is not immediately obvious whether previous techniques developed in concurrent/distributed languages and systems are applicable.

4.3 Inheritance Anomalies in the Previous Proposals

Recently, several proposals have been made for effectively allowing synchronization code to be inherited based on various synchronization schemes (examples are [2, 13, 22, 43, 35], among others). Some (although not all) of these proposals emphasized strong control over the conflicts a.k.a. inheritance anomaly, effectively claiming that synchronization code can be inherited for all common and/or necessary cases. Unfortunately, it is possible to show that such proposals still suffer from inheritance anomaly — in this section, we fortify this claim by presenting the actual (counter)examples of anomaly occurrence.

Before we proceed, however, we make a point that the proposals selected here are considered to be representative of certain classes of synchronization schemes, and the intention of the (counter)examples is to illustrate what type of inheritance anomaly would occur for such schemes. We do NOT intend to claim that a particular proposal is useless — as a matter of fact, some do embody good ideas that could be used as a basis of a more complete solution.

4.3.1 Simple Examples of Inheritance Anomaly — Caused by 'Body's, Explicit Message Reception within Methods, Path Expressions, Direct Key Specifications

In order to gain the reader's insight into the problem, we first present simple examples of inheritance anomalies occurring in OOCP languages. Some of these cases have already been pointed out by the previous researchers.

4.3.1.1 Bodies Some OOCP languages allow each object to have a so called '*body*', an internal method with its own thread of control. The body thread remains active irrespective of the external message reception. The body is typically used to control message receptions, usually in the fashion of Ada's **select** statement. After receiving a message, the body thread takes on the responsibility of invoking the method corresponding to the message. In some languages, the body thread suspends during method processing, while in others the body thread runs independently of the threads for message processing.

Some researchers refer to objects with body as *active objects*; by contrast, objects without body are called *passive objects*. There have been many variations of active objects in concurrent languages for distributed computing. The notable examples are SR[6], ADA, Mediators[18], and ALPS[46]. These languages have no generic support for inheritance; as a result, conflicts with inheritance naturally do not arise.

America[3] discusses the difficulty of integrating inheritance with languages that allow bodies: On defining a subclass from another class, the definition of the subclass usually require *total re-definition* of the body. This is rather obvious, because otherwise the newly added features cannot be used. America points out that this poses difficulty in programming because having a different body means that the dynamic behavior of such a new object may be totally different from the old ones, thus severely interfering with formal reasoning about the program. America states that, after initial experiments with inheritance in the OOCP language POOL/T, it was decided not to adopt inheritance as a primitive language feature[2]. Another related difficulty we point out is that such re-definitions require total knowledge of and access to the synchronization code of the ancestor classes. Thus, not only that they cannot be inherited, but also encapsulation of class implementation is broken with respect to synchronization constraints.

As an example of the 'body' anomaly, consider a first-in first-out bounded buffer class as illustrated in Figure 4.1. It has two public methods, `put()` and `get()`; `put()` stores an item in the buffer and `get()` removes the oldest one. Two instance variables `in` and `out` count the total numbers of items inserted and removed, respectively, and act as indices into the buffer — the location of the next item to be put is indexed by (`in` *mod* `size`) and that of the oldest item by (`out` *mod* `size`). Upon creation, the buffer is in the empty state, and the only message acceptable is `put()`; arriving `get()` messages are not accepted but kept in the message queue un-processed. When a `put()` message is processed, the buffer is no longer empty and can accept both `put()` and `get()` messages, reaching a 'partial' (non-empty and non-full) state. When the buffer is full, it can only accept `get()`, and after processing the `get()` message, it becomes partial again.

Figure 4.2 is a definition of class `b-buf` which implements the above described behavior, given with an extended syntax of C++ for reader familiarity. (Note that, some liberty is taken with the syntax and semantics — for instance, C++ does not provide the Smalltalk-80 style **super** pseudo variable, whose meaning should be obvious to those familiar in OO programming.). Explicit message reception is made within the body using the **select** and **accept** statements. The `get()` message is accepted by the first **accept** statement in the body if the buffer is not empty; then the actual `process_get()` method is invoked

---

[2]The recent version of POOL called POOL/I incorporates inheritance. Proper body re-definition is left as the responsibility of the programmer.

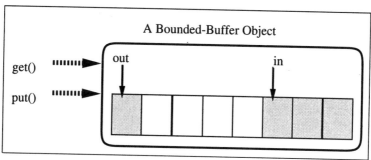

Figure 4.1
A Bounded Buffer Object

with the **start** statement. Upon its termination, the result of the method invocation is directly returned to the caller. Here, it is quite obvious that in any subclasses of **b-buf**, the entire **body()** must be re-defined in order to account for the newly added method definitions.

```
Class b-buf: ACTOR {// b-buf is an Actor
  int in, out, buf[SIZE];
public:
  void b-buf() { in = out = 0; }
  void process_put() { //store an item
    in++;
  }          //the argument of the call is omitted
  int process_get() {  //remove an item
    out++;
  }          //the return value of the call is omitted
  void body() {
    loop {
      select {
        accept get() when (!(in == out)) start process_get();
      or
        accept put() when (!(out = in + SIZE))
          start process_put();
}}}}
```

Figure 4.2
Definition of Bounded Buffer Class with Body (The code related to accessing the local array storage for insertion and removal is omitted for brevity.)

There are several languages that allow body within objects ([8, 13]. [15] also essentially allows bodies when the 'low level' scheme is utilized).

4.3.1.2 Explicit Message Receptions An analogous situation occurs if a language allows explicit (interior) reception of messages within a method, in that the newly added method definitions cannot be entirely accounted for. Therefore it would be difficult to incorporate inheritance into languages that allow interior message receptions. Examples of such languages are ABCL/1[51, 50] and CSSA[34].

There are also languages that extend existing sequential OO languages with explicit message reception statements in order to achieve inter-object concurrency, such as Concurrent C++[17], Buhr et. al.'s extension to C++[11], or Tuple Space Smalltalk[27]. For these languages, however, the messages explicitly received are not processed via the normal method dispatch mechanism of the base language. As a result, inheritance and communication are totally separated from the beginning, causing extensive breakage of encapsulation.

4.3.1.3 Path Expressions Again, a similar problem occurs for languages with synchronization schemes expressed in variants of Path Expressions[12]. Additionally, the original path expression suffers the limitation that is imposed by the expressive power of Path Expressions with respect to complex synchronization constraints of objects. For instance, the textual length of the path expression of the above bounded buffer example would be enormous for a large SIZE, because one must account for every possible combinations of interleaved puts and gets; more specifically, the expressive power of the original Path Expressions is limited to the regular expression, whereas the bounded buffer require a more powerful language class for concise description. This can be resolved with augmenting the terms in the path expression with guards and thereby allowing conditional synchronization[7]. An example OOCP language with augmented Path Expression is Procol[45]. Nevertheless, the original problem is not resolved, because one still cannot account for the newly added methods in the subclass unless the entire path expression is re-defined.

4.3.1.4 Direct Key Specifications One very important classification of inheritance anomaly is its occurrence in the synchronization schemes involving operations with message keys. We refer to this as the *direct key specification anomaly*. The primary reason for anomaly is that the newly added keys in the subclasses cannot be accounted for in the synchronization scheme of the methods inherited from the parent methods. Languages employing this type of synchronization schemes such as SINA[44][3] or OTM[19] would suffer from the inheritance anomaly if they were to be extended to incorporate inheritance. (For the example of the anomaly occurring with bounded buffers, see[22].)

4.3.2 Problems with *Behavior Abstractions*

Kafura et. al's proposal called the *behavior abstraction*[22] attempts to solve the above problems, especially the problem with direct key specifications, in the context of their

---

[3]Although SINA does not support inheritance, there is an extension called Sina/ST[2] which employs pattern matching of method names and arguments in the similar manner as the path expression. Inheritance and delegation are simulated using this scheme. The path expression anomaly we have discussed in Section 4.3.1.3 would occur for this scheme.

language ACT++. The essence of their proposal is to assign identifiers to *accept sets*, namely, the set of keys of messages that can be accepted by an object.

Figure 4.3 is the definition of the bounded-buffer object with behavior abstractions. We basically adopt a simple Actor-like language, whereby:

- Each object is single threaded i.e., an object can only accept one message at a time.

- Message passing is asynchronous, and pending messages are placed in the message queue.

- The next 'behavior' of the object is specified with the **become** primitive (see below).

The **behavior** statements declare three sets of keys named **empty**, **partial**, and **full** assigned to {put}, {put,get}, and {get}, respectively. The synchronization scheme employs the **become** statement to designate a set of method keys acceptable in the next state. We call such a set the *next accept set*. This set is not a first-class value; rather, another *key* is designated to each next accept set at the first part of a class definition.

Kafura describes in [22] how behavior abstraction serves as a clean solution to the anomaly exhibited in the **x-buf** example; there, **x-buf** has one additional method **last** that is similar to **get** — the difference is that it removes the last item previously put into the buffer instead of the first. In Figure 4.3, neither **put** nor **get** need to be re-defined in **x-buf**, whereas re-definitions of all the methods were necessary for the comparative language that could only specify the method keys.

Unfortunately, it is possible to create a non-trivial counterexample of inheritance anomaly with behavior abstractions. Consider creating a class **x-buf2**, a subclass of **b-buf**. **x-buf2** has one additional method **get2**, which removes the two oldest items from the buffer simultaneously. (Notice that this cannot be done with successive messages sends of **get**, because **get** messages from different objects may be interleaved.) The corresponding synchronization constraint for **get2** requires that at least two items exist. As a consequence, the partial state must be partitioned into two — the state in which exactly one item exists, and the remaining states. To maintain consistency with the new constraint, we need another accept set **x-one** that represents the former state (the **behavior** definitions in Figure 4.4). Then, the methods **get** and **put** *must be re-defined* (Figure 4.4). Here, notice that NONE of the methods (except the initializer) in **b-buf** can be inherited — the anomaly has occurred again[4].

4.3.3 Problems with First-Classing of Accept Sets — *Enabled Sets*

Tomlinson and Singh[43] propose a scheme that enhances Kafura's in their Actor-based reflective language called Rosette. In Rosette, the accept sets can be treated as first-class objects called *enabled sets*. We show that this difference is essential, because their proposal can localize (although not eliminate) the method re-definitions in some cases. We also show, however, that there are still other cases that would require a considerable amount of re-definitions.

---

[4]Recently, they have proposed a more advanced scheme called *behavior sets*, which is similar in essence to Tomlinson and Singh's enable sets we discuss next.

```
Class b-buf: ACTOR {// b-buf is an Actor
   int in, out, buf[SIZE];
behavior:
   empty   = {put};
   partial = {put, get};
   full    = {get};
public:
   void b-buf() {
      in = out = 0;
      become empty;
   }
   void put() {
      in++; //store an item
      if (in == out + size) become full;
      else                  become partial;
   }
   void get() {
      out++; //remove an item
      if (in == out) become empty;
      else           become partial;
   }
}

Class x-buf: b-buf {// extends b-buf
behavior:
   x_empty   =                renames empty;
   x_partial = {put,get,last} redefines partial;
   x_full    = {get,last}     redefines full;
public:
   void x-buf() {
   }
   int last() {
      in-- ; //remove the last item
      if (in == out) become x_empty;
      else           become x_partial;
   }
}
```

Figure 4.3
B-buf and x-buf with Behavior Abstractions

```
    Class x-buf2: b-buf { // x-buf2 is a subclass of b-buf
    behavior:
      x_empty   =                  renames empty;
      x_one     = {put,get};
      x_partial = {put,get,get2} redefines partial;
      x_full    = {get,get2}     redefines full;
    public:
      void x-buf2() { in = out = 0; become x-empty; }
      void get2() { out += 2; //definition of get2
        if (in == out)            become x_empty;
        else if (in == out + 1) become x_one;
        else                      become x_partial;
      }
      //The following re-defines the methods in b-buf.
      void get() { out++;
        if (in == out)            become x_empty;
        else if (in == out + 1) become x_one;
        else                      become x_partial;
      }
      void put() { in++;
        if (in == out + size)   become x_full;
        else if (in == out + 1) become x_one;
        else                      become x_partial;
      }
    }
```

Figure 4.4
Inheritance Anomaly with Behavior Abstractions

Here is a brief overview of Rosette with respect to synchronization schemes: although its original syntax is based on S-expressions, we will continue to use our C++ based syntax with the following extensions:

- The **become** statement now specifies the next state and the next enabled set of the object:

    become(⟨*enabled-set*⟩, (⟨*new-state*⟩))

- An enabled set is an instance of class **Enable**; here the constructor adopts a special syntax whereby a set of message keys to be enabled are specified:

    Enable(⟨*message keys*⟩)

    There are several operations defined for the enabled set, such as union (+), intersection (&), etc.

- In order to specify the next enabled set for an object, we typically define a private method for each enable-set:

```
Enable ⟨method⟩() {return Enable(⟨message keys⟩)}
```

- There are two kinds of methods, *public* and *private*. The public methods are invoked as a result of a message reception from an external object. Message sending is asynchronous, and only those messages whose corresponding methods are currently 'enabled' by the enabled set can be accepted. On the other hand, the private methods are internal to the object and can be only invoked from within the public and private methods of the same object as a function call.

Now, consider defining, in addition to get2, method empty? which checks whether the buffer is empty or not. The method is in effect stateless, that is, it does not affect the state of the buffer. Thus, this message should always be acceptable irrespective of object state (as long as other methods are not executing). Then, in principle its definition should be independent of definitions of other methods, since the effects on the object state by other methods are irrelevant to empty?. But this is not the case — in the definitions of b-buf and x-buf2 (Figure 4.5), we can observe the followings:

- We must override every single private methods that returns an enabled set so that it enables the empty? method (all the private methods of x-buf2 in Figure 4.5).

- We must perform extensive case analysis of object state for the newly added method — this is necessary even if the method itself does not affect the state of the object.

The advantage of enabled-sets over behavior abstractions is that re-definition of the *parent methods*, although unavoidable, can sometimes be *encapusulated* within private methods by inheritance. This is seen in Figure 4.5, where only the private methods such as empty and full are re-defined. This is due to the first-class nature of enabled sets derived naturally from the reflective language architecture of Rosette; by allowing first-class operations on the enabled sets, an instance of a subclass can extend its enabled set to include the methods included in the subclass, supplimented with necessary synchronization code. We feel that reflective architecture is essential in OOCP languages[52], and this is one example of how it can be used to enhance the descriptive power of OOCP languages. Still, as we can observe in this case, all the synchronization code needs to be re-defined, as opposed to method guards, in order to achieve the same functionality.

Here, let us illustrate this by generalizing the method re-definitions of the enabled-sets. The private methods returning an enable set correspond to the 'states' distinguished at class K. On defining a method m at class K-*sub*, a subclass of K, the user needs to check, for each 'state', whether addition of m incurs partitioning of that state. If so, the predicate which determines the state may need to be partitioned. In Figure 4.6, this is done for the private methods state_1 through state_n. In our empty? example, since the method was always acceptable, Enable(..., empty?, ...) had to be added to ALL the private methods of x-buf2. Furthermore, on specifying the next behavior of m, the programmer must judge which of the states among those labeled state_1 through state_n is appropriate, depending on the current state of the object (Figure 4.6).

Another practical limitation with Rosette is that it involves first-class operations on enable sets each time a message is received. Although the cost of such operations on

```
    Class b-buf: ACTOR { // b-buf is an Actor
      int in, out, buf[SIZE];
  private:
    Enable empty() { return enable([put]) };
    Enable partial() { return enable([put,get]) };
    Enable full() { return enable([get]) };
  public:
    void b-buf() { in = out = 0; become(empty(),(in,out,buf));}
    void put() {
      if (in == out + size) become(full(),(in,out,buf));
      else                   become(partial(),(in,out,buf));
    }
    void get() { // Similar to put()...
  }


  // The entire private methods must be re-defined
  Class x-buf2: b-buf {
  private:
    Enable empty() { return Enable(empty?) + super empty() };
    Enable one() { return Enable(get,put,empty?) };
    Enable partial() {
      if (in == out + 1)
         return super partial + Enable(empty?);
      else return super partial() + Enable(get2,empty?) };
    Enable full() {
      return super full() + enable(empty?) };
  public:
    void x-buf2() { in = out = 0; become x-empty; }
    void get2() { out += 2; // addition of get2()
      if (in == out)        become(empty(),(in,out,buf));
      else if (in == out + 1) become(one(),(in,out,buf));
      else                    become(partial(),(in,out,buf));
    }
    // Painstaking case analysis is necessary
    int empty?()[] { // addition of empty?()
      if (in == out)         become(empty(),(in,out,buf));
      else if (in == out + 1) become(one(),(in,out,buf));
      else if (in == out - 1) become(full(),(in,out,buf));
      else                    become(partial(),(in,out,buf));
    }
  }
```

Figure 4.5
X-buf2 with Enabled-Sets

```
   Class K-sub: K { //K-sub is a subclass of K
     ⟨Instance Variable Definitions⟩
   private:
     Enable state_1() {
       if (⟨method⟩  is acceptable)
         return Enable(⟨method⟩) + super state_1()
       else
         return super state1_() };
     //Repeat for state_2 through state_n
         ...
   public:
     ⟨type⟩ ⟨method⟩(⟨args⟩...) {
       return ⟨value⟩;
       if      (Object is in state 1) become(state_1(),⟨new state⟩);
       else if (Object is in state 2) become(state_2(),⟨new state⟩);
           ...
       else if (Object is in state n) become(state_n(),⟨new state⟩);
     }
   }
```

Figure 4.6
General Analysis of Enabled Set

Rosette could be kept relatively low for coarse-grained concurrency, it is nevertheless unavoidable, and could incur substantial overhead in fine-grain parallel computing (see [30] for discussions).

Despite its limitations, we do acknowledge the significance of Rosette in pointing out that some first-classing of elements of synchronization scheme provides the possibility of enlarging the class of synchronization code that can be safely inherited.

4.3.4   Problems with Method Guards

A natural synchronization scheme is to attach a predicate to each method as a guard, thus making each object a conditional critical region (for example, [16, 28] and indivisible objects in [24]). We illustrate this for b-buf and x-buf2 in Figure 4.7. Here, we employ the following syntax:

⟨method name⟩(⟨formal arguments⟩) when (⟨guard⟩) { ⟨body of method definition⟩ }

where *guard* is a boolean expression whose terms are either constants or instance variables bound to primitive values. Method m is invoked only when *guard* evaluates to True. For instance, in class b-buf, the guard (in < out + size) attached to put() assures that put() is not invoked when the buffer is full. As shown in Figure 4.7, all the methods defined at b-buf are inherited by x-buf2 without any changes to the methods or the guards.

```
    Class b-buf: ACTOR {
      int in, out, buf[SIZE];
    public:
      void b-buf()  { in = out = 0; }
      void put() when (in < out + size) { in++; }
      void get() when (in >= out + 1)   { out++; }
    }

    // x-buf is a subclass of b-buf
    Class x-buf2: public b-buf {
    public:
      void x-buf2()
      void get2() when (in >= out + 2) { out += 2; }
      void empty?() when (true) { return in == out; }
    }
```

Figure 4.7
B-buf and x-buf2 with Method Guards

This scheme does provide an elegant solution to the **get2/empty?** example. Furthermore, although a naive implementation of guards is not usually very efficient, it can be improved with the use of program transformation [28] and other optimization techniques; and since they are usually invisible to the programmer, the full benefit of inheritance can be attained without sacrifices in efficiency.

However, the problem is that the occurrence of inheritance anomaly still cannot be prevented. This is a different kind of anomaly from the ones we have so far discussed in this paper. We will give two examples: one is the definition of the **gget()** method, and the other is the definition of the class **Lock** as a *mix-in class*.

First we consider defining **gb-buf**, a subclass of **b-buf**, adding a single method, **gget()**. The behavior of **gget()** is almost identical to that of **get()**, with the sole exception that it cannot be accepted immediately after the invocation of **put**. Such a condition for invocation cannot be distinguished with method guards and the set of instance variables available in **b-buf** alone; we need to define an extra instance variable **after-put**. As a consequence, both **get()** and **put()** must be re-defined as in Figure 4.8. We note that the analogous situation also occurs for accept set based schemes.

The reason for the anomaly occurrence is that we cannot judge the state for accepting the **gget** message with the guard declarations in **b-buf**. To be more specific, **gget** is a *trace-only or history-only sensitive* methods with respect to instances of **b-buf**; we will defer the discussion until the next section.

We next consider the **Lock** class, which is an abstract *mix-in* class[9]. Direct instances of **Lock** are not created; rather, the purpose of **Lock** is to be 'mixed-into' other classes in order to add the capability of locking an object. In **Lock**, a pair of methods **lock** and **unlock** have the following functionality: an object, upon accepting the **lock** message,

```
    // gb-buf is a subclass of b-buf with gget()
    Class gb-buf: b-buf {
      bool after-put;
    public:
      void gb-buf() { after-put = False};

      // Definition of gget()
      void gget() when (!after-put && (in >= out + 1))
          { out++; after-put = False; }

      // The following methods must be re-defined
      void put() when (in < out + size) { in++; after-put = True; }
      void get() when (in >= out + 1) { out++; after-put = False; }
    }
```

Figure 4.8
Inheritance Anomaly with Guards — the `gget` method

will be 'locked', i.e., will suspend the reception of further messages until it receives and accepts the `unlock` message. Its synchronization constraint is *localized* i.e., it is not affected by methods of the class it is being mixed into.

When Lock is 'mixed-into' the definition of `b-buf` to create the class `lb-buf`, we are likely to assume that it would not affect the definition of other methods, since the state of the object with respect to `lock` and `unlock` is totally orthogonal to the effect of other messages. However, this is not the case — first, we must add an instance variable `locked` which indicates whether the object is currently 'locked' or 'unlocked'; this is obviously necessary since it is impossible to distinguish between the two states otherwise. Then, the inherited methods such as `put` or `get` must be overridden in order to account for `locked` (Figure 4.9). Furthermore, all methods which would be defined in the subclasses of `lb-buf` must also account for `locked`. This would not have been necessary if we were to be defining exactly the same methods in the subclass of `b-buf`. To summarize, the effect of mixing-in Lock cannot be localized in `b-buf`.

Why has anomaly occurred here? Again, `lock` and `unlock` are history-only sensitive methods. In addition, although neither of them cause partitioning of states, they modify the synchronization constraints of the methods that are already defined, in this case both `put` and `get`. Thus, method guards of `b-buf` had to be modified in order to maintain consistency with the new constraints.

4.4   Analysis of Inheritance Anomaly

We have seen through examples that the previous proposals are not sufficient for avoiding the inheritance anomaly. We believe that their shortcomings are due to insufficient

```
  Class Lock: ACTOR {
    bool locked;
public:
    void Lock() {locked = False};
    void lock() when (!locked} {lock = True};
    void unlock() when (locked) {lock = False};
}

// lb-buf is a subclass of b-buf with Lock mix-in
Class lb-buf: b-buf,Lock {
public:
    void lb-buf();
    // The following methods must be re-defined
    void put() when (!locked && (in < out + size)) { in++; };
    void get() when (!locked && (in >= out + 1)) { out++; };
}
```

Figure 4.9
Inheritance Anomaly with Guards — the Lock class

analysis of the situation; that is to say, the conflict we treat here is deeply rooted in the semantics of synchronization constraint/schemes verses semantics of inheritance, and analysis is first necessary for achieving a sufficiently clean solution.

There are three reasons why inheritance anomaly occurs, depending on what the sub-class definition entails on how the *state* of the object upon which the messages are acceptable are modified:

- **Partitioning of Acceptable States** — get2, gget
- **History-only Sensitiveness of Acceptable States** — gget, lock
- **Modification of Acceptable States** — lock

The three causes are relatively independent; for example, the gget partitions the states as well as being history-only sensitive.

4.4.1 Partitioning of States

The x-buf2 example in Figure 4.3.2 is a anomaly caused by *partitioning of acceptable states*. In object-oriented languages, an object is said to have some 'state'. Then, one can consider the 'set of states' an object can have. This set can be partitioned into disjoint subsets according to the synchronization constraint of the object; in the bounded buffer examples in Section 4.3, there are three distinguishable set of states, under which respective sets of acceptable messages can be defined: *empty*, *partial*, and *full*. This is conceptually illustrated by the left rectangle of Figure 4.10.

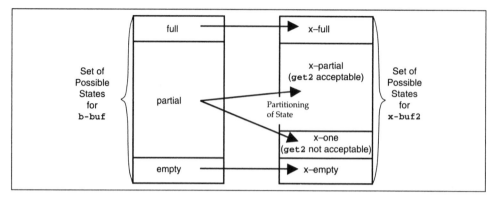

Figure 4.10
Conceptual Illustration of the State Partitioning Anomaly

Now, when a new method is added in the definition of the subclass, the partitioning of the set of states in the parent class may need to be further partitioned in the subclass; this is because the synchronization constraint of the new method may not be properly be accounted for in the partitioning of the parent class. In our example, when the get2() method was added in x-buf2, a partitioning of x-partial into x-one and x-partial was necessary in order to distinguish the state at which only one element is in the buffer.

For accept set based synchronization schemes, this state partitioning is usually distinguished at the termination of the methods with some conditional statements, upon which the objects 'become' that state. This is seen for example in the definitions of put and get methods in Figure 4.3. Requirement for method re-definitions follows naturally, as we have illustrated in Figure 4.4, because the new partitioning must be accounted for in all the methods. Note that, this is not resolved by making accept sets first-class values, because this partitioning cannot be affected by the operations upon the accept-set data.

This partitioning is not a problem for method guards, because they are able to directly judge whether the message is acceptable or not under the current state. Thus, even if the new methods were added, the guards would not need be re-defined, provided that it would not affect the partitioning of the methods in such a way that the condition denoted by a guard in a certain method would no longer be valid; this certainly holds for most cases of inheritance.

Localization of the synchronization schemes is possible via the use of private (localized) method definitions and first-classing of accept sets. This would in turn allow the sharing of synchronization schemes. The advantage here is that the re-definitions of methods that share and/or re-use the synchronization schemes could be localized to within a single method. However, it is not clear if there are situations where such schemes would be advantageous over method guards in the first place.

4.4.2 History-only Sensitiveness of States

When two different views in modeling the 'state' of objects. One is the *external view*, where the state is captured indirectly by the external observable behavior of the object.

This view is taken by the models of parallelism based on process calculi, such as CCS[33] and Actors[1]; there, the equivalence of two objects are determined solely with how they respond to external experiments, and not with how their internal structures are constructed[5]. Another is the *internal view*, where the state is captured by the valuation of the state variables in the implementation of the object; for example, a Cartesian point object can have a valuation such that its x-coordinate is 3, and its y-coordinate is 5. (The actual semantics is more complicated by the fact that the valuation could be another object, and that objects have methods with self and super references (see [38]).)

The two views on state are not identical; there are set of states whose elements can be distinguished under the external view, but is indistinguishable under the internal view. With method guards, in particular, only the latter states are distinguishable, because guards are usually boolean expressions consisting of constant object values, instance variables of the object, and various arithmetic/logical operators (other syntactic categories such as message keys are usually not allowed). Then, it follows that there exist some synchronization constraint that cannot be specified with a given set of instance variables and method guards: this is precisely the history information that do not manifest itself in the values of the instance variables.

When such a distinction becomes necessary, the state of the object under the internal view must be 'refined' in order to match the state of the external view. For this purpose, the methods in a parent class must be modified; that is to say, the state of the object is *history-only sensitive* with respect to the internally distinguishable ones. This is illustrated in our previous gget example in Section 4.8, where the state "immediately after accepting put" cannot be distinguished with the set of instance variables available in b-buf, requiring the addition of an instance variable after-put. Since the proper valuation of this variable must be done in all the methods, the requirements of method modification arose (The situation is similar for accept set based schemes in this respect, in that the gget example would require considerable re-definitions.). Also notice that gget partitions the state as well.

4.4.3 Modification of Acceptable State

The methods in the Lock example in Figure 4.9 are *history-only sensitive* in a similar manner as gget. The difference from gget is that the execution of the methods in Lock modifies the set of states under which the methods inherited from the parent could be invoked (Figure 4.11). That is to say, mixing-in of Lock introduces finer-grained distinction for the set of states under which get (or put) in lb-buf can be invoked. This would naturally require the modification of the method guards to account for the new synchronization constraint.

In addition, the lock method in class Lock is *orthogonally restricting* in the following sense: Lock imposes restriction to the set of states in which each method of the parent class can be invoked; this restriction is determined orthogonally to whether that method can be invoked when that instance is regarded as an instance of the parent class. For

---

[5]To be more precise, the equivalence relation of objects are typically defined by the *bisimulation* relation. One could define several classes of bisimulation relations, yielding weaker or stronger equivalences according to his requirements, e.g. whether object congruence is required, etc.

example, whatever the state of the object (i.e., whether the state is an element of full, partial or empty in the parent class), the question whether the instance is locked or not solely depends on the state of the variable locked. This may not always be the case in general; nevertheless, *orthogonally restricting* is an important subclassification in which the first-class accept set based schemes exhibit good characteristics.

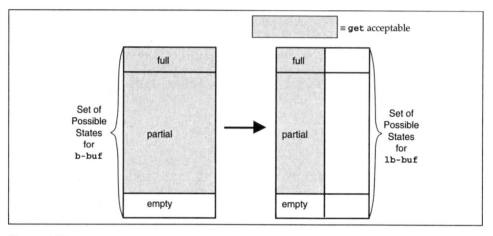

Figure 4.11
Conceptual Illustration of the State Modification Anomaly

4.4.4   Examples of Analysis of Anomaly Occurrence—Synchronizing Actions

Given the above categorizations, we can now analyze the effectiveness of the synchronization schemes, and create an example of anomaly occurence. Below is the brief analysis on *Synchronizing Actions* which was recently proposed[35]. The primary synchronization scheme in Synchronizing Actions is essentially the same as behavior abstractions, but it also supports method guards in the form of preconditions. Figure 4.12 is the definition of a bounded buffer in Synchronizing Actions. The four keywords in the method definition are as follows: matching, action, pre, and post specify the guard, the pre-actions, the method body, and the post-actions, and respectively. Synchronizing Actions supports intra-object concurrency, and behavior abstractions is used to exclude mutually interfering operations.

Since Synchronizing Actions utilize behavior abstractions, one could conjecture that the anomalies presented in Section 4.3.2 could occur. It is a little bit difficult, because most of the partitioning is absorbed in the guards; it is however, possible to create a mutual exclusion condition that cannot be reflected to the guards, thus requiring redefinitions. As an example, we define a class extended-bounded-buffer2, which extends the bounded-buffer class with a method read-middle, which returns the middle elements of the buffer excluding the head and tail. Thus, read-middle should not be invoked when the buffer consists of less than three elements. Furthermore, suppose that the implementation details require that there exist five or more elements for read-middle to be mutually independent from both put and get (this alternative partitioning cannot be reflected to the guards). Figure 4.12 is the resulting subclass definition of extended-bounded-buffer2. Here, notice that not only the concurrency-control part have to be extended, but also the methods themselves must also be re-defined (the precondition part). The required re-definition occurs for the same reason as the original behavior abstractions — the partitioning of states.

4.5 Recent Proposals for Solutions to the Inheritance Anomaly

Recently, there has been much research that have proposed to minimize the effect of inheritance anomaly in OOCP languages, allowing inheritance of synchronization code in various situations. We briefly review them in this section, discussing their advantages as well as their limitations.

4.5.1 Shibayama's Proposal

Shibayaba first proposed a scheme based on fine-grained inheritance of synchronization schemes, so that the amount of code that must be re-defined can be minimized. In the proposed extension of ABCL/1 to incorporate inheritance[40] , methods are categorized into *primary*, *constraint*, and *transition* methods. A method of one category may have its counterparts with identical method names in other categories, and each of them can be separately defined/inherited/overridden. The categorization of methods is as follows:

- A *primary method* is responsible for the task other than object-wise synchronization.

- A *constraint method* acts as a method guard. The difference from the guard in the previous sections is that the guards can be re-defined independently of the primary methods; thus, only the constraint methods need to be overridden when the guards of the methods of the parent class must be changed (the corresponding primary methods are unaffected).

- A *transition method* determines how the messages are delegated among the objects. Its re-definition allows dynamic modification of the delegation path. By encapsulating the state transitions of the object in the delegated object, re-definitions involving history-sensitive state transitions can be localized.

By separating the synchronization code from other parts of method definitions, the amount of re-definitions is minimized. Shibayama also shows in [40] that locking behavior of an object can be treat with a modest amount of code re-definitions in the concurrent implementation of a 2-3 tree.

The limitations of Shibayama's proposal include: (1) there was no way to operate upon *sets* of methods as abstract synchronization states of objects, resulting in lack of encapsulation as well as other drawbacks such as cumbersome re-definitions when multiple methods are affected, (2) almost identical inheritance rules were applied to each category, which made code re-use awkward, and (3) no implementation schemes nor benchmarks were given—in particular, Shibayama's proposal requires a number of

```
   class bounded-buffer;
private: const SIZE = 64; int in = 0, out = 0, buf[SIZE];
concurrency-control:  int N = 0;      //counts queued elements
   behavior-abstraction op-on-head = { get }  op-on-tail = { put }
public:
   method put(int elem);
      matching   ( N < SIZE ); pre   { exclude op-on-tail; }
      action     { in++; /* add element to tail of buf */ }
      post       { N++; }
   method int get();
      matching   ( N > 0 );      pre   { exclude op-on-head; }
      action     { /* return element from head of buf */ out++; }
      post       { N--; }
end bounded-buffer;
class extended-bounded-buffer2 inherits bounded-buffer;
concurrency-control:
   behavior-abstraction // new exclusion sets for read-middle
      op-on-head-and-tail-and-middle = { get, put, read-middle-elements }
      op-on-head-and-middle = { get, read-middle-elements }
      op-on-tail-and-middle = { put, read-middle-elements }
public:
   method int[] read-middle-elements();
      matching   ( N >= 3 );
      pre        { exclude op-on-head-and-tail-and-middle; }
      action     { /* return the middle elements of buf excluding two
                   elements from both head and tail */ }
      post       { N = 2; }
   // re-definitions of both put and get methods in bounded-buffer
   method put(int elem);
      matching   ( N < SIZE );
      pre        { if (N >= 5) exclude op-on-tail
                     else exclude op-on-tail-and-middle; }
      action     { in++; /* add element to tail of buf */ }
      post       { N++; }
   method int get();
      matching   ( N > 0 );
      pre        { if (N >= 5) exclude op-on-head
                     else exclude op-on-head-and-middle; }
      action     { /* return element from head of buf */ out++; }
      post       { N--; }
end bounded-buffer;
```

Figure 4.12
Inheritance Anomaly in Synchronizing Actions

successive method delegations to describe state transitions, whose execution could be a considerable overhead.

4.5.2 Caromel's Proposal

Caromel's proposal[14], based on the Eiffel II language, in effect provides different synchronization schemes as a set of library routines implemented in terms of more lower-level primitives. For this purpose, methods, bodies, messages, message queues, and guards (dubbed respectively as routines, LIVE routines, requests, request lines, and blocking conditions, in their terminology) are manipulated as first-class entities in the synchronization code. A concurrent object, by inheriting from a class called ABSTRACT_PROCESS, attains the ability to dynamically associate synchronization code to individual methods. By overriding this association in the synchronization routine of the child classes, it is often possible to localize the effect of inheritance with respect to object-wise synchronization.

Caromel has shown that (1) first-classing of elements of synchronization schemes, and (2) adopting different synchronization schemes according to the requirements of different synchronization constraints, promote code re-use of concurrent objects.

The proposal, unfortunately, does not sufficiently resolve the inheritance anomaly in general. The limitations are that, once a synchronization scheme is adopted in the superclass by concrete instantiation of the abstract class, it is often difficult to override it in a consistent way to adopt a different synchronization scheme. This is in a sense breakage of encapsulation, because once a user 'commits' by defining concrete classes, their subclasses must assume such commitments in their programming, and in the worst case, the entire synchronization scheme must be re-programmed as we have seen for the 'body' anomaly. Another problem is the overhead of the execution synchronization code itself: since the synchronization scheme is not built-in as a primitive of the language, and no special optimizations are performed for integrating user-level code, execution of the user-defined code would be a substantial overhead. This cost was not an issue in [14], since Eiffel II seems to be intended for coarse grained concurrent computing in an distributed environment. But for achieving medium to fine-grain concurrency, the cost is definitely intolerable.

4.5.3 Frølunds's Proposal

Frølund proposes a simple framework in which concentrates on re-use of synchronization code for the derived (i.e., overridden) methods[25]. The synchronization scheme is based on method guards, in which synchronization constraints get increasingly restrictive in subclasses. Basically, one specifies a guard that gives the condition under which the method *cannot be accepted*, i.e. a *negative* guard. Furthermore, the guard expressions are accumulated along the inheritance chain for a given method, so that, given a method with the name m, all the guards for the methods in the ancestor classes with the name m and were thus overridden must evaluate to *false* in order for the message m to be accepted. Thus, the re-use only works in the way to restrict the conditions under which the messages are acceptable. Frølunds points out that this is reasonable given that it should be possible for superclass operations to work on (all) subclass state, i.e., if an

ancestor operation is not enabled in a particular state, then a derived operation with
extended behavior will also incur inconsistency in that state. In addition, one could
refer to other methods within the guard expressions; in this case, the method itself is
not invoked, but instead, its guard(s) are evaluated and the resulting boolean value is
returned. This is similar to the abovementioned proposal by Shibayama.

Although the proposal works to avoid the state partitioning anomaly because it is
based on guards, and also allows re-use of guards to some degree, the scheme seems
limited in practice:

- The paper only focuses on the re-use of guards, and avoidance of other anomalies is
  not given enough consideration. Re-use and associated anomalies regarding history
  sensitiveness (represented by `gb-buf`) is not mentioned at all. State modification is
  considered to some degree with the `Lock` example, but the solution is with ad-hoc
  construct that is non-extensible in the subclass: one can only specify the synchronization constraints that should hold uniformly for all methods to be defined in subclasses
  except for a single exception method with the `all-except`(*method-name*) construct.
  This will allow for a very simple `lock` case, where only one particular method (i.e.,
  `lock`) needs to be excluded, with a declaration such as:

    (lock_var == 1) disables all-except(lock);

  However, is not possible to add a method which COULD be invoked under the same
  or more restrictive synchronization constraint as `lock`, because `all-except(lock)`
  prohibits any further extensions regarding the constraint on the `lock_var`, including
  the future definitions in the subclasses. For example, it is impossible to extend the
  class by adding a method `inquire-lock` which (1) inquires and returns the state of
  the lock, and (2) can be invoked irrespective of the condition of the lock itself.

- Another problem is that the scheme never seems to have been implemented. Although
  the proposed syntax for the separation of guards and their associated method is clean,
  it is not immediately obvious how one might implement it in an efficient way, because
  the guards and methods no longer have one-to-one correspondences.

Nevertheless, we feel that Frølund's work is noteworthy for pointing out issues of
encapsulation and consistency in re-use.

4.5.4   Meseguer's Proposal

Meseguer proposes a new formalism[31] for modeling concurrent systems, and an OOCP
language called Maude, which is based on this formalism. The language possesses the
flexibility to provide cleans solutions for (some of the) anomalous examples we have
presented in this paper[32].

Meseguer's formalism is a logic called the (concurrent) rewriting logic, which (Meseguer
states that) most models of concurrent computation can be regarded as its special instantiations. A concurrent system is derived from (instantiations of) *modules*, that are
composed of *terms* and rewrite rules. Computation proceeds by simultaneous simplification of terms when there are applicable rewrite rules. There are two types of modules,
functional and *system*. The rewriting in system modules are not equational, i.e., does not

exhibit the Church-Rosser property. This allows the modeling of phenomenon specific to concurrent computations, such as non-deterministic choice. The Maude language[31], based on this framework, provides *object-oriented modules* for ease of programming in concurrent object-oriented style. For actual execution, object-oriented modules are first translated into system modules; then, computation proceeds with concurrent rewriting according to the rewrite rules of the translated module. Inheritance is also supported in object-oriented modules directly with Maude's order-sorted type structures.

Inheritance anomaly is avoided in Maude in the following way[32]: the side conditions placed on the rewrite rules can serve as a guard; thus, state-partitioning anomaly does not occur. In addition, rewrite rules can be flexible, operating on the term structures as first class values. Thus, there is (albeit implicit) reflective capability in Maude, which allow history information to be encoded within the term structure of the class definition in a straightforward way. For example, it is simple to define a class which adds the locking capability to arbitrary classes. As an example, suppose we mix class `Lock` and class `A` to create class `Lockable-A`. The definition of the `Lock` class would "masquerade" the class identifier of `A` into a quoted one, `A'`. This quoted class can only accept the `unlock` message, and when it does, it restores the class identifier to `A`.

Although Maude does provides powerful language features to support several synchronization schemes, more work needed to be done to exploit the the extent of applicability of Maude to other classes of inheritance anomaly. One problem with proposal is that, because the solutions are based on the powerful pattern-matching capabilities of Maude, practical application of the proposal could be inefficient as a result in a fine-grain setting. Unless some good implementation scheme is devised, a single message send could take at the least several hundreds of instructions.

4.5.5 Ishikawa's Proposal

Ishikawa proposed a communication mechanism between concurrent objects that allows re-use of communication protocols more complex than the standard client-server protocol[21]. The proposal is similar to those based on enable sets; each class maintains a set of *method set*, a set of bindings between the method name and the method body itself. The programmer specifies which method set the method definition will belong to, allowing multiple definition of methods with the same name belonging to different method sets. Each object dynamically maintains a *visible set*, which dictates which methods are acceptable to the object. The user specifies operations on the visible set `include` and `exclude` with a method set name as an argument. In addition, *intensive sets* of an object dictates which methods could be subject to immediate (unqueued) execution.

The proposal has significance in pointing out that first class operations on method sets could be one important feature the language must support in order to allow re-use of synchronization code; however, it too has its limitations. Although the original intent of the proposed mechanism was not on solving the inheritance anomaly in the first place, Ishikawa nevertheless presents a solution to the `Lock` anomaly problem in the paper. However, the solution seems to be quite limited, as it works only for very simple locks, and not for more complex locks such as the `WRITE-LOCK` example which incorporate a hierarchy of locks, as is described in Section 4.7.3. As a matter of a fact, by our understanding the presented solution is not correct in a sense that the locking interferes with the synchronization behavior of the buffer—according to his definition, the visible set of an object, which holds the methods that are acceptable, is substituted with the `scope` construct in the combined subclass of `Buffer` and `Lock` without any regard to the previous state of the object. In other words, whatever information the object had on the synchronization information that corresponds to the object state prior to locking, is thrown away. This presents a serious problem: for example, if the buffer was full prior to locking, the visible set holding the information is thrown away because the after method of `unlock` in class `LockBuffer` replaces the visible set of the object to be the initial one of the object, namely, `#unlocked` and `#free` by the use of the construct `scope #visible` (See [21], Example 5.2 for details of the original solution).

Other problems with the proposal is that (1) the state partitioning anomaly easily occurs for the same reason as accept sets; secondly, (2) it seems that the mechanisms have never been implemented in practice; the basic mechanisms for the `import/export` seems quite inefficient to implement compared to simple guards or enable sets, with no immediate obvious means of optimizations.

4.5.6   Summary of Previous Proposals and Their Limitations

The previous proposals reviewed here have identified to some degree that (1) separation of synchronization codes to localize the changes in the synchronization code, and (2) first-class construction of synchronization schemes (possibly with reflective capability of a language), could potentially provide the necessary flexibility to keep code re-definitions to the minimum.

However, when one considers practice, we feel that they are not satisfactory for the following reasons:

- We have seen in the previous sections that no single synchronization scheme would serve as a panacea for all the cases of inheriting synchronization codes for satisfying the new synchronization constraints of the subclass; in particular, accept sets and guards each have their advantages as well as drawbacks. Instead, our premise is that the user should be able to choose whatever synchronization scheme deemed appropriate for particular synchronization constraints. With objects, the emphasis would then be on orthogonality/encapsulation property, that is, the principle that not only the synchronization code but also the synchronization scheme should be encapsulated, e.g., the scheme employed in the parent class is an implementation detail *that should not be exposed to the subclasses*. The proposals, however, restrict the user to a single synchronization scheme, thus limiting the expressiveness, and/or has not addressed the encapsulation issue at all. As a result, re-use that could lead to inheritance anomalies, which could otherwise be avoided using different synchronization schemes, become difficult.

- A related problem is that none of the schemes have properly considered avoiding the necessity of recompilation of parent methods, or encapsulation of their source code. In practice, it is strongly desirable to be able to separately compile the subclasses with a restricted set of static information exported from the superclasses. This is both due to (1) speed (avoiding long recompilation delays) and (2) propriety issues (many commercial class libraries comprising an application framework does not come with a source code). Although some of the simpler proposals in the previous sections could satisfy this requirement, the issue nevertheless has not been properly considered.

- Some proposals allow inheritance of synchronization code separately from main method bodies. The manner the synchronization code of the superclass is referenced, however, is done in a syntactically and conceptually different way compared to standard method inheritance. Thus, users are faced with two different inheritance systems, possibly with no obvious conceptual model of how they interact.

- The final and the most important issue is that, for all proposals, efficiency issues of the implementation of their schemes have been given little consideration, if implementation were considered at all. Implementation of efficient concurrent OO-languages is not at all trivial— in our recent work in implementing language ABCL on various architectures, developing software technologies for efficient implementation has been one of the primary focus of our research: for example on ABCLonAP1000[42], we have trimmed down the local *asynchronous* message sending overhead down to about 20 SPARC instructions in the best cases, nearly matching the (procedure calling) method invocation time of C++. Remote asynchronous invocation requires less than 10 μseconds, competing favorably with architectures that facilitate special message-passing hardware. On analyzing the previous solutions, none considers whether their implementation could be done with a comparable efficiency; in fact, the overhead for some of them could easily be hundreds of instructions per each method invocation, which would prohibit their usage in practical situations.

4.6 Our Proposed Solutions to Inheritance Anomaly

During the course of our research, we have proposed several solutions to minimize re-definitions and promote code re-use. Although the early ones have been totally superseded by our new proposal outlined in Section 4.6.3, they have nevertheless been precious steps worthy of introduction here.

4.6.1 Early Proposal 1 — First-Class Guards with a Reflective Architecture

Our first proposal was based on reflection and first-classing of method guards[29]. It facilitated guarded methods, since it avoids the state-partitioning anomaly. In addition, we attempted to minimize the anomaly for history-only sensitive cases by granting first-class status to a set of method guards. A OOCP language X0/R with a reflective architecture as shown in Figure 4.13 achieves this purpose. The *metaobject* of x, denoted as x.meta, is a meta-level representation of the structure and computation of x. Here, the metaobject is itself a (concurrent) object — this is basically the *individual-based* model of reflection as proposed in [48]. Given x, we can manipulate the guards as a first class-object via x.meta. Figure 4.14 illustrates how the Lock mixin class can be programmed with this strategy. (Note that '*object* <-- *message*' denotes a message send.)

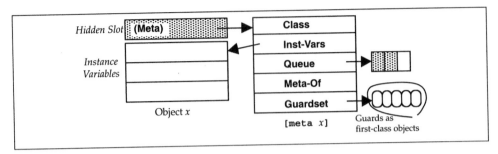

Figure 4.13
Object and its Metaobject in X0/R

Although further application of X0/R to other solutions were not investigated, the idea of 'replacing' the set of guards dynamically was valuable[6].

4.6.2 Early Proposal 2 — Eliminating Synchronization Code Syntactically

In our prototype OOCP language HARMONY[47], we took another approach of *eliminating* the need for synchronization code with automated concurrency control feature of the system, instead of inventing various new synchronization schemes which might cause yet another anomaly. Transactions supplemented with method guards are the basic synchronization scheme of objects, of which guards are usually only necessary for essential methods, because inter-object synchronization for maintaining integrity is now implicit in the transaction facility of the system. With such a strategy, inheritance anomaly is much less likely to occur, since there is little requirement for the methods whose synchronization code cause the anomaly. With bounded buffer, for example, only the essential (guarded) put and get methods are necessary; compound methods known to cause anomalies, such as get2 which removes two items from the buffer atomically, are no longer necessary in the first place. This is because with Harmony one can perform successive gets to the buffer with guarantee of atomicity without any programming of synchronization code such as locking. The details are found in a [47].

Application of HARMONY to fine-grain computing, however, was difficult due to extensive overhead of distributed transaction management among the objects. Nevertheless, the idea of making the synchronization scheme implicit, was valuable.

4.6.3 Our New Proposal

We have recently proposed a set of language OOCP languages primitives that provide high degree of efficient and encapsulated re-use of synchronization code[30]. The primitives are being incorporated into the new version of ABCL we are currently designing/implementing. The proposal is designed with high practicality in mind—it extends and extensively refines the ideas in the past proposals to (1) separate and localize the

---

[6]Some other ideas of X0/R, such as *dynamic progression of degree of reflectivity*[29], was employed in the actual efficient implementation of our OOC-Reflective language, ABCL/R2[26].

```
class lock {
   Guard_set saved_guards; //  saved set of first-class guards
methods:
   // replace the guards of the metaobject so that only unlock can be accepted.
   void lock() {
      saved_guards = self.meta <-- get_all_guards();
      self.meta <-- set_all_guards(FALSE_GUARDS);
      self.meta <-- set_guard("unlock", TRUE);
   }
   // not invoked until the guard is set to TRUE with :lock
   void unlock() when FALSE {
      self.meta <-- set_all_guards(saved_guards);
      // The guard for unlock is reset to  FALSE as a result.
   }
}
```

Figure 4.14
Definition of Lock Class with X0/R

synchronization schemes from the main bodies of methods, allowing fine-grained inheritance/overriding, and to (2) allow dynamic operations on the methods themselves, in order to control which messages are acceptable by an object. Furthermore, it has the following novel and favorable characteristics:

- Our proposal allows both guard-based and accept-set based synchronization schemes to coexist and be integrated, so that the best scheme can be chosen to program given synchronization constraints.

- The manner we re-use the synchronization code is syntactically similar to superclass method references in sequential OO-languages (e.g.,super). Thus, users with experience in OO-programming can readily adapt to our proposal. Inheritance rules are made to depend on each synchronization scheme, however, because the most 'natural' way of inheritance differs among the schemes.

- We offer a high degree of encapsulation and re-use for synchronization code. Furthermore, even synchronization schemes could be encapsulated in superclasses in many cases by proper exporting of class information by the user.

- Expressiveness is not our sole concern—we have also devised speed- and space-efficient incorporation into the software architecture of the aforementioned ABCL/onAP1000. In particular, all space/time-consuming data structure construction for object synchronization can be done at compile-time.

4.6.3.1 Overview of Execution Model of Concurrent Objects The execution model of our concurrent object is an extension of ABCM[50]. A rough overview is as

follows: an object sends messages asynchronously, either *past type* ("asynchronously send and no-wait", syntactically denoted by *Receiver* <- *Msg*) or *now type* ("asynchronously send and wait for a reply", syntactically denoted by *Receiver* <-- *Msg*). The transmission order of messages between two objects are preserved (*transmission order preservation law*). The now-type is similar to procedure call, except that (1) the receiver can continue its execution even after it has returned a reply message and (2) the *reply destination* (reply message box) of a now-type message is a first-class object, which can be passed around as message arguments.

Upon message reception, an object executes messages in a mutually exclusive manner. An object is *dormant* if it is not processing a message, and *active* if it is. All the messages received during active mode are placed in its message queue. When in dormant mode, the object scans its message queue from its head, and accepts the first message that satisfies its synchronization specification, which is the combination of *method sets*, *synchronizers*(extended form of guarded methods), and *transition specifications*(state transition directives of *accept-sets*): First, the object evaluates its set of *synchronizers* to determine, within its current *accept set* (i.e., the set of currently acceptable methods for the object) which messages are acceptable according to its current state. The object scans the message queue for an acceptable message, and executes the corresponding method. After its execution is completed, the object evaluates the *transition specification* associated with the method, and alters its accept set with the method sets specified in the transition.

Synchronization schemes specify operations on the accept sets with *method sets* to designate the set of methods to be enabled/disabled. Method sets are inherited and re-defined in subclasses. The programmer can choose and combine the synchronization schemes in the synchronization code to best express his synchronization constraints (i.e., with various forms of synchronizers and transition *types*). Altogether, the set of synchronization code is localized within the *synchronization specification* of a given class. The constituent primitives of synchronization specification can be individually inherited and re-used in a 'fine-grain' manner, using a similar syntax to standard method inheritance but with separate inheritance rules for each synchronization scheme. The main part of method that do not contain synchronization code (i.e., the method body) is totally separated from the synchronization specification, and are inherited and overridden separately from synchronization code.

4.6.3.2 Method Sets A *method set* is a set of methods (identifiers) bound with the corresponding method bodies. It is worthy to note in the outset that method sets are designed NOT to be full first class objects, in that they cannot be assigned to variables and such, and are only subject to restricted run-time extensions. This allows the *Virtual Function Table (VFT)* (the table that holds pointers to the compiled methods code according to their method identifiers) to be determined at compile time for efficient execution and low storage space.

Primitive method set constructor has the form #{*method name*,...}. There are also some primitive set operations, such as '|'(union). Other than within the method definitions, the method sets in the program must be assigned to explicit identifiers to be referenced, disallowing arbitrary run-time set operations. The basic definition form is:

```
mset name #{method name, ...};
```

Example 1 Consider the `b-buf` class with the two methods, `put` and `get`:

```
class b-buf {
method_sets:
     mset    EMPTY    #{put}             // only 'put' to empty buffer
     mset    FULL     #{get}             // only 'get' from full buffer
     mset    PARTIAL  EMPTY | FULL  // both possible otherwise
        :
}
```

A *method qualifier* is a limited form of qualifer expression to denote a constructor for a set of methods. The restriction on the qualifier is that the resulting set must be computable at compile time. Currently, the supported form is as follows:

- `all`—all the methods of the class including the inherited methods,

- `defined`—the defined methods of the class, excluding the inherited ones, and

- `all_except`(*method set*,...)—all the methods of the class except the ones of the specified method sets.

Example 2 The following constructs a pair of mutually exclusive method set: `LOCKED` is a singleton set containing `unlock`, while `UNLOCKED` contains all the methods defined at the class, except `unlock`.

```
class Lock {
method_sets:
   mset    LOCKED         #{unlock}
   mset    UNLOCKED       all-except(LOCKED)
        :
}
```

Method set definitions can be re-defined in subclasses. If the overridden definitions of the superclass needs to be referenced, the subclasses may refer to them using the `super` operator followed by the method set identifier[7] (see Example 3). All the method sets are recomputed in the subclass to account for re-definitions, so that any changes are propagated to the derived method sets.

One special case is as follows: when the name of a method is not syntactically manifest in any of the method set definitions, then the method is called a *synchronization free* method. Such a method is added implicitly and uniformly to all the method sets of the class. This is to allow non-constrained methods to be freely invokable by default. When

---

[7]In practice, matters are more complicated due to multiple inheritance.

the method is later explicitly used in a construction of a method set in a subclass, this implicit addition is nullified for that subclass and its siblings.

Also, the method qualifier is (re)computed when one defines a new method in the subclass: for example, if new methods are added in a subclass of `Lock`, they are added to the `UNLOCKED` method set for that class, because `UNLOCKED` is defined as `all-except(LOCKED)`.

Example 3 Consider defining a class `x-buf` as a subclass of `b-buf` of Example 1 by adding the following two methods: (1) `last`, which removes the last element that was `put`, and (2) `empty?` which checks whether the buffer is empty or not. Since the synchronization constraint for `last` is identical to that of `get`, it is added to the method set where `get` was a member, namely, `FULL`. Method `empty?` is a synchronization-free method, and is automatically added to all the method sets. Furthermore, the method sets that were derived from `FULL`, i.e., `PARTIAL`, are also automatically updated in `x-buf` as well.

```
    class x-buf: b-buf{
  method_sets:
      mset    FULL     super FULL | #{last}
      // PARTIAL  is automatically redefined.
        :
  }
```

Altogether, method set `PARTIAL` in `x-buf` is `#{put, get, last, empty?}`.

A method set can be statically bound to a guard expression, so that a method set in the superclass can be partitioned into multiple method sets, depending on runtime object states. Such *guarded method set* is introduced to cope with the state partitioning anomaly, allowing transitions to have (full) flexibility of guards. Below is the syntax:

mset *name* #{*method name*, ...} when *guard expression*;

Note, however, that we do not allow arbitrary run-time set operations on the method sets; the purpose of the guarded method set definitions is to maintain the encapsulation property without method sets being full first-class entities for efficiency reasons.

Example 4 The following definition of `PARTIAL` allows partitioning of the state in the subclass:

```
    class x-buf2: b-buf {
  method_sets:
      mset    PARTIAL    super PARTIAL            when (size == 1)
      mset    PARTIAL    super PARTIAL | #{get2} when (size > 1)
        :
  }
```

4.6.3.3 Synchronizers A *synchronizer* is a combination of *guard expressions, enabling specifier*, and a list of method sets. In essence, it is similar to a guarded method, but is more flexible in that a single guard can be assigned to multiple methods in method sets.

A guard expression is basically a side-effect free boolean expression involving instance variables and method arguments. Local variables of individual methods are not allowed in the guards to maintain encapsulation. The named method argument must exist in all the methods associated with the guard (both for synchronizers and transitions) or compile-time error will result. The guard expression also can contain *acceptance inquiry* function `enabled()` and `disabled()`, which takes either a method name or a method set as an argument. The guard expressions can be assigned symbolic names with `guard` definitions, so that they can be re-used and possibly redefined in subclasses.

> **guard**   *name*   *guard expression*

The synchronizer thus becomes:

```
synchronizers:
    guard enables method set name, ...;
```

A special keyword `initially` can be specified in place of a guard in order to indicate which method set is enabled initially upon object creation. Also, a synchronizer can be chosen NOT to be inherited for methods in a given method set with **override** *method set*.

Example 5 Synchronization specification for `b-buf` can be made with synchronizers in the following way:

```
    guards:
        guard   empty_guard    (size == 0)
        guard   full_guard     (size == MAX_SIZE)
        guard   partial_guard (!empty_guard && !full_guard)
    synchronizers:
        initially        enables EMPTY;
        partial_guard    enables PARTIAL;
        empty_guard      enables EMPTY;
        full_guard       enables FULL;
            :
```

4.6.3.4 Transition Specifications *Transition specification* can be used as an alternative synchronization scheme to synchronizers. A *transition* corresponding to a method is executed immediately after the completion of the method body. Its purpose is to specify the transitional behavior of an object's accept set, that reflects the synchronization constraint dictated by the internal state of the object. The transitions are specified on a method-by-method basis, via *transition specifications* for the method. Each transition of an object is associated with a *transition type*, which designates the effect of the method set upon the current accept set, and an optional *guard*, which governs the condition under which the transition is executed. The basic syntax of transition specification for a given method is as follows:

```
transitions:
 transition method name1 () {
   transition-type-1  method-set {when guard-expression 1};
                  :
   transition-type-n  method-set {when guard-expression n};
 }
 transition method name2 () {
                  :
```

Each line of the transition specification is simply called a *transition*. The guard expression of each transition is evaluated sequentially from transitions 1 to n, and the transition of the first guard to evaluate to **true** is executed exclusively. This not only automates the disambiguation of multiple possible transitions, but also allows for finer control of inherited transitions.

The currently available *transition types* are as follows: **become**, **push**, **enable**, **disable**, **restore**, **wait_once**, **enable_once**, **disable_once**, and **is**. Below is their brief description:

1. **Become:**   Replaces the accept set entirely.

2. **Push:**   Replaces the current accept set, but also 'pushes' it so that it can be restored with a subsequent **restore**.

3. **Enable:**   Enables the methods in the method set in addition to the ones in the current accept set. (Effectively, the new accept set is the set union of the old accept set and the specified method set).

4. **Disable:**   A complement to **enable**, disables the methods that are elements of the argument method set and the current accept set (effectively, the set difference is taken).

5. **Restore:**   Restores the method set to the one prior to performing **push**, **enable**, or **disable**.

6. **Wait_once:**   The current accept set is 'pushed' and replaced as is with **push**, but is subsequently restored with a forced **restore** transition in the next accepted message, just prior to execution of the real transition. This effectively allows handshaking-type protocol to be programmed easily, as is with the **wait-for** construct of ABCL/1.

7. **Enable_once, disable_once:**   A combination of **enable** or **disable** with automatic **restore**, as is with **wait_once**.

8. **Is:**   A special-purpose keyword to inherit the transitions of the parent class.

The transition specifications of the parent class are inherited, but overriding them can be done in a more sophisticated manner compared to overriding of method sets and synchronizers:

- Each class can have its *default transition specification*, indicated by a special keyword `default`. If the method does not have any transition specification in its class or its superclasses, the default transition specification is used *if one is defined*. The default transition specification can also be overridden along the inheritance chain.

- The transition `is self` *method-name* refers to the entire transition specification of that method, allowing sharing among the methods. The expression `super` *method-name* is the similar, except that the search for the corresponding reference starts from the immediate superclass as is with Smalltalk-80 (with disambiguation rules for multiple inheritance).

- There is an automatic inheritance rule to relieve the programmer from explicit declaration of inheritance of transition specifications: when one defines a transition for a method, if there are no lines with the `is` specification, an implicit `super` *method-name* is assumed to exist as the *last* transition in the specification, effectively inheriting the entire transition specification of the superclass for the method. (In order to prohibit this automatic inheritance, the last line of the transition specification can made into a special form `override`.)

- The guard expression can be substituted for `otherwise` to be the *otherwise transition*. This transition is selected when there are no guards that become true. When there are multiple otherwise transitions, the one in the most specific subclass supersedes the others in the superclasses.

Note that, combined with the ordered evaluation rule of the transitions, the above inheritance mechanism of transition specifications allows the programmer the freedom to define transitions that either precede or succeed the superclass transitions with arbitrary placement of the `super`. Default transitions can be referenced by `self` and `super` as well, so that individual methods can customized upon the default transitions of its superclass.

Example 6 Here is an alternative definition of `b-buf` using transitions.

```
   transitions:
transition get() {
    become EMPTY when (size == 0);
    become FULL  when (size == BUFSIZE);
    become PARTIAL otherwise;
}
transition put() {
    is get();  // transition of put the same as get
}
        :
```

4.6.4   Inheriting Synchronization Code in our New Proposal

When the programmer creates a new subclass, he (re)defines the new methods, and also (re)defines the method sets, synchronizers, and transitions to satisfy the new synchronization constraint, re-using much of the synchronization code of the superclasses. This is achieved in principle in a syntactically similar way as the re-use of normal methods in sequential object-oriented languages: syntactic references to method sets and other values in the superclasses are modified to be those of the inherited classes when they are re-defined, and superclass definitions can be referenced with `self` and `super`. However, inheritance rules are customized for each synchronization scheme according to their characteristics, as we have seen in the descriptions. The required updating of synchronization code is encapsulated within the synchronization specification of the class, i.e., the method sets, synchronizers and transition specifications. The main bodies of the methods in the superclasses, by contrast, are unaffected in the subclasses, avoiding the inheritance anomaly and achieving encapsulation.

In general, inheritance anomaly is avoided in the following way: state partioning anomaly does not occur when using synchronizers. For transition specifications, there are two ways of expressing the state partitioning in the subclasses: first is to augment the sets of transitions with the additional partitioning required. By appropriate placement of `super`, only the states that are partitioned for the new methods in the subclass need to be modified, and majority of the parent transitions are re-used automatically by the implicit inheritance rule of transition specifications. Second is to employ method sets bound with (dynamically computed) guards. By describing the new partition of the method sets with the guards, the transitions in the superclasses can be refined with re-definitions only for the relevant method sets. For state modifications such as `lock`, synchronizers can be re-defined, or alternatively, transitions can also be used effectively to 'switch' the method sets according to the state. We do not employ (expensive) higher-order term structure encodings and expensive pattern matchings as in Maude[32], but still provide comparable descriptive power.

Furthermore, as we exemplify in the next section, encapsulation is possible not only for the synchronization code of the superclass, but also possible to for the *synchronization scheme* of the superclass in many cases, if the user exports the appropriate information of the synchronization specification to the subclass; therefore, by careful design, the user can maintain the freedom of selecting the appropriate synchronization scheme irrespective of the scheme employed in the superclasses.

4.7   Examples of Avoiding Inheritance Anomaly

The inheritance anomaly examples are now programmed using our proposal. We show that (1) the synchronization code is encapsulated in the synchronization specifications and does not manifest in the main body of the methods, and (2) separate inheritance (rules) for method sets, synchronizers, and transitions allow fine-grain re-use of superclass synchronization code, keeping re-definitions very small. Furthermore (3) synchronization schemes are also encapsulated; separate solutions for the same problem are programmed using either synchronizers or transitions (except **gget**). We also emphasize that synchronization scheme of the superclasses are also encapsulated, i.e., the solutions would work irrespective of the choice of the synchronization scheme in the original **b-buf** first presented below:

- **Bounded Buffer with Synchronizers:**

```
Class b-buf {
  int size = in = out = 0; int item[MAX_SIZE];
method_sets:
  mset    EMPTY    #{put}          // only 'put' to empty buffer
  mset    FULL     #{get}          // only 'get' from full buffer
  mset    PARTIAL  EMPTY | FULL    // both possible otherwise
synchronizers:
  initially enables EMPTY;
  (0 < size && size < MAX_SIZE) enables PARTIAL;
  (size == 0) enables EMPTY;
  (size == MAX_SIZE) enables FULL;
methods:
  void put(int item)
       { size--; out = (out + 1) % max_size; return item[out];}
  int get(){ size++; in = (in + 1) % max_size; item[in] = x;}
}
```

- **Bounded Buffer with Transition Specifications:**

```
Class b-buf {
  int size = in = out = 0; int item[MAX_SIZE];
method_sets:
  mset    EMPTY    #{put}          // only 'put' to empty buffer
  mset    FULL     #{get}          // only 'get' from full buffer
  mset    PARTIAL  EMPTY | FULL    // both possible otherwise
methods:
  void put(int item)
       { size--; out = (out + 1) % max_size; return item[out];}
  int get(){ size++; in = (in + 1) % max_size; item[in] = x; }
transitions:
  transition default {  // the default transition specification
       become EMPTY when (size == 0);
       become FULL  when (size == BUFSIZE);
       become PARTIAL otherwise;
  }
}
```

4.7.1   State Partitioning Anomaly—Method `get2`:

The method obtains two elements atomically from the buffer. State partitioning in
the subclass is trivially satisfied with guards. With accept sets, there are two possible
solutions: One is to augment the transition specifications of each method to realize the
partition. The other is to use method sets bound with guards—method sets are 'refined'
with guards to dynamically add **get2** as an element depending on the internal state of
the object.

- **Solution with Synchronizers:**

```
Class x-buf2: b-buf { // x-buf2 is a subclass of b-buf
// Optional re-definitions of method sets,
//    necessary if the future subclasses are to use transitions.
  method_sets:
    mset    FULL    super FULL | #{get2}
    mset    PARTIAL super PARTIAL | #{get2}
    mset    ONE     super PARTIAL
  synchronizers:
    (size > 1) enables get2
  methods:
    int get2(){ // code to operate and return two elements; }
}
```

- **Solution with Transition Specifications (1):**

```
Class x-buf2: b-buf { // x-buf2 is a subclass of b-buf
method_sets:
  mset    FULL    super FULL | #{get2}
  mset    PARTIAL super PARTIAL | #{get2}
  mset    ONE     super PARTIAL
methods:
  int get2()
    { // code to operate and return two elements; }
transitions:
  transition default { // account for new state partitioning
    become ONE when (size == 1); //
    implicit 'is super default()'
  }
}
```

- **Solution with Transition Specifications (2):**

```
Class x-buf2: b-buf { // x-buf2 is a subclass of b-buf
  method_sets:
    mset    FULL      super FULL                  when (size == 1)
    mset    FULL      super FULL | #{get2}        when (size > 1)
    mset    PARTIAL   super PARTIAL               when (size == 1)
    mset    PARTIAL   super PARTIAL | #{get2}     when (size > 1)
    mset    ONE       super PARTIAL
  methods:
    int get2()
      { // code to operate and return two elements; }
  // Transitions need not be re-defined
}
```

4.7.2 History-Only Sensitiveness—Method gget in class gb-buf:

Although not all history sensitiveness can be resolved with our scheme, cases where only the previous message affects the accept set can be handled gracefully with the family of _once transitions. Here, we present a solution to the **gget** method in **gb-buf**; notice that the solution works irrespective of whether **b-buf** is specified with synchronizers or transitions. A more elaborate inter-object protocol can be designed by the combined use of both synchronizers and transitions.

- **Solution with Transition Specifications:**

```
class gb-buf: b-buf {
  method_sets:
    mset    AFTER-PUT     #{gget};
    mset    FULL          super FULL | AFTER-PUT
  methods:
    // gget identical to get except for synchronization constraint
    int gget() { return super get(); }
  transitions:
    transition put() { disable_once AFTER-PUT; } // Only once after put
    // gget automatically handled by the default: transition,
    //   if b-buf were specified with transitions.
}
```

4.7.3 State Modification Anomaly—Method Lock/Write-Lock/Unlock:

The **write-lock** class defines a two-level lock where the method **lock** locks the object exclusively so that no other methods can access it until it receives a corresponding **unlock** message, whereas the **write-lock** message allows side-effect free methods to be invoked. **Write-lock** is to be used as a mixin, so that the invokable methods under write-locked

state can be extended in the subclasses. It is also straightforward to refine the locks by
constructing a hierarchy of locks.

- **Solution with Synchronizers:**

```
typedef lock_state = {unlocked_lock,write_locked_lock,locked_lock};
class write-lock {
   lock_state lock_var = unlocked_lock;
   lock_stack lstatck = new(lock_stack);
method_sets:
   mset     LOCKED         #{unlock}
   mset     WRITE-LOCKED   self LOCKED   // redefined in subclass
   mset     UNLOCKED       all-except(LOCKED)
synchronizers:
   (lock_var == unlocked_lock) enables UNLOCKED;
   (lock_var == write_locked_lock) enables WRITE-LOCKED;
   (lock_var == locked_lock) enables LOCKED;
methods:
   void lock() {lstack.push(lock_var); lock_var = locked_lock;}
   void write-lock(){lstack.push(lock_var);lock_var = write_locked_lock;}
   void unlock() {lock_var = lstack.pop; }}
```

- **Solution with Transition Specifications:**

```
typedef lock_state = {unlocked_lock,write_locked_lock,locked_lock};
class write-lock {
   lock_state lock_var = unlocked_lock;
   lock_stack lstatck = new(lock_stack);
method_sets:
   mset     LOCKED         #{unlock}
   mset     WRITE-LOCKED   self LOCKED   // redefined in subclass
   mset     UNLOCKED       all-except(LOCKED)
methods:
   // Locking can be handled entirely with transitions,
   //   but we define the methods to maintain encapsulation
   void lock() {lstack.push(lock_var); lock_var = locked_lock;}
   void write-lock(){lstack.push(lock_var);lock_var = write_locked_lock}
   void unlock() {lock_var = lstack.pop;}
transitions:
   transition lock() { push LOCKED; }
   transition write-lock() { push WRITE-LOCKED; }
   transition unlock() { restore; }
}
```

- We give two examples of the use of `lock`: One is to add a method to the `lock`
  class itself which inquires the status of the lock, which is not possible with Frølund's

proposal[25]. Notice how the inheritance of method sets allows easy re-use of existing lock code.

```
class lock2: lock {
method_sets:
  mset    ALWAYS        #{inquire-lock}   // Always invokable.
  mset    LOCKED        super LOCKED | ALWAYS
  // WRITE-LOCK is automatically updated
  mset    UNLOCKED      super UNLOCKED | ALWAYS
methods:
  lock_state inquire-lock() { return lock_var; }
}
```

As an example of use of `write-lock` as a mix-in, we define a class `lb-buf`, which is a bounded buffer that allows locking; in particular, if the buffer is write-locked, then only the `empty?` method can be invoked. Further extensions to `lb-buf` is possible by augmenting the method set `READ-ONLY`. We note that this type of encapsulated extensibility is much more cumbersome with other proposed schemes:

```
class lb-buf: b-buf,write-lock {
method_sets:
  mset    READ-ONLY      #{empty?}  // Can be extended in subclasses
  mset    WRITE-LOCKED   super WRITE-LOCKED | READ-ONLY
  // No other definitions are necessary
  // Note that empty? is in both UNLOCKED and WRITE-LOCKED
}
```

4.7.4   Combining Synchronization Schemes

Recall that a message is accepted as a combined effect on the accept set by the synchronizers and transitions: for instance, after the accept set has been determined by the transitions, the guard in the synchronizer may further restrict the messages that could be received. This is illustrated in the following stream-communication example:

Example 7 Here, is a two-phase handshaking protocol for stream communication: the receiver waits for a `stream_open` message from an anonymous sender; when it receives the message, it sends an acknowledgement, and waits for subsequent `stream_put` messages only from the same sender—messages from other senders are not accepted. When it receives the `stream_close` message from the sender, it returns to the initial state.

```
    class stream-receiver {
    Object opener = NULL;
    method_sets:
      mset  STREAM_CLOSED    #{stream_open}
      mset  STREAM_OPEN      #{stream_put, stream_close}
    synchronizers:
      initially enables CLOSED;
      // Stream_put and stream_close received
      //   only if it matches the opener
      (message_sender == opener) enables STREAM_OPEN;
    methods:
      int stream_open(Object message_sender) {
        opener = message_sender;  // subsequent messages from opener
        opener <- ack(true);  // sends acknowledgement to sender  }
      int stream_put(Object message_sender, int data) {
        // consume data
        message_sender <- ack(true);  // acknowledgement to sender }
      int stream_close(Object message_sender) {
        message_sender <- ack(true);  // acknowledgement to sender
        opener = NULL; // close stream }
    transitions:
      transition stream_open() { become STREAM_OPEN; }
      transition stream_close() { become STREAM_CLOSED; }
    }
```

4.8   Conclusion and Future Work

The prime objective of OOCP languages is to provide maximum computational power through concurrency of objects. At the same time, OOCP languages allow the system to be flexible and dynamically configurable. This effectively captures the essential properties of concurrent computational systems, which are highly complex and must change and evolve to adapt to the requirements of the user. Some ideas that have flourished in the sequential OO world, particularly inheritance, have similar objectives; but unfortunately, as we have shown, synchronization constraints and inheritance have conflicting characteristics, and thus it is difficult to combine them in a clean way. We have analyzed various types of inheritance anomaly and discussed several previous approaches to its solution as well as their limitations. Our new proposal is to have multiple synchronization scheme constructs which allow proper encapsulation as well as efficient implementation.

One related research we should note is the event types for synchronization as first class values, in the concurrent version of language SML[39]. Another work towards the type theory for active objects[36] by Nierstrasz et. al. and also by Honda[20] are also interesting—although our work has not addressed the issues of types in OOCP languages and adhered to inheritance as means of reusing code, the relationship between the type theory and the semantics of inheritance is an active area of research for sequential OO languages. Recent works by America et. al. to separate the subtyping hierarchy from the inheritance hierarchy in the POOL family of OOCP languages such as POOL/I and POOL/S[5, 4] are also promising; in their formalism, subtyping relationship is determined solely by the observed external behavior and not the internal structure. Using this formalism, one can determine if the inheritance is actually correct in a sense that the behavior of the parent class is entirely preserved.

In conclusion, in order for OOCP languages to be usable for large-scale programming, the inheritance anomaly needs more theoretical analysis. We need to strive on the followings:

- Establishing a more precise and formal definition of classification of inheritance anomaly. Although [28] made some preliminary formal analysis, it was not complete in that it only treats the anomaly that occurs with state partitioning. The work on active object types mentioned above could serve as a basis of more comprehensive formalism.

- Further identification of a general class of synchronization schemes with respect to anomaly classifications. Although we tried to be as comprehensive as possible by categorizing and selecting representative synchronization schemes, formal analysis might provide more insights for further sub-categorization.

- Continuous development of languages features which respect the encapsulation and efficiency criteria, based on the above two analysis.

4.9 Acknowledgments

We would like to thank the following individuals for their discussions and contributions during the course of this work: Gul Agha, Peter Wegner, Pierre America, Jens Palsberg, José Meseguer, Oscar Nierstraz, Dennis Kafura, Mehmet Aksit, Lodewijk Bergmans, Etsuya Shibayama, Makoto Takeyama, Mario Tokoro, Yutaka Ishikawa, Ken Wakita, Masahiro Yasugi, Shigeru Chiba, and Kenjiro Taura. We would also like to thank the other members of the ABCL project group for many helpful comments and discussions.

References

[1] G. A. Agha. *ACTORS: A Model of Concurrent Computation in Distributed Systems*. The MIT Press, 1986.

[2] Mehmet Aksit and Anand Tripathi. Data abstraction and mechanism in Sina/ST. In *Proceedings of OOPSLA'88*, volume 23, pages 267–275. SIGPLAN Notices, ACM Press, September 1988.

[3] P. America. Inheritance and subtyping in a parallel object-oriented language. In *Proceedings of ECOOP'87*, volume 276 of *Lecture Notes in Computer Science*, pages 234–242. Springer-Verlag, 1987.

[4] Pierre America. A parallel object-oriented language with inheritance and subtyping. In *Proceedings of OOPSLA'90*, volume 25, pages 161–168. SIGPLAN Notices, ACM Press, October 1990.

[5] Pierre America. Designing an object-oriented programming language with behavioural subtyping. In *Proceedings of the REX School/Workshop on Foundations of Object-Oriented Languages (REX/FOOL), Noordwijkerhout, the Netherlands, May,1990*, number 489 in Lecture Notes in Computer Science, pages 60–90. Springer-Verlag, February 1991.

[6]   Gregory R. Andrews, Ronald A. Olsson, Michael Coffin, Irving Elshoff, Kelvin Nilsen, Titus Purdin, and Gregg Townsend. An overview of SR language and implementation. *ACM Transactions on Programming Languages and Systems*, 10(1):51–86, January 1988.

[7]   Gregory R. Andrews and Fred B. Schneider. Concepts and notations for concurrent programming. *ACM Computing Surveys*, 15(1):3–43, March 1983.

[8]   J. P. Bahsoun, L. Feraud, and C. Betourne. A "two degrees of freedom" approach for parallel programming. In *Proceedings of the 1990 IEEE International Conference on Programming Languages*, pages 261–270, 1990.

[9]   Gilad Bracha and William Cook. Mixin-based inheritance. In *Proceedings of OOPSLA'90*, volume 25, pages 303–311. SIGPLAN Notices, ACM Press, October 1990.

[10]   Jean-Piere Briot and Akinori Yonezawa. Inheritance and synchronization in concurrent OOP. In *Proceedings of ECOOP'87*, volume 276 of *Lecture Notes in Computer Science*, pages 33–40. Springer-Verlag, 1987.

[11]   P. A. Buhr, Glen Ditchfield, and C. R. Zarnke. Adding concurrency to a statically type-safe object-oriented programming language. In *Proceedings of the 1988 ACM SIGPLAN Workshop on Object-Based Concurrent Programming*, volume 24, pages 18–21. SIGPLAN Notices, ACM Press, April 1989.

[12]   R. H. Campbell and A. N. Habermann. The specification of process synchronization by path expressions. In *Lecture Notes in Computer Science*, volume 16, pages 89–102. Springer-Verlag, 1974.

[13]   Denis Caromel. A general model for concurrent and distributed object-oriented programming. In *Proceedings of the 1988 ACM SIGPLAN Workshop on Object-Based Concurrent Programming*, volume 24, pages 102–104. SIGPLAN Notices, ACM Press, April 1989.

[14]   Denis Caromel. Programming abstractions for concurrent programming — a solution to the explicit/implicit control dilemma. In B. Meyer, J. Potter, M. Tokoro, and J. Bezivin, editors, *Proceedings of TOOLS 3, Sydney*, pages 245–253, November 1990.

[15]   Antonio Corradi and Letizia Leonardi. Parallelism in object-oriented programming languages. In *Proceedings of the 1990 IEEE International Conference on Programming Languages*, pages 271–280, 1990.

[16]   D. Decouchant et. al. A synchronization mechanism for typed objects in a distributed system. In *Proceedings of the 1988 ACM SIGPLAN Workshop on Object-Based Concurrent Programming*, volume 24, pages 105–107. SIGPLAN Notices, ACM Press, April 1989.

[17]   Narain Gehani and William D. Roome. *The Concurrent C Programming Language*. Prentice Hall, 1989.

[18]   J. E. Grass and R. H. Campbell. Mediators: A synchronization mechanism. In *Proceedings of the 1986 IEEE International Conference on Distributed Computing Systems*, pages 468–477, 1986.

[19]   John Hogg and Steven Weiser. OTM: applying objects to tasks. In *Proceedings of OOPSLA'87*, volume 22, pages 388–393. SIGPLAN Notices, ACM Press, October 1987.

[20]   Kohei Honda. Interaction types. (unpublished manuscript), 1992.

[21]   Yutaka Ishikawa. Communication mechanisms on autonomous objects. In *Proceedings of OOPSLA'92*, volume 27, pages 303–314. SIGPLAN Notices, ACM Press, October 1992.

[22]   Dennis G. Kafura and Keung Hae Lee. Inheritance in Actor based concurrent object-oriented languages. In *Proceedings of ECOOP'89*, pages 131–145. Cambridge University Press, 1989.

[23]   Henry Lieberman. Concurrent object-oriented programming in Act/1. In Akinori Yonezawa and Mario Tokoro, editors, *Object-Oriented Concurrent Programming*, pages 9–36. The MIT Press, 1987.

[24]   Steven E. Lucco. Parallel programming in a virtual object space. In *Proceedings of OOPSLA'87*, volume 22, pages 26–34. SIGPLAN Notices, ACM Press, October 1987.

[25]   Svend Frølund. Inheritance of synchronization constraints in concurrent object-oriented programming languages. In *Proceedings of ECOOP'92*, 1992.

[26]   Hidehiko Masuhara, Satoshi Matsuoka, and Akinori Yonezawa. Object-oriented concurrent reflective languages can be implemented efficiently. In *Proceedings of OOPSLA'92*, volume 27, pages 127–144. SIGPLAN Notices, ACM Press, October 1992.

[27]   Satoshi Matsuoka and Satoru Kawai. Using Tuple Space communication in distributed object-oriented languages. In *Proceedings of OOPSLA'88*, volume 23, pages 276–283. SIGPLAN Notices, ACM Press, September 1988.

[28]   Satoshi Matsuoka, Ken Wakita, and Akinori Yonezawa. Synchronization constraints with inheritance: What is not possible — so what is? Technical Report 10, Department of Information Science, the University of Tokyo, 1990.

[29]   Satoshi Matsuoka and Akinori Yonezawa. Metalevel solution to inheritance anomaly in concurrent object-oriented languages. In *Proceedings of the ECOOP/OOPSLA'90 Workshop on Reflection and Metalevel Architectures in Object-Oriented Programming*, October 1990.

[30]   Satoshi Matsuoka and Akinori Yonezawa. Highly efficient and encapsulated re-use of synchronization code in concurrent object-oriented languages. (Submitted), 1993.

[31]   José Meseguer. A logical theory of concurrent objects. In *Proceedings of OOPSLA'90*, volume 25, pages 101–115. SIGPLAN Notices, ACM Press, October 1990.

[32]   José Meseguer. Solving the inheritance anomaly in concurrent object-oriented programming. In *Proceedings of ECOOP'93*, 1993. (to appear).

[33]   Robin Milner. *Communication and Concurrency*. Prentice Hall, Engle Cliffs, 1989.

[34]   Jürgen Nehmer, Dieter Haban, Friedemann Mattern, Dieter Wybraniez, and H. Dieter Rombach. Key concepts of the INCAS multicomputer project. *IEEE Transactions on Software Engineering*, 13(8):913–923, August 1987.

[35]   Christian Neusius. Synchronizing actions. In *Proceedings of ECOOP'91*, volume 512 of *Lecture Notes in Computer Science*, pages 118–132. Springer-Verlag, 1991.

[36]   Oscar Nierstrasz and Michael Papathomas. Towards a type theory of active objects. In *Proceedings of the 1990 ECOOP-OOPSLA Workshop on Object-Based Concurrent Programming, Ottawa, Canada, Oct. 1990*, volume 2 of *OOPS Messenger*, pages 89–93. ACM Press, April 1991.

[37]   M. Papathomas. Concurrency issues in object-oriented programming languages. In D. Tsichritzis, editor, *Object Oriented Development*, chapter 12, pages 207–245. Université de Geneve, 1989.

[38]   Uday S. Reddy. Objects as closures: Abstract semantics of object-oriented language. In *Proceedings of the ACM Conference on LISP and Functional Programming*, pages 289–297, 1988.

[39]   J. H. Reppy. Synchronous operations as first-class values. In *Proceedings of the SIGPLAN '88 Conference on Programming Design and Implementation*, pages 250–259, 1988.

[40]   Etsuya Shibayama. Reuse of concurrent object descriptions. In B. Meyer, J. Potter, M. Tokoro, and J. Bezivin, editors, *Proceedings of TOOLS 3, Sydney*, pages 254–266, November 1990.

[41]   Alan Snyder. Encapsulation and inheritance. In *Proceedings of OOPSLA'86*, volume 21, pages 38–45. SIGPLAN Notices, ACM Press, September 1986.

[42]   Kenjiro Taura, Satoshi Matsuoka, and Akinori Yonezawa. An efficient implementation scheme of concurrent object-oriented languages on stock multicomputers. In *Proceedings of 4th ACM Symposium on Principles and Practices of Parallel Programming (PPoPP'93), San Diego*, May 1993. (to appear).

[43]   Chris Tomlinson and Vineet Singh. Inheritance and synchronization with Enabled-Sets. In *Proceedings of OOPSLA'89*, volume 24, pages 103–112. SIGPLAN Notices, ACM Press, October 1989.

[44]   Anand Tripathi, Eric Berge, and Mehmet Aksit. An implementation of object-oriented concurrent programming language SINA. *Software—Practice and Experience*, 19(3):235–256, March 1989.

[45]   Jan van den Bos and Chris Laffra. PROCOL: a parallel object language with protocols. In *Proceedings of OOPSLA'89*, volume 24, pages 95–102. SIGPLAN Notices, ACM Press, October 1989.

[46]   Prasad Vishnubhotla. Synchronization and scheduling in ALPS objects. In *Proceedings of the 1988 IEEE International Conference on Distributed Computing Systems*, pages 256–264, 1988.

[47]   Ken Wakita and Akinori Yonezawa. Linguistic supports for development of organizational information systems. In *Proceedings of ACM COCS*, November 1991.

[48]   Takuo Watanabe and Akinori Yonezawa. Reflection in an object-oriented concurrent language. In *Proceedings of OOPSLA'88*, volume 23, pages 306–315. SIGPLAN Notices, ACM Press, September 1988.

[49] Masahiro Yasugi, Satoshi Matsuoka, and Akinori Yonezawa. ABCL/onEM-4: A new software/hardware architecture for object-oriented concurrent computing on an extended dataflow supercomputer. In *Proceedings of 6th ACM International Conference on Supercomputing*. ACM, 1992.

[50] Akinori Yonezawa, editor. *ABCL: An Object-Oriented Concurrent System*. Computer Systems Series. The MIT Press, 1990.

[51] Akinori Yonezawa, Jean-Pierre Briot, and Etsuya Shibayama. Object-oriented concurrent programming in ABCL/1. In *Proceedings of OOPSLA'86*, volume 21, pages 258–268. SIGPLAN Notices, ACM Press, September 1986.

[52] Akinori Yonezawa and Takuo Watanabe. An introduction to object-based reflective concurrent computations. In *Proceedings of the 1988 ACM SIGPLAN Workshop on Object-Based Concurrent Programming*, volume 24, pages 50–54. SIGPLAN Notices, ACM Press, April 1989.

5 Composing Active Objects

Oscar Nierstrasz

Many of the shortcomings of present-day object-oriented programming languages can be traced to two phenomena: (i) the lack of general support for software composition, and (ii) the semantic interference between language features addressing operational and compositional aspects of object-oriented programming. To remedy this situation, we propose the development of a "pattern language" for active objects in which objects and, more generally, applications, are constructed by composing software patterns. A "pattern" can be any reusable software abstraction, including functions, objects, classes and generics. In this paper we seek to establish both informal requirements for a pattern language and a formal basis for defining the semantics of patterns. First, we identify some basic requirements for supporting object composition and we review the principal language design choices with respect to these requirements. We then survey the various problems of semantic interference in existing languages. Next, we present a formal "object calculus" and show how it can be used to define the semantics of patterns in much the same way that the λ calculus can be used to give meaning to constructs of functional programming languages. We conclude by summarizing the principle open problems that remain to define a practical pattern language for active objects.

5.1 Introduction

Object-oriented programming languages can either be characterized in terms of the features they support, or in terms of the way these features are used to change the nature of programming. We shall argue in this paper that too much emphasis has traditionally been placed on the details of specific object-oriented features and not enough on the more general topic of software composition. This leads us to propose the development of a "pattern language" for active objects that generalizes the principles of object-oriented programming to the definition and composition of software patterns.

If we consider the way in which object-oriented programming languages (OOPLs) are used, we see two complementary, yet distinct roles they play:

1. Applications consist of systems of cooperating and communicating objects, each with well-defined responsibilities.

2. Applications are compositions of pre-packaged software components (i.e., classes, abstract classes, etc.) that fit together to define an object system.

The first of these roles is a natural extension of the principles of modularity and data abstraction, inspired by the world of modelling and simulation and introduced with the language Simula [7]. The second role emerged with the definition of the Smalltalk language and environment [18]. Here, the emphasis is on the composition of applications from reusable software, facilitated by the definition of standard interfaces and components.

Although Smalltalk has demonstrated with some degree of success the reuse potential offered by OOPLs, and other languages have duplicated or improved upon these efforts, object-oriented programming has not revolutionized software development. Aside from the fact that the development of a library of truly reusable software components for a new application domain can entail a significant investment of effort, we see two technical reasons why present-day OOPLs fall short in this area: First, existing OOPLs emphasize *programming* over software composition. Reuse, whether implemented by inheritance or by other mechanisms, is achieved only by programming new objects, not by functionally composing existing objects or object parts. Second, language features that support composition and reuse often *interfere* with other features and mechanisms concerned with operational aspects of objects, such as concurrency and persistence. Both these problems can also be seen as side-effects of viewing OOP features as "add-ons" to existing languages, rather than as a fundamentally different programming paradigm in which software composition plays the leading role.

We propose that an effective object-oriented programming language will support application construction from reusable software patterns much in the same way that architectural designs can be composed from established architectural patterns [2]. By a software *pattern*, we mean any reusable software abstraction, that is, any identifiable piece of software that may be fruitfully exploited in multiple contexts. By *software composition* we mean the construction of applications by means of operators that bind patterns to one another. Patterns, in order to be useful, typically contain free variables that will be bound by actual parameters or by the environment in which they are instantiated, but we shall not initially make any assumptions about what precise mechanisms are used to define them. Rather, we point out that existing programming languages typically provide some specific pattern definition mechanisms but usually not any general purpose ones. For example, expressions, statements, functions, procedures, macros, generics, packages, modules, classes, and so on, are all specific kinds of patterns, but very few languages arguably provide programmers with the ability to define new kinds of patterns appropriate for specific problem domains. Similarly, few languages provide support for software composition that goes beyond the composition of expressions and statements, which is to say, low-level programming.

We take it for granted here that the operational view of applications as collections of cooperating and communicating objects has clear advantages, and in particular that such systems are inherently concurrent (whether or not the concurrency is exploited by a parallel or distributed implementation). What we are more concerned with is how we can build such systems by composing software patterns. Our goal in this paper is to explore the theme of a pattern language for active objects by investigating the interplay between the operational and compositional aspects of objects. More specifically, in §2 we develop some informal requirements for OOPL design by considering the impact of the choice of the operational view of concurrent objects on software composition and reuse. Then, in §3 we shall review the more significant problems of semantic interference between OOPL features and argue that the root of these problems generally lies in the confusion between the operational and compositional issues. As a concrete example, we shall look at some of these problems as they are manifested in *Hybrid*, a concurrent OOPL whose design attempts to integrate various seemingly orthogonal OOPL features. Finally, in §4, we propose the development of a pattern language for active objects in which the semantics of higher-level patterns is given by a mapping to a formal "object calculus" called OC. We present OC through examples that illustrate the composition of active objects from more primitive patterns, and we conclude by identifying some of the key open research problems in the development of a pattern language for active objects.

5.2 Requirements for Composable Active Objects

The key features characterizing object-oriented languages are generally accepted to be [49]:

1. *Objects:* support for *encapsulation* of service and state as objects;
2. *Classes:* the ability to *instantiate* objects from class templates;
3. *Inheritance:* the ability to define new object templates by *incremental modification* of existing ones [50].

The operational view of objects is that of entities with private state which provide services to clients by exchanging messages. The compositional view is supported by classes and inheritance. A class is a software pattern that can be used to create an object by binding its instantiation parameters, or it can be used to derive a new (sub) class by binding self and super to a new environment including the instance variables and methods introduced by the subclass.

The operational view affects the compositional view in essentially two ways: First, the contexts in which an object may be instantiated should depend on the external message-passing interface of the object and not the internal details of the object's implementation. In particular, the way in which a client interacts with a given object should conform to a standard protocol that does not depend on the presence or absence of other clients. Second, classes should be composed of patterns representing object parts (i.e., instance variables, methods, interface specifications, constraints, etc.) in such a way that new classes can be derived without necessarily having to override (re-bind) inherited patterns. More specifically, the derivation interface should be abstract, so that a subclass can be derived without requiring detailed knowledge of the implementation of the superclass. In either case, compositionality is impaired if operational details are not sufficiently abstract.

In this section we will discuss a number of basic requirements on the operational view of concurrent objects that affect compositionality, and we will review various language design alternatives with respect to their compatibility with these requirements. We will concentrate on the client/server interaction, as these issues are somewhat better understood, and say less about the interplay between concurrency and inheritance, as this is a topic of much active research. The following requirements summarize the operational features that should be transparent in the client/server contract [40] (see also the dissertation of Papathomas [41]):

- *Object autonomy:* the internal state of an active object should be automatically protected from concurrent requests without the need for clients to explicitly synchronize with one another;

- *Internal concurrency:* it should be possible to replace a sequential implementation of an active object with a concurrent one without affecting clients;

- *Request scheduling transparency:* handling of local delays (i.e., scheduling the servicing of requests based on an object's internal state or on the nature of the request) should be transparent to the client;

- *Reply scheduling transparency:* handling of remote delays (i.e., scheduling of the receipt of a reply with respect to other ongoing tasks) should be transparent to the service provider.

A fifth requirement, which is not very well understood in the presence of inheritance, is a topic of much active research and study, as we shall see in §3:

- *Composable synchronization policies:* mechanisms for defining synchronization policies should support the composition of new policies from existing ones.

If we accept these requirements as evaluation criteria, we can compare and rank various OOPL design alternatives with respect to the degree to which they satisfy them. Papathomas [41] has proposed a classification scheme for object-based concurrent languages based on the following three aspects: (i) *Object Models:* How is object consistency maintained in the presence of concurrency? (ii) *Internal Concurrency:* What means do objects have to manage multiple threads of control? (iii) *Client-Server Interaction:* What degree of control do objects have over the interaction protocol?

We shall now summarize from the observations presented in [40] concerning the evaluation of various basic OOPL design choices.

5.2.1   Object Autonomy

As a first cut, concurrent object-based languages can be distinguished according to the kind of object model they support, i.e., the means by which objects protect their internal state in the presence of concurrent threads. There are basically three different approaches, but, in a few rare cases, different approaches may be combined in a particular object model:

- *The Orthogonal Approach:* Synchronization is independent of object encapsulation. Mechanisms such as locks or semaphores must be used to synchronize concurrent invocations or internal consistency may be violated [8, 18, 32];

- *The Heterogeneous Approach:* Both active and passive objects are provided. Passive objects are protected by virtue of being used only within single-threaded active objects [14, 20];

- *The Homogeneous Approach:* All objects are "active" and have control over the synchronization of concurrent requests [3, 34, 46].

The orthogonal approach fails to support object autonomy. Since no implicit protection of objects' states is provided, only specially designed objects can be safely used in the presence of concurrent clients. Objects that behave correctly in a sequential setting may "break" if exposed to concurrent requests. The heterogeneous approach suffers because one cannot typically interchange implementations of active and passive objects. The existence of two different kinds of objects limits code reusability, since it may either force duplicate (active and passive) implementations of essentially the same object, or unnatural decomposition of applications in order to maximally exploit active objects. In some cases, a mixed model is supported, as in Argus [27], where active objects (*guardians*) may be internally concurrent, and so must synchronize accesses to passive objects (*clusters*) as in the orthogonal approach. The homogeneous approach does not suffer from these defects, but there is a potential performance problem if active objects are too "heavyweight" in contrast to passive objects. It may be possible, however, for a compiler to generate automatically more efficient code for active objects occurring in contexts that require no synchronization [39].

5.2.2 Internal Concurrency

We can make various distinctions according to the means for coping with internal concurrency [49]:

- *Sequential Objects* have a single active thread of control [5, 3, 53];
- *Quasi-Concurrent Objects* explicitly interleave multiple threads of control [34];
- *Concurrent Objects* support internally concurrent threads. We can further distinguish the cases in which thread creation is either:
  - *Client-driven:* threads are implicitly created upon the receipt of a request, as in the orthogonal object model;
  - *Server-driven:* in which case objects must explicitly create a new internal thread (for example, using the *become* primitive of actor languages [1]).

Purely sequential objects that follow a strict RPC protocol overly restrict potential concurrency as they are unable to handle remote delays [28]. Additional concurrency can only be introduced by delegating tasks to proxy objects (e.g., Cboxes [52] and future variables [53]), that will reply to the original client (i.e., by abandoning the strict RPC protocol). Even quasi-concurrent objects must make use of additional active objects to achieve true concurrency. Client-driven concurrency has the disadvantages of the orthogonal object model. Server-driven internal concurrency has the clearest advantages in that concurrent activities are properly encapsulated: there is no need to artificially introduce additional *external* objects just to distribute the work load.

5.2.3 Client/Server Interaction

Finally, we can distinguish languages according to the forms of client/server interaction supported. The main concerns from the point of view of the client and the server are, respectively, reply scheduling (the control the client has over the delivery of the reply) and request scheduling (the control the server has over the acceptance of requests).

From the server's point of view, the key issue is whether requests are accepted unconditionally or not:

- *Unconditional acceptance:* No synchronization with the state of the object occurs [8, 18, 32].
- *Conditional acceptance:*
  - *Explicit acceptance:* An explicit *accept* statement is used to indicate which requests will be served [5, 3, 53].

- *Reflective computation:* The arrival of a message triggers a reflective computation in the associated "meta-object" which is capable of directly manipulating messages, mailboxes, etc. [11, 48].

- *Activation conditions:* Implicit or explicit conditions govern the acceptance of requests.

  * *Representation specific:* Conditions are expressed in terms of the object's internal state [24, 34, 47].

  * *Abstract:* Message acceptance depends on the *abstract state* of an object [10, 20, 46].

The various approaches to conditional acceptance are generally equivalent in expressive power, provided that there is some way to delay servicing of a request based on the contents of the request message. The main difference between these approaches from the point of view of composition is the extent to which the synchronization policy of the server can be understood in abstract terms to facilitate reusability and incremental modification. In this respect the approach of abstract states (whether by means of *enabled sets* [46], *behaviour abstraction* [20, 21] or *synchronizing actions* [33], etc.) appears to be the most promising, though it is not clear how best to accommodate (1) local delays based on message contents, which potentially entail an infinite number of "abstract" states, and (2) incremental modification, which extends and alters the graph of transitions between abstract states.

From the client's point of view, the most important distinction is the interaction protocol supported:

- *One-way Message-Passing:* higher-level protocols are explicitly programmed [10];

- *Request/Reply:* every request necessarily entails a reply.

  - *RPC:* a requesting thread blocks until a reply is received. Internal threads may be sequential [3], quasi-concurrent [34] or concurrent [47], as described above;

  - *Proxies:* sending of requests and receipt of replies may be delegated to (external) proxy objects [14, 52, 53].

Reply scheduling is essentially concerned with three issues: (1) the interleaving of client activities, (2) controlling the reply address, and (3) obtaining the reply. With one-way message-passing (whether synchronous or asynchronous) clients have complete control over all three issues, at the expense of abstraction. In particular, servers are obliged to keep track of the reply address. A protocol in which requests implicitly entail replies eliminates this problem. RPC in combination with purely sequential objects exhibits the problems mentioned earlier, but is quite flexible in combination with concurrent and quasi-concurrent objects. Concurrent RPC has the advantage over both proxies and quasi-concurrent RPC in that additional external objects do not need to be introduced in order to split up a logically concurrent task. Internally concurrent threads are properly encapsulated.

5.2.4   Observations

After eliminating approaches that fail to adequately support one requirement or another, we are left looking for: (i) a homogeneous model of active objects (ii) that supports server-driven internal concurrency (and hence hierarchical composition of active objects), (iii) a client-server interaction protocol that is by default one of remote procedure calls, (iv) but which provides both clients and servers transparent control over the scheduling of requests and replies. The main technical difficulty appears to be the specification of synchronization policies in such a way as to adequately support incremental modification.

5.3   Language Feature Integration

Now that we have established some basic requirements for OOPL design, let us consider the interplay between various language features.

Wegner [49, 51] has identified the following dimensions as a design space for object-based languages: objects, classes and types, inheritance and delegation, data abstraction, strong typing, concurrency and persistence. Semantic interference between object-oriented dimensions has been noted by numerous researchers. Let us simplify the problem space by considering only the following four dimensions: *encapsulation* (objects + classes), *inheritance*, *strong typing* and *concurrency*. As we shall see, several of the difficulties that arise are due to interference between the operational model, in which the client/server relationship is that of message-passing between objects, and the compositional model, which supports very different client/server relationships, such as inheritance between classes and containment for instance variables.

We shall first discuss interference in general, and then we will look at particular examples of interference of language features in Hybrid, a concurrent object-oriented language.

5.3.1   Orthogonality and Interference of Object-Oriented Dimensions

Inheritance vs.   Encapsulation   The main difficulty with inheritance in object-oriented languages is that, in order to define meaningful extensions to inherited behaviour, subclasses must "violate encapsulation" of their parent classes [44, 43] (i.e., they must be able to access instance variables otherwise hidden from clients of superclass instances). Furthermore, once an inheritance hierarchy has been defined, modifications to superclasses can affect subclasses in unexpected ways, thus limiting the freedom to modify the implementation of classes and, once again, "violating encapsulation".

In both cases the problem arises from a failure to distinguish between the *two* kinds of client of a class: other instances, and subclasses. Various solutions have been proposed, including:

- Provide a common interface to both kinds of client (which ignores the fact that different clients typically have different needs);

- Separate interfaces for ordinary clients and subclasses (including private class methods, etc.);

- Provide mechanisms to extend inherited behaviour in a controlled fashion, such as the *inner* construct of Simula [7] and Beta [25] and the "before" and "after" methods of CLOS [31];

- Adopt a more compositional approach as an alternative to inheritance, in which the dependencies of class templates (or *habitats* [43]) are made explicit.

As a general principle, we conclude that binding interfaces of any software pattern should be explicit, and different classes of clients should be distinguished.

Types vs. Encapsulation   Through types we mean to express the abstract interface of objects. Type-checking is a means to increase our confidence that we are using objects in a consistent way. It is convenient to view types as partial specifications of behaviour, that is, as *predicates* describing those properties of an object that we are interested in as clients. In this view, subtypes are simply stronger predicates. An object, which is an instance of a particular class, can thus be viewed as simultaneously belonging to all types whose properties it holds. This justifies dynamic binding in object-oriented languages that allow one to bind variables to any instance that satisfies the type constraint of the variable.

Various polymorphic type theories based on the λ calculus have been developed for type-checking programming languages (see, for example, [12]), but they consider a type to stand for a set of *values*. Such a theory can be applied to languages that support functional objects (i.e., in which "objects" are tuples of values and functions). Types may be refined to subtypes by applying the contra-variant rule: input parameters to functions may be generalized and return values may be refined. (This is the essence of polymorphism: that instances of the supertype may be replaced by instances of the refined type without causing surprises for clients).

In most OOPLs, however, objects are not values, but entities with changing state. The arguments to operations are used not only to compute return values, but may be used to change the state of the object. In languages with updatable attributes, for example, attribute types cannot be refined, as they serve as both inputs and outputs [13].

More difficult to handle is the problem of changing *roles* [42]: an object may have multiple roles with respect to different clients, and these roles may change during its lifetime. A type theory that would deal with state change and multiple roles must take into account certain temporal properties of objects.

Types vs. Inheritance   Most difficulties with types and inheritance are due to a confusion between types and classes. It is commonly assumed that the class (inheritance) hierarchy and the type hierarchy must correspond, and that the type of a subclass will always be a subtype of the type of the superclass. If we view types as interface specifications, then it is clear that classes unrelated by inheritance may share a common interface. In this case, we may have type equivalences and subtype relationships across the class hierarchy.

Conversely, in some languages, such as Eiffel, classes may be derived by applying the co-variant rule (which allows both input parameters as well as return values to be of a refined type). In this case subclasses will not satisfy the type constraint of the superclass, and there will be no subtyping relationship between the two classes. Furthermore, if it is possible for a subclass to "hide" part of an inherited interface, then there will also be no subtype relationship between superclasses and subclasses. For example, in Eiffel, one may use inheritance to define a FixedStack class that inherits its interface from the (abstract) class Stack and its internal representation from the (implementation) class Array and hiding the operations inherited from Array. But if we would now bind a FixedStack instance to a variable of type Array, the Array operations would be exposed and encapsulation of the FixedStack instance would be violated.

Inheritance and subtyping must therefore be seen as independent [16]. In some languages, such as POOL-I [4], types and classes are separate concepts.

Concurrency vs. Encapsulation   As we have seen already in §2, the view of objects as encapsulations of service and state must be treated delicately in the presence of concurrency. In the simplest case, encapsulation of passive objects is violated by concurrent clients that do not synchronize their requests. Conversely, encapsulation of clients is compromised if it is their responsibility to explicitly synchronize requests to shared, passive objects. We conclude that, at least, some model of active objects is desirable.

The situation is complicated by the need for objects that are capable of coping with local and remote delays by means of scheduling requests and replies. As we argued in §2, request and reply scheduling should be transparent to, respectively, clients and servers, as well as to "nearby" objects. In Hybrid [39], for example, objects that make use of such scheduling mechanisms cannot be used with impunity as instance variables, as the use of these mechanisms will also affect the enclosing object, possibly violating encapsulation.

Concurrency vs. Inheritance   A very similar situation exists when we consider inheritance, where the "nearby" objects are subclass instances. Here the difficulty is that inherited behaviour may be very sensitive to cooperation between methods making use of concurrency mechanisms to support request/reply scheduling. It can, in general, be very difficult to extend the inherited behaviour in a consistent way. Superclass encapsulation is thus violated by the need to expose implementation details, and reusability is compromised since inherited methods cannot synchronize with subclass methods [20].

Various approaches to address this problem essentially make the compositional (i.e., inheritance) interface more explicit. As mentioned in §2, such approaches are typically based on abstract states and the separation of the synchronization policy from the implementation of methods.

Concurrency vs. Types   If we indeed view types as partial specifications of behaviour, then it is clear that merely characterizing the message-passing interface of an object does not go very far. In particular, when we are concerned with software composition, we are interested in knowing when one object is substitutable for another in a given context, that is, when an object is "plug-compatible" with another. To this end, we must be able to characterize certain temporal and concurrent properties that can affect the various clients of an object. A short, non-exhaustive list would include:

- *Non-uniform service availability:* the fact that requests to perform certain operations may be delayed or rejected depending on the state of the object;

- *Non-client/server protocols:* active objects may conform to alternative message-passing protocols such as early reply [28] and send/receive/reply [17];

- *Multiple concurrent clients:* objects capable of handling multiple concurrent requests may not work correctly if placed in a sequential environment (e.g., a communication buffer), and, conversely, clients may not work correctly if they expect a strictly sequential behaviour from a service provider (e.g., if they do not expect the state to change in between one message exchange and another).

What is at issue is that the client/server contract cannot always be reduced to a static message-passing interface that specifies only the requests accepted, the consequent replies, and the types of values they may contain. In general, it will be necessary to express some temporal properties of the message-passing interface in order to reason about valid object compositions. Note that we do not seek to fully specify object behaviours and prove that their composition correctly implements an abstract specification. Rather, we only wish to verify some weaker safety and liveness conditions: when is it safe for an object to send certain messages, and what kind of replies can be expected. For example, a stack and a queue would both satisfy the type constraint that only specifies the possible orderings of put and get operations, though their fully abstract specifications would differ.

Understanding plug-compatibility in terms of the visible interactions an object may exhibit appears promising as a means to abstract away from implementation details [35, 37]. Modal logics [26] and propositional temporal logic [6] appear useful as formalisms for expressing abstract properties of concurrent systems, and can also be used to reason about changing roles [6], though it is not yet clear whether they will prove appropriate as a formalism for developing a type theory.

5.3.2   Semantic Interference in Hybrid

Let us briefly consider how some of these problems of semantic interference manifest themselves an a particular language. *Hybrid* is a concurrent OOPL whose design attempts to integrate cleanly various seemingly orthogonal language features [34]. In particular, the prototype implementation provides [22]:

- objects + classes + inheritance
- strong typing + genericity
- concurrency
- persistence

Features currently being implemented include:

- homogeneity ("everything" is an object)
- distribution (see [23])

Hybrid is based on a model of active objects. Active objects (as opposed to passive objects) have complete control over the scheduling of incoming requests. They may, therefore, not only ensure mutual exclusion of method activations (if required), but they may also exercise a fine degree of control over local and remote delays and internal concurrency.

Concurrent activity in Hybrid is delimited by *domains*. Each domain is essentially a quasi-concurrent process, that is, at most one thread of control may be running at any time within a domain, but mechanisms are provided for switching attention from one thread to another. Domains are always mapped to a single, autonomous active object (i.e., instance variables cannot have their own domain, nor can a group of autonomous objects belong to a single domain). A domain, by default, handles exactly one request at a time. A domain only accepts new requests while in the *idle* state. While servicing a request, a domain is either *busy* or *waiting* (if there is a pending call to another domain).

A logical thread of control that traces the logically connected requests and replies between domains is called an *activity*. (We introduce this term to avoid confusion with the term "thread," which is usually understood to be a property of a single process only.) Domains permit recursive calls as such requests will be associated to the currently running activity. In figure 1 we see an activity as a trace of *call* (white) and *reply* (black) messages between domains. New activities are created by calling special operations, called *reflexes*, that yield no return value. The effect of calling a reflex is to place a new request in the target's message queue, and then to continue without waiting for a reply.

Domains can exercise a fine degree of control over the acceptance of requests by associating services (operations) to *delay queues*. Such queues can be either *open* or *closed*. When a domain is idle, it will accept requests only from its open queues (figure 2). Local delays that do not depend on message contents are easy to capture using delay queues. For example, a bounded buffer can be modelled by associating the put and get operations to notFull and notEmpty delay queues.

Domains may be quasi-concurrent. By use of the mechanism of *delegated calls*, a domain may interleave the servicing of requests: a delegated call to another domain causes the calling domain to immediately become *idle* instead of waiting for its reply. The calling context is temporarily saved, and is restored when the reply is available. For example, in figure 3 we see an object servicing a request on behalf of activity α delegate a call to another domain, allowing it to switch its attention temporarily to request β.

Delegated calls are very expressive, and can be used to handle both remote delays and, in combination with delay queues, local delays that depend on message contents. Internal concurrency is not directly supported in Hybrid, but it is possible to simulate it by means of delegated calls to "worker" objects.

Although Hybrid succeeded in demonstrating that object-oriented features could be combined with concurrency, persistence and strong-typing in a single programming language, it cannot be claimed that these features were fully integrated. In particular, the central issues of composition and reuse have been addressed in only a limited way. Let us consider some of the problems encountered:

- *Homogeneity:* although it was intended that all objects should have the same first-class status, it is not at all clear how to treat active objects as first-class values; similarly, delay queues are object-like, but cannot be consistently treated as other objects;

- *Types:* strong-typing on the basis of signatures (operation names and argument and return types) tells us nothing about the behaviour of concurrent and mutable objects, and hence tells us very little of use concerning substitutability of objects with superficially similar interfaces [37];

- *Composition:* objects implemented in terms of delay queues and delegated calls cannot be (re)used in arbitrary contexts without potentially introducing deadlocks (through closed delay queues) or violating encapsulation (by exposing an enclosing object during a delegated call);

- *Inheritance:* by the same token, it can be difficult or impossible for a subclass to incrementally modify the synchronization policy of a superclass in a consistent way [20], since inherited methods have no way of accessing delay queues introduced by subclasses without being overridden;

- *Encapsulation:* it is not generally possible to define higher level patterns of behaviour using only classes, inheritance and genericity; for example, mechanisms to support internal concurrency, internal triggers, and transactions, although they can be programmed in Hybrid, apparently cannot be packaged in a general way.

Note that each of these issues is concerned with some aspect of *composition* of concurrent behaviour.

In a more practical vein, the Hybrid project suffered from (1) the lack of any generally accepted computational model for active objects suitable for defining the semantics of language constructs, and (2) the lack of good prototyping tools for experimenting with language design alternatives. These observations have led us to search for a computational model and notation for active objects that can be used as an executable target for language specifications [35, 36, 38]. At the same time, it is essential to be very clear about the informal goals and requirements for language design [40] and to study the problems of semantic interference from these viewpoints.

5.4   Towards a Pattern Language for Active Objects

We have presented the object-oriented paradigm as a two-level programming model in which an application can be viewed both operationally as a configuration of cooperating active objects, and functionally as a composition of software patterns that yields this configuration. A programming language to support this paradigm should therefore address equally well the operational aspects of active objects and the functional aspects of specifying and composing software patterns.

We propose the development of a pattern language for active objects which would be used according to the three levels of Figure 4:

1. *Computational Model:* at this level the operational behaviour of software patterns is specified by means of a formal "object calculus"; the object calculus gives meaning to patterns much in the same way that the λ calculus is used to give semantics to sequential programming languages [45]: it provides both a formal notation for

the semantics of language features and a possible operational interpretation of their behaviour;

2. *Language Primitives:* at the language level we identify the particular behavioural patterns that define our object model, the kinds of objects we can construct, and the kinds of abstractions that will be appropriate for composing objects;

3. *Software Components:* finally, in terms of the language primitives provided, we are able to define software components that can be composed to produce running applications.

Applications would be constructed by composing reusable software patterns much in the way that architectural designs can be composed from established architectural patterns [2]. Language designers would use the pattern language to develop the primitive patterns of object models. Designers of application frameworks and libraries would define the standard interfaces and patterns for particular application domains. Application developers would produce new applications by composing the pre-defined application patterns.

In this section we shall present a concrete object calculus, called OC, and we shall illustrate how higher-level patterns for composing active objects can be defined by a mapping to OC. We shall conclude by summarizing the principal research problems that remain to defining a practical pattern language.

5.4.1   OC — An Object Calculus

The object calculus that we shall present informally here is based on recent developments in process calculi. In particular, it extends the π calculus [30] to tuple-based communication, and to functional application and communication of expressions as in the λ calculus. For details on these extensions and a description of the formal semantics of OC, see [38].

The terms of OC consist of a set of expressions representing *agents*, $\mathcal{A}$. Agents are composed of a set of *names*, $\mathcal{N}$, a set of *input offers*, $\mathcal{X}$, and a set of output offers, or communicable *values*, $\mathcal{V}$. We let a, b, c range over $\mathcal{A}$, n, m over $\mathcal{N}$, x over $\mathcal{X}$, and v over $\mathcal{V}$.

An agent is an entity that may offer to (synchronously) input or output some message tuple, or may silently change state (if it is itself composed of communicating agents). A communication may take place if the input and output offers of two agents match. The syntax of input and output offers are, respectively:

$$x ::= n \mid n? \mid (x, ..., x)$$
$$v ::= n \mid a \mid (v, ..., v)$$

The notation "?" indicates the introduction of a new variable name. Input and output offers match if they correspond structurally and if values appearing in the input offer are equal to the corresponding values in the output offer. Variables match any value and are subsequently bound to the values they match. (So, x? matches y and (x,x?) matches (x,y), but (x,x) does not match (x,y).)

The syntax of agents is as follows (loosest to tightest binding):

$$a ::= a \& a \mid n := a \mid a|a \mid x \rightarrow a \mid v \wedge a \mid a@v \mid n\backslash a \mid n \mid \text{nil}$$

Concurrent composition is &, recursion is :=, (left-preferential) choice is |, abstraction (input) is →, output is ∧, (functional) application is @, restriction (of local names) is \ and the inactive agent is given by nil. A name n stands for an agent only if it has been bound to an agent expression by a communication or by a recursive definition.

As an example, consider the following specification of a counting semaphore:

csem := (p→nil & v→csem)

csem is a recursively defined composite agent. It consist of two concurrently composed agents, p→nil, which can accept the message p and become nil, and v→csem, which can accept v and become csem.

Note that csem accurately captures the semantics of a counting semaphore. A resource may be claimed by communicating a p, yielding the system:

nil & v→csem

To recover the original state of csem, a v must be sent. With each additional v communicated, a new copy of p→nil is introduced.

We can use the counting semaphore agent to restrict access to a resource that repeatedly accepts print messages:

resource := print → resource

Two clients synchronize via the semaphore before accessing the resource:

c1 := p∧print∧print∧v∧nil

c2 := p∧print∧print∧print∧v∧nil

So, c1 may output p and become print∧print∧v∧nil. In the system:

csem & resource & c1 & c2

either of c1 or c2 (non-deterministically) claims the resource, and the other must wait until the semaphore is released again.

A binary semaphore is very similar, but is a sequential rather than a concurrent agent:

bsem := p→v→bsem | v→bsem

The choice operator | selects either one input or the other. So bsem can input p to become v→bsem or v to become bsem.

Functional composition is achieved by means of the @ operator. It is similar to remote communication via ∧ except that no competition can take place. The left operand of @ is treated as though it were a function and its right operand as its argument. The target of @ may not communicate with any external agents but must eventually accept the argument as input (if it can), or deadlock.

To understand how @ works, let us now consider an agent that models the behaviour of the Linda *tuple space* [15]. Linda provides a small set of primitives to allow concurrent processes to communicate and synchronize by writing and reading tuples to a so-called tuple space. A process may write a tuple using the non-blocking *out* primitive, and may read a tuple either destructively with the *in* primitive, or non-destructively with the *rd* primitive. Both read primitives block if no matching tuple exists. The following agent, linda, supports these three primitives:

linda := (out,t?) → (linda & tuple@t)

tuple := t? → ((in,t)∧nil | (rd,t)∧tuple@t)

When linda receives a request to create a new tuple, it replaces itself by a system including a copy of itself and an agent that implements the behaviour of a tuple. The tuple is instantiated by forcing tuple to accept the value t as input, i.e., by treating it as a function. The resulting agent can either (destructively) output (in,t) and become nil, or (non-destructively) send (rd,t) and become tuple@t again.

The last operator to introduce is restriction ($\backslash$), which defines the scope of a new name. If that name is ever communicated outside that scope, then it must be distinguished by renaming (i.e., by α-conversion) to a unique name. For example, a generator of unique identifiers could be specified as:

idgen := x$\backslash$((new,x)$\wedge$idgen)

Since the name x occurs within its own local scope, it is guaranteed to be globally unique upon communication to clients.

5.4.2 Modeling Active Objects with OC

In much the same way that denotational semantics can be attributed to sequential programming languages by mapping their syntactic features to λ calculus terms [45], semantics can be given to concurrent languages by mapping their constructs to process calculi [29]. We shall illustrate this approach not by defining a complete programming language, but by defining some derived operators of OC that might correspond to constructs of a concurrent OOPL.

Let us start by considering the following example of a template for an object that recursively computes factorials (modelled after the standard example used to illustrate concepts of actor languages [1, 19]):

recFact := self? $\rightarrow$ [fact, n?] $\Rightarrow$ become(recFact) ;
$\qquad\qquad\qquad\qquad\qquad$ if (n=0)
$\qquad\qquad\qquad\qquad\qquad$ then return(1)
$\qquad\qquad\qquad\qquad\qquad$ else self $\Leftarrow$ [fact,n$-$1]
$\qquad\qquad\qquad\qquad\qquad\qquad\qquad$ $\gg$ (k? $\rightarrow$ (n$\times$k) $\gg$ (x? $\rightarrow$ return(x)))

The agent recFact accepts a name (standing for an object identifier) as input, and becomes an object with self bound to its oid. The body of the object is specified using a number of derived operators ($\Rightarrow$, ;, become, etc.). The object accepts requests ([fact,n?]) to compute factorials, and eventually replies to clients with the result. Upon receiving a request, it immediately "becomes" a copy of itself so that it may start to accept new requests concurrently with the processing of the pending request. This is possible since instances of recFact carry no state information other than that related to the pending request.

If the request is to compute the factorial of 0, it returns the result 1, otherwise it sends itself a request to compute the factorial of n$-$1. We may informally read the expression $E \gg (x? \rightarrow A)$ as let x = E in A. Then the result of the subexpression self $\Leftarrow$ [fact,n$-$1] is multiplied by n, and that result is in turn sent back to the client.

To create a new copy of recFact and ask it to compute the factorial of 10, we may now write:

new(recFact) $\gg$ (rf? $\rightarrow$ (rf $\Leftarrow$ [fact,10] $\gg$ done))

In the following encoding of the derived operators, we adopt the convention that requests from clients to objects are always of the form:

(oid, $request$, $args$, rid)

where oid is the object's oid, $request$ is the name of the service, $args$ its arguments, and rid the client's request identifier. Replies will be of the form:

(rid, result, val)

where val is the value returned. Furthermore, self and client will be reserved keywords standing respectively for an object's oid and the rid of the current request. Now let us consider the semantics of each of the derived operators.

The operator $\Rightarrow$ simply expands the request form $[M, A]$ to the appropriate input offer, binding client in the body:

$[\![\,[M,A] \Rightarrow S\,]\!] = (\text{self},M,[\![\,A\,]\!],\text{client?}) \rightarrow [\![\,S\,]\!]$

Statements are agents that take a continuation agent as input:

$[\![\,Stmt \; ; \; Cont\,]\!] = [\![\,Stmt\,]\!]@[\![\,Cont\,]\!]$

The become statement instantiates concurrent copies of its continuation and the object template O with self as the oid.

$[\![\,\text{become}(O)\,]\!] = \text{cont?} \rightarrow ([\![\,O\,]\!]@\text{self \& cont})$

The if then else construct applies two possible continuations to a Boolean agent that selects one of them:

$[\![\,\text{if } B \text{ then } C1 \text{ else } C2\,]\!] = [\![\,B\,]\!]@([\![\,C1\,]\!],[\![\,C2\,]\!])$

Booleans are encoded as follows:

$[\![\,\text{true}\,]\!] = (\text{a?},\text{b?}) \rightarrow \text{a}$
$[\![\,\text{false}\,]\!] = (\text{a?},\text{b?}) \rightarrow \text{b}$

The operators $+, -, \times, /, =$, and $\gg$ are just syntactic sugar for applying a binary tuple with the operator in the first position:

$[\![\,A \; Op \; B\,]\!] = [\![\,A\,]\!]@(Op, [\![\,B\,]\!])$, where $Op \in \{+, -, \times, /, =, \gg\}$

The representation of numbers is closely modelled after the standard encoding in the λ calculus. We shall not repeat the encoding here (see [38] for details) but remark only that n=0 returns a Boolean agent, n$-$1 and n$\times$k return integer agents, and n$\gg$econt evaluates to econt@n, where econt is an expression continuation of the form $n? \rightarrow \text{cont}$ for some name n. So $E \gg (\text{x?} \rightarrow \text{cont})$ eventually binds x to the value of E in cont.

The return operator is straightforward:

$[\![\,\text{return}(V)\,]\!] = (\text{client},\text{result},[\![\,V\,]\!])\wedge\text{nil}$

The request/reply protocol is encapsulated in the following construct:

$[\![\,X \Leftarrow [M,A]\,]\!] = (\gg,\text{econt?}) \rightarrow \text{rid}\backslash(\;([\![\,X\,]\!],M,[\![\,A\,]\!],\text{rid}) \wedge (\text{rid},\text{result},\text{value?}) \rightarrow \text{econt@value})$

$X \Leftarrow [M, A]$ takes as input the expression continuation that will eventually receive the result. A new request identifier rid is then specified so that the request can be distinguished from those of other clients. The request is then dispatched to the object with oid X, the return value is accepted, and the value is applied to the expression continuation econt.

Finally, we have:

$[\![\,\text{new}(O)\,]\!] = (\gg,\text{econt?}) \rightarrow \text{id}\backslash([\![\,O\,]\!]@\text{id \& econt@id})$

which instantiates an object with new oid id from template O and passes id to its expression continuation, and:

$[\![\,\text{done}\,]\!] = \text{x?} \rightarrow \text{nil}$

which can be used as an expression terminator.

It should be noted that the derived operators presented here are intended only to illustrate, through a simple, yet non-trivial example, the general approach of defining language constructs by means of a mapping to an object calculus. We do not mean to suggest that these operators are (or are not) especially well-suited for general-purpose composition of active objects.

5.4.3   Open problems

An object calculus would serve as only the lowest level of a pattern language. A pattern language would consist of a core language corresponding to an object calculus, a set of pre-defined syntactic patterns, and a pattern declaration mechanism for binding syntactic patterns to their interpretation as behavioural patterns. We can identify three main lines of activity towards developing a practical pattern language:

- *Theoretical:* When are two patterns behaviourally equivalent? Is there a simple "normal form" for patterns to which they can be transformed? What is an appropriate type theory for "plug-compatibility" of patterns?

- *Experimental:* What object models meet our requirements for composing active objects? What are suitable basic patterns at the language-level? What constitutes a well-designed pattern library?

- *Pragmatical:* What are effective strategies for implementing a pattern language on conventional hardware? How can parallel and distributed architecture be exploited? What are the interoperability issues when communicating with applications written in other languages?

Equivalence and Plug-compatibility   There is a well-developed body of literature on behavioural equivalences for process calculi. See, for example, [29] for an introduction. Nevertheless, this is an area of much active research, and it is far from clear what "tests" should determine when two terms of a process calculus specify the "same" behaviour.

Aside from purely theoretical concerns, a well-defined notion of equivalence has several important practical applications. Garbage collection can be performed if we can determine that a system is equivalent to another one with certain agents removed. Optimization is possible if we can determine that certain behavioural patterns are equivalent to other ones that can be implemented more efficiently. During compilation, certain expressions may be pre-evaluated if we can show that lazy and eager evaluation will give the same results.

A closely related subject is that of a type theory for composing patterns. If we consider a type as a partial specification of behaviour, that is, as a *contract* between a client and a provider of services, and if we can verify these contracts statically, then we can reason about the plug-compatibility of patterns. In the examples we have seen in OC, the composition of agents that do not "fit" simply results in a deadlocked agent. (For example, if 10 then a else b will deadlock since 10 is not a Boolean agent and will not be able to accept the message (a,b).) In general, an adequate type theory for pattern composition should take into account not just static aspects of services provided at a particular point in time, but also dynamic aspects of properties associated with future reachable states of agents. As such, we imagine that modal and temporal logics will be useful in developing such a theory (recall the discussion above in §3).

Object Models   An object model for a pattern language determines the kinds of messages exchanged by objects, the structure of objects and their constituent parts, and the primitive patterns that can be used to compose objects and to define higher-level patterns. A suitable object model should satisfy the various requirements we have posed in §2 and should address the problems of semantic interference identified in §3. Ultimately, the acid test of a good object model will be quality of the application-level patterns that can be developed and the ease with which applications can be built by composing such patterns.

Implementation   We have introduced OC as an executable specification language for the development, rapid prototyping and evaluation of OOPL design choices. We have also proposed that an object calculus like OC be used as the kernel of a pattern language. Although a prototype implementation of an OC interpreter exists [38], it is by no means efficient enough to use as the kernel of a real programming language. As there is much in common with the formal foundations of functional programming languages, we expect that much of the research that has been performed to develop efficient implementations of functional languages will also apply to the implementation of a pattern language.

There are, of course a number of traditional pragmatic issues to be studied: interpretation vs. compilation, type-checking, version management, interoperability with other languages, programming and debugging tools, and so on. In the arena of more exotic implementation issues, we may consider visual formalisms for active objects and composing software patterns, and interactive composition and monitoring of applications by means of "active graphics" whose formal semantics may be given by graphical transformation rules much in the same way that the structural operational semantics of process calculi are given by transition rules.

5.5   Concluding Remarks

We have presented the view that present-day object-oriented programming languages emphasize too much *programming* at the expense of *software composition*. To remedy this situation, we propose the development of a *pattern language* for active objects that addresses both the operational view of applications as collections of communication objects and the functional view of applications as compositions of plug-compatible software patterns.

As set of concrete steps towards this goal, we have (i) identified a number of language requirements for composing active objects, (ii) reviewed the principal classes of OOPLs with respect to these requirements, (iii) reviewed the principal difficulties of semantic interference between OOP language features, (iv) proposed an *object calculus* as a formal basis for specifying, understanding, prototyping and evaluating OOPLs, and (v) outlined a program for the development of a pattern language for active objects.

The key difficulties to be resolved appear to be (i) the development of an object model that supports well the composition of objects with non-trivial synchronization policies,

(ii) the development of basic language-level patterns to support composition and reuse, (iii) the development of a type theory for plug-compatibility of patterns.

Acknowledgements

The author would like to acknowledge the contribution of Michael Papathomas, whose work on evaluating language design alternatives is summarized in §2.

Sincere thanks are also due to Peter Wegner for his careful reading of various versions of the manuscript and for suggesting significant improvements to the presentation of this material.

References

[1]   G.A. Agha. *ACTORS: A Model of Concurrent Computation in Distributed Systems*, The MIT Press, Cambridge, Massachusetts, 1986.

[2]   C. Alexander, S. Ishakawa and M. Silverstein. *A Pattern Language*, Oxford University Press, New York, 1977.

[3]   P. America. "POOL-T: A Parallel Object-Oriented Language," in *Object-Oriented Concurrent Programming*, ed. A. Yonezawa, M. Tokoro, pp. 199-220, The MIT Press, Cambridge, Massachusetts, 1987.

[4]   P. America. "A Parallel Object-Oriented Language with Inheritance and Subtyping," Proceedings OOPSLA/ECOOP '90, ACM SIGPLAN Notices, vol. 25, no. 10, pp. 161-168, Oct 1990.

[5]   American National Standards Institute, Inc. *The Programming Language Ada Reference Manual*, LNCS 155, Springer-Verlag, 1983.

[6]   C. Arapis. "Temporal Specifications of Object Behaviour," in *Proceedings Third International Symposium on Mathematical Fundamentals of Database and Knowledge Base Systems*, ed. B. Thalheim, J. Demetrovics, H.-D. Gerhardt, LNCS 495, pp. 308-324, Springer-Verlag, Rostock, Germany, May 1991.

[7]   G. Birtwistle, O. Dahl, B. Myhrtag and K. Nygaard, *Simula Begin*, Auerbach Press, Philadelphia, 1973.

[8]   A. Black, N. Hutchinson, E. Jul and H. Levy. "Object Structure in the Emerald System," Proceedings OOPSLA '86, ACM SIGPLAN Notices, vol. 21, no. 11, pp. 78-86, Nov 1986.

[9]   T. Bloom. "Evaluating Synchronization Mechanisms," Proceedings of the Seventh Symposium on Operating Systems Principles, pp. 24-32, Pacific Grove, CA, Dec 10-12, 1979.

[10]   J. van den Bos and C. Laffra. "PROCOL – A Parallel Object Language with Protocols," ACM SIGPLAN Notices, Proceedings OOPSLA '89, vol. 24, no. 10, pp. 95-102, Oct 1989.

[11]   J-P. Briot. "Actalk: A Testbed for Classifying and Designing Actor Languages in the Smalltalk-80 Environment," in *Proceedings ECOOP '89*, pp. 109-129, Cambridge University Press, Nottingham, July 10-14, 1989.

[12]   L. Cardelli and P. Wegner. "On Understanding Types, Data Abstraction, and Polymorphism," ACM Computing Surveys, vol. 17, no. 4, pp. 471-522, Dec 1985.

[13]   L. Cardelli. "A Semantics of Multiple Inheritance," Information and Computation, vol. 76, pp. 138-164, 1988.

[14]   D. Caromel. "Concurrency and Reusability: From Sequential to Parallel," Journal of Object-Oriented Programming, vol. 3, no. 3, pp. 34-42, Sept/Oct 1990.

[15]   N. Carriero and D. Gelernter. "How to Write Parallel Programs: A Guide to the Perplexed," ACM Computing Surveys, vol. 21, no. 3, pp. 323-357, Sept 1989.

[16]   Wm. Cook. W. Hill and P. Canning, "Inheritance is not Subtyping," in *Proceedings POPL '90*, San Francisco, Jan 17-19, 1990.

[17]   W.M. Gentleman. "Message Passing Between Sequential Processes: the Reply Primitive and the Administrator Concept," Software – Practice and Experience, vol. 11, pp. 435-466, 1981.

[18]   A. Goldberg and D. Robson. *Smalltalk 80: the Language and its Implementation*, Addison-Wesley, May 1983.

[19]   C. Hewitt. "Viewing Control Structures as Patterns of Passing Messages," Artificial Intelligence, vol. 8, no. 3, pp. 323-364, June 1977.

[20]   D.G. Kafura and K.H. Lee. "Inheritance in Actor Based Concurrent Object-Oriented Languages," in *Proceedings ECOOP '89*, pp. 131-145, Cambridge University Press, Nottingham, July 10-14, 1989.

[21]   D.G. Kafura and G. Lavender. "Recent Progress in Combining Actor-Based Concurrency with Object-Oriented Programming," ACM OOPS Messenger, Proceedings OOPSLA/ECOOP 90 workshop on Object-Based Concurrent Systems, vol. 2, no. 2, pp. 55-58, April 1991.

[22]   D. Konstantas, O.M. Nierstrasz and M. Papathomas. "An Implementation of Hybrid, a Concurrent Object-Oriented Language," in *Active Object Environments*, ed. D. Tsichritzis, pp. 61-105, Centre Universitaire d'Informatique, University of Geneva, June 1988.

[23]   D. Konstantas. "A Dynamically Scalable Distributed Object-Oriented System," in *Object Management*, ed. D. Tsichritzis, pp. 245-254, Centre Universitaire d'Informatique, University of Geneva, July 1990.

[24]   S. Krakowiak, M. Meysembourg, H. Nguyen Van, M. Riveill, C. Roisin and X. Rousset de Pina. "Design and Implementation of an Object-Oriented Strongly Typed Language for Distributed Applications," Journal of Object-Oriented Programming, vol. 3, no. 3, pp. 11-22, Sept/Oct 1990.

[25]   B.B. Kristensen, O.L. Madsen, B. Møller-Pedersen and K. Nygaard. "The BETA Programming Language," in *Research Directions in Object-Oriented Programming*, ed. B. Shriver, P. Wegner, pp. 7-48, The MIT Press, Cambridge, Massachusetts, 1987.

[26]   K.G. Larsen and Liu Xinxin. "Compositionality Through an Operational Semantics of Contexts," in *Proceedings ICALP '90*, ed. M.S. Paterson, LNCS 443, pp. 526-539, Springer-Verlag, Warwick U., July 1990.

[27]   B. Liskov and R. Scheifler. "Guardians and Actions: Linguistic Support for Robust, Distributed Programs," ACM TOPLAS, vol. 5, no. 3, pp. 381-404, July 1983.

[28]   B. Liskov, M. Herlihy and L. Gilbert. "Limitations of Synchronous Communication with Static Process Structure in Languages for Distributed Computing," in *Proceedings POPL '86*, St. Petersburg Beach, Florida, Jan 13-15, 1986.

[29]   R. Milner. *Communication and Concurrency*, Prentice-Hall, 1989.

[30]   R. Milner. "Functions as Processes," in *Proceedings ICALP '90*, ed. M.S. Paterson, LNCS 443, pp. 167-180, Springer-Verlag, Warwick U., July 1990.

[31]   D.A. Moon. "The Common Lisp Object-Oriented Programming Language Standard," in *Object-Oriented Concepts, Databases and Applications*, ed. W. Kim and F. Lochovsky, pp. 49-78, ACM Press and Addison-Wesley, 1989.

[32]   J.E.B. Moss and W.H. Kohler. "Concurrency Features for the Trellis/Owl Language," in *Proceedings ECOOP '87*, pp. 223-232, Paris, France, June 15-17, 1987.

[33]   C. Neusius. "Synchronizing Actions," in *Proceedings ECOOP '91*, ed. P. America, LNCS 512, pp. 118-132, Springer-Verlag, Geneva, Switzerland, July 15-19, 1991.

[34]   O.M. Nierstrasz. "Active Objects in Hybrid," Proceedings OOPSLA '87, ACM SIGPLAN Notices, vol. 22, no. 12, pp. 243-253, Dec 1987.

[35]   O.M. Nierstrasz and M. Papathomas. "Viewing Objects as Patterns of Communicating Agents," Proceedings OOPSLA/ECOOP '90, ACM SIGPLAN Notices, vol. 25, no. 10, pp. 38-43, Oct 1990.

[36]   O.M. Nierstrasz. "A Guide to Specifying Concurrent Behaviour with Abacus," in *Object Management*, ed. D. Tsichritzis, pp. 267-293, Centre Universitaire d'Informatique, University of Geneva, July 1990.

[37]   O.M. Nierstrasz and M. Papathomas. "Towards a Type Theory for Active Objects," ACM OOPS Messenger, Proceedings OOPSLA/ECOOP 90 workshop on Object-Based Concurrent Systems, vol. 2, no. 2, pp. 89-93, April 1991.

[38]   O.M. Nierstrasz. "Towards an Object Calculus," in *Proceedings of the ECOOP '91 Workshop*

on Object-Based Concurrent Computing, ed. M. Tokoro, O.M. Nierstrasz, P. Wegner, LNCS, Springer-Verlag, Geneva, Switzerland, July 15-16, 1991, to appear.

[39] M. Papathomas and D. Konstantas. "Integrating Concurrency and Object-Oriented Programming – An Evaluation of Hybrid," in *Object Management*, ed. D. Tsichritzis, pp. 229-244, Centre Universitaire d'Informatique, University of Geneva, July 1990.

[40] M. Papathomas and O.M. Nierstrasz. "Supporting Software Reuse in Concurrent Object-Oriented Languages: Exploring the Language Design Space," in *Object Composition*, ed. D. Tsichritzis, pp. 189-204, Centre Universitaire d'Informatique, University of Geneva, June 1991.

[41] M. Papathomas. "Language Design Rationale and Semantic Framework for Concurrent Object-Oriented Programming," Ph.D. thesis, Dept. of Computer Science, University of Geneva, 1992, forthcoming.

[42] B. Pernici. "Objects with Roles," Proceedings ACM-IEEE Conference of Office Information Systems (COIS), Boston, April 1990.

[43] R.K. Raj and H.M. Levy. "A Compositional Model for Software Reuse," in *Proceedings ECOOP '89*, pp. 3-24, Cambridge University Press, Nottingham, July 10-14, 1989.

[44] A. Snyder. "Encapsulation and Inheritance in Object-Oriented Programming Languages," Proceedings OOPSLA '86, ACM SIGPLAN Notices, vol. 21, no. 11, pp. 38-45, Nov 1986.

[45] J.E. Stoy. *Denotational Semantics: The Scott-Strachey Approach to Programming Language Theory*, MIT Press, 1977.

[46] C. Tomlinson and V. Singh. "Inheritance and Synchronization with Enabled Sets," Proceedings OOPSLA '89, ACM SIGPLAN Notices, vol. 24, no. 10, pp. 103-112, Oct 1989.

[47] A. Tripathi and M. Aksit. "Communication, Scheduling and Resource Management in SINA," Journal of Object-Oriented Programming, vol. 2, no. 4, pp. 24-36, Nov/Dec 1988.

[48] T. Watanabe and A. Yonezawa. "Reflection in an Object-Oriented Concurrent Language," Proceedings OOPSLA '88, ACM SIGPLAN Notices, vol. 23, no. 11, pp. 306-315, Nov 1988.

[49] P. Wegner. "Dimensions of Object-Based Language Design," Proceedings OOPSLA '87, ACM SIGPLAN Notices, vol. 22, no. 12, pp. 168-182, Dec 1987.

[50] P. Wegner and S. B. Zdonik. "Inheritance as an Incremental Modification Mechanism or What Like Is and Isn't Like," in *Proceedings ECOOP '88*, ed. S. Gjessing and K. Nygaard, LNCS 322, pp. 55-77, Springer Verlag, Oslo, August 15-17, 1988.

[51] P. Wegner. "Concepts and Paradigms of Object-Oriented Programming," ACM OOPS Messenger, vol. 1, no. 1, pp. 7-87, Aug. 1990.

[52] Y. Yokote and M. Tokoro. "Concurrent Programming in ConcurrentSmalltalk," in *Object-Oriented Concurrent Programming*, ed. A. Yonezawa, M. Tokoro, pp. 129-158, The MIT Press, Cambridge, Massachusetts, 1987.

[53] A. Yonezawa, E. Shibayama, T.Takada and Y. Honda. "Modelling and Programming in an Object-Oriented Concurrent Language ABCL/1," in *Object-Oriented Concurrent Programming*, ed. A. Yonezawa, M. Tokoro, pp. 55-89, The MIT Press, Cambridge, Massachusetts, 1987.

II Programming Constructs

6 Supporting Modularity in Highly-Parallel Programs

Andrew A. Chien

The programming of massively concurrent MIMD machines challenges our programming technology in many ways. We are faced with two seemingly conflicting goals. We would like to build highly concurrent programs, in order to extract maximum performance from these new machines. On the other hand, we would like to use data abstraction tools in order to manage program complexity. Conventional data abstraction tools cause serialization. In practice, this serialization limits program concurrency, leaving the programmer with a choice of modularity or concurrency in his programs.

We have extended the Actor model to allow the construction of multi-access data abstractions. These abstractions have virtually unlimited potential for concurrency because they need not introduce serialization. This extended actor model, the *Aggregate Model*, introduces the notion of collections of actors (aggregates) – accessible by a single group name. Messages sent to the group are directed to one of the members of the collection. As each of the actors can receive messages concurrently, the abstraction implemented by the group need not be serializable.

We have designed an object-oriented language based on the *Aggregate Model* called Concurrent Aggregates. We have been evaluating the utility of aggregates for concurrent object-based programs by writing a series of application kernel programs. These studies explore the use of aggregates to express highly-concurrent programs and preserve modularity structures found in sequential versions of those programs. We summarize our experience by describing the four different usage paradigms for aggregates that emerged. In addition, we describe two program examples in detail and show how the introduction of aggregates can decrease serialization and increase program concurrency.

6.1 Introduction

We are interested in concurrent computing because it holds the promise of enabling us to solve larger and more complex problems. Concurrent computing is fast becoming a reality with advances in circuit technology allowing the construction of computer systems with thousands of powerful processors. The peak computing rate of these machines will exceed 500 billion instructions per second [13, 4]. Machines with such a high degree of concurrency will require exploitation of fine-grained concurrency in order to utilize the hardware.

Fine-grained message passing machines present new challenges in programming. We are interested in an object-oriented approach to programming, as it gives rise to locality, modularity and fine-grained concurrency. In research on concurrent object-oriented programming languages, the Actor model developed by Hewitt, Clinger and Agha [12, 1] has become the basis for much of the current research [21, 3, 17].

While the Actor model is appropriate for concurrent object-oriented languages targeted for distributed systems, it has one major drawback for fine-grained message passing computers. Generally, actors must receive messages serially – the semantics of the model depends on there being a unique total order on message receptions by each actor[1]. As

---

[1]Of course actors that are immutable and a few other cases can be implemented without serialization. One way to implement an immutable actor with little serialization is to replicate it.

actors are the only tool for building abstractions in the model, this means that all abstractions must be serializing – effectively ruling out abstractions in any place there is a large amount of concurrency. *Our solution is to augment the actor model with collections of actors – aggregates.* Each aggregate has a group name, and therefore can be used to build non-serializing abstractions. The actors in an aggregate can all receive messages concurrently, so the abstractions have the potential for virtually unlimited concurrency. This extension is simple and can be implemented efficiently.

Based on the Aggregate Model, we have designed a programming language called Concurrent Aggregates. In order to evaluate the practical utility of programming with aggregates, we have written a set of application kernels in this language. The purpose of these studies is three-fold: 1) to explore how data abstractions might be implemented using aggregates, 2) determine if program modularity structures can be preserved by substituting multi-access abstractions in appropriate places and 3) explore the levels of concurrency achievable by this approach.

Our programming experiments have uncovered four different ways that aggregates can be used to implement multi-access data abstractions. These four different paradigms are discussed in Section 6.5. In a number of cases, aggregates allow the original program modularity structures to be preserved, while increasing program concurrency. Since the sequential program's modularity structure presumably represents a lucid organization of the program, preserving the program's structure is desirable. This presumption is based on the notion that sequential programs are modularized with little distortion due to performance issues. To illustrate how a sequential program's modularity structure is preserved, we present two detailed examples where aggregates are used effectively to reduce serialization. Finally, we show concurrency profiles which characterize the concurrency exposed by the introduction of aggregates. We discuss these experiments in detail to give the reader a perspective from which to evaluate aggregates.

6.2   Background

We are primarily interested in programming fine-grain concurrent computers such as the J-machine [13, 16] and the Mosaic C [4]. These machines are characterized by massive concurrency ($\approx 10^5$ nodes), fast communication networks [14] (latency of $< 2\mu s$ from user process to user process – roughly 20 instruction times), small local memories ($\approx 64K$ words), and support for fine-grain computation (hardware support for message passing, fast context switching, fast task creation and dispatch). Each of the nodes executes instructions from its own local memory (i.e. this is an MIMD machine). Although there is a global shared address space, there is no shared memory. Nodes communicate via asynchronous message passing. Machines such as the J-machine have tremendous performance potential if we can develop effective ways of programming them. Of course, fine-grained programs can also be executed on medium-grained machines, and some interesting compiler research pursues techniques to make that efficient [8, 9].

This work was motivated by the complexity of writing large programs in existing concurrent object-oriented languages. Mechanisms for building massively concurrent abstractions in these languages all lead to serialization of message reception. This serialization reduced concurrency – unacceptable given the massive-concurrency in the target hardware. Experimentation with concurrent data abstractions in languages such as Concurrent Smalltalk [5, 18] influenced our ideas about programming massively-parallel machines. The design of Concurrent Aggregates [7, 11] builds on that work as a starting point. While our work with aggregates is related to the work on distributed aggregate objects described in [5, 6], our work is done in the context of an actor language which implies fine-grained concurrency. Bain's work embeds distributed aggregate objects in an SPMD or process-based message-passing model.

Aggregates are superficially similar to multi-ported objects in concurrent logic programming languages such as Janus [20]. However, objects in these languages are serialized, so multi-ported objects cannot be used to implement data abstractions which are truly multi-access (can accept more than one request at a time). In shared memory machines, regions of memory can be multi-access. While these regions can certainly be used to implement multi-access structures (typically dependent on knowledge of implementation details such as cache block size), these approaches typically provide no means for encapsulating the implementation and concurrency of the parallel data abstraction.

At the implementation level, caches and other dynamic replication techniques have been used to implement multiple access. While such techniques are effective in many cases, in many cases, customized coherence protocols for particular data abstractions can give improved performance. Further, this information may be difficult for the implementation to derive. Consequently, we have focused on providing the programmer with tools for building multi-access abstractions and allowing them to craft a partitioning and a coherence protocol which gives the best performance on their parallel data abstraction. This gives the programmer some measure of control, and allows him to give information on how to do this well for a particular abstraction. Our work on non-serializing abstraction tools is not meant as a substitute for efficient implementations which reduce implementations as much as possible. Rather, our work complements efforts reduce the serialization of a single object to the minimum, giving benefits which are a product of the two.

6.2.1   Overview

The remainder of the paper is structured as follows. In Section 6.3, we describe the serialization problem and describe how it can limit performance. A solution to the problem, the use of aggregates, is shown in Section 6.4. The required extensions to the actor model are clearly described. Section 6.5 summarizes our experience using an aggregates-based language, giving several detailed examples which demonstrate how aggregates can be used and showing their effectiveness in increasing program concurrency. Finally, we discuss the utility and drawbacks of using aggregates and summarize results presented in this paper in Section 6.6.

6.3   The Serialization Problem

Most concurrent object-oriented languages such as ACORE [19], ABCL/1 [21], CANTOR [3] and POOL-T [2], serialize data abstractions. When hierarchies of abstractions are

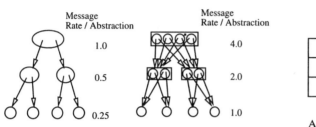

Message
Rate / Abstraction   Message
                                      Rate / Abstraction

1.0   4.0

0.5   2.0

0.25   1.0

Serializing Abstractions   Non-serializing Abstractions

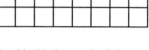

A grid with thousands of elements,
its single actor message rate = 1.0

Figure 6.1
Serialization in Data Abstractions

built, or the abstractions need to support massive concurrency, this serialization can cause reduce concurrency dramatically. These two scenarios are depicted in Figure 6.1. Many of these languages are based on the Actor model, which serializes message reception in order to provide a cleaner operational semantics for programs, freeing the programmer from consideration of finer-grained interaction between message executions.

Behavior replacement is the key element in simplifying reasoning about Actor programs, but limits concurrency unnecessarily as is shown in Figure 6.2. Consider a simple hash table which stores key-element associations and implements insert, delete, and query operations. Because the hash table interface object and the array can only have limited throughput (objects are serializing) a hash table can only have limited throughput. If we were to replicate the hash table interface part, (its pure function and interface), we would be unable to address it in the same way as other objects. Each replica would have a distinct name, so passing a reference to a highly concurrent hash table would involve passing a collection of names, not just a single acquaintance name.

While the Actor model provides a good foundation for the semantics of message-passing systems, it must be extended with non-serializing data abstraction tools to be suitable for for massively-concurrent message-passing machines. In such systems, traditional abstraction tools often cannot be used because they place far too great a constraint on program concurrency – even if the serialization for a single message is quite small. For example, it would be nice to use a grid abstraction in a multigrid relaxation algorithm, or a hash table in a highly-concurrent dictionary program. In both of these cases, adding a layer of abstraction increases program modularity – allowing the abstraction implementation to change without effecting the abstraction users. Using actors to build such abstractions has a disastrous effect on program concurrency – their serialization would become the limiting factor. This is unacceptable in many cases, as such a reduction in concurrency could dramatically reduce performance. In Section 6.4, we propose a simple

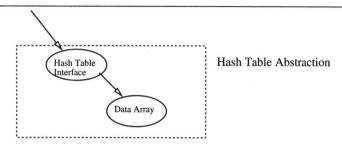

Figure 6.2
A Hash Table Abstraction in the Actor Model

extension to the Actor model – aggregates. Aggregates solve the serialization problem by allowing the programmer to use a collection of objects to implement abstractions.

6.4   A Solution: Aggregates – non-serializing data abstractions

Aggregates allow a programmer to use collections of objects to implement data abstractions. The key to this is that the objects in a collection share a single group name. This group name allows the abstraction to be manipulated in a fashion identical to ordinary actors. In order to make the interface multi-access, messages sent to the abstraction (the collection) are directed to an arbitrary member of the collection[2]. Each member of the collection is assigned a unique index in the aggregate and within the aggregate, members can be selected by index. The multi-access interface to an aggregate is depicted in Figure 6.3.

Varieties of such collections of objects have been proposed and implemented in languages described in [5, 18, 7]. Those collections were typically viewed as a means of spreading a few large data structures (in large PDE solvers, for example) over coarse-grained message passing machines. Only in [7] have we seen the conceptualization of these collections as a general means of reducing serialization due to abstraction boundaries. Previously, little effort has been made to unify the operational behavior these collections with the Actor model. We have proposed the addition of aggregates – collections of actors – as a solution to this serialization problem. The addition of aggregates requires only a few small changes to the Actor transition rules. We call the extended actor model, the aggregate model. The transition rules for the Aggregate Model are given below with the additions given in italics.

Aggregate Model

---

[2]The message direction may be more sophisticated in languages and their implementations, but in consonance with the Actor model spirit of efficiency and minimal constraint for the implementors, selecting an arbitrary member seems the least restrictive specification that is useful.

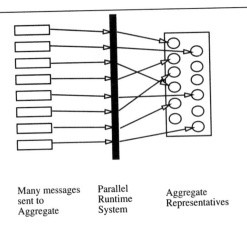

Many messages   Parallel   Aggregate
sent to   Runtime   Representatives
Aggregate   System

Figure 6.3
An Aggregate Interface is Multi-Access

Aggregates are collections of actors. Each aggregate has a group name. Each actor in an aggregate has its own actor name. Group names and actor names are manipulated uniformly.

Actor transitions: In response to a message, an actor can perform some number of the following operations.

1. Send messages to its acquaintances (these may include individual actors and aggregates)

2. Specify a new behavior (includes local state modification)

3. Create new Actors

System transitions: Messages sent to actors are delivered eventually, and in an indeterminate order. Messages that have arrived at an actor that is occupied are queued in its mail queue. Each actor repeatedly accepts message from its message queue, one at a time. Message execution can be overlapped, but conceptually the reception of a message must be sequential. *Messages sent to aggregates are delivered to an arbitrary actor in the collection. Reception at this actor is subject to the rules above. In addition, a distinguished operation SELECT can be applied to a group name to select actors out of a collection. Within an aggregate, this can be used to communicate and coordinate members in the implementation of a coherent abstraction.*

Aggregates can be used to implement abstractions with virtually unlimited concurrency (little serialization). The change to the Actor Model is slight and can be implemented quite efficiently (see [10] for a detailed investigation of this issue). The message distribution mechanism allows aggregates to present a uniform, yet non-serializing interface.

The group name can be used as the name of the abstraction and manipulated as any other object name. Because messages for the aggregate can be sent to any member, the actors in the aggregate must cooperate to implement the abstraction. In Section 6.5, we discuss some of the ways they can cooperate. Supporting aggregates requires an extension to the actor model because their implementation requires a change to the basic addressing structure. Within the Actor model, an aggregate could be emulated by using an immutable Actor which contained pointers to all the members of the aggregate. To get non-serializing behavior equivalent to an N-member aggregate, it would be necessary to have N copies of the immutable actor – an N^2 storage overhead!

6.5   Programming with Aggregates

In order to experiment with aggregates, we designed a programming language called Concurrent Aggregates (CA). More information on Concurrent Aggregates can be found in [7, 10]. CA has been used to construct a number of application programs including matrix multiplication, multigrid relaxation, N-body interaction, printed circuit board routing, a concurrent B-tree, a digital logic simulator, and a host of smaller programs. In this section, we first discuss how aggregates were used in these programs, classifying the types of usage into four categories. Subsequently, we describe the structure of two applications, a printed-circuit board router and a gate-level logic simulator in detail to give the reader insight into how the aggregates were actually used.

Our studies have revealed that the use of aggregates can be divided into the following four categories: consistent replication, loosely-consistent replication, partitioned state and structured cooperation. In each case, aggregates are used to reduce serialization. Because aggregates allow programmers to describe a distributed, concurrent implementation of a data abstraction, it is possible for programmers to manage the replication and consistency of data explicitly. While this poses a challenge, it also gives the programmers an opportunity to tailor replication and consistency to the requirements of the problem at hand, potentially leading to higher performance. We describe the four categories of usage below, citing examples of abstractions from our programming studies.

1. **Consistent Replication** In a consistent replication scheme, each actor in an aggregate holds identical copies of the state. To modify that state, all actors in the collection must be locked. Then for each member, the update is performed and the member unlocked. So long as writes are infrequent, replication will reduce serialization. Pure read sharing is included in this category. **Examples:** structural abstraction interfaces such as a FIFO queue interface, dynamic combining tree interface, and the net abstraction in the PC board router[3] (read-only) and leaf nodes in B-trees (read-mostly).

2. **Loosely Consistent Replication** Loosely-consistent replication reduces serialization by allowing some concurrency between read and write requests. Reads are allowed to access stale copies of data in order to increase the operation overlap. The

---
[3]See Section 6.5.1.

degree of consistency can be controlled by the update policy and whether writers wait
for write completion acknowledgements. Loose-consistency can significantly reduce
the cost of write (mutating) operations. **Examples:** intermediate nodes in a B-tree,
parallel event queue (see Section 6.5.2).

3. **Partitioned State** When an abstraction has state that can be partitioned into non-
   interacting parts, aggregates can be used effectively to reduce serialization. The state
   is partitioned over the actors in the aggregate and requests are received and redirected
   to the appropriate actor in the collection. **Examples:** arrays, grids, and hash tables
   such as the occupancy table in the PC board router.

4. **Structured Cooperation** Aggregates can also be used to build abstractions in which
   actors cooperate in a structured fashion. In many such cases, an aggregate's members
   are organized into a network with a particular interconnection pattern. When requests
   are received, the interconnection pattern shapes the resulting computation. Only the
   combined action of the collection of actors implements the abstraction. **Examples:**
   static and dynamic combining trees, broadcast trees, and structured grids for SOR
   computations and structured synchronization.

While the four categories above probably do not capture the full range of possibilities for aggregate-based programs, they represent an interesting variety of usage. The
first three are examples of programmers exploiting the ability to control replication and
consistency to improve program performance. The fourth category, structured cooperation, represents a new kind of abstraction entirely. These abstractions are inherently
multi-access (e.g. combining and broadcast) and consequently could not previously be
expressed as a data abstraction due to the resulting serialization. Thus aggregates can
be used to capture and modularize this distinct class of abstractions which are inherently
multi-access. In the next section, we describe two application kernels in detail to illustrate when and how aggregates can be used to reduce serialization. We hope that the
examples will provide a powerful argument as to the utility of aggregates for preserving
program modularity in the face of concurrency.

6.5.1   Example 1: Printed Circuit Board Router

A printed circuit board router is used to route a series of "nets", wires from one pin
to another. Routes must avoid obstacles on the board. A complex VLSI board might
have twenty thousand nets. One common approach is to route nets independently, so for
clarity our program runs consider only the routing of a single net. In an actual system,
a number of nets would be routed simultaneously. Our router uses A* search to find a
path for each net. Since short nets are generally desirable, partial paths are prioritized
by a distance estimate; their length plus the distance remaining to be traveled. At each
step, the path with the *lowest* total distance estimate, is extended. The basic algorithm
is outlined below:

1. Insert obstacles into grid database

2. Insert starting point into priority queue

3. Remove path with lowest total distance estimate

4. Extend path in each direction, subject to obstacles (check grid)

5. Merge it with other paths (check occupancy table), discarding the longer path to this point.

6. For each extended path, check if it has reached the destination, if yes, FINISH. If no, insert it into the priority queue.

7. goto step 3

Steps 2 through 6 are repeated for each net with steps 3 through 6 being done repeatedly. Our sequential implementation of the application uses a number of data abstractions: a grid database for obstacles, a priority queue, a net, and an occupancy table which detects convergent paths. We would like to increase the program's concurrency while preserving the same basic abstractions. Figure 6.4 shows the correspondence between steps in the routing algorithm and access to each data abstraction.

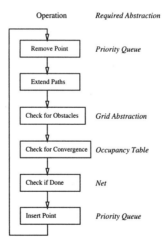

Figure 6.4
The sequence of operations for routing a net and the abstractions which must be accessed concurrently to support concurrent routing.

To increase the program's concurrency, we modified it to exploit the concurrent extension of paths in several directions and concurrent pursuit of several paths. This corresponds to having several concurrent executions of the loop shown in Figure 6.4 using the same set of data abstractions. Initially, the serialization imposed by the data abstractions prevented successful exploitation of the path-level concurrency. For example, the original occupancy table was an array in which the availability and path occupying a spot on the PC board was recorded as a value in an array element. Each active path extension involves a check for convergence. Since arrays are serialized objects, the occupancy table serialized checks for convergence, effectively eliminating much of the path-level concurrency.

By reimplementing each of the abstractions with non-serializing abstraction tools, we were ultimately able to expose path-level concurrency. However, even one serializing abstraction could eliminate much of the path-level concurrency. The one exception to this is our sequential implementation of the priority queue. If greater concurrency were desired, the priority queue could also be reimplemented for higher concurrency using aggregates. *How would one decide which abstractions to reimplement?* We proceeded by first introducing the concurrent path computations. For each bottleneck abstraction we found, we substituted an aggregate-based, non-serialized implementations of the abstraction. Due to identical modularity of all versions of the program, we were able to identify and modify each bottleneck abstraction separately. The interfaces of all of the abstractions (grid, occupancy table, net, etc.) remained the same, the new implementations simply increased the supportable levels of concurrency.

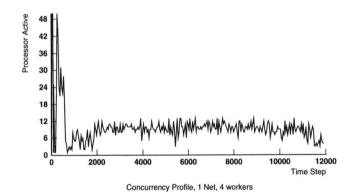

Concurrency Profile, 1 Net, 4 workers

Figure 6.5
A concurrency profile for the routing of a single net, with 4 concurrent path extensions allowed. The initial peaks before time step 1000 correspond to initialization of data structures.

Through the changes described above, the net routing program was transformed from a sequential program (concurrency of one) to a program with significant amount of concurrency. This is illustrated in the concurrency profile displayed in Figure 6.5. It is clear from the figure that significant concurrency (6-8 fold concurrency) was exposed.

The concurrency profile was produced by a simple simulation. The objects were first mapped to processors randomly and then the printed circuit board router was run. At each time step, each node can process, exactly one message is processed[4]. Message transmission latency is ignored. These simulations were done on a abstract message-passing machine simulator described in more detail in [10]. The router is routing a single net, routed from the lower left corner to the upper right hand corner of a very small (36x36 grid) printed circuit board. The board is covered with regularly spaced obstacles, and our program extends up to four paths simultaneously.

To demonstrate the importance of non-serializable abstractions at these key points in the PC board router, we varied the amount of serialization introduced at the abstraction boundaries of the grid, net and occupancy table. This can be done easily in a Concurrent Aggregates program[5], as reducing the number of representatives in an aggregate gradually increases the degree of serialization. When an aggregate has only one representative, its serialization is the same as a single object. The graphs shown in Figures 6.6 and 6.7 show that the concurrency limits can be attributed to serialization in a number of program abstractions. Removing this serialization increases program concurrency *and* decreases the critical path length.

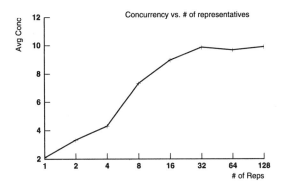

Figure 6.6
The concurrency change as the number of representatives in the key non-serializing abstractions is increased.

The average and peak concurrency of the printed circuit board router program improve as the degree of serialization is decreased. While decreasing the degree of serialization increased concurrency, it did not significantly increase the total amount of work. In fact, after removing the increased initialization overhead for the non-serialized versions, decreasing the serialization also reduced the total work slightly due to decreased contention

---

[4]Of course, each object can also only process one message, but this constraint is implied by that on nodes and the assumption that each object resides on only one node.
[5]Provided that the logical structure of the abstraction is not tied to the number of representatives.

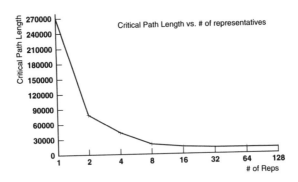

Figure 6.7
The change in critical path length as the number of representatives is increased. The majority of the
benefit has been received by 32 representatives.

until the cost of initializing the large number of members in an aggregate becomes large
enough to compensate.

6.5.2   Example 2: Logic Simulator

Logic simulation is often done via event-driven simulation. For each circuit node transition, an event is queued. At each time step, the simulator evaluates the node transitions,
causing more gates to switch and causing more events to be scheduled in the future. In
a large chip, it is not uncommon to have hundreds of thousands of logic gates. Most
logic simulators consist of a priority queue and a network of gates and circuit nodes. The
simulation proceeds as a series of event dequeues, event evaluations, gate evaluations and
event enqueues onto the priority queue. The basic simulation algorithm is given below:

1. Load the network

2. Load initial events into the event queue

3. Dequeue next event

4. Evaluate event

5. Enqueue resulting events, cancel unnecessary events

6. goto 3

Our goal was to exploit additional concurrency arising from two sources in the algorithm. First, events occurring at the same simulated time can be evaluated concurrently.
Second, since all events have a positive, finite delay, it's possible to evaluate the events

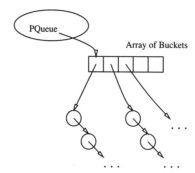

Figure 6.8
The object structure for a serial priority queue abstraction. The priority queue object uses an array of
buckets to keep track of events. Each bucket holds the events for one time step and is implemented with
a list.

for a number of time steps simultaneously. This effectively "software pipelines" event
evaluation for a sequence of time steps. Exposing this additional concurrency requires
that the event queue (a priority queue) be made concurrent. It also requires that the gate
evaluations and signal propagations be concurrent, but networks of gates are naturally
formulated as parallel interconnections of objects. In the sequential version, the basic
priority queue structure is shown in Figure 6.8. The relationship between algorithmic
steps and data abstraction access is given in Figure 6.9.

To exploit concurrent event processing, the priority queue must allow the simultaneous enqueueing of many events and the rapid "firing" of all the events scheduled for a
time step. The sequential priority queue implementation does not. First, because the
buckets for each time step were kept in an array (again, a single object) at least part of
every event enqueue operation must be serialized. Second, events are dequeued one at a
time, requiring one dequeue message for each event scheduled for a particular time. All
dequeue and enqueue calls are serialized by the priority queue, limiting event execution
concurrency.

To reduce the serialization due to the priority queue, we modified it by reimplementing the header structure with an aggregate and replicating the array of buckets.
These two changes allow event enqueues to be processed concurrently. To fire the
events in a time step more rapidly, we modified the priority queue to implement an
`execute_all_events(time)` operation, rather than a single event dequeue. This operation causes all the events in a time step to be executed, exposing the circuit's natural
concurrency.

To support the enqueueing many events simultaneously, we replicated the array of
buckets and also implemented each bucket with an aggregate. The new priority structure

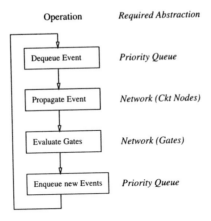

Figure 6.9
The sequence of invocations for the inner simulation loop of the logic simulator and the required abstractions.

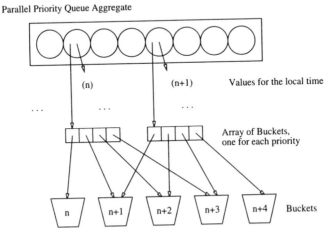

Figure 6.10
Removing unnecessary serialization from the priority queue involved replicating the header structures, the array of buckets, and making the buckets themselves concurrent. The resulting abstraction provides virtually the same interface, but supports much higher levels of concurrency.

is presented in Figure 6.10. Non-serializing buckets are pictured in Figure 6.11. Making the time-step buckets concurrent was absolutely essential as with the improved priority queue, many events can arrive at a particular bucket simultaneously.

Each bucket is implemented with a combining tree aggregate. As each request is received, it is linked into a dynamic broadcast tree as shown in Figure 6.11. Thus, an event becomes part of exactly one such tree when it is entered into the event queue. When the simulation is ready to fire that time step, the tree is used to fire all the events attached to the tree. Each node in a dynamic combining tree combines requests and links the events into small broadcast trees. The consolidated request is forwarded up the tree. The requests are further consolidated and the small broadcast trees linked into larger ones. Thus, the arrival order and arrival location of requests determines their place in the broadcast tree.

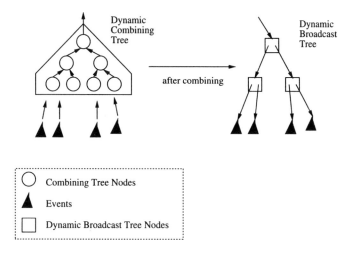

Figure 6.11
An aggregates-based implementation of a concurrent bucket, based on a simplified version of a dynamic combining tree. Enqueued events are collected into a broadcast tree, which is used to initiate their evaluation concurrently.

To further facilitate multi-access, our priority queue implementation uses loosely-consistent replication. Each representative in the priority queue keeps a local time. This allows event enqueues and execute_all_events messages to be executed concurrently by allowing each representative to update its local time and pointers independently. At the same time, other representatives could be processing enqueue requests. Software pipelining was achieved by using a sliding window of time steps; all of which are being evaluated concurrently. This technique further increased the importance of making the priority queue highly-parallel. The software pipelining was effective because our new implementation of the priority queue was able to support a very high rate of enqueue requests. The concurrency profile for the simulation of sixteen 8-bit counters ($\approx$ 900 gates) is illustrated in Figure 6.12.

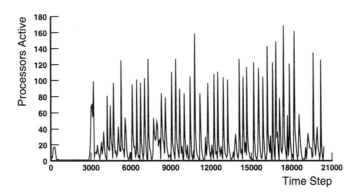

Processor Concurrency Profile

Figure 6.12
The concurrency profile for a logic simulation. The low concurrency before time 3000 is due to initialization of data structures.

Figures 6.13 and 6.14 show the increase in concurrency and decrease in critical path length as the serialization of the priority queue is reduced. Initial attempts to increase concurrency gave little benefit due to the serialization of a key data abstraction, the priority queue. As the number of representatives is increased, the serialization introduced by the priority queue abstraction decreases, improving program concurrency. The downturn in average concurrency which occurs beyond 32 representatives is due to some serialization in the initialization of the priority queue aggregate and could be removed with some recoding.

6.5.3   Discussion

Our changes to the printed circuit board router and the logic simulator removed unnecessary serialization, increasing program concurrency. In both cases, the program changes preserved the data abstraction interfaces with little change, maintaining the modularity structure of the program. This demonstrates that the modularity structure of some sequential programs can be preserved while supporting high levels of concurrency. While our simulation runs showed modest levels of concurrency, these levels are significant improvements over the programs with serializing abstractions. Higher levels of concurrency can be attained for the PC board router by routing a number of unrelated nets concurrently. With the logic simulator, the concurrency levels out as we reach the concurrency

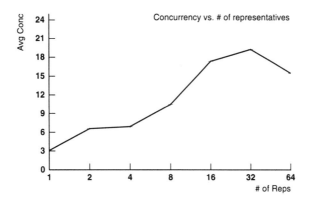

Figure 6.13
The achieved program concurrency as the number of representatives in the priority queue and buckets are increased. The number of bucket arrays is also increased with the number of priority queue representatives.

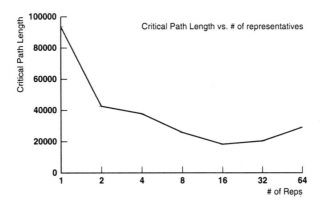

Figure 6.14
The critical path length of the logic simulation decreased, until we reached beyond 32 representatives.

limit imposed by the logic circuit. For larger circuits, much higher levels of concurrency would be expected and could be supported through the use of larger aggregates. The experience of reimplementing the priority queue in the logic simulator was typical of much of our experience for CA programs. The process involves a propagation of aggregates from a top-level down through levels of a hierarchy removing serialization as long as significant concurrency exist.

6.6   Summary

We have been working in the context of fine-grained message passing machines. The ability of these machines to efficiently exploit fine-grained concurrency, coupled with their massive hardware concurrency make constructing massively concurrent programs a high priority. The serialization embedded in the data abstraction tools available in most concurrent object-based languages limit the amount of concurrency a data abstraction can support. This limits the utility of abstractions in an environment where they are sorely needed to manage program complexity.

Our extended model, the *Aggregate Model* addresses the serialization problem by allowing actors to be collected and given a group name. This allows a collection of objects to be viewed as a single entity, implementing a single abstraction. This change is powerful because it allows the objects to cooperate with each other, forming the basis for non-serializing data abstractions.

We designed and implemented a language based on the aggregate model. Our experience writing programs has shown us that aggregates are a useful programming tool. In many cases, the introduction of aggregates allows us to preserve the sequential program's modularization, while exposing program concurrency. In a number of experiments, we have demonstrated that aggregates can be used to reduce serialization, directly reducing the critical path length, thereby increasing program concurrency.

Aggregates which allow the preservation of program modularization structures in the face of concurrency. This is a significant contrast to element-wise data-parallel languages or message-passing programs which force the embedding of sequential data abstractions within a single thread of a MIMD program. In contrast, aggregates allow the construction of abstractions which are concurrent, spanning multiple threads of execution. Thus, abstractions can have their natural form, and are not required to be reshaped due to the introduction of concurrency.

We have presented examples which show that serialization at abstraction interfaces can limit parallel performance and show how one might produce a non-serialized implementation of a data abstraction. These experiments demonstrate that multi-access abstraction tools can be useful in concurrent object-based languages. A corollary of this is that the *multi-access abstraction tools, aggregates, can be used to modularize programs with significant concurrency*. We further argue that multi-access abstraction tools are necessary, as it does not appear easy to find program modularizations for parallel programs which have serialized interfaces without fragmenting formerly sensible data abstractions. This means that serialized abstraction tools leave the programmer to choose between performance and modularity.

References

[1] G. A. Agha. *Actors: A Model of Concurrent Computation in Distributed Systems.* MIT Press, Cambridge, MA, 1986.

[2] P. America. Inheritance and Subtyping in a Parallel Object-Oriented Language. In *Proceedings of ECOOP*, pages 234–42. Springer-Verlag, June 1987.

[3] William C. Athas. *Fine Grain Concurrent Computations.* PhD thesis, California Institute of Technology, 1987. 5242:TR:87.

[4] William C. Athas and Charles L. Seitz. Multicomputers: Message-Passing Concurrent Computers. *IEEE Computer*, pages 9–24, August 1988.

[5] William L. Bain. Indexed Global Objects for Distributed Memory Parallel Architectures. In P. Wegner G. Agha and A. Yonezawa, editors, *Workshop on Object-Based Concurrent Programming*, pages 95–8. ACM Press, April 1988. SIGPLAN Notices Volume 24, Number 4.

[6] William L. Bain. Aggregate Distributed Objects for Distributed Memory Parallel Systems. In *Proceedings of the Fifth Distributed Memory Computers Conference*, Charleston, South Carolina, April 8-12 1990. SIAM.

[7] A. A. Chien and W. J. Dally. Concurrent Aggregates (CA). In *Proceedings of Second Symposium on Principles and Practice of Parallel Programming.* ACM, March 1990.

[8] A. A. Chien, W. Feng, V. Karamcheti, and J. Plevyak. Techniques for Efficient Execution of Fine-grained Concurrent Programs. In *Proceedings of the Fifth Workshop on Compilers and Languages for Parallel Computing*, pages 103–13, New Haven, Connecticut, 1992. YALEU/DCS/RR-915, Springer-Verlag Lecture Notes in Computer Science, 1993.

[9] Andrew Chien and Wuchun Feng. GST: Grain-Size Transformations for Efficient Execution of Symbolic Programs. Technical Report ANL-91/34, Argonne National Laboratory, 9700 South Cass Avenue, Argonne, IL 60439-4801, 1991.

[10] Andrew A. Chien. *Concurrent Aggregates: Supporting Modularity in Massively-Parallel Programs.* MIT Press, Cambridge, MA, 1993.

[11] Andrew A. Chien and William J. Dally. Experience with Concurrent Aggregates (CA): Implementation and Programming. In *Proceedings of the Fifth Distributed Memory Computers Conference*, Charleston, South Carolina, April 8-12 1990. SIAM.

[12] William D. Clinger. Foundations of Actor Semantics. Technical Report AI-TR-633, MIT Artificial Intelligence Laboratory, 1981.

[13] W. J. Dally, A. Chien, S. Fiske, W. Horwat, J. Keen, M. Larivee, R. Lethin, P. Nuth, S. Wills, P. Carrick, and G. Fyler. The J-Machine: A Fine-Grain Concurrent Computer. In *Information Processing 89, Proceedings of the IFIP Congress*, pages 1147–1153, August 1989.

[14] W. J. Dally and P. Song. Design of a Self-Timed VLSI Multicomputer Communication Controller. In *Proceedings of the International Conference on Computer Design*, pages 230–4. IEEE Computer Society, 1987.

[15] William J. Dally. *A VLSI Architecture for Concurrent Data Structures.* Kluwer Academic Publishers, Boston, Mass., 1987.

[16] William J. Dally, Linda Chao, Andrew Chien, Soha Hassoun, Waldemar Horwat, Jon Kaplan, Paul Song, Brian Totty, and Scott Wills. Architecture of a Message-Driven Processor. In *Proceedings of the 14th ACM/IEEE Symposium on Computer Architecture*, pages 189–196. IEEE, June 1987.

[17] P. Wegner, G. Agha and A. Yonezawa, editors. *Workshop on Object-Based Concurrent Programming.* ACM SIGPLAN, ACM Press, April 1988.

[18] W. Horwat, A. Chien, and W. Dally. Experience with CST: Programming and Implementation. In *Proceedings of the SIGPLAN Conference on Programming Language Design and Implementation*, pages 101–9. ACM SIGPLAN, ACM Press, 1989.

[19] Carl R. Manning. ACORE: The Design of a Core Actor Language and its Compiler. Master's thesis, Massachusetts Institute of Technology, August 1987.

[20]   V. Saraswat, K. Kahn, and J. Levy. Janus: A step towards distributed constraint programming. In *Proceedings of the North American Conference on Logic Programming*, Austin, Texas, October 1990.

[21]   A. Yonezawa, E. Shibayama, T. Takada, and Y. Honda. Object-Oriented Concurrent Programming – Modelling and Programming in an Object-Oriented Concurrent Language ABCL/1. In Aki Yonezawa and Mario Tokoro, editors, *Object-Oriented Concurrent Programming*, pages 55–89. MIT Press, 1987.

7 Multiple Concurrency Control Policies in an Object-Oriented Programming System

Gail E. Kaiser, Wenwey Hseush, Steven S. Popovich, and Shyhtsun F. Wu

Object-oriented systems have been generally recognized as a good choice for approaching a range of parallel and distributed programming problems. But different parallel and distributed applications have different consistency models, so *multiple concurrency control policies* are needed. When objects are shared among applications with different policies, multiple policies must operate simultaneously and compatibly. We have investigated two consistency models, critical sections on individual objects and classical serializable transactions, and the interactions both between these models and with "uncontrolled" concurrency, in the context of the MELD distributed object-oriented programming language. We present the relevant language constructs and discuss programming problems and implementation issues.

Keywords: Applications, database systems, distributed systems, parallel programming, programming languages, transaction processing.

7.1 Introduction

Object-oriented programming languages and data management systems have become very popular [25, 30]. Concurrent object-oriented programming systems (COOPS) are particularly attractive for intrinsically parallel and distributed applications [2], such as discrete event simulation and network management [3]. COOPS thus require support for *concurrency control*, to enforce data consistency within and across these applications.

It is sometimes suggested that the classical *transaction* model be integrated directly into COOPS facilities. This model permits applications to be defined in terms of serializable transactions: either all the operations carried out during a transaction complete or none of them do, and the effects of the transactions committed over the lifetime of the system appear to have occurred in some serial order [4].

The classical transaction model provides a good solution to many programming problems, but has been recognized as too strict for many applications [27]. Different parallel and distributed applications have different consistency requirements, so *multiple* concurrency control policies are needed. When data is shared among applications with different policies, then the policies must operate simultaneously and compatibly.

We have investigated the *interoperability* of classical transactions and a less strict consistency model, which we call *atomic blocks*, that provides exclusive access to an individual object during a sequence of statements. We have also explored the implications of "uncontrolled" concurrency within the same COOPS. Our work has been in the context of the MELD object-oriented programming language [21].

After briefly discussing the motivation for this work, we introduce MELD's classes and the basic concurrency-related facilities, which might execute without any control. We explain both atomic blocks and transactions, together with the corresponding language constructs and run-time support. We then discuss the insights obtained through our integration of the three policies. We describe our implementation and compare to other concurrent object systems, and conclude by summarizing the contributions of this work.

7.2   Motivation

There are many applications where classical serializable transactions unnecessarily restrict concurrency. One area is computer-supported cooperative work [14]. Collaboration involves long "transactions" carried out over hours or days, where participants *share* knowledge and data while their "transactions" are in progress, so the isolation enforced by serializability is inappropriate.

Real-time systems [35] are another domain where the classical transaction model does not work. For example, in an on-line stock trading system, the stock exchange feed writes the new values of prices as they are received and cannot be blocked even though there may be portfolio management computations concurrently reading the prices. Further, portfolio managers want to see the latest prices as they become available, so reading an old snapshot of the data (obtained, for example, using a multiversion concurrency control protocol) is unacceptable, as is blocking price updates (for example, using a locking concurrency control protocol).

We have previously proposed some specific approaches for both the cooperative work and real-time domains [31, 17, 20], but our goal in sketching these domains here is to motivate our claim that the classical transaction model alone is insufficient, and to demonstrate the need for different concurrency control policies specific to application functionality. Thus, a COOPS should provide language constructs for several distinct concurrency control policies, supporting different consistency requirements. Since applications with different consistency requirements sometimes share data, the policies must operate compatibly within an objectbase.

Such interoperability is related to the problem of executing transactions in heterogeneous database systems [33]. Global transactions consist of subtransactions, each of which executes on a different database, where each database may have a different scheme for implementing serializable transactions. One might use two-phase locking, another timestamps with multiple versions, and a third optimistic concurrency control, but the global transactions must be serialized. This might be enforced by requiring each database to support a particular predefined protocol, as in Superdatabase [32]. Elmagarmid and Du describe a methodology to construct local concurrency control schemes given a particular global mechanism and application-specific tradeoffs [10].

This problem is subtly different than ours, since each of the federated databases supports only a single implementation of transactions, so it is never the case that the *same* object is accessed by different threads of control operating according to different implementation schemes. In contrast, the Papyrus architecture does allow multiple threads employing different concurrency control schemes to access the same objects, with the interactions among schemes specified in a conflict matrix [29]. But again the divergence is with respect to implementation schemes, not the consistency models themselves, since they all enforce serializability. We are concerned with interoperability among implementations of different consistency models.

There has been much theoretical work on consistency models other than serializability. Lynch [24] and Garcia-Molina [13] have proposed consistency models in terms of multiple abstraction levels, where interleavings between steps at one level of abstraction depend on the semantics of the lower-level operations carried out by the steps. Weihl [36] describes three local atomicity properties for abstract data types, which exploit of the algebraic properties of the type's operations to ensure global consistency. Herlihy and Wing [15] describe a fine grain correctness condition called linearizability, which requires that each operation appear to "take effect" instantaneously, with the start order of non-concurrent operations preserved. Barghouti and Kaiser [5] survey the literature on transaction models for cooperative work. None of this work addresses the problems of interoperability among multiple consistency models applied to the same objects and possibly even the same operations.

7.3   Overview of MELD

In the MELD COOPS, each class defines instance variables and methods for every object of the class. Instance variables are strongly typed, where the type is primitive (integer, string, *etc.*), a programmer-defined class, or an array of variables of the same type (either primitive or programmer-defined). Instance variables and methods may be inherited from ancestor classes, using a multiple inheritance policy described in previous papers [19, 18]. MELD methods may call arbitrary C functions, for example, to support mathematical and/or graphic applications or reuse existing code.

Figure 7.1 depicts part of a class definition for simple printer spoolers. Keywords are given in **boldface** font. There are three instance variables, Q, P and L; in each case the type is another programmer-defined class, `FileQueue`, `Printer` and `AcctLog`, respectively. The Q variable is initialized by sending the **create** message to the `FileQueue` class,[1] while the other two variables are implicitly initialized to **nil**. A new `PrintSpooler` object is created by executing "PrintSpooler.**create**()".

Three methods are defined in the figure. The `QueueFile` method adds a file to the print queue, logs the user's request for accounting purposes, and then uses **send** to invoke the `Daemon` method. If the queue is non-empty, `Daemon` prints the first element of the queue and removes it from the queue; if the queue is empty, it does nothing. `CancelFile` cancels a print job when requested by the user.

MELD supports two granularities of parallelism, within an object and among objects (which may reside on the same or different machines). A method may send a message to its own object with "**send** message **to $self**" or to another object with "**send** message **to** receiver", where the "message" includes the name of a method and its actual arguments and the "receiver" is the name of a variable that references the other object. The original method continues execution without concern for whether its message has been received and does not wait for an acknowledgment, so **send** is asynchronous.

A method may also make a procedure call to its own object using "**$self**.message" or to another object using the "receiver.message" construct. In either case, the calling method blocks until the return, so procedure call is synchronous. A synchronously called method returns to its caller using the "**return** expression" construct, if a function, or by

---

[1]MELD does not actually represent classes as full-fledged objects, so this "message" is interpreted specially by the run-time support.

```
CLASS PrintSpooler ::=
        {* FIFO queue of Files *}
        Q: FileQueue := FileQueue.create();
        {* Printer managed by instance *}
        P: Printer;
        {* Log for usage of Printer *}
        L: AcctLog;
METHODS:
        Daemon () ⟶
            if (not Q.Empty())
            then begin
                    P.PrintFile(Q.First());
                    Q.RemoveFirst();
            end
        QueueFile (F: File; U: User) ⟶
            begin
                    Q.Enter(F);
                    L.LogUsage(F, U);
                    send Daemon() to $self;
            end
        CancelFile (F: File; U: User) ⟶
            begin
                    Q.RemoveEntry(F, U);
                    L.LogCancellation(F, U);
            end
            ...
END CLASS PrintSpooler
```

Figure 7.1
Printer Spooler Class

reaching the end of the method, if a procedure.[2]

When an object receives a message or a call, it (conceptually) spawns a new control thread to execute the method named in the message, and thus may execute multiple methods in parallel (some of which may be blocked awaiting returns from synchronous calls). The MELD implementation does not represent threads physically, but the effect achieved is the same as generating a new thread of control. When multiple methods execute in parallel, they may access the same instance variables.

Concurrency is thus maximized at the cost of nondeterminism and potential inconsistency since one method may view, or even overwrite, the intermediate values of instance variables written by another concurrently executing method. If the programmer knows that such read-write or write-write conflicts with never arise, due to the logic of the

---

[2]This is the only distinction between functions and procedures, except that the type of the return value of a function is declared in its method header.

program, then this is not a problem and maximum concurrency is desirable. But if the logic of the program permits race conditions, then the programmer can use either atomic blocks or transactions, as described in the next two sections, respectively. Both atomic blocks and transactions effectively isolate the protected code sequence, so such conflicts cannot arise.

```
{* Semaphore for mutual exclusion *}
CLASS Semaphore ::=
        {* no instance variables needed *}
METHODS:
        {* declaration *}
        response Available();
        {* initialize counting semaphore by
           generating N responses *}
        Init (N: integer)  ⟶
            if (N > 0)
            then begin
                    respond Available() to $self;
                    send Init(N-1) to $self;
            end
        {* wait until count is positive, and
effectively decrement count by matching
Available() response *}
        P()  ⟶  delayuntil Available();
        {* effectively increment count by generating another response *}
        V()  ⟶  respond Available() to $self;
END CLASS Semaphore
```

Figure 7.2
Semaphore Class

When strict isolation is not desirable, the programmer can explicitly program synchronization and information exchange between multiple on-going control threads. A method may send a message using the "**respond** message **to** receiver" construct, which is received when the recipient object (which may be the same object if the "receiver" is "**$self**") invokes a matching "**delayuntil** message". Alternatively, the **delayuntil** may happen first, and block until the corresponding **respond**. The **delayuntil** primitive will wait indefinitely if there is never a matching response (deadlocks are detected, and broken by halting the system). The names of responses must not conflict with method names, and are declared by "**response** name (arguments)". Figure 7.2 shows how these facilities could be used to implement a counting semaphore.

7.4 Atomic Blocks

An *atomic block* is a sequence of statements whose effects appear to be atomic with respect to the current object, that is, the entire object is locked for the duration of the atomic block. Any other code already executing within the object is suspended, and any arriving messages are queued until the atomic block terminates. Thus, no other code can read or update the instance variables of the object while the atomic block is executing. Atomic blocks combine the advantages of the critical sections common in operating systems to protect sequences of code, and the locking common in database systems to protect pieces of data. Atomic blocks represent a minimal concurrency control policy that protects both code and data.[3]

Figure 7.3 illustrates how atomic blocks might be used for the classical producer-consumer problem. The `Init` method invokes `Spacing`, which signals the N spaces available in the buffer using the `SpaceAvailable` response. The `Produce` method blocks according to the **delayuntil** construct until a space is available, and then enters its atomic block – the code surrounded by the **begin atomic** and **end atomic** keywords (uncontrolled sequential code is enclosed between simple **begin** and **end**, and is known as a *sequential block*).[4]

The atomic block manipulates the queue representation, and then signals that a space in the buffer has been filled using the `EntryAvailable` response. The `Consume` method blocks until a space has been filled, and then enters its atomic block. Although it responds `SpaceAvailable` before returning, intended to signal a waiting `Produce` method, `Consume` continues to hold a lock on the `ProducerConsumer` object until after the atomic block terminates with the **return**.[5] A waiting `Produce` method's **delayuntil** on `SpaceAvailable` is not matched until after the lock is released.

Thus an atomic block cannot be corrupted, since no other threads can read or write any instance variable of an object while an atomic block is executing on that object. However, an atomic block can begin executing on an object in the middle of one or more concurrent sequential blocks, suspending them, and thus can view the partial results of the sequential blocks. If atomicity of a sequential block is necessary for the application, then the programmer should write it as an atomic block.

The degree of consistency guaranteed by atomic blocks is insufficient in some cases. Consider Figure 7.1 again, and now assume that each operation on a `FileQueue` is implemented by an atomic block. Say the printer queue is empty, and a user invokes `QueueFile` to queue a file for printing. `Daemon` executes `Empty`, which returns **false**. The **if** statement then enters its **then** part, preparing to invoke `First`. But say that in the meantime, the same user executes `CancelFile`. Then it might be possible that

---

[3]We are not currently concerned with atomicity in the sense of crash recovery, although MELD does support a persistent objectbase, and selected classes may be declared persistent – instances of all other classes are by default transient and exist only in memory.

[4]The implementation actually encloses atomic blocks in parentheses "(...)" and uncontrolled sequential blocks in square brackets "[...]", following a minimalist style borrowed from C, but we employ keywords in this paper for improved readability.

[5]It is possible that the scheduler may switch contexts immediately after the **return**, in which case the lock will actually be released only when the scheduler next selects this (conceptual) thread of control.

```
CLASS ProducerConsumer ::=
      Q: array[1..N] of T;
      P, integer := 0;
METHODS:
      {* declaration *}
      response SpaceAvailable(), EntryAvailable();
      {* initialization *}
      Init () ⟶ send Spacing(N) to $self;
      {* create S spaces *}
      Spacing (S : integer) ⟶
         if (S > 0)
         then begin
               respond SpaceAvailable() to self;
               send spacing(S-1) to $self;
         end
      Produce (X : T) ⟶
         begin
               delayuntil SpaceAvailable();
               begin atomic
                     P := P % N + 1;
                     Q[P] X;
                     respond EntryAvailable() to self;
               end atomic
         end
      Consume () : T ⟶
         begin
               delayuntil EntryAvailable();
               begin atomic
                     C := C % N + 1;
                     respond SpaceAvailable() to self;
                     return(Q[C]);
               end atomic
         end
END CLASS ProducerConsumer
```

Figure 7.3
Producer-Consumer Program

the `RemoveEntry` called by `Cancelfile` is scheduled before the call to `First` executed by `QueueFile`, in which case `First` would find an empty queue and some erroneous condition would result.

```
Daemon ()  ⟶
      begin atomic
             if (not Q.Empty())
             then begin
                    P.PrintFile(Q.First());
                    Q.RemoveFirst();
      end
      end atomic
```

Figure 7.4
Atomic Daemon Method

It may seem that we could solve this problem by implementing the `Daemon` method as an atomic block surrounding all its procedure calls to the object referenced by its `Q` variable, as shown in Figure 7.4. But this would not work as desired, since the atomic block would lock only the `PrintSpooler` object and not any of the objects referenced by its instance variables. If there were any other access paths to these objects, such as a second `PrintSpooler` object sending files to the same printer (for instance, the "don't care" queue illustrated in the next section), then the inconsistency described above could still occur. The basic problem is that an atomic block only protects one object (**$self**), not any of the other objects that may be sent messages from within the atomic block.

Another problem with atomic blocks is that there is a high potential for deadlock. The simplest case is a recursive procedure call. Since all calls and messages for the same object are queued until an atomic block terminates, the atomic block would wait for itself forever.

7.5   Serializable Transactions

Transaction blocks solve these problems with atomic blocks, and should be used instead of atomic blocks for any applications that require consistency across multiple objects and/or where the logic of the program may lead to deadlock. A transaction block is a sequence of statements executed as a serializable transaction with respect to all other MELD code ever executed.

Returning to the `PrintSpooler` example, the inconsistency problem could be solved by defining the `Daemon` method as a transaction rather than an atomic block, as shown in Figure 7.5. Transaction blocks appear between the keywords **begin transaction** and **end transaction**.[6]. Transaction blocks guarantee serializability, so it could never happen that `Empty` returns **false** but the subsequent call to `First` finds an empty queue.

---

[6]Double angle brackets "≪ … ≫" are used in the implementation.

```
Daemon ()  ⟶
     begin transaction
          if (not Q.Empty())
          then begin
               P.PrintFile(Q.First());
               Q.RemoveFirst();
          end
     end transaction
```

Figure 7.5
Transaction Daemon Method

MELD implements transactions using a distributed optimistic concurrency control mechanism based on multiple versions, developed by Agrawal *et al.* [1]. Transactions read the versions of objects that existed at the time they started, and update shadow copies of these objects. After all its work has completed, the transaction is validated by checking that its reads and writes are serializable with respect to all previously validated transactions. In the case of distributed transactions involving objects residing in multiple processes on the same or different machines, two-phase commit is used. Only if validation succeeds are the shadow copies made public. If validation fails, the shadow copies are forgotten and the transaction may be restarted.[7]

Validation of transactions is done at the granularity of individual instance variables and array elements, rather than the entire object as protected by atomic blocks, in order to increase concurrency within an object.[8] In the original PrintSpooler example, this has no useful effect since the sets of variables accessed by the three methods overlap. However, in the extended example of Figure 7.6, a single PrintSpooler object supports N file queues and M printers, say with N one more than M to allow a "don't care" queue for as fast as possible printing by the first available printer. Now multiple copies of QueueFile and CancelFile can execute simultaneously for different users, and at the same time as Daemon, as long as these methods do not update the same file queue or spool to the same printer.

7.6   Interactions among Multiple Concurrency Control Policies

The integration of atomic blocks and serializable transactions in the same system with uncontrolled concurrency raises several interesting issues. First, in order to guarantee serializability, each transaction must be validated with respect to all atomic blocks and other MELD code executing over the same objectbase, not just all other transactions. We handle this by treating sequential and atomic blocks as sequences of "fake" transactions

---

[7]Restart of aborted transactions is treated as optional, with user confirmation required.
[8]Locking of individual instance variables and array elements by atomic blocks seemed highly likely to result in deadlock situations, so we decided against this alternative.

```
CLASS PrintSpooler ::=
        {* N = M+1 for first available *}
        Q: array[1..N] of FileQueue;
        P: array[1..M] of Printer;
        {* per queue *}
        L: array[1..N] of AcctLog;
METHODS:
        Init () ⟶ send BufferSpacing(N) to $self;
        BufferSpacing (B : integer) ⟶
           if (B > 0)
           then begin
                   Q[B] := FileQueue.create();
                   send BufferSpace(B-1) to $self;
           end
        Daemon () ⟶
           begintransaction
                   if (not Q.Empty())
                   then begin
                           P.PrintFile(Q.First());
                           Q.RemoveFirst();
                   end
           end transaction
        QueueFile (F: File; U: User; myQ: integer) ⟶
           begin
                   begintransaction
                           Q[myQ].Enter(F);
                           send LogUsage(F, U) to L[myQ];
                   end transaction
                   send Daemon() to $self;
           end
        CancelFile (F: File; U: User; myQ: integer) ⟶
           begintransaction
                   Q[myQ].RemoveEntry(F, U);
                   send LogCancellation(F, U) to L[myQ];
           end transaction
END CLASS PrintSpooler
```

Figure 7.6
Enforcing Serializability on Instance Variables

that appear, for the purposes of validation of real transactions, to have already committed. All statements in uncontrolled code and atomic blocks are immediately committed step-by-step as they execute, using fake transaction numbers, since transaction numbers are required by the optimistic concurrency control scheme.[9] If there is a conflict between non-transaction code and a transaction, the transaction is rolled back and may be restarted.

This adds a significant performance penalty to uncontrolled code and atomic blocks executing in the same system as transactions. In particular, each statement must first obtain a transaction number and then commit its read and write sets. The implementation recognizes the special case of non-transaction code and these processes are streamlined for the fake transactions (since no commit protocol is needed), but there does not seem to be any way to avoid some additional overhead. The compiler might check whether transactions are actually used in a given application, and generate optimized executables accordingly, but this could cause serious run-time errors with respect to separately compiled code operating on the same objectbase.

In addition to faking a transaction, each statement in a sequential block must also check the lock of the current object, to avoid conflicts with atomic blocks, but this is cheap by comparison. Each statement in a transaction block must check locks for the same reason. The code within atomic blocks does not need to check locks, since by definition if an atomic block is executing it holds the lock.[10]

Another cost imposed specifically by our optimistic implementation technique for implementing transactions is the maintenance of multiple shadow versions of instance variables. Each instance variable is represented as a sequence of public versions and a sequence of shadow versions. The public versions are ordered with the most recently committed first, and older versions following. The performance penalty here is negligible, except for the indirect effects of the additional memory space consumed.

Atomic blocks and other code not nested within a transaction access instance variables exactly as they would in a non-transactional system, except it is necessary to check for each statement whether its transaction number matches the first public version. It will, and that will be the end of the search. In the case of transaction code, including the code of an atomic block executed *within* a transaction, the transaction number is also used. Access to an instance variable involves a search through the sequence of shadow versions if this instance variable has been updated by that transaction, and through the sequence of public versions if not, since a corresponding shadow version will not exist if this instance variable has not been updated by that transaction.

MELD's support for asynchronous message passing means that multiple threads may execute on behalf of the same transaction. This is a problem independent of the need to interoperate with non-transaction code. Since all threads generated from within a transaction carry the same transaction identifier, there is no synchronization among these threads, and the same nondeterminism and potential inconsistency arises as with uncontrolled code. The conventional approach to multi-threaded transactions is to support

---

[9]It would be more efficient for an atomic block to execute as a single fake transaction, but this is not supported in the implementation.

[10]We should note that neither transactions nor atomic blocks prevent corruption by concurrent C code embedded within MELD programs, since C statements do not respect the protection conventions.

nested transactions [26], with each thread initiated as a subtransaction.

We did not do this in MELD because we found some ambiguity in the notion of nested transactions when an optimistic concurrency control implementation is used. For example, it is not clear whether a subtransaction should validate only against its siblings, only against other subtransactions in its "family" rooted by a single top-level transaction, or against all transactions in the system. Further, for any of these alternatives, the required overhead would be unnecessarily high when there is only one level of subtransactions, and the subtransactions are short and execute only on a single object. As a compromise, MELD allows atomic blocks to be executed by threads directly or indirectly spawned from transaction blocks, as a minimalist subtransaction facility. The atomic block (in effect) views the shadow version of the object belonging to the transaction, rather than the latest committed version of the object. However, the atomic block still locks the entire object independent of its context.

7.7 Implementation Status

MELD is translated into C and runs on SunOS 4.0.3 on Sun 3s and Sun 4s, Ultrix 3.1 on DecStation 3100s, and AIX 2.2.1 and Mach 2.5 on IBM RT 135s. The MELD implementation is organized into five subsystems: (1) mpp, the MELD preprocessor, which implements multiple inheritance; (2) sc, which supports static semantic checking across separately compiled MELD modules, called *features*; (3) mc, the MELD compiler, which translates preprocessed Meld programs into C; (4) ml, the MELD linker, which combines separately compiled MELD features and links them together with the MELD run-time kernel and existing C code called from within MELD methods; and (5) the run-time kernel, which supports concurrency control policies, persistent data, the distributed name service, and other facilities. The total is about 24,000 lines of C code and yacc and lex rules.

Several small example systems have been implemented in MELD, including a multi-user stock trading application. We have also developed a small information model for distributed network management, involving throughput as reported by (simulated) data sensors.

7.8 Related Work

In Section 7.2, we considered related work on multiple concurrency control schemes for the same concurrency control policy, serializability. Here we compare MELD to a few other systems concerned with multiple concurrency control policies.

Argus [23] has both atomic and non-atomic objects, binding concurrency control to one level of abstraction. In contrast, MELD supports concurrency control both within and among objects, and gives the programmer the freedom to combine different concurrency control policies on the same object.

Camelot [34] and Mach [16] together provide a transaction facility for objects, with a C language extension for programming [6]. Avalon, which is implemented on top of

Camelot, provides more complete language support for transactions, concentrating on fault tolerance rather than concurrency control, as extensions of C++ [9] and Common-Lisp [8]. Avalon's notion of consistency was influenced by Argus, and also binds atomicity to the object.

Hybrid [28] has an atomic block construct that provides atomicity across multiple objects, but blocks other code from executing within any of those objects until the atomic block terminates. MELD's atomic blocks work similarly, but on single objects only; MELD's transactions provide atomicity across multiple objects, but permit more concurrency because serializability is enforced at the granularity of individual instance variables rather than entire objects.

In Clouds, concurrency control is not bound to the object level, and *standard* (uncontrolled), *local consistency preserving* (analogous to atomic blocks) and *global consistency preserving* (analogous to transactions) threads may be executed across multiple objects [7]. However, when threads with different consistency levels access the same object, the *lowest* level of consistency is supported (that is, standard ¡ local ¡ global), exactly the opposite of MELD – and exactly the opposite of what we believe most programmers would expect. Thus no guarantees can be made for consistency actually being preserved by global consistency preserving threads!

In the *transaction group* paradigm, transactions are collected into groups, and concurrency control within each group of transactions may employ a different policy although serializability is maintained among transactions in different groups [22, 11]. But this work does not make clear whether it is necessary to statically determine "groups" and/or the objects they may access *a priori*. This is not possible in our context, since the same code may execute either uncontrolled or as part of a transaction and the set of objects shared among control threads with the same or different policies is determined dynamically as the applications execute at run-time.

7.9   Conclusions

We began by motivating the need for multiple consistency models, and thus multiple concurrency control policies, in concurrent object-oriented programming systems. We described our experimentation with three concurrency control policies in the MELD COOPS. Uncontrolled sequential blocks are unsafe, but relatively fast. Atomic blocks are lightweight and guarantee consistency within an object, but are not sufficient for applications requiring consistency among multiple objects and/or processes. Serializable transactions are relatively expensive.

To integrate the three policies, we extended the run-time support so all other code checks the locks manipulated by atomic blocks and also extended atomic blocks to operate on the shadow versions of instance variables maintained by transactions. The most significant performance penalty seems to be due to the necessity to execute all statements of uncontrolled code and atomic blocks as if they were fake transactions in order to detect conflicts between transactions and non-transaction code.

During our experience designing and implementing MELD, including the integration of these three concurrency control policies, and the development of several small systems using MELD, we have learned much about COOPS as well as concurrency control. We have recently redesigned MELD from scratch, with the new language named MELDC [12]. The primary goal of our new effort is high performance for distributed COOPS applications written in MELDC.

Acknowledgments

Ronald Chacar implemented the toy network management system in MELD. Quoc-Bao Nguyen ported MELD from SunOS to AIX, Mach and Ultrix, fixing several bugs in the concurrency control implementation in the process. David Staub developed MELD's distributed name service. David Garlan collaborated with the first author on the original design for a non-concurrent MELD.

The Programming Systems Laboratory was supported by National Science Foundation grants CCR-9000930, CDA-8920080 and CCR-8858029, by grants from AT&T, BNR, Citicorp, DEC, IBM, Siemens, Sun and Xerox, by the Center for Advanced Technology and by the Center for Telecommunications Research.

An extended abstract of this paper appeared in the *Second IEEE Symposium on Parallel and Distributed Processing*, Dallas TX, December 1990, pp. 623-626.

References

[1]   D. Agrawal, A. J. Bernstein, P. Gupta, and S. Sengupta. Distributed optimistic concurrency control with reduced rollback. *Journal of Distributed Computing*, 2(1):45–59, April 1987.

[2]   *ECOOP-OOPSLA Workshop on Object-Based Concurrent Programming*. ACM Press, October 1990. Special issue of *OOPS Messenger*, 2(2), April 1991.

[3]   Secretariat: USA (ANSI). Information retrieval, transfer and management for OSI, part 1: Management information model. Technical Report ISO/IEC JTC1/SC21 N, ISO International Organization for Standardization, May 1989.

[4]   Philip A. Bernstein, Vassos Hadzilacos, and Nathan Goodman. *Concurrency Control and Recovery in Database Systems*. Addison-Wesley, Reading MA, 1987.

[5]   Naser S. Barghouti and Gail E. Kaiser. Concurrency control in advanced database applications. *ACM Computing Surveys*, 23(3):269–317, September 1991.

[6]   Joshua J. Bloch. The Camelot library: A C language extension for programming a general purpose distributed transaction system. In *9th International Conference on Distributed Computing Systems*, pages 172–180, Newport Beach CA, June 1989. Computer Society Press.

[7]   Raymond C. Chen and Partha Dasgupta. Linking consistency with object/thread semantics: An approach to robust computation. In *9th International Conference on Distributed Computing Systems*, pages 121–128, Newport Beach CA, June 1989.

[8]   Stewart M. Clamen, Linda D. Leibengood, Scott M. Nettles, and Jeannette M. Wing. Reliable distributed computing with Avalon/Common Lisp. In *International Conference on Computer Languages*, pages 169–179, New Orleans LA, March 1990.

[9]   David Detlefs, Maurice Herlihy, and Jeannette Wing. Inheritance of synchronization and recovery properties in Avalon/C++. *Computer*, 21(12):57–69, December 1988.

[10]   Ahmed K. Elmagarmid and Weimin Du. A paradigm for concurrency control in heterogeneous distributed database systems. In *6th International Conference on Data Engineering*, pages 37–46, Los Angeles CA, February 1990.

[11]   Mary F. Fernandez and Stanley B. Zdonik. Transaction groups: A model for controlling cooperative work. In *3rd International Workshop on Persistent Object Systems: Their Design, Implementation and Use*, pages 128–138, Queensland, Australia, January 1989.

[12]   Howard Gershen and Erik Hilsdale. Navigating the MeldC: The MeldC user's manual. Technical Report CUCS-031-91, Columbia University Department of Computer Science, October 1991.

[13]   Hector Garcia-Molina. Using semantic knowledge for transaction processing in a distributed database. *ACM Transactions on Database Systems*, 8(2):186–213, June 1983.

[14]   Irene Greif, editor. *Computer-Supported Cooperative Work: A Book of Readings*. Morgan Kaufmann, San Mateo CA, 1988.

[15]   Maurice P. Herlihy and Jeannette M. Wing. Linearizability: A correctness condition for concurrent objects. *ACM Transactions on Programming Languages and Systems*, 12(3):463–492, July 1990.

[16]   Michael B. Jones and Richard F. Rashid. Mach and Matchmaker: Kernel and language support for object-oriented distributed systems. In *Object-Oriented Programming Systems, Languages and Applications Conference*, pages 67–77, Portland, OR, September 1986. Special issue of *SIGPLAN Notices*, 21(11), November 1986.

[17]   Gail E. Kaiser. A flexible transaction model for software engineering. In *6th International Conference on Data Engineering*, pages 560–567, Los Angeles CA, February 1990. IEEE Computer Society.

[18]   Gail E. Kaiser and David Garlan. MELDing data flow and object-oriented programming. In *Object-Oriented Programming Systems, Languages and Applications Conference*, pages 254–267, Orlando FL, October 1987. Special issue of *SIGPLAN Notices*, 22(12), December 1987.

[19]   Gail E. Kaiser and David Garlan. Melding software systems from reusable building blocks. *IEEE Software*, 4(4):17–24, July 1987.

[20]   Gail E. Kaiser and Brent Hailpern. An object-based programming model for shared data. *ACM Transactions on Programming Languages and Systems*, January 1992. In press. Available as IBM Research Report RC 16442 and Columbia University Department of Computer Science CUCS-046-90, December 1990.

[21]   Gail E. Kaiser, Steven S. Popovich, Wenwey Hseush, and Shyhtsun Felix Wu. MELDing multiple granularities of parallelism. In Stephen Cook, editor, *3rd European Conference on Object-Oriented Programming*, British Computer Society Workshop Series, pages 147–166, Nottingham, UK, July 1989. Cambridge University Press.

[22]   P. Klahold, G. Schlageter, R. Unland, and W. Wilkes. A transaction model supporting complex applications in integrated information systems. In *ACM-SIGMOD 1985 International Conference on Management of Data*, pages 388–401, Austin TX, May 1985. ACM.

[23]   Barbara Liskov, Dorothy Curtis, Paul Johnson, and Robert Scheifler. Implementation of Argus. In *11th ACM Symposium on Operating Systems Principles*, pages 111–122, Austin TX, November 1987. Special issue of *Operating Systems Review*, 21(5), 1987.

[24]   Nancy A. Lynch. Multilevel atomicity — a new correctness criterion for database concurrency control. *ACM Transactions on Database Systems*, 8(4):484–502, December 1983.

[25]   Norman Meyrowitz, editor. *OOPSLA ECOOP '90 Proceedings Object-Oriented Programming: Systems, Languages and Applications Conference European Conference on Object-Oriented Programming*, Ottawa, Canada, October 1990. ACM Press. Special issue of *SIGPLAN Notices*, 25(10), October 1990.

[26]   J. Eliot B. Moss. *Nested Transactions: An Approach to Reliable Distributed Computing*. Information Systems. The MIT Press, Cambridge MA, 1985. PhD Thesis, MIT LCS TR-260, April 1981.

[27]   Erich Neuhold and Michael Stonebraker (editors). Future directions in DBMS research. *SIGMOD Record*, 18(1):17–26, March 1989.

[28]   O. M. Nierstrasz. Active objects in Hybrid. In *Object-Oriented Programming Systems, Languages and Applications Conference Proceedings*, pages 243–253, Orlando FL, October 1987. Special issue of *SIGPLAN Notices*, 22(12), December 1987.

[29]   Marie-Anne Neimat and Kevin Wilkinson. Extensible transaction management in Papyrus. In Bruce Shriver, editor, *23rd Annual Hawaii International Conference on System Sciences*, volume II,

pages 503–511, Kona HI, January 1990.

[30]   Andreas Paepcke, editor. *OOPSLA '91 Conference on Object-Oriented Programming Systems, Languages, and Applications*, Phoenix AZ, October 1991. ACM Press. Special issue of *SIGPLAN Notices*, 26(11), November 1991.

[31]   Calton Pu, Gail E. Kaiser, and Norman Hutchinson. Split-transactions for open-ended activities. In Francois Bancilhon and David J. Dewitt, editors, *14th International Conference on Very Large Data Bases*, pages 26–37, Los Angeles CA, August 1988.

[32]   Calton Pu. Superdatabase for composition of heterogeneous databases. In *4th International Conference on Data Engineering*, pages 548–555, Los Angeles CA, February 1988.

[33]   S. Ram, editor. *Special Issue on Heterogeneous Distributed Databases Systems*, volume 24:12 of *IEEE Computer Magazine*. IEEE Computer Society, December 1991.

[34]   Alfred Z. Spector, Joshua J. Bloch, Dean S. Daniels, Richard P. Draves, Dan Duchamp, Jeffrey L. Eppinger, Sherri G. Menees, and Dean S. Thompson. The Camelot project. *Database Engineering*, 9(4), December 1986.

[35]   John A. Stankovic. Misconceptions about real-time computing: A serious problem for next-generation systems. *Computer*, 21(10):10–19, October 1988.

[36]   William E. Weihl. Local atomicity properties: Modular concurrency control for abstract data types. *ACM Transactions on Programming Languages and Systems*, 11(2):249–282, April 1989.

8 Ports for Objects in Concurrent Logic Programs

Sverker Janson, Johan Montelius, and Seif Haridi

We introduce *ports*, an alternative to streams, as communication support for object-oriented programming in concurrent constraint logic programming languages. From a pragmatic point of view ports provide efficient many-to-one communication, object identity, means for garbage collection of objects, and opportunities for optimised compilation techniques for concurrent objects. From a semantic point of view, ports preserve the monotonicity of the constraint store which is a crucial property of all concurrent constraint languages.

We also show that the Exclusive-read, Exclusive-write PRAM model of parallel computation can be realised quite faithfully using ports in terms of space and time complexity, thus allowing arbitrary parallel programs to be written efficiently.

Ports are available in AKL, the Andorra Kernel language, a concurrent logic programming language that provides general combinations of don't know and don't care nondeterministic computations.

8.1 Introduction

In this paper we introduce an alternative to streams as the communication medium for object-oriented programming in concurrent logic programming languages. This alternative will be seen to provide us with efficient many-to-one communication, object identity, means for garbage collection of objects, and optimised compilation techniques for objects. It will also provide us with means for mixing freely objects and other data structures provided in concurrent logic programming languages.

We regard *objects* for concurrent logic programming languages as processes, as first proposed by Shapiro and Takeuchi [16], and later extended and refined in systems such as Vulcan, A'UM, and Polka [11, 20, 3] (Figure 8.1).

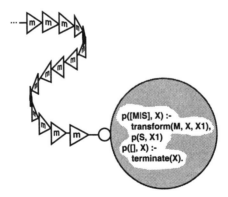

Figure 8.1
Objects as stream-consuming recursive processes

Some of these systems are embedded languages that make restricted use of the underlying language. We are interested in full-strength combinations of the underlying language with an expressive concurrent object-oriented extension, with all the problems and opportunities this entails.

In this paper, we present an approach to communication between objects (and processes in general), which is both efficient and useful in such a general setting. In the next section, we will remind the reader of a number of problems with previous approaches, and then, in the following sections, we introduce *ports* as a solution to these problems, one which also adds entirely new possibilities, such as a simple approach to optimised compilation of objects.

We will also show that the Exclusive-read Exclusive-write PRAM model of parallel computation can be realised quite faithfully, in terms of both space and time complexity, using ports. This indirectly demonstrates that arbitrary parallel algorithms can be expressed quite efficiently.

8.2   Background

In this section we present some of the background of our work. First we examine some requirements on object-oriented systems. Then we discuss the notion of a communication medium, and review a number of proposals that do not meet our requirements. We also discuss the limitations of some existing systems that are based on these proposals.

8.2.1   Requirements of Object-Oriented Systems

Our starting point is a number of requirements on object-oriented languages currently in use, such as Smalltalk and C++, and we will let these guide our work. In so doing, we here only consider requirements on the object-based functionality, including requirements on the interaction between the host language and the concurrent object-oriented extension. Other aspects of object-oriented languages, such as inheritance, can be realised in this setting in many different ways (e.g., [7]).

Since our goal is the integration of concurrent object and logic programming, we conform to the tradition of languages such as C++, where the object-oriented aspects are added to the underlying language and, in particular, allow objects and other data structures to be mingled freely. Thus, in a logic programming language, it should be possible to have objects *embedded* in a term data structure (Figure 8.2). Since terms can be shared freely in concurrent logic programming languages, the extra ability will allow concurrent objects to share, for instance, an array of concurrent objects.

Higher-level object-oriented languages provide automatic *garbage collection* of objects that are no longer referenced (Figure 8.3). Programmers do not have to think about when objects are no longer in use, nor do they have to deallocate them explicitly. The high-level nature of logic programming languages makes it desirable to provide garbage collection of objects, just as of other data structures.

Note that, in the goal-directed view of logic programming, an object is a goal, which has to be proved; it cannot just be thrown away. However likely the assumption that a goal is provable without binding variables, there is no such guarantee. In a concurrent object-oriented setting, another dimension is added, in that an object may still be active, and affect its environment, although it is no longer referred to by other objects. Even if

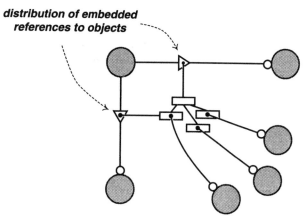

Figure 8.2
Objects embedded in terms

there are no incoming messages, an object may wish to perform some cleaning up before being discarded. Thus, garbage collection of objects in concurrent (logic) programs should involve notifying an object that it will no longer receive messages. It is up to the object to decide to terminate.

In addition, an implementation of objects should provide

- light-weight message sending and method invocation, the cost of which should preferably be similar to that of a procedure call,

- compact representation of objects, the size of which should be dominated by the representation of instance variables,

- memory conservative behaviour, which means that a state transition should only involve modifying relevant instance variables—objects are reused.

In this paper, we will address all but the last of the above requirements. The last requirement is generally solved in concurrent logic programming languages by providing a mechanism for detecting single references, and reusing the old instance variables.

8.2.2 Communication Media

A *communication medium* is a data type that carries messages between processes acting as objects (Figure 8.4).

The medium is used as a handle to an object, and is regarded as the *object identifier* from a programmer's point of view.

In the concurrent constraint view that we take, the communication medium is managed (described and inspected) using constraints [13]. All constraints are added to a shared *constraint store*. To *send* a message means to impose a constraint on the medium which allows a process to detect the presence of a message, and *receive* the message by inspecting its properties. A sender of messages is a *writer* of the medium. A receiver of messages is a *reader* of the medium. A message that is received once and for all is said to be *consumed*.

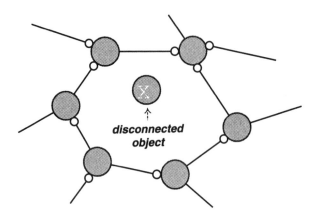

Figure 8.3
Garbage-collectable object

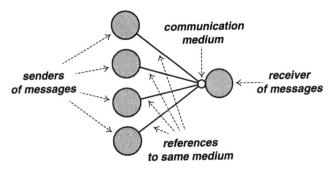

Figure 8.4
The communication medium

A medium can be *closed* by imposing constraints that disallow additional messages. A receiver can detect that a medium is closed.

An important property of the constraint store in concurrent logic programming languages is that it is monotonic. Addition of constraints will produce a new constraint store that entails all the information in the previous one. This property is important because it implies that once a process is activated by the receipt of a message, this activation condition will continue to hold until the message is consumed regardless of the actions of other processes.

8.2.2.1 Requirements on Communication Media The discussion above leads us to the following requirements on our communication medium.

- Any constraint-based solution should preserve the monotonicity of the constraint store.

- The number of operations required to send a message (make it visible to an end receiver) should be constant (for all practical purposes), independent of the number of senders. All senders should be given equal opportunity, according to a first come first served principle. We call this the *constant delay property*.

- When a part of the medium that holds a message has been consumed, it should be possible to deallocate or reuse the storage it occupied, by garbage collection or otherwise.

- To provide completely automatic garbage collection of objects, it should be possible to apply the closing operation automatically (when the medium is no longer in use).

- To enable sending multiple messages to embedded objects, it should be possible to send multiple messages to the same medium.

The last requirement seems odd in conventional object-oriented systems. It is however a problem in all single-assignment languages including the current concurrent logic programming languages.

8.2.2.2   Streams   The list is the by far most popular communication medium in concurrent logic programming. In this context lists are usually called *streams*.

A message m is sent on the stream S by constraining S to a *list pair* S=[m|S1]. The next message is sent on the stream S1. The stream is closed by constraining it to the *empty list* S=[]. The receiver, which should be waiting for S to become constrained to either a list pair or the empty list, will then either successfully match S against a list pair [M|R], whereupon M will be bound to m and R to S1, in which case the next message can be received on S1, or match S against [], in which case no further messages can be received. By the *end-of-stream* we mean a tail of the stream that is not yet known to be a list pair or an empty list.

To achieve the effect of several senders on the same stream, there are two basic techniques: (1) Several streams, one for each sender, are interleaved into one by a process called *merging*. (2) The language provides some form of atomic "test-and-set" unification, which allows *multiple writers* to compete for the end-of-stream.

Merging is typically achieved either by a tree of binary mergers, or by a multiway merger. The binary merge tree is built by splitting a stream as necessary (Figure 8.5).

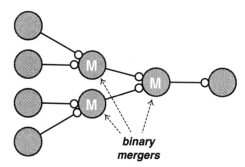

Figure 8.5
Binary merge network

Clearly, this technique does not have the constant delay property as the (best case) cost is $O(\log m)$ in the number of senders m. A *multiway merger* is a single merger process that allows input streams to be added and deleted dynamically (Figure 8.6).

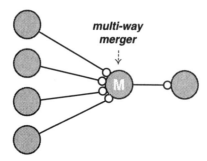

Figure 8.6
Multi-way merger

A *constant delay multiway merger* cannot be expressed in most concurrent logic programming languages (AKL is an exception [8]), but it is conceptually clean, and it is quite possible to provide one as a language primitive. We will assume that all multiway mergers have constant delay.

A number of disadvantages of merging follow.

- A merger process has to be created whenever there is the slightest possibility that several senders will send on the same stream. For many purposes this is not a problem. Once a multiway merger is created, adding and deleting input streams is fairly efficient. Yet, needing one feels like an overhead in an object-oriented context, where references to objects should be freely distributable.

- Explicit closing of all streams to all objects is necessary, since otherwise the program will either eventually deadlock, or at least some objects will continue to be suspended, forever occupying storage.

- The merger process itself occupies storage, it also wastes storage when creating a new merged stream, and if it uses the standard mechanisms for suspension, it is likely to be (comparatively) inefficient.

- Messages have to be sent on the current end-of-stream variable, which is changed for every message sent. To make it possible to use a stream that is stored in some other data structure, the new end-of-stream variable has to be stored in the data structure after one round of sending is completed. Usually this means copying parts of the data structure (but if some form of single reference optimisation is employed by the language implementation [2, 10, 4], this would not necessarily be the case). Even worse, to enable sharing of this data structure with another process/object, where the possibility of the other object sending messages on the embedded streams cannot be excluded, two copies of the data structure have to be created (allocating new memory for at least one). All the streams have to be split in two (by merging), one for each copy.

- A serious problem is the *transparent message-distribution problem*. A message is usually a term m(C1,..,Cn) where the Ci's are message components. Suppose we want to implement a transparent message-distributor object, which when it receives a message, of any kind, will distribute it to a list of other objects. Without prior knowledge of the components of messages, the distributor object cannot introduce the merging required for stream components.

An advantage with merging is that it allows list pairs to be reused in the merger and deallocated by the receiver as soon as a message has been consumed. In some cases, in a system with fairly static object-structure, explicit closing of all streams as a means for controlled termination of objects can be considered an advantage. Another general advantage of all stream communicating systems is the implicit sequencing of messages from a source object to a destination. This simplifies synchronisation in many applications.

Multiple writers can only be expressed in some languages with atomic test-and-unify. The drawbacks of multiple writers are summarised as follows:

- The cost for multiple writers is typically $O(m)$ per message, when there are m senders, and is therefore even further from the constant delay property than merging.

- The delay is proportional to the number of messages that have been sent.

- An inactive sender may hold a reference to parts of the stream that have already been consumed by the intended receiver, making deallocation impossible.

- It is difficult to close a stream. Some distributed termination detection technique, such as short-circuits or the like, has to be used. In practice, this outweighs the advantages of multiple writers.

An advantage with multiple writers is that no merger has to be created. Moreover, several messages can be sent on the same stream, and not only by having explicit access to the end-of-stream variable.

Neither merging nor multiple writers provide a general solution to the problem of automatic garbage collection of objects. There are special cases, as exemplified by A'UM (see Section 8.2.3), where (acyclic structures of) objects are terminated automatically.

It can be suspected that many of the problems described above are inherent in the use of streams as communication channels. Thus, people have looked for alternative data types.

8.2.2.3 Mutual References Shapiro and Safra [15] introduced *mutual references* to optimise multiple writers, and as an implementation technique for constant delay multiway merging. The mental model is that of multiple writers.

A shared stream S is accessed indirectly through a *mutual reference* Ref, which is created by the allocate_mutual_reference(Ref, S) operation. Conceptually, the mutual reference Ref becomes an alias for the stream S. The message sending and stream closing operations on mutual references are provided as built-in operations. The stream_append(X, Ref, New_Ref) operation will bind the end-of-stream of Ref to the list pair [X|S1], and New_Ref is returned as a reference to the new end-of-stream. The stream S can be closed using the close_stream(Ref) operation, which binds the end-of-stream to the empty list [].

An advantage of this is that the mutual reference can be implemented as a pointer the the end-of-stream. When a message is appended, the pointer is advanced and returned. If a group of processes are sending messages on the same stream using mutual references, they can share the pointer, and sending a message will always be an inexpensive, constant time operation. Mutual references can be used to implement a constant delay multiway merger. Another advantage is that an inactive sender will no longer have a reference to old parts of the stream. This makes it possible to deallocate or reuse consumed parts of the stream.

A disadvantage is that we cannot exclude the possibility that the stream has been bound from elsewhere, and that stream_append has to be prepared to advance to the real end-of-stream to provide multiple writers behaviour.

Otherwise, mutual references have the advantages of multiple writers, but the difficulty of closing the stream remains. It is also unfortunate that the mental model is still that of competition instead of cooperation.

8.2.2.4   Channels Tribble et al [17] introduced *channels* to allow multiple readers as well as multiple writers.

A channel is a partially ordered set of messages. The write(M, C1, C2) operation imposes a constraint that: (1) the message M is a member of the channel C1, and (2) M precedes all messages in channel C2. The read(M, C1, C2) operation selects a minimal (first) element M of C1, returning the remainder in a channel C2. The empty(C) operation detects that a channel C is empty. The close(C) operation imposes the constraint that a channel C is empty.

In the intended semantics, messages have to be labeled to preserve message multiplicity. Also, since the constraints do not specify which messages are not in the channels, only minimal channels satisfying the constraints are considered.

Channels seem to share most of the properties of multiple writers on streams. Thus, all messages have to be retained on an embedded channel, in case someone might read it. An inactive sender causes the same problem. Closing is just as explicit and problematic. The multiple readers ability can be achieved by other means. For example, a process can arbitrate requests for messages from a stream conceptually shared by several readers.

8.2.2.5   Bags Kahn and Saraswat [10] introduced *bags* for the languages Lucy and Janus.

Bags are multi-sets of messages. They are like streams in that subsequent messages are sent on subsequent bags, but there is no need for user-defined merging, as this is taken care of by the Tell constraint bag-union $B = B1 \cup \cdots \cup Bn$. A message is sent using the Tell constraint $B = \{m\}$. A combination of these two operations, $B = \{m\} \cup B1$, corresponds to sending a message on a stream, but without the order of messages given by the stream. A message is received by the Ask constraint $B = \{m\} \cup B1$.

Note that bags can be implemented as streams, with a multiway merger as bag-union. The single-reference property of Janus then makes it possible to reuse list pairs in the multiway merger, and to deallocate (or reuse) list pairs when a bag is consumed.

Therefore, it is not surprising that bags have most of the disadvantages of streams with multiway merging. The host languages Lucy and Janus only allow single-referenced objects and therefore suffer less from these problems.

8.2.3   Object-Oriented Concurrent Logic Programming

Most proposals for object-oriented embedded languages in, and object-oriented extensions of, concurrent logic programming languages, are limited by their communication medium, streams.

Vulcan   is a pure object-oriented embedded language [11]. It apparently does not allow embedding objects in terms, has no special provisions for termination, and suffers from the transparent message distributor problem.

A'UM   is also a pure object-oriented embedded language [20]. It provides automatic termination, by reference counting of objects implemented in the host language, and solves the transparent message distributor problem by restricting all components of a message to be streams to other objects. This, of course, restricts the language.

Polka   is a language extension of Parlog [3]. It does apparently allow arbitrary mixtures of objects and terms, in a style not entirely unlike what we are aiming for, but it does not solve any of the problems of stream merging.

8.3   Ports

We propose *ports* as a solution to the problems with previously proposed communication media.

8.3.1   Ports Informally

A *port* is a connection between a bag of messages and a corresponding stream of these messages (Figure 8.7). A bag which is connected via a port to a stream is usually identified with the port, and is referred to as a port.

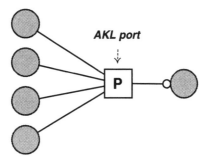

Figure 8.7
AKL port

The open_port(P, S) operation creates a bag P and a stream S, and connects them through a port. Thus, P becomes a port to S. The send(P, M) operation adds a message M to a port P. A message which is sent on a port is added to its associated stream with constant delay. When the port becomes garbage, its associated stream is automatically closed. The port(P) operation recognises ports. A first simple example follows.

?- open_port(P, S), send(P, a), send(P, b).

P = <some printed representation of a port>,
S = [a,b] ?

Here we create a port and a related stream, and send two messages. The order in which the messages appear could just as well have been reversed.

Ports solve all of the problems mentioned for streams and others.

- No merger has to be created; a port is never split.

- Several messages can be sent on the same port, which means that ports can be embedded.

- Message sending delay is constant.

- Senders cannot refer to old messages, and thus prevent garbage collection.

- A port is closed automatically when there are no more potential senders, thus notifying the consumer of messages.

- The transparent forwarding problem is solved, since messages can be distributed without inspection.

- Messages can be sequenced, as described in Section 8.4.

8.3.2   Ports as Constraints

We can provide a sound and intuitive interpretation of ports as constraints as follows. Ports are bags, in other words multi-sets. The open_port and send operations on ports are constraints with the following reading. The open_port constraint states that all members in the bag are members in the stream and vice versa, with an equal number of occurrences. The send constraint states that an object is a member of the bag.

Our method for finding a solution to these constraints is don't care nondeterministic. Like the commit operation in concurrent logic programming languages, we are happy with any solution. Therefore, the interpretation in terms of constraints is not a complete characterisation of the behaviour of ports, just as Horn clauses do not completely characterise the behaviour of commit guarded clauses. In particular, it does not account for message multiplicity, nor for their "relevance", i.e., it does not "minimise" the ports to the messages that appear in a computation.

A logic with resources could possibly help, e.g., Linear Logic [6]. The don't care nondeterministic and resource sensitive behaviour of ports can easily be captured by LL. The automatic closing requires much more machinery. If such an exercise would aid our understanding remains to be seen.

8.3.3   Solving Port Constraints

We now define the operational semantics of ports in terms of rewrites on (parts of) a constraint store.

Observe that the rewrite rules will strictly accumulate information in the constraint store; the right hand side always implies the left hand side. The first rule adds an annotation only. The second and third rules add constraints on the stream. Thus, we preserve the desirable monotonicity property.

The first rule annotates the open_port constraint, for control purposes. We need an index to keep track of where in the stream S we are putting new messages.

$$\text{open\_port}(P, S) \Rightarrow \text{open\_port}(P, S)_S$$

The second rule consumes a send to a port, moving the message to its associated stream. Observe that this rule monotonically adds information to the constraint store. Although the send constraint is removed, it is still implied by the presence of the message in the stream.

$$\text{open\_port}(P, S)_{S'}, \text{send}(P, m) \Rightarrow$$
$$S' = [m \mid S''], \text{open\_port}(P, S)_{S''}$$

The third and final rule closes the associated stream when the port P satisfies the *garbage condition* with respect to the computation state (see below).

$$\text{open\_port}(P, S)_{S'} \Rightarrow S' = [], \text{open\_port}(P, S)_{S'}$$

The garbage condition for a port holds in a computation state if there exists a *garbage collected* state in which the port only occurs in a single open_port constraint and in consumed send constraints.

We will attempt to give a definition of a kind of a garbage collected state, which, although quite an intuitive notion, is fairly operational in nature, and therefore difficult to fit into the notion of a constraint store.

Let us assume, to keep our definition simple, that our host language is a determinate concurrent constraint language, with ports and with syntactic equality constraints of the form $X = Y$ or $X = f(Y\Delta 1, \ldots, Y\Delta n)$, where variables may be ports. Note that this combination of ports and equality is not accounted for by the constraint solving rules, and that the system presented here is incomplete in this regard.

A *computation state* consists of a conjunction of constraints and agents. The idea is that we may throw away constraints that no longer restrict variables reachable from agents, because the resulting constraint store is logically equivalent.

A computation state A is *garbage collected* wrt another computation state B if (1) they have the same agents, (2) the constraints in A are a subset of the constraints in B, and (3) the conjunction σ of constraints in A is equivalent to the conjunction θ of constraints in B, modulo the existential quantification of variables $v_1, \ldots, v_n$ occurring in constraints but not in agents, i.e.

$$\exists v_1 \cdots \exists v_n.\sigma \equiv \exists v_1 \cdots \exists v_n.\theta$$

For example, if "p(X), X = f(Y), Z = g(W, X)" is a state, then "p(X), X = f(Y)" is garbage collected wrt that state, since

$$\exists Y \exists Z \exists W(X = f(Y) \; \& \; Z = g(W, X)) \equiv \exists Y \exists Z \exists W(X = f(Y))$$

This also corresponds to our intuition. Note that for some constraint systems a more involved notion of simplification than the deletion of individual constraints is necessary.

8.3.4 Implementation

There are advantages in the implementation of ports, and of objects based on ports, which we first discuss in this section and then return to in Section 8.4.

The implementation of ports can rely on the fact that a port is only read by the open_port/2 operation, and that the writers only use the send/2 and port/1 operations on ports, which are both independent of previous messages.

Therefore, there is no need to store the messages in the port itself. It is only necessary that the implementation can recognize a a port, and add a message sent on a port to its associated stream. This can be achieved simply by letting the representation of a port point to the stream being constructed. In accordance with the rewrite rules, adding a message to a port then involves getting the stream, unifying the stream with a list pair of the message and a new "end-of-stream", and updating the pointer to refer to the new end-of-stream. Closing the port means unifying its stream with the empty list. Note that the destructive update is possible only because the port is "write only".

In this respect, ports are similar to mutual references. But, for ports there is conceptually no such notion as *advancing* the pointer to the end-of-stream. We are constructing a list of elements in the bag, and if the list is already given, it is unified with what we construct.

Other implementations of message sending are conceivable, e.g., for distributed memory multi-processor architectures.

That a port has become garbage is detected by garbage collection, as suggested by the definition. If a copying garbage collector is used, it is only necessary to make an extra pass over the ports in the old area after garbage collection, checking which have become garbage (i.e., were not copied). Their corresponding streams are then closed.

From the object-oriented point of view, this is not optimal, as an object cannot be deallocated in the first garbage collection after the port becomes garbage, which means that it survives the first generation in a two-generation generational garbage collector. Note that for some types of objects, this is still acceptable, as their termination might involve performing some tasks, e.g., closing files. For other objects, it is not. In Section 8.4 we discuss compilation techniques based on ports that allow us to differentiate between these two classes of objects, and treat them appropriately.

Reference counting is more incremental, and is therefore seemingly nicer for our purposes, but the technique is inefficient, it does not rhyme well with parallelism, and it does not reclaim cyclic structures. MRB and compile-time GC are also of limited value [2, 4], as we often want ports to be multiply referenced.

8.4   Concurrent Objects

Returning to our main objective, object-oriented programming, we develop some programming techniques for ports, and discuss implementation techniques for objects based on ports.

Given ports, it is natural to retain the by now familiar way of expressing an object as a consumer of a message stream, and use a port connected to this stream as the object identifier.

```
create_object(P, Initial) :-
    open_port(P, S),
    object_handler(S, Initial).
```

In the next two sections we address the issues of synchronisation idioms, and of compilation of objects based on ports, as above.

8.4.1   Synchronisation Idioms

We need some synchronisation idioms. How do we guarantee that messages arrive in a given order? We can use continuations, as in Actor languages.

The basic sequencing idiom is best expressed by a program (which is written in AKL, using the conditional (if-then-else) guard operator "→").

```
open_cc_port(P, S) :-
    open_port(P, S0),
    call_cont(S0, S).

call_cont([], S) :-
    → S = [].
call_cont([(M & C)|S0], S) :-
    → S = [M|S1],
      call(C),
      call_cont(S0, S1).
call_cont([M|S0], S) :-
    → S = [M|S1],
      call_cont(S0, S1).
```

The (Message & Continuation) operator guarantees that messages sent because of something which happens in the continuation will come after the message. For example, it can be used as follows.

```
?- open_cc_port(P, S), send(P, (a & Flag = ok)), p(Flag, P).
```

The procedure p/2 may then choose to wait for the token before attempting to send new messages on the port P.

The above synchronisation technique using continuations can be implemented entirely on the sender side, with very little overhead. A goal send(P, (m & C)) is compiled as (send(P, m), C), with the extra condition that C should only begin execution after the message has been added to the stream associated with the port. It should be obvious that this is trivial, even in a parallel implementation.

Another useful idiom is the three-argument send, defined as follows.

```
send(P0, m, P) :-
    send(P0, (m & P = P0)).
```

which is useful if several messages are to be sent in sequence. If this is very common, a send-list operation can be useful.

```
send_list(P, []) :-
    → true.
send_list(P0, [M|S]) :-
    → send(P0, M, P1),
      send_list(P1, S).
```

8.4.2   Objects based on Ports

If messages are consumed one at a time by the object message-handler, and the input stream is not manipulated in other ways, as can be guaranteed by an object-oriented linguistic extension, then it is possible to compile the message handler using message oriented scheduling [19]. Instead of letting messages take the indirect route through the stream, this path can be shortcut by letting the message handling process pose as a special kind of port, which can consume its messages directly. There is then no need to save messages to preserve stream semantics. It is also easy to avoid creating the "top-level structure" of the message, with suitable parameter passing conventions. The optimisation is completely local to the compilation of the object.

Looking also at the implementation of ports from an object-oriented point of view, an object compiled this way poses as a port with a customised send-method. This view can be taken further by also providing customised garbage collection methods that are invoked when a port is found to have become garbage. If the object needs cleaning up, it will survive the garbage collection to perform this duty, otherwise the GC method can discard the object immediately.

Object-types in common use, such as arrays, can be implemented as built-in types of ports, with a corresponding built-in treatment of messages. This may allow an efficient implementation of mutable data-structures. Ports can also serve as interfaces to objects written in foreign languages.

Ports and built-in objects based on ports are available in the AKL Programming System (AKL/PS) [9]. An interesting example is that an AKL engine is provided as a built-in object. A user program can start a computation, inspect its results, ask for more solutions (AKL is don't know nondeterministic), and, in particular, reflect on the failure or suspension of this computation. This facility is especially useful in programs with a reactive part and a (don't know nondeterministic) transformational part, where the interaction with the environment in the reactive part should not be affected by nondeterminism or failure, as exemplified by the AKL/PS top-level and some programs with graphical interaction. In the future, this facility will also be used for debugging of AKL programs and for meta-level control of problem solving.

8.5 Modelling PRAM with Ports

Shapiro [14] discusses the adequacy of concurrent logic programming for two families of computer architectures by simulating a RAM (Random Access Machine) and a network of RAMs in FCP (Flat Concurrent Prolog). However, a simulator for shared memory multi-processor architectures, PRAMs (Parallel RAMs), is not given.

We conjecture that PRAMs cannot be simulated in concurrent logic programming languages without ports or a similar construct. This limitation could, among other things, mean that array-bound parallel algorithms, such as many numerical algorithms, cannot always be realised with their expected efficiency in these languages.

In the following we will show the essence of a simulator for an Exclusive-read Exclusive-write PRAM in AKL using ports.

8.5.1 PRAM with Ports

A memory cell is easily modelled as an object.

```
cell(P) :-
      open_cc_port(P, S),
      cellproc(S, 0)
cellproc([], _) :-
      | true.
cellproc([read(V0)|S], V) :-
      | V0 = V,
        cellproc(S, V).
cellproc([write(V)|S], _) :-
      | cellproc(S, V).
cellproc([exch(V1, V2)|S], V) :-
      | V2 = V,
        cellproc(S, V1).
```

PRAM is achieved by creating an array of ports to cells (Figure 8.8).

```
memory(M) :-
      M = m(C1, ..., Cn),
      cell(C1), ..., cell(Cn).
```

Any number of processes can share this array and send messages to its memory cells in parallel, updating them and reading them. The random access is achieved through the random access to slots in the array, and the fact that we can send to embedded ports without updating the array. Sequencing is achieved by the processors, using continuations as above.

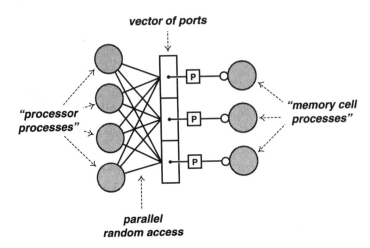

Figure 8.8
PRAM with AKL ports

8.5.2   RAM without Ports

Most logic programming languages do not even allow modelling RAM, as a consequence of the single-assignment property. Shapiro's simulator for a RAM depends on a built-in n-ary stream distributor to access cell processes in constant time as above. In KL1 the MRB scheme allows a vector to be managed efficiently, as long as it is single-referenced [2].

memory(M) :- new_vector(M, n).

A program may access (read) the vector using the

vector_element(Vector, Position, ^Element, ^NewVector)

operation (which preserves the single-reference property). Sequencing is achieved through continuing access on NewVector. Similarly, a program may modify (write) the array using the

set_vector_element(Vector, Position, ^OldElement, NewElement, ^NewVector)

operation (which also preserves the single-reference property). Sequencing can be achieved as above.

8.5.3   PRAM without Ports?

If MRB (or *n*-ary stream distributors) and multiway merging are available, they can be used to model PRAM, but with a significant memory overhead. Each processor-process is given its own vector of streams to the memory cells. All streams referring to a single memory cell are merged. Sequencing is achieved as above. Thus we need $O(nm)$ units of storage to represent a PRAM with n memory cells and m processors.

The setup of memories is correspondingly more awkward.

```
memories(M1, ..., Mm) :-
      memvector(M1, C11, ..., C1n),
      memvector(M2, C21, ..., C2n),
      ...,
      memvector(Mm, Cm1, ..., Cmn),
      cell(C1), ..., cell(Cn),
      merge(C11, ..., C1m, C1),
      merge(C21, ..., C2m, C2),
      ...,
      merge(Cn1, ..., Cnm, Cn).

cell(S) :- cellproc(S, 0).

memvector(M, C1, ..., Cn) :-
      new_vector(M1, n),
      set_vector_element(M1, 1, _, C1, M2),
      set_vector_element(M2, 2, _, C2, M3),
      ...,
      set_vector_element(Mn, n, _, Cn, M).
```

Memory is accessed and modified as in a combination of the two previous models (Figure 8.9). A stream to a memory cell is accessed using the KL1 vector operations. A message for reading or writing the cell is sent on the stream, and the new stream is placed in the vector. An isomorphic structure can also be achieved using n-ary stream distributors.

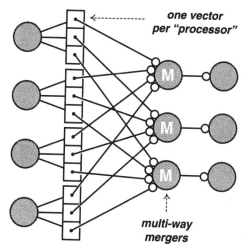

Figure 8.9
PRAM without AKL ports

8.6 Examples

In the following, examples are shown, due to Barth, Nikhil, and Arvind [1], which exhibit
the need for parallel random access functionality in a parallel programming language.
The two examples, histogramming a tree of samples and graph traversal, exemplify basic
computation structures common to many different settings.

Barth, Nikhil, and Arvind contrast random access solutions with pure functional programs, showing clearly that the former are an improvement both in terms of the total
number of computation steps and in terms of the length of the critical path (in "maximally" parallel executions). The compared programs can be expressed in AKL with
and without ports, respectively. Only the parallel random access solution with ports is
shown; its alternatives without ports can be expressed in many different ways.

8.6.1 Histogramming a Tree of Samples

Given a binary tree in which the leaves contain numbers in the range $1, \ldots, n$, count the
occurrences of each number.

In our solution, the number of occurrences are collected in a table of counters, with
indices in the given range. Assume that the memory agent defined in the previous section
returns a memory of this size. The program traverses the tree, incrementing the counter
corresponding to a number. To guarantee that all nodes have been counted, the program
performs the computation in a guard, and returns the table upon its completion.

```
hist(T, M) :-
      memory(M0),
      count(T, M0)
      → M = M0.


count(leaf(I), M) :-
      → arg(I, M, C),
         send(exch(K, K+1), C).
count(node(L,R), M) :-
      → count(L, M),
         count(R, M).
```

8.6.2 Graph Traversal

Given a directed graph in which the nodes contain unique identifiers and numbers, compute the sum of the numbers in nodes reachable from a given node. Assume that the
identifiers are numbers in the range $1, \ldots, n$. Any number of computations on the same
graph can be done concurrently.

In our solution, the nodes which have been traversed are marked in a separate array.
For simplicity we assume this to have the indices in the given range, whereas a better

solution would employ hashing to reduce its size. Assume that the memory agent returns a memory of this size. A graph node is an expression of the form

$$node(I, K, Ns)$$

where I is the unique node identifier, K is a number (to be summed), and Ns is a list of neighbouring nodes. (Note that cyclic structures are not a problem in the given constraint system of rational trees.)

```
sum(N, G, S) :=
      memory(M),
      traverse(N, G, M, S).


traverse(node(I, K, Ns), M, S) :-
      arg(I, M, C),
      send(exch(1, X), C),
      ( X = 1 → S = 0
      ; traverse_list(Ns, M, S) ).


traverse_list([], _, S) :-
      → S = 0.
traverse_list([N|Ns], M, S) :-
      → traverse(N, M, S1),
         traverse_list(N, M, S2),
         S = S1 + S2.
```

8.7 Discussion

We have argued that the communication medium *ports* solves a number of problems with the interpretation of processes as objects. It provides efficient many to one communication, object identity, means for garbage collection of objects, and opportunities for optimised compilation techniques for objects.

Ports are available in the AKL Programming System being developed at SICS. The prototype is available without charge for research purposes. (Contact any of the authors.)

The Andorra Kernel Language (AKL) is a general combination of search-oriented nondeterministic languages, such as Prolog, and the process-oriented committed-choice and concurrent constraint languages [18, 12, 13]. For an introduction to the language from this perspective, see [8]. For a formal treatment, see [5].

In AKL interesting combinations of object-oriented and constraint solving programs are possible, partly thanks to ports, but that is the topic of another paper.

Acknowledgements

This work was in part sponsored by ESPRIT Project 2471 ("PEPMA"). SICS is a non-profit research foundation, sponsored by the Swedish National Board for Industrial and Technical Development (NUTEK), Asea Brown Boveri AB, Ericsson Group, IBM Svenska AB, NobelTech Systems AB, the Swedish Defence Material Administration (FMV), and Swedish Telecom.

References

[1] Paul S. Barth, Rishiyur S. Nikhil, and Arvind. M-structures: extending a parallel, non-strict, functional language with state. In *Functional Programming and Computer Architecture '91*, 1991.

[2] T. Chikayama and Y. Kimura. Multiple reference management in flat GHC. In *Proceedings of the Fourth International Conference on Logic Programming*, volume 2, pages 276–293. MIT Press, 1987.

[3] Andrew Davison. *POLKA: A Parlog Object-Oriented Language*. PhD thesis, Department of Computing, Imperial College, London, May 1989.

[4] Ian Foster and Will Winsborough. Copy avoidance through compile-time analysis and local reuse. In *Logic Programming: Proceedings of the 1991 International Symposium*, San Diego, California, October 1991. MIT Press.

[5] Torkel Franzén. Logical aspects of the Andorra Kernel Language. SICS Research Report R91:12, Swedish Institute of Computer Science, October 1991.

[6] J.-Y. Girard. Linear logic. *Theoretical Computer Science*, 50(1):1–102, 1987.

[7] Yaron Goldberg and Ehud Shapiro. Logic programs with inheritance. In *Proceedings of the International Conference on Fifth Generation Computer Systems 1992*. Omsha Ltd, June 1992.

[8] Sverker Janson and Seif Haridi. Programming paradigms of the Andorra Kernel Language. In *Logic Programming: Proceedings of the 1991 International Symposium*, San Diego, California, October 1991. MIT Press.

[9] Sverker Janson and Johan Montelius. Design of a sequential prototype implementation of AKL. SICS research report, Swedish Institute of Computer Science, 1992.

[10] Kenneth M. Kahn and Vijay A. Saraswat. Actors as a special case of concurrent constraint programming. In Norman Meyrowitz, editor, *OOPSLA/ECOOP '90 Conference Proceedings*. ACM/SIGPPLAN, 1990.

[11] Kenneth M. Kahn, Eric Dean Tribble, Mark S. Miller, and Daniel G. Bobrow. Vulcan: Logical concurrent objects. In P. Shriver and P. Wegner, editors, *Research Directions in Object-Oriented Programming*. MIT Press, 1987.

[12] Michael J. Maher. Logic semantics for a class of committed choice programs. In *Proceedings of the Fourth International Conference on Logic Programming*. MIT Press, 1987.

[13] Vijay A. Saraswat. *Concurrent Constraint Programming Languages*. PhD thesis, Carnegie-Mellon University, January 1990.

[14] Ehud Shapiro. A test for the adequacy of a language for an architecture. In *Concurrent Prolog: Collected Papers*. MIT Press, 1987.

[15] Ehud Shapiro and Shmuel Safra. Multiway merge with constant delay in Concurrent Prolog. *Journal of New Generation Computing*, 4(3):211–216, 1986.

[16] Ehud Shapiro and Akikazu Takeuchi. Object-oriented programming in Concurrent Prolog. *Journal of New Generation Computing*, 1(1):25–49, 1983.

[17] Eric Dean Tribble, Mark S. Miller, Kenneth Kahn, Daniel G. Bobrow, Curtis Abbott, and Ehud Shapiro. Channels: A generalisation of streams. In *Proceedings of the Fourth International Conference on Logic Programming*. MIT Press, 1987.

[18] Kazunori Ueda. Guarded horn clauses. Technical Report TR-103, ICOT, June 1985.

[19]   Kazunori Ueda and Masao Morita. A new implementation technique for flat GHC. In *Proceedings of the Seventh International Conference on Logic Programming*. MIT Press, 1990.

[20]   K. Yoshida and T. Chikayama. A'UM—a stream-based concurrent object-oriented language. In *Proceedings of FGCS'88*, ICOT, Tokyo, 1988.

III Language Design

9   Specifying Concurrent Languages and Systems with Δ-Grammars*

Simon M. Kaplan, Joseph P. Loyall, and Steven K. Goering

This paper illustrates the use of graph grammars for specifying concurrent systems and languages. The model used in this paper, Δ-Grammars, is rooted in existing graph grammar theory and provides a convenient framework in which to specify both static and dynamic concurrent systems. Our approach is illustrated by three examples.

9.1   Introduction

This paper illustrates the use of graph grammars for describing and specifying concurrent systems and languages. Graph grammars are well suited for such specifications because they have a strong theoretical base, support a visual intuition, and support specification of dynamic systems.

The graph grammar model used in this paper, Δ-Grammars, is based on Ehrig's double-pushout categorical construction for generalized graph-to-graph transformations [4] and is very similar to Göttler's X- and Y-grammar models [7, 8, 9]. The major differences are the addition of a *restriction* region to productions (effectively a visual guard on production application) and a theory of Kleene-like *-groups for Δ productions. Concurrent systems and languages are specified in Δ by representing the state of a program as a graph and representing state transitions by Δ-productions.

This paper is structured as follows: First, we present an overview of Δ-Grammars and their relation to previous graph grammar research. Then we demonstrate the specification of concurrent systems and languages using Δ-Grammars with three examples. The first is a specification for the *remote client-server* problem, in which connections among clients must be established in an arbitrary, dynamically changing network of clients and servers. This example illustrates how complex dynamic concurrent systems can be specified in Δ. The second example presents a Δ solution to the *dynamic dining philosophers* problem. The major focus of this example is on abstraction mechanisms in Δ so that a solution can be specified at multiple interconnected levels of abstraction. The third example shows how a concurrent language, Actors [1], can have its semantics defined using a Δ-Grammar. The resulting semantics is lazy and highly concurrent.

9.2   Δ-Grammars

In this section, we informally describe Δ-Grammars. For the formal specifications and more detailed discussion, see [14, 6, 5, 15, 17]. We proceed in three parts. The first presents a brief informal overview; the second describes some of the features of Δ-Grammars; and the third describes how Δ-Grammars relate to existing graph grammar research.

The purpose of this section is not to give a formal overview of Δ-Grammars. Formal definition of the basic concepts and their use in Δ-Grammars can be found in the cited references.

---

*This research supported in part by the National Science Foundation under grant CCR-8809479, by the Center for Supercomputing Research and Development at the University of Illinois and by AT&T through the Illinois Software Engineering Project. Steve Goering is also supported as an IBM fellow.

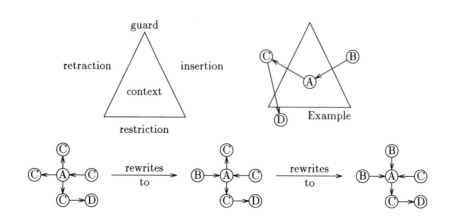

Figure 9.1
Form of Production

9.2.1   Informal Overview

A Δ-GRAMMAR consists of an initial graph and a set of Δ-productions. Execution of a program specified in Δ consists of repeatedly choosing a Δ-production and applying it to the graph resulting from the previous transformation. Production application is said to *rewrite* the current graph at each step.

A Δ-production consists of five sections, represented by the triangular notation of Figure 9.1 (thus the name Δ-GRAMMARS).

- The *retraction*, the fragment of the graph removed during the rewrite, is written to the left of the triangle.

- The *insertion*, the fragment that is created and embedded into the graph during the rewrite, is written to the right of the triangle.

- The *context*, the fragment that is identified but not changed during the rewrite, is written in the center of the triangle. The context is common to both the left and right-hand sides of the production, *i.e.* the left-hand side of the production is the union of context and retraction, and the right-hand side is the union of context and insertion. The context is used to help identify the retraction and to indicate the part of the host graph to which the insertion is embedded.

- The *restriction*, the fragment of the graph that must not exist for the rewrite to occur, is written beneath the triangle. If the subgraph matching the context and retraction can be extended to match the restriction, then the production cannot be applied to that subgraph.

- The *guard*, a textually expressed condition that must be true for the rewrite to occur, is written above the apex of the triangle. A guard is a boolean expression over the variable labels which appear in the production.

While guards and restrictions serve a similar purpose — control over the applicability of the productions — they operate in orthogonal domains. The restriction is a restriction on the topology of the graph to which the production is being applied (it prohibits production application where certain 'shapes' can be found in the graph), while the guard is a restriction on the values of the labels on the nodes and edges of the graph.

A Δ-production p is applied to a graph g by the following steps:

1. A subgraph isomorphic to the left-hand side of p is identified in g.

2. If no isomorphic subgraph exists or if the isomorphic subgraph can be extended to match the left-hand side plus the restriction (if one exists), p cannot be applied to g.

3. The guard, if it exists, is evaluated. If it is false, p cannot be applied to g.

4. The elements of the subgraph isomorphic to the retraction are removed from g, leaving the *host* graph.

5. A graph isomorphic to the insertion, called the *daughter* graph, is instantiated.

6. The daughter graph is embedded into the host graph as shown by the edges between the context and insertion in p.

A sample Δ-production and its application to a graph is illustrated in Figure 9.1. The application of a Δ-production to a host graph is atomic with regard to the subgraph matching the context and retraction. Since it does not affect any part of the host graph not connected to the matched graph[1], any other part of the host graph may be modified at the same time. Because of this, many applications can occur simultaneously.

9.2.2   Features of Δ

Δ has many features that make it convenient to specify programs. Detailed discussion of Δ and these features is given in [6, 15].

- Labels that may be used in a graph are either names that are declared *a priori* or values of other known domains such as integers. Nodes and edges in graphs and Δ-productions may be either labeled or not labeled. During a rewrite, non-labeled elements of a Δ-production unify to non-labeled elements of a graph, and labeled elements unify to elements with the same labels.

- Variable labels may also be used, where each variable is restricted by a type system to only take on values from a subset of all legal labels. When the same variable is used in several places in a Δ-production, it must unify to the same value in each place for the rewrite to occur. Variable labels appear in Δ-productions as names preceded by a "?", *e.g.* "?x", "?y". Usually an intricate type system is unneeded, so that all variable labels may take on values of all constant labels. Where more distinction is needed, it is specified textually as a restriction on the range of values which can

---

[1]Actually, just the part of the graph matched by the retraction.

be bound to the variable label. There is a distinguished variable "?" that may be
used multiple times in a Δ-production without requiring that those uses be unified
to the same label during a rewrite. Using this feature reduces the number of variable
names required and simplifies Δ specifications. Specific variable names are only used
where a type restriction is needed or where unification of several graph elements is
desired, *e.g.* where an element is retracted and an element of the same label is inserted
with different connectivity. The variable is bound by its matching to the retracted
element's label, and this binding is used to give the inserted element its label.

- Guards are boolean expressions over both type restrictions on variables and relations
  (predicates) on those variables.

- Subsets of elements in the contexts and retractions of Δ-productions can be grouped
  together into *folds*. During a rewrite multiple elements in a fold may map to the
  same graph element, as long as other restrictions (same label and same connectivity)
  are satisfied. Δ-productions are annotated by adding subscripts to labels such that
  elements with the same subscript belong to a common fold.

- Sets of elements in a Δ-production can be grouped together to form **-groups* (pro-
  nounced "star groups"). *-groups represent zero or more occurrences of the group
  of elements. A Δ-production p that contains a *-group is syntactic shorthand for an
  infinite sequence of Δ-productions with no *-groups, each with i occurrences of the
  group that is starred, $i = 0, 1, 2, \ldots$. Application of p to a graph g consists of applying
  the Δ-production from this sequence that matches a subgraph in g maximally. The
  semantic definition of *-groups is given in [5].

- Application of Δ-productions is *fair*. That is, if it is infinitely often possible to apply
  a Δ-production to a particular place in a graph, the Δ-production will be applied at
  that place an infinite number of times [5].

9.2.3   Relation to Graph Grammar Theory

Δ-GRAMMARS are based on the double pushout categorical definition of graph grammars
presented by Ehrig in [3, 4]. Variable labels and unification of labels during application
is based on the results in [17].

The restriction and guard regions are graphical and textual means of specifying the
"application conditions" described by Ehrig and Habel in [2].

Several concrete models of graph grammars have been developed. For example, NLC
grammars [13, 18] have been developed as a clean, efficiently executable model. The
major difficulties of executing graph grammars, graph isomorphism and specifying the
embedding, are simplified in NLC grammars. Because of its single node replacement,
establishing an isomorphism between the left-hand side of a production and a subgraph
of the graph being rewritten is simply the matter of matching the single node in the
left-hand side of the production to a single node in the graph and unifying their labels.
The embedding in NLC grammars is usually specified as n-NCE embedding, *i.e.* within a
neighborhood of distance n from the node being rewritten. NLC grammars are completely
encompassed by Δ-GRAMMARS (productions in NLC grammars are just Δ-productions
with a single node in the retraction), but there are many applications to which NLC

grammars are not suited. Any rewrites requiring the cooperation and deletion of several distant nodes requires the cooperation of several NLC productions and are difficult to represent in NLC grammars.

Hyperedge replacement grammars [10, 11, 16] emphasize edges as the important elements in graphs, using nodes merely as sockets to glue edges together. Hyperedge replacement grammars, therefore, center rewriting around the replacement of a hyperedge in a graph. Graphs contain two kinds of nodes, terminal nodes that can never be rewritten, representing "socket" nodes in a hypergraph, and nonterminal nodes, representing hyperedges, that can be rewritten corresponding to the way hyperedges can be rewritten. Embedding in the immediate neighborhood of a nonterminal node (or hyperedge) is simplified by the fact that no two nonterminal nodes are adjacent, *i.e.* no hyperedge can be connected to another hyperedge without being "glued" together by a "socket" node. Hyperedge replacement grammars can be represented by Δ-GRAMMARS in a similar way that NLC grammars can, but there are many Δ-GRAMMARS that are difficult or impossible to represent using hyperedge replacement grammars.

Δ-GRAMMARS are most similar in nature to Y-grammars [7, 8] and X-grammars [9]. Productions in a Y-grammar are written around a Y, with the left-hand side to the left of the stem, the right-hand side to the right of the stem, and the embedding specification between the uprights. During application of a Y-production, the embedding specification functions as *optional context*, *i.e.* matching the embedding specification portion of the production is optional.

Y-grammars suffer from a lack of *required context*. That is, if a portion of the graph *must* exist for the rewrite to occur but it is left unchanged, that portion must occur in the left-hand side and again in the right-hand side of the production being applied, effectively being removed and then reinserted by the rewrite. For the embedding to be correct, all elements connected to this portion must also be included in both the left- and right-hand sides, and so on. X-grammars solves this problem. X-productions are written around an X, with left-hand side, right-hand side, and optional context as in Y-productions, but with required context written in the bottom part of the X.

Δ-productions have required and optional context as specified by their context regions and *-groups, respectively, and therefore Δ-GRAMMARS encompass Y- and X-grammars. Δ-productions also have application conditions in the form of guards and *forbidden context* (restrictions).

9.3 Clients and Servers

The purpose of this paper is to show how graph grammars, specifically the Δ model, can be used to specify solutions to a range of problems in software engineering. Of particular interest here are problems involving the specification of concurrent systems and languages. We now turn our attention to showing how three such problems — the client/server problem, the dynamic dining philosophers problem and a semantics for the concurrent language Actors — can be specified in Δ.

In this section we focus on the client/server problem.

Concurrent problems intuitively lend themselves to graphical representations, such as

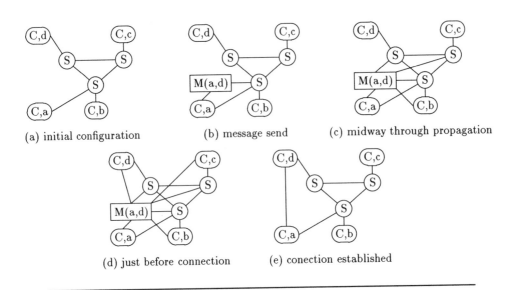

(a) initial configuration   (b) message send   (c) midway through propagation

(d) just before connection   (e) conection established

Figure 9.2
Client-Server Example: Making the Connection

a representation of processes as nodes in a graph and communication links as edges between nodes. Graphical representations easily capture the two-dimensional relationship between the flow of data between processes and the flow of control within processes.

A Δ-specification of a concurrent problem solution is composed of a representation of the state of the solution program as a graph and a representation of state transitions as graph transformations in the form of Δ-productions.

Here is an informal specification of the client/server problem:

> Consider a message based system with an arbitrary number of nameservers and clients. The number of nameservers and clients may change dynamically. Nameservers may be connected together in any arbitrary topology and clients are attached to exactly one nameserver each. A nameserver may take requests from any of its clients and may make requests for services to one or more other nameservers. A client may make a request to its nameserver to be connected to another client in order to exchange data. The nameserver problem is to allow clients to connect to other clients in order to facilitate this exchange.

In more detail, a graphical representation of an example system configuration (state) is shown in Figure 9.2(a). Client (C, a) (*i.e.* the client with attribute a) requests connection to the client with attribute d. Such a client does exist in the system – (C, d), but neither (C, a) or its nameserver know this because (C, d) is attached to a remote nameserver. The connection is requested by sending a message to client (C, a)'s nameserver (Figure 9.2(b)), which then propagates the request through the system until it reaches (C, d) (Figures 9.2(c) and (d)). When this client is identified, the connection is established (Figure 9.2(e)).

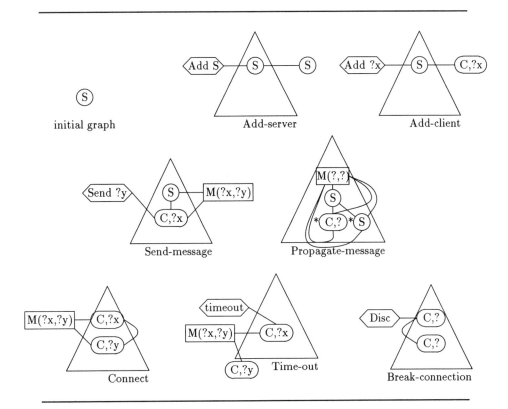

Figure 9.3
Client-Server Example: The Δ-specification

A problem of this complexity requires many levels of interaction. There is the *network* level, where clients and servers interact by propagating messages and establishing connections; there is a *global* level where external events, such as human interaction or node failure, triggers the addition or deletion of clients and servers; and there is a *machine* level, where computation internal to clients and servers occurs, possibly causing message sends, connection requests, and even timeouts and disconnections. We intend to specify only the network level here, ignoring the details of the other levels. In Section 9.4 we will explain how multiple levels and their interactions can be specified. Hexagonal nodes (triggers, explained in Section 9.4.1) will specify an interface point between levels.

The Δ-specification of the network level is shown in Figure 9.3. The initial configuration is just a single server with no clients. Δ-productions specify graph transformations that add clients to servers, add servers to servers, connect existing servers (so the server configuration can be more than just tree-like), and send connection requests from clients to servers. These productions are all straightforward.

The `Propagate-message` production propagates a message to all clients and servers connected to a particular client. Despite its seeming complexity, it is actually very simple:

- The client C with attribute a has sent a message indicating that it wants to connect to a client with attribute b. This message has reached server S.

- Server S has other servers and clients in its neighborhood.

- The effect of the production is to propagate the message to all clients and servers which have not already received it (the restriction ensures that clients and servers do not receive the message more than once). This is an example of the specification writer imposing a constraint on the implementation, and is necessary because an arbitrary topology of servers can include cycles.

- Notice the *-groups (one containing the (C,?)-node and its incident edges, the other containing an S-node and its incident edges) must match maximally, meaning that the message is propagated to *all* adjacent clients and servers that have not already received it.

The transformation that establishes a connection and halts all further message forwarding once a matching client has been found is represented by the production **Connect**. The unification in the graph matching phase of the rewriting ensures that the attribute of the message and that of the client match. The message is in the retraction; this indicates that the message vertex (and therefore all edges incident on it) are automatically removed as part of the connection establishment process. The actual connection is shown in the insertion part of the production.

Application of the **Break-connection** production produces the obvious results. Application of this production is triggered by a different level, either an internal event in one of the clients or an external (system) event.

The final production, **Time-out**, implements the requirement that if, after some amount of time, the match has not succeeded, the client (or an external event) might abort the connection request. The restriction of **Time-out** that the connection must not be about to succeed is placed for efficiency and to demonstrate the utility of restriction regions.

Note that many clients can be requesting connections at the same time (*i.e.* there is no restriction on the number of active messages in the system). It may be useful to restrict a client from requesting more than one connection at a time; placing a restriction on **Send-message** would accomplish this.

9.4 Dynamic Dining Philosophers

An informal specification of the static dining philosophers problem is:

> Consider a number of philosophers sitting at a table, with a single fork between each adjacent pair. Each philosopher spends his time at the table thinking (meditating) for some finite time and eating for some finite time, infinitely alternating between the two states. When a philosopher wants to start eating after he has been thinking for some time, he must pick up both adjacent forks (he is eating spaghetti). Since there is contention for each fork by the two philosophers it is between, the problem is to specify the system in such a way that there is no deadlock (a state in which no philosopher can eat).

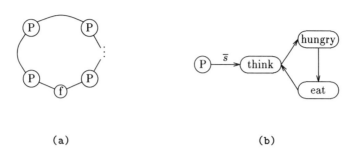

(a)   (b)

Figure 9.4
Two views of a dining philosophers system. The global view (a) expresses only the interaction
between philosophers while the internal view (b) shows the state of each individual philosopher.

We will extend this to the dynamic problem in Section 9.4.3.

The state of a solution program can be naturally expressed using a graph representing
the status of the table at a given time. P-nodes represent philosophers seated at the table
and f-nodes represent forks that are on the table and therefore available for use by an
adjacent philosopher. There is at most one fork between any two philosophers. A sample
state graph is illustrated in Figure 9.4(a).

Each philosopher is in one of three states; he is either thinking, hungry (waiting to
eat), or eating. This is also naturally expressed in graphical notation, as shown in
Figure 9.4(b). Each P-node has a finite state machine with those three states and an
$\bar{s}$-edge pointing to the current state of the philosopher.

This view of the state provides a nice modular division of the solution of the dining
philosopher problem. Dividing the functionality of the system in this way allows us to
graphically specify the interaction between philosophers separate from the state of an
individual philosopher. Doing so allows the system to be examined at different levels.
At the global level, philosophers pick up their forks, hold them a while, and put them
down. At the local level, a philosopher thinks for a while, gets hungry, and eats.

Remember that we divided the solution of the client-server problem into separate levels
in a similar way. For Δ to be useful for specifying solutions to concurrent problems,
we must be able to specify solutions in a systematic manner, dividing problems into
subproblems, building Δ-specifications for each subproblem separately, and combining
these specifications to provide a complete, modular solution to the main problem. Such
a solution would be able to be modified and upgraded by adding new modules or by
modifying specific modules without affecting other modules.

9.4.1   Platforms and Triggers

Although no one would argue that a program couldn't be written as one large unit, it
is much easier to write and to understand if it is divided into modules, each a part of

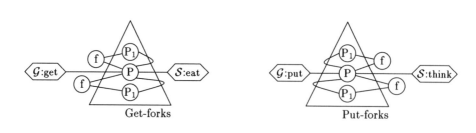

Figure 9.5
The $\mathcal{G}$ platform, representing interactions between philosophers.

some logical partition of the problem. Likewise, specifying a program in Δ is easier if the main problem is divided into smaller, more manageable subproblems, and a set of Δ-productions is developed for each of these subproblems. These independent sets of Δ-productions are called platforms and the interface between them is provided by triggers. A trigger is a node with a special shape that provides the interface between platforms (we use hexagons to represent triggers). An *input trigger* is a trigger that appears in the precondition of every Δ-production in the platform. A platform is *called* by placement of the platform's input triggers into the graph[2]. *Output triggers* are triggers that appear in the insertions of Δ-productions in the platform, indicating the platform *calling* another platform.

Since the labels of nodes in the graph can be tuples of arbitrary structure, the labels of triggers in a platform can contain variables. Parameters are passed to a platform by unification of the label of the trigger in the graph with the labels of triggers in the platform.

The placement of a trigger in the graph does not guarantee that a useful transformation of the graph will occur at the location of the trigger. The platform is called by placement of the trigger but elements isomorphic to the rest of the elements in the preconditions of some of the platform's Δ-productions must exist (and elements matching the corresponding restrictions must not exist) in order for the Δ-productions to be applicable.

9.4.2   A Modular Solution to the Dining Philosophers Problem

The Δ-productions to specify the dining philosophers system are broken into two platforms accordingly. The $\mathcal{G}$ platform, shown in Figure 9.5, performs the global graph transformations, *i.e.* picking up and putting down the forks. The $\mathcal{S}$ platform, shown in Figure 9.6, performs the local transformations, *i.e.* each philosopher's state changes. The two communicate by placing parameterized triggers into the graph. The shape (hexagonal) indicates that the node is a trigger and the label contains a key, $\mathcal{G}$ or $\mathcal{S}$, indicating

---

[2]This is using the function analogy of functional languages. To use an actors system analogy, we would say, "A message is sent to a platform by placing the platform's input trigger into the graph."

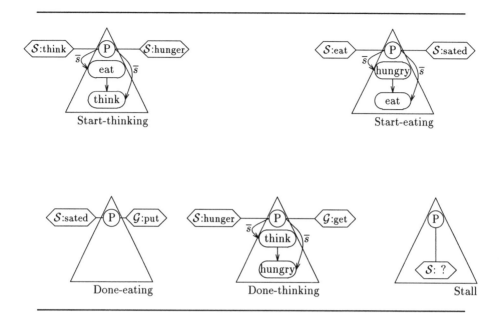

Figure 9.6
The S platform, representing state changes for an individual philosopher.

the platform being called and an actual parameter, *e.g.* get and think, indicating the action to be taken. The two platforms must communicate since some state changes cause a global action, *e.g.* transition to the hungry state requires that the philosopher try to pick up the forks, and some global actions cause a state change, *e.g.* picking up the forks allows the philosopher to eat.

The Stall production models the need for arbitrary time delays. It can always be applied in place of any of the other Δ-productions in the S platform but does nothing. Without this Δ-production, a philosopher would start eating and then immediately indicate that he is done eating and put down the forks. Likewise, thinking would take no time. The Stall production can be applied any finite number of times before another Δ-production in the S platform is applied, so that thinking and eating can take arbitrary time. The guarantee of fairness of production application in Δ [6] ensures that the Stall production can never be applied an infinite number of times.

The specification is deadlock-free since picking up both forks is an atomic action, *i.e.* at any time a philosopher is eating or one of his neighbors is eating, and fairness ensures that an eating philosopher eventually relinquishes his forks.

9.4.3   Stepwise Refinement of the Specification

Suppose we now extend the problem, making the dining philosophers system dynamic, *i.e.* allowing new philosophers to enter and sit at the table and allowing existing philosophers to leave the table. Since this affects the global state of the table, but not the internal

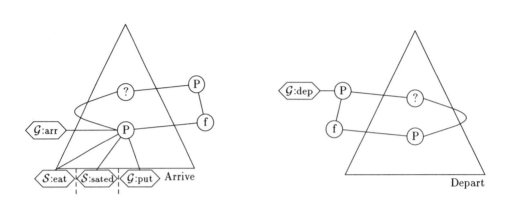

Figure 9.7
New productions to allow philosophers to enter and leave.

state of philosophers in the system, updating the specification only requires updating the
$\mathcal{G}$ platform.

The two Δ-productions that represent philosophers arriving at and leaving the system
are in Figure 9.7. These are in the $\mathcal{G}$ platform, since a $\mathcal{G}$ trigger is the only trigger that
appears in the precondition of each Δ-production. Notice that, except for the triggers,
the Δ-productions are mirror images of one another. This fits the intuitive notion that
leaving should be the opposite of arriving. **Arrive** inserts a new philosopher and fork
into the graph. The restrictions make sure that the fork is not placed adjacent to a
philosopher that is holding two forks (otherwise, when he replaces his forks there would
be two forks between a single pair of philosophers). **Depart** removes a philosopher and
a fork from the graph. It cannot be applied until there is at least one fork adjacent to
the departing philosopher, *i.e.* until it or one of its neighbors has relinquished its forks.

It is interesting to note a certain 'polymorphism' in the productions shown in Figure 9.7. When a new philosopher arrives, he must choose to sit next to a philosopher
who is not eating (call this philosopher s); however, one of s's neighbors may well be
eating. In our configuration, this means that s may not have an incident **eat**, **sated** or
put trigger. However, it does not require that s be adjacent to any forks (its neighbors
may be eating). The '?' match-anything variable marker is useful here, as it allows s
to be adjacent to either a fork or another philosopher, and guarantees that the correct
configuration will be maintained.

Similarly, when leaving, the departing philosopher must take one fork with him, but
need not care if his other neighbor is a fork or not (his other neighbor is busy eating).

9.5 Δ as Support for Concurrent Languages

In previous sections, we used Δ to specify solutions to problems in concurrency. In this section, we demonstrate how Δ is useful for specifying entire languages. Although Δ is powerful enough to specify any language, it is clear that it is more useful for specifying languages with a graphical intuition, such as concurrent languages and object-based languages. We illustrate this by presenting a specification for a most general object-based concurrent language, Actors [1]. First we briefly describe actor languages. Then we specify the actor language by giving a Δ-Grammar and initial graph that define the behavior of the language.

9.5.1 Overview of Actor Systems

An actor system, an actor program in execution, consists of a set of *actors* and a set of pending *tasks*. Each actor is a mail *address* and a *behavior function* mapping tasks to activities that the actor can perform. Each task is a pending message. It consists of an *essence* (called a "tag" in [1]) that distinguishes it from other tasks that might otherwise be identical, a *target* (the actor to which it must eventually be delivered), and a *communication* (the data being transmitted).

An *event* is the reception of a message by an actor. The task's target must match the actor's address. The task is removed from the set of pending tasks and the actor's behavior function is used to calculate the rest of the change that the event causes to the actor system: adding new tasks (by sending messages), adding new actors (by creating new addresses and giving each of them an initial behavior), and specifying the next behavior of the current actor (or more correctly, a new actor with the same mail address).

An event is atomic. The actor and task involved provide all the data to calculate the event's effect on the actor system. Both are deleted (although the actor is always replaced by another actor with the same address, and this is usually described as being the next behavior of the same actor) and new actors and tasks to add to the system state are computed functionally. Though formally events are atomic, any realization has to implement them as sets of discrete activities. There is a lot of internal concurrency possible because the model does not specify a sequence on these activities. There is also external concurrency, events can be processed in parallel so long as no actor is used more than once at any given time.

9.5.2 An Actor Language

In this section, we present a most general actor language (hereafter referred to simply as *actors*) that we are specifying, based on [1]. Throughout the remainder of this discussion, we use the following abbreviations:

n	name of any kind
B	behavior name
L	list of acquaintance names
S	statement

The abstract syntax for actors is:

Prog	$\Rightarrow$	B $\mid$ *Beh* *Prog*	[Behavior name and list of Beh]
Beh	$\Rightarrow$	B L L S	[Behavior definition]
L	$\Rightarrow$	ϵ $\mid$ n L	[List of actual/formal param names]
B	$\Rightarrow$	n	
S	$\Rightarrow$	ϵ	[no op]
		$\mid$ S S	[concurrent eval]
		$\mid$ n B L	[create actor]
		$\mid$ n n S S	[conditional]
		$\mid$ n L	[send message]
		$\mid$ B L	[becomes]

By the first production, an actor program is a single behavior name and a list of behavior definitions. Execution begins with a single actor called the receptionist with initial behavior as indicated by this behavior name. The receptionist is known, by definition, to the outside world so that the actor system can receive messages (*i.e.* input) from the outside. The initial receptionist behavior has no parameters so that the receptionist is instantiated with that behavior (without needing further data) to form the starting state for the actor program.

Each behavior definition is tagged with a name and has two lists of parameters and a statement. The first parameter list (elements called *creation acquaintances*) names the data received from an actor's creator when the actor is created. The second parameter list (elements called *message acquaintances*) names the data accompanying a message reception. The statement is the *body* of the behavior that is executed when an event occurs, *i.e.* a message is received.

Parameter passing is through a positional copying of data, where the length of the actual and formal parameter lists must match. All data are acquaintances with scope of one behavior instantiation. Besides creation and message acquaintances, there is the special acquaintance "**self**" that refers to the actor's own mail address, and there are *local acquaintances* bound by **create** statements to newly created actors.

Concrete syntax for actor programs is:

- **Receptionist** B; *Beh* ... *Beh* — A list of behavior definitions, one of which is designated as the initial behavior of the receptionist;

- **Beh** B := [(L) (L) S] — A behavior name is bound to a behavior. The statement is executed in the context of the two sets of formal parameter names;

- ϵ — The NULL statement does nothing;

- $S; S$ — Concurrent evaluation of several statements;

- **create** n = $B(L)$ — Instantiate a new actor with behavior B and actual parameters L and bind it to a local acquaintance name n;

- **if** $n_1 = n_2$ **then** S_1 **else** S_2 — Check whether two acquaintances are equal and branch accordingly;

- **send** n (L) — Send message L to the actor address stored in acquaintance n;

- **becomes** $B(L)$ — Specify the next behavior of the actor.

A-nodes	actor mail addresses. Exactly one per actor.
$\mathcal{X}$-nodes	execution contexts. Exactly one per behavior instantiation.
acq edges	named edges including **self**. Directed from $\mathcal{X}$-nodes to A-nodes.
$\overline{m}$-edges	messages, message acquaintance parameter passing.
$\overline{p}$-edges	context instantiation, creation acquaintance parameter passing.
$\overline{b}$-edges	behavior, threads of control for startup and statement execution.
$\overline{c}$-edges	threads of control to complete copying of one parameter list.

Figure 9.8
Elements in the state graph of an actor program.

To simplify presentation, we ignore error conditions and present a specification for only correct actor programs.

9.5.3 The Specification of Actors

The specification of actors consists of two parts:

- The *state graph* representing the state of the actor program, and
- The twelve productions (shown in Figures 9.9 and 9.10) that specify rules for transforming the state graph according to the actor execution model. Performing these transformations executes the actor program.

The initial state graph is a simple compilation of the abstract syntax tree of an actor program. Uses of behavior names (by **create** and **becomes** statements) are linked to the definitions of those behaviors and nodes representing the receptionist are created.

Each actor in the system is represented in the state graph by an A-node (its mail address), a set of $\overline{m}$-edges (its mailbag contents), and a set of $\mathcal{X}$-nodes (one for each message received and, hence, behavior instantiated). Since a **becomes** statement can be executed concurrently with other statements, a single actor can be executing several behaviors at once.

Each execution of a behavior by an actor is called an *execution context* and is represented by an $\mathcal{X}$-node and a set of outdirected edges. When a behavior is instantiated (by a **becomes** or **create** statement) there are three edges: a **self**-edge which is an acquaintance usable by the code that also gives the actor address from which a message must be received, a $\overline{b}$-edge recording the behavior the context must exhibit, and a $\overline{p}$-edge recording the actual parameters. $\overline{c}$-edges are used to control the copying of parameters[3]. The elements that appear in an actor state graph are summarized in Figure 9.8.

Execution of an actor program is performed by transformations of the state graph as specified by Δ-productions. The transformation rules represented by these Δ-productions are applied to the state graph to control interpretation of the actor system. The execution is explained in two parts. First, the way that parameters are passed so that an actor can start executing a behavior and receive a message is explained, and second, the execution of the six kinds of statements is described.

---

[3]The receptionist starts with two outdirected edges the first time. There are no actual parameters in the system and no formal parameters in its initial behavior definition, so the step of copying data to instantiate it is omitted. Thus the edge recording actual parameters is not used.

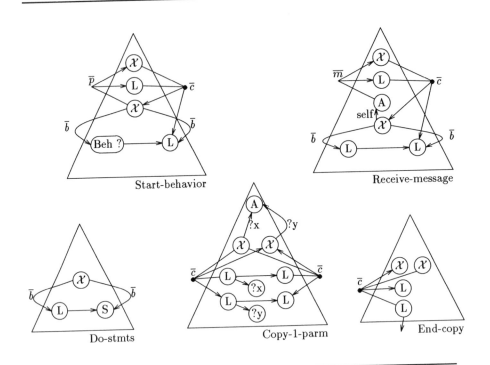

Figure 9.9
Starting a behavior and receiving a message.

Actor Behavior Startup   The Δ-productions specifying the rules to startup a behavior are shown in Figure 9.9. We describe each of the transformations they represent
individually.

  Start-behavior — The $\bar{p}$-edge indicating instantiation of a behavior is removed and
a $\bar{c}$-edge is inserted to control copying of parameters (of creation acquaintances). A
$\bar{c}$-edge has two sources and two targets. Its sources are an L-node giving the list of actual
parameter names yet to be copied and an execution context giving values for each of
these names. Its targets are an L-node giving the list of formal parameter names yet to
be copied and an execution context that will receive values for each of these names. The
$\bar{b}$-edge is advanced. Parameter copying is done concurrently with continued execution
controlled by the $\bar{b}$-edge.

  Copy-1-parm — The $\bar{c}$-edge is advanced one name down each of the parameter lists
and a new acquaintance edge is created in the receiving execution context. The new edge
is labeled with the name in the formal parameter list and its target is the acquaintance
of the actual parameter of the old execution context.

  End-copy — Removes the $\bar{c}$-edge when all parameters have been copied.

Receive-message — Removes one $\overline{m}$-edge (representing a message in the actor's mailbag). A $\overline{c}$-edge is inserted to copy the actual parameters (in the form of acquaintances) in the message to the receiving behavior's (execution context's) formal parameters (message acquaintances). The $\overline{b}$-edge is advanced so that execution of the body of the behavior is done concurrently with parameter copying.

Do-stmts — Advances the $\overline{b}$-edge to begin execution of the body of the behavior.

Statement Execution Productions representing statement execution are given in Figure 9.10. We now explain the transformations they represent individually. Each $\overline{b}$-edge represents a separate thread of execution in the behavior.

Null — the $\overline{b}$-edge is retracted. This terminates a thread of execution, reducing the amount of concurrency.

Concurrent-eval — execution proceeds concurrently on both sub-statements, each controlled by a separate $\overline{b}$-edge.

Send — the $\overline{b}$-edge is removed and an $\overline{m}$-edge is placed in the graph, representing delivery of a message to the actor pointed to by the named acquaintance. Delivery of messages is immediate, but arrival-order nondeterminism is achieved because delivered messages are not queued. Reception (*i.e.* arrival) may be in any (fair) order among messages that have been delivered to an actor.

To apply the **Send** production an acquaintance edge of the correct name must exist pointing from the $\mathcal{X}$-node to the target actor's A-node. If this edge has not yet been created, application of this production is blocked until parameter copying (of both creation and message acquaintances) has proceeded far enough. A similar situation exists with the **If-true** and **If-false** productions.

If-true — tests for equality of addresses. The production is only applicable if both of the named acquaintances point to the same actor address. The $\overline{b}$-edge controlling execution then proceeds down the "then" branch.

If-false — the production is only applicable if the named acquaintances point to different actor addresses. The two A-nodes cannot match to the same graph node. If it applies, execution continues down the "else" branch.

Create — create a new actor address and an execution context to instantiate the first behavior for that actor. Also create a $\overline{p}$-edge to pass actual parameters to the new actor. Bind the new actor to a named acquaintance and continue execution of the current context concurrently with the new context.

Adding the new acquaintance to the current execution context rather than creating a new execution context (to extend by the acquaintance) has two results. First, the name is visible outside the scope of the **create** statement; the scope of the **create**-bound name is the entire behavior. Thus the code fragment

```
create e = behavior(f); create f = behavior(e)
```

makes sense. Two actors are created and each is passed the other as a parameter. Neither will be able to finish initializing until the other has been created, but this is not a problem. All acquaintance names, **create**-bound names and formal parameters, must differ from each other in the scope of a behavior definition.

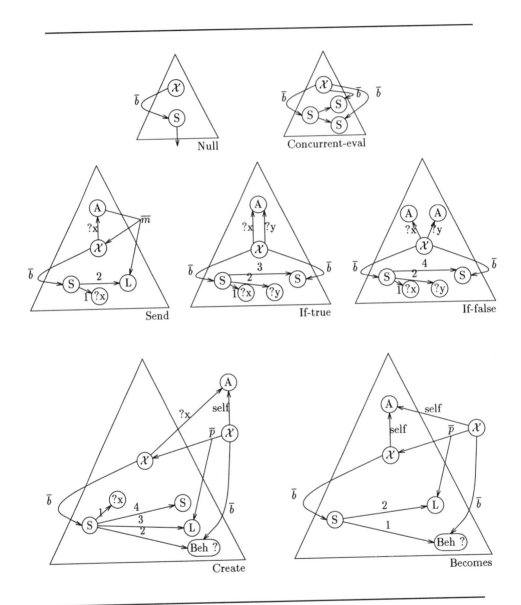

Figure 9.10
Actor Statement Execution.

The second consequence of handling **create** this way, is that the one-to-one correspondence between execution contexts ($\mathcal{X}$-nodes) and behavior instantiations is maintained.

Becomes — instantiate a new behavior for the current actor and begin execution in that context.

The specification is lazy and, as such, exhibits a high degree of concurrency. Parameter copying from the creation of an actor, parameter copying from the receipt of a message, and execution of the statements in the body of a behavior are all done concurrently.

9.5.4   Example–A Bank Account in Actors

As an example, we present a simple bank account in actors. To keep the example easy to understand, we present selected portions of the program and its execution in detail, while glossing over other portions. Consider the following actor program fragment (decorated with concrete syntax to make it easier to read):

```
Receptionist cust;
Beh cust := {customer's behavior}
Beh acct := [(bal, wd, dep) (req, amt)
    if req = wd
      become acct(bal - amt, wd, dep)
    else
      if req = dep
        become acct(bal + amt, wd, dep)
      else
        become acct(bal, wd, dep) ]
```

There are two behaviors, a customer (**cust**) and an account (**acct**). The customer is the receptionist and, although its behavior is not specified, creates bank accounts and withdraws from or deposits to them. The customer might interact with many other actors as well, but we consider it only as it interacts with its bank account(s).

To keep the example manageable, we have made some simplifying assumptions. The bank account does naive deposits and withdrawals. For example, it does not check for error conditions, such as overdrafts or invalid transactions. Also, we use + and − arithmetic expressions instead of implementing arithmetic using actors (see [5] for details).

Figure 9.11 illustrates the state graphs during the processing of a withdrawal transaction to this bank account. The clouds in the graphs represent parts of the graph that are unimportant to the execution at that step and are omitted to make the presentation simpler.

When a new account is created, it is sent three creation acquaintances, a balance (**bal**), a deposit actor (**dep**), and a withdrawal actor (**wd**). The deposit and withdrawal actors are used to identify transactions. The creation acquaintances are copied by applying **Start-behavior** once, **Copy-1-parm** for each acquaintance, and **End-copy** once. At this point, the bank account is awaiting a message receipt (a withdrawal or deposit transaction) and the state graph looks like Figure 9.11(a).

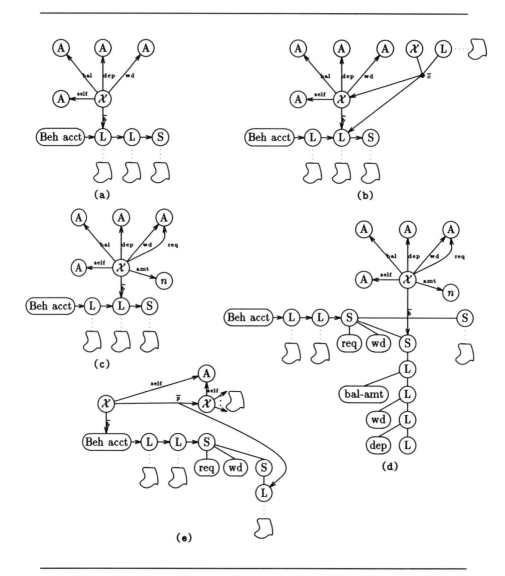

Figure 9.11
State graphs of bank account actor example.

When a withdrawal message is received, `Receive-message` is applied and the state graph looks like Figure 9.11(b). This triggers the application of `Copy-1-parm` for each message acquaintance followed by application of `End-copy` once. At this point, the state graph looks like Figure 9.11(c).

`Do-stmts` is applied, advancing the $\bar{b}$-edge to the S-node and triggering application of `If-true`. Since the request is a withdrawal (the `req` and `wd` acquaintances are the same actor), the $\bar{b}$-edge advances to the *then* clause. The state graph looks like Figure 9.11(d).

`Becomes` is applied, creating a new account (complete with a new execution context, X-node). The state graph looks like Figure 9.11(e).

`Start-Behavior` is applied to start the new behavior. The creation acquaintances are copied and the account actor awaits a withdrawal or deposit message (unless one has already been sent).

This is just a fragment of the execution of such an actor system. There could be many customers and accounts executing and interacting concurrently.

9.5.5   Relation to Actor Grammars

The idea of using graph grammars as a way of describing actor systems has also been investigated by Janssens and Rozenberg [12] who developed a formalism known as Actor Grammars for defining the behaviour of actor systems.

Actor Grammars consider the internal behaviour of an actor to be 'atomic'. Thus every event (in the sense of [1]) in an actor system is handled by a single monolithic production. While this is 'correct' semantically there is an important aspect of actor systems which is ignored in this formulation. Actors are meant to have internal concurrency, *i.e.* an actor can be processing many messages concurrently. As soon as an actor's 'next behavior' is known it should be allowed to process the next message, and not have to wait for completion of the processing of the current message (which could take arbitrarily long). This concept of an actor effectively processing several messages simultaneously (and therefore having several active behaviors at a given time) seems to be missing from the Actor Grammar formulation.

A second difference is that in the Δ solution there are a small fixed set of productions and the actor programs are compiled into 'state machines' which 'drive' the application of these productions, while in the Actor Grammar solution the grammar itself must be modified each time an actor behaviour is modified, deleted or added.

9.6   Conclusions

We have demonstrated the usefulness of graph grammars in specifying concurrent programs and languages. Using Δ-GRAMMARS, concurrent programs and languages can be specified in a simple, intuitive notation. Platforms allow us to describe any level of a specification without considering other (possibly lower) levels while triggers allow us to describe where a level interacts with other levels. With these tools, a specification can be as high-level or as low-level as the specification writer desires.

We illustrated the technique with three examples: the client-server problem, the dining philosophers example, and the object-based concurrent language Actors.

References

[1]   Gul Agha. *ACTORS: A Model of Concurrent Computation in Distributed Systems.* M.I.T. Press, Cambridge, Mass., 1986.

[2]   H. Ehrig and A. Habel. Graph grammars with application conditions. In G. Rozenberg and A. Salomaa, editors, *The Book of L.* Springer-Verlag, Berlin, 1986.

[3]   Hartmut Ehrig. Introduction to the algebraic theory of graph grammars (a survey). In Volker Claus, Hartmut Ehrig, and Grzegorz Rozenberg, editors, *Graph Grammars and their Application to Computer Science and Biology, LNCS 73*, pages 1–69, Heidelberg, 1979. Springer-Verlag.

[4]   Hartmut Ehrig. Tutorial introduction to the algebraic approach of graph-grammars. In Hartmut Ehrig, Manfred Nagl, Grzegorz Rozenberg, and Azriel Rosenfeld, editors, *Graph Grammars and their Application to Computer Science, LNCS 291*, pages 3–14. Springer-Verlag, 1987.

[5]   Steven K. Goering. *A Graph-Grammar Approach to Concurrent Programming.* PhD thesis, University of Illinois at Urbana-Champaign, 1990. Tech. report UIUCDCS-R-90-1576.

[6]   Steven K. Goering, Simon M. Kaplan, and Joseph P. Loyall. Theoretical properties of Δ. Book in preparation.

[7]   H. Göttler. Semantical description by two-level graph-grammars for quasihierarchical graphs. In *Proc. 'Workshop WG 78 on Graphtheoretical Concepts in Comp. Science', Applied Computer Science, 13*, Munich, 1979. Hanser-Verlag.

[8]   Herbert Göttler. Attributed graph grammars for graphics. In Hartmut Ehrig, Manfred Nagl, and Grzegorz Rozenberg, editors, *Graph Grammars and their Application to Computer Science, LNCS 153*, pages 130–142. Springer-Verlag, 1982.

[9]   Herbert Göttler. Graph grammars and diagram editing. In Hartmut Ehrig, Manfred Nagl, Grzegorz Rozenberg, and Azriel Rosenfeld, editors, *Graph Grammars and their Application to Computer Science, LNCS 291*, pages 216–231. Springer-Verlag, 1987.

[10]   Annegret Habel. *Hyperedge Replacement: Grammars and Languages.* PhD thesis, University of Bremen, 1989.

[11]   Annegret Habel and Hans-Jorg Kreowski. May we introduce to you: Hyperedge replacement. In Hartmut Ehrig, Manfred Nagl, Grzegorz Rozenberg, and Azriel Rosenfeld, editors, *Graph Grammars and their Application to Computer Science, LNCS 291*, pages 15–26. Springer-Verlag, 1987.

[12]   D. Janssens and Grzegorz Rozenberg. Basic notions of actor grammars. In Hartmut Ehrig, Manfred Nagl, Grzegorz Rozenberg, and Azriel Rosenfeld, editors, *Graph Grammars and their Application to Computer Science, LNCS 291*, pages 280–298. Springer-Verlag, 1987.

[13]   Dirk Janssens and Grzegorz Rozenberg. Graph grammars with node-label control and rewriting. In Hartmut Ehrig, Manfred Nagl, and Grzegorz Rozenberg, editors, *Graph Grammars and their Application to Computer Science, LNCS 153*, pages 186–205. Springer-Verlag, 1982.

[14]   Simon M. Kaplan. Foundations of visual languages for object-based concurrent programming. In Gul Agha, Peter Wegner, and Akinori Yonezawa, editors, *Object-Based Concurrent Programming.* Addison-Wesley, to appear 1989.

[15]   Joseph P. Loyall, Simon M. Kaplan, and Steven K. Goering. Δ working papers. Technical Report UIUCDCS-R-90-1597, University of Illinois Department of Computer Science, 1990.

[16]   Michael Main and Grzegorz Rozenberg. Fundamentals of edge-label controlled graph grammars. In Hartmut Ehrig, Manfred Nagl, Grzegorz Rozenberg, and Azriel Rosenfeld, editors, *Graph Grammars and their Application to Computer Science, LNCS 291*, pages 411–426. Springer-Verlag, 1987.

[17]   Francesco Parisi-Presicce, Hartmut Ehrig, and Ugo Montanari. Graph rewriting with unification and composition. In Hartmut Ehrig, Manfred Nagl, Grzegorz Rozenberg, and Azriel Rosenfeld, editors, *Graph Grammars and their Application to Computer Science, LNCS 291*, pages 496–514. Springer-Verlag, 1987.

[18]   Grzegorz Rozenberg. An introduction to the nlc way of rewriting graphs. In Hartmut Ehrig, Manfred Nagl, Grzegorz Rozenberg, and Azriel Rosenfeld, editors, *Graph Grammars and their Application to Computer Science, LNCS 291*, pages 55–66. Springer-Verlag, 1987.

10   Interaction Abstract Machines

Jean-Marc Andreoli, Paolo Ciancarini, and Remo Pareschi

Linear Objects (*LO*) is an abstract linguistic model for concurrent computation whose theoretical background is given by Linear Logic, a logic recently introduced by Jean-Yves Girard to provide a theoretical account for the notion of *action*. In this paper, we characterize *LO* computations in terms of *Interaction Abstract Machines* (IAMs), in the same vein of such metaphors as the Chemical Abstract Machine. The main point about IAMs is in allowing interactions among independent, locally defined subsystems — a crucial requirement for capturing the global behavior of open systems.

10.1   Introduction

The purpose of this paper is of characterizing computations in open systems — i.e. systems obtained via the interaction of autonomous, heterogeneous components — in terms of *Interaction Abstract Machines* (IAMs), in the same vein of such metaphors as the Chemical Abstract Machines (CHAMs) [6]. The main point about IAMs is in allowing interactions among independent, locally defined subsystems — a crucial requirement for capturing the global behavior of open systems. Thus, IAMs make a step forward with respect to CHAMs in that they move from pure "chemistry" to an elementary form of "socio-biology", concerning the interactions of certain simple organisms (agents whose structure is given by multisets of active atomic components). IAMs may be seen as a necessary, intermediate step in going towards a comprehensive "sociology" and "psychology" of open systems, which will be capable of capturing also higher-level aspects in the behavior of software agents [12, 15, 21].

The rest of the paper is structured as follows. Section 10.2 introduces the metaphor of IAMs, based on a naive view of wave mechanics; indeed, our societies are so simple that their behavior can be captured in a totally mechanistic fashion. Section 10.3 introduces the most direct formal counterpart of IAMs, incarnated in the computational model of Linear Objects (*LO*) [3], and provides, in terms of two *LO* programs, two programming examples of IAMs. Section 10.4 compares our approach with related work. Finally, Section 10.5 concludes the paper by discussing future directions of research.

10.2   Interaction Abstract Machines

The behavior of a IAM results of the concurrent activities of a system of communicating, autonomous, agents.

Here, we first show the case of single-agent IAMs, corresponding to systems behaving in a totally solipsistic manner, in that the global behavior of a system of this kind strictly coincides with the local one characterizing the single agent which lives in it. We then consider the general case of multiagent systems, corresponding to IAMs characterized by genuine social interaction.

$p \,\text{⅋}\, a \,\text{∘−}\, q \,\text{⅋}\, r \,\text{⅋}\, s$
$r \,\text{⅋}\, u \,\text{∘−}\, t$

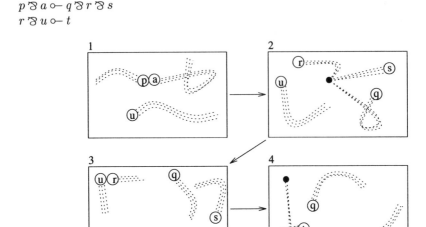

Figure 10.1
A single agent Interaction Abstract Machine

10.2.1   Single-agent IAMs: Tight Integration

In a single-agent IAM, the state of the agent is represented as a multiset of resources. It may evolve according to laws of the following form, also called "methods":

$$A_1 \,\text{⅋} \cdots \text{⅋}\, A_n \,\text{∘−}\, B_1 \,\text{⅋} \cdots \text{⅋}\, B_m$$

$A_1, \ldots, A_n$ and $B_1, \ldots, B_m$ are two (non-empty) multisets of resources, respectively called the "head" (on the left-hand side) and the "body" (on the right-hand side) of the method. The symbols ⅋ (read "par") and ∘− (read "become") are primitive operators of the model.

A method can be triggered by the agent if its state *contains* all the resources in the head of the method. In this case, the agent may perform a transition to a new state obtained by *replacing* in the old state the resources of the head with those of the body of the method. The remaining part of the state is left unchanged by the transition.

The different internal activities of the agent may be performed in parallel. In fact, if the state of the agent contains two *disjoint* submultisets of resources which match the heads of two methods, then these two methods can be triggered simultaneously. On the other hand, when two methods with *non disjoint* heads are applicable to a given state of the agent, they cannot both be applied at the same time, and there is no way, in the model, to control which one will effectively be applied: method selection is assumed to be totally fair.

In fact, a single-agent IAM can be seen as an elementary *blackboard system* [18]. The state of the agent captures the content of the blackboard at any time; the methods represent the different knowledge sources which interact through the blackboard: the head of a method specifies resources which are taken from the blackboard; conversely, the body specifies resources which are output to the blackboard. The communication via the blackboard is totally asynchronous: in fact, there is no requirement that, when a method outputs a resource to the blackboard, another method must necessarily make use of it.

10.2.1.1   The IAM metaphor in the Single-Agent Case   In the IAM metaphor, the state of the (single) agent is represented as a set of particles evolving within a determined (computational) space. Each particle represents a resource, and we assume that the particles are in a perpetual "Brownian" motion, so that they may randomly collide together. Methods in this metaphor are represented by laws of physics, governing particle interaction during the collisions: in a collision, some particles (those corresponding to the resources in the head of a method) disappear, while new particles (given by the resources in the body of the method) are released. In fact, in the single-agent case considered here, the IAM metaphor is completely analogous to that of the CHAM, where the evolution laws are interpreted in terms of chemical reactions instead of particle interactions.

Graphically, the space where the particles evolve is represented as a rectangular box, and each particle is itself represented as a circle inside this space, labeled with the name of the its associated resource. The random motion of the particles is represented by a trail (dashed lines) behind the particle and collision points are marked by a small black disk. A sample evolution of a single-agent IAM, which consists of a sequence of collision-replacements of particles, is illustrated by the sequence of diagrams of Fig. 10.1. In Diagram 1, the resources p and a, which form the head of the first method, collide, and in Diagram 2 they have been replaced by the resources q, r, s of the body of the method. Then in Diagram 3, the resource r just released collides with the resource u which was already there. At that time, the second method applies and, in Diagram 4, the resources r, u are replaced by the single resource t. Evolution may proceed forever in this way.

10.2.1.2   Competitive Behavior   Fig. 10.2 illustrates a case of competition for resources, typical of the internal behavior of IAMs agents. Given the two methods in the figure, *either* one can be applied to the state corresponding to Diagram 1, but not *both*, since application of one method consumes a resource (a) needed in the application of the other method. Depending on which method prevails (i.e. which collision occurs, p, a as in Diagram 2a or q, a as in Diagram 2b), the agent evolves as shown either in Diagram 3a or in Diagram 3b. This also illustrates the non-deterministic behavior of IAMs: since collisions occur at random, there is no way to control which method will prevail.

Thus, a single agent can itself be viewed as a bundle of different computational threads, corresponding to the different functionalities of the agent. Such functionalities are *tightly integrated* and indeed do not need to interact in terms of explicit communication, but just in terms of consumer/producer interdependencies; furthermore, they may overlap on determinate tasks, creating competing alternatives — just in the same way, human agents can consider different options to meet everyday life tasks and requirements (e.g. fighting or running away etc.). However, scaling up to real (albeit elementary) societies requires further expressive capabilities, which we illustrate in the next sections.

$p \,\mathfrak{B}\, a \,\circ\!\!-\, r$
$q \,\mathfrak{B}\, a \,\circ\!\!-\, s$

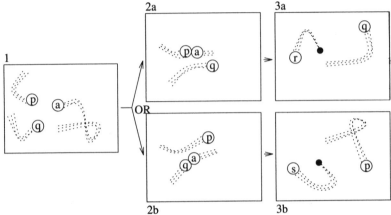

Figure 10.2
Competition for a resource a inside an agent

10.2.2 Multi-agent IAMs: Loose Integration

Indeed, to build multi-agent systems, we add new primitives for the *creation* and *termination* of agents, obtained via the following extension of the syntax of methods: the body of a method (right-hand side) may now be formed of *0 or more* multisets of resources instead of just one unique multiset. We use the symbol ⊤ (read "top") to denote the empty body and the symbol & (read "with") to connect several multisets of resources in the body.

As before, an agent can trigger a method if its state contains the resources of the head of the method. In this case,

(*i*)   if the body of the method is the empty multiset (⊤), then the agent terminates;

(*ii*)   if the body of the method corresponds to a single multiset then the body replaces the head in the new state of the agent, just as illustrated in the previous section;

(*iii*)   if the body contains n multisets of resources ($n > 1$), then $n - 1$ exact copies of the agent state are generated and, in each of the n clones thus obtained, the head of the method is replaced by the corresponding multiset of the body.

The main point here is that, in the third case above, the generated agents become completely independent and start evolving autonomously. Notice also the analogy with the mechanisms for creation (by cloning) and termination of processes in the Unix operating system, based on the primitives "fork" and "exit".

The IAM metaphor introduced in the previous section for the single agent case, can easily be extended to account for the new operators. The universe (of computation) now

$$p \, \Im \, a \, \circ\!\!-\, (q \, \Im \, r) \, \& \, s$$
$$r \, \Im \, u \, \circ\!\!-\, \top$$

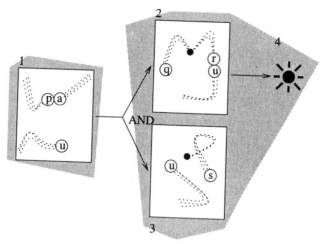

Figure 10.3
A multiagent Interaction Abstract Machine

consists of several concurrent spaces of the kind introduced previously:

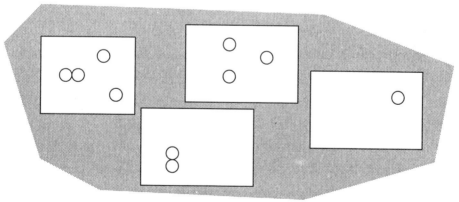

Each agent of the IAM can now perform its own, local transitions, without affecting the others. The system is completely dynamic and open, in that new agents may appear at any time, while others may disappear.

A sample evolution of a multi-agent IAM is illustrated by the diagrams of Fig. 10.3. In Diagram 1, the resources p and a collide, so that the first method applies: the agent is therefore duplicated (Diagrams 2 and 3); in one clone, p, a are replaced by q, r and in the other, p, a are replaced by s. Now, in Diagram 2, the resource r just produced collides with the resource u and the second method, which has an empty body, applies in this clone, which hence disappears (Diagram 4). The other clone is unaffected by this evolution.

Just as there can be internal parallel activities inside an agent, so different agents can evolve in parallel, since the triggering of methods in one agent does not interfere with what happens in another agent. Thus, multi-agent IAMs are characterized by multiple levels of concurrency. As opposed to the case of concurrent internal activities within an agent, concurrent agents capture the situation of independent, *loosely integrated* subsystems; as a matter of fact, their interaction must emerge through the explicit exchange of information, as described in the next section.

A conceptually different notion of multiple independent subsystems is also achieved in the CHAM metaphor, with the concept of "membranes" enclosing sub-solutions in a CHAM. The main difference here is that a IAM is a completely flat structure, i.e. all the agents are at the same level, whereas, in a CHAM, solutions can be enclosed within other solutions up to an arbitrary depth. This feature has a crucial consequence in terms of inter-agent communication, presented below.

10.2.3   Interagent Communication

As we have pointed out in section 10.2.1, we can consider what happens inside an agent as a form of interaction, involving different computational threads (the methods), which is however achieved without any form of explicit linguistic communication; what we have is instead a kind of interdependence induced by the production/consumption of resources: consumers depend on producers for satisfying their needs, and competition arises as a consequence of the same resource being usable by two or more consumers. But agents are encapsulated entities, separated from each other; therefore, if interaction *among* agents there has to be, this can only come from the explicit willingness of an agent to *communicate* something to its fellow creatures. Hence, in order to program IAMs as effectively interactive devices, we must endow agents with some elementary capabilities for performing speech acts.

10.2.3.1   Property-driven Communication   This is the way communication among agents is characterized in IAMs. The traditional message sending scheme relying on system addresses to identify the specific recipient of a message does not apply here, since the very notion of an agent's address is missing. Indeed, when a new agent is created, it does not get a name, nor any sort of identity; it simply comes into life as an aggregation of computational properties directly inherited from the agent it was cloned from. Thus, communication must be itself *property*-driven (as opposed to *address*- or *name*-driven): agents who are listening on given communication channels receive information broadcast on such channels by other agents; if the broadcast messages match the properties of the receiving agents then they react consequently, otherwise they simply ignore the message. Property-driven communication appears as a highly attractive feature in providing linguistic support for open systems, since the dynamic reconfigurability of such systems implies that agents may change their roles with respect to each other (e.g. who is supplying which services to whom); hence the desirability of making agents communicate

$p \,\wideparen{8}\, a \,\wideparen{8}\, {}^{\wedge}b \,{\circ}{-}\, q \,\wideparen{8}\, r$

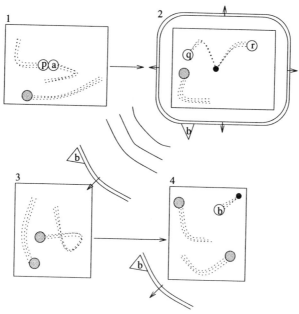

Figure 10.4
Broadcasting of resources

directly on the basis of their properties, rather than of their name. For instance, suppose that the agent with name A acts as a printer manager, i.e. is in charge of assigning printing requests to available printers, and that all printing requests must explicitly be addressed to the name of the agent currently acting as printer manager; then the event of replacing agent A with an agent B in the role of printer manager must be communicated to all the other agents, so as to allow them to properly reroute their requests. No such complication arises in case agents are permitted to send their requests away without specifying an address, but simply requiring whoever is in charge to process them.

10.2.3.2 Broadcasting Property-driven communication is realized in the IAM model through *broadcasting*. This functionality is obtained by the following extension of the syntax of methods: in the head of a method (left-hand side), some, but not all, resources may be prefixed with the special symbol $\wedge$ (called the "broadcast" marker). Now, the operational semantics of method triggering gets modified as follows: if all the non-marked resources of the head of a method are found in an agent's state, then the marked ones are *assumed* as being there — i.e., they are added to the state, and then immediately deleted by the application of the method. However, when a resource is added in an agent's state in this way, a copy of that resource is also added to the state of all the other agents in the system living at the time the method is triggered.

The main characteristic of this communication mechanism is that, when a message is broadcast, there is no need to freeze the whole system, then add the broadcast message in all the agents states and then unlock the system again (which would of course be unrealistic in a truly open system). In fact, it can be shown that the broadcast operation can be performed in a totally asynchronous and localized fashion. This property of broadcasting is captured in the IAM metaphor by introducing "waves" spreading across the system of agents. Each wave is a *potential* form of a particle, which becomes *actual* in an agent's space when the wave hits that space. Furthermore, it is assumed that the waves propagate "regularly" through the network of agents, which means that (*i*) a wave never hits twice the same agent, and (*ii*) it ultimately reaches all the agents in the system (except the one from which it is emitted as well as the descendent spawn from this one). The transmission times between agents are assumed to be randomly and uniformly distributed, i.e. we do not consider in this basic model of IAMs any form of topology of the agent network, nor communication failures or delays: the agents evolve in a purely isotropic "ether".

Graphically, a wave is represented as an ever growing closed curve (the "wave-front") labeled with some resource name for the particle it holds. Arrows show the direction of growth of the wave front. This mechanism is illustrated in Fig. 10.4. In Diagram 1, the resources p, a of the head of the method collide. There is also a resource b in the head of the method, but it is prefixed with the broadcast marker, so that it is immediately added to the agent state. The method is then triggered in the usual way, i.e. its head is replaced by its body; but, at the same time, a wave-front labeled with the broadcast resource b starts growing around the agent (Diagram 2). When this wave hits another agent, as in Diagram 3, a copy of b appears in this agent (Diagram 4). All the agents in the system thus receive the broadcast resource.

10.2.3.3 Non-competition and Cooperation Notice how, with respect to the *competitive* interaction among computational threads within an agent, the mechanism of interaction among agents induced by broadcast communication is essentially *non-competitive*, in the sense that separate copies of the same resource are distributed to the different agents, who are left completely free to make different use of their own copy. Specifically, compare Fig. 10.2 with Fig. 10.5; while in the case of Fig. 10.2 *either* one of the methods can be applied to transform the internal state of an agent, in the case of Fig. 10.5 *both* methods can be applied, one in each of the agents represented in Diagrams 1. Indeed, each of them receives a separate copy of the resource a which is broadcast (Diagrams 2) and processes it independently (Diagrams 3).

Thus, broadcast communication induces different responses to shared stimuli. From *non-competition* to *cooperation*, it is then quite an easy step; indeed, broadcast communication can be handily exploited to model the situation where complex problems need to be viewed by different cooperating "experts", each providing a specific response addressing one particular aspect of a common problem.

10.2.3.4 Forums and Subforums Another way to look at this approach to interagent communication is by viewing the different agents in the system as sharing a common

$$p \,\mathfrak{F}\, a \multimap r$$
$$q \,\mathfrak{F}\, a \multimap s$$

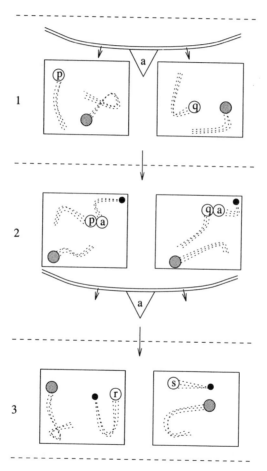

Figure 10.5
Cooperation among agents over a resource a

part which gets incrementally specified as they evolve; in [3] we have called this common interface the *forum*, as it plays the role of allowing global interactions among agents. An agent can communicate with other agents by making assumptions on the content of the forum; such assumptions are transmitted to all the other agents, who may then use them or not.

Without going into details, it is worth pointing out that general broadcasting can be easily restricted to "multicasting" by exploiting the fact that an agent, upon triggering a method, can generate unique constants which then may or may not be shared by the descendents of that agent, depending on their independent evolutions. Those agents which share a given constant can form a "subforum" by having each sender pass the constant as argument in the messages and each recipient match this argument against the constant: in this way, even though the messages are seen by all the agents in the forum, only those acquainted with the constant will be able to make use of them. In the case of a subforum with only two agents, we obtain a point-to-point bidirectional communication channel. For details about how this mechanism for generating unique identifiers is embedded as a primitive operation in the pattern matching mechanism of methods, see below and [3].

10.3 Examples

We present here two concrete instances, of quite different nature, of Interaction Abstract Machines. The first example corresponds to a distributed solution of a classical problem of operations research, namely the determination of the shortest path in a graph [5]. In this case, the problem itself is not distributed *per se*, but the solution we propose makes use of multiple communicating agents. The second example, on the other hand, is a simulation of an intrinsically distributed system, namely an airline reservation system, where multiple agents (airline companies, travel agencies) communicate through a network; their interaction is indeed obtained via an elementary incarnation of the "contract net" protocol [22], which assumes itself broadcast communication.

10.3.1 From the Metaphor to the Computational Model

The metaphor of IAMs has been incarnated in the computational model of Linear Objects (*LO* [3]), whose operational semantics is given in terms of the proof theory for Linear Logic [14]; one of the main motivations behind Linear Logic is of providing a background for the study of concurrent systems through a theoretical account of the notions of (inter)action and of resource-based computation. In the *LO* model, the resources are represented as tagged tuples of the form $p(v_1, \ldots, v_n)$, where the tag p ranges over a (finite) set of predicates and the arguments $v_1, \ldots, v_n$ of the tuple are of various types (numbers, strings, identifiers, lists...). In methods, these arguments may contain variables, whose names scope only over the method in which they occur. When a method is applied, its variables must first be instantiated, i.e. replaced by actual values. This is achieved by pattern matching with the elements in the state of the agent where the method is triggered. The variables which cannot be instantiated by pattern matching, i.e. those which occur in broadcast resources but not in the other resources of the head, are instantiated with new unique identifiers, which can be used as mail addresses in broadcast communication. This mechanism is used in the second example, to connect requests and corresponding answers which circulate through the forum.

In this section, we use the keyboard typable symbols @,&,#t and <>- (actually used in the LO implementations) instead of, respectively $\mathfrak{F}$, &, $\top$ and $\circ$-. Furthermore, we follow the usual convention of starting variable names with an uppercase letter.

"Raw" computations (such as arithmetics, string manipulation, and, more generally, any procedure irrelevant to the interaction machinery) are not accounted for in the IAMs model. There are various ways to integrate them in LO, without deeply affecting the basic model. First, there is the "server" approach, where a server is an agent among others, capable of interpreting and answering requests as any agent, except that its behavior is not described in terms of LO methods. Thus, one could think of an arithmetic server, receiving messages of the form sum(3,4,r) (where r is a unique identifier of the request) and answering back messages of the form r=7. But this approach involves too much communication overhead for an operation which should precisely not be handled through communication. The other approach consists of considering that each agent contains implicitly in its state resources of the form, say, sum(3,4,7) (as many such resources as needed in the computation). For example, the following method defines a simple counter capable of receiving messages of the form inc(X) incrementing its current value (hold in the resource val(V)) by a value X:

```
val(V) @ inc(X) @ {sum(V,X,V')} <>- val(V').
```

The curly brackets around the resource sum(V,X,V') mean that this resource must be searched in the implicit part of the agent's state (containing all the arithmetic information); in an execution, it would be actually implemented as a machine invocation of the addition. In fact, in the case of usual arithmetic operations, we use the following shorthand:

```
val(V) @ inc(X) <>- val(V+X).
```

which can easily be mapped into the previous form. In the operations research example below, we heavily make use of this shorthand notation for arithmetics operations. In the other example, we make use of operations manipulating more symbolic data; we do not explicitly program these procedures (other languages than LO are more appropriate for this task), but each time such a procedure occurs in a method, its role is explained.

LO can be implemented as a "coordination language", which extends, that is, preexisting programming environment with agent-oriented capabilities. To date there exist two implementations of LO, one as an extension of Modula-3 and the other as an extension of Prolog.

10.3.2 An Operations Research Algorithm

We consider here a directed acyclic graph, as, for example, the following one:

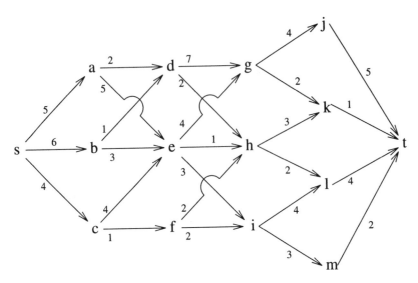

Each edge is labeled with a "cost", which is a positive integer. A path in the graph is a sequence of contiguous edges and the cost of a path is the cumulated sum of the costs of its edges. Two nodes in the graph are distinguished: the source (s) and the target (t). We assume that they are connected by some path and the problem is to find the lowest cost of the paths from s to t. For simplicity, the algorithm proposed below computes only the lowest cost from source to target, but, with a slight modification, it could also produce the actual path(s) corresponding to this lowest cost.

The graph is represented by a system of communicating agents, each of which corresponds to a node in the graph. Diagram 1 of Fig. 10.6 shows the initial state of the agent corresponding to node e. It contains exactly 5 resources: `node(e)` holds the name of the node (e); there is one resource of the form `edge(C,M)` for each outgoing edge of cost C from e to a node M. Finally, the resource `count(3)` holds the number of outgoing edges. We assume that similar agents are created for all the other nodes in the graph.

At run time, the system computes, for each node N, the minimal cost C of the path(s) from N to the target (node t). This information, encoded in the resource `mcost(N,C)`, is broadcast, so as to make it available to all the agents. The computation of the minimal cost C from node N to the target is done locally by the agent corresponding to node N in the following way:

- When the agent receives an information `mcost(M,C)` where M is a node such that there is an outgoing edge of cost C' from N to M, then it creates a resource encoding the cost of the path thus found from N to the target via M, which is of cost C+C'. This is a candidate value for the lowest cost from N to the target and it is stored in the resource `pcost(C+C')` simply produced within the agent space by the following method.

  ```
  edge(C',M) @ mcost(M,C) <>- pcost(C+C').
  ```

- When two candidate values for the minimal cost are produced by the previous method, they are compared and the lowest one is kept, while the other is discarded. As we

```
edge(C',M) @ mcost(M,C) <>- pcost(C+C').

pcost(C1) @ pcost(C2) @ count(Q) <>-
    pcost(min(C1,C2)) @ count(Q-1).

node(N) @ pcost(C) @ count(1) @ ^mcost(N,C) <>- #t.
```

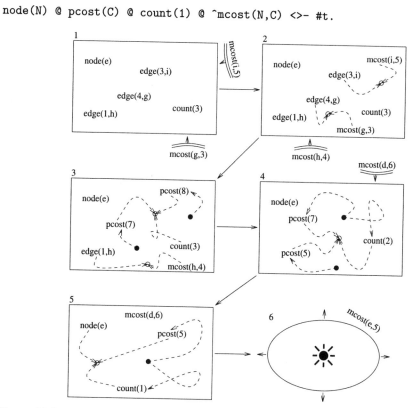

Figure 10.6
The program and a possible scenario of execution at node *e*

need to keep track of the number of such comparison-eliminations, the counter `count`
is decreased at the same time. This is achieved by the following method:

```
pcost(C1) @ pcost(C2) @ count(Q) <>-
    pcost(min(C1,C2)) @ count(Q-1).
```

- Finally, when all the candidate values for the minimal cost have been eliminated,
  except one (i.e. when the counter reaches 1), then we know that we have reached the
  actual minimal cost from N to the target, and the agent broadcasts this information,
  and terminates, using the following method.

```
pcost(C) @ count(1) @ node(N) @ ^mcost(N,C) <>- #t.
```

A possible scenario of execution of the methods above is shown in Fig. 10.6 for the agent
corresponding to node e. In Diagrams 1 and 2, the agent receives broadcast resources,
resp. `mcost(i,5)`, `mcost(g,3)` and `mcost(h,4)`, which are exactly the resources needed
by this agent to perform its local computation. Other resources of the same kind may
also be received at any stage in the execution (e.g. `mcost(d,6)` in Diagram 4), but
they will not be used and do not interfere with the computation. In Diagram 2, the two
received resources `mcost(i,5)` and `mcost(g,3)` are processed and produce two candidate
values for the lowest cost, namely `pcost(7)` and `pcost(8)` which appear in Diagram 3.
These values are compared together and `pcost(8)` (the highest) is discarded, as shown
in Diagram 4. At the same time, the counter is decreased. Meanwhile, the resource
`mcost(h,4)` has been received and produced `pcost(5)` (in Diagram 4). At this point,
`pcost(7)` is discarded and the counter is again decreased (Diagram 5) so that the resource
`pcost(5)` remains alone, while the counter has reached 1. Hence, the agent terminates
and broadcasts its result `mcost(e,5)` (Diagram 6). Of course, this scenario is possible
only because the agent has indeed received all the resources it needs (from adjacent
nodes) to perform its computation; this is always the case as long as the graph is acyclic.

The overall behavior of this Interaction Abstract Machine consists of two phases. In
the first phase (which has not been described above), the graph is activated, i.e. one
agent is created and initialized for each node in the graph. This typically involves the
use of the primitive & which allows creation of new agents by cloning. Then, in a second
phase, the actual computation is started by broadcasting the resource `mcost(t,0)` which
simply informs that the the empty path from the target node t to itself has a null cost
(which is obviously the lowest cost). This enables nodes j, k, l, m to react. They in
turn compute and broadcast their own lowest cost, triggering reactions in nodes g, h, i.
Results are then propagated in the same way to the layers d, e, f and a, b, c, and finally
to s. Some agent spawn at the beginning of the computation can then collect the result
broadcast by s, which is the solution of the problem, and display it to the terminal or
use it in some other computation.

The figure below shows the propagation of the results; the abbreviation `N:C` stands for
`mcost(N,C)`.

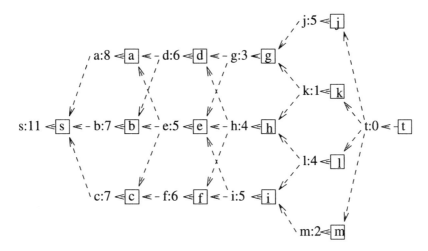

For each agent (node in the graph) there is an outgoing arrow to the resource which it broadcasts (its minimal cost to the target) and there are incoming arrows from each of the broadcast resources which it actually uses. The same resource may be used by several agents (e.g. $d : 6$ by both a and b); this is not a problem, since, due to the cooperative behavior of the agents on broadcast resources, they do not compete for shared resources but get individual copies of them.

10.3.3   Simulation of a Distributed System

We consider here a classical example of physical distribution of resources, in an airline reservation system. Two kinds of agents are involved: travel agencies and airline companies. We use *LO* here to simulate the activity of each of these agents and their interactions. We want to simulate the following scenario:

- Each agency submits requests to all the companies, searching for flights satisfying some constraints defined by a client: typically, the origin and the destination of the flight are specified, together with the maximal budget the client can afford.

- The companies receive the requests and may (or may not) send back flight offers matching the specifications.

- Each agency collects the offers corresponding to the request it has emitted, and sorts them according to some criterion provided by the client.

- After a certain time, the agency stops collecting offers and starts sending reservation requests to the companies. Each offer is tried in the order determined in the previous step.

- Each company receives reservation requests and checks whether they can be satisfied. This might not be the case if the selected flight is already fully booked. In any case, the answer (accept or reject) is returned to the agency.

- When a reservation request is accepted, the agency stops the reservation process and terminates the treatment of the current client request. The same happens if all reservations have been rejected, and the client is invited to submit another, less constrained, request.

The simulation program is initiated by

```
simul <>-
    agency_1 & ... & agency_n &
    company_1 & ... & company_m.
```

Each of the agents thus created is expanded, initiating the different agencies and companies.

We first describe the methods simulating the agencies activity. We assume that the state of each agency contains resources of the form

```
client_request(Specs,Criterion,Seat)
```

which represent client requests: these requests may occur asynchronously, and we are not interested here by how they are generated. The first argument in a request, Specs, encodes the client's description of the flight he requests (including, e.g. the origin, the destination, the desired dates, the maximal budget which the client can afford, etc...). The second argument specifies the criterion to be used to sort the companies offers (e.g. sort by price, or by travel time, etc...) and the third argument is the number of seats required. We also assume that each agency's state contains initially the resource agency (meaning that it is ready to process clients requests). The agency spawns a specialized agent to process each client's request, so that several client requests can be processed simultaneously:

```
agency @ client_request(Specs,C,S) <>-
    agency_process(Specs) @ criterion(C) @ nseat(S) &
    agency.
```

Processing a request starts with getting information from companies about the requested journey:

```
agency_process(Specs) @ ^info(Q,Specs) <>-
    agency_collect(Q) @ start_timer @
    count(0) @ sorted(0).
```

Thus, an invitation to tender info(Q,Specs) containing the specifications of the requested journey is broadcast to all the companies. At runtime, the variable Q above is instantiated with a fresh unique identifier[1] which is then used to identify in a unique way the broadcast message info(Q,Specs) so that only answers corresponding to this message are collected by agency_collect(Q). The resource start_timer starts the countdown for the flight offers from the companies to be considered. The resource count(X) holds the number of offers received so far. The resource sorted(X) holds the number of offers sorted so far. Indeed, as flight offers are received, they must be sorted:

---

[1]This specific treatment of the variable Q is determined by the fact that this variable occurs in the broadcast resource info(Q,Specs) but not in the other resources of the head of the method.

```
agency_collect(Q) @ offer(Q,F) @ count(X) <>-
    agency_collect(Q) @ sort(F) @ count(X+1).

sort(F) @ sorted(0) <>-
    next(best,F) @ next(F,worse) @ sorted(1).

sort(F) @ next(F1,F2) @ sorted(X)
criterion(C) @ {between(C,F,F1,F2)} <>-
    next(F1,F) @ next(F,F2) @
    sorted(X+1) @ criterion(C).
```

Thus, the sorting process generates resources of the form `next(F1,F2)`, meaning that offer F2 should be considered immediately after offer F1, should the latter fail on booking. The resource `{between(C,F,F1,F2)}` represents a call to some "raw" computation local to the agency (maybe involving some discussion with the client), which determines whether the offer F ranks between offers F1 and F2 according to criterion C. The dummy offers `best` and `worse` are introduced to enclose the ordered list of offers (it is assumed that any offer is between `best` and `worse`).

When the countdown initiated by `start_timer` is finished, i.e. the deadline for offers is reached, the agency stops collecting offers and enters the reservation process:

```
agency_collect(_) @ timer_ended @ count(X) <>-
    agency_reserve(X).
```

The flight offers are scanned in the order defined in the sorting process, and a reservation is tried for each of them, until one is accepted.

```
agency_reserve(X) @ sorted(X) @ next(best,F) <>-
    agency_try(F).

agency_try(F) @ {F != worse} @
nseat(S) @ ^book(Q,F,S) <>-
    agency_wait(Q,F) @ nseat(S).

agency_wait(Q,F) @ rejected(Q) @ next(F,F') <>-
    agency_try(F').

agency_wait(Q,F) @ accepted(Q) <>- #t.

agency_try(worse) <>- #t.
```

Notice that the first method enforces that all the offers have been sorted before starting reservations (indeed, for this method to apply, the count of received offers, held in the resource `agency_reserve(X)`, must be equal to the number of sorted offers, held in the resource `sorted(X)`). The second method broadcasts the booking request corresponding to the best flight offer not yet rejected (other than the dummy offer `worse`). Notice again that the variable Q is used to uniquely identify the broadcast message, so that only answers to that message are considered in the next two methods. If the answer is negative (third method), the next offer is considered. Otherwise (fourth method), the current agent, processing the initial client request, is terminated. It is also terminated when all the offers have been rejected, i.e. when the dummy offer worse is reached (fifth method).

We now describe the methods simulating companies activity. We assume that the initial state of a company contains the resource company (meaning that it is ready to process requests from agencies).

```
company @ info(Q,Spec) @
{satisfy(Spec,F)} @ ^offer(Q,F) <>-
    company.
```

The resource {satisfy(Spec,F)} represents a call to some "raw" computation local to the company, which determines whether the specification Spec can be matched with one of its flight offers F.

For the booking process, we assume that each company contains initially a database of resources of the form number(F,N) holding, for each of its flight offers F, the number N of available seats for this offer. Each booking order from the agencies may modify that number:

```
company @ book(Q,F,S) @
number(F,N) @ {S <= N} @ ^accepted(Q) <>-
    company @ number(F,N-S).
```

```
company @ book(Q,F,S) @
number(F,N) @ {S > N} @ ^rejected(Q) <>-
    company @ number(F,N).
```

Fig. 10.7 illustrates the Interaction Abstract Machine at work, while processing one client request. The dashed lines, labeled with resources, show the messages which are broadcast: they link the sender of each message to its potential receivers (even though the message is sent to all agents, only some of them will make use of it). The plain lines show the agent transitions. For clarity purpose, the content of each agent state is not drawn completely: only the relevant resources are displayed. Furthermore, in the state of the agency, we abbreviate the sorted list of offers as AA802:BA105:TWA732 which stands for the set of resources

```
next(best,AA802), next(AA802,BA105),
next(BA105,TWA732), next(TWA732,worse)
```

built by the program. Besides, the actual transitions corresponding to the computation of this sorted list are omitted (broken line on the figure), as they do not involve inter-agent communication. The (randomly named) constants q230,q934 and q937 are created at runtime and allow unique identification of the messages they appear in.

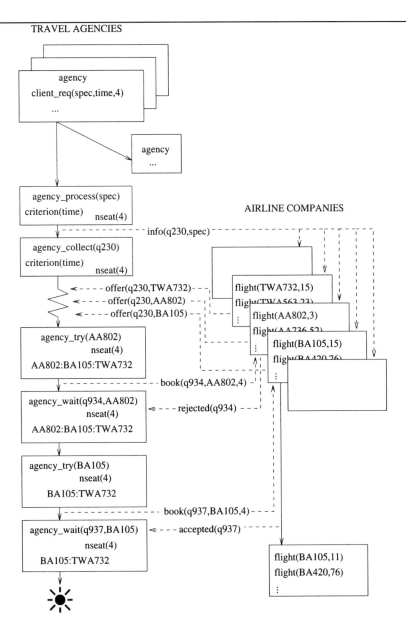

Figure 10.7
Simulation of an airline reservation system

10.4   Comparison to Other Models

Various programming languages or abstract computational models, often themselves supported by some implicit or explicit metaphor, have been proposed in the past for concurrent and distributed computing. Specifically, we focus on the three following paradigms: blackboards, constraints and actors.

10.4.1   Blackboards

We have seen how internal computations inside a single agent of a IAM can be seen as transformations on a blackboard: the resources in the agent's computational space correspond to the messages on the blackboard, and the methods which retract and assert resources correspond to different knowledge sources in the blackboard model. There are a number of parallel languages which are based on a similar concept, such as Associons [19], Gamma [8], Linda [13], Shared Prolog [7], and Swarm [11]. Actually both Associons and Gamma are abstract computing models more than full-fledged programming languages: they are based on multiset rewriting operators. Linda is a coordination language, i.e. a set of primitives for parallelism and communication that can be easily added to any sequential imperative language. Shared Prolog is a logic programming based counterpart of Linda. Swarm is a logic for parallel programming in the style of Unity [9]. Conditional Rewriting Logic [17], a recent development in this direction, extends this notion of concurrent computation as transformation of a shared data-space to the general domain of term-rewriting systems.

The Chemical Abstract Machine metaphor [6] applies quite naturally to blackboard-based concurrent computations, and it has been shown in this paper how this metaphor overlaps with that of Interaction Abstract Machines in the single-agent case. In fact, the notions of (chemical) solution (in the sense of the CHAMs), computation space (of IAMs), tuple space (in Linda or Shared Prolog), blackboard etc. all support the same idea that a shared, open and unordered data-structure (multiset) is an appropriate medium for communication in a concurrent or distributed data-driven system.

10.4.2   Constraints

A recent offspring from the family tree of concurrent logic programming languages is Concurrent Constraint Programming [20], a linguistic framework where concurrent agents communicate via a global store seen as a set of constraints. There is no competition between processes for the constraints in the store, so that the use of the store as a common interface through which agents communicate bears a close relationship with that of the forum in a IAM (see section 10.2.3.4), rather than with a blackboard. However, there are crucial differences as well: in Concurrent Constraint Programming languages, constraints are never removed from the store, which gets incrementally refined via the monotonic accumulation of new elements; by contrast, pieces of information exchanged through the forum are ephemeral, in that they can effectively be removed, but only locally, from the scope of the consuming agent (without interference with the other agents).

Also, there is no notion of consistency (and failure) in a IAM, whereas the Concurrent Constraint framework does not preclude it a priori (some syntactic restrictions [16] may however ensure that the store of constraints always remain consistent). The traditional logic programming notion of global inconsistency, which makes inconsistency in one branch of the computation responsible for the inconsistency of the whole computation tree appears undesirable and unrealistic from the point of view of distributed open systems, where failure in one node should only partially degrade the performance of the whole system.

Furthermore, the fact that the information units (constraints) which accumulate in the store are never removed decreases, to a large extent, the encapsulation and the locality of the agents, in that all actions concerning the manipulation of constraints performed by an agent are directly reflected on the store, and thus are visible to all the other agents. In fact, a Concurrent Constraint Programming computation could be simulated in terms of a single-agent IAM, where the head of each method would consist of a unique "active" atom — the predicate in Concurrent Constraints terminology — and a set of "passive" atoms — corresponding to the asked constraints — which also occur in the body of the method, so that they are never actually consumed. This restriction to a unique active head, typical of traditional logic programming languages, is incompatible with the IAMs model's ontology where multiple activities occur not only at the global level, stemming from the existence of multiple agents, but also locally, within each agent.

On the other hand, the Concurrent Constraint framework, and especially the notion of entailment among constraints, offers a flexible and elegant tool for declaratively expressing algorithmic computations, where the real concern is not on coordinating distributed agents, but on desequentializing algorithm execution.

10.4.3 Actors

The Actors model [1] provides a well-defined framework for specifying and reasoning about systems of concurrent communicating processes. Actors are encapsulated entities interacting with each other only via asynchronous message passing. Each actor has a unique system address, to which messages aimed at this actor are sent; a receiving actor reacts to a sent message by applying a method from its own script (set of associated methods). The Actor model has been very influential on the work on LO, among whose starting motivations there has been that of logically reconstructing the main features of Actor computations, while at the same time improving on others: specifically, by withdrawing the notion of agents identity (address) we have made communication property-driven, and by viewing agents as blackboards we have added a built-in form of dynamic inheritance (the behavior of an agent is compositionally obtained by summing up the behaviors of the computational threads which participate in it) missing from the original Actor model (see [2, 4] for an illustration of the capabilities of this inheritance mechanism).

However, there have been also other evolutions from the original Actor model which have been pointing, with different means, in similar directions. Specifically, the distributed actor language ABCL [25] comes also in a "reflective" flavor ABCL/R [24], where each object x has a meta-object $\uparrow x$ with direct read-write access to the state of x (x is called the denotation of $\uparrow x$). The communication between a meta-object and its denotation is therefore not only achieved by message passing but also by direct competitive access to their shared resources (the state of the denotation). In IAMs terminology, the meta-object and its denotation can be seen as different computational threads running within the same blackboard, so that they effectively compete for the resources in this blackboard. Thus, we can simulate through a IAM agent the whole "meta-ancestry" of an ABCL/R object, i.e. the set of objects consisting of the object, its meta-object, its meta-meta-object etc. In general, however, IAM agents have a less restricted behavior with respect to ABCL/R objects: in fact, the relation between an object and its meta-object in ABCL/R is not symmetric (the meta-object controls its denotation, and not the other way round) while, in a IAM agent, no component has, *per se*, a priority role (agents methods are unordered). Moreover, when a sent message reaches a IAM agent, it can then be consumed by any of the agent's components, while, in ABCL/R, messages are sent specifying which level in the meta-ancestry of an object is the recipient of the message.

Thus, although the two levels of concurrency (inside and across agents), implicit in the IAMs model, could be used to characterize ABCL/R computations, probably closer to the ABCL/R model would be abstract machines where the relationship among different subsystems is *hierarchically* organized, like, for instance, in the CHARM [10] model, another recently proposed extension of the Chemical Abstract Machine.

10.5   Conclusion and Future Work

We have introduced the metaphor of *Interaction Abstract Machine* to conceptually characterize concurrent multiagent worlds, where each computational agent itself is viewed as structured entities, whose behavior results from the concurrent activity of different components. These two levels of concurrency correspond to two basic mechanisms of communication, competitive (blackboard-style) and cooperative (forum-style). The model has been incarnated in a computational model, christened *LO*.

In the course of the paper, we have made an over-simplifying assumption, namely that all the agents are speaking the same language, so that there is no problem of converting heterogeneous data representations in inter-agent communication (nor within the same agent). Indeed, the evolution of all the agents in a IAM is determined by the same set of methods, which is assumed to be written in a homogeneous language, so that the occurrence of a constant, say 4, in two distinct methods, has the same meaning in both of them, while the same constant cannot appear in two different forms in two different methods. However, in real life, this is clearly not a very realistic assumption (see [23] for discussion on this subject): an essential part of our future research will be devoted to tackle this problem.

Acknowledgements

We thank Gerard Comyn and Alexander Herold for their encouragement and support. We are indebted to Mike Reeve for discussions on the importance of property-driven communication in open information systems.

References

[1] G. Agha and C. Hewitt. Actors: a conceptual foundation for concurrent object-oriented programming. In B. Shriver and P. Wegner, editors, *Research Directions in Object-Oriented Programming*. MIT Press, Cambridge, Massachussetts, 1987.

[2] J-M. Andreoli and R. Pareschi. LO and behold! concurrent structured processes. In *Proc. of OOPSLA/ECOOP'90*, Ottawa, Canada, 1990.

[3] J-M. Andreoli and R. Pareschi. Communication as fair distribution of knowledge. In *Proc. of OOPSLA'91*, Phoenix, Az, U.S.A., 1991.

[4] J-M. Andreoli and R. Pareschi. Linear objects: Logical processes with built-in inheritance. *New Generation Computing*, 9(3+4):445–473, 1991.

[5] J-M. Andreoli, R. Pareschi, and M. Bourgois. Dynamic programming as multi-agent programming. In *Proc. of the OOPSLA'90/ECOOP'91 workshop on Object-based concurrent computing*, Lecture Notes in Computer Science (612), Genève, Switzerland, 1991. Springer Verlag.

[6] G. Berry and G. Boudol. The chemical abstract machine. In *Proc. of the 17th ACM Symposium on Principles of Programming Languages*, San Francisco, Ca, U.S.A., 1990.

[7] A. Brogi and P. Ciancarini. The concurrent language shared prolog. *ACM Transactions on Programming Languages and Systems*, 13(1):99–123, 1991.

[8] J-P. Banâtre, A. Coutant, and D. Le Metayer. A parallel machine for multiset transformation and its programming style. *Future Generation Computer Systems*, 4(2):133–145, 1988.

[9] M. Chandy and J. Misra. *Parallel Programming Design: A Foundation*. Addison-Wesley, 1988.

[10] A. Corradini, U. Montanari, and F. Rossi. Concurrency and hiding in an abstract rewrite machine. In *Proc. of the International Conference on 5th Generation Computer Systems*, Tokyo, Japan, 1992.

[11] H.C. Cunningham and G.-C. Roman. A shared dataspace model of concurrency. In *Proc. of the 9th International Conference on Distributed Computing Systems*, 1989.

[12] L. Gasser. Social conceptions of knowledge and action: DAI foundations and open systems semantics. *Artificial Intelligence*, 47(1-3), 1991.

[13] D. Gelernter. Generative communication in Linda. *ACM Transactions on Programming Languages and Systems*, 7(1):80–113, 1985.

[14] J-Y. Girard. Linear logic. *Theoretical Computer Science*, 50:1–102, 1987.

[15] C. Hewitt. Open information systems semantics for distributed artificial intelligence. *Artificial Intelligence*, 47(1-3), 1991.

[16] K. Kahn, J. Levy, and V.A. Saraswat. Janus: A step towards distributed constraint programming. In *Proc. of NACLP'90*, Austin, Tx, U.S.A, 1990.

[17] J. Meseguer. Conditional rewriting logic as a unified model of concurrency. *Theoretical Computer Science*, 93:73–155, 1992.

[18] H. Penny Nii. Blackboard systems. In A. Barr, Cohen P., and Feigenbaum E., editors, *The Handbook of Artificial Intelligence, vol. 4*, pages 1–82. Addison-Wesley, 1989.

[19] M. Rem. Associons: A program notation with tuples instead of variables. *ACM Transactions on Programming Languages and Systems*, 3, 1981.

[20] V.A. Saraswat. *Concurrent Constraint Programming Languages*. PhD thesis, Carnegie-Mellon University, Pittsburg, Pa, U.S.A., 1989.

[21] Y. Shoam. Agent-oriented programming. Technical report, Standford University, Robotics Laboratory, Stanford, Ca, U.S.A., 1991.

[22] R.G. Smith. The contract net protocol: High level communication and control in a distributed problem solver. *IEEE Trans. Comput.*, 29(12):1104–1113, 1980.

[23] G. Wiederhold, P. Wegner, and S. Ceri. Towards mega-programming. Technical report, University of Stanford, Dept. of Computing, Standford, Ca, U.S.A., 1990.

[24] T. Watanabe and A. Yonezawa. Reflection in an object-oriented concurrent language. In

A. Yonezawa, editor, *ABCL, an Object-Oriented Concurrent System*. MIT Press, Cambridge, Massachusetts, 1990.

[25]   A. Yonezawa, E. Shibayama, Y. Honda, T. Takada, and J-P. Briot. An object-oriented concurrent computation model ABCM/1 and its description language ABCL/1. In A. Yonezawa, editor, *ABCL, an Object-Oriented Concurrent System*, pages 13–45. MIT Press, Cambridge, Massachusetts, 1990.

11   CC++: A Declarative Concurrent Object-Oriented Programming Notation

K. Mani Chandy and Carl Kesselman

CC++ is Compositional C++ , a parallel object-oriented notation that consists of C++ with six extensions. The goals of the CC++ project are to provide a theory, notation and tools for developing reliable scalable concurrent program libraries, and to provide a framework for unifying:

1. distributed reactive systems, batch-oriented numeric and symbolic applications, and user-interface systems,

2. declarative programs and object-oriented imperative programs, and

3. deterministic and nondeterministic programs.

This paper is a brief description of the motivation for CC++, the extensions to C++ , a few examples of CC++ programs with reasoning about their correctness, and an evaluation of CC++ in the context of other research on concurrent computation. A short description of C++ is provided.

11.1   Introduction

Compositional C++ , or CC++ is a concurrent object-oriented programming notation. CC++ is C++ with six extensions for writing declarative and concurrent programs. The declarative extensions are particularly suited for rapid prototyping. These extensions are used to *compose* programs to execute on distributed environments; the emphasis in compositional programming is on methods for putting programs together to execute concurrently so that the specification for a composed parallel program can be proved, in a simple way, from specifications of its components.

CC++ is a notation for reactive systems executing on heterogeneous distributed environments as well as for applications executing on parallel supercomputers.

The extensions of CC++ are based, in part, on ideas from Concurrent Logic Programming [23], Strand [10], PCN [7, 12], and dataflow languages [1]. Methods for reasoning about correctness are based on UNITY [6].

Organization of the Paper The next section presents the motivation for CC++. Since CC++ consists of a small number of extensions to C++ , some understanding of C++ is helpful in reading this paper; therefore, a very brief overview of C++ is provided in Section 11.3, for those unfamiliar with it. Section 11.4 describes the extensions in CC++, and Section 11.5 presents examples of parallel programs with methods for reasoning about their correctness. A description of an implementation of CC++ is given in Section 11.6. Section 11.7 compares CC++ with other object-oriented notations. Section 11.8 is a summary of the main points of the paper.

11.2   Motivation

The motivation for CC++ is given in this section. We conclude each topic in this section with a line, in *emphasis* font stating the relevance of each issue to CC++ design.

11.2.1   Integrating Different Approaches to Concurrency

Integration of Parallel and Reactive Systems   Within a decade, parallel super-computers will be integrated into reactive systems such as command and control systems, communication systems, process-control systems, and perhaps even automobiles. The same program may deal with differential equations, receive data from distributed sensors, control distributed processes, and interact with people.

Such a system has three main parts:

1. distributed control,

2. core numeric and symbolic computing,

3. user interfaces.

Parallel supercomputing usually deals with only the second of the three parts.

User-interface systems are thought of as sequential programs in which an event-manager schedules many objects such as windows and queues. Treating such systems as concurrent systems, with concurrently executing objects, simplifies design even if the computing platform is a sequential machine.

A common thread that unites all three parts of reactive systems is concurrency. Therefore, *a unified framework should be provided to manage concurrency in distributed control, core numeric and symbolic computation, and in user interfaces.*

Integration of Data Parallel and Asynchronous Computation   Data parallelism has been shown to be a powerful model of computation for scientific computing. The data-parallel model allows programmers to treat a distributed object — such as an array distributed across several nodes of a multicomputer — as a single object. Programmers can think of their programs as sequential programs in which certain operations are implemented as concurrent operations. Data parallel programs are attractive because they allow programmers to execute sequential programs on parallel machines by using distributed objects.

By contrast, the model of computing in reactive systems is that of asynchronous communicating objects. Programmers do not have the luxury of thinking of their programs as sequential programs in which some operations are executed concurrently because reactive systems, by their very nature, have multiple independent threads of control.

Both the data parallel model and the asynchronous model of computation are useful. The integration of parallel supercomputing with reactive computing requires *notations and tools for integrating data parallel and asynchronous computation models.*

Integration of Deterministic and Nondeterministic Programs   Most batch-oriented numeric and symbolic programs are deterministic. Determinism has several advantages, including repeatability of execution. Reactive programs, however, interact with their environment which is essentially unpredictable and uncontrollable. Therefore, reactive programs are nondeterministic in nature. The integration of parallel supercomputing with reactive computing requires *a unified framework that allows programmers to develop deterministic programs or nondeterministic programs, as needed. Demonstrating that a program is deterministic should be straightforward.*

Nonuniform Memory Access The time required to access data in a reactive system will vary depending on where the data is located. Though arguments can be made in favor of uniform memory access in parallel supercomputers, these arguments do not apply to distributed reactive systems. The integration of supercomputing with reactive systems requires that programmers pay attention to data locality in some cases (where data is geographically distributed). *The compiler, run-time system and to (some extent) the programmer must be cognizant of nonuniform access times of a distributed system.*

11.2.2 Developing Correct Concurrent Programs

Demonstrating Correctness Since debugging reactive programs is even more difficult than debugging sequential programs, *methods for developing reactive programs should include techniques for reasoning about program correctness.*

Exception Handling and Debugging One way to help in producing reliable code, is to provide mechanisms for inserting assertions (including invariants, and variant functions or metrics) into objects, and having the assertions checked at run-time. Run-time checks of assertions are particularly important in the development of libraries: the programmer who builds an object library can state the assertions to which users of the libraries must adhere, and run-time checks help protect the library builder from incorrect usage of the library [19]. Violation of an assertion causes an exception that is then handled in some suitable way. *Exception handling mechanisms are ideal vehicles for including assertions into objects.* Also, determinism in execution simplifies debugging — and CC++ programs can be written in a way that guarantees determinism.

Strong Typing or No Typing? Some concurrent notations, such as Strand [10], PCN [7], Concurrent Smalltalk [30], and HAL [16] have untyped variables. This has several advantages including the ability to use the same program for different types of arguments; for instance the same program can be used, without change, for lists of integers and lists of floating point numbers. An advantage of strong typing is that many errors can be detected at compile time. One reason for detecting errors of concurrent programs at compile time is that errors in concurrent systems can manifest themselves in strange ways such as starvation of some processes and these errors can be hard to detect and pinpoint at run-time. Programmers making the transition from sequential to concurrent programming find the development of concurrent programming to be difficult, and therefore, we think that *the advantages of strong typing outweigh its disadvantages.*

Some of the disadvantages of strong typing can be overcome by using C++ templates which are discussed later.

11.2.3 Software Engineering of Concurrent Programs

Objects Abstract data types, represented as objects, provide a clean interface between the use of the object and its implementation. An object can be implemented in different ways for different architectures, without changing the interface to the object. In particular, an object (such as an array) can be implemented in a distributed manner, and users of the object need not be concerned whether operations on the object are sequential or concurrent. Libraries of objects can be tailored, where necessary, for different kinds of architectures, without modifying programs that use the libraries. *An object-oriented language is an ideal vehicle for the development of concurrent programs.*

Declarative Programs   In many cases, declarative programs are easier to develop and verify than imperative programs because declarative programs are closer to specifications. Therefore, declarative programs are well-suited for rapid prototyping. One way to develop reliable programs is to develop a program in a declarative style and then transform those parts of the program that are used frequently into efficient imperative programs. *The integration of declarative and imperative programming supports step-wise development of programs.*

Portability   Computing platforms of reactive systems will be diverse, including loosely-coupled networks of tightly-coupled shared-memory machines. Programs must be portable (to some degree) across the diversity of platforms to reduce the amount of effort required to port a program from one platform to another. Therefore, *constructs for concurrency should not be based on a particular class of machines.* For instance, the method by which processes synchronize should not depend on whether the hardware platform uses message-passing or shared memory, but should employ an abstraction of both mechanisms.

Language support should be provided for heterogeneous computing. In CC++ this support is provided by processor objects (or logical processors). There can be different classes of processor objects corresponding to different types of processors. The scheduler attempts to map a processor object on to the most appropriate physical processor. The semantics of a program are in terms of processor objects, and the implementation uses the semantic construct to obtain efficient implementations on heterogeneous networks.

Templates   Some computational structures appear repeatedly in many different applications. Such computational structures can be represented as templates, and programs can be developed by "filling in" templates with different objects.

Examples of templates include parameterized objects in C++ , higher-order functions in functional programming, and source-to-source program transformation notations in PCN [8].

Templates can be re-used in different situations by suitably setting template parameters; thus template re-use improves productivity. *Use of template libraries will reduce program development time.*

Transforming Sequential Programs   Many, though not all, parallel programs can be constructed by putting sequential programs together. *Methods that help in constructing concurrent programs by modifying existing sequential programs, will remain useful.*

New Language or Extension?   There are two basic approaches to designing a concurrent notation: propose a new notation or extend an existing sequential notation. The advantage of a new notation is that it can be kept simple. The disadvantages of a new notation are that programmers have to learn a new language to use concurrent computers, and a new set of tools have to be developed for the new notation.

Our goal is to help programmers use concurrent constructs quickly; the obstacle of learning a new notation, even a small notation, is overwhelming for many programmers. Therefore, we decided to implement a small extension to a sequential notation. To help programmers learn the extension quickly, and to allow easy adaptation of tools for the sequential notation to the concurrent notation, *the extension must be* **tiny** *and* **fit** *the base notation.* In particular, the extended notation must not restrict the base notation in any way: every program in the base notation must also be a program in the extended notation. Also, the programming paradigms of the base notation must be applicable in the extended notation, as well; for instance, if iteration is used in the base notation then the extended notation should allow iteration to be used to construct parallel programs as well.

Single Paradigm for Concurrency or Many Paradigms?   One approach to developing parallel extensions to sequential languages is to insist that programmers use a single approach to obtain concurrency; the approach can be use of single-assignment variables, or monitors, or communicating processes, or functional programming. Another approach is to construct a *small* foundation that supports all of these approaches; if all these approaches for parallelism can be implemented on the small foundation, then programs using all these approaches are perforce programs written using the small foundation. We feel that a small foundation that supports a variety of parallel programming paradigms is useful to more programmers than a notation that only supports a single paradigm.

Multilingual Programming   A reactive system may employ programs in many notations. For instance it may use Fortran for numeric computation, Lisp or Prolog for symbolic computation, and C for process management. *Notations for concurrent programming should be able to call programs in other notations.*

11.2.4   Why CC++?

Why Use C++ as a Base Language?   Our goal of helping many programmers migrate to concurrent computing suggests that we extend a widely-used notation. The goal of investigating the use of sequential libraries for concurrent program development suggests that we use a base language that has a substantial collection of libraries.

Our primary interest is not in the broad (and important) area of language design; we focus our interest on the narrow issue *of an extension to a sequential notation that helps in developing correct efficient concurrent programs.* Therefore, though our extensions should be simple, the underlying sequential notation can be arbitrary.

Sequential notations, that we could have considered for the base language include Fortran, C, C++ , Cobol, Lisp, Pascal, Oberon and Smalltalk. Our goals of integrating symbolic and numeric programming; integrating user-interfaces, batch-oriented programs and reactive programs; providing support for multilingual programming; and investigating the potential re-use of sequential program libraries in concurrent programming suggested C or C++ in preference to the other notations. Our need for objects, templates, exception-handling, and type checking made C++ an obvious choice.

Since C is a subset of C++ , and since our extensions are compatible with C, we have, in effect, defined two extensions: Compositional C and Compositional C++.

The central ideas of the extensions can be used with other languages that have user-defined data structures and classes.

Libraries have been developed recently in C++ , for a variety of applications including numerics, combinatorics and user-interfaces. This supports the view that C++ can form a basis for integrating the development of the three parts of reactive systems: distributed control, core symbolic and numeric computation, and user-interfaces.

One of the disadvantages of C++ as a base language is that C++ is a very rich notation: it has a wealth of features useful in a variety of situations. Giving the formal semantics for such a rich notation is difficult. A small notation with a complete axiomatic semantics is preferable for program verification. After weighing the tradeoffs, we decided to use C++ , and reason about the correctness of *some* programs, rather than attempt to give proof rules that define the semantics of C++ .

Declarative Programming   A set of equations of the form:

$$(x = f(y)) \wedge (y = g(x))$$

where f and g are functions that satisfy certain properties, (and $\wedge$ is *logical and*) can be executed to determine x and y. The advantage of a program which is a set of equations is that in many cases, the specification is the program, and therefore the proof obligation — demonstrating that the program satisfies its specification — is straightforward.

Nondeterministic programs can be specified by a set of relations, such as: produce any x, y that satisfy:

$$p(x \downarrow, y \uparrow) \wedge q(y \downarrow, x \uparrow)$$

where p and q are treated as both relations and procedures. The arrows $\downarrow$ and $\uparrow$ indicate data flow into or out of procedures; thus, given x the procedure $p(x \downarrow, y \uparrow)$ computes any y that satisfies relation p. For example, x and y may be lists where y_0 is a a constant; y_{i+1} and x_i satisfy some relation specified in p; and x_i and y_i satisfy some other relation specified in q (and where the subscripts index the list).

Such a formula can be executed, with p producing y_i, followed by q producing x_i, for increasing i. Demonstrating correctness of a predicate calculus formula is often simpler than demonstrating correctness of an imperative program because the specification is often closer to the formula than to an imperative program.

Many specifications can be cast as conjunctions of implications and such specifications can also be transformed, in some cases almost syntactically, into declarative programs.

Our problem is to design a small declarative extension of C++ that allows programmers to write declarative programs such as these. The central design issue is to make the declarative extension a "natural" extension to C++ .

The declarative extension is implemented by using data flow and single-assignment variables. Single assignment variables can be found in concurrent logic programming languages [13, 10], dataflow languages [1, 18] and others [7]. Single-assignment variables were proposed at least as early as the 1960s. A contribution of CC++ is to employ single-assignment variables in the context of a strongly-typed, object-oriented imperative language.

The effect of message-passing, semaphores, monitors [21, 15], barriers and **await** commands [20], can be obtained by using objects and sync variables. Thus programs that use these constructs can be used, with little change, in CC++.

11.3   A Brief Overview of C++

We present a brief overview of the C++ programming language. With a few exceptions, C++ is a pure extension of ANSI C. Most valid ANSI C programs are also valid C++ programs. C++ extends C by adding strong typing and language support for data abstraction and object-oriented programming.

11.3.1   Strong Typing

Strong typing is essential to the construction of reliable programs. C++ has a more complete type-checking system than **C**. Function prototypes are required for all function definitions. A type-safe linkage mechanism is used to link together modules. Also, a type-safe dynamic data allocation mechanism is used which eliminates the need for implicit casting of **void** pointers. C++ includes a template facility that allows generic (or parameterized) functions to be defined in a type-safe manner. Experience has shown that when converting a program from C to C++, the type system of C++ uncovers errors at compile time that are undetected in the C program.

11.3.2   Data Abstraction and Encapsulation

C++ provides support for data abstraction and encapsulation by introducing the concept of a *class*, which is a generalization of a C structure. Classes are defined by the C++ keyword **class** as well as the C keywords: **struct** and **union**. A class is like a C structure that can contain function members as well as data members. Thus for a class C, member access can take the form: C.d for data members or C.f(a1,...,an) for function members. The syntax for declaring a class is basically the syntax used to declare a structure in C.

A class object may reference itself by means of the **this** pointer. Within a member function, the compiler arranges for the keyword **this** to point to the object to which the member function belongs.

Program reliability is increased by ensuring that data objects are always properly initialized when they are created and destroyed when they are no longer needed. A C++ class can provide a member function, called a constructor, that initializes a class object and a member function, called a destructor, that destroys an object. The compiler automatically invokes a constructor whenever a new class object is created and a destructor whenever a class object is destroyed.

11.3.2.1   Encapsulation   Classes are a unit of encapsulation; a class declaration defines a new scope. The type system ensures that member functions of a class can only be applied to instances of a class, thus encapsulating a data structure and the functions that manipulate that structure into a single entity.

The interface to a class is defined by designating members of a class as being either `public` or `private`. A `public` class member can be used without restriction by any program that has a reference to an instance of a class: public data members can be read or written and public member functions may be called. However, a private member can only be accessed from within the class object itself. Private data members can only be accessed by a class member function and private member functions can only be called from within another member function of the class.

11.3.2.2   Constant and Volatile Objects   C++ , as well as ANSI C, allows an object to be declared constant or volatile. A constant object (declared `const`) is one that cannot be changed, a volatile object (declared `volatile`) is one whose value can change without being explicitly written to. Constant and volatile can be combined to indicate a location that cannot be written to, yet whose value can change, for example, a nonsettable, memory mapped clock.

A class object can be declared to be constant or volatile. For example, the declaration:
   `const C x;`
creates a constant object of class `C` named `x`. Each data member of `x` is a constant object. The semantics of operations on a `const` object are defined by member functions that are explicitly designated as being `const`; only these member functions are allowed to be called in a constant object. Constant member functions allow a programmer to specify the elements of an object's interface that manipulate that object in a manner consistent with a constant declaration. The mechanism used for creating a volatile class object is much like that used for a constant object.

11.3.3   Overloading

A user-defined C++ class, can be used in any situation a language-defined type can be used. This is facilitated by allowing almost all C++ operators to be overloaded so that they apply to user defined types as well as system defined types. Arithmetic operators, comparison operators and data conversion operators (i.e. type casts) are among those operators that can be extended to apply to user-defined data types. Thus one can define the + operator to apply to a user defined vector type, string type or matrix type, and to define conversions between each of these types. Conversion between types can be specified in the program via an explicit type cast or automatically applied by the compiler.

11.3.4   Object-Oriented Programming

C++ supports object-oriented programming via two mechanisms: inheritance and virtual functions. Inheritance is used to support *is-a* relationships between objects. That is relationships such as: *a rat is a rodent*, can be expressed by defining a `rat` class (called a derived class) that inherits a `rodent` class (called a base class). A `rat` object will inherit all behavior specific to `rodent`.

Virtual functions provide for a degree of polymorphism in which the actual behavior of an aspect of an inherited class is defined by the derived class and not the base class. For example, all rodents get food, but the way a rat gets food is different than the way a guinea pig gets food. This type of relationship is represented via a virtual function.

11.4   The CC++ Language

A sequential C++ program can be converted into a parallel program by using the new constructs provided in CC++. The constructs are:

1. Parallel block.
2. Spawn.
3. Atomic functions.
4. Logical processors.
5. Global pointers.
6. Sync (for synchronizing) variables.

CC++ is a complete notation for writing distributed or parallel programs; there are no constructs such as fair merge, messages, or locks that are outside the notation.

C and C++ programs are valid (albeit sequential) programs in CC++. Therefore, programs in languages (such as Fortran) that can be called from C or C++ can also be called from CC++.

11.4.1   Control Flow

Constructs for sequential execution in CC++ are the same as in C++ . CC++ has two constructs for concurrent execution: **parallel blocks**, and **spawn**. A statement in CC++

1. has the syntax of a statement in C++ , or,
2. is a parallel block, or,
3. is a spawn statement.

11.4.2   Parallel Blocks

A **parallel block** has the syntax:

par *parblock*

where *parblock* has the syntax of a block in C++ with some restrictions given later.

Let B be the parallel block: par { S0 S1 ...   Sn } where S0 ... Sn are statements. When execution of B is initiated, execution of each of the component statements S0, ... , Sn of B is initiated. Execution of B terminates when execution of all its component statements terminate. Therefore, B is in execution if and only if at least one of its component statements is in execution.

Thus B has the same meaning as the following statement in [20]

cobegin S0; S1; ... ; Sn **coend**

and the following statement in PCN [7]:

{|| S0, S1, ... , Sn }

   The order in which component statements of a parallel block appear within the block is immaterial. For example, `par {S0 S1}` has the same meaning as `par {S1 S0}`.

Restrictions

1. A parallel block cannot have local variables (with the scope of the parallel block). Therefore, the component statements of a parallel block cannot be declaration statements. (Of course, a component statement `Si` of a parallel block can be a sequential block that has local variables with scope `Si`.)

2. The component statements of a parallel block cannot be labeled.

     There can be no jumps (using `goto`, for instance) from a statement outside a parallel block to a statement within the parallel block. Likewise, there can be no jumps from within a parallel block to statements outside the block. Moreover, there can be no jumps from one component statement `Si` of B to a different component statement `Sj` of B.

     Control can pass to a component statement of B in one and only one way: when execution of B is initiated, execution of each of the component statements S0, ... , Sn is initiated. Likewise, control can pass from a component statement of B in one and only one way: when all of the component statements of B terminate execution, B terminates execution. Thus the parallel block is a construct for creating structured parallel programs.

     Jumps entirely within one of the component statements `Si` of B are permitted if `Si` is a sequential block.

3. A statement in a parallel block must not execute a `return`. Therefore, we place the restriction that a parallel block cannot be a `return block`, where a `return block` is defined (recursively) as a block that contains (i) a `return` statement or (ii) a `return block`.

11.4.2.1   Sequential Block   The syntax of a sequential block in CC++ is the same as the syntax of a block in C++ except that a statement in CC++ can also be a parallel block or a spawn statement. Thus, statements S0 ... Sn are executed in sequence in the sequential block {S0 ... Sn} whereas they are executed concurrently in the parallel block `par {S0 ... Sn}`.

11.4.2.2   Spawn   The syntax of a spawn statement is:

spawn *function-call*

where *function-call* has the syntax of a function call in C++ .

   The execution of a spawn statement creates a new process which executes concurrently with the process executing the spawn. The process created by executing the spawn statement is called the *spawned* process. The process that executes the spawn statement is called the *spawning* process.

Execution of the spawning process continues with the statement (if any) that follows the spawn statement. The spawned process executes the function call specified in *function-call* component of the spawn statement. Values returned by the function are discarded, and not used in the computation.

A difference between **par** blocks and spawn statements is that the **par** block terminates when all its component statements terminate, whereas a spawning process can terminate before or after the spawned process terminates.

Examples   Consider the blocks:

```
{S0; f(x); S1;}
```

and

```
{S0; spawn f(x); S1;}
```

where S0; and S1; are statements. In the first block, S0, f(x) and S1 are executed sequentially. In the second block, S0 is executed, and after S0 terminates execution, **spawn f(x)** is executed. The spawn statement creates a process — the spawned process — and execution of the spawning process continues with S1. The spawned process executes f(x).

Thus in the second block, f(x) and S1 are executed concurrently whereas in the first block S1 is executed after f(x) terminates execution.

Restrictions   Care must be taken in designing the spawned process because it can continue execution even after the spawning process terminates execution. For instance, a process must not throw exceptions to be handled by a process that has terminated execution. Likewise, a process must not reference variables that are local to a terminated process.

11.4.3   Atomicity

An interleaving model of computation is used in CC++: a computation is a *sequence* of operations. A computation of a CC++ program is an arbitrary interleaving of computations of its concurrent processes subject to the requirement of atomicity specified next.

A function can be declared to be an **atomic function** by using the keyword **atomic** in the declaration, as in:

```
atomic void f(int x);
```

An execution of an atomic function is an atomic action: between the initiation of a call to an atomic function and its termination, no other operation occurs in a computation.

Restrictions

1. The only data that can be referenced by an atomic member function of an object
   p are member data fields of p. An atomic member function of p cannot reference
   members of other objects, nor can it reference static (i.e., global) variables.

   The only data that can be referenced by an atomic static function (i.e., a function
   that is not a member of an object) are static variables. An atomic static function
   cannot reference members of objects.

2. An atomic function cannot read a sync value. Therefore, an atomic function cannot
   suspend execution.

3. Atomic functions must terminate execution in a finite number of steps. Of course,
   this cannot be checked by the CC++ implementation. The programmer must ensure
   termination.

Concurrency of Execution of Atomic Functions   A computation is a *sequence* of
operations, and if two atomic operations occur at the "same time" we assume that one
of the atomic operations (chosen arbitrarily) occurs before the other in the computation.
In practice, many atomic functions can execute at the same time; for instance there
can be concurrent execution of atomic functions p.f(x) and q.f(y) where p and q are
different objects. Concurrently executing atomic functions are independent because one
function cannot reference variables referenced by the other. Independent operations can
be serialized (in arbitrary order) in the computation.

11.4.4   Fairness

A process is either **executable** or **suspended** at a point in a computation. In CC++,
an executable process remains executable until it is executed; the execution of some
other process cannot make an executable process become suspended. Executable and
suspended processes are discussed later.

Program initiation and termination in CC++ are the same as in C++: program execution starts with initiation of its **main** procedure, and the program terminates execution
when **main** terminates execution or when an **exit** or **abort** is called.

The fairness rule implemented by C++ is as follows. At all points t in the computation,
the following holds:

1. The program terminates (within a finite number of steps from t), or

2. for every process r that is executable at point t: the computation of r will progress
   (within a finite number of steps from t).

11.4.5   Sync, Const and Mutable Data

Introduction   Define a **data unit** as the memory occupied by a fundamental type (e.g.
char, int, short int, long int, float, double) or a pointer in C++ . Each data unit
is **mutable**, **const** (for constant) or **sync**. A mutable data unit has an arbitrary initial
value, and can be read and modified an arbitrary number of times. A constant data
unit has an unchanging value (unless it is cast as a nonconstant). A sync data unit is

a single-assignment or **worm** — write once read many times — data unit. A sync data unit can be assigned a value *at most once* in a computation of a correct CC++ program; an assignment to the same sync data unit more than once in a computation is an error.

Relationship between Sync and Constant   Sync can be thought of as a constant whose initialization can be delayed, in contrast to a `const` which must be initialized at the point of declaration.

Assigning a value to a sync is called initializing it, in analogy with initializing constants. A sync data unit is defined to be **uninitialized** before it is assigned a value, and **initialized** after it has been assigned a value.

Process Suspension   A process is either executable or suspended. Associated with each suspended process is a single uninitialized sync data unit; when this data unit becomes initialized the process becomes executable. An executable process p can become suspended in one and only one way: p is suspended if it reads an uninitialized sync data unit; p becomes executable again when the data unit becomes initialized .

Once a sync data unit becomes initialized it remains initialized forever thereafter. Therefore, if a suspended process p becomes executable, p remains executable until execution of p is resumed, and p next reads another uninitialized sync data unit.

The value of an uninitialized sync data unit is immaterial since a process that reads an uninitialized sync data unit is suspended until the data unit becomes initialized . The value of an initialized sync data unit is unchanging.

Aggregate Types   We restrict attention to initialization of sync data units — memory occupied by **fundamental** types or pointers in C++ . We do not define initialization of memory occupied by **aggregate** sync types such as `arrays` or `classes`. This is because reading and writing of aggregate types are carried out element-by-element. Thus, some elements of an aggregate sync type can be initialized, while others are uninitialized. A *bit* of an integer cannot be initialized while another bit is uninitialized; an integer is a fundamental type and either the entire integer is initialized or the entire integer is uninitialized.

Constants and Syncs in Concurrent Computing   An advantage of constants in concurrent computing is that copies of a constant can be made without violating multiple-copy consistency requirements, because a constant remains unchanged. Similarly, copies of syncs — constants with delayed initialization and with flags indicating initialization — can be made, with multiple copy consistency handled in a straightforward way. The only possible inconsistency for sync data is that one copy is uninitialized and the other copy is initialized. In this case, a process that reads the uninitialized copy waits for it to become initialized. The implementation need only guarantee that if one copy is initialized then all copies will become initialized.

11.4.6   Allocation and Deallocation of Storage

In C++ , memory is allocated when an object is defined, or when **new** t is executed where t is a type, or when memory is allocated by the operating system (by calling `malloc` for instance). Allocation of memory in CC++ is identical to that in C++ except that the memory allocated can be sync (in addition to being constant or mutable). The memory allocated to store a sync object (discussed later) consists of sync data units, and memory allocated to store a mutable object consists of mutable data units.

Storage for sync data units are deallocated (by a garbage collector) some finite time after there are no references to them. The garbage collector collects only sync storage; memory management for mutable and constant storage is as in C++ .

Programmers can deallocate storage (by using `delete` for example) but they should do so only if they can prove that there are no references to this storage at the point in the computation at which they are deallocated. Local storage of a block is deallocated when execution of the block terminates (as in C++). Therefore, one block should not reference local variables of a terminated block.

11.4.7 Sync Types

A type in CC++ is either a type in C++ or a **sync version** of a type in C++ . A variable that is declared to be a C++ type is a mutable variable or a constant. A variable that is declared to be a sync version of a C++ type is a sync variable.

The type modifier `sync` is used to declare a type to be a sync type. The use of the type modifier `sync` is syntactically identical to the use of the type modifier `const` in C++ .

A declaration:

```
sync T A[];
```

where T is a C++ type declares A to be an array each element of which is of type `sync` T. Programmers cannot declare an array to be partially sync and partially mutable, just as they cannot declare an array to be partially constant and partially mutable.

11.4.7.1 Sync Classes and Structures   In C++ , some fields of a structure can be constant types and other fields can be mutable types. Likewise, in CC++, some fields of a structure can be sync types and other fields can be mutable types.

In C++ , some member functions of a class can be constant functions (that should not modify data members of the class) and other member functions can be ordinary (non-const) functions. Likewise, in CC++, some member functions of a class can be sync functions and other member functions can be ordinary (non-sync) functions.

Restrictions

1. Sync unions are not permitted. Also, no part of a union can be sync.

2. Sync bit fields are not permitted. For instance,

```
sync struct flags{
               unsigned flagA : 1;
               unsigned flagB : 1;
           }
```

is not permitted.

Sync bit fields are not allowed because they would be of marginal use and complicate the implementation of CC++. The use of unions is restricted to prevent accessing sync data types as mutable and to avoid initializing only part of a sync structure, i.e. a union between characters and an integer.

11.4.7.2   Sync Objects   Since `sync` and `const` are type modifiers, we can declare `sync` versions of objects in the same way that we can declare `const` versions of objects. If `CLS` is a class, then

`const CLS x`

declares `x` to be a constant version of an object of class `CLS` in C++ . Likewise,

`sync CLS y`

declares `y` to be a `sync` version of an object of class `CLS` in CC++.

(An object can be declared to be `const sync`, or equivalently, to be `sync const`, which declares the object to be a const object with the restriction that it cannot be cast as a nonconstant object.)

11.4.7.3   Restrictions on Casting Pointers to Sync   There are several restrictions on how pointer to a `sync` can be cast. These restrictions are to prevent a `sync` object from being used as a non-`sync` object.

1. A pointer to `sync` `T` cannot be cast as a pointer to a nonsync type.

2. A pointer to `sync` `T` can be cast as a pointer to `sync` `D` if and only if casting a pointer to `T` as a pointer to `D` is legal in C++ .

3. A pointer to a fundamental sync type (`int`, `char`, `float`, ...) cannot be cast as a pointer to any other type. Likewise, a pointer to a type `T` cannot be cast as a pointer to a fundamental sync type different from `T`.

11.4.8   Logical Processor Objects

Introduction   Thus far, we have specified constructs for specifying parallel execution: the (par block, `parfor` statement and `spawn` statement), and a mechanism by which parallel program components can communicate and synchronize: (`sync` objects). These constructs are sufficient for constructing parallel programs. There are, however, pragmatic issues that are not addressed by these constructs. In particular, we need to provide:

- a means of abstracting processing resources in the programming language,
- a mechanism for separating algorithmic concerns from resource allocation issues,
- a way to express locality,
- a means for describing heterogeneous computation, and
- a mechanism by which existing C++ codes can be properly composed from within a parallel block.

To resolve these issues, CC++ introduces **logical processor objects**. Logical processor objects are very similar to objects in C++ : they have member functions and data members. Logical processor objects are different from C++ objects in one fundamental way: a collection of C++ objects can share information through global and static variables where as every instance of a logical processor object is completely self contained and can interact with other objects only through its public interface.

Logical processor objects address our concerns in the following ways:

- By definition, a logical processor object is an abstraction of the physical processing resources available in a computer system.

- Processor objects are built on the foundation of C++ objects. Therefore, abstract data type and object-oriented programming techniques facilitate the abstraction and separation of algorithmic and resource allocation concerns.

- Each processor object is mapped indivisibly onto a physical processing resource. Thus by programming with processor objects, a CC++ program has an explicit means of expressing locality.

- Because each instance of a logical processor object is self contained, existing C++ programs can be composed in parallel without them interacting unintentionally through shared, global variables.

The Logical Processor Class   A C++ computation consists of a single instance of a single program. We loosely define a program to be a stand-alone entity that performs a complete task. While a program in CC++ is the same as a program in C++ , a CC++ computation can contain multiple instances of multiples programs. Each instance of a program is represented by a logical processor object. As with any C++ object, a logical processor object has a type associated with it. We call this type the logical processor class.

A C++ program consists of a collection of compilation modules (files) that are linked together, generally by a system utility such as a linker. As part of the linking process, a processor object class is assigned to a program. Existing C++ modules can be linked into a processor object without modification. Since the processor object encapsulates all global and static variables within a program, multiple instances of a pure C++ processor object can be created and execute in parallel without interference.

If one wishes to manipulate a processor object from within a program, then a declaration for the processor object must be provided. A processor object class declaration is just like a regular class declaration, except the keyword `global` is used in combination with the `class` keyword to indicate that the declaration is for a processor object. For example:

```
global class worker {
public:
    int do_work(task);
    int status;
}
```

declares a processor object with one member function and one data member. The public members of a processor object correspond to globally defined symbols in the corresponding program. In our example, `status` must be a global variable and `do_work` must be a globally accessible function defined when the program is linked.

Accessing Logical Processors   One of the logical processors is designated the **initiator**. Computation of a CC++ program is initiated by initiating the `main` program on the **initiator** logical processor, and with no other function in execution. It is not possible to execute the `main` program on any logical processor other than the `initiator`.

Additional processor objects can only be created through the use of the C++ dynamic allocation operator: `new`. Initialization of a processor object requires knowing the location of the program text from which the processor object is to be constructed. This information is provided via the C++ constructor argument mechanism. Thus the statement:

```
worker * wPtr = new worker ("~carl/worker");
```

creates a new processor object of class worker and initializes it with the executable found in a file named `worker`. A pointer to the newly created processor object is returned by `new` and placed into the variable `wPtr`. In addition, the global variable `::this` always points to the processor object from which a reference the `::this` is evaluated.

As with any other CC++ object, members of a processor object can be accessed though a pointer to that object. Upon executing the variable declaration shown above, the statements:

```
wPtr->status++;
wPtr->do_work(task(23));
```

will increment the value of status in the newly created `worker` processor object and call the `do_work` function with an argument that is an object of type `task` initialized to the value 23. Note that the `->` operator can be overloaded, eliminating the need for an application program to ever refer directly to a processor object. This provides a flexible, user-defined scheme for addressing logical processors (for examples, see [9]). Examples of how a user might view logical processor ids include an integer, a pair of integers (if the logical processors form a two-dimensional mesh), or an enumerated type.

Logical Processors and Physical Processors   In addition to providing an argument to the initialization function (i.e. constructor) of an object, C++ allows an argument to be passed to the `new` operator itself. This *placement* argument is used by the CC++ runtime system to specify the low level mapping of logical resources (processor objects) to physical resources (processors). When combined with operator overloading and objects, the placement option to the `new` operator provides the framework from which many mapping strategies can be constructed. For example the statement:

```
worker * wPtr = new (NextNode) worker ("~carl/worker");
```

will create a new processor object of type **worker** and place that processor object on the physical node indicated by the object **NextNode**. The set of physical resource names that are available to a program are implementation specific.

Linkage The logical processor class is specified by the collection of linked files that constitute a logical processor object. *All linkage is within a single logical processor object.* There is no name space outside logical processor objects. In C++ , one can always refer to a global object named x with the expression

```
::x
```

However, in CC++, this expression is interpreted as meaning

```
::this->x
```

that is the value of x in the logical processor executing the expression.

A name that has external linkage in the collection of linked files is a *public* member of the processor object. A public member of one object can be referred to in other objects by using the -> operator. For example if **int x** has external linkage, then **int x** is a public data field of the processor class; a logical processor object can refer to member x of another logical processor object jPtr as jPtr->x.

A name that has internal linkage in the collection of linked files is not a public name of the processor object. For example, if **static int y** appears in a file **f**, then its linkage is internal to **f**, and a logical processor object cannot reference y local to file **f** in another logical processor object.

11.4.9   Global Pointers

In C++ , a reference to an object can be stored in a pointer variable or a reference variable. In CC++, pointers and references can be used as well. However, in CC++ we must distinguish between the situations in which a pointer or reference variable resides in the same logical processor as the object being referenced or a different logical processor from the object being referenced. The first case is referred to as a *local* pointer or reference, the second case is referred to as a *global* pointer or reference. Thus in CC++, a pointer is a local pointer, a global pointer or a **sync** pointer. For clarity, the following discussion will be limited to pointers, however, it applies to references as well.

A pointer that is not declared to be a global pointer or a sync pointer is a local pointer. In C++ , they type of a pointer can be modified with the keyword **const** or **volatile**, to indicate a pointer whose value cannot be changed or one whose value might change spontaneously. In CC++, the type modifiers for a pointer include the keyword **global**. Thus, the statement:

```
int * global g_ptr;
```

declares g_ptr to be a global pointer to an integer. Likewise, a **sync** pointer is declared using the keyword **sync** as in:

```
int * sync s_ptr;
```

which declares s_ptr to be a sync pointer to an integer. More than one modifier can be used in a declaration, thus the statement:

```
int * global const g_ptr;
```

declares a variable that is a constant, global pointer (i.e. an inter-logical processor pointer whose value cannot be changed).

Global and sync pointers contain two pieces of information: a logical processor id, and an address within that logical processor . A local pointer is the address within a logical processor object, and has no information about the id of the logical processor object itself.

A pointer in one logical processor object that points to a location in another logical processor object must be a global pointer or a sync pointer. A pointer in one logical processor object that points to a location within the same logical processor object can be any pointer: a local pointer, a global pointer, or a sync pointer.

A variable of type global pointer or sync pointer cannot be assigned to a variable of type local pointer. A variable of type local pointer can be assigned to a variable of type global pointer or sync pointer.

A global pointer cannot be cast as a local pointer.

11.5 Programming examples in CC++

This section presents a few examples that demonstrate the relationship between CC++ and approaches to parallel programming such as concurrent logic programming, functional programming, dataflow languages, monitors, and message-passing. The first three examples show how sequential programs in C can be transformed into C++ programs that execute in parallel.

11.5.1 Transforming Sequential Programs

Consider the sequential C function in Figure 11.1. The body of this function is a block consisting of a sequence of assignments. Each variable, a, b, *x, *y and *z, is assigned a value at most once, and a variable does not appear on the right-hand side of an assignment until it has been assigned a value.

Figure 11.2 shows another sequential version of the function f0. In this function, f1, the variables that are modified in the function body have been made into sync variables.

Function f2() in Figure 11.3 is identical to f1() except that

1. variables that are both read and modified are declared to be sync variables, and
2. the sequential block is replaced by a par block.

The transformed parallel program is equivalent to the sequential program.

```
void f0(int w,  *x,  *y,  *z)
{
  int a,b;
  a = w + 1;
  b = w * 2;
  *x = a-b;
  *y = a*b;
  *z = (*x) + (*y);
}
```

Figure 11.1
A sequential C++ program.

```
void f1(int w,  sync int *x,  *y,  *z)
{
  sync int a,b;
  {
    a = w + 1;
    b = w * 2;
    *x = a-b;
    *y = a*b;
    *z = (*x) + (*y);
  }
}
```

Figure 11.2
CC++ sequential program with sync variables

11.5.2   A Discrete-Event Simulation

We begin with a C++ program to simulate a tandem queueing network as shown in Figure 11.4.

The program:

```
generate_arrivals(int n, float mean, randm rand, cell* p)
```

takes inputs n, mean and rand and makes p->next a list of n arrival times with the mean interarrival time equal to mean and using a random number generator specified by object rand.

The program

```
generate_service(int n, float mean, randm rand, cell* p)
```

is similar to generate_arrivals except that it sets p->next to be a list of service times.

```
void g(int w, sync int *sync x,  *sync y,  *sync z)
{
  sync int a, b;
  par { a = w + 1;
b = w * 2;
*x = a-b;
*y = a*b;
*z = (*x) + (*y);
      }
}
```

Figure 11.3
A parallel CC++ version of the sequential function f0

The program void `simulate_queue(cell* a, cell* s, cell* d)` simulates a first-come-first-served queue with arrival times specified by list `*a`, service times specified by list `*s`, and it computes the departure times from the queue and stores them in list `*d`. The program to simulate a queue uses the following equation:

$$departure_i = service_i + max(departure_{i-1}, arrival_i)$$

where $departure_i$, $service_i$, and $arrival_i$ are the departure time, service time, and arrival time of the i-th job in the queue.

The program is given below.

The main program simulates a sequence of queues, with departures from one queue becoming arrivals to the next. The variables d0, and d1 represent departures from queues 0 and 1, respectively, and variables s0 and s1 represent service times at queues 0 and 1, respectively.

The main program is given below:

From Sequential to Parallel First, consider the sequential program. The initial values of lists a, s0, d0, s1, d1, are arbitrary, and elements of the lists are assigned values once. Therefore, we can safely convert these variables into sync variables. For example, we can change the declaration of a from

```
cell * a;
```

   to

```
cell * sync a;
```

Pointers to sync must be global pointers, therefore we change q in generate_arrivals and pa, ps, pd in simulate_queue to global. For example, we can change the declaration of q from

```
cell * q;
```

```
void generate_arrivals(int n, float mean, randm rand, cell * p)
{
  cell * q = p;
  float t = 0.0;
  int i;

  for (i=0; i<n; i++) {
    t = t+rand.generate(mean);
    q->next = new cell(t);
    q = q->next;
  }
  q->next = (cell*) NULL;
}
```

Figure 11.4
Sequential function for arrival time generation

to

```
cell * global q;
```

Finally change the sequential block in `main` to a parallel block:

11.5.3   How A Process Can Halt Another

Consider the following modification of **generate_arrivals**. In the program given earlier, n arrivals are generated where n is an input variable. Now, we want to modify the program to continue generating arrivals until some process initializes a `sync` variable done to TRUE.

We introduce a boolean (mutable) variable **over** which is initially FALSE and becomes TRUE after **done** is initialized.

```
main()
{
  int over = FALSE;
  sync int done;
  par {
    over = done;
    generate_arrivals(..,over,..);
    process_that_sets_done( $\ldots$, done, $\ldots$);
    $\ldots$
    }
  $\ldots$
}
```

Replace the **for** loop in **generate_arrivals** by the **while** loop:

```
void simulate_queue(cell* a, cell* s, cell* d)
{
  float t = 0.0;

  cell* pd = d; cell* pa = a->next;  cell* ps = s->next;

  while( (pa != (cell*) NULL) && (ps != (cell*) NULL)) {
    t = (ps->value) + max(t,pa->value);
    pd->next = new cell(t);

    pa = pa->next; ps = ps->next; pd = pd->next;
  };

  pd->next = (cell*)NULL;
}
```

Figure 11.5
Sequential function for computing simulation times

```
while(!over){ ...  }
```

11.5.4 Parafunctional Programming

The next program is a divide-and-conquer algorithm that produces a list of cells. An example of such a program is one that produces a list of cells whose data fields are the sequence of integers from low to high.

Consider the evaluation of a statement:

```
x = h(f(0,10),f(30,50));
```

where h is a function that has two arguments both of which are of type sync cell *sync. The evaluation of f(0,10) will return a pointer, say p to a sync cell, and have the side effect of spawning a statement that will create the list *p. Likewise, the evaluation of f(30,50) will return a pointer, say q to a sync cell, and have the side effect of spawning a statement that will create the list *q. Thus, the evaluation of the arguments of h have the side effect of spawning statements that "fill in" the values these arguments.

Think of program f in a parallel function library. We can write a sequential program, that calls functions from this library. The user of the library doesn't have to be concerned with sequential programming at all, but nevertheless function arguments will be evaluated in parallel.

11.5.5 Distributed Abstract Data Types

Consider:

```
main()
{
  cell *a, *s0, *d0, *s1, *d1;

  a = new cell(0.0);
  generate_arrivals(n, mean_interarrival, rand, a);

  s0 = new cell(0.0);
  generate_service(n, mean_service0, rand, s0);

  d0 = new cell(0.0);
  simulate_queue(a,s0,d0);

  s1 = new cell(0.0);
  generate_service(n, mean_service1, rand, s1);

  d1 = new cell(0.0);
  simulate_queue(d0,s0,d1);

}
```

Figure 11.6
Main program for sequential simulation

```
array class {
public:
  increment();
private:
  int size;
  int a[size];
}

void array::increment()
{
  for( int i=0; i < size; i++)
    a[i]++;
}
```

and another class:

```
array distributed_class {
public:
  void increment();
private:
```

```
main()
{
  cell *sync a, *sync s0, *sync d0, *sync s1, *sync d1;
  // begin parallel block
  par {
    a = new cell(0.0);
    generate_arrivals(n, mean_interarrival, rand, a);

    s0 = new cell(0.0);
    generate_service(n, mean_service0, rand, s0);

    d0 = new cell(0.0);
    simulate_queue(a,s0,d0);

    s1 = new cell(0.0);
    generate_service(n, mean_service1, rand, s1);

  } // end parallel block
}
```

```
  int size;
  int number_of_blocks;
  int size_of_block;
  int *a[number_of_blocks];
}

void array::increment()
{
  parfor(int i=0; i < number_of_blocks; i++)
    for(int j=0; j < size_of_block; j++)
      a[i][j]++;
}
```

Consider the following program stub:

```
array x;
distributed_array y;
x.increment();
y.increment();
```

The function calls `x.increment()` and `y.increment()` have the same effect, though the former call is implemented by a sequential algorithm, and the latter by a distributed algorithm.

```
sync cell * sync f(int low, high)
{
  int middle = (high-low)/2;
  if (high==low)
    return g(middle);
  else if (high-low <= threshold)
    return merge(f(low,middle), f(middle+1,high));
  else {
    sync cell *sync result = (sync cell *sync) new sync cell;
    spawn *result = *merge(f(low,middle),f(middle+1,high));
    return result;
  }
}
```

Here is another example, where the user of a library can write a sequential program, and have the program execute in parallel.

11.5.6 Monitors

Let us implement a message-passing channel with asynchronous sends and asynchronous receives. This example demonstrates the use of atomicity.

```
struct msg_cell{
  msg *data;
  msg_cell *next; }
```

We will create a list of msg_cell where the data field of each cell will point to a message.

```
struct ptr_cell{
  msg *sync *global data;
  ptr_cell *next; }
```

We use a list of ptr_cell where the data field of each cell points to a sync pointer to a message.

```
class channel{
  private:
    ptr_cell *recv_front, *recv_back;
    msg_cell *sent_front, *sent_back;

  public:
    atomic void send(msg m);
    atomic void receive(msg *sync *p);
}
```

Here `recv_front` and `recv_back` point to the front and back of the receive queue which is a queue of `ptr_cell`. Likewise `sent_front` and `sent_back` point to the front and back of the sent queue which is a queue of `msg_cell`.

Both sending and receiving are asynchronous. The sender does not block if there is no pending receive. Likewise, the receiver does not block if there is no message for it. The receiver executes `receive(p)` where p is of type `msg *sync *`; if `*p` is uninitialized then there is no message corresponding to this receive; if `*p` is initialized then `*p` is the address of the message that is received.

An empty queue is represented by a single *sentinel* cell that has an arbitrary data field. Thus, in an empty queue, `recv_front` = `recv_back` and both point to the sentinel cell. The last cell in the queue points to NULL; thus, `recv_back->next` = NULL.

An invariant of the program is that the receive queue or the sent queue is empty. Initially, both queues are empty. The sent queue contains the sequence of messages that have been sent and not yet received. The receive queue contains the sequence of pointers that will be assigned to messages when they arrive.

```
atomic void channel::send(msg m)
{
  msg *q = new msg(m);
  // q points to an area of memory containing a copy of m.

  // if the receive queue is empty, append m to the sent queue
  if(recv_front->next = (ptr_cell *) NULL) {
    sent_back->next = new msg_cell(q,(msg_cell*) NULL);
    // sent_back ->next points to a msg_cell whose data field
    // points to msg m, and whose next field is NULL.
    sent_back = sent_back->next;
  } else {
    // Since the receive queue is not empty, there is at least one
    // pending receive; so make the first pending receive pointer
    // point to m.
    ptr_cell *r = recv_front->next;
    // r points to first pending receive.
    recv_front->next = r->next;
    // r is no longer in the receive queue.
    *(r->data) = (msg *sync) q;
    delete r;
  }
}
```

The receive operation is the analog of the send operation, interchanging the use of receive queues and sent queues.

```
atomic void channel::receive(msg *sync *p)
{
    // if the sent queue is empty, append p to the receive queue
    if(sent_front->next = (msg_cell *) NULL) {
        recv_back->next = new ptr_cell(p,(ptr_cell*)NULL);
        // recv_back-¿next points to a ptr_cell whose data field
        // is p, and whose next field is NULL.
        recv_back = recv_back->next;
    } else {
        //  Since the sent queue is not empty, there is at least one
        //  unreceived message; so make p point to the first unreceived
        //  message.
        msg\_cell *r = sent\_front->next;
        //  r points to cell pointing to first unreceived message.
        sent\_front->next = r->next;
        //  r is no longer in the sent queue.
        *p = (msg *sync) r->data;
        delete r;
    }
}
```

11.6   Implementing CC++

An initial implementation of CC++ has recently been completed. In this section, we will discuss the significant aspects of the implementation. The goal of our implementation is functionality, not performance; there are clearly many avenues for optimization that can and will be pursued. At the present time, we do not have any performance data on our CC++ implementation.

Since the relationship between CC++ and C++ is so close, any implementation of CC++ should be based on an existing C++ implementation. Our strategy is to preprocess a CC++ program into a proper C++ program. The resulting C++ program is then translated into an executable form by an unmodified C++ compiler. The components of the implementation that are specific to CC++ consist of: 1) a CC++ to C++ translator, 2) a set of C++ class definitions that are used by the C++ compiler and 3) a CC++ runtime library.

The primary mechanisms that the CC++ implementation must provide are:

- multiple threads of control (for **par** blocks and **spawn** statements,

- global references, and

- single assignment semantics for all fundamental data types (integer, character, floats, etc.) and pointers.

Multiple threads of control are provided by any lightweight process library; an existing C++ thread package such as [5, 24] could also be used. The minimal capability required by the thread library is the ability to create new threads, uniquely identify a thread via an identifier and suspend and resume thread execution via its identifier. Certain execution environments, such as shared memory multiprocessors, also require the ability to perform an atomic action.

The implementation of CC++ global references varies greatly depending on the target architecture. Some parallel computers have hardware support for a single shared address space. On such machines, the CC++ implementation maps global references into regular references. However, many scalable parallel architectures do not directly support shared address spaces. While operating systems can support a global address space with page level sharing [17], finer resolutions are required for CC++.

On machines that don't provide a global address space, global pointers must be implemented in software. A global pointer is represented by an identifier for the address space being pointed into and the address within that address space. Operator overloading is used to convert a request for the contents of a global pointer into a message requesting its value from the appropriate processor. If the global pointer is to a sync object, the entire object can be cached on the processor on which the global pointer located. Obviously, using a global pointer to reference an object between logical processor objects will cost more that a local reference. However, as discussed in Section 11.2.1, locality of reference cannot be ignored.

Like global references, the implementation of sync objects will depend on the underlying hardware support. Some parallel computer architectures, such as the Dally' J-Machine and Smith's Tera, have hardware support for determining if a memory location has been written. However, on most computers, sync objects must be implemented in software. The CC++ implementation does this by associating a tag with every sync data element.

11.6.1 Converting CC++ to C++

To convert CC++ into C++ , the CC++ program is parsed, constructing a parse tree. The parse tree is then modified, converting it into a C++ parse tree and then written out in textual form. The CC++ parser is a modified version of the GNU C++ (G++) [28] parser. There are some minor syntactic limitations on the C++ accepted by G++ and the current CC++ implementation inherits these.

The hardest part of the transformation process is to ensure that the semantic restrictions outlined in Section 11.4 are checked as carefully as possible. The actual transformations required are straight forward.

11.7 Related Research

In our work, we have focused on language mechanisms that facilitate the design of interfaces for parallel composition. The design of CC++ draws ideas from a wide range of parallel programming languages. These include data flow languages with single-assignment variables [27, 1], remote procedure calls [25], message passing [22], actors [2], concurrent logic programming [11, 29, 23] and compositional languages, particularly PCN [7]. In this section, we discuss how significant aspects of CC++ relate to other parallel programming notations.

Parallel composition as defined by **par** blocks can be found in a number of other parallel programming notations. For example, a **par** is equivalent to the use of *cobegin* and *coend* in [20] and the parallel composition operator in PCN [7].

The use of **par** blocks differs from most other concurrent object-oriented languages in that with a **par** block, multiple threads of control exist within a single object. Other languages tend to associate thread creation with object creation [5, 14, 24, 2]. Consequently, only one thread of control is ever associated with an object. The **spawn** statement in CC++ can be used to achieve the same effect.

The advantage of **par** blocks and **parfor** statements over the tying thread creation to object creation approach is twofold. First, these statements are block-oriented, and they make parallelism within a block explicit; there is no question as to which statements execute in parallel and which in sequence. The second advantage is that one can associate a post condition with a **par** block or a **parfor** statement. When the statement terminates, the post condition can be asserted. This simplifies the process of reasoning about the behavior of the program.

Reasoning about the behavior of a program containing a **spawn** statement is more difficult. Because there is no way of knowing when the thread started by the **spawn** starts or completes, assertions about the **spawn** statement must state that a condition will hold at some unknown point in the future. Thus one has no choice but to resort to a temporal operator such as the *leads-to* operator.

No doubt, some readers will have recognized sync variables as being single assignment variables from dataflow languages [18] or from languages based in concurrent logic programming [10]. A reference to a structure which contains **sync** objects behaves much like an I-Structure in the dataflow language ID [4]. **sync** variables differ in that the **sync** attribute can be extended to abstract and concrete data types as definable in C++. In addition, **sync** variables differ from variables in programming languages such as Strand [10] and PCN [7] in that the blocking rule for **sync** variables prohibits the use of variable-to-variable assignment found in these languages.

Many concurrent object-oriented languages [2, 3, 30] use function call as the basis for communication. In actor based languages, a function call is interpreted as sending a message to the target object to perform the requested operation. The arguments in the function call are passed to the target object as well. The function call terminates immediately, without a waiting for a response from the target object. Applying this approach to C++ is problematic in that this approach changes the meaning of function call. By associating communication with shared variables and assignment, the semantics of all of the underlying operations in C++ are preserved. Finally, we note that actor type semantics of function call can be achieved either through the use of the **spawn** statement within the body of a member function or assignment to a **sync** variable whose value is read by a nondeterministic fair merger.

It is important to recognize that a **sync** variable in CC++ is a pure single assignment variable and not a logical variable as found in concurrent logic programming languages such as Strand [11], FCP [23], GHC [29] or Parlog [13] or compositional languages such as PCN [7]. In particular, the assignment x = y suspends until y has a value; variable-to-variable assignments are not made. Consequently, structured `sync` data behaves more like an I-Structure [4] from the dataflow language Id [1] than a tuple from a logic programming language. The use of single assignment variables in place of logical variables has the advantages that assignment semantics are completely consistent with C++ , and that pointer dereferencing is not required prior to variable use. The disadvantage is that some concurrent logic programming techniques, such as the short circuit technique [26] become sequentialized. This is not a significant drawback, however, because termination of parallel blocks is easily determined.

CC++ has many ideas in common with the parallel programming language PCN [7] which in turn draws heavily from committed choice concurrent logic programming languages such as Strand [11]. There are, however, fundamental differences between them. These include:

- CC++ provides a general shared-memory programming model. This includes having pointers to data objects anywhere in distributed memory.

- CC++ is a tiny extension to an object-oriented language whereas PCN is a new language. Indeed, most of the power of CC++ derives from C++ .

- Remote procedure call is a primitive operation in CC++.

- There are no nondeterministic language constructs in CC++ as opposed to PCN. Nondeterminism in CC++ can be obtained only through interleaving of atomic actions.

- PCN permits x = y as an equality. CC++ treats all assignment operators as assignment of value.

11.8   Summary

The six additions to C++ allow for the systematic development of concurrent programs. The central thesis of this effort is that it is possible to derive correct efficient parallel programs and support a variety of parallel programming paradigms in C++, using C++ tools such as programming environments and libraries, and six new constructs that are similar to existing constructs in C++.

11.9   Acknowledgment

The implementation of CC++ was done with the assistance of Mei Su, Tal Lancaster, Pete Carlin, Marc Pomerantz, Julia George and Ranjit Mathews. Thanks to Ian Foster and Craig Lee for their suggestions and for reviewing various versions of this document.

The research on C++ object libraries for concurrent computation is funded by DARPA under grant N00014-91-J-4014. The research on compositional concurrent notations is funded by the NSF Center for Research on Parallel Computing under grant CCR-8809615.

References

[1] William B. Ackerman. Data flow languages. *Computer*, 15(2):15–25, feb 1982.

[2] Gul Agha. *ACTORS: A Model of Concurrent Computation in Distributed Systems*. MIT Press, 1986.

[3] William C. Athas and C.L. Seitz. Multicomputers: Message-passing concurrent computers. *IEEE Computer*, aug 1988.

[4] Arvind and R.E. Thomas. I-Structures: An efficient data structure for functional languages. Technical Report TM-178, MIT, 1980.

[5] Brian Bershad, Edward Lazowska, and Henry Levy. Presto: A system of object-oriented parallel programming. *Software: Practice and Experience*, 18(8):713–732, aug 1988.

[6] K. Mani Chandy and Jayadev Misra. *Parallel Program Design*. Addison-Wesley, 1988.

[7] K. Mani Chandy and Stephen Taylor. *An Introduction to Parallel Programming*. Bartlett and Jones, 1991.

[8] Ian Foster. Program transformation notation: A tutorial. Technical Report ANL-91/38, Argonne National Laboratory, 1991.

[9] Ian Foster. Information hiding in parallel programs. Technical Report MCS-P290-0292, Argonne National Laboratory, 1992.

[10] Ian Foster and Stephen Taylor. *STRAND: New Concepts in Parallel Programming*. Prentice Hall, 1989.

[11] Ian Foster and Stephen Taylor. *Strand: New Concepts in Parallel Programming*. Prentice Hall, 1990.

[12] Ian Foster and Steve Tuecke. Parallel programming with PCN. Technical Report ANL-91/32, Argonne National Laboratory, 1992.

[13] Steve Gregory. *Parallel Logic Programming in PARLOG*. International Series in Logic Programming. Addison-Wesley, 1987.

[14] Andrew S. Grimshaw. An introduction to parallel object-oriented programming with Mentat. Computer Science Report TR-91-07, University of Virginia, 1991.

[15] C.A.R Hoare. Monitors: An operating system structuring concept. *cacm*, 17(10):549–557, oct 1974.

[16] C. Houck. Run-time system support for distributed actor programs. Master's thesis, University of Illinois at Urbana-Champaign, 1992.

[17] Kai Li and Richard Schaefer. A hypercube shared virtual memory system. In *Proceedings of the 1989 International Conference on Parallel Processing*, pages 125–132, aug 1989.

[18] J. McGraw et al. SISAL: Streams and iteration in a single assignment language, language reference manual, version 1.2. Technical Report M-146, LLNL, mar 1985.

[19] Bertrand Meyer. *Object-oriented Software Construction*. Prentice Hall International, 1988.

[20] S. Owicki and D. Gries. An axiomatic proof technique for parallel programs I. *Acta Informatica*, 6(1):319–340, 1976.

[21] Per Brinch Hansen. *The Architecture of Concurrent Programs*. Prentice-Hall, 1977.

[22] Charles Seitz. *Developments in Concurrency and Communication*, chapter 5, pages 131–200. Addison Wesley, 1991.

[23] Ehud Shapiro. Concurrent Prolog: A program report. *IEEE Computer*, 19(8):44–58, aug 1986.

[24] Bjarne Stroustrup and Jonathan Shopiro. A set of C++ classes for co-routine style programming. In *Proceedings of the USENIX C++ Workshop*, nov 1987.

[25] B. H. Tay and A. L. Ananda. A survey of remote procedure calls. *ACM Operating Systems Review*, 24(3), jul 1990.

[26] Akikazu Takeuchi. How to solve it in Concurrent Prolog. Unpublished note., 1989.

[27]   L. Tesler and H. Enea.   A language for concurrent processes.   In *Proceedings of AFIPS SJCC*, number ANL-91/38, 1968.

[28]   Michael D. Tiemann. *User's Guide to GNU C++*. Free Software Foundation, Inc., oct 1991.

[29]   Kazunori Ueda. Guarded horn clauses. In *Logic Programming '85*, pages 168–179. Springer-Verlag, 1986.

[30]   Andrew A. Chien, Waldemar Horwat and William J. Dally. Experience with CST: Programming and implementation. In *SIGPLAN 89 Conference on Programming Language Design and Implementation*, 1989.

12 A Logical Theory of Concurrent Objects and Its Realization in the Maude Language*

José Meseguer

A new theory of concurrent objects is presented. The theory has the important advantage of being based directly on a simple logic called *rewriting logic* in which concurrent object-oriented computation exactly corresponds to logical deduction. This deduction is performed by *concurrent rewriting* modulo structural axioms of associativity, commutativity and identity that capture abstractly the essential aspects of communication in a distributed object-oriented configuration made up of concurrent objects and messages. This axiomatization of objects, classes, and concurrent object-oriented computations in terms of rewriting logic is proposed as a general semantic framework for object-oriented programming. A direct fruit of this theory is a new language, called Maude, that can be used to program concurrent object-oriented systems in an entirely declarative way using rewriting logic. Modules written in this language are used to illustrate the main ideas with examples. Maude supports a highly modular and parameterized programming style, contains OBJ3 as a functional sublanguage, and provides a simple and semantically rigorous unification of functional programming and concurrent object-oriented programming. A sublanguage called Simple Maude that can be implemented with reasonable efficiency on a wide variety of parallel architectures is described. The relationship with Actors and with other models of concurrent computation is discussed. An extension of Maude called MaudeLog is sketched; MaudeLog is also based on rewriting logic and unifies the paradigms of functional, relational, and concurrent object-oriented programming. The model theory of rewriting logic and an initial model semantics for Maude modules are also discussed.

12.1 Introduction

An important feature that makes object-oriented programming very attractive as a programming language paradigm is its conceptual support for structuring programs as systems made up of objects that interact with each other. Object-oriented concepts fit well with our intuitive ideas about ordinary objects and their interactions in the world and allow us to conceive of a program as either a *simulation* or model of some aspects of the world, or—when actual interaction with the world is desired, as for example in a robotics application—as the addition of a subsystem of *artificial objects* as artifacts that interact with other objects in the world.

Since interactions between objects in the real world are concurrent, it would seem to follow that concurrency should be viewed as an *intrinsic* property of object-oriented systems. Although this idea was certainly present in the Simula 67 language [32, 16] and was partially realized there within the constraints of a sequential implementation by means of the notion of "quasi-parallel" execution, the notion that concurrency is intrinsic to object-oriented programming seems to have been deemphasized or forgotten to a considerable extent in the subsequent evolution of the field, as the existence of the term "concurrent object-oriented programming" to indicate a delimited subfield concerned with "adding concurrency" to object-oriented programming seems to point out.

*Supported by Office of Naval Research Contracts N00014-90-C-0086 and N00014-92-C-0518, and by the Information Technology Promotion Agency, Japan, as a part of the R & D of Basic Technology for Future Industries "New Models for Software Architecture" sponsored by NEDO (New Energy and Industrial Technology Development Organization).

Contents

This is an unsatisfactory state of affairs, especially when the following considerations are added:

1. At present it is considered very difficult to have both concurrency and inheritance in an object-oriented language. This difficulty is referred to as the "inheritance anomaly" [67, 90, 38].

2. Type-theoretic approaches to object-oriented programming, which are sometimes put forward as providing a semantics for the field, seem at present to be altogether silent on concurrency issues.

3. There seems to exist no agreement on a semantic basis for concurrent object-oriented programming. Wildly varying proposals to graft all sorts of concurrency constructs and models quite alien to the concepts of object-oriented programming into existing or new languages in an ad-hoc way are not only made, but are in some cases followed up with actual implementations. Certainly, Actors [3, 1] seems the best proposal so far, since actors do not suffer from the incoherence of other approaches and message passing is a very flexible communication mechanism, but the addition of inheritance to actor languages still seems to run into the difficulties already mentioned above.

4. Since just adding concurrency is at present somewhat of a stumbling block, it is not surprising that there is even less agreement on how concurrent object-oriented programming could be unified in a multiparadigm fashion with functional programming and with relational programming in a coherent and semantically rigorous way.

Regarding the last consideration, there are very good reasons for seeking a unification of these three paradigms or "perspectives" as Kristen Nygaard likes to call them. As Nygaard himself points out [89],

> "It seems obvious to the author that all these three perspectives should be supported within any new general programming language in the future. No perspective will "win" as some seem to believe."

Indeed, there is much to be gained in a unification of this kind if it is done right. By "done right" I mean that the overall unification should be based directly on an adequate logic so that programs become theories in that logic and computation becomes logical deduction. This, however, is not an easy task. The main difficulty has to do with logic, because the logics on which functional and relational programming are based—namely, equational logic (in either a first-order or a higher-order version) and first-order Horn logic, respectively—describe unchanging Platonic structures such as sets, functions and relations, as is fitting for logics originally introduced to develop logical foundations for mathematics. Such logics, however, deal very poorly with action and change, and deal particularly poorly with the type of change typical of concurrent object-oriented systems. This has many manifestations in practice, including among others the long-term embarrassment of the frame problem[1] in artificial intelligence.

This work proposes a simple logic of action called rewriting logic [70, 69, 72] as a general semantic framework for object-oriented programming with the following characteristics:

---

[1] For a detailed discussion of why rewriting logic entirely avoids the frame problem see [63].

1. Concurrency is intrinsic and therefore the semantic framework formalizes *concurrent* object-oriented programming. However, concurrency is *implicit* and does not require any special extralogical constructs; this agrees with the view that concurrency is inherent to object-oriented systems and should therefore be directly supported by an adequate semantic framework.

2. A rigorous semantics for multiple class inheritance is provided in such a way that the so-called inheritance anomaly blocking the integration of concurrency and inheritance disappears completely.

3. A declarative version of the actor model appears as a special case, and is given a new logical and truly concurrent semantics based on rewriting logic.

4. Rewriting logic provides not only a semantic framework, but also a *computational model* for concurrent object-oriented programming. This allows a fully declarative programming style for concurrent object-oriented systems that can be programmed as theories in rewriting logic and whose concurrent computations correspond to logical deductions in such a logic. All this is realized in a language called Maude that is directly based on rewriting logic, and makes possible a natural integration of specification, programming, and formal reasoning within such a language.

5. Maude naturally unifies the functional programming paradigm with concurrent object-oriented programming and contains a slight linguistic variant of the OBJ language [45, 53] as its functional sublanguage. An extension of Maude called MaudeLog [73]—also based entirely on rewriting logic—unifies the three paradigms of functional, relational, and concurrent object-oriented programming.

6. Rewriting logic is sound and complete and has initial models. The mathematical semantics of Maude modules is based on such initial models which intuitively correspond to concurrent systems[2].

7. Like OBJ [53], Eqlog [48], and FOOPS [49], Maude has modularity and parameterization mechanisms à la Clear [20]. This, together with its support for multiple class inheritance and with two new module operations proposed in this paper, endows Maude with powerful mechanisms for program reuse and for programming-in-the-large by adapting and composing modules together in very flexible ways.

8. A sublanguage of Maude called Simple Maude [83] provides a machine independent parallel programming language that can be implemented with reasonable efficiency on a wide variety of parallel architectures. In addition, Simple Maude can be used to incorporate modules written in conventional code into parallel programs, and to integrate open heterogeneous systems in a parallel computing environment.

The paper discusses in more detail all the aspects just mentioned about rewriting logic as a semantic framework for concurrent object-oriented programming and about the Maude language, and illustrates many of the ideas with examples. Section 2 introduces Maude's functional and system modules and their concurrent rewriting computation, and

---

[2]However, the denotational semantics of *functional* modules is given by the usual initial algebra semantics as in OBJ [51].

discusses some basic order-sorted algebra concepts used throughout the paper. Section 3 introduces rewriting logic, identifies concurrent rewriting computation with deduction in such a logic, and discusses the intended meaning of the logic. Section 4 presents a logical theory of concurrent objects based on rewriting logic, introduces Maude's object-oriented modules, and discusses class and module inheritance, object creation and deletion, message broadcasting, reflection, and actors. A brief discussion of the generality of rewriting logic as a model of concurrency is also included at the end of the section. Section 5 introduces Simple Maude, summarizes implementation ideas for several parallel architectures, and briefly discusses support for multilingual extensions and open heterogeneous systems. Section 6 presents and discusses two longer Maude examples. Section 7 gives a brief sketch of Maude and MaudeLog as multiparadigm logic programming languages and discusses the multiparadigm unification of functional and concurrent object-oriented programming, and of functional, relational, and concurrent object-oriented programming that they respectively provide. Section 8 discusses the model theory of rewriting logic, including initial and free models, gives a computational interpretation of such models as concurrent systems, and defines the mathematical semantics of Maude modules in terms of initial models. Section 9 discusses related work. The paper ends with some concluding remarks in Section 10.

12.2   Maude and Concurrent Rewriting

Concurrent rewriting is motivated with examples of *functional* and *system* modules in Maude. The system module examples show that the traditional interpretation of rewrite rules as equations must be abandoned and that a new logic and model theory are needed. Rewriting logic—introduced in Section 12.3—provides the answer; in it, concurrent computation by rewriting coincides with logical deduction. Discussion of object-oriented aspects, and in particular of Maude's *object-oriented* modules, is deferred to Section 12.4.

12.2.1   Functional Modules

The idea of concurrent rewriting is very simple. It is the idea of *equational simplification* that we are all familiar with from our secondary school days, *plus* the obvious remark that we can do many of those simplifications independently, i.e., in *parallel*. Consider for example the following Maude functional modules written in a notation entirely similar to that of OBJ3 [45, 53]:

```
fmod NAT is                         fmod NAT-REVERSE is
  sorts Nat NzNat .                     protecting NAT .
  subsort NzNat < Nat .                 sort Tree .
  op 0 : -> Nat .                       subsort Nat < Tree .
  op s_ : Nat -> NzNat .                op _^_ : Tree Tree -> Tree .
  op p_ : NzNat -> Nat .                op rev : Tree -> Tree .
  op _+_ : Nat Nat -> Nat [comm] .      var N : Nat .
  vars N M : Nat .                      vars T T' : Tree .
```

```
eq p s N = N .                          eq rev(N) = N .
eq N + 0 = N .                          eq rev(T ^ T') =
eq (s N) + (s M) = s s (N + M) .            rev(T') ^ rev(T) .
endfm                                   endfm
```

The first module defines the natural numbers in Peano notation with successor, prede-cessor and addition functions, and the second defines a function to reverse a binary tree whose leaves are natural numbers. Each module begins with the keyword **fmod** followed by the module's name, and ends with the keyword **endfm**. A module contains sort and subsort declarations introduced by the keywords **sort(s)** and **subsort(s)** stating the different sorts of data manipulated by the module and how those sorts are related. As in OBJ3, Maude's type structure is *order-sorted* [51]; therefore, sorts form a partially ordered set and it is possible to declare one sort as a *subsort* of another; for example, the declaration NzNat < Nat states that every nonzero natural number is a natural number, and the declaration Nat < Tree states that every natural number is a tree consisting of a single node. It is also possible to *overload* function symbols for operations that are defined at several levels of a sort hierarchy and agree on their results when restricted to common subsorts; for example, an addition operation _+_ may be defined for sorts Nat, Int, and Rat of natural, integer, and rational numbers with

Nat < Int < Rat .

Each of the functions provided by the module, as well as the sorts of their arguments and the sort of their result, is introduced using the keyword **op**. The syntax is user-definable, and permits specifying function symbols in "prefix," (in the NAT example the functions s_ and p_), "infix" (_+_) or any "mixfix" combination as well as standard parenthesized notation (**rev**).

A *functional* model for such an order-sorted syntax is called an *order-sorted algebra* [51] and consists of a set A_s for each sort symbol s, so that if $s \leq s'$ then $A_s \subseteq A_{s'}$, together with a function $f_A : A_{s_1} \times \ldots \times A_{s_n} \longrightarrow A_s$ for each operator declaration $f : s_1 \ldots s_n \longrightarrow s$ in such a way that if another operator declaration $f : s'_1 \ldots s'_n \longrightarrow s'$ has been given, with $s'_i \leq s_i$, $i = 1, \ldots, n$, and $s' \leq s$, then the function $f_A : A_{s'_1} \times \ldots \times A_{s'_n} \longrightarrow A_{s'}$ is just the restriction of the function $f_A : A_{s_1} \times \ldots \times A_{s_n} \longrightarrow A_s$ to the subset $A_{s'_1} \times \ldots \times A_{s'_n}$. The number hierarchy from the naturals to the rationals (and of course beyond) provides a good example of an order-sorted algebra.

Variables to be used for defining equations are declared with their corresponding sorts, and then equations are given; such equations provide the actual "code" of the module. Deduction with such equations is a typed variant of equational logic called *order-sorted equational logic*. However, operationally, only deduction from left to right by rewriting is performed, as explained below. As in OBJ3, the *mathematical semantics* of a Maude functional module is the *initial* order-sorted algebra [51] satisfying the equations declared in the module. For the two modules above, such initial algebras are just what we would expect, namely the natural numbers—with zero, successor, predecessor and addition—for the NAT module, and binary trees with natural numbers on their leaves—with tree

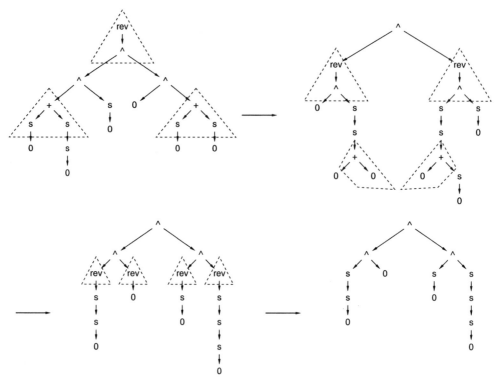

Figure 12.1
Concurrent rewriting of a tree of numbers.

reversal and binary tree constructor operators—for the **NAT-REVERSE** module, in which
the natural numbers are viewed as the subset of trees consisting of a single node.

The statement **protecting NAT** imports **NAT** as a *submodule* of **NAT-REVERSE** and
asserts that the natural numbers are not modified in the sense that no new data of sort
Nat is added, and different numbers are not identified by the new equations declared in
NAT-REVERSE.

To compute with such modules, one performs equational simplification by using the
equations from left to right until no more simplifications are possible. Note that this
can be done *concurrently*, i.e., applying several equations at once, as in the example of
Figure 12.1, in which the places where the equations have been matched at each step
are marked. Notice that the function symbol _+_ was declared to be commutative by the
attribute[3] [comm]. This not only asserts that the equation N + M = M + N is satisfied in
the intended semantics, but it also means that when doing simplification we are allowed
to apply the rules for addition not just to *terms*—in a purely syntactic way—but to
equivalence classes of terms *modulo* the commutativity equation. In the example of

---

[3]In Maude, as in OBJ3, it is possible to declare several attributes of this kind for an operator, including
also associativity and identity, and then do rewriting modulo such properties.

Figure 12.1, the equation `N + 0 = N` is applied (modulo commutativity) with 0 both on the right *and* on the left.

A particularly appealing feature of this style of concurrent programming is the *implicit* nature of the parallelism. Since in the two modules above the equations are *Church-Rosser* (also called *confluent*) and *terminating* (see Section 12.3.3 for a definition of these notions, [56, 33] for further background on the subject, and [59] for corresponding order-sorted versions of such notions) the *order* in which the rules are applied does not at all affect the final result. This agrees with the usual functional programming expectations, since it would be quite strange to obtain different results for the same functional expression. Indeed, in Maude, the rules in a *functional* module are always assumed to be Church-Rosser, but as we shall see later this is not assumed for either system modules or object-oriented modules, which do *not* have a functional interpretation.

12.2.1.1 Parameterized Functional Modules   As in OBJ3, functional modules can be *parameterized*. For example, we can define a parameterized module by generalizing the `NAT-REVERSE` module to a parameterized `REVERSE[X :: TRIV]` module in which the set of data that can be stored in tree leaves is a parameter. In parameterized modules, the properties that the parameter must satisfy are specified by one or more *parameter theories*. In this case, the (functional) parameter theory is the trivial theory `TRIV`

```
fth TRIV is
  sort Elt .
endft
```

which only requires a set `Elt` of elements. We can then define

```
fmod REVERSE[X :: TRIV] is
  sort Tree .
  subsort Elt < Tree .
  op _^_ : Tree Tree -> Tree .
  op rev : Tree -> Tree .
  var E : Elt .
  vars T T' : Tree .
  eq rev(E) = E .
  eq rev(T ^ T') = rev(T') ^ rev(T) .
endfm
```

Such a parameterized module can then be instantiated by providing an interpretation—called a *view*—mapping the parameter sort `Elt` to a sort in the module chosen as the actual parameter. For example, if we interpret `Elt` as the sort `Nat` in the `NAT` module, then we can obtain an instantiation equivalent to the module `NAT-REVERSE` in our first example by writing

```
make NAT-REVERSE is REVERSE[Nat] endmk
```

Another example of a parameterized functional module is the following module for lists whose elements belong to a set of elements. The set of elements is a parameter that can be instantiated to any set; therefore, as in the previous example, the parameter theory is the trivial theory `TRIV`.

```
fmod LIST[X :: TRIV] is
  protecting NAT BOOL .
  sort List .
  subsort Elt < List .
  op __ : List List -> List [assoc id: nil] .
  op length : List -> Nat .
  op remove_from_ : List List -> List .
  op _in_ : Elt List -> Bool .
  vars E E' : Elt .
  vars L L' : List .
  eq length(nil) = 0 .
  eq length(E L) = (s 0) + length(L) .
  eq remove nil from L = L .
  eq remove L from nil = nil .
  eq remove E from (E' L) = if E == E' then
      remove E from L else E' remove E from L fi .
  eq remove E L' from L = remove L' from (remove E from L) .
  eq E in nil = false .
  eq E in (E' L) = if E == E' then true
      else E in L fi .
endfm
```

Note that the "empty syntax" operator __ has been declared *associative* and has the constant nil as its *identity* element. The boolean operator == compares two terms and evaluates to true if they both evaluate to the same result and to false otherwise; this operator is built-in, but for modules with Church-Rosser and terminating equations it is always possible to define it equationally[4]. Rewriting with this module is performed *modulo* associativity and identity; this means that we can disregard parentheses and that a List variable can match nil. For example, if we instantiate this module to form lists of natural numbers by writing

```
make NAT-LIST is LIST[Nat] endmk
```

then the second equation for length will match the expression length(s s 0) modulo associativity and identity by matching E to s s 0 and L to nil.

12.2.1.2 Sort Constraints The expressiveness of the order-sorted type structure can be further increased by the declaration of axioms called *sort constraints* [78] (declared by the keyword sct) stating that a given functional expression has a sort smaller than anticipated. We illustrate this notion—which also appears in OBJ3 with a different syntax [53]—by the (parameterized) definition of sets as a subsort of multisets using a sort constraint. The example reuses the parameterized LIST module, adapting it to the present context by renaming the nil list to the null multiset and the List sort to the MSet sort using a module renaming construct, and by turning list concatenation into multiset union thanks to the addition of a commutativity attribute. Such reuse illustrates

[4]Cf. Theorems 54 and 71 in [77].

a flexible form of *module inheritance* that is available in Maude through its submodule, parameterization, and module expression mechanisms and is further discussed in Section 12.4.3. However, as it was also done in the FOOPS language [49], such inheritance at the module level is sharply distinguished from *class inheritance*, which will be discussed in Section 12.4.2 and which is a special case of *subsort inheritance*.

```
fmod MSET[X :: TRIV] is
  using LIST[X]*(sort List to MSet, op nil to null) .
  sort Set .
  subsorts Elt < Set < MSet .
  op __ : MSet MSet -> MSet [comm] .
  op null : -> Set .
  op set : MSet -> Set .
  op _U_ : Set Set -> Set .
  op |_| : Set -> Nat .
  var E : Elt .
  var MS : MSet .
  vars S S' : Set .
  sct (E S) : Set if not(E in S) .
  eq set(null) = null .
  eq set(E) = E .
  eq set(E MS) = if (E in MS) then set(MS) else E set(S) fi .
  eq S U S' = set(S S') .
  eq | S | = length(S) .
endfm
```

The keyword using asserts that, in this importation of the (renamed) LIST module, semantic modifications are being introduced so that the original equality relation between data elements will be altered[5]. The renaming expression

```
LIST[X]*(sort List to MSet, op nil to null)
```

changes the syntax of the LIST[X] module by renaming its sort List to MSet and its operator nil to null.

The original list concatenation operator is now understood as a multiset union operator; the original operator was already associative and had nil (now renamed to null) as an identity. Now we add a *commutativity* axiom, so that two multisets are equal if one is a permutation of the other; this is accomplished by adding a [comm] attribute declaration to the imported multiset union operator. Of course, this changes the equality relation between data elements. It also changes the rewriting relation in the sense that concurrent rewriting in this module is performed *modulo* the associativity, commutativity and identity axioms for the operator __. Therefore, we can disregard parentheses and the order of the arguments. We call rewriting modulo associativity, commutativity and identity *ACI-rewriting*.

---

[5]In general, further modifications by addition of new data elements to old sorts could also occur in a module imported with a using declaration; i.e., both addition of "junk" (new data elements) and of "confusion" between old data elements can take place in a using module importation.

The subsort Set of sets is defined as the subsort of all multisets with no repeated elements. This is accomplished by means of four declarations: the subsort declaration Set < MSet; an operator declaration stating that null is a set; a subsort declaration Elt < Set stating that singleton multisets are sets; and a sort constraint stating that the addition of an element to a set yields also a set provided that the element was not already inside the original set.

In general, a *sort constraint* [78] is a conditional assertion of the form

$$t(x_1, \ldots, x_n) : s$$

$$\text{if} \quad u_1(x_1, \ldots, x_n) = v_1(x_1, \ldots, x_n) \wedge \ldots \wedge u_k(x_1, \ldots, x_n) = v_k(x_1, \ldots, x_n)$$

where s is a sort and $t(x_1, \ldots, x_n)$ and the u_j, v_j are terms whose variables have sorts, say, $x_i : s_i$, $i = 1, \ldots, n$. We say that an order-sorted algebra A *satisfies* such a sort constraint if, for any assignment of values $a_i \in A_{s_i}$ to the variables x_i, such that for each $j = 1, \ldots, k$ the elements $u_{j_A}(a_1, \ldots, a_n)$ and $v_{j_A}(a_1, \ldots, a_n)$—obtained by evaluating the terms u_j and v_j in the algebra A under the assignment—are equal, then the element $t_A(a_1, \ldots, a_n)$ obtained by evaluating the term t in the algebra A under the assignment belongs to the set A_s. For the sort constraint in the above example, $k = 1$, with u_1 the term not(E in S), and v_1 (left implicit) the term true. If the sort constraint's condition is empty ($k = 0$) we speak of an *unconditional sort constraint* and adopt the notation

$$t(x_1, \ldots, x_n) : s$$

It is a fortunate fact that the class of order-sorted algebras satisfying a given set of equations and sort constraints has an initial algebra [76]. Of course, the *mathematical semantics* of (unparameterized) functional modules containing such sort constraint declarations is precisely such an initial algebra; a parameterized version of such an initiality result is what applies to the above multiset and set example. This means what we would naturally expect, i.e., that for each instantiation of the above module to a given set X of elements, the sort MSet consists of finite multisets of elements of X, the sort Set consists of finite sets of elements of X, and the data type operations between such sorts behave as desired.

In particular, the following additional operations have been defined: a function set that turns each multiset into a set by removing duplicated elements; a set union function _U_; and a set cardinality function |_|. Of course, a variety of other set-theoretic operations could have been defined similarly if desired.

12.2.2 System Modules

Maude system modules perform concurrent rewriting computations in exactly the same way as functional modules; however, their behavior is not functional. Consider the following module, NAT-CHOICE, which adds a nondeterministic choice operator to the natural numbers.

```
mod NAT-CHOICE is
    extending NAT .
    op _?_ : Nat Nat -> Nat .
```

```
    vars N M : Nat .
    rl N ? M => N .
    rl N ? M => M .
  endm
```

The intuitive *operational behavior* of this module is quite clear. Natural number addition remains unchanged and is computed using the two rules in the NAT module. Notice that any occurrence of the choice operator _?_ in an expression can be eliminated by choosing either of the arguments. In the end, we can reduce any ground expression to a natural number in Peano notation. The *mathematical semantics* of the module is much less clear. If we adopt any semantics in which the models are algebras satisfying the rules as equations—in particular an initial algebra semantics—it follows by the rules of equational deduction with the two equations in NAT-CHOICE that

```
    N = M
```

i.e., everything collapses to one point. Therefore, the declaration extending NAT, whose meaning is that two distinct natural numbers in the submodule NAT are not identified by the new equations introduced in the supermodule NAT-CHOICE, i.e., that no "confusion" is introduced in the old data, is violated in the worse possible way by this semantics; yet, the operational behavior in fact respects such a declaration. To indicate that this is not the semantics intended, system modules are distinguished from functional modules by means of the keyword mod, instead of the previous fmod. Similarly, a new keyword rl is used for rewrite rules—instead of the usual eq before each equation—and the equal sign is replaced by the new sign "=>" to suggest that rl declarations must be understood as "rules" and not as equations in the usual sense. At the operational level the equations introduced by the keyword eq in a functional module are also implemented as rewrite rules; the difference however lies in the *mathematical semantics* given to the module, which for modules like the one above should *not* be the usual initial algebra semantics. We need a logic and a model theory that are the perfect match for this problem. For this solution to be in harmony with the old one, the new logic and the new model theory should *generalize* the old ones.

System modules can also be parameterized. For example, we could have defined a parameterized module with a nondeterministic choice operator

```
  mod CHOICE[X :: TRIV] is
    op _?_ : Elt Elt -> Elt .
    vars A B : Elt .
    rl A ? B => A .
    rl A ? B => B .
  endm
```

and could have obtained a module equivalent to NAT-CHOICE by means of the module expression

```
    make NAT-CHOICE is CHOICE[Nat] endmk
```

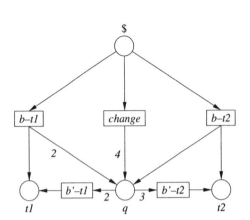

Figure 12.2
A Petri net and its code in Maude.

```
mod TICKET is
   sorts Place Marking .
   subsort Place < Marking .
   ops $,q,t1,t2 : -> Place .
   op __ : Marking Marking
            -> Marking
            [assoc comm id: null] .
   rl b-t1 : $ => t1 q q .
   rl b-t2 : $ => t2 q .
   rl change : $ => q q q q .
   rl b'-t1 : q q => t1 .
   rl b'-t2 : q q q => t2 .
endm
```

Another interesting example of a system module that illustrates both Maude's expressiveness and the generality of the concurrent rewriting model is the Petri net in Figure 12.2, which represents a machine to buy subway tickets. With a dollar we can buy a ticket $t1$ by pushing the button $b-t1$ and get two quarters back; if we push $b-t2$ instead, we get a longer distance ticket $t2$ and one quarter back. Similar buttons allow purchasing the tickets with quarters. Finally, with one dollar we can get four quarters by pushing *change*. The corresponding system module, TICKET, is given in the same figure. Note that the rules in this module are *labelled* by the name of the transition which they represent. A key point about this module is that the operator __—corresponding to *multiset union*—has been declared *associative*, *commutative*, and having an *identity* element null, and that rewriting is performed modulo those axioms, i.e., it is *ACI-rewriting*. In this example, *ACI*-rewriting captures exactly the concurrent computations of the Petri net. Suppose, for example, that we begin in a state with four quarters and two dollars. Then, by first concurrently pushing the buttons $b'-t1$ and $b-t2$, and then concurrently pushing the buttons $b'-t2$ and $b-t2$ we end up with a ticket for the shorter distance, three tickets for the longer distance and a quarter, as shown in the two steps of concurrent *ACI*-rewriting below:

$$q\ q\ q\ q\ \$\ \$ \longrightarrow q\ q\ t1\ t2\ q\ \$ \longrightarrow t2\ t1\ t2\ t2\ q.$$

As in the NAT-CHOICE example, this example also shows that initial algebra semantics is entirely inadequate to handle system modules with a nonfunctional behavior. In this case, interpreting the rules as equations would force the nonsensical identification of the three states above. System modules denote *concurrent systems*, not algebras, and rewriting logic is a logic that expresses directly the concurrent computations of such systems.

Indeed, the passage from functional modules to system modules involves a fundamental change in perspective, so that basic notions that previously had a very familiar interpretation in functional terms have now to be reinterpreted in a very different way. In

$$
\begin{array}{lcl}
State & \longleftrightarrow & Term \\
Transition & \longleftrightarrow & Rewriting \\
Distributed\ Structure & \longleftrightarrow & Algebraic\ Structure
\end{array}
$$

Figure 12.3
System-oriented interpretation of concurrent rewriting.

this new interpretation, *terms* are no longer understood as *functional expressions*, but as *structured states*, where the structure of the state is given by the operators that happen to appear in the term and by the structural axioms that they enjoy. For example, a Petri net marking is a state having a multiset structure given by a binary multiset union operator that enjoys *ACI* structural axioms. Similarly, an expression such as (3 ? 5) ? (7 ? 12) is a state having a binary tree structure. The algebraic structure of the state—as a multiset, binary tree, or whatever—is precisely what makes the state *distributed*, i.e., coincides with its *distributed structure*, and makes concurrency possible.

In the same way, *rewriting* is no longer seen as *functional evaluation* by equational deduction, but as *transition in a system*. This is clearly illustrated by the rewrite rules for the Petri net example, and also by the nondeterministic choice rules for the NAT-CHOICE example, where the final states are numbers. The states' algebraic—and therefore distributed—structure makes possible for many rewritings to occur *concurrently*, i.e., rewritings are *local* transitions of a distributed state that happen independently of each other. Figure 12.3 summarizes this discussion.

12.3 Rewriting Logic

Rewriting logic is defined, and concurrent rewriting is formalized as deduction in such a logic.

12.3.1 Basic Universal Algebra

For the sake of simplifying the exposition, we treat the *unsorted* case; the many-sorted and order-sorted cases can be given a similar treatment. Therefore, a set Σ of function symbols is a ranked alphabet $\Sigma = \{\Sigma_n \mid n \in \mathbb{N}\}$. A Σ-algebra is then a set A together with an assignment of a function $f_A : A^n \longrightarrow A$ for each $f \in \Sigma_n$ with $n \in \mathbb{N}$. We denote by T_Σ the Σ-algebra of ground Σ-terms, and by $T_\Sigma(X)$ the Σ-algebra of Σ-terms with variables in a set X. Similarly, given a set E of Σ-equations, $T_{\Sigma,E}$ denotes the Σ-algebra of equivalence classes of ground Σ-terms modulo the equations E (i.e., modulo provable equality using the equations E); in the same way, $T_{\Sigma,E}(X)$ denotes the Σ-algebra of equivalence classes of Σ-terms with variables in X modulo the equations E. Let $t =_E t'$ denote the congruence modulo E of two terms t, t', and let $[t]_E$ or just $[t]$ denote the E-equivalence class of t.

Given a term $t \in T_\Sigma(\{x_1, \ldots, x_n\})$, and terms $u_1, \ldots, u_n$, $t(u_1/x_1, \ldots, u_n/x_n)$ denotes the term obtained from t by *simultaneously substituting* u_i for x_i, $i = 1, \ldots, n$. To simplify notation, we denote a sequence of objects $a_1, \ldots, a_n$ by $\bar{a}$, or, to emphasize the length of the sequence, by $\overline{a}^n$. With this notation, $t(u_1/x_1, \ldots, u_n/x_n)$ can be abbreviated to $t(\overline{u}/\overline{x})$.

12.3.2   The Rules of Rewriting Logic

We are now ready to introduce the new logic that we are seeking, which we call *rewriting logic*. A *signature* in this logic is a pair (Σ, E) with Σ a ranked alphabet of function symbols and E a set of Σ-equations. Rewriting will operate on equivalence classes of terms modulo the set of equations E. In this way, we free rewriting from the syntactic constraints of a term representation and gain a much greater flexibility in deciding what counts as a *data structure*; for example, string rewriting is obtained by imposing an associativity axiom, and multiset rewriting by imposing associativity and commutativity. Of course, standard term rewriting is obtained as the particular case in which the set E of equations is empty. The idea of rewriting in equivalence classes is well known (see, e.g., [56, 33]).

Given a signature (Σ, E), *sentences* of the logic are sequents of the form $[t]_E \longrightarrow [t']_E$ with t, t' Σ-terms, where t and t' may possibly involve some variables from the countably infinite set $X = \{x_1, \ldots, x_n, \ldots\}$. A *theory* in this logic, called a rewrite theory, is a slight generalization of the usual notion of theory—which is typically defined as a pair consisting of a signature and a set of sentences for it—in that, in addition, we allow rules to be labelled. This is very natural for many applications, and customary for automata—viewed as labelled transition systems—and for Petri nets, which are both particular instances of our definition.

Definition 8   A (*labelled*) *rewrite theory*[6] $\mathcal{R}$ is a 4-tuple $\mathcal{R} = (\Sigma, E, L, R)$ where Σ is a ranked alphabet of function symbols, E is a set of Σ-equations, L is a set of *labels*, and R is a set of pairs $R \subseteq L \times (T_{\Sigma,E}(X)^2)$ whose first component is a label and whose second component is a pair of E-equivalence classes of terms, with $X = \{x_1, \ldots, x_n, \ldots\}$ a countably infinite set of variables. Elements of R are called *rewrite rules*[7]. We understand a rule $(r, ([t], [t']))$ as a labelled sequent and use for it the notation $r : [t] \longrightarrow [t']$. To indicate that $\{x_1, \ldots, x_n\}$ is the set of variables occurring in either t or t', we write[8] $r : [t(x_1, \ldots, x_n)] \longrightarrow [t'(x_1, \ldots, x_n)]$, or in abbreviated notation $r : [t(\overline{x}^n)] \longrightarrow [t'(\overline{x}^n)]$. $\square$

---

[6]We consciously depart from the standard terminology, that would call $\mathcal{R}$ a *rewrite system*. The reason for this departure is very specific. We want to keep the term "rewrite system" for the *models* of such a theory, which will be defined in Section 12.8 and which really are systems with a dynamic behavior. Strictly speaking, $\mathcal{R}$ is not a system; it is only a static, linguistic, *presentation* of a class of systems—including the initial and free systems that most directly embody our dynamic intuitions about rewriting.
[7]To simplify the exposition the rules of the logic are given for the case of *unconditional* rewrite rules. However, all the ideas and results presented here have been extended to conditional rules in [72] with very general rules of the form

$$r : [t] \longrightarrow [t'] \ \ if \ \ [u_1] \longrightarrow [v_1] \wedge \ldots \wedge [u_k] \longrightarrow [v_k].$$

This of course increases considerably the expressive power of rewrite theories, as illustrated by several of the Maude examples presented in this paper.
[8]Note that, in general, the set $\{x_1, \ldots, x_n\}$ will depend on the representatives t and t' chosen; therefore, we allow any possible such qualification with explicit variables.

Given a rewrite theory $\mathcal{R}$, we say that $\mathcal{R}$ *entails* a sequent $[t] \longrightarrow [t']$ and write $\mathcal{R} \vdash [t] \longrightarrow [t']$ if and only if $[t] \longrightarrow [t']$ can be obtained by finite application of the following *rules of deduction*:

1. **Reflexivity.** For each $[t] \in T_{\Sigma,E}(X)$,

$$\overline{[t] \longrightarrow [t]}$$

2. **Congruence.** For each $f \in \Sigma_n$, $n \in \mathbb{N}$,

$$\frac{[t_1] \longrightarrow [t_1'] \quad \ldots \quad [t_n] \longrightarrow [t_n']}{[f(t_1,\ldots,t_n)] \longrightarrow [f(t_1',\ldots,t_n')]}$$

3. **Replacement.** For each rewrite rule $r : [t(x_1,\ldots,x_n)] \longrightarrow [t'(x_1,\ldots,x_n)]$ in R,

$$\frac{[w_1] \longrightarrow [w_1'] \quad \ldots \quad [w_n] \longrightarrow [w_n']}{[t(\overline{w}/\overline{x})] \longrightarrow [t'(\overline{w'}/\overline{x})]}$$

4. **Transitivity.**

$$\frac{[t_1] \longrightarrow [t_2] \quad [t_2] \longrightarrow [t_3]}{[t_1] \longrightarrow [t_3]}$$

Equational logic (modulo a set of axioms E) is obtained from rewriting logic by adding the following rule:

5. **Symmetry.**

$$\frac{[t_1] \longrightarrow [t_2]}{[t_2] \longrightarrow [t_1]}$$

With this new rule, sequents derivable in equational logic are *bidirectional*; therefore, in this case we can adopt the notation $[t] \leftrightarrow [t']$ throughout and call such bidirectional sequents *equations*.

12.3.3 Concurrent Rewriting as Deduction

A nice consequence of having defined rewriting logic is that concurrent rewriting, rather than emerging as an operational notion, actually *coincides* with deduction in such a logic.

Definition 9 Given a rewrite theory $\mathcal{R} = (\Sigma, E, L, R)$, a (Σ, E)-sequent $[t] \longrightarrow [t']$ is called:

- a 0-*step concurrent $\mathcal{R}$-rewrite* iff it can be derived from $\mathcal{R}$ by finite application of the rules 1 and 2 of rewriting deduction (in which case $[t]$ and $[t]'$ necessarily coincide);

- a *one-step concurrent $\mathcal{R}$-rewrite* iff it can be derived from $\mathcal{R}$ by finite application of the rules 1-3, with at least one application of rule 3; if rule 3 is applied exactly once, we then say that the sequent is a one-step *sequential $\mathcal{R}$-rewrite*;

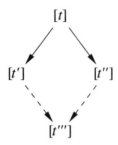

Figure 12.4
The Church-Rosser property.

- a *concurrent* $\mathcal{R}$-*rewrite* (or just a *rewrite*) iff it can be derived from $\mathcal{R}$ by finite application of the rules 1-4.

We call the rewrite theory $\mathcal{R}$ *sequential* if all one-step $\mathcal{R}$-rewrites are necessarily sequential. A sequential rewrite theory $\mathcal{R}$ is in addition called *deterministic* if for each $[t]$ there is at most one one-step (necessarily sequential) rewrite $[t] \longrightarrow [t']$. □

Example 10 All rewrite steps in Figure 12.1 are one-step concurrent rewrites, but none are sequential. For example, the first such step can be obtained by first applying replacement twice for the second rule in NAT to 0-step rewrites given by the substitutions $(N \mapsto 0, M \mapsto s0)$, and $(N \mapsto 0, M \mapsto 0)$, to get sequents

$$[s0+ss0] \longrightarrow [ss(0+s0)], \qquad [s0+s0] \longrightarrow [ss(0+0)];$$

then, applying congruence to each of these sequents and appropriate 0-step rewrites to get sequents

$$[(s0+ss0)\verb|^|s0] \longrightarrow [ss(0+s0)\verb|^|s0], \qquad [0\verb|^|(s0+s0)] \longrightarrow [0\verb|^|ss(0+0)];$$

and finally, applying replacement to those two sequents for the second rule in the REVERSE module. Note that transitivity was never used. □

The usual notions of confluence, termination, normal form, etc., as well as the well known Church-Rosser property of confluent rules, remain unchanged when considered from the perspective of concurrent rewriting [72].

Specifically, we call a rewrite theory $\mathcal{R}$ *terminating* if there is no infinite chain of one-step rewrites (whether sequential or concurrent)

$$[t] \longrightarrow [t_1] \longrightarrow \ldots \longrightarrow [t_n] \longrightarrow \ldots$$

We say that $[t']$ is an $\mathcal{R}$-*normal form* of $[t]$ if $[t] \longrightarrow [t']$ is an $\mathcal{R}$-rewrite and there does not exist any one-step $\mathcal{R}$-rewrite of the form $[t'] \longrightarrow [t'']$. If each $[t]$ has at least one normal form, we call the theory $\mathcal{R}$ *weakly terminating*.

We say that a rewrite theory $\mathcal{R}$ is *Church-Rosser* or *confluent* if given any two concurrent rewrites $[t] \longrightarrow [t']$, $[t] \longrightarrow [t'']$, there is a $[t''']$ and concurrent rewrites

$[t'] \longrightarrow [t''']$, $[t''] \longrightarrow [t''']$. This situation is shown in Figure 12.4. Likewise, we call $\mathcal{R}$ *ground Church-Rosser* when the property is only asserted for equivalence classes of ground terms. As already mentioned, the equations in Maude's functional modules are expected to be Church-Rosser, but system modules and object-oriented modules (see Section 12.4.1) are not expected to be Church-Rosser and typically they are not so. Indeed, the Church-Rosser property is a mark of functionality, since it guarantees that any term has at most one normal form, which can be interpreted as the result of its functional evaluation.

12.3.4   The Meaning of Rewriting Logic

A logic worth its salt should be understood as a method of correct reasoning about some class of entities, not as an empty formal game. For equational logic, the entities in question are sets, functions between them, and the relation of identity between elements. For rewriting logic, the entities in question are *concurrent systems* having *states*, and evolving by means of *transitions*. The *signature* of a rewrite theory describes a particular structure for the states of a system—e.g., multiset, binary tree, etc.—so that its states can be distributed according to such a structure. The *rewrite rules* in the theory describe which *elementary local transitions* are possible in the distributed state by concurrent local transformations. What the rules of rewriting logic allow us to reason correctly about is which *general* concurrent transitions are possible in a system satisfying such a description. Clearly, concurrent systems should be the *models* giving a semantic interpretation to rewriting logic, in the same way that algebras are the models giving a semantic interpretation to equational logic. A precise account of the model theory of rewriting logic, giving rise to an initial model semantics for Maude modules and fully consistent with the above system-oriented interpretation, is given in Section 12.8.

Therefore, in rewriting logic a sequent $[t] \longrightarrow [t']$ should not be read as "$[t]$ *equals* $[t']$," but as "$[t]$ *becomes* $[t']$." Clearly, rewriting logic is a logic of *becoming* or *change*, not a logic of equality in a static Platonic sense. The apparently innocent step of adding the symmetry rule is in fact a *very strong* restriction, namely assuming that *all change is reversible*, thus bringing us into a timeless Platonic realm in which "before" and "after" have been identified.

A related observation is that $[t]$ should not be understood as a *term* in the usual first-order logic sense, but as a *proposition*—built up using the *propositional connectives* in Σ—that asserts being in a certain *state* having a certain *structure*. However, unlike most other logics, the logical connectives Σ and their structural properties E are entirely *user-definable*. This provides great flexibility for considering many different state structures and makes rewriting logic very general in its capacity to deal with many different types of concurrent systems. This generality is further discussed in Section 12.4.8, and is treated in greater length in [72].

In summary, the rules of rewriting logic are rules to reason about *change in a concurrent system*[9]. They allow us to draw valid conclusions about the evolution of the system

---

[9]Since rewriting logic is a logic of change, it has some similarities with Girard's linear logic [39, 40] (see also [65] for a survey of work on the relationship between linear logic and concurrency). In fact, from the perspective of rewriting logic the quantifier-free fragment of linear logic appears as a particular choice

$$
\begin{array}{ccccc}
State & \leftrightarrow & Term & \leftrightarrow & Proposition \\
Transition & \leftrightarrow & Rewriting & \leftrightarrow & Deduction \\
Dist.\ Struct. & \leftrightarrow & Alg.\ Struct. & \leftrightarrow & Prop.\ Conn.
\end{array}
$$

Figure 12.5
The meaning of rewriting logic.

from certain basic types of change known to be possible thanks to the rules R. Our present discussion is summarized in Figure 12.5, which extends Figure 12.3 by adding each concept's logical counterpart.

12.4   A Logical Theory of Concurrent Objects

We are now ready to present a logical theory of concurrent objects based on rewriting logic deduction modulo ACI. The key idea is to conceptualize the distributed state of a concurrent object-oriented system—called a *configuration*—as a multiset of objects and messages that evolves by concurrent ACI-rewriting using rules that describe the effects of *communication events* between some objects and messages. Therefore, we can view concurrent object-oriented computation as *deduction* in rewriting logic; in this way, the configurations S that are *reachable* from a given initial configuration S_0 are exactly those such that the sequent $S_0 \longrightarrow S$ is *provable* in rewriting logic using the rewrite rules that specify the behavior of the given object-oriented system.

An *object* in a given state is represented as a term

$$\langle O : C \mid a_1 : v_1, \ldots, a_n : v_n \rangle$$

where O is the object's name or identifier, C is its class, the a_i's are the names of the object's *attribute identifiers*, and the v_i's are the corresponding *values*. The basic syntax and sort structure for attributes, objects, messages and configurations are given by the modules **ATTRIBUTES** and **CONFIGURATION** below; the first is a functional module defining the data type of attributes, and the second is a system module comprising all the entities that make up configurations. Before introducing such modules, we introduce an auxiliary parameterized module **MAP** that iterates a given parameter function over a multiset. This auxiliary module is used later to extract the set of attribute identifiers occurring in a set of attributes.

```
fth FUNCTION is
   sorts A B .
   op f: A -> B .
endft

fmod MAP[F :: FUNCTION] is
```

---
of user-definable connectives that are expressed in a very direct and natural way within rewriting logic in a conservative way [63].

```
    protecting MSET[A]*(sort MSet to AMSet, sort Set to ASet) .
    protecting MSET[B]*(sort MSet to BMSet, sort Set to BSet) .
    op map : AMSet -> BMSet .
    var X : A .
    var AMS : AMSet .
    eq map(null) = null .
    eq map(X AMS) = f(X) map(AMS) .
  endfm
```

We assume an already existing functional module ID of identifiers containing the sorts OId, CId and AId of object, class and attribute identifiers respectively (all of which are particular subsorts of the very general sort Value).

```
  fmod ATTRIBUTES is
    protecting ID . *** provides OId, CId and AId
    sorts Attribute Attributes Value .
    subsorts OId CId AId < Value .
    op (_:_) : AId Value -> Attribute .
    op aid : Attribute -> AId .
    var A : AId .
    var V : Value .
    eq aid(A : V) = A .

    protecting MAP[aid]*(sort AMSet to AttMSet, sort ASet to AttSet,
        sort BMSet to AIdMSet, sort BSet to AIdSet,
        op (__) : AMSet AMSet -> AMSet to (_,_)) .

    subsorts Attribute < Attributes < AttSet .
    op null : -> Attributes .
    var ATT : Attribute .
    var ATTS : Attributes .
    sct (ATT, ATTS) : Attributes if not aid(ATT) in map(ATTS) .
  endfm
```

The key sort being defined in the above module is the sort **Attributes** that will be used for the attributes of an object. A data element of that sort is a set of attributes[10]— where we have now adopted a notation that separates the different elements in the set by commas, as described in the renaming for the instantiation MAP[aid] of the MAP module that maps the parameter operator f to aid—but it must in addition satisfy the condition that *no attribute identifier can ever appear twice*; this would for example be violated by the set of attributes

    a: 3, b: true, a: 7

---

[10]The convenience of making the "union of attributes" operator _,_ into an *ACI*-operator will become apparent when we discuss inheritance issues in Section 12.4.2 and is also illustrated by the rules for CONFIGURATION below.

This condition is guaranteed by means of three assertions: the subsort declaration `Attribute < Attributes`; the operator declaration `null : -> Attributes`; and the sort constraint.

We are now ready for introducing objects, messages and configurations in the module `CONFIGURATION` described below. Some attributes of an object can be *hidden*. Messages belong to a sort `Msg`; some very general messages that can be used to query objects and to get responses are also defined below.

```
mod CONFIGURATION is
  protecting ATTRIBUTES .
  sorts Configuration Object Msg .
  subsorts Object Msg < Configuration .
  op __ : Configuration Configuration -> Configuration
                               [assoc comm id: null] .
  op <_:_|_> : OId CId Attributes -> Object .
  op _._replyto_ : OId AId OId -> Msg .
  op to_,_._is_ : OId OId AId Value -> Msg .
  var C : CId .
  var ATTS : Attributes .
  var AIDST : AIdSet .
  vars A B : OId .
  var AID : AId .
  var V : Value .
  rl (A . AID replyto B) < A : C | AID : V, ATTS > =>
      < A : C | AID : V, ATTS > (to B, A . AID is V)
      if not(hidden in map(AID : V, ATTS)) .
  rl (A . AID replyto B) < A : C | AID : V, hidden : AIDST, ATTS > =>
      < A : C | AID : V, hidden : AIDST, ATTS >
      (to B, A . AID is V) if not(AID in AIDST) .
endm
```

The *ACI*-operator `__` plays a role entirely similar to that played by the operator with the same syntax used for Petri nets, namely that of structuring the distributed state as a multiset. Objects with hidden attributes have an attribute of the form (`hidden : AIDST`) with `AIDST` a set of attribute identifiers specifying what attributes are hidden. Two very general kinds of messages are introduced. One that permits requesting that the value of an attribute identifier of a given object is sent to another object, and another for honoring such a request. The two rewrite rules specify the behavior of an object upon receiving a request for the value of one of its attributes. If the attribute in question does not appear in the object, or is among those hidden in the object, or is itself the attribute identifier `hidden`, then nothing happens, i.e., no rewrite rule applies[11]; otherwise, the attribute's value is sent to the requesting object.

---

[11]If desired, one could of course specify additional rules to send back an appropriate error message instead.

The type structure provided by the above signature is still rather unconstrained. For example, the definition of a class C of objects introduced in a given object-oriented module (see Section 12.4.1) will have the effect of constraining the attribute identifiers of objects in that class to contain a specific set $\{a_1, \ldots, a_n\}$ of attribute identifiers, and a subclass definition enlarges such a set. Similarly, the sort Value is typically the supersort of a possibly quite complex collection of (functional) algebraic data types, whose computations can also be specified by rewrite rules introduced in appropriate functional submodules of the system, but could in some cases contain also nonfunctional entities such as objects or entire configurations (see Section 12.4.6). In a class definition, the values v over which an attribute a ranges are typically forced to be in a given subsort of Value. Such tightening of the type structure to exactly reflect the type requirements of a given object-oriented system is discussed in Section 12.4.2.

12.4.1   Object-Oriented Modules

In Maude, concurrent object-oriented systems can be defined by means of *object-oriented modules*—introduced by the keyword omod—using a syntax more convenient than that of system modules because it assumes acquaintance with basic entities such as objects, messages and configurations, and supports linguistic distinctions appropriate for the object-oriented case; however, the syntax and semantics of object-oriented modules can be reduced to that of system modules as explained in Section 12.4.2.

For example, the ACCNT object-oriented module below specifies the concurrent behavior of objects in a very simple class Accnt of bank accounts, each having a bal(ance) attribute, which may receive messages for crediting or debiting the account, or for transferring funds between two accounts. We assume an already given functional module REAL for real numbers with a subsort relation NNReal < Real corresponding to the inclusion of the nonnegative reals (i.e., reals greater or equal than zero) into the reals, and with an ordering predicate _>=_.

```
omod ACCNT is
  protecting REAL .
  class Accnt | bal: NNReal .
  msgs credit debit : OId NNReal -> Msg .
  msg transfer_from_to_ : NNReal OId OId -> Msg .
  vars A B : OId .
  vars M N N' : NNReal .
  rl credit(A,M) < A : Accnt | bal: N > => < A : Accnt | bal: N + M > .
  rl debit(A,M) < A : Accnt | bal: N > => < A : Accnt | bal: N - M >
      if N >= M .
  rl transfer M from A to B
      < A : Accnt | bal: N > < B : Accnt | bal: N' > =>
      < A : Accnt | bal: N - M > < B : Accnt | bal: N' + M >
      if N >= M .
endom
```

After the keyword class, the name of the class—in this case Accnt—is given, followed by a "|" and by a list of pairs of the form a: S separated by commas, where a is an

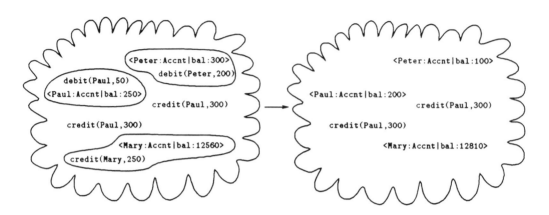

Figure 12.6
Concurrent rewriting of bank accounts.

attribute identifier and S is the sort inside which the values of such an attribute identifier must range in the given class. In this example, the only attribute of an account is its bal(ance), which is declared to be a value in NNReal. The three kinds of messages involving accounts are credit, debit, and transfer messages, whose user definable syntax is introduced by the keyword msg. The rewrite rules specify in a declarative way the behavior associated with the credit, debit, and transfer messages.

The multiset structure of the configuration provides the top level distributed structure of the system and allows concurrent application of the rules. For example, Figure 12.6 provides a snapshot in the evolution by concurrent rewriting of a simple configuration of bank accounts. To simplify the picture, the arithmetic operations required to update balances have already been performed. However, the reader should bear in mind that the values in the attributes of an object can also be computed by means of rewrite rules, and this adds yet another important level of concurrency to a concurrent object-oriented system, which might be called *intra-object concurrency*[12]. Intra-object concurrency seems to be absent from the standard models and languages for concurrent object-oriented programming, where only *inter-object concurrency* is considered.

The system evolves by concurrent rewriting (modulo *ACI*) of the configuration using the rewrite rules of the system, whose lefthand and righthand sides may—as illustrated in the example above—involve patterns for several objects and messages. Intuitively, we can think of messages as "travelling" to come into contact with the objects to which they are sent and then causing "communication events" by application of rewrite rules. In the model, this travelling is accounted for in a very abstract way by the *ACI* axioms. This

---

[12]The eight queens example in Section 12.6.1 provides a good illustration of intra-object concurrency.

abstract level supports both synchronous and asynchronous communication and provides great freedom and flexibility to consider a variety of alternative implementations at lower levels. Such abstraction from implementation details makes possible high level reasoning about concurrent object-oriented programs and their semantics without having to go down into the specific details of how communication is actually implemented.

Another example of an object-oriented module is a module for FIFO buffers of bounded size. The set of elements to be stored in the buffer is a parameter; the other parameter is the size of the buffer which is specified by the (functional) parameter theory

```
fth NAT* is
  protecting NAT .
  op k : -> NzNat .
endft
```

whose models are choices of a nonzero natural number **k**. The bounded buffer module is as follows

```
omod BD-BUFF[X :: TRIV, K :: NAT*] is
  protecting LIST[X] .
  class BdBuff | contents: List [hidden] .
  msg put_in_ : Elt OId -> Msg .
  msg getfrom_replyto_ : OId OId -> Msg .
  msg to_elt-in_is_ : OId OId Elt -> Msg .
  vars B I : OId .
  var E : Elt .
  var Q : List .
  rl (put E in B) < B : BdBuff | contents: Q > =>
       < B : BdBuff | contents: E Q >
       if length(Q) < k .
  rl (getfrom B replyto I)
       < B : BdBuff | contents: Q E > =>
       < B : BdBuff | contents: Q >
       (to I elt-in B is E) .
endom
```

The only attribute of a buffer is its **contents**, which is a list of elements. Since the contents should not be visible outside the buffer, this attribute has been declared [hidden]; this means that no other object can send a message requesting the entire contents of the buffer because messages of that kind are ruled out for hidden attributes. The two types of communication events that are possible are specified by the two rules of the module. If an arbitrary object I possesses the name B of a buffer, then it is possible for that object to either send a message (put E in B) to put the element E in B, or to send a message (getfrom B replyto I) to B, and the last rule specifies that, when B has a nonempty queue, it will send the first element of its queue to I by means of the message (to I elt-in B is E).

The two rules in the bounded buffer module provide a simple declarative solution to the problem of specifying the appropriate behavior of a bounded buffer that receives a put message when it is full or a get message when it is empty. The implicit effect of the rules is that the corresponding messages "float" in the configuration until the appropriate conditions for the buffer hold; if additional error handling is desired, this can be specified by adding more rules. By contrast, a language like ABCL/1 [104] requires introducing a special "waiting mode" for objects and a corresponding "select construct" to reactivate the object appropriately after such waiting. The simplicity of the treatment afforded by rewrite rules in this example exemplifies a general fact, namely that using rewrite rules there is no need for any explicit "synchronization code." This permits avoiding the "inheritance anomaly" [74], a subject further discussed in Section 12.4.2.

Specific instances of the bounded buffer module can then be obtained by providing appropriate *views* for its two parameter theories. For example, a buffer of length 4,096 holding characters of sort Char that we assume already introduced in a module CHAR can be defined by

```
make
BD-CHAR-BUFF is BD-BUFF[Char,view to NAT is op k to 4096 . endv]
endmk
```

where the first abbreviated view maps Elt to Char, and the second view sets the value of the bound k to be 4,096 (we assume standard notation for numbers here).

12.4.1.1   General Form of the Rules   In Maude, the general form required of rewrite rules used to specify the behavior of an object-oriented system is as follows:

$$(\dagger) \quad M_1 \dots M_n \, \langle O_1 : C_1 \,|\, atts_1 \rangle \dots \langle O_m : C_m \,|\, atts_m \rangle$$

$$\longrightarrow \langle O_{i_1} : C'_{i_1} \,|\, atts'_{i_1} \rangle \dots \langle O_{i_k} : C'_{i_k} \,|\, atts'_{i_k} \rangle$$

$$\langle Q_1 : D_1 \,|\, atts''_1 \rangle \dots \langle Q_p : D_p \,|\, atts''_p \rangle$$

$$M'_1 \dots M'_q$$

$$if \ C$$

where $k, p, q \geq 0$, the Ms are message expressions, $i_1, \dots, i_k$ are different numbers among the original $1, \dots, m$, and C is the rule's condition. A rule of this kind expresses a *communication event* in which n messages and m distinct objects participate. The *outcome* of such an event is as follows:

- the messages $M_1, \dots, M_n$ disappear;
- the *state* and possibly even the *class* of the objects $O_{i_1}, \dots, O_{i_k}$ may change;
- all other objects O_j vanish;
- new objects $Q_1, \dots, Q_p$ are created;
- new messages $M'_1, \dots, M'_q$ are sent.

Notice that, since some of the attributes of an object—as well as the parameters of messages—can contain object names, very complex and dynamically changing patterns of communication can be achieved by rules of this kind. Notice also that when $k = p = q = 0$ all the objects vanish, and no new objects or messages are created.

In addition, all rules must satisfy the property that *rewriting of a configuration without repeated object names leads to a configuration without repeated object names*. In other words, we are only interested in configurations in which there is a *set* of objects, not a multiset, and we never want to reach a configuration in which two objects have the same name; however, there is no problem in allowing configurations in which identical copies of a message have been sent, perhaps as the outcome of different communication events. A *necessary condition* required for this property to hold for a rule is that if in a *ground instance* of the rewrite rule the instances of the object names $O_1, \ldots, O_m$ are all different, then the instances of the object names $Q_1, \ldots, Q_m$ are also all different and different from the Os. Sufficient conditions to guarantee the uniqueness of objects are discussed in Section 12.4.4.

Although the above discussion suffices for the moment, more has to be said on the rules of object-oriented systems. Section 12.4.2 explains how rules are inherited and gives notational conventions that simplify the writing of rules. Also, since the above form of rules is very general, it is important to identify useful commonly occurring subcases that allow much more efficient implementation; this is the theme of Section 12.5 in which the Simple Maude sublanguage is introduced.

12.4.1.2 Synchrony, Asynchrony, and Autonomous Objects Given the general form (†) of rewrite rules representing communication events in an object-oriented system, it is possible for one, none, or several objects to appear as participants in the lefthand sides of rules. If only one object appears in the lefthand side, we call such a communication event *asynchronous*, whereas if several objects are involved we call it *synchronous* and say that the objects in question are forced to *synchronize* in the event. For example, the rules for crediting and debiting accounts describe asynchronous communication events, whereas the rule for transferring funds between two accounts forces them to synchronize.

Note that a particular case allowed by the general form (†) of the rewrite rules is that in which no messages at all appear in the lefthand side. This gives rise to a rather striking mode of activity, namely that of objects that—on their own or synchronizing with other objects—change their state and/or send messages to other objects *without any external prompting by messages*. We call objects that can evolve without receiving messages by means of rules of this type *autonomous objects*.

Note that objects, whether autonomous or not, can in some cases exhibit a never-ending pattern of activity. For example, a *clock* object having a *time* attribute (say, a natural number) may update its time by sending a `tick` message to itself and having a "ticking rule" that increases the time by one unit and sends another `tick` message each time a `tick` message is received.

```
tick(C) < C : Clock | time: T > => < C : Clock | time: T + 1 > tick(C) .
```

Of course, we could define clocks in a different way as autonomous objects by eliminating the `tick` message and giving instead a rule

```
< C : Clock | time: T > => < C : Clock | time: T + 1 > .
```

The general form (†) of rules is too general for efficient implementation purposes and we may very well wish to seek additional restrictions under which an efficient implementation can be attained at the expense of some loss in expressiveness. This topic, and a particular set of restrictions leading to a sublanguage called Simple Maude having only asynchronous communication that we have studied jointly with Timothy Winkler in [83], are discussed in Section 12.5. The general idea is to consider Maude as a wide-spectrum language such that more expressive specification and rapid prototyping can be carried out in Maude, but where efficient execution assumes the restrictions in Simple Maude. One can then adopt a transformational approach to move from specifications to—possibly inefficient—prototypes, and from prototypes to efficient code. We are currently investigating techniques of this kind in joint work with Patrick Lincoln and Timothy Winkler.

12.4.2 Class Inheritance and Reduction to System Modules

Class inheritance is directly supported by Maude's order-sorted type structure. A subclass declaration C < C' in an object-oriented module omod $\mathcal{O}$ endom is just a particular case of a subsort declaration C < C'[13]. As we shall see, the effect of a subclass declaration is that the attributes, messages and rules of all the superclasses as well as the newly defined attributes, messages and rules of the subclass characterize the structure and behavior of the objects in the subclass.

For example, we can define an object-oriented module CHK-ACCNT of checking accounts introducing a subclass ChkAccnt of Accnt with a new attribute chk-hist recording the history of checks cashed in the account.

```
omod CHK-ACCNT is
  extending ACCNT .
  dfn ChkHist is LIST[2TUPLE[Nat,NNReal]] .
  class ChkAccnt | chk-hist: ChkHist .
  subclass ChkAccnt < Accnt .
  msg chk_#_amt_ : OId Nat NNReal -> Msg .
  var A : OId .
  vars M N : NNReal .
  var K : Nat .
  var H : ChkHist .
  rl (chk A # K amt M) < A : ChkAccnt | bal: N, chk-hist: H >
      => < A : ChkAccnt | bal: N - M, chk-hist: H << K ; M >> >
      if N >= M .
endom
```

Adopting the same convention as in OBJ3, the statement

```
  dfn ChkHist is LIST[2TUPLE[Nat,NNReal]] .
```

is an abbreviation for the statement

---

[13]The reason why classes, although conceptually distinguished from other sorts, have in essence the same treatment for their subsort relations as any other sorts will become clearer after we discuss the reduction of object-oriented modules to system modules later in this section.

```
protecting LIST[2TUPLE[Nat,NNReal]]*(sort List to ChkHist) .
```

which imports a data type of lists of 2-tuples (pairs denoted `<<_;_>>`) consisting of a natural number and a nonnegative real, and renames the principal sort `List` to `ChkHist`. The checking history of the account is then represented as a list of such pairs with the first number in the pair corresponding to the check number, and the second number corresponding to the check's amount.

The best way to understand classes and class inheritance in Maude is by making explicit the full structure of an object-oriented module which is left somewhat implicit in the syntactic conventions adopted for them. Indeed, although Maude's object-oriented modules provide a convenient syntax for programming object-oriented systems, their semantics can be reduced to that of system modules; in a sense we can regard the special syntax reserved for object-oriented modules as syntactic sugar. In fact, each object-oriented module `omod` $\mathcal{O}$ `endom` can be translated into a corresponding system module `mod` $\mathcal{O}\#$ `endm` whose semantics *is* by definition that of the original object-oriented module[14].

However, although Maude's object-oriented modules can in this way be reduced to system modules, there are of course important conceptual advantages provided by the syntax of object-oriented modules, because it allows the user to think and express his or her thoughts in object-oriented terms whenever such a viewpoint seems best suited for the problem at hand. Those conceptual advantages would be lost if only system modules were provided.

In the translation process, the most basic structure shared by all object-oriented modules is made explicit by the `CONFIGURATION` system module defined at the beginning of this section. The translation of a given object-oriented module extends this structure with the classes, messages and rules introduced by the module. For example, the following system module `ACCNT#` is the translation of the `ACCNT` module introduced earlier. Note that a subsort `<Accnt` of `CId` is introduced. The purpose of this subsort is to range over the class identifiers of the subclasses of `Accnt`. For the moment, no such subclasses have been introduced; therefore, at present the only constant of sort `<Accnt` is the class identifier[15] `Accnt`.

```
mod ACCNT# is
  extending CONFIGURATION .
  protecting REAL .
  sorts <Accnt Accnt .
  subsort Accnt < Object .
  subsort <Accnt < CId .
```

---

[14]For the moment, consider the semantics of the module in terms of concurrent rewriting. Section 12.8 gives a model-theoretic semantics for Maude modules that makes completely precise their intended semantics.

[15]Notice the slight ambiguity introduced by this notation, since now `Accnt` denotes *two different things*: a *sort name* in the sort structure of a module, and a *data element* in a subsort of a data type of class identifiers. However, this ambiguity is harmless—the context will always make explicit the intended sense—and could in any case be easily avoided by an appropriate notational convention; for example, by adopting quotes for the identifier use.

```
subsort NNReal < Value .
op Accnt : -> <Accnt .
ops credit,debit : OId NNReal -> Msg .
op transfer_from_to_ : NNReal OId OId -> Msg .
vars A B : OId .
vars M N N' : NNReal .
var X : <Accnt .
vars ATTS ATTS' : Attributes .
sct < A : X | bal: N, ATTS > : Accnt .
rl credit(A,M) < A : X | bal: N, ATTS >
     => < A : X | bal: N + M, ATTS > .
rl debit(A,M) < A : X | bal: N, ATTS >
     => < A : X | bal: N - M, ATTS >  if N >= M .
rl transfer M from A to B
     < A : X | bal: N, ATTS > < B : X | bal: N', ATTS' > =>
     < A : X | bal: N - M, ATTS > < B : X | bal: N' + M, ATTS' >
     if N >= M .
endm
```

Objects of sort Accnt are defined by a sort constraint requiring that its class identifier has sort <Accnt and that one of its attributes is of the form (bal : N), with N of sort NNReal. Note that the rewrite rules originally introduced in the ACCNT module have been modified to make them applicable not only to objects whose class identifier is exactly Accnt, but also to other objects with class identifiers for subclasses of Accnt, which may in addition have other attributes, i.e., indeed to all the objects of the class Accnt. In other words, whenever a class identifier C appears in the lefthand side of a rule declared in an object-oriented module, we implicitly understand that a variable ranging over <C is meant instead. This way of inheriting rules was pointed out in Section 4.4 of [69]; I am indebted to Timothy Winkler for later suggesting to me the elegant sort structure of the sorts <C as a better alternative to a more cumbersome identifier data type definition.

Note that the convention just described also involves leaving implicit a variable ATTS, ranging over the additional attributes that may appear in a subclass. In fact, we can further simplify the notation used in object-oriented modules by adopting, in addition, the convention of not mentioning in a given rule those attributes of an object that are not relevant for that rule. To explain this additional convention, let $\overline{a : v}$ denote the attribute-value pairs $a_1 : v_1, \ldots, a_n : v_n$, where the $\overline{a}$ are the attribute identifiers of a given class C having $\overline{s}$ as the corresponding sorts of values prescribed for those attributes. In this context, the v_i can be either terms (with or without variables) or variables of sort s_i.

The general convention is that in object-oriented modules we allow rules where the attributes appearing in the lefthand and righthand side patterns for an object O mentioned in the rule need not exhaust all the object's attributes, but can instead be in any two arbitrary subsets of the object's attributes[16]. We can picture this as follows

---

[16]We assume that, as it is usually but not exclusively the case, the class of the object O does not change

$$\ldots \langle O : C \mid \overline{al : vl}, \overline{ab : vb} \rangle \ldots \longrightarrow \ldots \langle O : C \mid \overline{ab : vb'}, \overline{ar : vr} \rangle \ldots$$

where $\overline{al}$ are the attributes appearing only on the *left*, $\overline{ab}$ are the attributes appearing on *both* sides, and $\overline{ar}$ are the attributes appearing only on the *right*. What this abbreviates in the corresponding reduction to a system module notation is a rule of the form

$$\ldots \langle O : X \mid \overline{al : vl}, \overline{ab : vb}, \overline{ar : x}, atts \rangle \ldots \longrightarrow \ldots \langle O : X \mid \overline{al : vl}, \overline{ab : vb'}, \overline{ar : vr}, atts \rangle \ldots$$

where X is a variable of sort $<C$, the $\overline{x}$ are new "don't care" variables and *atts* matches the remaining attribute-value pairs. The attributes mentioned only on the left are preserved unchanged, the original values of attributes mentioned only on the right don't matter, and all attributes not explicitly mentioned are left unchanged[17]. We can illustrate this convention with a simple example, namely a rule for a new type of message requesting the highest check number already cashed in a checking account

```
(highest-chk# A reply to B) < A : ChkAccnt | chk-hist: H >
   => < A : ChkAccnt | chk-hist: H >
      (to B highest-chk# A is max.1st(H))
```

where `max.1st` is an appropriately defined function that computes the highest number among those in the first components of pairs in the list. Note that the `bal` attribute is not mentioned at all, although of course it must be present in all objects in a subclass of `Accnt`. The rewrite rule for which the above rule is just a shorthand notation is

```
(highest-chk# A reply to B) < A : Y | bal: M, chk-hist: H, ATTS >
   => < A : Y | bal: M, chk-hist: H, ATTS >
      (to B highest-chk# A is max.1st(H))
```

where `Y` is a variable of sort `<ChkAccnt`, `M` is a variable of sort `NNReal`, `H` is a variable of sort `ChkHist`, and `ATTS` is a variable of sort `Attributes`.

Note that, since the `CONFIGURATION` module has been imported, besides the messages for crediting and debiting accounts, and for transferring funds between accounts, an account `A` with balance `N` can also receive messages of the form (`bal . A replyto O`) and will then respond to `O` by sending the message (`to O bal . A is N`). Since this capability is built in for arbitrary objects—unless the requested attribute has been declared `hidden`—it is never mentioned in the definition of an object-oriented module.

We are now ready to consider the full structure of subclasses. We can illustrate that structure by means of the reduction of the `CHK-ACCNT` module to its system module form.

```
mod CHK-ACCNT# is
   extending ACCNT# .
   sorts <ChkAccnt ChkAccnt  .
   subsort ChkAccnt < Accnt .
```

---

due to the rewrite; however, it should be possible to extend the present convention to some cases of interest in which the class does change.

[17]This notational convention generalizes a similar convention in [69] and has been developed in joint work with Timothy Winkler [83].

```
      subsort <ChkAccnt < <Accnt .
      dfn ChkHist is LIST[2TUPLE[Nat,NNReal]] .
      subsort ChkHist < Value .
      op ChkAccnt : -> <ChkAccnt .
      op chk_#_amt_ : OId Nat NNReal -> Msg .
      var A : OId .
      var Y : <ChkAccnt .
      var ATTS : Attributes .
      vars M N : NNReal .
      var K : Nat .
      var H : ChkHist .
      sct < A : Y | bal: N, chk-hist: H, ATTS > : ChkAccnt .
      rl (chk A # K amt M) < A : Y | bal: N, chk-hist: H, ATTS >
         => < A : Y | bal: N - M, chk-hist: H << K ; M >>, ATTS >
            if N >= M .
   endm
```

Note that—in addition to a subsort declaration `ChkAccnt < Accnt` stating that checking accounts are accounts, i.e., the subclass relation—a subsort `<ChkAccnt < <Accnt` has been declared, having a class identifier `ChkAccnt` (introduced in a later operator declaration) in that subsort; i.e., the sort hierarchy for class identifiers mimics the class hierarchy, and has a class identifier constant (with the same name as that of the class) for each class in the corresponding point of the hierarchy.

An object in the class `ChkAccnt` must satisfy the sort constraint that its class identifier has sort `<ChkAccnt` and that it has at least two attributes, one called `bal` with a `NNReal` value, and another called `chk-hist` with a `ChkHist` value. The rewrite rule given in the original `CHK-ACCNT` module is interpreted here—according to the conventions already explained—in a form that can be inherited by subclasses of `ChkAccnt` that could be defined later. `ChkAccnt` itself inherits the rewrite rules for crediting and debiting accounts, and for transferring funds between accounts that had been defined for `Accnt`, and also the rules for requesting the value of its attributes which had been defined in the `CONFIGURATION` module.

In this example, there is only one class immediately above `ChkAccnt`, namely, `Accnt`. In general, however, a class C may be defined as a subclass of several classes $D_1, \ldots, D_k$, i.e., *multiple inheritance* is supported. Each class C has associated with it a family of pairs $\overline{a : s}$ each consisting of a different attribute identifier and a sort for its values. In case hidden attributes have been declared, we also associate with the class C the subset $a_{i_1}, \ldots, a_{i_j}$ of those attribute identifiers that are *hidden*. The objects of a class C not having any hidden attributes are then defined by a sort constraint of the form

$$\langle O : X \mid \overline{a : Y},\ ATTS \rangle : C$$

where the variable O has sort `OId`, X has sort $<C$, the variables $\overline{Y}$ have sorts $\overline{s}$, and the variable $ATTS$ has sort `Attributes`. If hidden attributes $a_{i_1}, \ldots, a_{i_j}$ have been declared, the above sort constraint must be made *conditional* on having all the hidden attribute identifiers $a_{i_1}, \ldots, a_{i_j}$ inside the set denoted by the variable Y_q, where $a_q = $ `hidden`. For

example, the sort constraint for the class `BdBuff` of bounded buffers in the parameterized module `BD-BUFF`, which has its `contents` attribute hidden is

```
sct < 0 : X | contents: Q, hidden: S, ATTS > :
     BdBuff if (contents in S) .
```

with `0` of sort `OId`, `X` of sort `<BdBuff`, `Q` of sort `List`, and `ATTS` of sort `Attributes`.

If an attribute and its sort have already been declared in a superclass, they should not be declared again in the subclass. Indeed, all such attributes—whether hidden or not—are *inherited*, and if they were hidden in a superclass they remain hidden in the subclass. In the case of multiple inheritance, the only requirement that is made is that if an attribute *a* occurs in two different superclasses, then the sort attributed to it in each of those superclasses is the same[18]. In summary, a class inherits all the attributes, messages, and rules from all its superclasses. An object in the subclass behaves exactly as any object in any of the superclasses, but it may exhibit additional behavior due to the introduction of new attributes, messages and rules in the subclass.

One caveat: in the case of *multiple* inheritance, it is in principle possible for a specific kind of message to have been introduced in two different superclasses, with quite different rules for handling such messages in each of them. As already mentioned, if a new class is defined as a subclass of each of those two superclasses, it will inherit the rules from both of them. In some cases this may be unproblematic, in the sense that everything behaves as expected because either the rules for one superclass specify the same behavior for that message as the rules of the other, or each set of rules specifies behavior for mutually exclusive circumstances, or, more generally, the two sets of rules agree on some cases and do not overlap on the remaining cases. The problem may arise when genuinely different behavior can result in the same situation depending on whether the rule applied belongs to one superclass or another, since this difference in behavior may be unintended. What this could probably indicate is a wrong use of the class inheritance mechanism on the part of the user. The right solution in such a situation may be to use *module inheritance* mechanisms instead (see Section 12.4.3) to obtain the desired behavior. In any case, the system should always warn the user whenever a potential source of unintended behavior arises due to the inheritance of messages from two unrelated superclasses.

Rule inheritance in Maude solves the so-called *inheritance anomaly* [67, 90, 38] blocking the combination of inheritance and concurrency in object-oriented languages. The anomaly has to do with the serious difficulties often found for reusing in a subclass the code that handles the messages received by an object of a given class and performs appropriate actions. Typically, if a new kind of message is later introduced for a subclass, it may not be possible to reuse the original code as given so that the new messages can also be handled. The simplicity of the solution provided by Maude, which does not require any explicit code for synchronization, is due to its declarative character and to the very fine granularity of its code, where the basic program units are rewrite rules. The

---

[18]This condition could be relaxed to just requiring that the sorts in question have some common subsorts, and we could similarly allow that in a subclass the sort of an inherited attribute is restricted to a subsort. However, although somewhat more expressive, these relaxations would introduce some complications in the inheritance of rewrite rules. To simplify the exposition we do not treat here this more general case and restrict ourselves to the simpler sort assumptions just explained.

code for a class is therefore an unstructured *set* of rewrite rules, with each rule acting independently of the others. For a subclass, this set of rules is typically enlarged by adding some new rules, but this in no way alters the previously given rules which remain exactly as before and are inherited from the superclass or superclasses. There is no room here for a more detailed discussion of this solution, which can be found in [74], except to mention that cases where the rules of a superclass cannot be used as originally given but must be modified in order to obtain a somewhat different behavior can be handled with similar ease using the module inheritance techniques described in Section 12.4.3.

12.4.3 Module Inheritance

There are indeed cases in which one does actually want to *modify* the original code to adapt it to a somewhat different situation. The above class and rule inheritance mechanisms will typically *not* help in such cases. Rather than doing violence to class inheritance and rule inheritance in order to force upon them the job of modifying code, the solution adopted in Maude is to insist on keeping what can be described as an *order-sorted* semantics for class inheritance, and then to provide different *module inheritance* mechanisms to do the job of code modification. An example already discussed in the functional case is the modification of the LIST module to obtain the MSET module, and other examples illustrating module inheritance by importation, parameterization, renaming or their combination have already been given as well. This distinction between the level of classes (more generally sorts) and the level of modules was already clearly made in the FOOPS language (besides the original paper [49], see also [54] for a very good discussion of inheritance issues and of the class-module distinction in the context of FOOPS), and indeed goes back to the distinction between sorts and modules in OBJ [53].

In Maude, code in modules can be modified or adapted for new purposes by means of a variety of module operations—and combinations of several such operations in *module expressions*—whose overall effect is to provide a very flexible style of software reuse that can be summarized under the name of *module inheritance*. Module operations of this kind include:

1. *importing* a module in a `protecting`, `extending`, or `using` way;

2. *adding new equations or rules* to an imported module;

3. *renaming* some of the sorts or operations of a module;

4. *instantiating* a parameterized module by means of *views*;

5. *adding modules* to form their union;

6. *redefining* an operator so that its syntax and sort requirements are kept intact, but its semantics can be changed by discarding previously given rules or equations involving the operator so that new rules or equations can be then given in their place;

7. *removing* a rule or an equational axiom, or removing an operator or a sort altogether along with the rules or axioms that depend on it so that it can be either discarded or replaced by another operator or sort with different syntax and semantics.

The operations 1–5 are all exactly as in OBJ3 [53]. The operations 6–7 are new and permit giving a simple solution to the thorny problem of *message (or method) specialization* without in any way complicating the class inheritance relation, which remains based on an order-sorted semantics. The need for message specialization, i.e., for providing a somewhat different behavior for a message already defined in an old class when received by objects in a new class arises frequently in practice. For example, a bank may at some point want to introduce a new kind of checking accounts in which there is a charge of 50 cents for each cashed check, and then the updating of an account's balance upon receipt of a message of type (chk A # K amt M) has to be modified by the extra 50 cents charge. The problem is that if the new class of checking accounts with checking charges is defined as a subclass of the old, then the nice property of rule inheritance derived from subclass inheritance as defined in Section 12.4.2 is completely destroyed, because the rules for the superclass should *not* be inherited in the new subclass and would in fact produce the wrong behavior.

The solution given to this problem in Maude is to understand this as a module inheritance problem, and to carefully distinguish it from class inheritance. In this case, it is the *modules* in which the classes are defined that stand in an inheritance relation, not the classes themselves. The *redefine* operation, with keyword rdfn, provides the appropriate way of modifying and inheriting the CHK-ACCNT module in the definition of the CHK(0/.50)ACCNT module that introduces the new class of checking accounts with charges and also keeps around the previous class of checking accounts without charges.

```
omod CHK(0/.50)ACCNT is
  extending CHK-ACCNT .
  using CHK-ACCNT*(class ChkAccnt to Chk.50Accnt,
      rdfn(msg chk_#_amt_)) .
  var A : OId .
  vars M N : NNReal .
  var K : Nat .
  var H : ChkHist .
  rl (chk A # K amt M) < A : Chk.50Accnt | bal: N, chk-hist: H > =>
      < A : Chk.50Accnt | bal: N - (M + .50), chk-hist: H << K ; M >> >
      if N >= (M + .50) .
endom
```

What the module expression

```
using CHK-ACCNT*(class ChkAccnt to Chk.50Accnt,
    rdfn(msg chk_#_amt_)) .
```

indicates is that a new copy of the CHK-ACCNT module is created and imported (but without copying its submodules, for example ACCOUNT, which are *shared*) in such a way that the class ChkAccnt is renamed to Chk.50Accnt and the message (msg chk_#_amt_) is *redefined*, i.e., its syntax and sort information are maintained, but the rule defining the behavior of the message is discarded. The new behavior is then introduced in the new rule given at the end of the module. Space limitations preclude giving a detailed account of the `rdfn` and `rmv` (remove) commands; this will be done elsewhere. However, we can give a fully detailed account of the use of the `rdfn` command in the above example by presenting a corresponding system module reduction:

```
mod CHK(0/.50)ACCNT# is
  extending CHK-ACCNT# .
  sorts Chk.50Accnt <Chk.50Accnt .
  subsort Chk.50Accnt < Accnt .
  subsort <Chk.50Accnt < <Accnt .
  op Chk.50Accnt : -> <Chk.50Accnt .
  var A : OId .
  var Z : <Chk.50Accnt .
  var ATTS : Attributes .
  vars M N : NNReal .
  var K : Nat .
  var H : ChkHist .
  sct < A : Z | bal: N, chk-hist: H, ATTS > : Chk.50Accnt .
  rl (chk A # K amt M) < A : Z | bal: N, chk-hist: H, ATTS >
    => < A : Z | bal: N - (M + .50), chk-hist: H << K ; M >>, ATTS >
      if N >= (M + .50) .
endm
```

The essential point is that, although both `ChkAccnt` and `Chk.50Accnt` are subclasses of `Accnt`, the class `Chk.50Accnt` is *not* a subclass of `ChkAccnt`. Therefore, in the context of the new module, the old rule for messages of the form (`chk A # K amt M`) and the new rule charging 50 cents *coexist without interference*, because they apply to different objects in two different classes that are *incomparable* in the class hierarchy. By contrast, the rules for crediting and debiting accounts and for transferring funds between accounts apply, thanks to rule inheritance, to all classes of accounts, precisely because all of them are subclasses of `Accnt`.

The distinction between class inheritance and module inheritance can be illustrated in this example by means of the diagrams in Figure 12.7, where the diagram on the left expresses the class inheritance relation between the three classes involved, and the diagram on the right expresses the module inheritance relation between the modules used to define those classes. Note that the arrows in the subclass relation have a very specific meaning, namely that of a *subsort* relation, whereas the inheritance arrows between modules can have a much more flexible—yet precise—variety of meanings, because of the variety of module operations that can be involved. In this case, the solid arrows correspond to inheritance by `extending` importation, whereas the dotted arrow involves sort renaming, message redefinition, and a `using` importation; note also that the module `CHK-ACCNT` is inherited in *two* different ways by the module `CHK(0/.50)ACCNT`. In this way we can have great flexibility of code reuse *and* a precise and satisfactory semantics for subclasses that respects the intuitions of what it means to *classify* objects. By contrast, in approaches that conflate these two equally laudable goals, flexibility of code reuse is achieved at the heavy price of emptying the notion of class of most of its conceptual value.

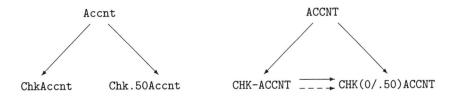

Figure 12.7
Class inheritance vs. module inheritance for bank accounts.

To illustrate the many possibilities for module inheritance that Maude's module operations permit we show below a different, and in fact more general, way of obtaining the two checking account classes in our example. The idea is to define a parameterized module for checking accounts with a checking charge, where the amount of the charge is a parameter, and then to inherit it by two different instantiations to obtain the two desired classes.

```
fth NNREAL* is
  protecting REAL .
  op c : -> NNReal .
endft

omod CHRG-CHK-ACCNT[C :: NNREAL*] is
  extending ACCNT .
  dfn ChkHist is LIST[2TUPLE[Nat,NNReal]] .
  class ChkAccnt | chk-hist: ChkHist .
  subclass ChkAccnt < Accnt .
  msg chk_#_amt_ : OId Nat NNReal -> Msg .
  var A : OId .
  vars M N : NNReal .
  var K : Nat .
  var H : ChkHist .
  rl (chk A # K amt M) < A : ChkAccnt | bal: N, chk-hist: H >
    => < A : ChkAccnt | bal: N - (M + c), chk-hist: H << K ; M >> >
      if N >= (M + c) .
endom
```

then we can define the module with our two desired classes as follows,

```
omod CHK(0/.50)ACCNT is
  extending CHRG-CHK-ACCNT[view to REAL is op c to 0 . endv] .
  extending CHRG-CHK-ACCNT[view to REAL is op c to .50 . endv]*(
                  sort ChkAccnt to Chk.50Accnt) .
endom
```

12.4.4   Object Creation and Deletion

In Maude, object creation and deletion can be treated very simply. In fact, a variety of approaches are possible to ensure the key property required, namely that, under appropriate initial conditions, we never reach a configuration in which two different objects have the same name. One possibility is to make object generation *indirect*, in the sense of being mediated by messages of one of the two types below

```
new(C | ATTS)      (new C | ATTS ack A req R)
```

where the first type of message requests that a new object of class C with attributes ATTS is created, and the second makes the same request but also requires sending an acknowledgement to object A with the name of the new object corresponding to its request called R. What we must assume is that in the initial configuration we only have a collection of *different* objects in class ProtoObject and having a single attribute counter whose value is a natural number. Then the rules for creating objects are

```
new(C | ATTS) < O : ProtoObject | counter: N >
   => < O : ProtoObject | counter: N + 1 > < O.N : C | ATTS >

(new C | ATTS ack A req R) < O : ProtoObject | counter: N >
   => < O : ProtoObject | counter: N + 1 > < O.N : C | ATTS >
      (to A : R is O.N)
```

This scheme will of course guarantee that all the names of created objects are different. Since there is in principle no bound on the number of proto-objects in the initial configuration, this scheme can be highly distributed so that object creation does not become a bottleneck. For example, in a multicomputer implementation it would be natural to provide one proto-object per processor in a built-in fashion.

The above scheme for indirect object creation can be slightly modified in order to force some of the attributes of an object to always have fixed initial values (this can be required by means of an initially declaration [74] fixing the initial value of an attribute). A more flexible but similar idea is to allow any initial value for an attribute, but to provide a *default* value when the value is not explicitly mentioned in the new message; such default values could either be declared explicitly or, as in FOOPS [49], could be automatically computed by the system following some conventions. What is required to support both default and fixed initial attribute values is to make the state of proto-objects richer—so that they contain the appropriate default and initially information for the relevant attributes in each class—and to make the above rules for new messages conditional to the outcome of checking such information.

A similarly indirect approach to object deletion is to use messages of one of the two types below

```
delete(A)      (delete A ack B)
```

with corresponding rules

```
delete(A) < A : X | ATTS > => null

(delete A ack B) < A : X | ATTS > => (to B : A deleted)
```

We can however allow *direct* generation or deletion of objects in a variety of very general circumstances, including situations in which both direct and indirect schemes are used without conflicting with each other. For example, a very easy scheme for direct object generation that is compatible with the indirect scheme just presented is to assume that one of the objects, call it O, matched by the lefthand side of a rule of the form (†) and surviving in the righthand side of the rule in question has a counter, say with value N. Then, the p new objects created by the righthand side are given names $O.N.1, \ldots, O.N.p$, and O's counter is increased. An example of direct object deletion where objects garbage-collect themselves is given in the eight queens example of Section 12.6.1.

In summary, there are many ways by which the *uniqueness* of objects can always be guaranteed in an object-oriented system so that the requirement that the rules preserve this uniqueness is satisfied. In addition, object creation can be realized in a highly distributed way. The particular choice of mechanisms and the corresponding choice of data representations for object identifiers may depend on particular characteristics of the given application.

12.4.5 Broadcasting Messages

Besides the communication that objects can perform among themselves, it is often very desirable to provide more global types of communication so that, for example, all the objects in a given class receive a certain message. In [69] a scheme for such broadcast communication was proposed based on the idea of having a "metaobject" for each class containing the list of all the current objects in the class. This metaobject could broadcast a message to all such objects when appropriate. However, for massively parallel computations involving large numbers of objects distributed across many processors this scheme would be undesirable, although it could be improved by splitting the class metaobject into a hierarchy of metaobjects.

A better approach, developed in joint work with Timothy Winkler and to be further expanded elsewhere, will be briefly sketched below. The key idea is to absorb broadcast communication within the *structural axioms* E of the rewrite theory in question. This means that a broadcast can be viewed at this abstract level as happening "by magic" in the sense that structural axioms are supported by what might be called an "invisible infrastructure" which of course in practice will require some concrete architectural implementation.

Since broadcasting is a global operation, it should be understood as having an entire *configuration* as one of its arguments, for example the configuration making up the global state of all objects and messages at a particular stage of a concurrent computation. The other two arguments can for example be a message and a class identifier C indicating the class to which the message should be broadcast. Since the message's addressee is not unique, it is best to assume a generic address denoted by the constant "*" that can later be replaced by the real address, so that our message will initially be of the form

M(*). In Maude, the keyword ax is reserved for equations that are part of the structural axioms E of the rewrite theory specified in a module. Here are the structural axioms for broadcast communication:

```
vars S S' : Configuration .
var MSG : Msg .

ax broadcast(M(*),C,S S') = broadcast(M(*),C,S) broadcast(M(*),C,S') .
ax broadcast(M(*),C,MSG) = MSG .
ax broadcast(M(*),C,< O : D | ATTS >) = if (D : <C)
    then (subst * by O in M(*)) < O : D | ATTS >
    else < O : D | ATTS > fi .
ax broadcast(M(*),C,null) = null .
```

where the predicate (D : <C) is a special instance of the notion of a *sort predicate* $t : s$, testing whether a given term t has sort s, that is built-in but can be equationally axiomatized using "retract operators" [51]. The term (subst * by O in M(*)) corresponds to the application of a substitution operator whose result is M(O), and can be equationally axiomatized for each type of message.

The effect of the above structural axioms is that the broadcast will travel as if by magic across the entire configuration, but its only effect will be that a message is created for each object in the class C. This treatment of broadcasting shows the advantage of rewriting logic's great freedom of choice for the appropriate structural axioms of a rewrite theory, which makes possible giving an account of broadcast in purely logical terms. By way of related work, Andreoli and Pareschi [9] consider broadcast in the context of their linear logic based language LO.

12.4.6 Reflection

The idea of a broadcast suggests the presence of a "master" or "controller" on whose behalf the broadcast is performed. Since such a master has access to an entire configuration, it is natural to conceptualize it as a type of "metaobject" having a configuration as one of its attributes, say

```
< M : Master | configuration: S, ATTS >
```

that can then initiate a broadcast for the configuration S under appropriate conditions specified by rewrite rules for the class Master. Rewrite rules for this class may also specify many other actions, such as those involved in detecting global termination, in reacting to various types of feedback from objects in the configuration, or in performing communication with the "outside world." In particular, actions taken by "reflecting" on the global state of the computation seem naturally expressible in this way. All this means that, in general, we should not think of the sort Value for the values of attributes as involving only data in sorts of functional modules, but as being capable of involving at times entire configurations, with a subsort relation Configuration < Value.

This leads to a more structured view of the concurrent state of an object-oriented system, not as a single configuration, but instead as a possibly quite complex ensemble of configurations and objects that can contain each other like Russian dolls. This view seems closely related the notion of "group objects" proposed by Watari et al. [102], and to Matsuoka et al.'s notion of "hybrid group reflective architecture" [66]. In this way, reflection can be used to better exploit resources at different levels and to respond dynamically to changes in a concurrent computation. Since not one but many "metaobjects" can exist and can even contain other metaobjects, this permits a very distributed style of reflection and allows division of labor, so that higher level metaobjects may only have to deal with simpler and more abstract representations of the distributed state that they control, perhaps indirectly, at lower levels.

For example, besides a master object controlling an entire parallel execution, there can be a *group object* associated with each processor of the parallel machine in which the execution is taking place. Under the control of such a group object there can be a set of ordinary objects for which the group object provides services such as scheduling, sending and delivering messages to and from objects in other processors, etc. For some purposes, including for example broadcasting, the master metaobject may only have to communicate with these group objects, without having to directly involve the objects contained inside each group object. In general, this style of concurrent reflection may involve messages going up and down an entire hierarchy of metaobjects. We can therefore refine more and more our previous view of the master object in the way sketched below

```
< M : Master | configuration: (< G1: Group | configuration: S1, ATTS1 > S
                    < Gn: Group | configuration: Sn, ATTSn >), ATTS >
```

One way in which rewriting logic seems promising in the context of concurrent object-oriented reflection is that it could provide a simple and uniform semantic basis to deal with metaobjects. It appears that they could be dealt with in exactly the same way as ordinary objects, with appropriate rewrite rules specifying the behavior of different metaobject classes such as `Master`, `Group`, etc.

A related topic—discussed also in [69]—is that entities such as classes, modules, etc. can also be represented as metaobjects. This can lead to very flexible and adaptable language implementations using the *metaobject protocol* methodology [58], a methodology that has been adapted to the concurrent case by Matsuoka et al. in [66].

Finding a simple and rigorous semantics for concurrent object-oriented reflection is considered an important open problem, because this area is undergoing rapid development and seems very promising in order to better control the execution of concurrent systems so as to use the computational resources in an optimal way. We refer the reader to [99] for a recent collection of papers on reflection, including object-oriented approaches. In future work we hope to further explore the use of rewriting logic in reflection.

12.4.7 Actors

Actors [3, 1] provide a flexible and attractive style of concurrent object-oriented programming. However, their mathematical structure, although already described and studied by previous researchers [28, 1], has remained somewhat hard to understand and, as a consequence, the use of formal methods to reason about actor systems has remained limited. The present logical theory of concurrent objects sheds new light on the mathematical structure of actors and provides a new formal basis for the study of this important approach.

Actors	OOP
Script	Class declaration
Actor	Object
Actor Machine	Object State
Task	Message
Acquaintances	Attributes

Figure 12.8
A dictionary for Actors.

Specifically, the general logical theory of concurrent objects presented in this paper directly yields as a special case an entirely declarative approach to the theory and programming practice of actors. The specialization of our model to that of actors can be obtained by first clarifying terminological issues and then studying their definition by Agha and Hewitt [3].

Actor theory has a terminology of its own which, to make things clearer, we will attempt to relate to the more standard terminology employed in object-oriented programming. To the best of our understanding, the table in Figure 12.8 provides a basic terminological correspondence of this kind.

The essential idea about actors is clearly summarized in the words of Agha and Hewitt [3] as follows:

> "An actor is a computational agent which carries out its actions in response to processing a communication. The actions it may perform are:
>
> • Send communications to itself or to other actors.
>
> • Create more actors.
>
> • Specify the *replacement behavior*."

The "replacement behavior" is yet another term to describe the new "actor machine" produced after processing the communication, i.e., the new state of the actor.

We can now put all this information together and simply conclude that a logical axiomatization in rewriting logic of an actor system—which is of course at the same time an *executable* specification of such a system in Maude—exactly corresponds to the special case of a concurrent object-oriented system in our sense whose rewrite rules instead of being of the general form (†) are of the special asynchronous and unconditional form

$$M \ \langle O : C \mid atts \rangle$$
$$\longrightarrow \langle O : C' \mid atts' \rangle$$
$$\langle Q_1 : D_1 \mid atts_1'' \rangle \ldots \langle Q_p : D_p \mid atts_p'' \rangle$$
$$M_1' \ldots M_q'$$

Therefore, the present theory is considerably *more general* than that of actors. In comparison with existing accounts about actors [3, 1] it seems also fair to say that our theory is *more abstract* so that some of those accounts might be now regarded as *high level architectural descriptions* of particular ways in which the special case of the abstract model corresponding to actors can be implemented. In particular, the all-important *mail system* used in those accounts to buffer communication is the implementation counterpart of what in our model is abstractly achieved by the *ACI* axioms.

Another nice feature of our approach is that it gives a *truly concurrent* formulation—in terms of concurrent *ACI*-rewriting—of actor computations, which seems most natural given their character. By contrast, Agha [1] presents an interleaving model of sequentialized transitions. Agha is keenly aware of the inadequacy of reducing the essence of true concurrency to nondeterminism and therefore states (pg. 82) that the correspondence between his interleaving model and the truly concurrent computation of actors is *"representationalistic, not metaphysical."*

Yet another contribution of rewriting logic is its simple and unproblematic support for class inheritance in a concurrent context. It seems to be a generally accepted folklore opinion that it is very difficult to support both concurrency and class inheritance in actor languages; in fact, a number of actor languages do not support inheritance for this reason, and the whole matter is considered an open problem for which only partial or tentative solutions seem to have been suggested so far. Maude's simple solution to this "inheritance anomaly" [67, 90] was already mentioned in Section 12.4.2 and is discussed in full detail in [74].

It is also important to point out that, in our account, the way in which an object changes its state as a consequence of receiving a message may involve many concurrent rewritings of its attributes, i.e., objects exhibit *intra-object concurrency*; by contrast, typical actor languages treat change of object state as a sequential computation, and formal models of concurrency for actors such as that in [1] only deal with message-passing inter-object concurrency. In this sense, the concurrent rewriting model is considerably more fine grained, and when implemented on an appropriate architecture such as the RRM (see Section 12.5.3) directly supports the massive exploitation of both inter-object parallelism (typically by interprocessor communication) and intra-object parallelism (typically by SIMD data parallelism). A good example exhibiting these two types of parallelism is the search for solutions to the eight queens problem in Section 12.6.1.

There is one additional aspect important for actor systems and in general for concurrent systems, namely *fairness*. For actors, this takes the form of requiring *guarantee of mail delivery*. The issue of fairness for term rewriting has already received attention by several authors, including Francez and Porat [92] and Tison [100]. Indeed, it is possible to state precisely a variety of fairness conditions for concurrent rewriting; in particular, one could express the guarantee of mail delivery for the special case of actors in these terms. However, a detailed treatment of this topic is outside the scope of this paper and will have to wait for a future occasion.

12.4.8 Generality of the Concurrent Rewriting Model

Concurrent rewriting is a very general model of concurrency from which many other models—besides those discussed in this paper—can be obtained by specialization. Space limitations preclude a detailed discussion, for which we refer the reader to [72]. However, we can summarize such specializations using Figure 12.9, where CR stands for concurrent rewriting, the arrows indicate specializations, and the subscripts $\emptyset$, *AI*, and *ACI* stand

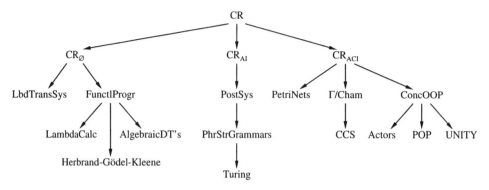

Figure 12.9
Unification of concurrency models.

for syntactic rewriting, rewriting modulo associativity and identity, and ACI-rewriting respectively. Within syntactic rewriting we have labelled transition systems, which are used in interleaving approaches to concurrency; functional programming (in particular Maude's functional modules) corresponds to the case of *confluent*[19] rules, and includes the λ-calculus (see Section 12.5.2) and the Herbrand-Gödel-Kleene theory of recursive functions. Rewriting modulo AI yields Post systems and related grammar formalisms, including Turing machines. Besides the general treatment by ACI-rewriting of concurrent object-oriented programming that contains Actors as a special case [3], rewriting modulo ACI includes Petri nets [93], the Gamma language of Banâtre and Le Mètayer [13] and Berry and Boudol's *chemical abstract machine* [15], CCS [84] (which can be naturally expressed in rewriting logic [75], and can also be obtained as a special case of the *cham* [15]), as well as Unity's model of computation [26]; another special case is Engelfriet et al.'s POPs and POTs which are higher level Petri nets for actors [36, 35].

The ACI case is quite important, since it contains as special subcases a good number of concurrency models that have already been studied. In fact, the associativity and commutativity of the axioms appear in some of those models as "fundamental laws of concurrency." However, from the perspective of this work the ACI case—while being important and useful—does not have a monopoly on the concurrency business. Indeed, "fundamental laws of concurrency" expressing associativity and commutativity are only valid in this particular case. They are for example meaningless for the tree-structured case of functional programming. The point is that the laws satisfied by a concurrent system cannot be determined *a priori*. They essentially depend on the actual distributed structure of the system, which is its algebraic structure.

More importantly—and this is a key advantage of Maude's object-oriented modules— an ACI operator, even when present, does account only for *some* of the concurrency of a system when other operators not having that property are also present. For example, an object may communicate with other objects in an ACI distributed state, but its attributes can also have a distributed structure—typically a tree structure—so that their updating can be performed in parallel. Concurrent rewriting does not discriminate between one

---

[19]Although not reflected in the picture, rules confluent *modulo* equations E are also functional.

level of parallelism (*ACI* communication between objects) and another (parallel attribute updating); instead, it integrates both levels within the same formal framework supporting concurrency *at all levels*.

Of course, the general claim that a system's distributed structure coincides with its algebraic structure applies also here. The *ACI* axioms lead to a state structure that is distributed as a *commutative word*, *multiset*, or *bag*, all these being different expressions for the same idea. This is a very fluid and flexible structure which, in particular, is an ideal abstract structure for *communication*; as already pointed out, this may only account for the *top-level structure* of a system, which in the framework of rewriting logic is seamlessly integrated with any other distributed structures at lower levels.

12.5   Simple Maude

This section summarizes joint work with Timothy Winkler [83] on the design of a sublanguage of Maude called Simple Maude chosen with the purpose of being implementable with reasonable efficiency on a wide variety of parallel machines. The present summary will focus primarily on Simple Maude and will touch more briefly on implementation issues and on the use of Maude as glue to parallelize conventional programs and to put together heterogeneous systems; more details are given in the joint paper [83].

12.5.1   Maude as a Wide Spectrum Language

Although concurrent rewriting is a general and flexible model of concurrency and can certainly be used to reason formally about concurrent systems at a high level of abstraction, it would not be reasonable to implement this model for programming purposes in its fullest generality. This is due to the fact that, in its most general form, rewriting can take place *modulo* an arbitrary equational theory E which could be undecidable. Of course, a minimum practical requirement for E is the existence of an algorithm for finding all the matches modulo E for a given rule and term; however, for some axioms E, this process, even if it is available, can be quite inefficient, so that its implementation should be considered a theorem proving matter, or at best something to be supported by an implementation for uses such as rapid prototyping and execution of specifications, but probably should not be made part of a programming language implementation. A good example is general AC-rewriting, which can be quite costly for complicated left-hand side patterns; this can be acceptable for rapid prototyping purposes—in fact, the OBJ3 interpreter [45, 53] supports this as well as rewriting modulo other similar sets of axioms E—but seems to us impractical for programming purposes even if a parallel implementation is considered[20].

In this regard, it is useful to adopt a *transformational* point of view. For specification purposes we can allow the full generality of the concurrent rewriting model, whereas for programming purposes we should study subcases that can be efficiently implemented; executable specifications hold a middle ground in which we can be considerably more

---

[20]Of course, even in a case like this there can be different opinions. Banâtre, Coutant, and Le Mètayer have in fact considered parallel machine implementations of AC-rewriting for their Gamma language [12].

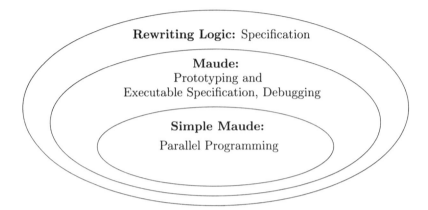

Figure 12.10
Maude and Simple Maude as subsets of Rewriting Logic.

tolerant of inefficiencies in exchange for a greater expressiveness. The idea is then to develop program transformation techniques that are semantics-preserving and move us from specifications to programs, and from less efficient programs—perhaps just executable specifications—to more efficient ones. This transformational approach fits in very nicely with the design of Maude which, as with OBJ3 in the functional case, can be regarded as a wide spectrum language that integrates both specification and computation. Indeed, Maude *theories*, whether functional, system, or object-oriented, are used for specification purposes—for example, to specify the semantic requirements of the parameters of a parameterized module—and therefore need not be executable[21]. For Maude *modules*, which are of course executable, a distinction should be made between use for rapid prototyping and executable specification, and use for programming, with more stringent restrictions imposed in the latter case.

This suggests considering two subsets of rewriting logic. The first subset gives rise to Maude—in the sense that Maude modules are rewriting logic theories in that subset—and can be supported by an interpreter implementation adequate for rapid prototyping, debugging, and executable specification. The second, smaller subset gives rise to Simple Maude, a sublanguage meant to be used for programming purposes for which a wide variety of machine implementations can be developed. Program transformation techniques can then support passage from general rewrite theories to Maude modules and from them to modules in Simple Maude. Figure 12.10 summarizes the three levels involved.

Regarding Maude and its implementation as an interpreter, we plan to support rewriting modulo all the axioms supported by OBJ3, where a binary operator can be declared to be associative and/or commutative and/or having a neutral element, and rewriting

---

[21]In fact, for the sake of greater expressiveness they may even be theories in logics different from rewriting or equational logic; details will appear elsewhere.

modulo a combination of those axioms is supported by the implementation. In particular, all the modules in this paper are executable Maude modules. The Maude interpreter will support rapid prototyping and debugging of system designs and specifications that, if desired, could also be used to derive an efficient system by applying to them a series of semantics-preserving transformations and refinement steps bringing the entire program within the Simple Maude sublanguage; some program transformations can be automated so that a user can write certain types of programs in a more abstract way in Maude and could leave the task of transforming them into Simple Maude programs to a compiler.

12.5.2   Simple Maude

Simple Maude represents our present design decisions about the subset of rewriting logic that could be implemented efficiently in a wide variety of machine architectures. In fact, we regard Simple Maude as a *machine-independent parallel programming language*, which could be executed with reasonable efficiency on many parallel architectures. As discussed briefly later, Simple Maude can also support multilingual extensions and can be used as the glue for putting together open heterogeneous systems encompassing many different machines and special I/O devices. This section summarizes the language conventions for functional, system, and object-oriented modules in Simple Maude.

12.5.2.1   Rewriting Modulo Church-Rosser and Terminating Equations   As work on compilation techniques for functional languages has amply demonstrated, syntactic rewriting, i.e., rewriting modulo an empty set of structural axioms, can be implemented efficiently on sequential machines; our experience with parallel compilation techniques for syntactic rewriting in the Rewrite Rule Machine (RRM) project [50, 6, 5] leads us to believe that this can be done even more efficiently on parallel machines. Therefore, functional or system modules with an empty set of structural axioms are among the easiest to implement and belong to Simple Maude.

A closely related class of modules also allowed in Simple Maude is that of functional or system modules having an associated rewrite theory $\mathcal{R} = (\Sigma, E, L, R)$ such that the set E of structural axioms is Church-Rosser and terminating and has the additional property that, for the rewrite theory $\mathcal{R}' = (\Sigma, \emptyset, L, R)$, whenever we have $\mathcal{R}' \vdash t \longrightarrow t'$ we also have $\mathcal{R}' \vdash can_E(t) \longrightarrow t''$ with $can_E(t') = can_E(t'')$, where $can_E(t)$ denotes the (canonical) normal form to which the term t is reduced by the equations E used as rewrite rules. Under such circumstances we can implement rewriting modulo E by syntactic rewriting with the rewrite theory $\mathcal{R}'' = (\Sigma, \emptyset, L, R \cup E)$ provided that we restrict our attention to sequents of the form $can_E(t) \longrightarrow can_E(t')$ which faithfully simulate $\mathcal{R}$-rewritings in E-equivalence classes. For modules of this kind the structural axioms $u = v$ in E are introduced by the syntax

```
ax u = v .
```

A functional module defined by a rewrite theory $\mathcal{R}$ of this kind has the same initial algebra as the functional module defined by the associated rewrite theory $\mathcal{R}''$. However, the semantics of both modules as defined in Section 12.8 are different. For system modules of this kind, the semantics associated with $\mathcal{R}$ and with the rewrite theory $\mathcal{R}''$ that simulates it are even more different.

Even for functional modules, the possibility of allowing a distinction between rules and structural axioms is quite convenient and meaningful. For example, we can in this way avoid all the fuss with variables and substitution in the standard lambda calculus notation by defining a functional module LAMBDA corresponding to the $\lambda\sigma$-calculus of Abadi, Cardelli, Curien, and Lévy [1] in which we interpret their *Beta* rule as the only rule, and their set σ of Church-Rosser and terminating equations for explicit substitution as the set E of structural axioms. The point is that σ-equivalence classes are isomorphic to standard lambda expressions (modulo α conversion), and rewritings in σ-equivalence classes correspond to β-reductions.

There are of course a variety of strategies by which we can interleave E-rewriting and R-rewriting in the implementation of modules of this kind, and some strategies can be more efficient than others. It could also be possible to generalize the class of modules that can be implemented by syntactic rewriting by giving weaker conditions on the relationship between R and E that are still correct assuming a particular strategy for interleaving R- and E-rewritings.

12.5.2.2 Object-Oriented Modules In Maude, the essence of concurrent object-oriented computation is captured by concurrent ACI-rewriting using rules of the general form (†) described in Section 12.4.1.1. In a sequential interpreter this can be *simulated* by performing ACI-rewriting using an ACI-matching algorithm. However, in a parallel implementation ACI-rewriting should be realized exclusively by means of *communication*. The problem is that realizing general AC- or ACI-rewriting in this way can require unacceptable amounts of communication and therefore can be very inefficient, even for rules of the form (†) introduced in object-oriented modules that make a somewhat limited use of ACI-rewriting because no variables are ever used to match multisets. For this reason, our approach to the object-oriented modules of Simple Maude is to only allow conditional rules of the form

(‡) $M \ \langle O : F \mid atts \rangle$

$\longrightarrow (\langle O : F' \mid atts' \rangle)$
$\langle Q_1 : D_1 \mid atts_1'' \rangle \ldots \langle Q_p : D_p \mid atts_p'' \rangle$
$M_1' \ldots M_q'$
if C

involving only one object and one message in their lefthand side, where $p, q \geq 0$, and where the notation $(\langle O : F' \mid atts' \rangle)$ means that the object O—in a possibly different state—is only an optional part of the righthand side, i.e., that it can be omitted in some rules. We allow as well conditional rules for autonomous objects of the form (again, with $p, q \geq 0$)

(§) $\langle O : F \mid atts \rangle$

$\longrightarrow (\langle O : F' \mid atts' \rangle)$

$\langle Q_1 : D_1 \mid atts_1'' \rangle \ldots \langle Q_p : D_p \mid atts_p'' \rangle$

$M_1' \ldots M_q'$

$if \ C$

Specifically, the lefthand sides in rules of the form (‡) should fit the general pattern[22]

$M(O) \ \langle O : C \mid atts \rangle$

where O could be a variable, a constant, or more generally—in case object identifiers are endowed with additional structure—a term. Under such circumstances, an efficient way of realizing AC-rewriting by communication is available to us for rules of the form (‡), namely we can associate object identifiers with specific addresses in the machine where the object is located and send messages addressed to the object to the corresponding address. For example, a rule to credit money to an account can be implemented this way by routing the credit message to the location of its addressee so that when both come into contact the rewrite rule for crediting the account can be applied. Rules of the form (§) are even simpler to implement, since their matching does not require any communication by messages; however, both types of rules assume the existence of a basic mechanism for sending the messages generated in the righthand side to their appropriate destination.

How should the gap between the more general rules (†) allowed in Maude modules and the more restricted rules (‡) and (§) permitted in Simple Maude modules be mediated? Our approach to this problem—in forthcoming joint work with Patrick Lincoln and Timothy Winkler—has been to develop program transformation techniques that, under appropriate fairness assumptions, guarantee that rewriting with rules of the form (†) can be simulated by rewriting using rules of the form (‡) and (§). The basic idea is that a (†) rule in general requires the synchronization of several objects—what in some contexts is called a *multiparty interaction*—but this synchronization can be achieved in an asynchronous way by an appropriate sending of messages using rules of the form (‡). Transformations of this kind can be automated and relegated to a compiler, so that a user could write object-oriented modules in Maude and not have to worry about the corresponding expression of his program in Simple Maude. However, Simple Maude is already quite expressive—in particular, more expressive than Actors—and many programs will fall naturally within this class without any need for further transformations.

The strategy described in this section for Simple Maude's object-oriented modules can be generalized to system modules[23] so that they can also perform concurrent AC-rewriting by asynchronous message-passing communication; this generalization is discussed in [83].

---

[22] However, the rules for object creation using proto-objects given in Section 12.4.4 which do not fit this pattern are also allowed in Simple Maude.

[23] As discussed before, we also allow Simple Maude system modules where the structural axioms E are given by Church-Rosser and terminating equations.

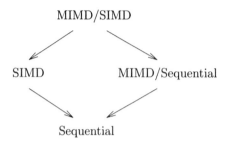

Figure 12.11
Specialization relationships among parallel architectures.

12.5.3   Sequential, SIMD, MIMD, and MIMD/SIMD Implementations

Simple Maude can be implemented on a wide variety of parallel architectures. The diagram in Figure 12.11 shows the relationship among some general classes that we have considered. There are two orthogonal choices giving rise to four classes of machines: the processing nodes can be either a single sequential processor or a SIMD array of processors, and there can be either just a single processing node or a network of them. The arrows in the diamond denote specializations from a more general and concurrent architecture to degenerate special cases, with the sequential case at the bottom. The arrows pointing to the left correspond to specializing a network of processing nodes to the degenerate case with only one processing node; the arrows pointing to the right correspond to specializing a SIMD array to the degenerate case of a single processor.

Each of these architectures is naturally suited for a different way of performing rewriting computations. Simple Maude has been chosen so that concurrent rewriting with rules in this sublanguage should be relatively easy to implement in any of these four classes of machines; the paper [83] discusses this matter in greater detail; here we limit ourselves to a brief sketch. In the MIMD/Sequential (multiple instruction stream, multiple data) case many different rewrite rules can be applied at many different places at once, but only one rule is applied at one place in each processor. The implementation of object-oriented rules of the form (‡), involving a message and an object, can be achieved by *interprocessor communication*, sending the message to the processor in which the ad- dressee object is located, so that when the message arrives the corresponding rules can be applied. The sequential case corresponds to a single conventional sequential processor and can be viewed as the degenerate case of a MIMD/Sequential machine with only one processor. In this case, at most one rule is applied to a single place in the data at a time. Since there is only one processor in which all objects are located, implementing rules of the form (‡) does not require any interprocessor communication. The SIMD (single instruction stream, multiple data) case corresponds to applying rewrite rules one at a time, possibly to many places in the data. The implementation of rules of the form (‡) will require special SIMD code for message passing in addition to the SIMD code for performing the rewriting. The MIMD/SIMD case is at present more exotic; the Rewrite Rule Machine (RRM) [52, 7, 6, 5] is an architecture in this class in which the processing nodes are two-dimensional SIMD arrays realized on a chip and the higher level structure is a network operating in MIMD mode. This case corresponds to applying many rules to many different places in the data, but here a single rule may be applied at many places simultaneously within a single processing node. The message passing required for rules of the form (‡) can be performed in a way entirely similar to the MIMD/Sequential case. From the point of view of maximizing the amount and flexibility of the rewriting that can happen in parallel, the MIMD/SIMD case provides the most general solution and offers the best prospects for reaching extremely high performance in many applications.

12.5.4 Multilingual Extensions and Open Heterogeneous Systems

Simple Maude will support the integration of modules written in conventional languages such as Fortran and C; this will allow reusing and parallelizing code originally developed for sequential machines. More generally, not only conventional code, but entire systems and special-purpose hardware devices can be integrated in a similar way. The joint paper [83] provides a more detailed discussion of this aspect of the language, which is briefly summarized below.

The way in which this integration can be accomplished generalizes a facility already available in Maude's functional sublanguage (OBJ) for defining *built-in sorts* and *built-in rules* [45, 53]. This facility has provided valuable experience with multilingual support, in this case for OBJ and Common Lisp, and can be generalized to a facility for defining *foreign interface modules* in Maude. Such foreign interface modules have abstract interfaces that allow them to be integrated with other Maude modules and to be executed concurrently with other computations; however, they are treated as "black boxes." In particular, Maude's model of computation and its modular style provide a simple way of gluing a concurrent program together out of pieces that can be either written in Simple Maude or can be sequential code written in conventional languages. Foreign interface modules may provide either a functional data type, or an object-oriented class. In the first case, the treatment will be extremely similar to that provided in OBJ. In the second case, the abstract interface will be provided by the specification of the messages that act upon the new class of objects. This second case is also the approach used to interface to existing systems or applications and to special-purpose hardware devices; they are treated as, possibly quite complex, black boxes.

Future computing environments will be heterogeneous, involving many different machine architectures, and evolving, with components being attached and removed over time. It has long been recognized that message-passing models provide one of the best ways to integrate distributed heterogeneous systems. Designs based on message passing also make it relatively easy to add or remove resources, and to deal with variations in the size of parallel architectures (the number of processing nodes). The advantage of the concurrent rewriting model is that it integrates message passing within a simple and mathematically precise abstract model of computation and can therefore be used as both a semantic framework and as a language for the integration of heterogeneous systems. In order to incorporate something (whether it be a special-purpose processor, an I/O device, a database, or a program written in C) into the abstract model, it is just necessary to treat it as a black box and to specify its interface to the system, i.e., the message protocol that is used for interacting with it.

Related efforts in multilingual support for parallel programming include: the *Linda* language developed by D. Gelernter and his collaborators at Yale [25], the *Strand* language designed by I. Foster and S. Taylor [37], the *Program Composition Notation* (PCN) designed by K. M. Chandy and S. Taylor at Caltech [27], and the *GLU* language developed by R. Jagannathan and A. Faustini at SRI International [57].

12.6   More Examples

This section presents two somewhat longer Maude examples: a module for autonomous objects that search all the solutions to the eight queens problem in parallel, and a fault-tolerant communication protocol.

12.6.1   Eight Queens

The following example illustrates several Maude features, including autonomous objects, object creation and deletion, the convenience of the notational conventions for rules involving objects introduced in Section 12.4.2 that allow omitting mention of attributes irrelevant for a particular rule, extensive use of intra-object concurrency, and parameterization. The example is the well-known eight queens problem of finding all board configurations on an 8×8 board in which eight queens are placed on the board in such a way that no queen is able to capture any other queen. According to the rules of chess, a queen can capture any other piece along its same row, column, or diagonals. An actor treatment of this problem has appeared in [11]. The idea in both [11] and in the example below is to search all the solutions in parallel without any backtracking.

We make the size of the board a parameter, and represent a *partial solution* as a list of pairs of nonzero natural numbers $(1, n_1), \ldots, (i, n_i)$, indicating that i queens have already been placed successfully on the first i columns of the board, in the positions contained in the list. Of course, since only one queen can be placed per row (or per column) in a solution, the only rows that remain free as potential candidates for placing new queens are in the set $\{1, \ldots, k\} - \{n_1, \ldots, n_i\}$, with $k \times k$ the assumed size of the board. This is the set of row positions in column $i + 1$ that we have to examine to try to expand the partial solution $(1, n_1), \ldots, (i, n_i)$ by adding a new queen in column $i + 1$. Since, by construction, there will be only one queen per row and per column in this expanded partial solution, the only thing that we have to check is that the row position chosen in the set of free rows to place the queen on the $i + 1$-th column is not in the same diagonal as any of the previous queens. This can be done by applying the predicate `in-diag` defined in the auxiliary functional module `DIAG` below; we can then gather together all successful row positions failing the `in-diag` test by means of the function `good-rows`. We assume that the `INT` module has a sort `NzNat` of nonzero natural numbers, and an absolute value function `|_|`.

```
fmod DIAG is
```

```
      protecting INT .
      protecting BOOL .
      protecting LIST[2TUPLE[NzNat,NzNat]*(sort 2Tuple to NzNatPair)]*(
                   sort List to PairList) .
      protecting LIST[NzNat]*(sort List to NzNatList) .

      op in-diag : NzNat NzNat PairList -> Bool .

      *** arguments to in-diag: a row position, the column being
      *** considered, and a partial solution up to the previous column

      vars C R C' R' : NzNat .
      var P : NzNatPair .
      var L : NzNatList .
      var Q : PairList .

      eq in-diag(R,C,P Q) = in-diag(R,C,P) or in-diag(R,C,Q) .
      eq in-diag(R,C,<< C' ; R' >>) = (| R - R' | == | C - C' |) .
      eq in-diag(R,C,nil) = false .

      op good-rows : NzNatList NzNat PairList -> NzNatList .

      ***   arguments to good-rows: a list of free rows, the column being
      ***   considered, and a partial solution up to the previous column

      eq good-rows(R L,C,Q) = good-rows(R,C,Q) good-rows(L,C,Q) .
      eq good-rows(nil,C,Q) = nil .
      eq good-rows(R,C,Q) = if in-diag(R,C,Q) then nil else R fi .
  endfm
```

The search for all the solutions will use objects in a class QAgent having attributes caller (the name of the external object that requested the eight queens solutions), psol (a partial solution), column (the last column in the partial solution), free-rows (the unoccuppied rows), good-rows (the rows in the next column that can expand the partial solution), and tested (whether or not the free rows have been tested as expansions of the solution). The search will begin in a configuration involving the set of k objects

```
  < N : QAgent | caller: B, psol: << 1 ; N >>, column: 1,
    free-rows: remove N from (1 ... K), good-rows: nil, tested: false >
```

for N varying from 1 to k, with object N beginning the search at row N in the first column and searching for good rows in column 2. The module defining QAgent has the functional theory NAT* of Section 12.4.1 as its parameter, to specify the side size k of the $k \times k$ board.

```
  omod K-QUEENS[K :: NAT*] is
```

```
protecting DIAG .
class QAgent | caller: OId, psol: PairList, column: NzNat ,
           free-rows: NzNatList, good-rows: NzNatList, tested: Bool .
msg to_sol_ : OId PairList -> Msg .
vars A B : OId .
vars R C : Nznat .
var Q : PairList .
vars L L' : NzNatList .

*** the agent tests which free rows are good for placing a queen
*** in the next column, and records the information

rl < A : QAgent | psol: Q, column: C, free-rows: L,
       tested: false > =>
     < A : QAgent | good-rows: good-rows(L,C + 1,Q), tested: true > .

*** for each good row found, a new object continuing the search
*** with that row in the expanded partial solution is created, except
*** in case the good row is in the last column, where the solution
*** is sent to the caller and the agent garbage-collects itself

rl < A : QAgent | caller: B, psol: Q, column: C, free-rows: L,
       good-rows: N L' > =>
   if (C + 1) < k then
     < A : QAgent | good-rows: L' >
     new(QAgent | caller: B, psol: Q << C + 1 ; N >>, column: C + 1,
         free-rows: remove N from L, good-rows: nil, tested: false)
   else (to B sol Q << k ; N >>) fi .

*** if no good row is left, the agent garbage-collects itself

 rl < A : QAgent | good-rows: nil, tested: true > => null .
endom
```

The classical eight queens case can be obtained by a simple instantiation

```
make 8-QUEENS is K-QUEENS[view to NAT is op k to 8 . endv] endmk
```

12.6.2   A Communication Protocol Example

If a communication mechanism does not provide reliable, in-order delivery of messages, it may be necessary to generate this service using the given unreliable basis. The following example, developed jointly with Timothy Winkler and borrowed with slight modifications from [83], shows how this might be done. Since unreliable communication is a more serious issue across different machines, this example illustrates the application of Maude to heterogeneous open systems (see Section 12.5.4). This was derived from the alternating bit protocol as presented in Lam and Shankar [60], although, since we do not assume in-order delivery, we cannot use the alternating bit protocol. The same kind of example is discussed in a somewhat different way in Chandy and Misra [26]. The following definition creates a generic, fault-tolerant connection between a specific sender and receiver pair. Notice that—thanks to the abstractness of the concurrent rewriting model and to the parameterization mechanisms of the language—the module is very general in several respects:

- it makes very few assumptions about the communication between sender and receiver;
- the parameter ELT can be instantiated to any type of data to be sent;
- the parameters S and R can be instantiated to any two previously defined classes of objects.

The requirement that the parameters S and R have to satisfy is expressed by the object-oriented theory CLASS below, whose Cl sort can be instantiated to any class of an object-oriented module. To disambiguate the use of the parameter sort Cl in S and R, we use the notation Cl.S and Cl.R.

```
oth CLASS is
  class Cl .
endoth

omod PROTOCOL[ELT :: TRIV, S :: CLASS, R :: CLASS] is
  protecting LIST[ELT] .
  protecting NAT .

  sort Contents .
  subsort Elt < Contents .
  op empty : -> Contents .
  msg to:_(_,_) : OId Elt Nat -> Msg . *** data to receiver
  msg to:_ack_ : OId Nat -> Msg . *** acknowledgement to sender

  class Sender | rec: OId, sendq: List, sendbuff: Contents ,
                 sendcnt: Nat .
  subclass Sender < Cl.S .

  *** rec is the receiver, sendq is the outgoing queue, sendbuff
  *** is either empty of the current data, sendcnt is the sender
  *** sequence number

  vars S R : OId .
  var N : Nat .
  var E : Elt .
  var L : List .
  var C : Contents .
```

```
rl produce :
   < S : Sender | rec: R, sendq: E . L,
       sendbuff: empty, sendcnt: N > =>
   < S : Sender | rec: R, sendq: L, sendbuff: E, sendcnt: N + 1 > .

rl send :
   < S : Sender | rec: R, sendq: L, sendbuff: E, sendcnt: N > =>
   < S : Sender | rec: R, sendq: L, sendbuff: E, sendcnt: N >
   (to: R (E,N)) .

rl rec-ack :
   < S : Sender | rec: R, sendq: L, sendbuff: C, sendcnt: N >
   (to: S ack M) =>
   < S : Sender | rec: R, sendq: L,
           sendbuff: (if N == M then empty else C fi),
           sendcnt: N > .

class Receiver | sender: OId, recq: List, reccnt: Nat .
subclass Receiver < Cl.R .

*** sender is the sender, recq is the incoming queue,
*** and reccnt is the receiver sequence number

rl receive :
   < R : Receiver | sender: S, recq: L, reccnt: M > (to: R (E,N)) =>
   (if N == M + 1 then
      < R : Receiver | sender: S, recq: L . E, reccnt: M + 1 >
    else
      < R : Receiver | sender: S, recq: L, reccnt: M >
    fi)
   (to: S ack N)
endom
```

Under reasonable fairness assumptions, these definitions will generate a reliable, in-order communication mechanism from an unreliable one. The message counts are used to ignore all out-of-order messages. The fairness assumption will ensure that the **send** action and corresponding **receive** actions will be repeated until a **rec-ack** can be performed; thus each **produce** necessarily leads to a corresponding **rec-ack**. Note that the **send** operation is enabled until the corresponding **rec-ack** occurs.

We can explicitly model the fault modes of the communication channel as in the following definition:

```
omod PROTOCOL-IN-FAULTY-ENV[ELT :: TRIV, S :: CLASS, R :: CLASS] is
   extending PROTOCOL[ELT,S,R] .
```

```
    var M : Msg .

    rl duplicate :
      M => M M .

    class Destroyer | sender: OId, rec: OId, cnt: Nat .

    var N : Nat .
    var E : Elt .
    vars S R D : OId .

    rl destroy1 :
      < D : Destroyer | sender: S, rec: R, cnt: N > (to: R (E,N)) =>
      < D : Destroyer | sender: S, rec: R, cnt: N > .

    rl destroy2 :
      < D : Destroyer | sender: S, rec: R, cnt: N > (to: S ack N) =>
      < D : Destroyer | sender: S, rec: R, cnt: N > .

    rl limited-injury :
      < D : Destroyer | sender: S, receiver: R, cnt: N > =>
      < D : Destroyer | sender: S, receiver: R, cnt: N + 1 > .
  endom
```

Messages may be duplicated or destroyed. The `limited-injury` rule, under an assumption of fair application of the total set of rules, will ensure that messages are not always destroyed. The new system, with the `Destroyer`, will also satisfy the same correctness condition regardless of messages being duplicated, being destroyed, or arriving out of order.

12.7   Maude and MaudeLog as Multiparadigm Logic Programming Languages

The statement made in the Introduction about Maude being a language directly based on a logic—namely rewriting logic—so that programs in Maude are logical theories and concurrent Maude computation is logical deduction has by now been explained and illustrated with examples in great detail. Calling Maude a "logic programming language" is therefore entirely justified, provided that we use this term in a broad sense that allows choosing among many logics the one that best suits our particular needs. In addition, Section 12.8 will discuss how initial models for rewriting logic can be used to give a denotational semantics to Maude programs in agreement with the logic programming nature of Maude.

In fact, although this has been kept implicit in the exposition, Maude's design is based on a general axiomatic notion of "logic programming language" which is itself based on a general axiomatic theory of logics. This theory of "general logics" and the associated general notion of "logic programming language" were developed in [68], and were inspired by previous work of Goguen and Burstall on "institutions" [44]. The paper [73] introduces these general concepts, discusses general methods for designing multiparadigm logic programming languages using such concepts, and explains how Maude and MaudeLog were designed according to those methods. We briefly sketch here some of the ideas of [73] to give the reader a better insight about the multiparadigm aspects of Maude and of MaudeLog.

For designing multiparadigm logic programming languages, a key technical tool is the use of *mappings between logics* that relate the syntax, sentences, entailments, and models of two different logics by appropriate translations. Technically, a unification of paradigms is achieved by mapping the logics of each paradigm into a richer logic in which the paradigms are unified.

In the case of Maude and MaudeLog, what is done is to define a new logic—rewriting logic—in which concurrent computations—and in particular concurrent object-oriented computations—can be expressed in a natural way, and then to formally relate this logic to the logics of the functional and relational paradigms, i.e., to equational logic and to Horn logic, by means of maps of logics that provide a simple and rigorous unification of paradigms. As it has already been mentioned, we actually assume an order-sorted structure throughout, and therefore the logics in question are: order-sorted rewriting logic, denoted *OSRWLogic*, order-sorted equational logic, denoted *OSEqtl*, and order-sorted Horn logic, denoted *OSHorn*.

At first sight one might conjecture that in order to extend functional programming to handle concurrent systems and object-oriented computations one has to *complicate* the logic, by embedding equational logic inside a more involved formalism. Maude's solution to this problem, provided by rewriting logic, achieves a very simple unification of functional programming within the broader context of concurrent systems programming and concurrent object-oriented programming by doing *just the opposite*. That is, rewriting logic actually has *simpler* rules of deduction than equational logic; indeed, as has already been mentioned, it can be obtained from equational logic by dropping the symmetry rule. The point, however, is that rewriting logic has a much broader class of models than equational logic (see Section 12.8), and the new models, corresponding to concurrent systems, are just what we need.

Rather than trying to force nonfunctional applications within a functional world, what it is done in this solution is to abandon any such attempts altogether, i.e., to leave the functional world untouched, and then to show that the logic of functional programming—in the particular variant discussed here of order-sorted equational logic—can be embedded within (order-sorted) rewriting logic by means of a map of logics

OSEqtl $\longrightarrow$ *OSRWLogic*.

The details of this map of logics are discussed in Appendix B of [73]. At the programming language level, such a map corresponds to the inclusion of Maude's *functional modules* (essentially identical to OBJ3 modules) within the language. The key point of having a map of this kind is that it relates both the proof-theoretic and the model-theoretic aspects of both logics. This permits maintaining intact the standard *initial algebra semantics* as the mathematical semantics of Maude's functional modules, just as in OBJ3, while allowing for a different semantics—based on the model theory of rewriting logic (see Section 12.8)—for Maude's system modules and object-oriented modules.

Since the power and the range of applications of a multiparadigm logic programming language can be substantially increased if it is possible to solve queries involving *logical variables* in the sense of relational programming, as in the Prolog language, we are naturally led to seek a unification of the three paradigms of functional, relational and concurrent object-oriented programming into a single multiparadigm logic programming language. This unification can be attained in a language extension of Maude called MaudeLog.

As before, the method used to achieve a unification of this kind in a simple and rigorous manner is to combine the logics involved by means of mappings. In addition to the mapping from equational logic to rewriting logic just discussed, which provides the integration of the functional facet, what remains is the integration of Horn logic. Such an integration is achieved by a map of logics

OSHorn $\longrightarrow$ *OSRWLogic*

that systematically relates order-sorted Horn logic to order-sorted rewriting logic. The details of this map are discussed in Appendix C of [73].

The difference between Maude and MaudeLog does not consist in any change in the underlying logic; indeed, both languages are based on rewriting logic, and both have rewrite theories as programs. It resides, rather, in an enlargement of the set of *queries* that can be presented, so that, while keeping the same syntax and models, in MaudeLog we also consider queries involving existential formulas of the form

$$\exists \overline{x} \quad [u_1(\overline{x})] \longrightarrow [v_1(\overline{x})] \wedge \ldots \wedge [u_k(\overline{x})] \longrightarrow [v_k(\overline{x})].$$

Therefore, the sentences and the deductive rules and mechanisms that are now needed require further extensions of rewriting logic deduction. In particular, solving such existential queries requires performing *unification*, specifically—given Maude's typing structure—order-sorted unification [79].

The above map of logics means that, after a simple translation, we can view a (pure) Prolog program as a MaudeLog program. We illustrate this translation by means of a simple example of family relations.

Here is the example in terms of Horn clauses:

```
Parent(X,Y) :- Father(X,Y)
Parent(X,Y) :- Mother(X,Y)
Grandparent(X,Z) :- Parent(X,Y), Parent(Y,Z)
Father(Peter,Paul)
Mother(Mary,Paul)
Father(Arthur,Peter)
Mother(Claire,Peter)
Father(Robert,Mary)
Mother(Louise,Mary)
```

This is the MaudeLog translation[24]:

```
mod FAMILY is
   extending PROP .
   sort People .
   ops father mother parent grandparent : People People -> Prop .
   ops peter paul mary arthur claire robert louise : -> People .
   vars X Y Z : People .
   rl father(X,Y) => parent(X,Y) .
   rl mother(X,Y) => parent(X,Y) .
   rl parent(X,Y), parent(Y,Z) => grandparent(X,Z) .
   rl true => father(peter,paul) .
   rl true => mother(mary,paul) .
   rl true => father(arthur,peter) .
   rl true => mother(claire,peter) .
   rl true => father(robert,mary) .
   rl true => mother(louise,mary) .
endm
```

The imported module PROP has a conjunction operator `_,_: Prop Prop -> Prop` as a multiset operator (i.e., it is associative and commutative) with identity `true`. In addition, it has the rule `rl X => true`.

Then the query

```
grandparent(X,Paul)?
```

is translated into the existential formula

```
∃X : People .  true => grandparent(X,Paul)
```

To solve this, we do backward search from the goal using the rewrite rules. In fact, because there exists an endomorphism of rewriting logic mapping the theory FAMILY to a version with all =>'s reversed, this could be reformulated in terms appropriate for forward search if desired.

Although the basic relationship formalized by the map of logics between Horn logic and rewriting logic is well understood, the design of MaudeLog is at a more preliminary stage than that of Maude and much work remains to be done at the theoretical level, in the deduction and operational semantics aspects, at the language design level, and eventually in an actual implementation.

12.8 Semantics

In this section we discuss models for rewriting logic and explain how such models are used to give semantics to modules in Maude. We will focus on the basic ideas and intuitions and leave out some of the details, which can be found in [72].

---

[24]Although the clauses are translated as illustrated below, the rewrite theory obtained by this translation makes additional requirements on the models, as explained in Appendix C of [73].

12.8.1   The Models of Rewriting Logic

We first sketch the construction of initial and free models for a rewrite theory $\mathcal{R} = (\Sigma, E, L, R)$. Such models capture nicely the intuitive idea of a "rewrite system" in the sense that they are systems whose states are E-equivalence classes of terms, and whose transitions are concurrent rewritings using the rules in R. Such systems have a natural *category* structure [62], with states as objects, transitions as morphisms, and sequential composition as morphism composition, and in them dynamic behavior exactly corresponds to deduction.

Given a rewrite theory $\mathcal{R} = (\Sigma, E, L, R)$, the model that we are seeking is a category $\mathcal{T}_{\mathcal{R}}(X)$ whose objects are equivalence classes of terms $[t] \in T_{\Sigma, E}(X)$ and whose morphisms are equivalence classes of "proof terms" representing proofs in rewriting deduction, i.e., concurrent $\mathcal{R}$-rewrites. The rules for generating such proof terms, with the specification of their respective domain and codomain, are given below; they just "decorate" with proof terms the rules 1-4 of rewriting logic given in Section 12.3.2. Note that we always use "diagrammatic" notation for morphism composition, i.e., $\alpha; \beta$ always means the composition of α *followed by* β.

1. **Identities**. For each $[t] \in T_{\Sigma, E}(X)$,

$$\overline{[t] : [t] \longrightarrow [t]}$$

2. **Σ-structure**. For each $f \in \Sigma_n$, $n \in \mathbb{N}$,

$$\frac{\alpha_1 : [t_1] \longrightarrow [t'_1] \quad \ldots \quad \alpha_n : [t_n] \longrightarrow [t'_n]}{f(\alpha_1, \ldots, \alpha_n) : [f(t_1, \ldots, t_n)] \longrightarrow [f(t'_1, \ldots, t'_n)]}$$

3. **Replacement**. For each rewrite rule $r : [t(\overline{x}^n)] \longrightarrow [t'(\overline{x}^n)]$ in R,

$$\frac{\alpha_1 : [w_1] \longrightarrow [w'_1] \quad \ldots \quad \alpha_n : [w_n] \longrightarrow [w'_n]}{r(\alpha_1, \ldots, \alpha_n) : [t(\overline{w}/\overline{x})] \longrightarrow [t'(\overline{w'}/\overline{x})]}$$

4. **Composition**.

$$\frac{\alpha : [t_1] \longrightarrow [t_2] \quad \beta : [t_2] \longrightarrow [t_3]}{\alpha; \beta : [t_1] \longrightarrow [t_3]}$$

Convention and Warning. In the case when the same label r appears in two different rules of R, the "proof terms" $r(\overline{\alpha})$ can sometimes be *ambiguous*. We assume that such ambiguity problems *have been resolved* by disambiguating the label r in the proof terms $r(\overline{\alpha})$ if necessary; with this understanding, we adopt the simpler notation $r(\overline{\alpha})$ to ease the exposition.

Each of the above rules of generation defines a different operation taking certain proof terms as arguments and returning a resulting proof term. In other words, proof terms form an algebraic structure $\mathcal{P}_{\mathcal{R}}(X)$ consisting of a graph with nodes $T_{\Sigma, E}(X)$, with identity arrows, and with operations f (for each $f \in \Sigma$), r (for each rewrite rule), and

_;_ (for composing arrows). Our desired model $\mathcal{T}_{\mathcal{R}}(X)$ is the quotient of $\mathcal{P}_{\mathcal{R}}(X)$ modulo the following equations[25]:

1. **Category**.

   (a) *Associativity.* For all α, β, γ

   $$(\alpha; \beta); \gamma = \alpha; (\beta; \gamma)$$

   (b) *Identities.* For each $\alpha : [t] \longrightarrow [t']$

   $$\alpha; [t'] = \alpha \quad and \quad [t]; \alpha = \alpha$$

2. **Functoriality of the Σ-algebraic structure**. For each $f \in \Sigma_n$, $n \in \mathbb{N}$,

   (a) *Preservation of composition.* For all $\alpha_1, \ldots, \alpha_n, \beta_1, \ldots, \beta_n$,

   $$f(\alpha_1; \beta_1, \ldots, \alpha_n; \beta_n) = f(\alpha_1, \ldots, \alpha_n); f(\beta_1, \ldots, \beta_n)$$

   (b) *Preservation of identities.*

   $$f([t_1], \ldots, [t_n]) = [f(t_1, \ldots, t_n)]$$

3. **Axioms in E**. For $t(x_1, \ldots, x_n) = t'(x_1, \ldots, x_n)$ an axiom in E, for all $\alpha_1, \ldots, \alpha_n$,

   $$t(\alpha_1, \ldots, \alpha_n) = t'(\alpha_1, \ldots, \alpha_n)$$

4. **Exchange**. For each $r : [t(x_1, \ldots, x_n)] \longrightarrow [t'(x_1, \ldots, x_n)]$ in R,

   $$\frac{\alpha_1 : [w_1] \longrightarrow [w'_1] \quad \ldots \quad \alpha_n : [w_n] \longrightarrow [w'_n]}{r(\overline{\alpha}) = r(\overline{[w]}); t'(\overline{\alpha}) = t(\overline{\alpha}); r(\overline{[w']})}$$

Note that the set X of variables is actually a parameter of these constructions, and we need not assume X to be fixed and countable. In particular, for $X = \emptyset$, we adopt the notation $\mathcal{T}_{\mathcal{R}}$. The equations in 1 make $\mathcal{T}_{\mathcal{R}}(X)$ a category, the equations in 2 make each $f \in \Sigma$ a functor, and 3 forces the axioms E. The exchange law states that any rewriting of the form $r(\overline{\alpha})$—which represents the *simultaneous* rewriting of the term at the top using rule r *and* "below," i.e., in the subterms matched by the variables, using the rewrites $\overline{\alpha}$—is equivalent to the sequential composition $r(\overline{[w]}); t'(\overline{\alpha})$, corresponding to first rewriting on top with r and then below on the subterms matched by the variables with $\overline{\alpha}$, and is also equivalent to the sequential composition $t(\overline{\alpha}); r(\overline{[w']})$ corresponding to first rewriting below with $\overline{\alpha}$ and then on top with r. Therefore, the exchange law states that rewriting at the top by means of rule r and rewriting "below" using $\overline{\alpha}$ are processes that are independent of each other and can be done either simultaneously or in any order. Since $[t(x_1, \ldots, x_n)]$ and $[t'(x_1, \ldots, x_n)]$ can be regarded as functors $\mathcal{T}_{\mathcal{R}}(X)^n \longrightarrow \mathcal{T}_{\mathcal{R}}(X)$, from the mathematical point of view the exchange law just asserts that r is a *natural transformation* [62], i.e.,

---

[25] In the expressions appearing in the equations, when compositions of morphisms are involved, we always implicitly assume that the corresponding domains and codomains match.

LEMMA 12.1 For each $r : [t(x_1, \ldots, x_n)] \longrightarrow [t'(x_1, \ldots, x_n)]$ in R, the family of morphisms

$$\{r(\overline{[w]}) : [t(\overline{w}/\overline{x})] \longrightarrow [t'(\overline{w}/\overline{x})] \mid \overline{[w]} \in \mathcal{T}_{\Sigma,E}(X)^n\}$$

is a natural transformation $r : [t(x_1, \ldots, x_n)] \Longrightarrow [t'(x_1, \ldots, x_n)]$ between the functors $[t(x_1, \ldots, x_n)], [t'(x_1, \ldots, x_n)] : \mathcal{T}_\mathcal{R}(X)^n \longrightarrow \mathcal{T}_\mathcal{R}(X)$.

□

What the exchange law provides in general is a way of *abstracting* a rewriting computation by considering immaterial the order in which rewrites are performed "above" and "below" in the term; further abstraction among proof terms is obtained from the functoriality equations. The equations 1-4 provide in a sense the *most abstract* "true concurrency" view of the computations of the rewrite theory $\mathcal{R}$ that can reasonably be given. In particular, we can prove that all proof terms have an equivalent expression as a composition of one-step rewrites:

LEMMA 12.2 For each $[\alpha] : [t] \longrightarrow [t']$ in $\mathcal{T}_\mathcal{R}(X)$, either $[t] = [t']$ and $[\alpha] = [[t]]$, or there is an $n \in \mathbb{N}$ and a chain of morphisms $[\alpha_i]$, $0 \le i \le n$, whose terms α_i describe one-step (concurrent) rewrites

$$[t] \xrightarrow{\alpha_0} [t_1] \xrightarrow{\alpha_1} \ldots \xrightarrow{\alpha_{n-1}} [t_n] \xrightarrow{\alpha_n} [t']$$

such that $[\alpha] = [\alpha_0; \ldots; \alpha_n]$. In addition, we can always choose all the α_i corresponding to sequential rewrites, i.e., we can decompose $[\alpha]$ into an interleaving sequence. □

The category $\mathcal{T}_\mathcal{R}(X)$ is just one among many *models* that can be assigned to the rewrite theory $\mathcal{R}$. The general notion of model, called an $\mathcal{R}$-system, is defined as follows:

Definition 11 Given a rewrite theory $\mathcal{R} = (\Sigma, E, L, R)$, an $\mathcal{R}$-*system* $\mathcal{S}$ is a category $\mathcal{S}$ together with:

- a (Σ, E)-algebra structure given by a family of functors

  $$\{f_\mathcal{S} : \mathcal{S}^n \longrightarrow \mathcal{S} \mid f \in \Sigma_n, n \in \mathbb{N}\}$$

  satisfying the equations E, i.e., for any $t(x_1, \ldots, x_n) = t'(x_1, \ldots, x_n)$ in E we have an identity of functors $t_\mathcal{S} = t'_\mathcal{S}$, where the functor $t_\mathcal{S}$ is defined inductively from the functors $f_\mathcal{S}$ in the obvious way.
- for each rewrite rule $r : [t(\overline{x})] \longrightarrow [t'(\overline{x})]$ in R a natural transformation $r_\mathcal{S} : t_\mathcal{S} \Longrightarrow t'_\mathcal{S}$.

An $\mathcal{R}$-*homomorphism* $F : \mathcal{S} \longrightarrow \mathcal{S}'$ between two $\mathcal{R}$-systems is then a functor $F : \mathcal{S} \longrightarrow \mathcal{S}'$ such that it is a Σ-algebra homomorphism—i.e., $f_\mathcal{S} * F = F^n * f_{\mathcal{S}'}$, for each f in Σ_n, $n \in \mathbb{N}$—and such that "F preserves R," i.e., for each rewrite rule $r : [t(\overline{x})] \longrightarrow [t'(\overline{x})]$ in R we have the identity of natural transformations[26] $r_\mathcal{S} * F = F^n * r_{\mathcal{S}'}$, where n is the number of variables appearing in the rule. This defines a category $\mathcal{R}$-*Sys* in the obvious way. □

---

[26]Note that we use diagrammatic order for the *horizontal*, $\alpha * \beta$, and *vertical*, $\gamma; \delta$, composition of natural transformations (see [62]).

What the above definition captures formally is the idea that the models of a rewrite theory *are systems*. By a "system" we of course mean a machine-like entity that can be in a variety of *states*, and that can change its state by performing certain *transitions*. Such transitions are of course transitive, and it is natural and convenient to view states as "idle" transitions that do not change the state. In other words, a system can be naturally regarded as a *category*, whose objects are the states of the system and whose morphisms are the system's transitions.

For *sequential* systems such as labelled transition systems this is in a sense the end of the story; such systems exhibit *nondeterminism*, but do not have the required algebraic structure in their states and transitions to exhibit true concurrency [70, 72]. Indeed, what makes a system *concurrent* is precisely the existence of an additional *algebraic structure*. Ugo Montanari and I first observed this fact for the particular case of Petri nets for which the algebraic structure is precisely that of a commutative monoid [81, 80]; this has been illustrated by the TICKET example in Section 12.2.2 where the commutative monoid operation $\_\_$ made possible the concurrent firing of several transitions. However, this observation holds in full generality for *any algebraic structure whatever*.

What the algebraic structure captures is twofold. Firstly, *the states themselves are distributed according to such a structure*; for Petri nets the distribution takes the form of a *multiset* that we can visualize with tokens and places; for a functional program involving just syntactic rewriting, the distribution takes the form of a *labelled tree structure* which can be spatially distributed in such a way that many transitions (i.e., rewrites) can happen concurrently in a way analogous to the concurrent firing of transitions in a Petri net. A concurrent object-oriented system as specified by a Maude module combines in a sense aspects of the functional and Petri net examples, because its configuration evolves by multiset *ACI*-rewriting but, underneath such transitions for objects and messages, arbitrarily complex concurrent computations of a functional nature can take place in order to update the values of object attributes as specified by appropriate functional submodules. Secondly, *concurrent transitions are themselves distributed according to the same algebraic structure*; this is what the notion of $\mathcal{R}$-system captures, and is for example manifested in the concurrent firing of Petri nets, the evolution of concurrent object-oriented systems and, more generally, in any type of concurrent rewriting.

The expressive power of rewrite theories to specify concurrent transition systems[27] is greatly increased by the possibility of having not only transitions, but also *parameterized transitions*, i.e., *procedures*. This is what rewrite rules—with variables—provide. The family of states to which the procedure applies is given by those states where a component of the (distributed) state is a substitution instance of the lefthand side of the rule in question. The rewrite rule is then a *procedure*[28] which transforms the state *locally*, by replacing such a substitution instance by the corresponding substitution instance of the righthand side. The fact that this can take place concurrently with other transitions "below" is precisely what the concept of a *natural transformation* formalizes. The table of Figure 12.12 summarizes our present discussion.

A detailed proof of the following theorem on the existence of initial and free $\mathcal{R}$-systems

---

[27] Such expressive power is further increased by allowing *conditional* rewrite rules, a more general case to which all that is said in this paper has been extended in [72].

[28] Its *actual parameters* are precisely given by a substitution.

System	$\longleftrightarrow$	*Category*
State	$\longleftrightarrow$	*Object*
Transition	$\longleftrightarrow$	*Morphism*
Procedure	$\longleftrightarrow$	*Natural Transformation*
Distributed Structure	$\longleftrightarrow$	*Algebraic Structure*

Figure 12.12
The mathematical structure of concurrent systems.

for the more general case of conditional rewrite theories is given in [72], where the soundness and completeness of rewriting logic for $\mathcal{R}$-system models is also proved. Below, for $\mathcal{C}$ a category, $Obj(\mathcal{C})$ denotes the set of its objects.

THEOREM 12.1 $\mathcal{T}_{\mathcal{R}}$ is an initial object in the category $\mathcal{R}$-Sys. More generally, $\mathcal{T}_{\mathcal{R}}(X)$ has the following universal property: Given an $\mathcal{R}$-system $\mathcal{S}$, each function $F : X \longrightarrow Obj(\mathcal{S})$ extends uniquely to an $\mathcal{R}$-homomorphism $F^{\natural} : \mathcal{T}_{\mathcal{R}}(X) \longrightarrow \mathcal{S}$. $\square$

12.8.2   Preorder, Poset, and Algebra Models

Since $\mathcal{R}$-systems are an "essentially algebraic" concept[29], we can consider classes Θ of $\mathcal{R}$-systems defined by the satisfaction of additional equations. Such classes give rise to full subcategory inclusions $\Theta \hookrightarrow \mathcal{R}$-$Sys$, and by general universal algebra results about essentially algebraic theories (see, e.g., [14]) such inclusions are *reflective* [62], i.e., for each $\mathcal{R}$-system $\mathcal{S}$ there is an $\mathcal{R}$-system $R_{\Theta}(\mathcal{S}) \in \Theta$ and an $\mathcal{R}$-homomorphism $\rho_{\Theta}(\mathcal{S}) : \mathcal{S} \longrightarrow R_{\Theta}(\mathcal{S})$ such that for any $\mathcal{R}$-homomorphism $F : \mathcal{S} \longrightarrow \mathcal{D}$ with $\mathcal{D} \in \Theta$ there is a unique $\mathcal{R}$-homomorphism $F^{\diamond} : R_{\Theta}(\mathcal{S}) \longrightarrow \mathcal{D}$ such that $F = \rho_{\Theta}(\mathcal{S}); F^{\diamond}$. The assignment $\mathcal{S} \longmapsto R_{\Theta}(\mathcal{S})$ extends to a functor $\mathcal{R}$-$Sys \longrightarrow \Theta$, called the *reflection functor*.

Therefore, we can consider subcategories of $\mathcal{R}$-Sys that are defined by certain equations and be guaranteed that they have initial and free objects, that they are closed by subobjects and products, etc. Consider for example the following equations:

$\forall f, g \in Arrows, \; f = g \; if \; \partial_0(f) = \partial_0(g) \wedge \partial_1(f) = \partial_1(g)$

$\forall f, g \in Arrows, \; f = g \; if \; \partial_0(f) = \partial_1(g) \wedge \partial_1(f) = \partial_0(g)$

$\forall f \in Arrows, \; \partial_0(f) = \partial_1(f).$

where $\partial_0(f)$ and $\partial_1(f)$ denote the source and target of an arrow f respectively. The first equation forces a category to be a preorder, the addition of the second requires this preorder to be a poset, and the three equations together force the poset to be *discrete*, i.e., just a set. By imposing the first one, the first two, or all three, we get full subcategories

$\mathcal{R}$-$Alg \subseteq \mathcal{R}$-$Pos \subseteq \mathcal{R}$-$Preord \subseteq \mathcal{R}$-$Sys$.

A routine inspection of $\mathcal{R}$-$Preord$ for $\mathcal{R} = (\Sigma, E, L, R)$ reveals that its objects are preordered Σ-algebras $(A, \leq)$ (i.e., preordered sets with a Σ-algebra structure such that all

---

[29]In the precise sense of being specifiable by an "essentially algebraic theory" or a "sketch" [14]; see [72].

the operations in Σ are monotonic) that satisfy the equations E and such that for each rewrite rule $r : [t(\overline{x})] \longrightarrow [t'(\overline{x})]$ in R and for each $\overline{a} \in A^n$ we have, $t_A(\overline{a}) \geq t'_A(\overline{a})$. The poset case is entirely analogous, except that the relation $\leq$ is a partial order instead of being a preorder. Finally, $\mathcal{R}$-Alg is the category of ordinary Σ-algebras that satisfy the equations $E \cup unlabel(R)$, where the $unlabel$ function removes the labels from the rules and turns the sequent signs "$\longrightarrow$" into equality signs.

The reflection functor associated with the inclusion $\mathcal{R}$-$Preord \subseteq \mathcal{R}$-$Sys$ sends $\mathcal{T}_\mathcal{R}(X)$ to the familiar $\mathcal{R}$-*rewriting relation*[30] $\rightarrow_{\mathcal{R}(X)}$ on E-equivalence classes of terms with variables in X. Similarly, the reflection associated to the inclusion $\mathcal{R}$-$Pos \subseteq \mathcal{R}$-$Sys$ maps $\mathcal{T}_\mathcal{R}(X)$ to the partial order $\geq_{\mathcal{R}(X)}$ obtained from the preorder $\rightarrow_{\mathcal{R}(X)}$ by identifying any two $[t], [t']$ such that $[t] \rightarrow_{\mathcal{R}(X)}[t']$ and $[t'] \rightarrow_{\mathcal{R}(X)}[t]$. Finally, the reflection functor into $\mathcal{R}$-Alg maps $\mathcal{T}_\mathcal{R}(X)$ to $T_\mathcal{R}(X)$, the free Σ-algebra on X satisfying the equations $E \cup unlabel(R)$; therefore, the classical *initial algebra semantics* of (functional) equational specifications reappears here associated with a very special class of models which—when viewed as systems—have only trivial identity transitions.

12.8.3   The Semantics of Maude

This paper has shown that, by generalizing the logic and the model theory of equational logic to those of rewriting logic, a much broader field of applications for rewrite rule programming is possible—based on the idea of programming *concurrent systems* rather than *algebras*, and including, in particular, concurrent object-oriented programming. The same high standards of mathematical rigor enjoyed by equational logic can be maintained in giving semantics to a language like Maude in the broader context of rewriting logic. We present below a specific proposal for such a semantics having the advantages of keeping functional modules as a sublanguage with a more specialized semantics. Another appealing characteristic of the proposed semantics is that the operational and mathematical semantics of modules are related in a particularly nice way. As already mentioned, all the ideas and results in this paper extend without problem[31] to the *order-sorted* case; the unsorted case has only been used for the sake of a simpler exposition. Therefore, all that is said below is understood in the context of order-sorted rewriting logic.

We have already seen that object-oriented modules can be reduced to equivalent system modules having the same behavior but giving a more explicit description of the type structure. Therefore, of the three kinds of modules existing in Maude, namely functional, system and object-oriented, we need only provide a semantics for functional and system modules; they are respectively of the form fmod $\mathcal{R}$ endfm, and mod $\mathcal{R}'$ endm, for $\mathcal{R}$ and $\mathcal{R}'$ rewrite theories[32]. Their semantics is given in terms of an *initial machine* linking the module's operational semantics with its denotational semantics. The general notion of a machine is as follows.

---

[30]It is perhaps more suggestive to call $\rightarrow_{\mathcal{R}(X)}$ the *reachability relation* of the system $\mathcal{T}_\mathcal{R}(X)$.

[31]Exercising of course the well known precaution of making explicit the universal quantification of rules.

[32]Note that, although in a functional module fmod $\mathcal{R}$ endfm, $\mathcal{R}$ is an *equational* theory, we can regard $\mathcal{R}$ as a rewrite theory whose rules are its Church-Rosser equations, and whose structural axioms E are those axioms modulo which we are rewriting, such as associativity, commutativity, identity .... Note also that in the case of system modules having functional submodules, which is treated in [70], the semantics given below would be inaccurate, because we must "remember" that the submodule in question is functional.

Definition 12 For $\mathcal{R}$ a rewrite theory and $\Theta \hookrightarrow \mathcal{R}\text{-}Sys$ a reflective full subcategory, an $\mathcal{R}\text{-}machine\ over\ \Theta$ is an $\mathcal{R}$-homomorphism $[\![\_]\!] : \mathcal{S} \longrightarrow \mathcal{M}$, called the machine's *abstraction map*, with $\mathcal{S}$ an $\mathcal{R}$-system and $\mathcal{M} \in \Theta$. Given $\mathcal{R}$-machines over Θ, $[\![\_]\!] : \mathcal{S} \longrightarrow \mathcal{M}$ and $[\![\_]\!]' : \mathcal{S}' \longrightarrow \mathcal{M}'$, an $\mathcal{R}$-machine *homomorphism* is a pair of $\mathcal{R}$-homomorphisms (F, G), $F : \mathcal{S} \longrightarrow \mathcal{S}'$, $G : \mathcal{M} \longrightarrow \mathcal{M}'$, such that $[\![\_]\!]; G = F; [\![\_]\!]'$. This defines a category $\mathcal{R}\text{-}Mach/\Theta$; it is easy to check that the initial object in this category is the unique $\mathcal{R}$-homomorphism $\mathcal{T}_\mathcal{R} \longrightarrow R_\Theta(\mathcal{T}_\mathcal{R})$. $\square$

The intuitive idea behind a machine $[\![\_]\!] : \mathcal{S} \longrightarrow \mathcal{M}$ is that we can use a *system* $\mathcal{S}$ to *compute* a result relevant for a *model* $\mathcal{M}$ of interest in a class Θ of models. What we do is to perform a certain computation in $\mathcal{S}$, and then output the result by means of the abstraction map $[\![\_]\!]$. A very good example is an *arithmetic machine* with $\mathcal{S} = \mathcal{T}_{\mathtt{NAT}}$, for $\mathtt{NAT}$ the rewriting theory of the Peano natural numbers corresponding to the module $\mathtt{NAT}^{33}$ in Section 12.2, with $\mathcal{M} = \mathbb{N}$, and with $[\![\_]\!]$ the unique homomorphism from the initial $\mathtt{NAT}$-system $\mathcal{T}_{\mathtt{NAT}}$; i.e., this is the initial machine in $\mathtt{NAT}\text{-}Mach/\mathtt{NAT}\text{-}Alg$. To compute the result of an arithmetic expression t, we perform a terminating rewriting and output the corresponding number, which is an element of $\mathbb{N}$.

Each choice of a reflective full subcategory Θ as a category of models yields a different semantics. As already implicit in the arithmetic machine example, the *semantics of a functional module*[34] fmod $\mathcal{R}$ endfm is the initial machine in $\mathcal{R}\text{-}Mach/\mathcal{R}\text{-}Alg$. For the *semantics of a system module* mod $\mathcal{R}$ endm not having any functional submodules, we propose the initial machine in $\mathcal{R}\text{-}Mach/\mathcal{R}\text{-}Preord$, but other choices are also possible. On the one hand, we could choose to be as concrete as possible and take $\Theta = \mathcal{R}\text{-}Sys$ in which case the abstraction map is the identity homomorphism for $\mathcal{T}_\mathcal{R}$. On the other hand, we could instead be even more abstract, and choose $\Theta = \mathcal{R}\text{-}Pos$; however, this would have the unfortunate effect of collapsing all the states of a cyclic rewriting, which seems inappropriate for many "reactive" systems. If the machine $\mathcal{T}_\mathcal{R} \longrightarrow \mathcal{M}$ is the semantics of a functional or system module with rewrite theory $\mathcal{R}$, then we call $\mathcal{T}_\mathcal{R}$ the module's *operational semantics*, and $\mathcal{M}$ its *denotational semantics*. Therefore, the operational and denotational semantics of a module can be extracted from its initial machine semantics by projecting to the domain or codomain of the abstraction map. This makes Maude a *logic programming language* in the general axiomatic sense of [68] mentioned in Section 12.7.

12.9   Related Work

Within the limits of this paper it is impossible to do justice to the wealth of related literature on concurrent object-oriented programming, term and graph rewriting, abstract data types, concurrency theory, Petri nets, linear and equational logic, ordered, continuous and nondeterministic algebras, etc. The paper [72] contains 125 such references. In the area of concurrent object-oriented programming alone there are many references; one may start with [105, 4, 103, 101] and references there, plus papers in recent OOPSLA

---

[33]In this case E is the commutativity attribute, and R consists of the two rules for addition.
[34]For this semantics to behave well, the rules R in the functional module $\mathcal{R}$ should be *confluent* modulo E.

and ECOOP proceedings, and of course this volume. Here the attempt will be much
more restricted, and will only try to briefly discuss a limited amount of work in some
related areas.

FOOPS.   Since the work on FOOPS and FOOPLog [49] was the first attempt, in joint
work with Joseph Goguen, to achieve the two ends of providing a semantic framework for
object-oriented programming and of unifying functional, relational, and object-oriented
programming, and since in fact the ideas and experience of FOOPS have had an important influence on Maude, a few remarks should be made by way of comparison between
the two languages.

   Although both projects share the two ends just mentioned, their semantic frameworks—
which provide the means to attain those ends—are quite different. There are indeed
important similarities, such as the use of order-sorted techniques, the sharing of OBJ
as a functional sublanguage, the basic agreement on modularity and parameterization
techniques, and the shared distinction between the levels of sorts, classes and modules.
However, the semantic frameworks actually developed are so different that a comparison
amounting to something like an explanation of one framework in terms of the other seems
quite difficult.

   The original semantic framework of FOOPS given in [49] used two different semantic
accounts. One based on order-sorted equational logic with hidden sorts—using the ideas
of [47] and [77] about algebraic data types with state which have been further developed
in [42, 54]—and another based on reflective equational logic. The two accounts com-
plemented each other well, but neither of them was comprehensive enough to warrant
abandoning the other. For example, creation and deletion of objects and interactions
between objects are not covered by the hidden sort account but have a good explanation
in terms of reflective equational logic. Recent work by Joseph Goguen and his coworkers
at Oxford has developed a third semantic account of FOOPS in terms of sheaves [43, 55]
which is very useful for treating concurrency aspects not covered in [49].

   In spite of the many good contributions provided by FOOPS, the reason that motivated the present work was a vague dissatisfaction with the somewhat limited way in
which the two goals of providing a semantic framework for object-oriented programming
and of unifying functional, relational, and object-oriented programming were achieved by
the FOOPS framework. On the one hand, the need to rely on several semantic accounts
suggested seeking a simple logical framework that could fully account for all aspects of
object-oriented systems, including their concurrency; on the other, having a logic on
which concurrent object-oriented programming could be defined as logic programming in
the strict axiomatic sense of [68] and on which the functional and relational paradigms
could be unified by maps of logics seemed the most satisfactory way of achieving the
desired unification of paradigms. Although FOOPS and FOOPLog are certainly declarative languages, for the moment they fall short of being logic programming languages
in the precise axiomatic sense of [68], although this does not exclude that they could be
shown to be so in the future.

Algebraic Approaches to Object-Oriented Programming.   Besides the recent
work on FOOPS at Oxford already discussed, there is also important work on the semantics of object-oriented programming using algebraic techniques by members of the

ESPRIT research group IS-CORE including Amílcar Sernadas, Hans-Dieter Ehrich, Udo Lipeck, Tom Maibaum, Robert Meersman, and their collaborators (see [95] for a collection of papers), and there is joint work by Hans-Dieter Ehrich, Joseph Goguen and Amílcar Sernadas relating Goguen's sheaf semantics to ideas in the IS-CORE group [34]. Although we can generally say that this body of work makes use of algebraic data type techniques and aims at a conceptual clarification of the notion of object, a detailed comparison of the work of the IS-CORE group with the present work is beyond the scope of this paper.

There is also important work by Milner, Parrow and Walker on the π-calculus [86] giving a semantics to actors in a generalization of Milner's CCS. As the recent work of Milner shows [85], the π-calculus, or at least a good part of it, seems to be naturally expressible in terms of Berry and Boudol's Chemical Abstract Machine [15] and therefore by rewrite rules modulo *ACI*. This suggests that the π-calculus, or important fragments of it, can be viewed naturally as a specialization of the concurrency model provided by rewriting logic; however, a more detailed comparison will have to wait for a future occasion.

More generally, there is a broad body of work using a variety of algebraic approaches in the specification of concurrency that has been recently surveyed thanks to the efforts of Egidio Astesiano and Gianna Reggio [10].

Type Theory Approaches.   In recent years there has been a steady increase in the use of constructive type theory to give semantics to some aspects of object-oriented programming. Early important references include the original work of Reynolds on subtypes [94], Cardelli's paper on the semantics of inheritance [21], and the paper of Cardelli and Wegner on the FUN language [24]; a good number of other papers by a variety of authors have been written since then. For the most part, work in this area seems to take what might be described as a "translational" approach in which, by using increasingly more powerful constructive type theories, aspects and features of object-oriented programming are translated into type-theoretic accounts of them. In this way, a number of aspects have been studied, such as, for example, applicative models of inheritance (e.g., [22, 19, 17, 91]), record operations (e.g., [23]), reuse aspects of inheritance (e.g., [29, 88, 18]), and type-checking issues (e.g., [87, 31, 61]).

Although valuable contributions clarifying some aspects of object-oriented programming have been made by proponents of this approach, it seems for the moment uncertain whether the general approach of translating object-oriented programming features into type-theoretic formulations will ultimately succeed in covering in a satisfactory way all the aspects of object-oriented programming. Judging from the experience of previous work on the denotational semantics of imperative languages—of which these type-theoretic approaches are in a sense a further development—one might be inclined to think that the addition of concurrency, on which these approaches seem to be silent, could prove quite hard. Since most constructive type theories have their origins in the foundations of mathematics and were designed to deal with unchanging mathematical entities[35], the difficulties in dealing with action and change in most of them can be quite intrinsic. In addition, a difficulty with some of the current work in this area is the sheer complexity

---

[35]One notable exception is Girard's Linear Logic [39].

of the formalisms into which object-oriented concepts are sometimes translated, which makes at times difficult to understand whether a given account does justice to and sheds light on the original problem, and raises some doubts about whether a simpler account should instead be sought. One of the proponents of this approach seems to acknowledge to some extent this difficulty in the statement [18],

"While the semantics of our language is rather complex, involving fixed points at both the element and the type level, we believe that this complexity underlies the basic concepts of object-oriented programming languages."

Maude—and for that matter FOOPS [49] and OBJ [53]—shares with type-theoretic approaches the use of *subtypes*. In those three languages the typing is order-sorted and uses ideas that go back to the original paper by Goguen [41] and have been further developed by several authors (see [51] and references there), whereas the theories of subtypes used in type-theoretic approaches can be traced back to the work of Reynolds on implicit conversions and generic operators [94]. Although there are some differences between both approaches—for example, the notion of subtype as inclusion tends to be lost in type-theoretic approaches—the two are in fact closely related, as recent joint work with Narciso Martí-Oliet [64] has demonstrated by extending the logic and the model theory of order-sorted algebra to higher types in an approach that subsumes those of [51] and [94] while maintaining a distinction between inclusive and coercive notions of subtype. However, by making the option of having higher-order types orthogonal to subtyping issues, the order-sorted approach is in fact a considerably simpler formalism and affords a simpler treatment of object-oriented concepts.

In the case of Maude, one essential difference is that order-sortedness pervades not only equational logic, which is used for functional modules, but also rewriting logic which is the logic used to give semantics to system modules and to object-oriented modules; therefore, concurrent actions—which would be problematic in a functional context—mesh very well with subclasses in a rewriting logic account that, as shown in this paper, provides a simple semantic framework for object-oriented programming.

Logic Programming Approaches. The theoretical work ahead should include an exploration of how the approach presented here for MaudeLog can be precisely related to other recent (relational) logic programming approaches such as *concurrent logic programming* (see the survey [97]), which is in a sense related to object-oriented programming [98], the work of Corradini and Montanari [30] which addresses concurrency issues and also belongs to this general area, the work of Saraswat and others on *concurrent constraint programming* [96], and the work of Andreoli and Pareschi on *linear logic programming* [8, 9], which is directly aimed at supporting concurrent object-oriented computations. Since quantifier-free linear logic can be regarded as a special case of rewriting logic [63], this last approach, though different, is somewhat closer in spirit to Maude and MaudeLog. Detailed comparisons of this kind may also provide additional semantic insights on issues hitherto addressed in a more operational or proof-theoretic way in some of these other approaches.

12.10   Concluding Remarks

This paper has presented a general semantic framework for object-oriented programming based on rewriting logic that is intrinsically concurrent and provides a simple and rigorous account of key concepts such as objects, classes and class inheritance, concurrent object-oriented synchronous and asynchronous communication, autonomous objects, and object creation and deletion. A declarative version of the actor model has been obtained as a special case of the framework. In addition, the Maude language—based on rewriting logic—which unifies in a fully declarative way the functional and concurrent object-oriented paradigms has been introduced, and its features and expressive power have been illustrated with examples. It has been explained that in Maude the simultaneous support of concurrent communication and class inheritance is entirely unproblematic. The parameterization and modularity mechanisms of Maude have been illustrated with examples and it has been shown how such mechanisms can support flexible ways of code reuse that complement those of class inheritance. The Simple Maude sublanguage has been described, and its capabilities as a machine independent parallel language with support for multilingual extensions and open heterogeneous systems, as well as implementation ideas for mapping it on several parallel architectures have been discussed. The logic and model theory of rewriting logic have been presented and have been used to give a mathematical semantics to Maude modules. Finally, an extension of Maude called MaudeLog that is also based on rewriting logic has been proposed as a fully declarative unification of the functional, relational, and concurrent object-oriented paradigms.

The present paper is a report of work in progress. Although the logical foundations of Maude are well established, much remains to be done to move the ideas forward in several directions, including the following:

- More experience should be gained with examples to advance the language design and to further explore the capabilities of the language. This will also help in sharpening and expanding the boundaries of Maude and Simple Maude.

- Applications of Maude and MaudeLog and of the rewriting logic formalism to a number of areas such as distributed artificial intelligence[36], object-oriented databases[37], communication protocols, and discrete event simulation should be investigated and illustrated with examples.

- Specification and verification aspects should be studied and should be illustrated with examples. The specification logics should not be limited to equational and rewriting logic. Rewriting logic should be embedded within a richer logic to be used for specification purposes. This will increase the expressiveness of Maude's functional, system and object-oriented theories.

- The study of parameterization and modularity issues, already initiated in [71] and [70] respectively, and of the module inheritance techniques discussed in this paper should be advanced.

---

[36] For a Maude example of distributed coordination between agents see Section 7 of [75].

[37] A first step in applying rewriting logic to the semantics of object-oriented databases has been taken in [82].

- The work on program transformations to derive more efficient and more easily implementable modules from less efficient ones or even from specifications should be continued and advanced. More generally, the design of machine-independent program analysis and program optimization tools based on the concurrent rewriting model should be explored.

- Implementation and compilation techniques for various classes of parallel architectures should be studied in more detail, trying to achieve the greatest possible degree of portability and genericity across different machine implementations. A Maude interpreter should be developed, as well as a portable parallel implementation of Simple Maude.

- Multilingual extensions and uses of Maude in the context of open heterogeneous systems should be studied in greater detail.

- All aspects of MaudeLog should be further developed; much work remains to be done on its language design, on its underlying theory and relations to other approaches, on its deduction and operational semantics, and eventually on an actual implementation.

Acknowledgements

It is a pleasure to thank my fellow members of the Declarative Languages and Architecture Group at SRI International, especially Timothy Winkler, Narciso Martí-Oliet and Patrick Lincoln. The present exposition has benefited very much from many discussions with them, from their comments, and from their technical contributions to Maude. In addition, Timothy Winkler has kindly allowed me to summarize our joint work on Maude [83] and on broadcasting communication and has suggested many improvements; Narciso Martí-Oliet has caught many small errors, has suggested many improvements to the text, and has influenced the rewriting logic ideas through our joint work on linear logic and its relationship to Petri nets [65], and on action and change in rewriting logic [63]; and Patrick Lincoln's contributions to program transformations for Maude's object-oriented modules as well as his comments and suggestions have also influenced the paper.

It is also a pleasure to thank Joseph Goguen for our long term collaboration on the OBJ, Eqlog and FOOPS languages [45, 53, 49], concurrent rewriting [46] and its implementation on the RRM architecture [50, 6], all of which have directly influenced this work, and Prof. Ugo Montanari for our joint work on the semantics of Petri nets [80, 81] that was an important early influence on rewriting logic.

I cordially thank Akinori Yonezawa and Satoshi Matsuoka for kindly explaining to me the difficulties involved in the "inheritance anomaly" along several conversations, and Peter Wegner, Gul Agha, and Kristen Nygaard for their kindness and interest in listening to my ideas about object-oriented programming and for their helpful comments and suggestions.

References

[1]   M. Abadi, L. Cardelli, P.-L. Curien, and J.-J. Lévy. Explicit Substitutions. In *Proc. POPL'90*, pages 31–46. ACM, 1990.

[2]   G. Agha. *Actors*. MIT Press, 1986.

[3]   G. Agha and C. Hewitt. Concurrent programming using actors. In A. Yonezawa and M. Tokoro, editors, *Object-Oriented Concurrent Programming*, pages 37–53. MIT Press, 1988.

[4]   G. Agha, P. Wegner, and A. Yonezawa, editors. *Proceedings of the ACM-SIGPLAN Workshop on Object-Based Concurrent Programming*. ACM Sigplan Notices, April 1989.

[5]   H. Aida, J. Goguen, S. Leinwand, P. Lincoln, J. Meseguer, B. Taheri, and T. Winkler. Simulation and performance estimation for the rewrite rule machine. In *Proceedings of the Fourth Symposium on the Frontiers of Massively Parallel Computation*, pages 336–344. IEEE, 1992.

[6]   Hitoshi Aida, Joseph Goguen, and José Meseguer. Compiling concurrent rewriting onto the rewrite rule machine. In S. Kaplan and M. Okada, editors, *Conditional and Typed Rewriting Systems, Montreal, Canada, June 1990*, pages 320–332. Springer LNCS 516, 1991.

[7]   Hitoshi Aida, Sany Leinwand, and José Meseguer. Architectural design of the rewrite rule machine ensemble. In J. Delgado-Frias and W.R. Moore, editors, *VLSI for Artificial Intelligence and Neural Networks*, pages 11–22. Plenum Publ. Co., 1991. Proceedings of an International Workshop held in Oxford, England, September 1990.

[8]   Jean-Marc Andreoli and Remo Pareschi. LO and behold! Concurrent structured processes. In *ECOOP-OOPSLA'90 Conference on Object-Oriented Programming, Ottawa, Canada, October 1990*, pages 44–56. ACM, 1990.

[9]   Jean-Marc Andreoli and Remo Pareschi. Communication as fair distribution of knowledge. In *OOPSLA'91 Conference on Object-Oriented Programming, Phoenix, Arizona, October 1991*, pages 212–229. ACM, 1991.

[10]   Egidio Astesiano and Gianna Reggio. Algebraic specification of concurrency. To appear in *Proceedings of the ADT'91 Workshop*, Springer LNCS, 1992.

[11]   W. Athas and C. Seitz. Multicomputers: Message-passing concurrent computers. *Computer*, pages 9–24, August 1988.

[12]   J.-P. Banâtre, A. Coutant, and D. Le Mètayer. Parallel machines for multiset transformation and their programming style. *Informationstechnik* **it**, 30(2):99–109, 1988.

[13]   J.-P. Banâtre and D. Le Mètayer. The Gamma model and its discipline of programming. *Science of Computer Programming*, 15:55–77, 1990.

[14]   M. Barr and C. Wells. *Toposes, Triples and Theories*. Springer-Verlag, 1985.

[15]   Gérard Berry and Gérard Boudol. The Chemical Abstract Machine. In *Proc. POPL'90*, pages 81–94. ACM, 1990.

[16]   Graham Birtwistle, Ole-Johan Dahl, Bjorn Myhrhaug, and Kristen Nygaard. *Simula Begin*. Charwell-Bratt Ltd, 1979.

[17]   V. Breazu-Tannen, T. Coquand, C.A. Gunter, and A. Scedrov. Inheritance and explicit coercion. In *Proc. LICS'89*, pages 112–129. IEEE, 1989.

[18]   Kim Bruce. A paradigmatic object-oriented programming language: design, static typing and semantics. Technical Report CS-92-01, Williams College, January 1992.

[19]   Kim Bruce and Giuseppe Longo. A modest model of records, inheritance and bounded quantification. *Information and Computation*, 87:196–240, 1990.

[20]   Rod Burstall and Joseph Goguen. The semantics of Clear, a specification language. In Dines Bjorner, editor, *Proceedings of the 1979 Copenhagen Winter School on Abstract Software Specification*, pages 292–332. Springer LNCS 86, 1980.

[21]   Luca Cardelli. A Semantics of Multiple Inheritance. In G. Kahn, D. MacQueen, and G. Plotkin, editors, *Semantics of Data Types, LNCS 173*, pages 51–67. Springer LNCS 173, 1984.

[22]   Luca Cardelli. Structural Subtyping and the Notion of Power Type. In *Proc. POPL'88*. ACM, 1988.

[23]   Luca Cardelli and John Mitchell. Operations on records. *Math. Struct. in Comp. Sci.*, 1:3–48, 1991.

[24]   Luca Cardelli and Peter Wegner. On understanding types, data abstracton and polymorphism. *Computing Surveys*, 17:471–522, 1985.

[25]   N. Carriero and D. Gelernter. Linda in context. *Communications of the Association for Computing Machinery*, 32:444–458, April 1989.

[26]   K. Mani Chandy and Jayadev Misra. *Parallel Program Design: A Foundation*. Addison-Wesley, 1988.

[27]   K. Mani Chandy and Stephen Taylor. *An Introduction to Parallel Programming*. Jones and Bartlett Publishers, 1992.

[28]   Will Clinger. Foundations of actor semantics. Technical report AI-TR-633, Massachusetts Institute of Technology, Artificial Intelligence Laboratory, 1981.

[29]   William Cook, Walter Hill, and Peter Canning. Inheritance is not Subtyping. In *Proc. POPL'90*, pages 125–135. ACM, 1990.

[30]   Andrea Corradini and Ugo Montanari. An algebraic semantics of logic programs as structured transition systems. In S. Debray and M. Hermenegildo, editors, *North American Conference on Logic Programming*, pages 788–812. MIT Press, 1990.

[31]   Pierre-Louis Curien and Giorgio Ghelli. Coherence and subsumption. To appear in *Mathematical Structures in Computer Science*, 1991.

[32]   Ole-Johan Dahl, Bjorn Myhrhaug, and Kristen Nygaard. The simula 67 common base language. Technical report, Norwegian Computing Center, Oslo, 1970. Publication S-22.

[33]   N. Dershowitz and J.-P. Jouannaud. Rewrite systems. In J. van Leeuwen, editor, *Handbook of Theoretical Computer Science, Vol. B*, pages 243–320. North-Holland, 1990.

[34]   Hans-Dieter Ehrich, Joseph Goguen, and Amílcar Sernadas. A categorical theory of objects a observed processes. In J. W. de Bakker, W. P. de Roever, and G. Rozenberg, editors, *Foundations of Object-Oriented Languages, Noordwijkerhout, The Netherlands, May/June 1990*, pages 203–228. Springer LNCS 489, 1991.

[35]   J. Engelfriet, G. Leih, and G. Rozenberg. Parallel object-based systems and Petri nets, I and II. Technical Report 90-04,90-05, Dept. of Computer Science, University of Leiden, February 1990.

[36]   J. Engelfriet, G. Leih, and G. Rozenberg. Net-based description of parallel object-based systems, or POTs and POPs. In J. W. de Bakker, W. P. de Roever, and G. Rozenberg, editors, *Foundations of Object-Oriented Languages, Noordwijkerhout, The Netherlands, May/June 1990*, pages 229–273. Springer LNCS 489, 1991.

[37]   Ian Foster and Stephen Taylor. *Strand: New Concepts in Parallel Programming*. Prentice Hall, 1990.

[38]   Svend Frølund. Inheritance of synchronization constraints in concurrent object-oriented programming languages. In O. Lehrmann Madsen, editor, *Proc. ECOOP'92*, pages 185–196. Springer LNCS 615, 1992.

[39]   Jean-Yves Girard. Linear Logic. *Theoretical Computer Science*, 50:1–102, 1987.

[40]   Jean-Yves Girard. Towards a geometry of interaction. In J.W. Gray and A. Scedrov, editors, *Proc. AMS Summer Research Conference on Categories in Computer Science and Logic, Boulder, Colorado, June 1987*, pages 69–108. American Mathematical Society, 1989.

[41]   Joseph Goguen. Order sorted algebra. Technical Report Semantics and Theory of Computation Report 14, UCLA, 1978.

[42]   Joseph Goguen. Types as theories. In G.M. Reed, A.W. Roscoe, and R. Wachter, editors, *Topology and Category Theory in Computer Science*, pages 357–390. Oxford University Press, 1991.

[43]   Joseph Goguen. Sheaf semantics for concurrent interacting objects. *Mathematical Structures in Computer Science*, 2(2):159–191, 1992.

[44]   Joseph Goguen and Rod Burstall. Institutions: Abstract model theory for specification and programming. *Journal of the ACM*, 39(1):95–146, 1992.

[45]   Joseph Goguen, Claude Kirchner, Hélène Kirchner, Aristide Mégrelis, José Meseguer, and Timothy Winkler. An introduction to OBJ3. In Jean-Pierre Jouannaud and Stephane Kaplan, editors, *Proceedings, Conference on Conditional Term Rewriting, Orsay, France, July 8-10, 1987*, pages 258–263. Springer LNCS 308, 1988.

[46]   Joseph Goguen, Claude Kirchner, and José Meseguer. Concurrent term rewriting as a model of computation. In R. Keller and J. Fasel, editors, *Proc. Workshop on Graph Reduction, Santa Fe, New Mexico*, pages 53–93. Springer LNCS 279, 1987.

[47]   Joseph Goguen and José Meseguer. Universal realization, persistent interconnection and implementation of abstract modules. In M. Nielsen and E. M. Schmidt, editors, *Proceedings, 9th International Conference on Automata, Languages and Programming*, pages 265–281. Springer LNCS 140, 1982.

[48]   Joseph Goguen and José Meseguer. Eqlog: Equality, types, and generic modules for logic programming. In Douglas DeGroot and Gary Lindstrom, editors, *Logic Programming: Functions, Relations and Equations*, pages 295–363. Prentice-Hall, 1986. An earlier version appears in *Journal of Logic Programming*, Volume 1, Number 2, pages 179-210, September 1984.

[49]   Joseph Goguen and José Meseguer. Unifying functional, object-oriented and relational programming with logical semantics. In Bruce Shriver and Peter Wegner, editors, *Research Directions in Object-Oriented Programming*, pages 417–477. MIT Press, 1987.

[50]   Joseph Goguen and José Meseguer. Software for the rewrite rule machine. In *Proceedings of the International Conference on Fifth Generation Computer Systems, Tokyo, Japan*, pages 628–637. ICOT, 1988.

[51]   Joseph Goguen and José Meseguer. Order-sorted algebra I: Equational deduction for multiple inheritance, overloading, exceptions and partial operations. *Theoretical Computer Science*, 105:217–273, 1992.

[52]   Joseph Goguen, José Meseguer, Sany Leinwand, Timothy Winkler, and Hitoshi Aida. The rewrite rule machine. Technical Report SRI-CSL-89-6, SRI International, Computer Science Laboratory, March 1989.

[53]   Joseph Goguen, Timothy Winkler, José Meseguer, Kokichi Futatsugi, and Jean-Pierre Jouannaud. Introducing OBJ. Technical Report SRI-CSL-92-03, SRI International, Computer Science Laboratory, 1993. To appear in J.A. Goguen, editor, *Applications of Algebraic Specification Using OBJ*, Cambridge University Press.

[54]   Joseph Goguen and David Wolfram. On types and FOOPS. To appear in *Proc. IFIP Working Group 2.6 Working Conference on Database Semantics: Object-Oriented Databases: Analysis, Design and Construction, 1990*.

[55]   Joseph Goguen and David Wolfram. A sheaf semantics for FOOPS expressions (extended abstract). In M. Tokoro, O. Nierstrasz, and P. Wegner, editors, *Object-Based Concurrent Computing*, pages 81–98. Springer LNCS 612, 1992.

[56]   Gerard Huet. Confluent reductions: Abstract properties and applications to term rewriting systems. *Journal of the Association for Computing Machinery*, 27:797–821, 1980. Preliminary version in *18th Symposium on Mathematical Foundations of Computer Science*, 1977.

[57]   R. Jagannathan and A.A. Faustini. The GLU programming language. Technical Report SRI-CSL-90-11, SRI International, Computer Science Laboratory, November 1990.

[58]   Gregor Kiczales, Jim des Riviers, and Daniel G. Bobrow. *The Art of the Metaobject Protocol*. MIT Press, 1991.

[59]   Claude Kirchner, Hélène Kirchner, and José Meseguer. Operational semantics of OBJ3. In T. Lepistö and A. Salomaa, editors, *Proceedings, 15th Intl. Coll. on Automata, Languages and Programming, Tampere, Finland, July 11-15, 1988*, pages 287–301. Springer LNCS 317, 1988.

[60]   Simon S. Lam and A. Udaya Shankar. A relational notation for state transition systems. *IEEE Transactions on Software Engineering*, SE-16(7):755–775, July 1990.

[61]   Patrick Lincoln and John Mitchell. Algorithmic aspects of type inference with subtypes. In *Proc. POPL'92*. ACM, 1992.

[62]   Saunders MacLane. *Categories for the working mathematician*. Springer-Verlag, 1971.

[63]   Narciso Martí-Oliet and José Meseguer. Action and change in rewriting logic. Paper in preparation. Given as a talk at the ESPRIT Workshop on Logics of Action and Change, Lisbon, January 1993.

[64]   Narciso Martí-Oliet and José Meseguer. Inclusions and subtypes. Technical Report SRI-CSL-90-16, SRI International, Computer Science Laboratory, December 1990. Submitted for publication.

[65]   Narciso Martí-Oliet and José Meseguer. From Petri nets to linear logic through categories: a survey. *Intl. J. of Foundations of Comp. Sci.*, 2(4):297–399, 1991.

[66]   Satoshi Matsuoka, Takuo Watanabe, Yuuji Ichisugi, and Akinori Yonezawa. Object-oriented concurrent reflective architectures. In M. Tokoro, O. Nierstrasz, and P. Wegner, editors, *Object-Based Concurrent Computing*, pages 211–226. Springer LNCS 612, 1992.

[67]   Satoshi Matsuoka and Akinori Yonezawa. Analysis of inheritance anomaly in object-oriented concurrent programming languages. Dept. of Information Science, University of Tokyo, January 1991. To appear in G. Agha, P. Wegner, and A. Yonezawa, editors, *Research Directions in Object-Based Concurrency*, MIT Press, 1993.

[68]   José Meseguer. General logics. In H.-D. Ebbinghaus et al., editor, *Logic Colloquium'87*, pages 275–329. North-Holland, 1989.

[69]   José Meseguer. A logical theory of concurrent objects. In *ECOOP-OOPSLA'90 Conference on Object-Oriented Programming, Ottawa, Canada, October 1990*, pages 101–115. ACM, 1990.

[70]   José Meseguer. Rewriting as a unified model of concurrency. In *Proceedings of the Concur'90 Conference, Amsterdam, August 1990*, pages 384–400. Springer LNCS 458, 1990.

[71]   José Meseguer. Rewriting as a unified model of concurrency. Technical Report SRI-CSL-90-02, SRI International, Computer Science Laboratory, February 1990. Revised June 1990.

[72]   José Meseguer. Conditional rewriting logic as a unified model of concurrency. *Theoretical Computer Science*, 96(1):73–155, 1992. Also Technical Report SRI-CSL-91-05, SRI International, Computer Science Laboratory, February 1991.

[73]   José Meseguer. Multiparadigm logic programming. In H. Kirchner and G. Levi, editors, *Proc. 3rd Intl. Conf. on Algebraic and Logic Programming*, pages 158–200. Springer LNCS 632, 1992.

[74]   José Meseguer. Solving the inheritance anomaly in concurrent object-oriented programming. Technical Report SRI-CSL-92-14, SRI International, Computer Science Laboratory, 1992. To appear in *Proc. ECOOP'93*, Springer LNCS.

[75]   José Meseguer, Kokichi Futatsugi, and Timothy Winkler. Using rewriting logic to specify, program, integrate, and reuse open concurrent systems of cooperating agents. In *Proceedings of the 1992 International Symposium on New Models for Software Architecture, Tokyo, Japan, November 1992*, pages 61–106. Research Institute of Software Engineering, 1992.

[76]   José Meseguer and Joseph Goguen. Order-sorted algebra II. In preparation.

[77]   José Meseguer and Joseph Goguen. Initiality, induction and computability. In Maurice Nivat and John Reynolds, editors, *Algebraic Methods in Semantics*, pages 459–541. Cambridge University Press, 1985.

[78]   José Meseguer and Joseph Goguen. Order-sorted algebra solves the constructor-selector, multiple representation and coercion problems. *Information and Computation*, 103(1):114-158, 1993.

[79]   José Meseguer, Joseph Goguen, and Gert Smolka. Order-sorted unification. *J. Symbolic Computation*, 8:383–413, 1989.

[80]   José Meseguer and Ugo Montanari. Petri nets are monoids: A new algebraic foundation for net theory. In *Proc. LICS'88*, pages 155–164. IEEE, 1988.

[81]   José Meseguer and Ugo Montanari. Petri nets are monoids. *Information and Computation*, 88:105–155, 1990. Appeared as Technical Report SRI-CSL-88-3, SRI International, Computer Science Laboratory, January 1988.

[82]   José Meseguer and Xiaolei Qian. A logical semantics for object-oriented databases. Technical

Report SRI-CSL-92-15, SRI International, Computer Science Laboratory, 1992. To appear in *Proc. International SIGMOD Conference on Management of Data*, May 1993, ACM.

[83]   José Meseguer and Timothy Winkler. Parallel programming in Maude. In J.-P. Banâtre and D. Le Mètayer, editors, *Research Directions in High-level Parallel Programming Languages*, pages 253–293. Springer LNCS 574, 1992. Also Technical Report SRI-CSL-91-08, SRI International, Computer Science Laboratory, November 1991.

[84]   Robin Milner. *Communication and Concurrency*. Prentice Hall, 1989.

[85]   Robin Milner. Functions as processes. *Mathematical Structures in Computer Science*, 2(2):119–141, 1992.

[86]   Robin Milner, Joachim Parrow, and David Walker. A calculus of mobile processes I and II. Technical Report ECS-LFCS-89-85&86, Dept. of Computer Science, University of Edinburgh, 1989.

[87]   John Mitchell. Coercion and type inference. In *Proc. POPL'84*, pages 175–185. ACM, 1984.

[88]   John Mitchell. Toward a Typed Foundation for Method Specialization and Inheritance. In *Proc. POPL'90*, pages 109–124. ACM, 1990.

[89]   Kristen Nygaard. Basic concepts in object-oriented programming. Lecture and paper delivered at the Object-Oriented Programming Workshop held at Yorktwon Heights, New Yor, June 9-13, 1986; abstract in *Sigplan Notices*, 21, No. 10, page 187, October 1986, 1986.

[90]   M. Papathomas. Concurrency issues in object-oriented programming languages. In D. Tsichritzis, editor, *Object Oriented Development*, pages 207–246. Université de Geneve, 1989.

[91]   Wesley Phoa. Using fibrations to understand subtypes. To appear in M. Fourman, P. Johnstone, and A. Pitts (eds.) *Proc. Symp. on Applications of Categories in Computer Science, Durham, 1991*, Cambridge University Press, 1992.

[92]   Sara Porat and Nissim Francez. Fairness in term rewriting systems. Manuscript, Technion, May 3, 1990.

[93]   Wolfgang Reisig. *Petri Nets*. Springer-Verlag, 1985.

[94]   John Reynolds. Using category theory to design implicit conversions and generic operators. In Neal D. Jones, editor, *Semantics Directed Compiler Generation*, pages 211–258. Springer LNCS 94, 1980.

[95]   G. Saake and A. Sernadas, editors. *Information Systems—Correctness and Reusability*. Technische Universität Braunschweig, Information-Berichte 91-03, 1991.

[96]   Vijay Saraswat. *Concurrent constraint programming languages*. PhD thesis, Computer Science Department, Carnegie-Mellon University, 1989.

[97]   E. Shapiro. The family of concurrent logic programming languages. *ACM Computing Surveys*, 21:413–510, 1989.

[98]   Ehud Shapiro and Akikazu Takeuchi. Object oriented programming in concurrent Prolog. *New Generation Computing*, 1:25–48, 1983.

[99]   Brian Smith and Aki nori Yonezawa, editors. *Proc. of the IMSA'92 International Workshop on Reflection and Meta-Level Architecture, Tokyo, November 1992*. Research Institute of Software Engineering, 1992.

[100]   Sophie Tison. Fair termination is decidable for ground systems. In Nachum Dershowitz, editor, *Rewriting Techniques and Applications, Chappel Hill, North Carolina*, pages 462–476. Springer LNCS 355, 1989.

[101]   M. Tokoro, O. Nierstrasz, and P. Wegner, editors. *Object-Based Concurrent Computing*. Springer LNCS 612, 1992.

[102]   S. Watari, S. Kono, E. Osawa, R. Smoody, and M. Tokoro. Extending object-oriented systems to support dialectic worldviews. In *Symposium on Advanced Database Systems, Kyoto, Japan, December 1989*, 1989.

[103]   Peter Wegner. Concepts and paradigms of object-oriented programming. *OOPS Messenger*, 1:7–87, 1990.

[104]   A. Yonezawa, J.-P. Briot, and Etsuya Shibayama. Object-oriented concurrent programming in ABCL/1. In *OOPSLA '86 Conference on Object-Oriented Programming, Portland, Oregon, September-October 1986*, pages 258–268. ACM, 1986.

[105]   A. Yonezawa and M. Tokoro, editors. *Object-Oriented Concurrent Programming*. MIT Press, 1988.

IV Operating Systems

13   CHOICES: A Parallel Object-Oriented Operating System[*]

Roy H. Campbell and Nayeem Islam

The *Choices* parallel object-oriented operating system design is a collection of interconnected frameworks. A framework is refined into subframeworks. Each subframework's design specifies the possible concurrent messages, control flow, and synchronization between a dynamic number of component objects. In addition, objects within a subframework have other dependency relationships that vary dynamically. In this paper, we describe the concurrency and parallelism in *Choices* in terms of subframeworks, dynamic entity relationship diagrams and concurrent control flow graphs.

Choices has a number of implementations on different hardware platforms with different resource allocation and management algorithms. Classes are used to inherit common interfaces and implementations following an object-oriented design methodology. Of particular help in building and understanding the *Choices* subframeworks, the relationships and control flows between the abstract classes defined in a subframework are inherited by the concrete implementations of the classes. We describe, therefore, the problem-oriented models of concurrency and communication implemented in *Choices* as attributes that are defined for an abstract subframework and inherited by more concrete subframeworks.

13.1   Introduction

Choices is an operating system designed for distributed and shared memory multiprocessor systems. To accommodate diverse parallel applications, it supports a large set of components that may be combined to support different models of parallel and concurrent programming. Generic components are customized through object-oriented inheritance and specialization to match the specific concurrency requirements of applications. We refer to this customization as problem-oriented concurrent programming.

Problem-Oriented Concurrent Programming The notion of specializing parallel programming primitives to support better the behavior of different applications has attracted much research interest. It is difficult to port parallel applications to new multiprocessor architectures and subsequently to modify them to take advantage of their particular features. Instead, it is proposed to modify the support for the parallel processing primitives. For example, Cheriton introduced the notion of problem-oriented shared-memory[7] in which the consistency of shared data is tailored towards the needs of a particular application. We advocate a similar approach for message passing systems, process management and concurrent access to objects. This flexible approach permits *Choices* to run applications with different concurrency requirements efficiently. Further, because object-oriented programming supports the dynamic binding of different implementations to a common interface, it is possible to alter an implementation to better suit the concurrent aspects of a program during a particular phase of its execution. In order to simplify the modification of the support for parallel processing primitives, we have taken care to structure the design of *Choices* so that it may easily be specialized.

[*]This work was supported in part by NSF CDA 8722836 grant number 1-5-30035 and the second author was supported in part by an IBM Graduate Fellowship.

Object-Orientation The object-oriented operating system approach builds system software that models system resources and resource management as an organized collection of objects that encapsulate mechanisms, policies, algorithms, and data representations. A class defines a collection of objects that have identical behavior. Class hierarchies define relationships between classes that share common behavioral properties. Inheritance and inclusion polymorphism permit the methods of a concrete subclass to implement operations specified for an abstract class.

In the design of *Choices*, the concept of a framework subsumes the conventional organization of an operating system into layers[22]. Frameworks not only allow the design of layers, but they also permit the construction of more complex structures. The use of frameworks permits design and code reuse and the consistent imposition of design constraints on all software, independent of the level at which it may be used. In particular, *Choices* provides frameworks for both application and system level concurrency that impose a small number of consistency and coherency constraints on the possible specializations of the parallel and concurrent system primitives.

Frameworks A framework is an architectural design for object-oriented systems. It describes the components of the system and the way they interact. The components of the system are defined as classes within the framework. The interactions in the system are defined in terms of classes, instances, constraints, inheritance, inclusion polymorphism, and rules of composition. *Choices* frameworks use single inheritance to define class hierarchies and C++ subtyping to express inclusion polymorphism. In practice, we have found that the design of a complex system such as an operating system is itself best defined as a framework that guides the design of the subframeworks of the subsystems. A subsystem is a functional component of a system. The subframeworks refine the general operating system framework, as it applies to a specific subsystem.

The framework for the system provides generalized components and constraints to which the specialized subframeworks must conform. Conformance is enforced in the subframeworks by reusing the classes and constraints defined in the framework. The subframeworks introduce additional components and constraints and subclass components of the framework. Recursively, these subframeworks may be refined further. Frameworks simplify the construction of a family of related systems by providing an architectural design that has common components and interactions. An instance of a framework is a particular member of the family of systems. The frameworks defining parallel processing primitives in *Choices* include the **Process**, **Message Passing**, and **Virtual Memory** subsystems.

Implementation *Choices* was designed from the beginning as an object-oriented operating system implemented in C++. The system runs stand-alone on the Sun SPARC-station II and Encore Multimax and can also run in a virtual operating system mode on top of SUN-OS and MS/DOS. It supports distributed and shared memory multiprocessor applications, virtual memory, and has both conventional file systems and a persistent object store. The system has over 300 classes and 150,000 lines of source code.

Comparison To Other Operating Systems *Choices* is different from operating systems such as Mach [21], UNIX and V [8] in several regards. Whereas as Mach and V are object-based, where a server may be regarded as an object, *Choices* is object-oriented in addition to being object-based. An object-oriented operating system encourages customization of interfaces and the operating system itself through inheritance. This customization is encouraged for both applications and new hardware architectures.

Contents of Paper   In Section 13.2 we describe the modeling of concurrency in the *Choices* operating system. In Section 13.3 we discuss the techniques for describing the concurrency and dynamic relationships in the frameworks of *Choices*. Section 13.4 introduces the frameworks in the *Choices* object-oriented operating system. In Sections 13.5, 13.6 and 13.7, we discuss the design of the Process, Message Passing and Virtual Memory subframeworks. We then discuss how these subframeworks affect the design of the Persistent Storage framework in Section 13.8, and the device management subframework in Section 13.9. In Section 13.10 we discuss the *Choices* application programming model and in Section 13.11 we show examples of concurrent applications on *Choices*. In Section 13.12, we conclude by reviewing the lessons we have learned from using frameworks to design a parallel object-oriented operating system.

13.2   Model of Concurrency

An operating system implements various system concepts, including the concept of concurrency, in order to manage the resources of a computer system. Although it is convenient to program a concurrent system in a programming language that has concurrent programming primitives, an operating system must implement different specializations of concurrency for application and system use and for shared memory multiprocessors and distributed memory multicomputers. In the *Choices* operating system, we model concurrency using objects and specialize the concept of concurrency using subclassing. We apply the appropriate concurrency specialization to a concurrent program at runtime using reflection. A concurrent program is a function that is bound to a particular concurrency specialization and dispatched on a processor by invoking methods on an appropriate subclass of Process.

Object-oriented languages like Actors [1] and ConcurrentSmalltalk [28] model concurrency as a thread of control that is intimately tied to an object. For example, each method invocation on an Actor spawns a thread of control in the Actor. Multiple threads of control may be active at an Actor address and these threads are independent of the threads of control at other Actors. Each thread is part of the private state of an Actor. Similarly, each ConcurrentSmalltalk object is a self-contained module and a unit of concurrent execution. However, method invocations are similar to remote procedure calls [4] except that:

1. An object receiving a message may continue concurrent execution after replying to the message.

2. An object sending a message may continue concurrent execution without receiving a reply. A special synchronization construct is used for reply messages.

In essence, Concurrent Smalltalk supports both synchronous and "asynchronous" remote procedure calls. Unlike Actors or ConcurrentSmalltalk, C++, the language in which *Choices* is programmed does not have concurrency primitives. Instead, *Choices* provides a "model" for a *thread of control* that executes a C++ function. The model supports the creation, interrupting, dispatching, preempting, blocking and destruction of the thread of control that executes the function.

Central to the *Choices* concurrency model are Process objects. A C++ function is bound to a Process using the initialization message. Subsequent messages may start, suspend, resume, or terminate the thread of control and the associated concurrent execution of the C++ function. The notion of a thread of control and the concept of a Process are distinct. The thread of control and the execution of the C++ function occur as a "side-effect" of invoking methods on Process. A thread of control must have an associated Process but a Process may not have a thread of control. For example, when a thread of control reaches the end of its C++ function, it ceases to exist. However, its corresponding Process will still respond to messages and it is used to release any resources, like memory, that were associated with the execution of the C++ function.

The abstract class Process defines a common interface that is inherited by all the different realizations of a thread of control that are supported by *Choices*. Subclasses of Process implement low-level interrupt processing, system and application threads of control.

Conceptually, the control flow that executes the C++ function bound to a process flows through *Choices* application and system objects by invoking methods on these objects. We refer to the sequence of transformations that result from a thread of control flowing through objects as a *Choices* process. For the purposes of this paper we need not distinguish between a process and a thread of control.

Explicit control of a process is not available directly nor required in Actor systems or in ConcurrentSmalltalk. However, it is important for an operating system to have explicit control over which processes are running on which processors. Therefore, *Choices* provides facilities for both involuntarily and voluntarily changing the execution of a process on a processor. For example, a process may be timesliced, may block on a semaphore or may voluntarily relinquish the processor it is executing on. *Choices* also provides explicit scheduling support for parallel programming such as gang scheduling, which may be thought of as a collection of processes that are dispatched, blocked or suspended on a collection of processors, one process to a processor.

Reflection has also been used for customizing concurrency in Muse [27]. In Muse, reflection allows for the explicit control of processes. However, in *Choices*, we provide direct facilities to manipulate a Process. *Choices* uses reflection [15] in a restricted manner and only in a few key places. With respect to concurrency, reflection allows a C++ function to be bound to a Process and thereby implicitly made into a process. Muse has reflection built into the operating system and uses reflection extensively.

13.3   Techniques for Documenting Frameworks

In this section, we describe the approach we have adopted for documenting our object-oriented system. The approach uses conventional software engineering design documentation techniques that are coupled with an object-oriented approach. In later sections, we will use the approach to describe the concurrency and synchronization in *Choices*.

We will use the following terminology to describe an object-oriented system. The terminology is based on the *Choices* system implementation language C++ [24]. An *object* contains data and has a predefined set of methods or operations. An object has public, protected and private methods. We refer to the public methods of a class as its interface, or signature. A *class* is a generator or template for objects. An *abstract* class is often used as a template for other classes.

A description of a framework serves to document the specification, implementation, use and reuse of the design and the code in a system. Framework descriptions are often found in graphical user interfaces. Examples include the Model/View/Controller [14] and Unidraw [26] frameworks.

In the following sections we use three techniques to describe frameworks: class hierarchies, entity relationship diagrams and control flow graphs. We use these techniques to describe the *Choices* parallel object-oriented operating system. We present information about subframeworks at the abstract class level. By presenting information about abstract classes we are able to provide a concise, yet high level description of the system. In any complete description of the system concrete classes will replace abstract classes. We often omit concrete class descriptions because they are too detailed for the purposes of this paper.

Class hierarchies depict the classification of system objects into categories. They describe code sharing and interface inheritance in the system design. Class hierarchies consist of abstract classes, often at the root of the hierarchy and concrete subclasses, often at the leaves. Figure 13.1 is an example of three trees with abstract and concrete classes. Each subframework in *Choices* has a set of class hierarchies that define the abstract and concrete classes in the system.

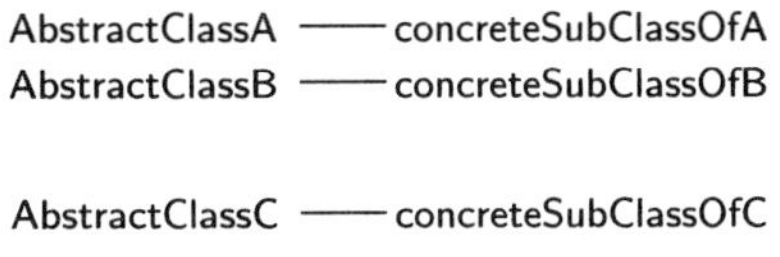

AbstractClassA ——— concreteSubClassOfA
AbstractClassB ——— concreteSubClassOfB

AbstractClassC ——— concreteSubClassOfC

Figure 13.1
Example Class Hierarchies

The description of the graphical user interface framework in [26] uses object communication diagrams to depict how data flows between objects, as these objects invoke methods on each other. Instead of data flow we model control flow transitions in object-oriented systems. In particular, the nodes are objects, and an edge from a node A to a node B labeled o, represents an invocation of the o method of B from within A.

Control flow diagrams can depict the runtime behavior of the system. For an object-oriented system, such a diagram represents an ordering on $object-> method$ invocations.[1] Each subframework in *Choices* has a control flow graph that describes the most important control flow through that subsystem. We will describe *abstract* control flow graphs, that represent an abstraction of the control flow through the instances of classes in the framework. As abstractions, these control flows may only pass through classes that are abstract. In any implementation of the operating system there will be a concrete control flow, representing the control flow through a series of objects that are instances of concrete classes. A concrete control flow is a refinement of an abstract control flow. We will provide examples of this refinement in *Choices* in section 13.4. When we describe abstract control flow graphs we will often use the terminology that method m is invoked on an instance of class A even though class A may not be instantiable. We take this liberty since we are describing an abstract property of the system. In an implementation of *Choices* some concrete subclass of A will have its m method invoked on it as part of a concrete control flow that is a refinement of the abstract control flow.

Control flow graphs have often been used for intermediate program representations [2]. A control flow graph is a directed graph $CFG =< N_{CFG}, E_{CFG}, \textbf{Entry}, \textbf{Exit} >$. In traditional representations, the nodes, N_{CFG}, represent basic blocks of a program. The two additional nodes, **Entry** and **Exit** represent points of transfer into and out of the control flow graph, respectively. The edges, E_{CFG}, represent transfers of control (jumps) between the basic blocks. There is an edge to any basic block from which the program may be entered from **Entry** and there is a edge from any basic block that can leave a program to the special node **Exit**. The edges are numbered showing the order of flow through the system from **Entry** to **Exit**. Thin arrows show the call of the method only whereas a thick arrows represents call and return. Arrows with disconnected line segments are used to signify a flow in a distributed environment where the dashed arrows are in response to a control flow elsewhere in the network. The presence of these types of arrows indicates the that two control flows in separate machines may communicate.

Figure 13.2 shows this control flow relationship between three abstract classes. The graph is entered when method m, is invoked on abstractClassA. The point of entry is denoted by the dashed rectangle labeled **Entry**. The control flows through the graph in the following sequence.

1. Method m is invoked on abstractClassA.

2. Method n is invoked on abstractClassB. (both method call and return are shown).

3. Method o is invoked on abstractClassC.

4. The control flow then leaves the system through the node labeled **Exit**.

Abstract entity relationship diagrams are similar to abstract control flow graphs, in that they can be used to express the relationships between abstract classes in the system. We will often refer to these abstract entity relationship diagrams as abstract class relationship diagrams. We will use a modified version of Pressman's [20] entity-relationship

---

[1]We attempt to capture the major flow of control through each of the subframeworks. The decomposition into subframeworks make the flow of control through the different subframeworks much simpler. Each subframework flow of control is then combined to describe the flow of control of *Choices*.

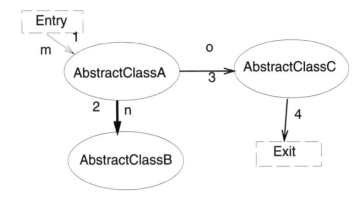

Figure 13.2
Abstract Flow of Control between three abstract classes A, B and C

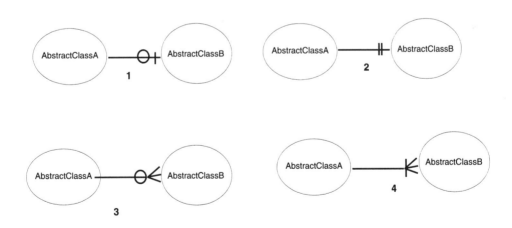

Figure 13.3
Entity Relationship Links between Abstract Classes

and instance connection notation to describe abstract class relationships. We may also annotate the links between the abstract classes with labels to make the type of relationship between classes more explicit. The abstract class relationships are *generalizations* of relationships maintained by instances of concrete subclasses. These generalizations specify common relationships that are inherited by the entities it generalizes. A concrete class may refine an entity relationship defined in a superclass. An abstract class may have an instance name attached to it. This is necessary when an abstract class appears in a diagram more than once. These names represent instances in an implementation of *Choices* that are instantiations of a concrete subclass of the abstract class. Figure 13.3 shows the notation we will use to represent one-to-one and one-to-many relationships. A single bar denotes a one-to-one relationship, and a three-pronged fork indicates a one-to-many relationship. These relationships may be mandatory (denoted by an additional line) or optional (denoted by a additional small circle). Figure 13.3 depicts the possible entity relationships between two abstract classes. In Figure 13.3, diagram **1** shows a one-to-one optional connection, diagram **2** shows a one-to-one mandatory connection, diagram **3** shows a one-to-many optional connection and diagram **4** shows a one-to-many mandatory connection. An optional **D** indicates whether or not the entities at the end of a link may vary dynamically, that is the instances corresponding to that end of the link may change as the system runs.

Specialization   Both control flow graphs and entity relationship diagrams have similar specialization rules. The control flow or entity relationship diagram is inherited by copying it into the new diagram. The three rules of specialization are given below.

1. An abstract class may be replaced by a concrete class.

2. New abstract and concrete classes may be added.

3. Relations and control flows may be added.

However, previously defined relations or control flows may not be removed.

These rules ensure substitutability: the new entity relationship or control flow diagram may be reused wherever the old one was expected since it obeys all the relationships and control flows of the old diagram but may possibly have added more [12].

Composition   Control flow graphs may be combined in one of two ways. First, an **exit** node in one graph may be connected to an **entry** node of another graph. This entails sequential composition. When there are no arcs between the two graphs these graphs may be concurrently composed. The graphs are independent and hence concurrent. Concurrent composition is shown in Figure 13.4 where graphs 1 and 2 are concurrent. The dashed line in between the graphs indicates concurrent composition.

Entity relationship diagrams may be composed by adding entity relationships between the two classes in two separate diagrams. Concurrency is not relevant to these diagrams.

A more detailed discussion of these relationships and their refinements can be found in Campbell and Islam [5, 12].

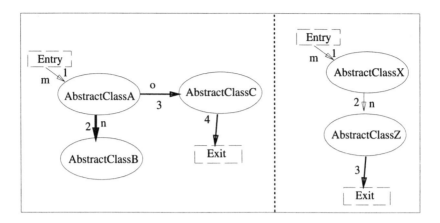

Figure 13.4
Concurrent Composition of two Control Flow graphs

13.4 Choices Frameworks

The framework for *Choices* defines abstract classes that represent the fundamental components of an operating system. Subframeworks specialize these components for use in the context of a subsystem of the operating system. The *Choices* framework imposes design constraints upon the subframeworks, which ensure that they may be integrated into a coherent system. These design constraints are specified through the use of control flow graphs and entity relationship diagrams.

The *Choices* framework consists of three abstract classes:

1. MemoryObject, storage for data.

2. Process, a thread of control which executes a sequential algorithm.

3. Domain, an environment that binds the names processed by the threads of control to storage locations.

Figure 13.5
An abstract class relationship diagram for the three fundamental components of Choices

Figure 13.5 shows an abstract class relationship diagram that defines how these three fundamental components interact. The figure shows that a Process must have a Domain and that several Processes may have the same Domain. The **D** in the abstract class relationship diagram next to the Process shows that the number and instances of Processes associated with a particular Domain varies dynamically over time. However, once a Process is started it cannot change the Domain it is associated with. Hence there is no **D** at the other end of the relation. The Domain has several MemoryObjects that store program code and data. A MemoryObject may be associated with one or more Domains. MemoryObjects may be dynamically removed from domains and added to new Domains as the system runs. Hence this relation is annotated by **D** at both ends. Specializations of the components are required in order to implement the different subsystems of an operating system. For example, the MemoryObject is specialized in the virtual memory subsystem to represent both physical memory and virtual memory. In the file system, the MemoryObject is specialized to represent disks and files. The constraints imposed between the abstract classes of the *Choices* framework are inherited by the subframeworks though refinements of the entity relationship diagrams and control flow graphs. Thus, in either case one or more Domains may be associated with a file, virtual memory, or with physical memory. Similarly, Processes are associated with a Domain.

The basic *Choices* entity relationship diagram may be *refined*. Figure 13.6 shows two possible refinements to the basic *Choices* entity relationship diagram (shown inside Box 1). Box 3 shows a refinement where concrete classes are used instead of abstract classes. In particular, Process has been replaced by a concrete class ApplicationProcess and its related ApplicationContext is shown. This diagram has another refinement. An ApplicationProcess is related to both a kernel domain and a user domain. The refinement shows the transformation from 1-1 to 1-many. ApplicationProcesses execute application programs in "user mode." They may also execute operating system procedures in the kernel in "supervisor mode." When an AppilcationProcess executes in user mode, it is associated with a user Domain. When an ApplicationProcess executes in supervisor mode, it is associated with the kernel Domain. The virtual memory used by an ApplicationProcess is divided into regions represented by MemoryObjects or data stores that are associated with the Domain of the application. In Box 2, two concrete classes have been added as refinements to Process, that is InterruptProcess and SystemProcess. The InterruptProcess is shown with its associated UninterruptibleSystemContext. SystemProcesses execute operating system programs. InterruptProcesses execute interrupt routines for networks communication and disk devices. Physical memory is mapped into virtual memory one-to-one and is represented by a MemoryObject associated with the Domain. Storage associated with a running Process is allocated by the kernel Domain from this MemoryObject. A particular region of virtual memory can be shared between two or more concurrent applications. In this case, the MemoryObject representing the region is associated with two or more user Domains. A region of virtual memory can also be shared between applications and the operating system code. In this case, the MemoryObject is associated with both the kernel and user Domains.

Figure 13.7 shows the abstract control flow in the creation of a Process which will result in a new thread of control. It shows the control flow graph for process creation. In this particular case it shows the order and sequence of calls to C++ object constructors. The following list shows the order of invocations of the methods in *Choices*.

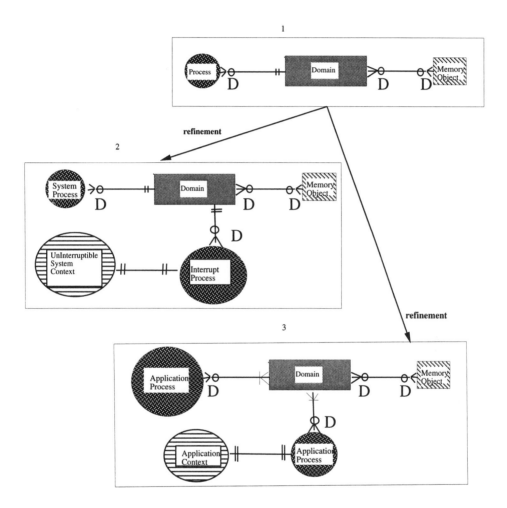

Figure 13.6
Refinement of the basic *Choices* entity relationship diagram. Box 1 is an Abstract Entity relationship diagram and Boxes 2 and 3 show refinements

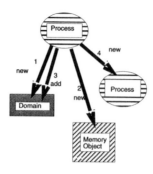

Figure 13.7
Abstract Control Flow Graph for Process Creation in *Choices*

1. A new Domain is created.

2. New MemoryObjects corresponding to the data, text and initialized data segments of the program are created.

3. These MemoryObjects are then added to the new Domain.

4. A new Process is created and is given the new domain, an entry point as well as the initial arguments for the entrypoint as arguments to the Process constructor.

Figure 13.8 shows two possible refinements to the basic *Choices* control flow graphs. In these refinements, new concrete classes have been introduced and concrete subclasses of ProcessContext have been added.

The components of the subsystems of *Choices* refine these basic relations in the various subframeworks. For example, the virtual memory subframework inherits the constraints imposed upon MemoryObject and Domain, defines specializations of these classes. It also introduces new abstract classes to define the necessary additional components that are required to implement a virtual memory system.

In this section, we have described how an abstract class diagram may be refined. In the following sections we will present abstract class diagrams and class hierarchies without explicitly showing all the refinements in detail.

There are four parts to the description of a *Choices* subsystem and its subframework. First, a generalized set of orthogonal **component**s is defined. Second, an **architectural overview** of the subframework is given. The architectural overview consists of the abstract classes corresponding to the components. A set of concrete classes that are implementations of the abstractions are also described. Instances of these concrete classes constitute the *Choices* operating system at runtime. The abstract class relationship diagram for the subframework specifies the *constraints* between the various classes. Third, a **design overview** provides detailed accounts of the methods of the classes. Fourth, a **control flow graph** describes the flow of threads of control through the most important objects in the system. Finally, the interaction of this subframework with the rest of *Choices* is provided.

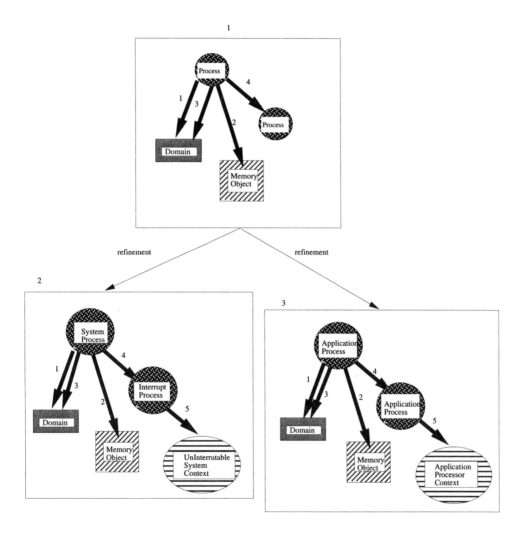

Figure 13.8
Box 1 shows the basic abstract control flow graph of *Choices*. Boxes 2 and 3 show refinements into concrete control flow graphs.

In the next few sections we describe the subframeworks of *Choices* that support concurrency. These are the Process, Message Passing and Virtual Memory subframeworks. We then discuss how these subframeworks are used in writing applications and in designing the Persistant Storage and Device Management subframeworks.

13.5 Process Management

Choices is a multitasking operating system that supports multiple threads of control or Processes. Processes provide the *active* computational part of an operating system. We model a process as an object that has methods that may be invoked to change its state. *Choices* supports grouping a number of Processes together into a Gang. Gang scheduling permits the Processes in a Gang to be dispatched on a multiprocessor simultaneously. A variety of other process scheduling policies are also supported.

Components The process management framework of *Choices* has the following components:

1. The Process
   is a control path through a group of C++ objects. A SystemProcess runs in the kernel and is non-preemptable. An ApplicationProcess runs in user and kernel space. An InterruptProcess is used to handle the occurrence of an interrupt. Each Process is associated with exactly one Domain, and it executes in that Domain. Processes may share a Domain with other Processes. Context switching is light-weight between Processes in the same domain and is heavy-weight between Processes in different domains.

2. The ProcessorContext
   saves and restores the machine dependent state of a Process. Every Process has exactly one ProcessorContext, and each ProcessorContext belongs to exactly one Process.

3. The Processor
   encapsulates the processor dependent details of the hardware central processing unit (CPU) including the hardware CPU identification numbers and the state of the hardware interrupt mechanism.

4. The Gang
   is a group of Processes that should be gang scheduled, or run simultaneously, on the processors of a multiprocessor. The Gang allows the collection of Processes to be manipulated as a single unit.

5. The ProcessContainer
   implements scheduling in *Choices*. Subclasses of ProcessContainer perform scheduling, and inherit the uniform interface for scheduling. Processes are run by inserting them into instances of subclasses of ProcessContainer. The Processor removes a Process from its ready queue before dispatching the Process. For multilevel feedback queues and other scheduling disciplines, the ProcessContainer insertion and removal methods are specialized to provide a given scheduling policy.

Architectural Overview The process management system has the following class hierarchy and relationships between its abstract classes. The class hierarchies for the process system are shown in Figure 13.9 with the abstract classes distinguished by bold font. A Process has subclasses SystemProcess, PreemptableSystemProcess and Interrupt-Process that are kernel processes associated with the kernel Domain. The subclass ApplicationProcess is a user process associated with a user Domain and the subclass Gang represents a group of ApplicationProcesses that are dispatched simultaneously on multiprocessors. The ProcessorContext class hierarchy manages the processor-dependencies associated with implementing a Process. The Processor hierarchy shows a variety of central processing units that are supported. The ProcessContainer has concrete subclasses for FIFO scheduling, round robin scheduling and two corresponding schedulers that handle Gangs as well as regular Processes.

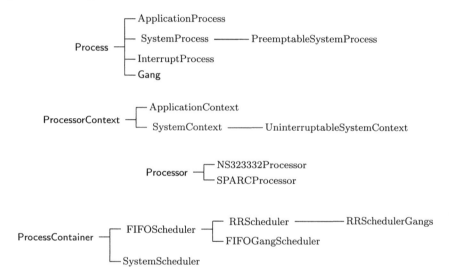

Figure 13.9
Process System Class Hierarchies

Figure 13.10 is an abstract class relationship diagram for the process subframework. Each Processor has exactly one running Process and one SystemScheduler ready queue from which it dispatches Processes. The running process and the ready queue associated with the Processor may change dynamically. The SystemScheduler gives priority to the SystemProcesses in the ready queue over ApplicationProcesses. When the currently running Process blocks or voluntarily relinquishes its Processor, the Processor retrieves a new Process to run from its ready queue. A particular ProcessContainer may be a ready queue of more than one, but not necessarily all, the Processors in a multiprocessor system allowing such systems to have scheduling partitions. The Processors associated with a ProcessContainer may change dynamically. A ProcessContainer may contain more than one Process or Gang. These Processes and Gangs may be different instances at different times.

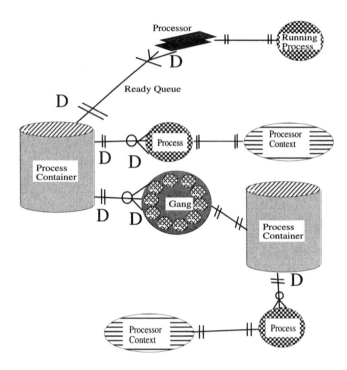

Figure 13.10
Abstract class relationship diagram for Process Management

Each Process has a ProcessorContext and a ProcessContainer which is the ready queue to which it should be added when it is ready to run. A Process may be added to different ProcessContainers at different times. This is particularly helpful for multiprocessors where a Processor may run a different group of Processs at different times. A Gang has a FIFOGangScheduler and a special ProcessContainer for holding its Process members. When a Gang is first dispatched from the ready queue, the SystemScheduler notes the number of Gang members and assigns the processor to dispatch an actual Gang Process member from the FIFOGangScheduler. The FIFOGangScheduler is empty and the Processor busy waits for the scheduler to fill. When the required number of Processors have been collected, the SystemScheduler adds the Gang members in the Gang ProcessContainer to the FIFOGangScheduler. The Processors then dispatch Gang members from the FIFOGangScheduler one by one. A more detailed description may be found in [11, 10].

Design Overview Some of the more important methods of the classes of the process system are described in this section. A Process has methods block to block the process, giveProcessorTo to give the Processor to a specified process, relinquish to return the process to the ready queue in order to allow the Processor to run other processes, and ready to put the Process on its ready queue. The methods block and relinquish are implemented using giveProcessorTo. The methods becomeUninterruptable and becomeInterruptable are used to turn processor interrupts off and on.

ProcessorContext implements processor dependent methods including checkpoint for saving and restore for restoring processor dependent state including registers, the frame pointer, stack pointers and the program counter. The checkpoint and restore methods are called by the giveProcessorTo method of the Process class. Processor has chip specific methods and the method idleContainer that returns the ready queue ProcessContainer.

A ProcessContainer has methods add, remove and isEmpty. The Gang class has methods addMemberto add Processes to it, scheduleMembers to schedule the Gang members by adding them to the FIFOGangScheduler, ready to add the Gang to the ready queue and returnProcessor to relinquish the Gang processes' processors.

Object Flow Diagram of the Process Management System In this subsection, we trace how a process is moved between the various process containers and processors in the system. We describe the movement of the process using an Object Flow Diagram [12], which is a variant of data flow graphs. The diagram depicts how a particular object, in this case an instance of the class Process is passed between various system objects. Figure 13.11 traces the movement of an instance of class Process from creation, to blocking and finally to deletion. The diagram also identifies the state of a process when it is in different ProcessContainers. For example, a Process is in the **blocked** state when it is in a Semaphore's ProcessContainer. The following transitions are shown in Figure 13.11.

1. a Process is created using the C++ operator **new**.

2. The ready method is invoked on the Process which puts the process on the System-Scheduler.

3. The Process is taken off the SystemScheduler in FIFO order (or some other discipline) and the restore method is invoked on it and on Process B's ProcessorContext. The process is now said to be **Running** on a Processor.

4. A Process may become blocked: that is, it invokes the P method on a Semaphore, or invokes the relinquishProcessor method on itself, or puts itself on a specialized ProcessContainer and then invokes the block method on itself.

5. While it is blocked if another process invokes the V method on the Semaphore that this process is waiting for, and it is the next Process to be chosen from the ProcessContainer it is put on the SystemScheduler.

6. If the Process was waiting on a GraciousSemaphore it will directly run on the Processor without being inserted into the SystemScheduler when the V method is invoked on the GraciousSemaphore.

7. If a Process invokes the die method on itself it is put into the GarbageCan Process-Container.

8. A WasteManagerProcess will remove this zombie Process from the garbage can and invoke the **delete** operator on it.

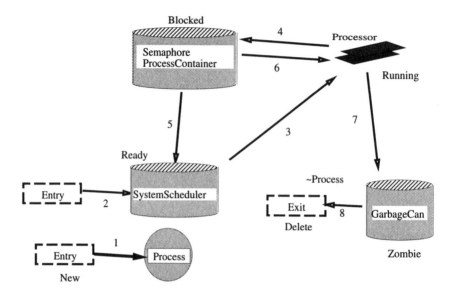

Figure 13.11
Object Flow Diagram of the Process Management System

Multiprocessor Context Switching In this subsection, we describe the steps involved in context switching between processes. In general, this a difficult problem to implement correctly [19]. In the *Choices* scheduling model, a process adds itself to its ready container, and a Processor will take it from the ready container and start running it. In a multiprocessor there is the possibility of a Process running on two or more Processors at the same time. In this section, we describe the algorithm for context switching on *Choices*.

There are three ways in which a Processor may switch from running one Process to running another.

1. The currently running Process may wait by invoking the P method on a Semaphore or the block method on itself.

2. The currently running Process is preempted or interrupted.

3. The currently running Process voluntarily calls relinquishProcessor on itself.

In each of these cases, the thread of control giving up the Processor picks the next Process to run by calling the remove method on the SystemScheduler. It then invokes the giveProcessorTo method with the next Process to run as a parameter. The code for the giveProcessorTo and restore methods is shown in Figure 13.13. The giveProcessorTo method is the low level routine where actual transfer of control takes place between Processes. The restore method restores the page tables of the newly running Process. The code for the methods relinquishProcessor and block is shown in Figure 13.12. These are high level methods that eventually call the giveProcessorTo method. The code for Semaphores is shown in Figure 13.15. An important aspect of correctness is when a Process stack is locked and released. A key aspect of the performance of the system is to minimize the time between locking and releasing a Process stack. The following algorithm is correct and efficient.

```
void
Process::relinquishProcessor()
{
        int wasInterruptable = becomeUninterruptable();
        Process * nextProcess = thisCPU()→idleContainer()→remove();
        /* If there is another process, give the processor to it.
         * Put the current process into its idleContainer(). Otherwise, just
         * run last process */
        if( nextProcess ≠ 0 ) {
                ready();
                giveProcessorTo( nextProcess );
        }
        if( wasInterruptable ) {
                becomeInterruptable();
        }
}
void
Process::block()
{
/* block suspends this process and runs the next process from SystemScheduler.
 * The caller of block() should have put this process on some ProcessContainer*/
int wasInterruptable = becomeUninterruptable();
Process * nextProcess = thisCPU()→getNextReadyProcess();
Assert( ! isInterruptable() );
giveProcessorTo( nextProcess );
if( wasInterruptable ) {
        becomeInterruptable();
}
}
```

Figure 13.12
The code for the relinquishProcessor and block method of the Process class. These methods are used for context switching.

The giveProcessorTo method locks the stack of the Process to which the Processor is about to be given. This ensures that *no other processor is using this stack*. The current Processor busy-waits if another Processor is using the stack. When it gets the lock on the Process's stack the giveProcessorTo method invokes the checkPoint method on the related ProcessorContext which is used to save the machine dependent state of Process. The call to checkpoint appears to return twice and this is where the transfer of control actually takes place between two processes. The first time the call to checkpoint will return NULL, as can be seen in Figure 13.13, and the new Process's machine dependent context is restored, by invoking restore on the restore method on its related ProcessorContext. The machine dependent context of the Process is also saved in the first call. When this same Process is later resumed (when another process calles checkpoint on itself, and invokes restore on this Process's context) the checkpoint returns a second time, providing

```
/* This gets called by restarted interrupt processes and by method giveProcessorTo */
void
Process::restore( Process * previousProcess )
{
/* Release old process's stack for use by other processor's
 * Note Interrrupt processes get here but previousProcess is nil */
        if (previousProcess ≠ 0)
                        previousProcess→releaseStack();
/* Switch Processor to correct Domain */
        if( thisCPU()→MMU()→currentlyActiveDomain() ≠ domain() )
                thisCPU()→MMU()→activate( domain() );
        basicRestore();/*Perform subclass specific restoring. */
}


void
Process::giveProcessorTo( Process * anotherProcess )
{
        save();
/* Lock the stack of the Process to which this Processor is switching
 * in order to make sure that no other processor is using that stack.
 * The Processor busy waits if another Processor is still using the stack. */
        anotherProcess→getStack();
/* Checkpoint the current state of this process/context.
 * context()->checkpoint() will return a 0 when the checkpoint
 * is first taken. The process that resumed this process
 * is returned when the checkpoint is resumed. */
        Process * processWhoResumedUs;
        if( ( processWhoResumedUs = context()→checkpoint() ) == 0 ) {
                thisCPU()→_currentProcess = anotherProcess;
                anotherProcess→context()→restore( this );
        }

/* This is where you get after the process is rolled
 * back to the spot it was checkpointed.
 * Since we are now running on a new stack, free the old process
 * stack and let another processor use it, if required by calling restore. */

        restore( processWhoResumedUs );
}
```

Figure 13.13
The code for the restore and giveProcessorTo methods of the Process class. These methods are used for context switching.

```
void Process::getStack()
{
        stackBusy.wait(); /* lock stack during context switch to avoid race for stacks
*/
        _stackBusy = 1;
}
void Process::releaseStack()
{
        if (_stackBusy) {
                _stackBusy = 0;
                stackBusy.releaseNextWaiter(); /* unlock stack at end of context
switch */
        }
}
```

Figure 13.14
The code for context switching locking stack of a Process

a pointer to the process that restarted the current process and puts the flow of control out of the if statement. When the checkpoint returns for the second time the machine dependent state of the process has been already been restored. The Process will be restarted, and it will have its restore method invoked, with a pointer to the previously running Process passed in as an argument. The restore method will release the stack of the previous Process, allowing it to be run on other Processors. The restore method then activates the page tables for the new domain of the newly running Process. Any object that interacts with scheduling such as TimeSliceTimer and Semaphore must perform one of the following two sequences to correctly schedule a Process.

```
1. currentProcess -> ready();
 currentProcess->giveProcessorTo( nextProcess );
```

or

```
2. SemaphoreProcessContainer.add( currentProcess );
currentProcess->block();
```

The block method calls the giveProcessorTo method which will call the restore method. The restore method will free the stack of the previous Process.

The control flow graph for the *Choices* multiprocessor context switching algorithm is shown in Figure 13.17. This helps to clarify the description given earlier on context switching. We now itemize the steps to clarify the multiprocessor context switching algorithm.

1. Process A is readied for execution.

2. It is added to the SystemScheduler

3. Another thread of control corresponding to Process B calls block on itself.

4. Another thread of control, corresponding to Process B, removes Process A from the SystemScheduler.

```
void
Semaphore::P()
{
Process * process = thisProcess();
int wasInterruptable = process→becomeUninterruptable();
lock.wait();
count--;
if( count < 0 ) {
            /* We have to block so get another process to run next*/
                    queue.add( process );
                    lock.releaseNextWaiter();
                    process→block( );
        }
        else {
                    lock.releaseNextWaiter();
        }
        if( wasInterruptable )
                    process→becomeInterruptable();
}

void
Semaphore::V()
{
        Process * process = thisProcess();
        int wasInterruptable = process→becomeUninterruptable();
        lock.wait();
        count++;
        Assert( count ≤ maxCount );
        if( count ≤ 0 ) {
                    Process * waiter = queue.remove();
                    lock.releaseNextWaiter();
                    Assert( waiter ≠ 0 );
                    waiter→ready();
        }
        else {
                    lock.releaseNextWaiter();
        }
        if( wasInterruptable )
                    process→becomeInterruptable();
}
```

Figure 13.15
Semaphore code for correct scheduling. The implementation of he P and V methods are shown

```
void
TimeSliceException::basicRaise( char * )
{
        Process * current = thisProcess();
        CPU * currentCPU = thisCPU();
        /* Force the timer to return a 0 residual when the process * reads it next.
*/
        currentCPU→timesliceTimer()→set( 0 );
        int wasInterruptable = current→becomeUninterruptable();
        Process * nextProcess = currentCPU→idleContainer()→remove();
        /* If there is another process, give the processor to it; put this process in
         * its idleContainer(). Otherwise, continue running*/
        if( nextProcess ≠ 0 ) {
                current → ready();
                current→giveProcessorTo( nextProcess );
        }
        else { /*Start the timer for another timeslice */
                currentCPU→timesliceTimer()→start( current→quantum() );
        }
        if( wasInterruptable ) {
                current→becomeInterruptable();
        }
}
```

Figure 13.16
Time slice interrupt code for correct scheduling

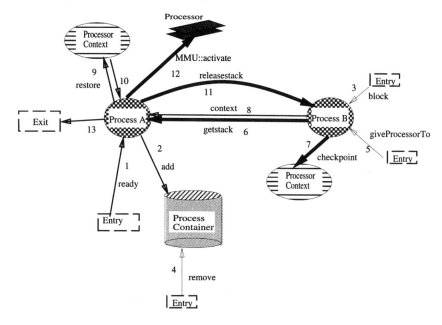

Figure 13.17
Control Flow through the Process subsystem: context switching

5. block calls the giveProcessorTo method and passes Process A to it as an argument.

6. The stack of Process A is locked.

7. giveProcessorTo calls the machine dependent method checkpoint on its related ProcessorContext.

8. The context of Process A is retrieved.

9. The context of Process A is restored.

10. The control flow is now in Process A.

11. The stack of Process B is now released. This Process may now be run on another Processor.

12. The pages tables of Process A are restored if its Domain was different from that of Process B.

13. Process A continues executing.

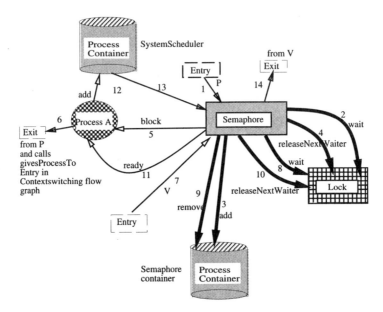

Figure 13.18
Control Flow through the Process subsystem: Semaphores

13.5.1 Synchronization

The *Choices* operating system provides three abstract classes for basic synchronization of processes. These classes are Locks, Semaphores and Barriers.

There are two types of locks in *Choices*: SpinLocks and BusyWait locks. SpinLocks disable interrupts while spinning on a shared variable. BusyWaits are similar but do not disable interrupts. A Semaphore has an integer variable that can only be accessed through the two methods P and V. Semaphores in *Choices* may block the Process that uses it. *Choices* supports six types of semaphores: Semaphore, GraciousSemaphores, Lazy-Semaphore, MutexSemaphore, BinarySemaphore and MultiVSemaphore. These semaphores vary in their initialization methods and the semantics of the V method: each concrete subclass reimplements the V method for a different semantics. The class hierarchy shown in Figure 13.19 is a simple example of interface and code reuse in *Choices*. Semaphore is abstract and all the other classes are concrete.

Regular semaphores are implemented by the class Semaphore and they can be initialized to an arbitrary value. When the V method is invoked on a Semaphore and another Process is waiting on that Semaphore the resumed Process is put on the SystemScheduler. For GraciousSemaphores an invocation of the V method will directly put the resumed Process on the Processor and the currently running Process is put on the SystemScheduler. A BinarySemaphore allows alternate sequences of P and V methods. A MutexSemaphore is a BinarySemaphore initialized to one. It is used for mutual exclusion [18]. A LazySemaphore allows the V method to be safely invoked more than the number of times the P method is invoked. The method V of a MultiVSemaphore takes as an argument the number of blocked Processes to be put on the ready queue at once as the result of an invocation of the V method.

Figure 13.19
Synchronization Class Hierarchies

There is currently one type of Barrier that allows N processes to synchronize at a particular point in a program.

Control Flow Graph for the Process Management System : Semaphores The control flow graph for a process blocking on a semaphore and then being restarted by another process is shown in Figure 13.18. In this control flow graph, Process A blocks and is later readied for execution. The diagram depicts the following flow of control:

1. The P method is invoked on a Semaphore by code executed by Process A.

2. The Semaphore waits to acquire the BusyWait lock on the Semaphore ProcessContainer.

3. If the process cannot enter the critical section, it is added to the Semaphore Process-Container.

4. The lock is released by invoking the releaseNextWaiter method on the BusyWait lock.

5. The block method is invoked on Process A.

6. Control flows into the context switching flow graph shown in Figure 13.17 at the entry point labeled block.

7. The V method is invoked on a Semaphore by code being executed by Process B.

8. The Semaphore ProcessContainer BusyWait lock is acquired again.

9. The remove method is invoked on the Semaphore ProcessContainer and Process A, the waiting process, is removed from the Semaphore ProcessContainer.

10. The BusyWait lock is relased.

11. The ready method is invoked on Process A.

12. The add method is invoked on the SystemScheduler.

13. Control returns to the Semaphore.

14. This Control Flow Graph is exited. When the Process is removed from the system scheduler it is run again.

The *Choices* Framework and Process Management   The implementation of a process is encapsulated completely within the process management framework and provides abstractions for many of the other subframeworks such as the message passing system and device driver system.

13.6   Message Passing System

This section describes a subframework for message passing designed to support parallel message-based applications. It describes facilities for creating structured messages and sending and receiving messages. This message passing system has been ported to a variety of hardware architectures. In *Choices* messages are sent to MessageContainers that are similar to Mach ports [21]. A message may be sent to a MessageContainer in the same address space, in a different address space (or a different protection domain) on the same machine or on different machines. The message system provides several reliability models including unreliable and "exactly once" message transmission [9].

Components   The message passing system has the following components:

1. The MessageContainer
   is a named communication entity for buffering messages. A MessageContainer can have multiple senders and multiple receivers. Once a MessageContainer has been created, it is registered with a NameServer using an appropriate name. A process intending to send a message to a MessageContainer must look the name up in the NameServer. On lookup, a sender is given a handle called a ContainerRepresentative that forwards messages to the MessageContainer. The ContainterRepresentative acts as a capability for the MessageContainer.

2. The Message System Interface
   is an adaptation layer encapsulating features specific to a particular parallel or distributed programming paradigm. The Kernel Message System Interface and User

Message System Interface support two alternate implementations of the message passing system, the former in the kernel and the latter in user space.

3. The Transport

   class specifies the mechanism that is used to move a message from a sender to a receiver. A local message may be transported by a separate process or copied by the sender and receiver processes. A remote message is transmitted across the network.

4. The Data Transfer

   class concerns the buffering strategies used in sending a message. On a shared memory multiprocessor, message sends may be double buffered, single buffered, or passed by reference. In a distributed system, messages are buffered for the message transport mechanism.

5. The Reliability

   class allows messages to be sent unreliably, with at-most-once semantics, and exactly-once [9] semantics.

6. The Flow Control

   class uses rate based flow control to ensure that the sender and the receiver are not overrunning one anothers data buffers.

Architectural Overview   The message passing system class hierarchies and the relationships between its abstract classes are as follows.   Figure 13.20 shows the class

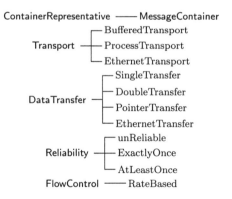

Figure 13.20
Message Passing System Class Hierarchies

hierarchies for the message passing system.

Transport has subclasses ProcessTransport that transports messages using a separate process, BufferedTransport that provides single or double buffering for a message, and EthernetTransport that delivers the message across an Ethernet.

DataTransfer has subclasses DoubleTransfer in which a sender process copies the message into a temporary buffer and a receiver process copies it from that buffer into a receiver buffer, SingleTransfer in which the receiver process copies the message from the sender buffer to a receiver buffer in a shared memory region, PointerTransfer in which the sender and receiver exchange buffer pointers but message data is not physically copied, and EthernetTransfer in which the sender and receiver copy the message data to and from Ethernet driver buffer regions.

Figure 13.21 is an abstract class relationship diagram for the message passing system framework.

Each Domain may have a KernelMessageSystemInterface or a UserMessageSystemInterface [2] and possibly several MessageContainers. ApplicationProcesses use ContainerRepresentatives to send messages to remote MessageContainers.

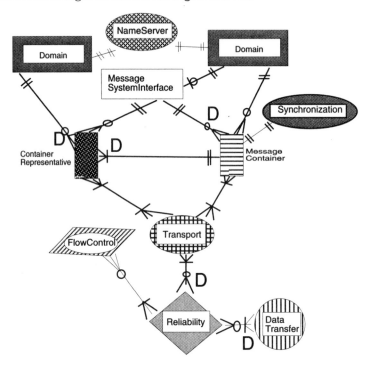

Figure 13.21
Abstract class relationship diagram for the Message Passing System

Each ContainerRepresentative communicates with only one MessageContainer through the Transport scheme. However, each MessageContainer may have several ContainerRepresentatives that know how to send messages to it. The ContainerRepresentative provides for asynchronous sends, from which synchronous message sends and remote procedure call type interfaces may be built. Both synchronous and asynchronous gets are available through the MessageContainer class.

---

[2] It will be a KernelMessageSystemInterface for the kernel Domain and a UserMessageSystemInterface for a user Domain.

The ContainerRepresentative delivers messages using the Transport with which it is associated. The MessageContainer buffers incoming messages received from its associated Transport. Each MessageContainer is associated with exactly one Synchronization object. Each Synchronization object is associated with exactly one MessageContainer.

For shared memory, Transport transfers control between the sending process activating ContainerRepresentative and the receiving process activating MessageContainer. This incurs little overhead.

For distributed systems, the ContainerRepresentative and MessageContainer and their two associated Transports are located on different machines. The Transports use the Reliability mechanism to send the messages through the DataTransfer scheme across the network using the appropriate reliability model. Reliability selects from an appropriate FlowControl policy. Currently, only rate based flow control is used.

Design Overview   The important methods of the message system classes are described in this section. MessageContainer has methods get, put and isEmpty to provide concurrent access to its internal message queue. put is used by Transport to add a message to the message queue. get and isEmpty are used by ApplicationProcesses to retrieve messages from the queue. MessageContainers are created by ApplicationProcesses, are associated with a particular Domain, and can be registered with a *Choices* NameServer so that ApplicationProcesses in other Domains and on other machines can send messages to it. All Processes in the same Domain may retrieve messages from any MessageContainer in its Domain. If a MessageContainer is associated with the kernel Domain, any Process in any Domain on the same machine may retrieve messages from it. However, a particular message system interface may impose further restrictions on which Processes can access a MessageContainer. Similarly, a ContainerRepresentative associated with a Domain can be used by any Process. Also, if the ContainerRepresentative is associated with the kernel Domain, then Processes in any Domain on the same machine may use it to send messages.

A process intending to send a message to a MessageContainer must look up its name in the NameServer. The NameServer returns a handle called a ContainerRepresentative. A ContainerRepresentative has the information to locate and deliver messages to the MessageContainer for which it is a representative. The ContainerRepresentive has a send method, that invokes the appropriate method on a Transport object.

The Transport has methods send and receive. The send method is called by the MessageContainer and the receive method is called by the Reliability class.

The reliability model used for sending messages is implemented by the Reliability class. Reliability has methods send, receive, sendWithNotification, and setTimeout. The receive is called by an instance of a Transfer class. The method for sending is invoked by the Transport class. The subclass UnReliable provides unreliable delivery of messages and is the basis for many protocols. The AtLeastOnce guarantees that a packet is delivered at least once but possibly more. The ExactlyOnce guarantees that a packet is delivered once and once only. Flow Control provides information about packet loss and changes the interpacket gap if necessary. It exports the method regulate to regulate the flow control.

The Transfer has method send and receive. The send method calls a network driver and the receive method is called by a network driver.

Control Flow through the Message Passing System   In this example, a process sends a message through the KernelMessageSystemInterface. A second process then performs a receive on the KernelMessageSystemInterface. The solid arrows show the direction of the flow of control on the sender side and the dashed arrows show the flow of control on the receiver. The double lined arrow, labeled **Error**, shows the possible redirection of flow of control when a packet is not delivered and a notification is returned. A detailed account of the abstract control flow trace for a send/receive interaction pair is given below for the distributed implementation of the message passing system. In the following trace, the numbers correspond to the numbers on the arrows in Figure 13.22.

1. At the top level an application process makes a call into the KernelMessageSystemInterface to send a message.

2. The KernelMessageSystemInterface looks up the appropriate MessageContainer in the NameServer. The NameServer returns a handle called a ContainerRepresentative. A ContainerRepresentative delivers messages to the MessageContainer which it represents.

3. The KernelMessageSystemInterface invokes the send method on the ContainerRepresentative.

4. The send method of the ContainerRepresentative invokes the send method on the Transport object.

5. The Transport generates transport headers and creates a network packet and invokes the send method on the Reliability object to send the packet across the network with the appropriate recovery semantics. Transport performs fragmentation for network packets.

6. The Reliability object calls the regulate method of the FlowControl object when too many packets are lost.

7. The Reliability object then invokes the send method on the Transfer object.

8. The control then flows into the Device subframework that attempts to deliver the packet across the network.

9. The Device subframework at the receiving end invokes the receive method on the Transfer object on the receiver machine.

10. The Transfer object at the receiving machine picks up the data. It passes the packet up to the Reliability object by invoking the receive method on the Reliability object.

11. The Reliability object sends the packet up to the Transport object. It may or may not generate an acknowledgement packet depending upon which subclass of the Reliability object is in use.

12. The Transport invokes the put method on the MessageContainer. It may perform re-assembly of network packets.

13. The MessageContainer will enter a critical section for queuing messages.

14. The MessageContainer will then exit the critical section for queuing messages.

15. A KernelMessageSystemInterface performs a get on the MessageContainer.

16. The message is then passed onto the ApplicationProcess.

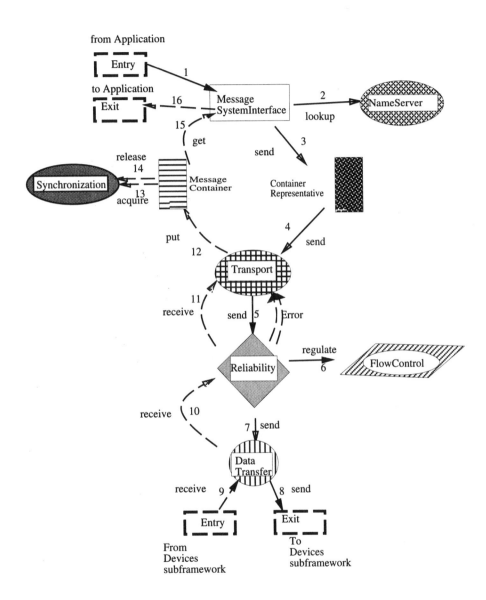

Figure 13.22
Control Flow Graph for the Message Passing System

Experiments versus Parameters				
Experiment	Location	Transport	Synchronization	DataTransfer
1 ◇	Kernel	Buffered	Spinlock	Single copy
2 ▽	Kernel	Buffered	Spinlock	Pointer
3 ⊗	Kernel	Process	Semaphore	Double copy
4 ×	Kernel	Buffered	Semaphore	Double copy
5 ⊕	Userlevel	Buffered	Spinlock	Single copy
6 ○	Kernel	Buffered	Spinlock	Double copy

Figure 13.23
List of the Problem-Oriented Message Passing Systems

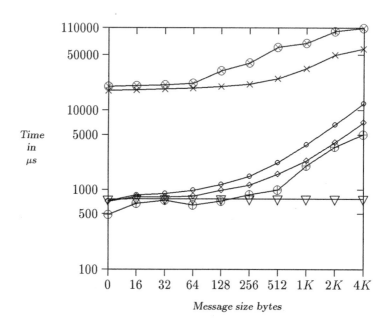

Figure 13.24
Round trip message passing times for different Message Passing Systems

Problem Oriented Message Passing Using Object-Oriented design techniques we were able to rapidly create and experiment with a wide variety of schemes for message passing. Once the key abstractions and abstract classes were designed, if classes are programmed only using the abstract class interfaces then little code has to be changed to experiment with different concrete subclasses. For example, we were able to combine different transfer, transport and protection implementations and evaluate the performance of each implementation. In a recent paper [13] we measured the performance of a variety of our message passing schemes on a shared memory multiprocessor. We did not find a single scheme that performed equally well on our sample of benchmarks and applications. In addition, we found that a particular application may perform better with different message passing systems depending on the number of processors available to it. For our tests we used several applications, including a ring message passing program commonly used for benchmarking message latency, a Fast Fourier Transform (FFT) adapted to the iPSC/2 [17] and a Simplex program that has been analyzed in detail[25]. Figure 13.23 is a list of the experiments that were evaluated using the ring benchmark. The column headers are the abstract classes described earlier and the column entries show the specific subclasses used. For the sake of clarify the exact subclass names are not used, instead descriptive names where chosen. Figure 13.24 shows the performance of each experiment in μs (microseconds) per round trip for different message sizes. These six experiments are actually a representative list of a large number of experiments done. The graphs show that a variety of message passing parameters may be combined to implement radically different message passing performance.

The *Choices* Framework and the Message Passing System Various parts of the *Choices* framework interacts with the message passing subframework. The KernelMessageSystemInterface and UserMessageSystemInterface provide interfaces for parallel and distributed computing for ApplicationProcesses. The *Choices* DistributedNameServer uses it for maintaining a consistent view of the name space. The message passing system control flow graph is sequentially composed with the Device subframework. It is concurrently composed with the Persistent Storage framework.

13.7 Virtual Memory

The *Choices* virtual memory system supports multiple 32 bit virtual memory address spaces, one and two level paging and shared memory. The system is implemented by representing the components of the system as objects. Each virtual memory space is supported by a Domain which provides the mapping between the virtual memory addresses used by Processes and physical storage. A virtual memory space can provide access to multiple different data stores. Each data store is mapped into a region of virtual memory and is represented by a MemoryObject. The data store represented by each MemoryObject is paged and may be larger than physical memory. Multiple applications may share the data in a MemoryObject by mapping it into each of their Domains.

Components The virtual memory system of *Choices* has the following components:

1. The MemoryObject

    represents a data store. The store might contain a process stack, code, heap, or data area of a program. Any one of several subclasses of MemoryObject may be used, including subclasses of PersistentStore that represent various kinds of disks and files. When a MemoryObject is cached in memory, virtual memory addresses may be used to reference the contents of the store. The MemoryObjectCache that caches the MemoryObject pages the contents of the store to and from the data store into physical memory.

2. The Domain (Address Space)

    maintains the mapping between virtual addresses and data stores. When a MemoryObject is added to a Domain, the Domain assigns a virtual address range to the contents of the data store and builds a MemoryObjectCache to cache the contents of the data store in physical memory. Processes accessing the data store use virtual memory addresses. If the data in the data store is not resident in physical memory, a page fault will occur. The Domain maps a page fault virtual address into an offset within the data store and sends a message to the appropriate MemoryObjectCache to fetch the appropriate page of data from the data store.

3. The PageFrameAllocator

    allocates and deallocates physical memory. It is used by the virtual memory system to reserve pages for paging.

4. The AddressTranslation

    encapsulates the address translation hardware of the computer. The virtual memory system makes requests to AddressTranslation to add and remove virtual memory to physical memory page mappings.

5. The MemoryObjectCache

    stores the mapping between virtual memory pages of a MemoryObject and the physical memory pages in which the data are actually stored. The mappings in the MemoryObjectCache are maintained in a machine independent form.

Architectural Overview   This section describes the virtual memory system class hierarchy and the relationships between its abstract classes. The class hierarchies for the virtual memory system are shown in Figure 13.25. These hierarchies show the abstract classes and their concrete subclasses. The abstract class interfaces are preserved in the subclasses and superclass code is reused in the subclasses.

The TwoLevelPageTable provides two level page tables. The PremappedMemoryObjectCache pre-maps all its virtual memory into one large contiguous space of physical memory. This is useful for memory mapped I/O. The PagedMemoryObjectCache is a concrete class of MemoryObjectCache. It implements cached data using page frame sized physical memory storage units.

Figure 13.26 is an entity diagram showing the relationship between the abstract classes of the virtual memory subframework. The diagram shows one or more Domains sharing one or more MemoryObjects. The MemoryObject reads and writes data from and to a data store represented by a File (see Section 13.8 on Persistent Storage.) Each

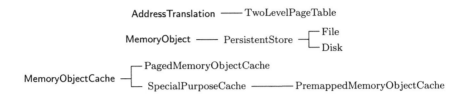

Figure 13.25
Virtual Memory System Class Hierarchies

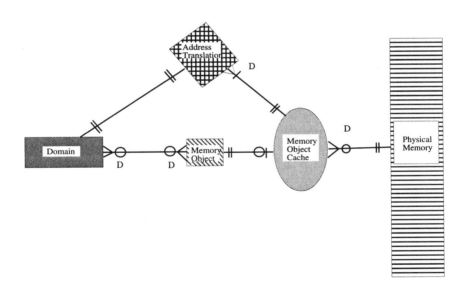

Figure 13.26
An abstract class relationship diagram for the virtual memory subframework

MemoryObject that is mapped into virtual memory has a corresponding MemoryObject-Cache that records in a machine independent manner the page mappings of the data store that have been copied into physical memory. The Domain handles page faults by requesting the MemoryObject to read the page into physical memory. The MemoryObject returns the page frame that contains the data to the Domain which then adds a virtual memory mapping for that page frame to its AddressTranslation object. Each Domain has its own AddressTranslation object but in a single processor system, only one of the AddressTranslation objects will be active at any one time. Page replacement algorithms may free physical memory pages for reuse. For each physical page, the MemoryObject-Cache records all the AddressTranslations that map virtual addresses to that page. The page replacement algorithm selects pages of information to return to the data store and removes the hardware virtual memory mapping by making requests to the appropriate AddressTranslation.

Design Overview   This section discusses the methods of particular classes in more detail. A MemoryObject supports access to an array of equal-sized logical units, where each unit is a block of bytes. A unit corresponds to a disk block, physical memory page frame, or number of bytes. The main access methods for a MemoryObject are read and write. The buildCache method of a MemoryObject returns a MemoryObjectCache. The MemoryObjectCache uses page frame units to read and write physical page frames that cache the contents of the MemoryObject. The MemoryObject converts page frame unit requests from its cache into units that are appropriate for its permanent storage. This allows, for example, the virtual memory system to page from a disk in blocks or a file in bytes.

A Domain maps a set of MemoryObjects or data stores into a virtual address space so that the contents of the data in the stores can be accessed by a virtual address. A Domain associates protection with each MemoryObject and it ensures that the virtual addresses that it uses for each memory object do not overlap. Domains have operations to add and remove MemoryObjects to lookup or find the MemoryObject at a particular virtual address and to handle a page fault repairfault. Each Domain has an AddressTranslation object which, when activated, controls the hardware memory management unit of the processor.

The Disk specifies the behavior of permanent storage in *Choices*. Its subclasses are device drivers. It exports the methods read, write, sizeOfUnits and numberOfUnits.

The MemoryObjectCache caches all, part, or none of the data of a   MemoryObject in physical memory. It keeps track of the physical address of each unit that has been cached. Its main methods are cache, release and protect. The cache method ensures that a particular unit is in the cache and returns the corresponding physical memory address. The release method removes a unit from the cache. Each unit is given a protection level when it is cached; protect sets the maximum protection level of a unit and can change the protection of an already cached unit.

The machine dependent code associated with the page mapping hardware is encapsulated in AddressTranslation. On a shared memory multiprocessor, several AddressTranslation may be active, one for each processor. AddressTranslation has methods addMapping, removeMapping and changePermission. addMapping is invoked by the Domain after querying MemoryObjectCache for a physical address using the cache method.

The PhysicallyAddressableUnit (PAU), is a machine-independent page descriptor associated with a MemoryObjectCache. Dirty and referenced bits are maintained in the PAUs by the MemoryObjectCache and are used in machine independent paging algorithms. The PageFrameAllocator manages physical memory page allocation and has allocate and free methods. PAUs corresponding to free pages that are not in use by any MemoryObject-Cache are kept in the PageFrameAllocator.

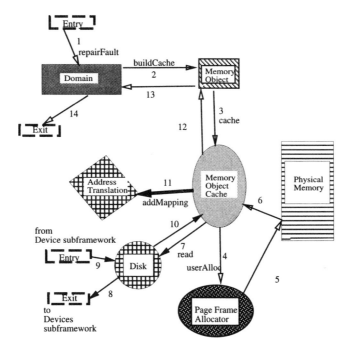

Figure 13.27
Flow of control through the Virtual Memory System

Flow of Control through Virtual Memory System   The most important control flow path in the system occurs during a page fault. We describe the processing of a page fault in detail in this section. A page fault involves the following flow of control. [3]

1. The faulting Domain's repairFault method is invoked.

2. The domain locates the MemoryObject that corresponds to the faulting address. It then invokes the buildCache method on that MemoryObject. This method makes a new MemoryObjectCache.

---

[3]We have omitted the flow of control when a page has to be paged out to make room for the new page

3. The MemoryObject invokes the cache method on the MemoryObjectCache, passing it the AddressTranslation of the faulting Domain.

4. The MemoryObjectCache invokes userAlloc on the PageFrameAllocator to get a new page.

5. The PageFrameAllocator consults physical memory.

6. A space is freed in physical memory for the new page. A new PAU is acquired and returned to the MemoryObjectCache.

7. The MemoryObjectCache asks the Disk for the page by invoking the read method on it.

8. The control flow enters the Device subframework to acquire the page.

9. The control flow returns from the Device with the new page from the physical device.

10. The page is given to the MemoryObjectCache.

11. The MemoryObject then invokes the addMapping method on the AddressTranslation passing the new PAU as a parameter. The AddressTranslation then makes this range of addresses accessible with the appropriate protection rights to the faulting domain.

12. Control returns to the MemoryObject.

13. Control returns to the Domain.

14. The faulting process is resumed.

The *Choices* **Framework and Virtual Memory**   The virtual memory framework interfaces to many of the other subsystems in *Choices* through the protocols it inherits from the *Choices* framework. The Domain provides an interface through which System-Processes manipulate virtual memory. The MemoryObject allows the memory mapping and caching of many different data stores, supports sharing, and allows policies and mechanisms involved in paging to be customized for a specific region of virtual memory.

13.8   Persistent Storage

The *Choices* persistent storage framework[16] introduces a hierarchy of classes that can be combined to build both standard and customized storage systems. It is flexible enough to efficiently support both persistent storage systems and traditional file systems[23].

Components   The framework contains the following major components:

1. The PersistentStore
   stores and retrieves blocks of persistent data and has random access methods. A PersistentStore is a subclass of MemoryObject.

2. The PersistentObject
   encapsulates and provides an operational interface to the data managed by a persistent data store.

3. The Persistent Store Container

divides the contents of a PersistentStore into an indexed collection of nested, smaller PersistentStores (i.e. a collection of Files). The PersistentStoreContainer shares storage devices by dividing a PersistentStore into smaller ones. Its methods create, make accessible, and delete these nested PersistentStores. PersistentStoreContainers supports the multiple levels of storage management in the framework and can be nested to an arbitrary depth. The PersistentStoreContainer in the lowest layer divides a disk into several partitions. The PersistentStoreContainer in the next layer subdivides partitions into logical storage for various types of files.

4. The Block Allocator

manages the allocation of the PersistentStores within a PersistentStoreContainer. In particular, it keeps track of which data blocks are currently allocated to a PersistentStore and which blocks are free. Subclasses encapsulate various mechanisms to manage block allocation, including free-lists or bit-maps.

5. The Persistent Store Dictionary

maps symbolic names to the indices used by PersistentStoreContainers. The indices may be used to refer unambiguously to the contents of a PersistentStore. While Files must be contained in exactly one container, they can be named by several dictionaries. Within any dictionary, the keys must be unique, but several keys may map to the same logical name.

6. The Persistent Array, Record File, and Autoload Persistent Objects

are three different models for structuring the data within files: as arrays of bytes or words (defined by subclasses of PersistentArray), as collections of records (defined by subclasses of PersistentRecordFile), and as data structures encapsulated by persistent objects (defined by subclasses of AutoloadPersistentObject).

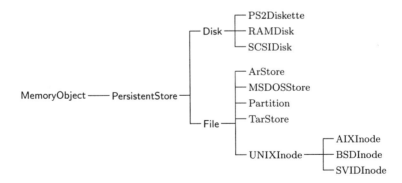

Figure 13.28
Persistent Store Class Hierarchy

Architecture Overview   The persistent storage system has the following class hierarchies and relationships between its abstract classes. The persistent storage framework
categorizes most persistent data into two fundamental classes: PersistentStores and PersistentObjects shown in Figure 13.28 and Figure 13.29, respectively. A PersistentStore
provides random access to an uninterpreted sequence of blocks of data while a PersistentObject interprets the data as having a format. For example, a UNIX inode is a
PersistentStore, while a UNIX directory is a PersistentObject. A disk is a PersistentStore,
but a table of descriptors for the files stored on a disk is a PersistentObject. All PersistentStores have the same interface, much of which is inherited from MemoryObject, but
the interfaces of different subclasses of PersistentObject differ greatly.

The concept of a PersistentStore is used both for physical and logical storage devices,
allowing reuse of code. The concrete subclasses of PersistentStore, shown in Figure 13.28,
belong to one of two categories represented by the following subclasses:

- Disks that encapsulate physical storage devices like hard disk drives, floppy disk drives,
  and RAM disks. Disks communicate with objects in the I/O subsystem.

- Files that encapsulate logical storage devices like UNIX inodes and disk partitions.
  Each file has a source PersistentStore that supplies it with data from a lower level of
  the file system. Files provide a *window* into their source PersistentStore. The size of
  this window can be fixed or variable and can range from zero up to the size of the
  source PersistentStore. The window can be contiguous or divided into discontiguous
  regions of blocks. Ultimately, the data read from and written to a File is also read
  from and written to a Disk.

The PersistentObject class defines objects that encapsulate and provide operations on
the data managed by a persistent store. Subclasses of PersistentObject, shown in Figure 13.29, abstract the organization, sharing, naming, and data structuring properties of
the persistent storage framework.

Figure 13.29
Persistent Object Class Hierarchy

A user Domain must have one or more FileSystemInterfaces to access persistent storage.
The FileSystemInterface allows the process to open zero or more PersistentObjects which
include RecordStreams and to examine the contents of one or more PersistentStoreDictionaries. Multiple processes in the same Domain may share the same FileSystemInterface.

The middle layer contains PersistentStoreDictionaries, PersistentArrays, and PersistentRecordFiles that structure the data that can be accessed through Files and Persistent-
StoreContainers.

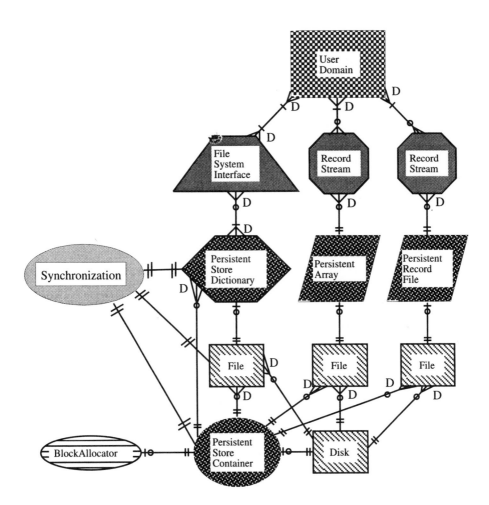

Figure 13.30
Abstract class relationships for the Persistent Storage System

PersistentArrays give read/write access to bytes of data and PersistentRecordFiles give read/write access to variable or fixed length records. Each RecordStream user interface has either a corresponding PersistentArray or PersistentRecordFile. A PersistentArray or PersistentRecordFile may be opened and shared by many different RecordStreams, some of which may have been opened by processes in different Domains.

The lowest layer contains Files, PersistentStoreContainers, BlockAllocators, and Disks. Each File has a PersistentStoreContainer and a Disk. PersistentStoreDictionaries access a PersistentStoreContainer as part of the implementation of opening a storage object and access dictionary information that is stored in a File. The classes in this layer have concrete subclasses which, for example, format physical data on disk as a System V UNIX file system. In this case, the File would behave like a System V UNIX inode, the PersistentStoreContainer would behave like a System V UNIX inode system, and the Disk would behave like a disk partition.

Design Overview Some of the more important methods of the file system classes are as follows. PersistentStores provide access to raw data, but other interfaces are also needed to satisfy the requirements of the clients of a file system. Some examples include: a container, which treats the data as a collection of files; a dictionary, which treats the data as a collection of file names; and a record file, which treats the data as a collection of records. Subclasses of PersistentObject define these and other customized interfaces to a PersistentStore's data. The PersistentObject class and its abstract subclasses provide methods that control the activation and deactivation of persistent objects, how these objects are mapped into memory, and how they are garbage collected. Each PersistentStore has an associated PersistentObject class that provides a data abstraction and encapsulation of the persistent data in the store. At run-time, there is a one-to-one correspondence between an instance of a PersistentStore and its associated PersistentObject.

The PersistentStore asA method returns a reference to the store's PersistentObject. If the PersistentObject has not yet been instantiated, the method instantiates the object by mapping the store's data into memory. The PersistentObject encapsulates this data as its state data. The PersistentStore thus provides the underlying data for its associated PersistentObject. PersistentObjects and their underlying PersistentStores provide the foundation for the *Choices* persistent storage framework. They implement *object-oriented* access to persistent data using the asA method (see [6]).

Several file system clients may access the same persistent data. To provide data consistency for concurrent updates to persistent data through the methods of a persistent object, the PersistentStore ensures that there is, at maximum, only one instance of its associated PersistentObject. When a PersistentObject is no longer needed in primary memory, its finalization code calls the close method on its underlying PersistentStore to inform the PersistentStore that it is also no longer needed in primary memory. A further asA request will instantiate a new PersistentObject that uses the existing persistent data.

PersistentStores also provide methods to report the size of their blocks and records and to report and set their length in both blocks and records. Block and record sizes are given as numbers of bytes. In general, records may span blocks.

The major methods supported by PersistentStoreContainers are create, open, and close. The create method returns a newly created File. The open method takes an index as an argument and returns the corresponding File. The close method informs a Persistent-StoreContainer that a currently open File is no longer being used by any other object in the system.

Files whose size can change, e.g. those that represent variable-length files, use the allocate and free methods of BlockAllocators to request and release the blocks of storage. Allocate reserves a block of storage and returns its index, and free releases a block of storage that is no longer needed.

Naming is orthogonal to storage organization. Using symbolic names, PersistentStores can be opened from, created in, added to, and removed from PersistentStoreDictionaries. The open method takes a key as an argument and returns the named PersistentStore. It obtains the PersistentStore by invoking the open method on its PersistentStoreContainer using the id-number that corresponds to the key. Two methods, create and add, allow PersistentStores to be added to dictionaries. The create method performs the same function as open for existing keys; if the key does not exist, however, the operation creates and returns a new PersistentStore. The add method takes a symbolic key and a PersistentStore as arguments. It inserts the key and the id-number of the PersistentStore into the dictionary. The remove method deletes a mapping from a key to an id-number.

Concurrent access to PersistentStoreDictionaries, PersistentStoreContainer and Files is mediated by the Synchronization class. A detailed description of the application interface is given in [6]. We provide a brief description here. A FileSystemInterface object unifies the name-spaces provided by PersistentStoreDictionaries by parsing sequences of symbolic keys, called *pathnames*, and resolving them to PersistentObjects. The public methods of the FileSystemInterface are similar to several UNIX system calls including: open, stat, link, unlink, mkdir, and chdir. These methods manipulate or return references to RecordStreams, PersistentObjects, or PersistentStores.

Subclasses of the RecordStream class provide stream-oriented application interfaces for both PersistentArrays and PersistentRecordFiles. RecordStreams provide the concept of a *current file position*, i.e. the location within the file where the next read or write will occur. Each instance of RecordStream gets data from or sends data to an underlying PersistentObject.

Control Flow through the Persistent Storage System   In this section, we describe the flow of control between the objects in the Persistent Storage subframework that occurs when opening and reading a RecordStream. The flow of control for these two important operations is shown in Figure 13.31.

The solid lines show the flow for the open, and the dashed lines show the flow for the read.

1. The ApplicationProcess invokes the open operation on the FileSystemInterface giving it two arguments. The first argument is the symbolic name of the object that will be opened; the second argument is the name of a class that presents the interface required by the application program. In this example a PersistentArray is opened, and the RecordStream class is used as the interface, since the application program will use its sequential read operation.

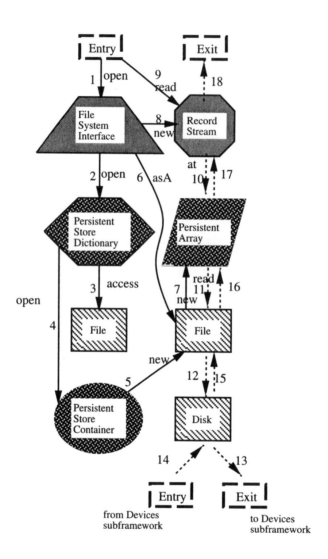

Figure 13.31
Flow control diagram for the Persistent Storage System

2. The FileSystemInterface then invokes the open operation on the PersistentStoreDictionary passing the symbolic name as an argument.

3. The access for rights for the File that contains the underlying data for the directory are then checked.

4. If the access check succeeds, the dictionary determines the idNumber corresponding to the named object. It then invokes the open operation of its PersistentStoreContainer, passing it the idNumber.

5. The PersistentStoreContainer creates a File object to manage the data that corresponds to the idNumber.

6. The FileSystemInterface then invokes the asA operation on the File to turn it into a PersistentArray. This is what the ApplicationProcess interacts with.

7. The File creates a PersistentArray object that provides a character array interface to the data of the File.

8. Then the FileSystemInterface creates a RecordStream object, passing it the PersistentArray object. Finally, the RecordStream is returned to the application.

9. The ApplicationProcess performs a read on the RecordStream specifying the number of bytes it wants to retrieve.

10. The RecordStream then invokes the method at on the PersistentArray, providing both the *offset* within the array and the number of bytes to be retrieved.

11. If the PersistentArray does not have the data cached, it invokes the method read on the File to retrieve the blocks of the file that would satisfy the request.

12. The File invokes read on the Disk after mapping its logical block numbers to the physical block numbers of the Disk.

13. The control flow enters the Device subframework to acquire the data from the physical disk.

14. The control flow returns from the Device with the data from the physical device.

15. The data is returned to the ApplicationProcess in steps 15, 16, 17, and 18. The data also will be cached by the PersistentArray.

The *Choices* Framework and the Persistent Storage Framework   The persistent storage framework interfaces to all the other *Choices* subsystems through the protocols it inherits from the MemoryObject. The MemoryObject allows physical and logical storage like disks and files to be used interchangeably, allowing redirection. This framework may be concurrently composed with Message Passing subframework. It is sequentially composed with the Device subframework.

13.9   Device Management

The I/O architecture of *Choices* allows a Process to communicate with peripheral devices. Several different I/O devices were examined before a set of abstract classes were designed

to provide a uniform interface for device management. Although the *Choices* device
drivers were influenced by those of UNIX, there are some notable differences. First,
Choices devices drivers have an object-oriented design. Second, the device management
subframework does not use the file system for naming nor does it use the file system
interface.

Components   The device management subframework of *Choices* has the following major components:

1. The Device

   acts as a server for components of other *Choices* subframeworks. For example, the
   concrete class DiskDevice acts as a server of the classes of the file system subframework.
   In turn, most of the Devices act as clients of DevicesController objects. For instance,
   two DiskDevices representing disks attached to the same hardware controller act as
   clients of the same DiskController.

2. The DevicesControllers

   represent hardware I/O controllers. A DevicesController acts as a server for possibly several Devices. A DevicesController is not visible to the user of a device. I/O
   operations should only be requested from a Device.

3. The DevicesManager

   supports the addition and removal of devices and controllers. Each system has only
   one object of this class. When a DevicesController is loaded into the system it registers
   itself with the DevicesManager object. Hardware controllers and devices that are
   added to the system are also registered with the DevicesManager. In addition, for each
   physical device a Device is constructed and returned when the method attachDevice
   is invoked on the DevicesController. The new Device is then bound to the NameServer.

Architectural Overview   The device system class hierarchy and the relationships between its abstract classes are described in this section. The class hierarchies of the device
management system are shown in Figure 13.32. These hierarchies show the abstract and
concrete classes of the device management subframework. The class hierarchies show
subclasses of Devices and DevicesController for handling disks and character devices such
as keyboards and serial lines.

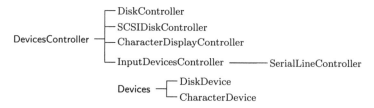

Figure 13.32
Device Management Class Hierarchies

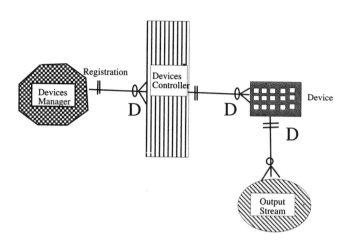

Figure 13.33
Abstract Class Relationship diagram for the Device Managment subframework

Figure 13.33 is an abstract class relationship diagram for the device management subframework. DeviceControllers register themselves on creation with a DeviceManager and are associated with one DeviceManager. The DeviceControllers associated with the DeviceManager change dynamically. There is a DeviceController for each type of device. A DeviceController controls a group of Devices of the same type. A class of Devices may be used with more than one class of DevicesControllers, and are thus highly reusable. A Device may be dynamically used with different DevicesControllers. User Processes interact with Devices which translate the user commands to controller specific commands. As a result, Devices may need to perform buffering between the user Process and a particular DevicesController. High level object such as OutputStream interact with devices. A particular OutputStream is associated with only one Device at a time, but an OutputStream may have different Devices at different times. There may be more than one OutputStream associated with the same Device.

Design Overview The more important methods of the Device management subsystem classes are described in this section. The protocol of a Device depends on the physical device it represents. For instance, DiskDevices have read and write methods that transfer a number of disk blocks. On the other hand, a CharacterDevice has additional methods to transfer strings of characters, such as stringArrived, and control methods such as setBaudRate to set control parameters. When a newly created concrete subclass of Device is created it is bound to a NameServer. Processes may access this device after looking it up in the NameServer. An appropriate interface to Devices may be chosen by invoking the asA on Devices. This is often necessary since the default interface to Devices may be of too low a level. Because Devices act as intermediaries between higher level I/O objects and the DeviceControllers, they need to buffer input and output requests to peripheral devices.

Devices and a DevicesControllers interact by exchanging Command objects. Requests for reads and writes on Devices cause the construction of one or more Commands which are then sent to a DevicesController object using the sendCommand method. There is an extensive class hierarchy of Commands. Examples of Commands include, FlushOutputCommand, to flush output to a character device, and setParityCommand to set the parity on a serial line. The Command based interface is very flexible for two reasons. The first is that a Device can be reused with different DevicesControllers. For example, a DiskDevice can be used as the Device of a machine-dependent DiskController and a machine-independent SCSIDiskController. The second advantage of this interface is that it does not force a DevicesController to have a specific interface that depends on its devices. The protocol of a DevicesController subclass can change without requiring a change to existing Devices.

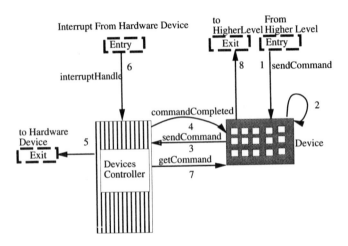

Figure 13.34
Control Flow Graph for the Device Managment Subframework

Control Flow Through the Device Management Subframework Devices are often used by higher level classes to perform input and output. For example, OuputStream may use a CharacterDevice for printing characters on the screen. The file system may use DiskDevices for accessing files on disk. The Device has three responsibilities: it accepts commands from higher layers (other subframeworks), it receives input for higher layers (other subframeworks) from a DevicesController and it may queue commands for a DevicesController. In the control flow graph of Figure 13.34 we show a typical output command.

1. A higher level subframework invokes the sendCommand method on a Device.

2. If the Device is busy the command is queued.

3. Otherwise, it is sent to the DevicesController using the sendCommand method of the DevicesController.

4. The DevicesController may ask for additional information from the Device by invoking the getCommand method on the Device.

5. The DevicesController initiates a hardware dependent transfer.

6. When an interrupt from a hardware device occurs the interruptHandle of the DevicesController is invoked.

7. DevicesController then invokes the commandCompleted method on the Device. It then polls the other Devices for further commands by invoking the getCommand method on all the Devices.

8. The Device returns the data to the higher level subframework.

The *Choices* **Framework and Device Management**   Other subframeworks use the Device Management subframework with the help of classes that provide communication between the two subframeworks. For instance, a Disk is a PersistentStore that does Input/Output using a DiskDevice. Devices are converted to objects in other hierarchies using the *Choices* conversion mechanism. The Device subframework may be sequentially composed with the Persistent Storage, Virtual Memory and Message Passing subframeworks.

13.10   Programming Model

Choices is an object-oriented operating system that has an object oriented interface for application programming. In this section, we describe the application interface for writing concurrent object oriented applications. As we have already noted, hypercube applications can be supported on *Choices* without any changes to the application. There are five aspects to writing parallel applications in *Choices*.

1. The Process interface: basic unit of concurrency.

2. The NameServer interface: locating and sharing objects.

3. The Message Passing interface: sending and receiving structured messages.

4. The Shared Memory interface: sharing memory between processes.

5. The Synchronization interface: synchronizing processes.

13.10.1   Process Interface

Processes are created by calling the appropriate constructor shown in Figure 13.35. All constructors require the entryPoint parameter, which is a pointer to the function that will be executed when the Process runs. arg1 and arg2 are the arguments to be passed to the entryPoint function when the new Process begins execution. When the Process returns from the function, it will automatically be terminated. The domain parameter specifies the Domain that should be used for running the Process. The first ApplicationProcess

```
SystemProcess (PFV entryPoint, Domain *domain, StackSize stackSize,
      int arg1)
PreemptableSystemProcess (PFV entryPoint, Domain *domain, StackSize
      stackSize, int arg1)
InterruptProcess (PFV entryPoint, Domain *domain, StackSize
      stackSize, int arg1)
ApplicationProcess (PFV entryPoint, int arg1 = 0,
      char ** arg2 = 0, StackSize userStackSize = normal)
ApplicationProcess (PFV entryPoint, Domain *domain, int arg1,
      int arg2, StackSize userStackSize = normal)
ApplicationProcess (PFV entryPoint, Domain *domain, int arg1,
      int arg2, char *userStackPointer)
PerCPUIdleProcess (PFV entryPoint, Domain *domain, StackSize
      stackSize, int arg1)
```

Figure 13.35
Process constructors

constructor, which does not have a domain parameter, assumes that the current Domain
will be used for executing the new ApplicationProcess. The parameters stackSize and
userStackSize specify the sizes of the kernel and user stacks, respectively, for use by the
new Process.

The third ApplicationProcess constructor is different from the other two in that it does
not create a user stack for the new Process. Instead, it uses the memory region pointed
by userStackPointer as the user stack.

Application programs are not permitted to create any type of Processes except ApplicationProcesses. Only the first two ApplicationProcess constructors are exported to
application programs. The first constructor is typically used by an application program
to create a lightweight Process, while the second constructor is used by the application
dispatcher library to dispatch heavyweight Processes.

None of the Process constructors add the newly-created Process to the System Scheduler — the programmer should do so explicitly. This is done by calling ready. The Process
will be added to the System Scheduler and will be executed at a time as determined by
the scheduling policy. When a Process is running, the Process may terminate itself by
calling die.

The utility function thisProcess() returns a pointer to the Process that is currently
running. The domain method is used to return a pointer to the Domain in which the
Process is running. The relinquishProcessor method may be called to give up the processor
voluntarily to the next Process waiting in the System Scheduler. The Process that called
relinquishProcessor is put back into the System Scheduler.

The function createAndRunProcess() in Figure 13.36 shows how a kernel programmer
may create a PreemptableSystemProcess that displays a message on the console and terminates itself. Note that the program will work correctly even when the call to die is
omitted; the new Process will terminate properly when it exits printMessageAndDie().

13.10.2   NameServer Interface

Objects are registered with a NameServer. Each Domain has a NameServer associated with
it and there is a NameServer in the kernel for all application running on the same machine.

```
void printMessageAndDie (int input)
{
    /* pring on console */
    Console () ≪ "Input is " ≪ input ≪ "\n" ≪ eor;
    thisProcess () → die ();
}

void createAndRunProcess ()
{
    /* Create a Process that will run the function * printMessageAndDie() with
argument 42. The new process
        * will run in the same Domain (i.e. the kernel Domain) as the current
Process. */
    Process* process = new PreemptableSystemProcess
        ((PFV) printMessageAndDie, thisProcess () → domain (),
            normal, 42);
    /* Add the new Process to the SystemScheduler. */
    process → ready ();
}
```

Figure 13.36
Creating and running a PreemptableSystemProcess

Each application gets a pointer to the StandardNameServer which is the NameServer in the applications Domain.

Access to objects is obtained by looking them up the appropriate NameServer. In general, each subframework provides a specialized name service that is appropriate for the functionality it provides. For example, applications intending to use the file service usually query the StandardNameServer for the FileSystemInterface. The application will then interact with the FileSystemInterface to open and create files. Similarly, the MessageSystemInterface and the DistributedNameServer may be obtained from the StandardNameServer to obtain naming facilities for message passing.

Figure 13.37 shows the methods of the StandardNameServer.

Interface Protocol of the Name Server Object		
return value	method name	paramaters
Object	lookup	const char *, Class *
const ProxiableObject *	bind	const char*,const ProxiableObject *, int * shared)
void	unbind	const char *
void	unbind	const ProxiableObject*
void	alias	const char * , const char *
int	mount	const char * , NameServer *
int	unmount	const char *

Figure 13.37
The StandardNameServer Interface

13.10.3 Message Passing Interface

In section 13.6 we defined the structure of the kernel subsystem that supports application message passing. In this section, we describe the application interface for message passing.

Choices provides a rich set of message types for communication including asynchronous sends/receives and synchronous sends/receives. These message types may be used to build most desired types of protocols for communicating between processes. The class hierarchies of these message are shown in Figure 13.38. The interface protocols for these message are shown in Tables 13.39, 13.40 and 13.41. Table 13.39 shows the basic primitives for asynchronous message sends, Table 13.40 shows the basic primitives for synchronous communication and Table 13.41 shows the primitives for communication that allows asynchronous receives. These message management classes use Message-Containers and ContainerRepresentatives to perform the communication. As described in section 13.6 MessageContainers and ContainerRepresentatives are kernel protected entities.

Applications may choose to develop their own subclasses of these basic message classes. They may not, however, alter the semantics of the basic communication entities such as MessageContainer and ContainerRepresentatives since these are located in the kernel.

These basic facilities may be used to develop abstract protocol interfaces. Concrete subclasses will be used to develop specific implementations. The communicating entities do not need to know about the specific abstract class used by the each other.

```
           ┌─ SyncMessage
Message ──┤
           └─ AsyncRMessage ───── iPSCMessage
```

Figure 13.38
Message Class hierarchies for communication

Concrete subclasses will provide different implementations of the protocol. The sender and receiver may have different protocols. For each protocol, a new abstract type must be created. Therefore sender and receiver may actually use different concrete subclasses. A wide range of protocols may be built using this technique. As long as the abstract interface is preserved any two entities may communicate.

13.10.4 Shared Memory Interface

Choices provides four separate mechanisms for sharing memory. First, Processes created in the same Domain share memory. Second, *Choices* provides a special method on Processes called clone that is similar to the traditional UNIX fork [3]. In this version all memory allocated from a shared memory allocator by a parent process is shared between all process related by a clone hierarchy (which is a series of parent/child clones). During the cloning process copies are made of all the memory objects in the original domain. All memory objects that are denoted as shared are mapped into the new Domain and not copied. The operator **new** may be overloaded to provide shared memory semantics. This means that the memory associated with this memory object will remain shared

Interface Protocol of an Asynchronous Message		
return value	method name	paramaters
constructor	Message	char* data, int size, int deldata =1
constructor	Message	int deldata=1
void	setReceivePort	MessageContainer *
void	setDestinationPort	ContainerRepresentative*
void	setSize	int
int	getSize	null
ContainerRepresentative *	getDestination	null
MessageContainer *	getReceiver	null
void	setData	char*
void	setUserData	char*,int
char *	getData	null
void	send	null
void	receive	null

Figure 13.39
Interface Protocol for Asynchronous sends and synchronous receives

Interface Protocol of a Synchronous Messages		
return value	method name	paramaters
–	MessageConstructor	char* data, int size, int deldata =1
–	MessageConstructor	int deldata=1
void	setReplyContainer	MessageContainer *
void	sync	null
void	reply	null
void	syncRecieve	null

Figure 13.40
Interface Protocol for synchronous sends and synchronous receives

Interface Protocol of an Asynchronous receives and sends		
return value	method name	paramaters
–	MessageConstructor	char* data, int size, int de ldata =1
–	MessageConstructor	int deldata=1
int	asyncRecv	null
int	probe	null
void	wait	null
int	done	null

Figure 13.41
Interface Protocol for asynchronous sends and asynchronous receives

upon cloning. Third, shared memory objects may be named and stored in the kernel NameServer. Processes unrelated by a cloning hierarchy may share these memory objects by adding them to their domain. These are all privileged operations that must be done in 'supervisor' mode. Fourth, Processes may use memory mapped PersistentObjects (similar to traditional UNIX memory mapped files) for sharing data. The difference between this mechanism and the third mechanism is that any changes to shared files in this option appear on disk, in files or persistent objects named explicitly by the sharing entities.

13.10.5 Synchronization Interface

Semaphores are created by calling the Semaphore constructor, passing the initial value of the Semaphore's counter as the argument. MutexSemaphore is a subclass of Semaphore whose internal counter is initially set to one. This semaphore is used for mutual exclusion.

GraciousSemaphore is a subclass of Semaphore that represents a type of Semaphore with a special property — when Process A is unblocked as a result of Process B calling the V method, Process A is resumed immediately (it is run immediately on the Processor) while Process B is put into the SystemScheduler for later execution. This is different from the semantics of regular Semaphores, which dictates that upon unblocking, Process A should be put into the SystemScheduler and Process B should continue to run.

To wait for a Process to terminate, the notifyUponCompletion method may be called by the kernel or application programmer. Suppose it is desired for Process A to wait for Process B to terminate. Process A may invoke the notifyUponCompletion method on B, passing a Semaphore as the argument. When B terminates, it will invoke the V method on the Semaphore. Therefore in order to wait for B, Process A should invoke the P method on the Semaphore, provided that the Semaphore has an initial count of 0.

All the types of synchronization classes described in section 13.5.1 are available to application programmers.

13.11 Examples

In this section, we describe two sample *Choices* applications. These applications highlight some of the features discussed in the last section on Programming in *Choices*. With the large set of functionality available in *Choices*, it is possible to experiment with different concurrent and communication paradigms. In particular, both shared memory and message passing may be combined to write parallel applications.[4]

The first example application shows how to set up two asymmetric Processes: a client and a server. Figure 13.42 shows the code for this application. In this example, the server process creates a MessageContainer which automatically registers it with the Distributed-NameServer. It then creates a Message specifying the size of the data and a user buffer pointer to the constructor of the Message. This application uses the basic message class for communication. This class supports asynchronous sends and synchronous receives. The server then invokes the receive on the message and blocks, waiting for its message request to be satisfied.

---

[4]The Message Passing system may use shared memory for local communication

```
/* Server Process */
serverProcess(int, char **)
{
DistributedNameServer *StandardDistributedNameServer =
          (DistributedNameServer *)(ProxiableObject *)StandardNameServer→
lookup("StandardDistributedNameServer", "DistributedNameServer");
MessageContainer *mport = new MessageContainer ("Server");
char * buf = new char[1024];
Message msg(buf,1024,0);
while(1) {
        msg.setReceivePort(mport);
        msg.setUserData(buf,1024);
        msg.receive();
        Console() ≪ " \n Received " ≪ (char *) msg.data() ≪ eor;
}
return 0;
}
int
main(int, char **) {
ProcessStar p = new ApplicationProcess(serverProcess);
p→setName( "#serverProcess");
p→ready();
}
/* Client Process */
clientProcess( int, char ** )
{
DistributedNameServer *StandardDistributedNameServer = (DistributedNameServer
*)(ProxiableObject *)StandardNameServer→
lookup("StandardDistributedNameServer", "DistributedNameServer");
ContainerRepresentative *myServer = StandardDistributedNameServer → lookup
("Server", "ContainerRepresentative");
Assert (myServer ≠ 0);
char programName [] = "MessagePassingDemo";
Message msg;
msg.setDestination (myServer);
msg.setSize (strlen (programName) + 1);
msg.setData (programName);
msg.send ();
}
int
main(int, char **) {
        ProcessStar p = new ApplicationProcess (clientProcess);
        p→setName( "#clientProcess");
        p→ready();
}
```

Figure 13.42
Asynchronous Message send and synchronous receive Example

```
/* Server Process*/
serverProcess(int, char **)
{
    DistributedNameServer *StandardDistributedNameServer =
            (DistributedNameServer *)(ProxiableObject *)StandardNameServer→
lookup("StandardDistributedNameServer", "DistributedNameServer");
        MessageContainer *mport = new MessageContainer ("Server");
        char * buf = new char[1024];
        SyncMessage msg(buf,1024,0);
        while(1) {
                msg.setReceivePort(mport);
                msg.setUserData(buf,1024);
                msg.rpcRecieve();/* wait for message*/
                Console() ≪ " Received " ≪ (char *) msg.data() ≪ "\n"≪ eor;
                strcpy(buf,"thanks");
                msg.setUserData(buf,strlen(buf) +1);
                msg.reply(); /*Send reply to the client*/
        }
        return 0;
}

int
main(int, char **) {
        ProcessStar p = new ApplicationProcess(serverProcess);
        p→setName( "#serverProcess");
        p→ready();
}

/* Client Process */
clientProcess( int, char ** )
{
    DistributedNameServer *StandardDistributedNameServer = (DistributedNameServer
*)(ProxiableObject *)StandardNameServer→
lookup("StandardDistributedNameServer", "DistributedNameServer");
        ContainerRepresentative *Server = StandardDistributedNameServer → lookup
("Server", "ContainerRepresentative");
    MessageContainer *recport = new MessageContainer ("Client");
        char * buf = new char[1024];
        SyncMessage rmsg(buf,1024,0);
        rmsg.setReplyPort(recport);
        rmsg.setDestination(Server);
        strcpy(buf,"SYNCdemo");
        rmsg.setUserData (buf,strlen (buf) + 1);
        rmsg.rpc();/* block until reply is in buffer*/
}
int
main(int, char **) {
        ProcessStar p = new ApplicationProcess (clientProcess);
        p→setName( "#clientProcess");
        p→ready();
}
```

Figure 13.43
Synchronous message and and receive Example

The client application asks the DistributedNameServer for a ContainerRepresentative for the name "Server". It creates a Message, sets the destination to the ContainerRepresentative it received from DistributedNameServer. It sets the size of the message by invoking the method setSize, which allocates memory of the requested size. The subsequent call to setData will copy the application's buffer to a library buffer. When the client invokes the send method, the message moves down to the network driver and is sent. When the message arrives at the server the receive method returns and the server can inspect the buffer of its message for client data.

In the second example application, shown in Figure 13.43, a client sends a message to a server but also passes a reply port in the message it sends. The server uses this to send a reply to the client. The server does not need to explicitly locate a MessageRepresentative to communicate with the client.

13.12   Conclusions

In this paper, we have described the design of a parallel object-oriented operating system that is capable of supporting highly parallel applications. We have discussed the *Choices* model of concurrency and communication, and how it has been used to design operating system services as well as applications. Our experience has shown that the use of an object-oriented framework is an effective technique for designing complex parallel software systems such as an operating system. In particular, the use of entity relation diagrams and flow graphs along with refinement techniques are extremely useful for documenting the design of an object-oriented operating system. We have also shown how a framework for a system can be used to help design the subframeworks required for subsystems. Parts of the framework are refined and specialized for the subframework. Refinement rules specify how the concrete implementations of each subframework are constrained. The use of an object-oriented prgramming language to design an operating system does not seem to the adversely affect the performance of the operating system [23, 13].

Acknowledgements   We would like to thank Peter Madany of SunLabs for his help in preparing the section on the Persistent Storage subframework. Many people have been involved in the coding of *Choices* including Vince Russo, Aamod Sane, David Raila and Panayotis Kougioris. We would like to thank Amitabh Dave and Svend Frolund for reading this paper.

References

[1]   Gul Agha. *ACTORS: A Model of Concurrent Computation in Distributed Systems*. MIT Press, Cambridge,Massachusetts, 1986.

[2]   Alfred Aho, Ravi Sethi, and Jeffrey Ullman. *Compilers, Principles, Techniques and Tools*. Addison Wesley, Reading,Massachusetts, 1987.

[3]   Maurice J. Bach. *The Design of the UNIX Operating System*. Prentice Hall, Englewood Cliffs, New Jersey, 1986.

[4]   Andrew D. Birell and Bruce J. Nelson. Implementing Remote Procedure Calls. In *ACM Transactions on computer systems*, February 1984.

[5]   31 Roy H. Campbell and Nayeem Islam. A Technique for Documenting the Framework of an Object-Oriented System. In *Second International Workshop on Object-Orientation in Operating Systems*, Paris, France, October 1992. IEEE Computer Society Press.

[6]   Roy H. Campbell, Nayeem Islam, and Peter Madany. *Choices*, Frameworks and Refinement. *Computing Systems*, 5(3), 1992.

[7]   David Cheriton. Problem Oriented Shared Memory: A Decentralised Approach to Distributed System Design. *6th International Conference on Distributed Computing Systems*, 1986.

[8]   David Cheriton. The V Distributed System. *Communications of the ACM*, pages 314–334, 1988.

[9]   A. Goscinski. *Distributed Operating Systems: The Logical Design*. Addison-Wesley, Sydney, Australia, 1991.

[10]   Nayeem Islam and Roy H. Campbell. "Uniform Co-Scheduling Using Object-Oriented Design Techniques" . In *International Conference on Decentralized and Distributed Systems*, Palma de Mallorca, Spain, September 1993.

[11]   Nayeem Islam and Roy Campbell. Design Considerations for Shared Memory Multiprocessor Message Systems. Technical Report UIUCDCS-R-91-1764, University of Illinois Urbana-Champaign, December 1991.

[12]   Nayeem Islam and Roy H. Campbell. " Reusable Data flow diagrams". Technical Report UIUCDCS-R-92-1770, University of Illinois Urbana-Champaign, Urbana, Illinois, November 1992.

[13]   Nayeem Islam and Roy H. Campbell. "Design Considerations for Shared Memory Multiprocessor Message Systems". In *IEEE Transactions on Parallel and Distributed Systems*, pages 702–711, November 1992.

[14]   Glen E. Krasner and Stephen T. Pope. A Cookbook for Using the Model-View-Controller Paradigm in Smalltalk-80. *Journal of Object-Oriented Programming*, pages 26–49, 1988.

[15]   Peter Madany, Nayeem Islam, Panayotis Kougiouris, and Roy H. Campbe ll. "Practical Examples of Reification an d Reflection in C++". In *International Workshop on Reflection and MetaLevel Architecture*, November 1992.

[16]   Peter W. Madany. *An Object-Oriented Framework for File Systems*. PhD thesis, Department of Computer Science, University of Illinois at Urbana-Champaign, June 1992.

[17]   H. Miyata, T. Isonishi, and A. Iwase. Fast Fourier Transformation using Cellular Array Processor. In *Parallel Processing Symposium JSPP 1989*, pages 297–304, February 1989.

[18]   James L. Peterson and Abraham Silberschatz. *Operating System Concepts*. Addison-Wesley, Reading, Massachusetts, 1985.

[19]   Rob Pike, Dave Presotto, Ken Thompson, and Gerard Holzmann. Process sleep and wakeup on a shared-memory multiprocessor. In *Proc. Spring EurOpen Conf.*, pages 161–166, Tromsø, Norway, May 1991.

[20]   Roger Pressman. *Software Engineering*. McGraw Hill, New York, New York, 1987.

[21]   Richard Rashid. Threads of a New System. *UNIX Review*, 1986.

[22]   Vincent F. Russo. *An Object-Oriented Operating System*. PhD thesis, University of Illinois at Urbana-Champaign, October 1990.

[23]   Vincent F. Russo, Peter W. Madany, and Roy H. Campbell. C++ and Operating Systems Performance: A Case Study. In *Proceedings of the USENIX C++ Conference*, pages 103–114, San Francisco, California, April 1990.

[24]   Bjarne Stroustrup. *The C++ Programming Language*. Addison-Wesley, Reading, Massachusetts, 1986.

[25]   Craig B. Stunkel. Linear Optimization via Message-Based Parallel Processing. In *Proceedings of 1988 International Conference on Parallel Processing*, pages 264–271, August 1988.

[26]   John M. Vlissides and Mark Linton. Unidraw: A Framework for Building Domain-Specific Graphical Editors. In *User Interface Software Technologies*, pages 81–94. ACM SIGGRAPH/SIGCHI, 1989.

[27]   Yasuhiko Yokote, Atsushi Mitsuzawa, Nobuhisa Fujinami, and Mario Tokoro. Reflective Object

Management in the Muse Operating System. In *International Workshop in Object Orientation in Operating Systems*, pages 16–23, Palo Alto, California, October 1991.

[28] Yasuhiko Yokote and Mario Tokoro. Concurrent Programming in ConcurrentSmalltalk. In Akinori Yonezawa and Mario Tokoro, editors, *Object-Oriented Concurrent Programming*, pages 129–158. MIT Press, 1987.

14 COSMOS: An Operating System for a Fine-Grain Concurrent Computer*

Waldemar Horwat, Brian Totty, and William J. Dally

COSMOS [9] is an operating system for the J-Machine, a fine-grain message-passing concurrent computer [3]. COSMOS provides a global virtual namespace, object-based memory management, support for distributed objects, and low-overhead context switching. Its memory management system provides fast, transparent access to storage distributed across the machine. COSMOS is designed to efficiently support fine-grain concurrent computation where tasks are very short (32 user instructions) and data objects are very small (8 words) on machines with up to 64K processing nodes. It is tailored for an environment where local computation is inexpensive. Communication bandwidth and memory capacity are the limiting resources.

COSMOS provides a shared global name space across the nodes of a message-passing concurrent computer. In COSMOS, all data and code are stored in objects. Each object is assigned a unique global ID that can be used to reference the object from any node. Objects are free to migrate between nodes to balance load or to exploit locality. The system supports distributed objects [10]. A distributed object is a single object that has its data distributed across many nodes of the machine.

To handle the short tasks typical of fine-grain computation, COSMOS provides a set of fast task management services. Using the hardware task scheduling and dispatching mechanisms of the message-driven processor (MDP) [6], creating a task, suspending a task, resuming a task, and destroying a task each require between four and sixty instructions. This quick task management is provided without sacrificing protection. Each task executes in its own addressing environment.

COSMOS is implemented in 3500 lines of MDP assembly code taking 1.5K words of storage on each node of a multicomputer. It has been running on a simulated multicomputer since May 1989 and on small J-Machines since Fall 1991. Although the task management services are quick in absolute terms, they are also heavily used by the fine-grain user programs; initial performance measurements indicate that the average fine-grain program spends 25% of its time in the COSMOS kernel. This ratio is acceptable because local computation is inexpensive compared to the costs of communication and memory.

Keywords: Operating systems, Memory management, Process management, Concurrent computers, Parallel computers, Message-passing, Multicomputers, Multiprocessors, Shared memory.

14.1 Introduction

14.1.1 Fine-Grain Computing

Fine-grain concurrent computers such as the MIT J-Machine [3] offer the potential of large speedups and improved cost/performance for many demanding problems. These machines also present several challenges to the operating system that are not met by conventional systems technology. The operating system for a fine-grain machine must handle many short tasks that are switched frequently and many small objects that must

*The research described in this paper was supported in part by the Defense Advanced Research Projects Agency under contracts N00014-88K-0738 and N00014-87K-0825, in part by a National Science Foundation Presidential Young Investigator Award, grant MIP-8657531, with matching funds from General Electric Corporation and IBM Corporation, and in part by an ONR fellowship.

be independently relocated and protected. These services must be provided in an environment where the costs differ considerably from those of a sequential computer.

The *grain size* of a program refers to the size of the tasks, objects, and messages that make up the program. Coarse-grain programs have a few long ($\approx 10^5$ instruction) tasks, while fine-grain programs have many short (≈ 10 to 100 instruction) tasks. With more tasks that can execute at a given time, fine-grain programs theoretically result in faster solutions than coarse-grain programs.

To achieve the high levels of concurrency possible with fine-grain programs, heavy demands are placed on the operating system. In the Concurrent SmallTalk (CST) programming system, for example, 16 user instructions are executed between each task switch, and a new task is created every 32 user instructions. The average object size is 8 words and objects must be individually relocatable [9]. To simplify programming and debugging it is desirable to provide a separate protected address space for each task with tasks sharing access to objects when required. Both local and remote interprocess communication is very frequent, once every 16 user instructions, and very fast, $\approx 1\mu s$ average end-to-end latency.

The *grain size* of a machine refers to the physical size and the amount of memory in one processing node. A coarse-grain processing node requires tens or hundreds of chips (one or more boards) and has $\approx 10^8$ bits of memory while a fine-grain node fits on a few chips and has $\approx 10^6$ bits of memory. Fine-grain nodes cost less and have less memory than coarse-grain nodes; however, because so little silicon area is required to build a fast processor, they need not have slower processors than coarse-grain nodes.

Memory in a fine-grain machine is more expensive relative to processing than in a sequential computer. With several thousand processors, processor cycles are not the scarce resource they are in a machine with a small number of processors. Also, in a machine where both processors and memory are incrementally extensible, the relative cost of processor and memory approaches the ratio of the silicon area devoted to each. By this measure, one MIP of integer processor has the same *cost* as 10^5 bits of memory [3]. This ratio of memory to processor capacity is two orders of magnitude lower than the 10^7 bits/MIP typical of sequential computers and coarse-grained parallel machines. It is not that the memory is more expensive in a fine-grain machine, but rather that processing cycles are much less expensive since the fixed costs of the machine are amortized across a large number of processors. To operate efficiently, the operating system for a fine-grain machine should trade processing cycles for memory where possible to exploit the inexpensive processing cycles and conserve the relatively expensive memory. Moreover, once a computer gets large enough, communication becomes the most critical resource and must be conserved as well.

Sequential computer operating systems such as UNIX [13] are not matched to the needs of fine-grain computers. These systems have been tuned to handle sequential programs that execute 10^4 instructions between task switches, have relatively slow I/O, and handle memory in large pieces (e.g., 1K-word pages). They require thousands of instructions to create a task, and hundreds of instructions to context switch between tasks. Many parallel operating systems [15] [16] are variants of sequential operating systems with similar memory management and task management functions augmented with low-overhead (lightweight) tasks or send and receive system calls to pass messages between nodes. These extended sequential systems, while adequate for coarse-grained parallel computers, are not suited for supporting fine-grained concurrency. Other systems, such as Emerald [11] and Amber [1] provide an object-oriented parallel paradigm, but they also emphasize sequential performance at the expense of communication–remote function call times in Emerald are on the order of tens of milliseconds [11].

14.1.2 Background

COSMOS has been written as part of the J-Machine project at MIT [3]. It is based in part on an earlier J-Machine operating system called JOSS [17].

The J-Machine is a fine-grain, MIMD (Multiple-Instruction/Multiple-Data) concurrent computer that provides low-overhead primitive mechanisms for communication, synchronization, and translation. The hardware is an ensemble of up to 65,536 nodes (message-driven processors or MDPs), each containing a 36-bit processor, 260K 36-bit words of memory (4K on-chip and 256K off-chip), and a router. The nodes are connected by a high-speed (360Mbit/s) 3-D mesh network. The worst-case message travel time on an unloaded, 4096-node J-Machine is $2.4\mu s$. On message arrival, an MDP automatically writes the message into memory and creates and dispatches a task in $< 1\mu s$.

The MDPs operate on 36-bit words, which are comprised of 32 data bits and 4-bit tags. The tags distinguish among primitive data types such as integers, Booleans, virtual IDs, segment descriptors, instructions, futures and c-futures[1], and others and assist in protection and debugging. An MDP provides four general-purpose data registers and four sets of virtual ID/segment registers at each of three levels of priority (background, priority 0, and priority 1); COSMOS uses only priority 0, with the other levels reserved for debugging and custom applications. User code on an MDP can access memory only through bounds-checked segment descriptors. In addition to the usual core of instructions, the MDPs provide instructions to maintain a general-purpose associative cache, used by COSMOS to efficiently support a global virtual address space. For sending messages, the MDPs provide instructions to inject words into the network, which is more convenient and faster than setting up direct-memory access buffers.

COSMOS was built to provide runtime support for the Concurrent Smalltalk (CST) programming system [9] [10]. CST is an object-oriented programming language evolved from Smalltalk-80 [7]. In CST, concurrency is achieved using asynchronous messages and controlled using locks. CST also includes distributed objects to allow a single object to process many messages simultaneously.

COSMOS has borrowed concepts from a number of previous multiprocessor and multicomputer operating systems including Hydra [18], Medusa [14], and the Cosmic Kernel [16].

14.1.3 COSMOS Overview

COSMOS (COncurrent Smalltalk Operating System) was designed to efficiently support the execution of fine-grain programs on a fine-grain concurrent computer. It uses structures and algorithms that minimize communication and memory use. Its task and memory management functions are tuned to handle short ($\approx$ 10 to 100 instruction) tasks and

---

[1]See subsection 4.4.

small objects. It provides a global address space for objects, giving the programmability of a shared-memory machine, while retaining the locality inherent in message-passing hardware.

Global Object Namespace   Most message-passing multicomputers have a separate memory address space on each node. Nodes interact only by sending messages between processes [16]. Separate address spaces make it difficult to construct distributed data structures [5], limit the size of a process' address space to the memory size of a node, and require entire processes to be relocated to balance memory use. Also, because storage on remote nodes cannot be directly accessed, these machines replicate the operating system and application code on each node.

COSMOS overcomes these limitations by providing a global object namespace. All data and code are stored in objects. Each object is assigned a unique global ID. Given an object ID, the corresponding object can be referenced from any node. Objects are free to migrate between nodes without changing their global IDs. Accesses to objects are bounds checked and protected. The system supports distributed objects [9]. Large distributed objects are implemented as a collection of small constituent objects accessed via a single ID. A one-to-many translation service prevents the single ID from becoming a bottleneck.

Task Management   COSMOS provides low-overhead task management services that efficiently support fine-grain programs. Using the hardware task scheduling and dispatching mechanisms of the J-machine's message-driven processors [6], creating a task, suspending a task, resuming a task, and destroying a task each require between four and sixty instructions. This inexpensive task management is provided without sacrificing protection.

Abstractions   COSMOS provides a set of abstractions that support concurrent object-oriented programming languages such as CST [9] [10]. These abstractions are constructed from objects and include the following:

- A *Method* is an object containing code. The system performs hierarchical distribution of methods and caches methods locally on each node.

- A *Context* is an object containing the state of a task. The system provides special allocation and deallocation of contexts to speed task creation and provides services for suspending and resuming contexts.

- A *Class* is an object that defines the properties of a specific class (or type) of object.

- A *Selector* is an object that defines an action that can be performed on objects of one or more classes. The system maintains a sparse mapping from class-selector pairs to methods.

An example of how COSMOS supports these abstractions during the execution of a CST program is shown in Figure 14.1. Figure 14.1A shows a task (context C_1) on node N_1 sending an increment message to a counter object on node N_2. Initially, C_1 is active on node N_1 executing method M_1 on object A. When the execution reaches the

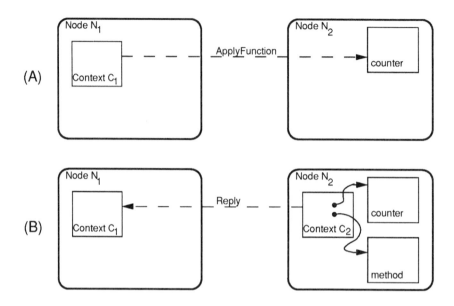

Figure 14.1
Example of CST executing on COSMOS

code corresponding to the source statement (increment counter), an ApplyFunction message[2] with argument increment is sent to the object counter on node N_2. The COSMOS ObjectNode system call (Section 3) is used to look up the node on which counter resides to determine the message's destination. The task with context C_1 then continues to execute on N_1 until it needs the result from the increment call, at which time it suspends execution if the result has not yet arrived.

Figure 14.1B illustrates the handling of the increment message by the counter object and the reply message to context C_1. When the ApplyFunction message arrives at N_2, the increment method is found, possibly on a third node (Section 5), and a task with context C_2, is created (Section 4) to apply this method to object counter. After the counter is incremented, it sends a reply message back to context C_1 on node N_1 containing the result of the increment operation, and context C_2 is destroyed. This message restarts context C_1 if it was blocked awaiting the result of the increment.

In this simple example, COSMOS services were used six times: to locate an object, to suspend a task, to find a method, to create a task, to destroy a task, and to restart a task. Careful design was required to allow COSMOS to support this heavy level of use

---

[2]The ApplyFunction message is used when the compiler is able to infer the type of the receiver (in this case counter) and thus can specify a method directly. COSMOS also provides an ApplySelector message that looks up the method based on the class of the receiver.

with acceptable overhead.

14.1.4 Outline

The remainder of this paper describes the operating system mechanisms in more detail. Section 2 presents the structure and layering of the operating system services. Section 3 describes the object-based memory model and object name resolution. Section 4 describes the machinery and data structures for performing low-overhead task control. Section 5 describes services to distribute code efficiently. Section 6 outlines a mechanism to support distributed objects where large objects are broken up into many segments and distributed across many nodes. Section 7 describes the performance of COSMOS as measured on a multicomputer simulator.

14.2   System Structure

COSMOS is an operating system kernel. It includes facilities for allocation, naming, relocation, and migration of objects and creation, scheduling, and management of tasks. It does not include an I/O system, file system, or user interface. Instead, it provides a substrate on top of which these facilities can be built.

14.2.1   Layers and Modules

COSMOS provides these kernel services using a collection of system calls, fault handlers, message handlers, and remote-procedure call (RPC) code. System calls and fault handlers are similar to their counterparts in sequential systems. A message handler is a physically addressed system routine that is executed each time a particular type of message is received. For each arriving message, the J-Machine hardware allocates a segment to hold the message and schedules a message handler to process it. The global services in COSMOS are constructed primarily from message handlers.

Using these components, COSMOS is constructed from a collection of modules as shown in Figure 14.2. These modules build up the kernel services in three layers:

Local Services: The boot code and a set of fault handlers run on the raw hardware and provide a set of abstractions that allow each node to function as an independent sequential computer, accessing memory by physical addresses.

A local memory management system provides for relocatable, protected memory within an individual processing node. Each object is allocated in a separate bounds-checked segment. Local objects are referenced by globally unique identifiers (IDs) that are translated into segment descriptors using a local translation table. Object IDs are tagged with special tags; user code can only access objects for which it has IDs; in user mode the MDP will fault on attempts to access an object through a non-ID word or to perform arithmetic/logical operations on IDs.

The J-Machine hardware performs most translations in a single instruction. The memory management in this layer is provided by the heap manager, the local object manager, and the name manager modules in Figure 14.2. Task management is provided by the context manager.

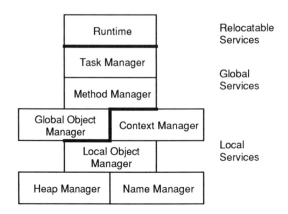

Figure 14.2
COSMOS Structure

Global Services: The global memory system provides for reference to and relocation of objects across the network. A remote object is accesed by translating its ID into a node number and then sending a message to that node. The translation from ID to node number is maintained in a distributed table composed from the translation tables on each node. The node on which an object is created, its *home* node, is responsible for knowing the node on which the object resides at all times. Objects are free to migrate from node to node as long as their home node is notified of their new location. The global object manager builds on the facilities of the local object manager and name manger to provide the memory management for this layer. The task manager provides for remote execution of tasks.

Relocatable Services: The facilities of this layer permit code to be accessed over the network and cached locally on a node only when needed. Some portions of COSMOS, labeled *Runtime* in Figure 14.2, are accessed in this manner, obviating the need to replicate this code on each node. Only code that is required to implement this layer or which would be inefficient if called as a function is locked down in memory. This layer is implemented by the method manager, which maintains the association between classes, selectors, and methods, in concert with the global object manager's facilities for distributing copies of immutable objects.

14.2.2   Criticalities

Most of the COSMOS code below the relocatable services layer is not re-entrant because it uses machine services such as the network, global variables[3], and physical memory addresses. Yet this code is richly connected, particularly when fault handlers are consid-

---

[3]The J-Machine hardware lacks stacks, so registers are saved in global or context variables when necessary

Criticality	Allowed Actions
0	All actions permitted (e.g., user code)
1	Caller's registers must be preserved.
2	No suspending faults, no modification of any context state.
3	Level 2 and no object migration.
4	Level 3 and no message sends.
5	Level 4 and no heap compaction.
6	Level 5 and no faults or system calls.
7	Level 6 and no priority 1 interrupts.

Table 14.1
Criticalities in COSMOS

ered. To ensure that non-re-entrant routines do not overwrite valid globals or the heap or attempt to send a message while another message send is in progress, a system of *criticalities* was used. Each routine and fault is assigned a criticality from Table 14.1 and is restricted not to call routines or cause faults with lower criticalities. Criticalities significantly simplified the bookkeeping involved in making this non-re-entrant code work correctly and efficiently.

14.2.3 Memory Map

Figure 14.3 shows the memory map of a single node in a J-Machine running COSMOS. The primary structures are the heap and the translation table. The heap uses most of the memory and is used to allocate objects including contexts. The heap is allocated from the top of the free area downward. The translation table is a hash table that holds associations including those used to support object naming. It consists of a fixed size root table combined with linked list hash buckets with entries allocated from the bottom of the free area upward. Each node also includes two hardware-managed incoming message queues (for priority 0 and priority 1), and a hardware-assisted translation table. The remaining memory blocks include the locked-down system code, fault vectors, and operating system variables.

The resident portion of the COSMOS kernel consists of 3500 lines (1122 words) of MDP assembly code. Fixed system tables bring the size of the resident operating system to about 1.5K words per node leaving 258.5K words per node for the heap and translation table. Additional operating system code written in both MDP assembly language and in CST is relocatable and need not be replicated on each node.

14.3 Object-Based Memory Management and Virtual Addressing

The J-Machine manages its memory in relocatable heap segments called *objects*. Each object is given a virtual name (ID) to allow relocation within the heap or across the

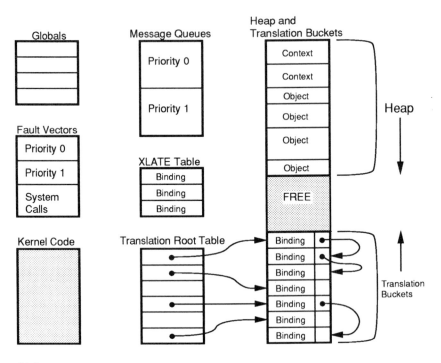

Figure 14.3
COSMOS Memory Map

network. The machinery to provide this memory model falls into two categories: the
services to allocate and deallocate contiguous segments of physical memory, and the
virtual addressing abstractions that allow location independence across the J-Machine
system. At the heart of the object-based system are the `NewLocalObject` system call and
`NewObject` message, which create local and remote objects. The heap, name, and object
managers outlined in Figure 14.2 participate in object creation. `NewLocalObject` first
allocates a segment of memory from the heap manager and then calls the name manager
to assign it a unique object ID. The length, ID, and class of each object are stored in a
two-word header shown in Figure 14.4.

14.3.1   The Heap Manager

Each node of a J-Machine has its own local memory that can be accessed very rapidly.
Part of this local memory is reserved by the memory manager as a heap for allocating
protected segments. The `AllocObject` heap manager call handles the allocation requests.
Memory is allocated starting from the current top of free memory. A simple sweeping
compactor reclaims fragmented storage. As the segments are swept, the local virtual

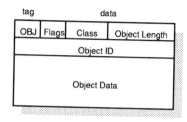

Figure 14.4
Each heap segment consists of header and ID words followed by user-defined data. The flags are used to indicate free, copyable, purgeable, and locked segments.

translation tables are updated with the segments' new locations. Compaction is very fast because local memory is small and fast, all processors can sweep in parallel, and relocation of a segment requires a translation table update on that node only. This *node autonomy* helps to reduce network traffic.

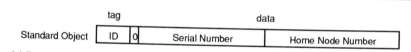

Figure 14.5
Virtual Name Format: An object's virtual name (ID) is a single word containing the object's 16-bit home node number and a 15-bit serial object number for that node.

14.3.2   The Name Manager

The use of virtual names for referencing segments allows segments to transparently relocate in the heap or even across nodes. The name manager is responsible for associating virtual names with physical memory segments and for resolving the current location of virtually named objects.

The format of a virtual name (or virtual ID) is shown in Figure 14.5. It is composed of two fields: a home node field and a serial number field. This format has two advantages: (1) The home node field allows access to objects that may relocate across the network because the home node always remembers where the object currently resides (except while an object is in the process of relocating). If another node wishes to know where an object currently resides, it can query the home node which can be determined from the virtual name. (2) Virtual IDs can be allocated very rapidly on each node without worry of name duplication, since the home nodes of each ID are unique. This way serial numbers can be generated consecutively on each node without any question of uniqueness. COSMOS's object naming scheme is similar to the assignment of object identifiers in [2], except that objects can migrate between nodes and still remain accessible through their virtual IDs.

Each node's name manager maintains an associative translation table that holds ID-to-physical-address bindings for all objects residing on the node, and ID-to-node-number assignments for all objects that were created on the node but have migrated elsewhere. To expedite the virtual-to-physical translation process, the translation table is cached by a hardware-accessible, two-way set-associative translation buffer (the XLATE Table in Figure 14.3) accessed by the XLATE machine instruction. The boundary between the name manager's table and the heap is movable, avoiding the need to statically estimate the percentage of memory needed for bindings.

14.3.3   Accessing an Object

A program that wishes to reference an object uses the XLATE instruction to attempt to translate a virtual ID to a physical address. If the binding is not in the translation buffer, the instruction faults and enters a fault handler which searches the name manager's translation table for the binding. Four possible conditions can occur in the object lookup:

The ID is bound to a segment address: This happens when the segment is local. A segment descriptor for the local segment is returned.

The ID is bound to a node number: The segment is not on the local node, but it is *rumored* to be on the node specified on the node number[4]. A request is made to the node specified for the segment in question. The segment will be migrated or copied (based on mutability) across the network from the specified node to this node. When the segment arrives, the segment descriptor will be returned. The current task is suspended to let other tasks run before the object arrives on this node. It will be restarted when the segment arrives, thus guaranteeing progress on the computation.

The ID is not bound: When the ID is not in the local table, a query is made to the home node of the object to find where it currently resides[5]. The home node can be found from the ID. The request for the segment is sent to the home node and the current task suspended. When the segment arrives, the task is resumed and the segment descriptor is returned.

This node is already waiting for the object: In this case no further requests for the object are made. Instead, this task is added to the local list of tasks waiting for the object.

When an object is migrated, the move is synchronized to be sure the home node is updated before the object moves again to allow the home node to track the object. Whenever objects are relocated by compaction or migration, all segment registers on the

---

[4]This node number is a *hint*. If it is incorrect, the requesting node invalidates the hint and requests the object from its home node. No attempt is made to follow forwarding pointers.

[5]If no binding for this ID exists on the home node, an error is signalled indicating that a deleted object was referenced.

node are invalidated[6]. Any subsequent access through an invalid segment register causes a fault which retranslates the new address from the corresponding virtual ID.

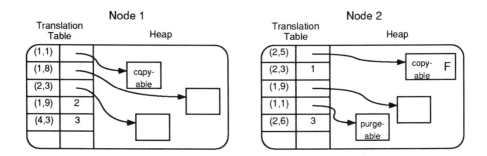

Figure 14.6
Sample Translation Tables: Node 1 holds three objects, a pointer to a fourth which is residing at node 2, and a hint to a fifth object at node 3. Node 2 also holds three objects, one of which is a copy of an object on node 1, as well as two pointers. Object (2,5) is a method that will be used in a later example.

14.3.4 Translation Table Example

Figure 14.6 shows an abstract view of two nodes and their translation tables. Node 1 has three resident objects. Their virtual IDs are listed symbolically in (home node, serial number) format. Since objects with IDs (1,1), (1,8), and (2,3) are resident, they have translation table entries. The object with ID (1,9) is not resident, but since this is its home node, it has an ID-to-node binding, indicating that the object is currently residing on node 2. There is also an ID-to-node binding for object (4,3) in the table. Since Node 1 is not the home node for this object, this binding is just a *hint* and is not guaranteed to be correct.

Node 2 has bindings for its local objects as well, including (1,9), and it has a node number binding indicating that (2,3) is currently residing on node 1. Node 2 also has a purgeable copy of the copyable object (1,1).

If node 1 accesses the (1,9) object, it sends a message to node 2 because it knows that object (1,9) resides on node 2. However, if node 1 accesses object (3,1) it has no *hint* as to the whereabouts of the object so it sends a request to node 3, the object's home node.

14.4 Task Control

The COSMOS task manager provides a set of low-overhead mechanisms to start a task, to suspend and restart it as necessary, and to destroy the task and *clean up* when done.

---

[6]Other nodes' segment registers need not be invalidated because nodes are not allowed to send physical segment addresses to other nodes.

Code is stored in *method* objects, taking advantage of the storage system described in the previous section.

14.4.1   A Sample Execution

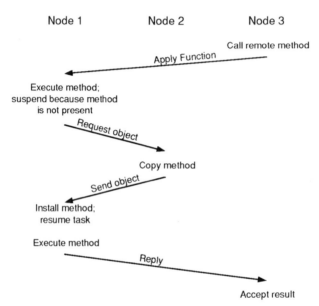

Figure 14.7
Example Method Call:

Figure 14.7 shows a simple example that illustrates the task execution process. Assume that node 3 just asked node 1 to call a method, F, with ID (2,5), on some arguments. The ApplyFunction message, including the arguments, arrives in the queue on node 1. When node 1 finishes its previous waiting messages, it dispatches on the message's header word which directs execution to the ApplyFunction message handler. The message handler then allocates a new task with a new context C, takes the ID (2,5) from the message, and attempts to translate the ID into a segment descriptor using the J-Machine's XLATE instruction.

If object (2,5) is non-local as shown in Figure 14.6, the translation faults, and node 1 sends a message to node 2 asking for the method object. Then, since the task cannot proceed, it suspends, saving its state, the processor registers, and the contents of the incoming message, in a *context* object. Sometime later a copy of method (2,5) will arrive from node 2 in another message. The method is then installed in the local heap and the suspended task is resumed from the context C.

Since a local copy of the method, object (2,5), now exists, the translation succeeds when it is retried and returns the segment descriptor for method F. The restarted task then jumps to the beginning of method F. As it executes, F may access arguments from the message (through a *message segment*[7]) or data objects in memory for which it holds segment descriptors or IDs. Any attempt to access a non-local object will fault in the same manner as above. Just before suspending, F sends the result to the caller on node 3 using a `Reply` message. The context C is then deallocated and its message flushed from the queue. Node 1 then dispatches on the next message in the input queue.

14.4.2 Scheduling

All process scheduling is via two hardware message queues, one for priority 0 and one for priority 1. Incoming messages are enqueued by the network hardware. When the queues are empty, the processor idles at a low *background* priority. A message arriving at priority 0 preempts a background task and can dispatch a message handler such as `ApplyFunction` or `Reply` as described above. Priority 1 messages preempt priority 0 tasks and are reserved for handling global system exceptions such as node memory overflow. Once a task is initiated, it is run without interruption until it completes, suspends to wait for an event, or is preempted by a priority 1 message. Thus message handlers run atomically without special arrangement. By convention the code executed in response to a message should execute in a bounded amount of time. The bound is enforced by the compiler, which will break any potentially unbounded loops into code which periodically yields the processor.

14.4.3 Context Management

Since tasks frequently suspend on accesses to non-local objects, a context is always allocated for a task. The context contains a task's local variables and provides space for the task's message and registers to be saved if the task suspends. Task allocation and deallocation are highly optimized since they are performed very frequently (once every 32 user instructions). A few free contexts are initially linked together on a context free list. When a context is requested it is provided from the free list unless the list is empty. If the free list is empty, a context is allocated from the heap, a significantly more expensive process. When contexts are deallocated they are returned to the free list[8]. With these optimizations, allocating a context from the free list takes 5 instructions and deallocating one takes 4 instructions.

14.4.4 Synchronization on Results

A task does not suspend when it calls a remote method. Instead, it stores a specially-tagged word known as a *context future (c-future)* in the local context variable that will hold the result. If the task accesses the result variable before its value has been computed,

---

[7]By convention one segment register is used to refer the the incoming message. Initially this segment references a portion of the message queue. After a tasks suspends it is relocated to reference the message stored in a task's context. The method has transparent access to message arguments regardless of the message location.

[8]The free list can optionally be truncated and the storage reclaimed the next time the heap is compacted.

the processor hardware detects the *c-future* and enters a fault handler that suspends the task. When the result does arrive in a `Reply` message, it is stored in the result local variable. The task is then resumed if it had been waiting for that particular result variable.

C-futures differ from full futures [8] in that c-futures are placeholders for values; they cannot be moved or read without waiting for the result. This makes c-futures very inexpensive. CST and COSMOS also have provisions for full futures, but they are not implemented in the current system.

This future synchronization facility takes good advantage of concurrency and makes it easy for a task to spawn multiple processes. All a task has to do is call several remote methods before accessing any of the results.

14.5   Code Distribution

To conserve memory, COSMOS maintains a single global copy of all code. Only a small amount of operating system code is permanently replicated on each node. The remaining code is cached locally on demand in a per-node method cache. A distribution tree is used to prevent accesses to shared code objects from becoming a bottleneck[9].

Consider the example from Section 14.1.3. If the `increment` method for class `counter` is not resident on node N_2, the translation from the method ID to a code segment descriptor fails with a *translate fault*. The translate fault handler suspends the current task, inserts a binding in the translation table that will cause the task to be restarted when the method arrives, and sends a `RequestObject` message into a distribution tree to fetch the method. The tree returns a copy of the method with the `MigrateObject` message. Upon receipt of this message, a copy of the `increment` method is allocated in the heap and marked copyable and purgeable. The translate table is then consulted to find any contexts that are waiting for the object, and these contexts are restarted. One waiting context is restarted immediately. The remainder are restarted by N_2 sending `RestartContext` messages to itself.

Parts of the heap are used as an instruction cache, storing local copies of methods, to prevent instruction fetches from being performed over the network. There is no explicit replacement of cached methods. Instead, method copies are reclaimed by the heap compactor. All method copies have the *purgeable* flag set in their object header. The compactor marks the method (by setting the *marked* flag in the object header) each time it compacts the heap. The first reference to the method will clear the mark. If the method is not referenced before the next compaction, the compactor seeing both the *marked* and *purgeable* flags set discards the copy.

Keeping a single master copy of all code results in significantly more efficient use of memory than the common practice of replicating the code on each node of a parallel computer [16]. However, a naive implementation of the code distribution mechanism described above can result in a serious serial bottleneck. Many parallel programs achieve

---

[9]Multi-level code distribution trees were implemented in JOSS and are planned for COSMOS; however, the current release of COSMOS only supports two-level code distribution trees without intermediate distributor nodes.

concurrency through data parallelism – viz. they apply the same function to many data elements simultaneously. In such programs, it is not unusual for several thousand nodes to request a copy of a method at the same time. If all requests were sent directly to the master copy of the method, considerable time would be spent processing them serially. Also, such a high volume of messages would probably overflow the input queue of the node on which the master copy resides, invoking a costly fault handler.

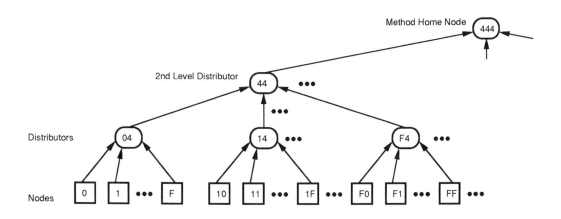

Figure 14.8
A Code Distribution Tree: Nodes request methods from a regional distributor that combines requests and forwards them up the tree to the master copy. This figure shows a three-level radix-16 tree for a method with home node 444_{16}. All node numbers are in hexadecimal.

COSMOS will use distribution trees to avoid the code distribution bottleneck. As shown in Figure 14.8, nodes request methods from a regional distributor. The address of the regional distributor is computed by substituting some bits from the method's home node number into the current node number. The distributor performs one of the following three actions:

1. If the distributor has a copy of the method it provides a copy immediately with a MigrateObject message.

2. If the distributor does not have a copy of the method and there is no outstanding request for the method, it records the request and requests a copy of the method from the next level of the distribution hierarchy.

3. If the distributor does not have a copy but has already requested one from up the hierarchy, it adds the requesting node to a list of nodes awaiting the method and suspends. When the method arrives, a copy is sent to all waiting nodes.

In effect the distributor *combines* requests for the same method. At each level of the hierarchy, only the first request for a particular method is propagated to the next level of the hierarchy. All subsequent requests are combined with the first request. A radix k distribution tree can handle requests from all nodes in an N node machine in $O(\text{Max}(k, \log_k N))$ time, much less than the $O(N)$ time required without combining.

14.6   Distributed Objects

A single object can only be directly accessed by the node on which it resides, and that node can only run one task at a time, implying that an object can only be involved in one computation at a time[10]. In the absence of coherent caching strategies, this one-object-one-task constraint can severely limit parallelism. In order to provide more concurrency when accessing large objects and to balance the memory usage more evenly across processing nodes, an object may be broken into several constituent pieces, though still identified by the same global name. This special type of object is called a *distributed object*.

The system supports distributed objects by providing allocation and constituent lookup services. When a distributed object is allocated, the system creates a number of constituent objects and distributes them across the processing nodes. Each constituent object has a normal object ID which is unique to the constituent, and a distributed ID or DID which is the same for all constituents of a distributed object.

The DID contains all of the information necessary to locate any constituent. The translation procedure is very efficient, avoiding the need for any remote operations such as those used to translate group identifiers in [2].

14.6.1   The Distribution Problem

To distribute objects a function is needed to map each constituent of the object to a node number. Using this function it must be easy to compute (1) the node on which a particular constituent resides and (2) the node on which the nearest constituent resides. The function should also distribute objects across the nodes of the machine in an acceptable manner. The DID should fit in a single word to allow a distributed object to be referenced in the same manner as a normal object.

The distribution function must simultaneously satisfy the two conflicting goals of load balancing and locality. The distribution scheme should distribute the objects uniformly across the network to balance load. At the same time it is desirable to concentrate the objects on a few nearby nodes to reduce network traffic. If the constituents of a distributed object are scattered uniformly across the machine, the data may lie very far away from the majority of the computation, resulting in many messages traversing a large distance. While network latency is relatively insensitive to distance, network throughput is degraded by many long distance messages. On the other hand, if the constituent objects are concentrated together to reduce network traffic, a local *hotspot* may result with this portion of the machine becoming overloaded.

---

[10]This does not apply to immutable objects that may be replicated and thus involved in many computations simultaneously.

14.6.2   A Distribution Scheme

COSMOS uses a simple uniform distribution function for constituent objects. If the N nodes of a J-Machine are numbered from 0 to $N-1$, the M constituents of a distributed object are located every S^{th} node, where the stride of the object, S, is a power of two, $S = N/M = 2^l$.

	tag			data	
Standard Object	ID	0	Serial Number	Home Node Number	
Dist. Obj. Constituent	ID	1	Serial Number	Home Node Number	
Dist. Obj. Group Name	DID	1	Serial Number	LogStride	Home Node Number

Figure 14.9
Distributed ID (DID) Format: The DID contains the distributed object's serial number, home node number, and a signed base-2 logarithm of the distributed object's stride

Figure 14.9 shows the format of a distributed ID. The DID encodes the number of constituent objects, the home node of the first object, and a node-unique serial number. The number of constituents is restricted to be a power of two to allow the number of constituents to be encoded in the DID as l, the log of the object's stride, S. With the DID format of Figure 14.9, only addition and bit shifting are required to find the nth constituent of a distributed object or to find the closest constituent to a given node[11].

The log of the stride, l may range from -16 to 15. When l is negative, there are several constituents on each node. This logarithmic encoding allows S to range from 2^{-16} (65536 constituents on each node of a J-Machine) to 2^{15} (2 constituents on a 64K-node J-Machine) in powers of two. The home node number H must be less than S. The kth constituent, counting from $k=0$, is located on the node numbered $H + \lfloor kS \rfloor$.

If the stride is 1 or greater, each constituent object has the same serial number as the group object. If S is less than 1, several constituents reside on every node in the J-Machine, and more than one serial number is required to distinguish them. Hence, the distributed object reserves $1/S$ consecutive constituent serial numbers, and the kth constituent has serial number $H + (k \bmod 1/S)$, where H is the DID's serial number. Except for their association with a group name (DID), the constituents are just like normal objects and may migrate. To avoid name conflicts with standard objects, constituents have a 1 in bit 31.

14.7   Performance Data

This section presents some measurements of COSMOS' performance on a simulated J-Machine running Concurrent Smalltalk code. COSMOS' overhead and the grain size

---

[11]A variety of definitions of "closest" can be used by changing one routine in COSMOS. The current one picks the closest node in a linear (dictionary) ordering of the J-Machine nodes.

of the benchmark programs are discussed followed by experimental measurements. The network load for these benchmarks is calculated. All data was collected from static analyses of COSMOS code and from timings done on an instruction simulator of a J-Machine.

14.7.1 COSMOS Kernel Performance

The instruction counts for selected COSMOS services are shown in Table 14.2. These counts assume that the required information and objects are found in the local caches. When a task is saved, a 6-word incoming message is assumed.

One factor that affects timing is the two kinds of memory attached to each node of the J-Machine. When running from the fast internal memory, the J-Machine nodes execute instructions in about two cycles for the instruction mix used in the COSMOS trials. All of COSMOS resides in the fast internal memory, while most of the user programs and data reside in the slow external memory, which is about five times slower. Thus, at 20 MHz, the J-Machine instructions that are part of COSMOS take an average of 100 ns to execute, while user program instructions take an average of about 500 ns each. Table 14.2 shows that user code calling a function or a method takes 13 instructions to send a two-argument call message and about 9 instructions to reply to a message.

14.7.2 Theoretical Performance Analysis

To calculate operating system overhead, a figure representing the typical amount of work in a function is needed. Although this number varies greatly depending on the application, assume for now that a function does about 10 instructions' worth of useful computation not counting call/return overhead[12]. Also assume that the program is compute-bound; viz., the processors always have something to do. With these assumptions, the information in table 1 is sufficient to estimate the percentage of processor time spent in the Cosmos kernel.

A couple of typical function calls is outlined in Figure 14.10. COSMOS executes $9 + 9 + 42 + 12 + 27 = 99$ instructions on node 1 and 4 instructions each on nodes 2 and 3, for a total of 107 instructions and 10.7 μs, while the user program executes $11 + 2 + 11 + 2 = 26$ instructions on node 1 and, assuming $n=10$, $10 + 8 + 1 = 19$ instructions each on nodes 2 and 3, for a total of 64 instructions and 32.0 μs. Thus, this program would execute 63% of its 171 instructions in the kernel and 37% in the user code. However, it would only spend 25% of its time in the kernel. Since four messages were sent, the grain size (the number of instructions executed per message) is 42.75.

There are a number of factors which can affect these estimates in either direction:

Concurrent function calling: The numbers in Figure 14.10 correspond to node 1 making two function calls and then waiting for the results. If node 1 were to make only one or more than two function calls in parallel, it would have more or fewer function calls over which to amortize the 42+27-instruction context suspend/resume cost, resulting in a different overhead ratio.

---

[12]Most tasks do considerably more work than this. We assume a low number here to calculate an upper bound on operating system overhead.

Service	Instructions
User Program Activities	
Call a function or a method with n arguments. The time does not include the *c-future* fault or reply time.	$11+n$
Return a reply to the caller and terminate function	9
Task and Method Managers	
Dispatch a function call (creates a task)	4
Dispatch a method call (looks up method based on class)	≥ 23
Suspend a task explicitly	28
Suspend a task on a context future fault	42
Unconditionally restart a task	20
Resume a task on a reply message	27
Global Object Manager	
Return the class of an object	15 to 25
Return the node *rumored* to contain the object: primitive objects	9
ordinary user objects	4
distributed objects	32
Return the ID of the nth constituent of a distributed object	38 or 49
Return the ID of a nearby constituent of a distributed object	12 or 27
Receive and install an n-word object and restart one task waiting for it	$101 + 2n$
Local Object Manager	
Allocate a local object	58
Deallocate a local object	39
Name Manager	
Allocate a new binding	26
Look up a binding if missed in the XLATE table	19
Delete a binding	28
Heap Manager	
Allocate a segment on the heap	20
Compact an N-word heap	$2N$ to $10N$

Table 14.2
Median Instruction Counts for COSMOS Services

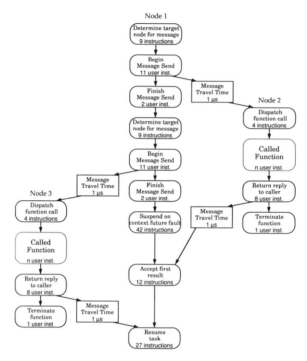

Figure 14.10
Remote Function Call Timing: This figure outlines the processing time spent in executing two function calls. The latency of the network is estimated at 20 cycles (1 μs) to send a message between two randomly chosen nodes on a 4096-node machine. The biggest components of the overhead are task suspending and resuming (42 and 27 instructions).

Tail forwarding: In many cases a function A calls another function B and then immediately passes the result back to A's caller. In this case B can send the result directly to A's caller, eliminating one message and the 77 instructions it would take A to suspend, resume, and send the result to its caller. Thus, a high fraction of tail-forwarded functions in a program will significantly reduce the operating system overhead by eliminating unnecessary context switches and synchronizations.

Method dispatching: An extra 19 instructions are required for method lookup if the class of the receiving object (the first argument) could not be resolved at compile time.

14.7.3   Experimental Results

The results of running several programs on a simulated J-Machine are summarized in Table 14.3.

No.	Program	Nodes	Input	Total Insts	Node Use(%)	Insts/Msg Word	Grain size	Avg Msg Size
1	factorial	4	10	5949	34	30.8	71.5	6.89
2	rangesum	4	50	17017	68	12.7	54.7	6.32
3	rangesum2	4	50	27971	70	13.4	59.3	6.33
4	sort	4	4	57939	41	30.3	123.6	9.87
5	sort	4	29	351144	77	14.9	77.6	6.82
6	sort	16	4	201681	12	95.9	116.6	10.21
7	sort	16	29	868586	34	32.6	81.2	7.33
8	sort	16	100	2612981	56	18.6	71.1	6.79
	Avg of All			4143268	49	31.2	82.0	7.57
	Avg of 2,3,5,8			3009113	68	14.9	65.7	6.57

Table 14.3
Experimental Results

The Total Instructions column includes the idle *background* code. The Node Use(%) column gives the percentage of time the processors spent executing foreground code. The Instructions/Message Word column contains the ratio of the total number of instructions executed to the number of network words sent; the reciprocal is the offered network load. The Grain Size is the number of *foreground* instructions executed to the number of network messages sent. Unless tail-forwarding is used extensively, the number of instructions needed to process one method invocation is twice the grain size.

Factorial is a simple recursive factorial program. Rangesum adds the numbers between 0 and n using a divide-and-conquer technique. Rangesum2 does the same except that it builds and traverses a tree data structure while doing the computation. Sort generates and sorts an array of n pseudo-random numbers using the Batcher parallel sort technique described in [12]. The "average of all" row gives the arithmetic mean for each column except instruction count where it gives a total. The "average of 2,3,5,8" row gives the same information for the four experiments that ran long enough not to be dominated by cache loading startup effects.

The grain size is comparable with the value derived in the previous subsection after accounting for additional compiler overhead and cache misses. The experimental number is higher, especially on small problem sizes, because the effects of method and translate cache misses are ignored in the analysis above. In the experiment, additional instructions are spent in fault handlers requesting methods and distributing them throughout the J-Machine. Also, for more complex methods, more than 10 useful instructions are executed on each method invocation. Furthermore, the CST compiler [9] inlines methods to increase the amount of work per method invocation.

Depending on whether the user program is located in internal or external memory, a 20 MHz J-Machine node will process a message once every 6.5 to 13.0 μs (more for small problem sizes), and a remote function call will take 13.0 to 26.0 μs.

14.7.4   Network Load

The message traffic generated by a typical program comes very close to the J-Machine network capacity. As seen in Table 14.3, after startup the network loading is usually one word every 12-20 instructions, with the lower figures dominating as the J-Machine is used more fully. In fact, on larger examples the programs could inject one word into the network approximately every 10 instructions. This implies that a program could inject words into the network as fast as one word every 20 cycles (1 μs) on every node[13].

Consider such a program running on a J-Machine organized as a $k \times k \times k$ mesh. Let $N = k^3$ be the number of nodes. To a first-order approximation, the capacity of the network is $3N$ half-word-hops/cycle[14], or $1.5N$ word-hops/cycle. Assuming random sources and destinations, a message will have to travel an average of $k/3$ hops on each of the three dimensions, so the expected distance the message has to travel is $3k/3 = k$ hops. Hence, the network's theoretical capacity is $1.5N/k = 1.5k^2$ words per cycle. The program offers $N/20$ words/cycle to the network, which means that unless locality is exploited, node utilization drops, or the program slowed down, there will be an upper bound on the size of the J-Machine which can run COSMOS.

A mesh loaded at about 30% of its theoretical capacity should be able to route messages without excessive delays [4]. This gives a maximum k of:

$$0.3 \times 1.5k^2 = k^3/20$$
$$k = 9. \tag{14.1}$$

Network loading should not become an important issue until a J-Machine with over $9^3 = 729$ nodes is built. Should Cosmos be sped up somehow, the critical size might fall lower. This is one of the reasons for building 1024-node or larger J-Machine prototypes – it will permit study of load management issues.

14.8   Conclusion

COSMOS provides low overhead task and memory management services to support fine-grain programs running on large-scale MIMD multicomputers such as the MIT J-Machine. The system is designed to make best use of a system in which processing is relatively inexpensive and communication bandwidth and memory must be conserved. Careful system organization and coding of critical system functions such as context allocation results in acceptable system overhead with tasks as small as 32 user instructions. Measurements of system performance on a simulated multicomputer indicate that fine-grain programs spend 25% of their time in the COSMOS kernel.

The COSMOS memory manager handles the creation, destruction, relocation, naming, and referencing of objects. It provides a global virtual address space on a message-passing multicomputer. The system is object-oriented. All code and data are contained

---

[13]Unlike the previous subsection, in this subsection the user program is assumed to be small enough to lie in fast memory to calculate the maximum load it could exert on the network. Moreover, even large programs could have small components that strain the network.

[14]The J-Machine's network can transmit an 18-bit half word between every pair of adjacent nodes on every cycle.

in objects. To conserve memory, a single copy of all but a small portion of the OS kernel code is distributed across the machine. To conserve communication bandwidth, code is cached on each node, and instructions are never fetched across the network. A code distribution tree is used to avoid bottlenecks in accessing shared code. Distributed objects are supported to balance the load of large objects and to avoid bottlenecks in accessing *popular* objects.

The COSMOS task manager creates, suspends, resumes, and destroys tasks. Through careful design and coding, these operations have been made very fast (0.4 to 6.0 μs on a 20MHz J-Machine) without compromising protection. Each task executes in its own protected addressing environment and interacts with other tasks only via messages or shared objects. This protection simplifies parallel program debugging by eliminating the unexpected interactions that may occur between tasks sharing a single address space. These low-overhead task management services enable the execution of fine-grain parallel programs with acceptable overhead.

Typical Concurrent Smalltalk (CST) programs spend 63% of their instructions and 25% of their time in the COSMOS kernel. Both the derived and measured data indicate that the grain size, the number of instructions executed in response to each message, is about 50 instructions (16 user instructions and 34 kernel instructions). The average number of instructions needed to process a function call (two messages) is 100 (32 user and 68 kernel instructions). The largest part of the overhead is due to suspending and resuming the task.

COSMOS has been operational on a J-Machine simulator since May 1989 and on small (128 nodes) prototype J-Machines since Fall 1991. We expect the first 1024-node J-Machine to be operational in the Summer of 1992. We are also currently working on collecting data on the performance of COSMOS on larger programs; this was made difficult by hardware errors in the early MDP chips.

Our experiments with COSMOS have identified a number of areas where improved hardware support is required to reduce overhead. We are currently investigating hardware support for task switching that will reduce task switching overhead to a few instructions per suspend/resume combination from the current 80 instructions. The current J-Machine hardware allocates its message queues in a FIFO manner forcing a task to copy its message out of the queue the first time its suspends. This overhead can be eliminated by building a message buffer with a more flexible allocation policy. Finally, our simulations suggest that our networks are operating dangerously close to saturation. Networks with higher throughput will be required to build larger machines or to run programs with a finer grain size.

Many challenges remain in the design of programming systems to support fine-grain parallelism. To prevent network bandwidth from limiting concurrency, resource allocation policies that exploit locality are required. Efficient algorithms must be developed for parallel garbage collection and load balancing. Parallel I/O systems, hardware and software, are needed to provide concurrent programs with user interfaces and file access. Perhaps the greatest challenge is one of education. Our experience suggests that fine-grain parallel programs are not difficult to write. However, designing such programs requires a set of skills for which few programmers today are trained. If these challenges can be met, fine-grain concurrent computers offer the potential of an order of magnitude improvement in cost/performance for high performance computer systems.

References

[1]   Chase, Jeffrey S., Amador, Franz G., Lazowska, Edward D., Levy, Henry M., and Littlefield, Richard J., *The Amber System: Parallel Programming on a Network of Multiprocessors,* University of Washington Department of Computer Science Technical Report 89-04-01, April 1989.

[2]   Cheriton, David R., "The V Distributed System," *Communications of the ACM,* Vol. 31, No. 3, March 1988, pp. 314-333.

[3]   Dally, William J. et.al., "The J-Machine: A Fine-Grain Concurrent Computer," *Information Processing 89,* Elsevier, 1989, pp. 1147-1153.

[4]   Dally, William J. "Performance Analysis of k-ary n-cube Interconnection Networks," *IEEE Transactions on Computers,* to appear.

[5]   Dally, William J., *A VLSI Architecture for Concurrent Data Structures.* Kluwer, 1987.

[6]   Dally, William J. et.al., "Architecture of a Message-Driven Processor," *Proceedings of the 14th ACM/IEEE Symposium on Computer Architecture,* June 1987, pp. 189-196.

[7]   Goldberg, Adele and Robson, David, *Smalltalk-80: The Language and its Implementation,* Addison-Wesley, Reading, Mass., 1983.

[8]   Halstead, Robert Jr., "Multilisp: A Language for Concurrent Symbolic Computation," *ACM Transactions on Programming Languages and Systems,* Vol. 7, No. 4, October 1985, pp. 501-538.

[9]   Horwat, Waldemar. *Concurrent Smalltalk on the Message-Driven Processor,* MIT Artificial Intelligence Laboratory Technical Report 1321, 1991.

[10]   Horwat, Waldemar, Chien, Andrew A., and Dally, William J., "Experience with CST: Programming and Implementation," *Proceedings of the ACM SIGPLAN '89 Conference on Programming Language Design and Implementation,* 1989.

[11]   Jul, Eric, Levy, Henry, Hutchinson, Norman, and Black, Andrew, "Fine-Grained Mobility in the Emerald System," *ACM Transactions on Computer Systems,* Vol. 6, No. 1, February 1988, pp. 109-133.

[12]   Knuth, Donald E., *The Art of Computer Programming, Volume 3: Sorting and Searching,* Addison-Wesley, 1973, p. 112.

[13]   Leffler, S.J., McKusik, M.K., Karels, M.J., and Quarterman, J.S., *The Design and Implementation of the 4.3BSD UNIX Operating System,* Addison-Wesley, 1989.

[14]   Ousterhout, J., Scelza, D., and Sindhu, P., "Medusa: An Experiment in Distributed Operating System Structure," *CACM,* Vol. 23, No. 2, February 1980, pp. 92-105.

[15]   Rashid, R. et.al., "Machine-Independent Virtual Memory Management for Paged Uniprocessor and Multiprocessor Architectures," *IEEE Transactions on Computers,* Vol. C-37, No. 8, August 1988, pp. 896-908.

[16]   Su, W., Faucette, R., and Seitz, C.. *C Programmer's Guide to the Cosmic Cube.* Technical report 5203:TR:85, California Institute of Technology, September 1985.

[17]   Totty, Brian, *An Operating Environment for the Jellybean Machine,* MIT Artificial Intelligence Laboratory Memo No. 1070, 1988.

[18]   Wulf, W. et. al., "HYDRA: The Kernel of a Multiprocessor Operating System," *CACM,* Vol. 17, No. 6, June 1974, pp. 337-345.

V Performance Monitoring

15 Monitoring Concurrent Object-Based Programs[*]

Bruce A. Delagi, Nakul P. Saraiya, and Sayuri Nishimura

15.1 Introduction

The operation of concurrent applications involving hundreds of processors can be difficult to understand. Our intuition about the performance of both simple and relatively complex applications on multiprocessor systems of this scale has often proven to be weak. Our first, naive implementations have routinely demonstrated poor performance. We have ultimately been able to better utilize the available system resources only because we could study how our implementations made use of these resources—by means of the extensive instrumentation provided by the general purpose multiprocessor simulation facility that we were led to develop.

Our investigations have been accomplished by simulating multiprocessor architectures executing concurrent applications. We have focussed on the communication and scheduling support facilities of the architecture, as defined by hardware models and communication topologies representing a hypothesized machine. The monitoring facilities of the simulator have then aided in identifying bottlenecks—both in the application and in the underlying multiprocessor system—leading to refined implementations with better performance.

Our architectural simulation system covers a range of detail. It is fine enough to deal with each of the many operations that comprise cut-through message transmission of a packet of data through the elements of a torus. It is also coarse enough, and thereby fast enough, to simulate complete applications—by ignoring the detail of simple processor operations that affect system operations only through their timing. This timing information is captured during the simulated execution of concurrent applications by dynamically running purely sequential segments of the application code directly on the simulation vehicle and measuring their execution times.

Our applications are programmed in a concurrent, object-oriented extension of Lisp called LAMINA [6]. In this programming model, an application is organized as pipelines of asynchronously communicating objects executing data-driven, run-to-completion tasks in response to messages.

Our instrumentation facility directly exploits this programming model, monitoring the critical operations performed on messages, both by application objects and by the resources of the underlying multiprocessor system. The facility then provides a comprehensive library of modules for aggregating this information, for organizing it along various dimensions, and for presenting it visually. The facility provides a number of predefined 'instruments' that dynamically display key measures of the system under study; however, all aspects of the instrumentation—data capture, aggregation, and visualization—are fully programmable, so that applications programmers or multiprocessor system designers can, if required, customize instrumentation to suit their needs.

In this article, we describe our approach to understanding the performance of concurrent object-based programs in simulation. By way of background, we introduce our

[*]This work was supported by Digital Equipment Corporation, by DARPA Contract F30602-85-C-0012, by NASA Ames Contract NCC 2-220-S1, and by Boeing Contract W266875.

simulation system in the remainder of this section. In sections 15.2 and 15.3, we describe our object-based programming model and the ensemble architecture [21] to support it. We follow up on this in section 15.4 by providing examples of how the data collected through monitoring can aid in understanding the operation of the application. In section 15.5 we give a more detailed portrait of the instrumentation architecture. Thereafter, in section 15.6, as a concrete example of our experience, we present a performance study of an application written in LAMINA. Finally, we summarize in section 15.7.

Simulation System Overview

Perhaps the most distinguishing characteristic of our investigation is the generality of the simulation and instrumentation tool that we undertook to create. It was evident at the outset that there was indeed much that we did not know about the effective operation of large scale multiprocessors running complex applications. We therefore engineered a system in which we could study a variety of language interfaces (and higher level frameworks) on alternative multiprocessor systems. The level of language interfaces and frameworks was kept separate from the level of information exchange protocols so that when we refined our multiprocessor system models (for example, to study alternative communication protocols [4]) application programs still worked. Further, we were able to support new language interface styles without redefining major parts of the system.

Our simulation system, called SIMPLE/CARE [7, 19], is based on a high performance object programming system with efficient and comprehensive capabilities for method combination [26]. SIMPLE, the general-purpose modelling substrate, allows system models to be built up incrementally through composition, that is, by aggregating component simulation objects into other such objects [2, 9, 15, 23]. We have used this facility to create a library of parameterized multiprocessor components, called CARE.

System instrumentation is also based on objects, and revolves around probe, panel and instrument abstractions. Probes 'connect' to components to monitor their individual operation, and dynamically capture data. Panels collect together the outputs of probes, transform these outputs, and compute derived measures that are used to dynamically drive presentations: SIMPLE display types such as histograms, intensity maps, strip charts and line plots. New panels are defined by customizing existing presentations and panels to specify probe types, data transforms, legends and the like. A set of panels is then aggregated into an instrument, which associates a name and a screen layout policy with it. We have defined a family of probes, panels and instruments corresponding to particular CARE system architectures and LAMINA programming models.

In summary, through a set of language extensions to Lisp—using an underlying object system—we have provided a facility for concurrent object programming (LAMINA) in a general purpose interactive simulation system (SIMPLE). This system features flexible, comprehensive instrumentation and rapid prototyping. We have built up a library of component and system models in this system (CARE) to support our parallel language extensions. This library can be also used as a starting point for the design of alternative hardware models.

We have used SIMPLE, CARE, and LAMINA to study the operation of a number of concurrent applications in simulation [14, 16, 17, 18]. SIMPLE/CARE is implemented in

Common Lisp [25] and uses the X window system [20].

15.2   The Lamina Object Model

In this section, we describe the LAMINA object-based programming model, illustrate its programming constructs through example code, and, finally, show how we monitor LAMINA applications by monitoring application objects.

15.2.1   Lamina Computations

The LAMINA object programming model [6] is founded on the notion of asynchronously communicating objects. An object, as used here, is a collection of variables—its state variables—manipulated by (and only by) a set of procedures—the methods associated with that object. Objects may be defined within a compiled class inheritance network; the current implementation uses the inheritance facilities of *Flavors* [26].

Objects communicate via *streams* [13, 22], that are a generalization of futures [10, 11], which represent the promise for a value. Unlike futures, which represent single values, streams represent sequences of values. The information sent to a stream over time builds the sequence associated with it. A consumer accesses the sequence by removing individual items from the front of the stream.

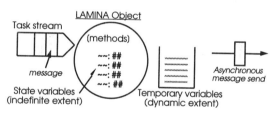

Figure 15.1
A LAMINA Object

As illustrated in figure 15.1, each object has associated with it a distinguished stream that serves as its *task stream*. The information placed on this stream specifies tasks to be executed by the object; each unit of information is a message. A message names a method to execute and includes the parameter values for the execution. An object that sends a message neither waits for the requested task to be performed, nor for an acknowledgement of the receipt of the message. Communication between objects is thus completely asynchronous.

Most parameters included in a message are passed by copying; only streams and global-ly-shared static constants (e.g., keyword symbols, procedures, read-only data arrays) are passed by reference. A sender may provide parameter values that are arbitrarily structured graphs composed of lists and arrays, and they are isomorphically reproduced at the receiving stream. This necessitates the encoding and decoding of messages at the sender and receiver, respectively, and the mechanism through which this is efficiently accomplished is discussed in section 15.3.

15.2.1.1   Computational Flow   The messages arriving on an object's task stream specify tasks to be performed by that object. Every object has a *dispatch process* associated with it which removes and executes each message on its task stream in turn. Tasks usually mutate the state variables of the object and generate new messages. They have exclusive access to their environment (i.e., state and temporary variables) during execution.

LAMINA tasks are data driven in that they are started when (and only when) all the information needed for their execution is available. Typically, a single message, in conjunction with the object's state variables, is sufficient for a task to begin execution. LAMINA also has a mechanism for efficiently scheduling tasks that depend upon multiple message arrivals from disparate sources [6].

Tasks in LAMINA are generally intended to be performed as the stages of pipelines that organize the work of the application objects. Therefore, in order to keep the pipelines flowing, a task that is started is run to completion (i.e., it cannot block). However, pipelines may also be used to emulate a traditional procedure call and return style by decomposing the original code into a pair of messages: one to make the remote call and the other to continue the computation when the values are returned. The application discussed in section 15.6 uses this approach to deal with object creation.

15.2.1.2   Providing Atomicity   Although LAMINA provides the programmer with a run-to-completion model, there may be reasons for preempting a task that are outside the application programmer's normal purview (e.g., to handle a debug trap or because the task's run quantum has expired). When this occurs, the object does not execute any other tasks until the preemption is resolved. This prevents other tasks on that object from gaining access to the environment of the suspended task. However, since other objects may execute tasks during this time, true atomicity can only be enforced if no mutable state is shared between environments. The mechanism by which objects communicate ensures this.

LAMINA objects can never mutate shared state because they only communicate by exchanging messages containing *independent* copies of local structures. Furthermore, the state variables of an object are only visible to its own methods and are therefore only accessible within a private task. Thus the atomicity of operations on an object is preserved even in the presence of preemptions.

15.2.1.3   Continuations   A LAMINA message specifies a transfer of control to the named method in the destination object along with data relevant to continuing the computation at that point. It may thus be usefully viewed as specifying a continuation [24] for the task that originates the message.

A LAMINA continuation is most often determined and invoked explicitly. The continuation is determined either via computation within the originating task or by virtue of being passed in as a 'client' parameter. In either case, its invocation is visible within the method code, as a message with the appropriate selector (and, perhaps, still another client) that is explicitly sent to the chosen object.

When an explicit continuation is not convenient (e.g., in performing a remote function call) an implicit, anonymous continuation can be used to capture the code and environment needed to later finish the local computation. LAMINA forms the continuation by copying any required bindings that are on the stack into a closure [25], which is deferred until further information (e.g., the return value from the remote function call) is available.

An implicit continuation is not part of the original task's atomic execution; the task and its continuation are independently atomic. The original task is first completed, and its continuation is run some time later, when the requirements for additional information have been met. In the meantime other tasks are executed by the object, keeping the pipeline flowing. Since the continuation shares its spawning task's execution environment, its environment may be altered by other tasks on the same object while it awaits execution. In this situation, the programmer must ensure that invariants are reestablished by the completion of each task and continuation.

15.2.1.4   Scheduling   The order of messages on an object's task stream dictates the order in which its tasks are scheduled. Task streams may be specialized to override their default first-in-first-out behavior, and to impose either prioritization or sequencing on messages (and, thereby, on task activations).

Prioritized, or ordered, task streams merge arriving messages with those already on the stream according to numeric 'order keys' included in messages. Thus, the highest priority pending task is scheduled first. Sequenced task streams additionally restrict message removals (and, hence, task activations) according to their order keys, deferring out-of-order messages until after intermediate messages in the sequence have arrived and their tasks have been executed. In both cases, scheduling is programmer-specified and cooperative because the order keys must be supplied by the tasks originating the messages.

15.2.1.5   Storage Considerations   We have focussed our attention on machines of the scale of several hundred processors, each with several megabytes of local storage. In this context, we expect the internal state of a LAMINA object (contained in its state variables) to occupy on the order of hundreds to thousands of bytes, and task execution to require on the order of hundreds to thousands of machine cycles. This perspective on granularity is important when considering means of supporting the LAMINA object model.

For example, if we assume that the support layer includes a virtual memory system, then high-performance, physically-addressed caches imply a page size of several kilobytes. If we further assume a page-protection-based stack-limit mechanism, then by maintaining a stack for each object we pay a factor of between ten and hundred in the (physical) space overhead associated with task execution.

Since LAMINA tasks and their explicit or implicit continuations normally run to completion, their control and binding stacks are non-empty only during execution. Furthermore, since task preemption is an exceptional condition, stack storage space is generally reusable among all the tasks on a processor. This allows the underlying system to manage relatively fine-grained objects without forgoing efficient virtual memory and cache mechanisms.

15.2.1.6   Actors and Lamina   The ACTORS [1] and the LAMINA object models are similar in that message arrival triggers computation and message arrival order is nondeterministic. However, LAMINA departs from ACTORS in a number of ways, primarily by trading off flexibility for efficiency.

- Not everything is an object in LAMINA. Predefined data types such as numbers, symbols, arrays and pairs exist as primitives, and operations on them do not entail message-passing. Although structures are passed by copying, they are locally mutable.

- Mutation is explicit in LAMINA. The overhead that we anticipate for creating and scheduling the 'lightweight' processes associated with task execution mitigates against efficient partitioning of the methods of LAMINA objects. Therefore, unlike actors, LAMINA objects do not deal with state changes by specifying a *replacement* [1] for themselves, but rather explicitly manipulate their own state variables through assignment.

- In LAMINA, the default execution model is serial command execution in the definition of an object's behavior. Thus, to the degree to which structures can be determined to have dynamic extent, they may be allocated and deallocated with a simple, efficient, stack discipline.

- Streams are first-class entities independent of objects in LAMINA, and they may include a scheduling discipline overriding arrival order. Objects may also establish communications over streams other than their task streams. Streams may be shared between objects; the system provides primitives for remotely accessing stream values [6].

- The inheritance system underlying LAMINA provides compiled inheritance for message combination and performs instantiation by compiled template.

15.2.2 Lamina Programs

In this section, we will briefly discuss the LAMINA programming extensions in the context of a simple example program; a more exhaustive treatment of the language extensions may be found in [6]. Our program is to compute the dynamics of N bodies that interact in 3-space through gravity. The LAMINA code is shown in figure 15.2.[1]

LAMINA objects are declared using the *Flavors* defflavor construct [26] and specializing the predefined lamina class, which defines the Self-Stream instance variable that contains the task stream of the object. An object is referenced by other objects by means of this stream. The lamina class also provides the basic functionality for dispatching tasks when messages arrive on the task stream, as discussed in section 15.2.1. The system-provided sequenced-self-stream mixin class specializes this behavior to maintain a sequenced task stream for the object.

We represent each body by a body object that is given an initial position and velocity (each of which is represented by a 3-element list). A simulation proceeds for a given number of time steps. During each step, each body multicasts its mass and current position to all other bodies in a :step message. Whenever a body receives a :step message, it computes and saves the incremental acceleration on itself due to the sending body. When it determines that it has received data from all other bodies for the current step,

---

[1]LAMINA constructs have been shown in uppercase for clarity.

```
(defflavor Body (ID Mass Position Velocity Bodies Steps Simulate-Clients
                 (Step 0) Expected Received (Acceleration (list 0 0 0)))
  (SEQUENCED-SELF-STREAM LAMINA)            ; inheritance
  (:initable-instance-variables ID Mass Position Velocity))

(DEFTRIGGER (body :simulate) ((all-bodies n-steps) clients)
  (setf Bodies (delete Self-Stream all-bodies :test #'REMOTE-ADDR-EQ)
        Expected (length Bodies) Steps n-steps Simulate-Clients clients)
  (SENDING Self-Stream :initiate-step () :by Step)) ; step=0
(DEFTRIGGER (body :initiate-step) ()        ; reset, inform others
  (setf Received 0) (fill Acceleration 0.0)
  (SENDING Bodies :step (list Mass Position) :by (+ Step 0.5)))
(DEFTRIGGER (body :step) ((m p))
  (send self :update-acceleration m p)      ; procedure call
  (when (= (incf Received) Expected)        ; all in?
    (send self :integrate)                  ; procedure call
    (if (< (incf Step) Steps)               ; bump step, done?
        (SENDING Self-Stream :initiate-step () :by Step)
                                            ; trigger (next) step
        (POSTING (list ID Position) :to Simulate-Clients))))
                                            ; return result

(defflavor Nbody-Simulator (Bodies-Spec Steps Simulate-Clients)
  (LAMINA) :initable-instance-variables)
(defmethod (nbody-simulator :after :init) (ignore) ; start simulation
  (declare (ignore ignore))
  (let ((client1 (NEW-STREAM)) (nbodies (length Bodies-Spec)))
    (dolist (spec Bodies-Spec)              ; create bodies
      (CREATING 'body
                (list :id (first spec) :mass (second spec)
                      :position (third spec) :velocity (fourth spec))
                :for client1))
    (let ((counter 0) (bodies ()))
      (WITH-POSTINGS ((body client1))       ; continuation
        (push body bodies)                  ; collect body task streams
        (when (= (incf counter) nbodies)    ; all in?
          (let ((client2 (NEW-STREAM)) (results ()))
            (SENDING bodies :simulate (list bodies steps) :for client2)
                                            ; go!
            (WITH-POSTINGS ((result client2)) ; continuation
              (push result results)         ; collect results
              (when (= (decf counter) 0)    ; all in?
                (POSTING results :to Simulate-Clients)))))))))
```

Figure 15.2
LAMINA Code for *N*-body Simulation

it integrates the total acceleration during this step to determine its new velocity and position. Finally, the body either initiates another step on itself (via an :initiate-step message send to its own task stream) or terminates and returns its position to the calling client (via posting).

Object creation is accomplished via the creating construct, which asynchronously creates a new instance of the specified class with the specified initialization property list, somewhere in the system.[2] Since object creation is asynchronous and since LAMINA methods run to completion, the nbody-simulator specifies a new stream, client1, as the client of each creation request, and then forms an implicit continuation to wait on the stream (via with-postings). When a remote body is created, the system returns its task stream to the client; this awakens the continuation, which incrementally builds its list of body task streams. When all the body task streams have been received, the nbody-simulator initiates a simulation by multicasting a :simulate message to all the bodies, and specifying a new stream, client2, as the client. It then spawns another continuation to collect results as they arrive and incrementally build the result list, which it finally returns to its original clients.

We use a sequenced task stream for the body class to ensure that :step messages relevant to the next step are not consumed during the current step. This works cooperatively. First, the sequenced stream steps by integer values starting from 0 (this is the default, and may be overridden). Second, each :step message is sent with an order key that is greater than the current step number but less than the next step number (using the :by option to sending). Finally, the :initiate-step message is ordered by the integer representing the (now) current step, which allows messages for that step to be consumed, but not for any step greater than it. This scheme also ensures that no body will process its first :step message until it has dealt with its first :initiate-step message, which provides the order key of 0; this is sent after a body has initialized its simulation parameters in :simulate.

15.2.3   Monitoring Lamina Computations

We have seen that LAMINA programs consist of fine-grained tasks that are executed by objects in response to messages arriving on their task streams. This means that these applications can be effectively monitored by simply monitoring the critical operations performed on messages by LAMINA objects, namely, the *generation* of messages by an object, the *arrival* of messages at the task stream of a target object, and the *dispatch* of such messages—which causes computation to be performed by the target object and perhaps further messages to be generated.

All application objects inherit from the lamina class, which defines a common format for messages and provides the method that dispatches operations from the task stream of an object. This allows us to to capture important information about a message (such as the method name, its parameters, the task stream of the originator of the message, the clients of the task specified by the message, and so forth) non-intrusively: by examining an object's task stream.

Messages also get timestamps when they are generated and when they are received at critical intermediate points on their way to the target dispatching process, thus providing

---

[2]A preferred location can also be specified by providing an appropriate site or stream reference [6].

access to performance indicators such as message latencies.

Other data available are: the time taken executing particular methods, the number of messages backed up on the task stream of an object, the number of tasks executed by an object, the number of tasks associated with a particular method executed, and so forth. Such information can then be presented either by object instance—sorting on key parameters to focus on the most 'interesting' objects—or aggregated by object class and method type. With additional effort, it can also be correlated in an application-specific grouping that represents the structure of a distributed sub-computation, such as an application pipeline or a distributed loop. Again, this is non-intrusive from the point of view of the application programmer and the running application.

15.3 A Message-Passing Machine Model

In this section, we describe a message-passing architecture to support the LAMINA object model. This architecture has been modelled using the CARE component library introduced in section 15.1.

15.3.1 Architectural Components

LAMINA is targeted to an multiprocessor system consisting of several hundreds of independent processing sites that are interconnected by a direct communications network. The network supports a low-latency, cut-through, point-to-point routing protocol that supports multicast transmissions [3, 4].

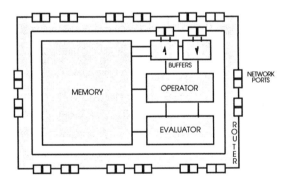

Figure 15.3
A processing site

A site is shown in figure 15.3, and it consists of:

- an *evaluator*, a general-purpose processor that is responsible for executing application code;

- an *operator*, a dedicated co-processor that is responsible for creating and accepting messages, for scheduling evaluator processes, and for managing storage;

- some *buffers*, which interface the operator to the communications facility;

- some *memory*, which is shared by the evaluator, the operator and the buffers at the site; and,

- some *network ports* and a dedicated *router*, which together form the communications hardware of the site.

These components are described in more detail below.

15.3.1.1   Communications Support   The processing sites are typically embedded in a low-dimensional network, such as a mesh or torus, with routing decisions independently made at each site.

The communications hardware at each site implements a dynamic, cut-through routing algorithm [3]. Cut-through routing means that a router makes (and acts upon) a routing decision as soon as the first few bytes of a packet have been received [12], rather than after the entire packet has been buffered as in store-and-forward schemes. The decision is dynamic in our system because it is based on the availability of output ports at that time, thus adapting to prevailing network load conditions. In the exceptional case that no suitable port is available due to congestion, the router instead initiates a connection to the local buffer and the message is stored in its entirety in local memory for later retransmission by the operator.[3]

With cut-through routing, the latency of a message is proportional to the sum of its length and the distance it covers in the network [5], as opposed to being proportional to the product of the two as with store-and-forward schemes. This results in a significant reduction in latency, making finer-grain LAMINA tasks cost-effective. It also makes locality less of an issue in object allocation.

Finally, the router provides direct support for multicast packets [3, 4], allowing low-latency transmission of the same packet to multiple destinations while using common channels when possible. This is a useful feature for LAMINA applications because it provides an efficient mechanism for messages that are multicast to replicated objects.

15.3.1.2   Message-Handling Support   The operator provides the message handling facilities at a processing site. It is primarily responsible for accepting and generating messages in the form of packets. It also enables and schedules processes for execution in the evaluator, and manages site storage.

As described earlier, LAMINA messages may contain values with arbitrary internal structure. These are to be passed by copying, and must be encoded before transmission. This function is performed by the operator. When the process running in the evaluator needs to transmit a message, it passes the operator a pointer to the data to be transmitted. The operator recursively traverses the data, linearizing it and relativizing internal pointers to produce a coded, relocatable copy. It forms this into a packet and transfers it to the network buffer for transmission to the remote site.

When the packet arrives at its destination, the operator at that site performs the reverse mapping, decoding: offsetting the relativized pointers to produce an isomorphic

---

[3]Our model assumes that virtual memory is managed on a system-wide basis. This means that sufficient local storage can be obtained to buffer incoming messages that have been misrouted. The mechanisms by which this storage is made available is not modelled.

copy of the original data in local memory, within the address space of the receiving object.

The evaluator at the transmitting site is free to continue processing once it has passed the message data pointer to the operator. However, it must not mutate the data until the encoding is completed. Similarly, the evaluator at the destination site is not involved in message reception. The operator places the message on the targeted stream, and, if it is for a dormant LAMINA object, enables the appropriate dispatch process and passes it to the evaluator for execution.

15.3.1.3 Simulation Model and Parameters

CARE simulates the communications subsystem just described at approximately the register-transfer level. The operator is functionally simulated and the evaluator uses the machine running the simulation to actually execute and time the application code. The storage associated with evaluators and operators in not explicitly modelled; nor is the operator's management of this storage. Most components are parameterized, allowing a wide range of architectures to be modelled with little effort.

For typical experiments, the base system cycle is set at $100ns$, so the evaluator is assumed to deliver up to 10 MIPS performance.[4] Task switching is assumed to take 150 cycles in each direction. Message creation and acceptance costs 100 cycles to interrupt the operator and set up internal registers and an additional 16 cycles per 32-bit word of data for encoding or decoding. Network channels are 4 bits wide, giving a channel bandwidth of 40 Mb/s. Finally, the system is configured as a torus with eight bidirectional channels at each site.

15.3.2 Monitoring Components

One characteristic of the monitoring environment that has proven critical to the development of useful instrumentation is consistency between the LAMINA computation model, the CARE machine model, and the SIMPLE measurement model. For LAMINA, objects interact by passing messages. For CARE, message arrival triggers machine operations. For SIMPLE, simulations are performed and monitored in terms of message traffic. Monitoring communications is thus equivalent to monitoring process interactions and monitoring process interactions is equivalent to monitoring the computation.

This approach allows us to provide a consistent view in the instrumentation of system operations involving both LAMINA application objects and CARE component objects. The measurements of message activity and network activity are easily related. This approach also has the additional attraction of allowing us to accomplish fast, flexible, and accurate simulations by the expedient of merely timing real execution between communication events: the only events we need to explicitly simulate are those that involve component communications.

A LAMINA application is therefore monitored in terms of the messages passed between LAMINA objects. The performance of the application can then be understood by monitoring the actions performed by the underlying system resources in supporting this

---

[4]Depending on the expected ratio between peak and average pipeline occupancy, this might realistically represent approximately 7 MIPS delivered instruction execution rate.

message traffic, namely, the *creation*, *communication* and *receipt* of message packets, and the *scheduling* and *execution* of tasks. The impact of the system design, its operating parameters, and its finite resources can be studied in terms of measures such as resource utilization, service latencies, resource conflicts, load imbalances, and resource bottlenecks.

15.4   Understanding Performance

In this section, we will describe some representative panels to illustrate how the operation of a concurrent application can be understood through the cooperative interaction of SIMPLE, CARE, and LAMINA.

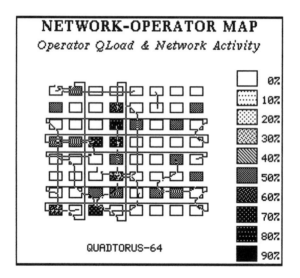

Figure 15.4
Mapping Panel

15.4.0.1   Activity and Load Maps   One of the most intuitive kinds of displays is the 'mapping' presentation. It provides an animation of activity in the design in terms of the spatial arrangement the system designer laid out when the structural organization of the design was defined. The 'Network Operator Map' panel shown in figure 15.4 uses this topology to display loads on the operator resources in the system and the activity in the interconnection network. The panel is driven by probes connected to the network output ports and operators of a 64-site system.

The boxes in figure 15.4 correspond to operators in the system. Their shading indicates how many packets are queued up for service by the corresponding operator. The panel is driven by probes monitoring operator queue lengths. Each such probe (one per operator in the system) is triggered whenever its host operator's status changes (indicating its activity) or when a packet arrives either from the network or from the evaluator at the site. Thus, the load depicted by this panel shifts as the simulation proceeds so that bottlenecks in operator resources stand out as visual 'hot spots'. Load imbalances show up as more or less constant utilization of only certain operators.

The lines between boxes correspond to connections made for packet transmission between the network ports of neighboring sites, so that a qualitative view of the degree to which the network is utilized at a given time in the simulation is available. This display is driven by probes monitoring network output components, each of which is triggered when a connection is either made or terminated at its site. We have found this panel useful in debugging the network protocols that we have experimented with—certain types of deadlocks and thrashing are often immediately apparent; for example, as connections that, once formed, are never broken, or as cyclical patterns of packets between sets of sites.

In CARE, mapping presentations have been specialized to create a number of different panels. We have found it useful for seeing object load (the number of LAMINA objects at a site), message load (the sum of the lengths of all LAMINA task queues at the site—an indication of the amount of processing work pending), or, simply, evaluator status.

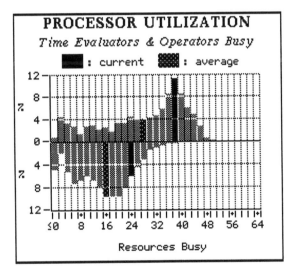

Figure 15.5
Utilization Histogram

15.4.0.2 Utilization Histograms A more statistical view of the operation of the system over time is provided by the depiction of, for example, the utilization of operator and evaluator resources as histograms. The 'Processor Utilization' panel shown in figure 15.5 shows the percentage of time that a given number of evaluators, displayed on the top half of the panel, and a given number of operators, displayed on the bottom half of the panel, have been used. Highlighting shows what the current situation is (37–38 evaluators are busy) as well as what the average situation has been through the current time of the simulation (27–28 evaluators have been busy simultaneously on average).

The data driving this panel is provided by probes that monitor transitions between 'busy' and 'idle' states at each of the operators and evaluators in the system. This data is aggregated by the panel to determine the periods of time in which each of these resources are used. The overlaps in utilization among operators (and separately among evaluators) of the system are determined from this information. From these calculated overlaps, the utilization of system resources for each of the overlapping periods is determined.

If this panel indicates that only a few evaluators are concurrently active, it may be either that the application is not generating enough concurrency, or that the processing load is unevenly balanced so that the potential concurrency is not being exploited.

We have used specializations of histograms in CARE to show quantities such as packet size distributions, network latency distributions and so forth.

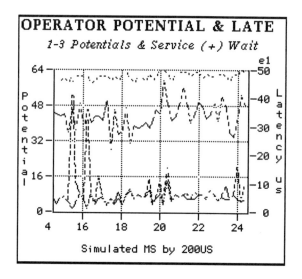

Figure 15.6
Activity Stripchart

15.4.0.3 Load and Latency Strip Charts A 'strip chart' presentation is a useful way to see the history of some measure of system activity. There are four such measures plotted in the 'Operator Potential & Latency' panel shown in figure 15.6.

This panel accepts data from probes attached to each of the operators in the system; these probes report the service queue depths and various latencies (based on packet timestamps) whenever their host operator performs a service.

Two of the measures are plotted on the scale at the right side of the strip chart, and they show the latency being experienced by operators in the system as they receive and service packets from the network. The time to service packets is the lower of the two plots, and it generally ranges from 20 to 80 microseconds in this case.[5] There are occasional delays between the time a packet is received and service on it is begun. This delay is shown as an incremental plot on top of the plot depicting packet service latencies; the

---

[5]Note the displayed 'e1' multiplier for the axis tick marks.

worst spike shows a queueing delay of approximately 400 microseconds, 15 milliseconds or so into the simulation.

If the latencies shown by this panel have a periodic character with unacceptable peak times, it may be that there are load imbalances that can be addressed to improve this situation. Alternatively, more or less monotonically increasing latencies indicate application pipelines that are not keeping up with their inputs. If the affected pipelines can be replicated and work spread among them, or if the grain size of the larger pipeline stages can be reduced—and the resources are adequate to the demand—the bottlenecks causing the increasing latencies may be broken.

The two upper measures plotted in figure 15.6 refer to the 'potential' for additional work remaining in the system. Their scale, indicating the number of idle operators in the system, is shown on the left side of the strip chart. The lower of the two plots indicates the number of operators that have no packets in their service queues. The remaining measure plotted is similar, and it indicates the number of operators that have less than three packets in their service queues.

The values of these 'potential' plots is an indication of resource utilization over time. The distance between them is an indication of load balance: if they are well spread, most of the operator resources have one to three packets to handle, which is an indication of good load balance. Alternatively, both plots close together toward the middle of the axis indicate that half of the resources described have more than three packets to handle and half have none: an indication of poor load balance. Both plots drawn down toward the bottom of the panel may indicate an overloaded system: all the resources being monitored have several packets in their service queues.

As shown in figure 15.9, similar panels have been defined for the communications subsystem (the 'Network Load & Latency' panel) and the processing subsystem (the 'Evaluator Potential & Latency' panel). These can be used in conjunction with the one described here to see the relative granularity among the subsystems and their relative utilization so as to discover the critical resources in the system.

15.4.0.4 Activity Tables

Often the most informative way to present data is as text tables. The two panels shown in figure 15.7 use 'scrolling text' presentations to dynamically summarize the activity of LAMINA application objects in the system.

These panels are driven by probes that are attached to the evaluators in the system. These probes monitor every task execution, reporting various metrics associated with the task and the object that executed it.

In the 'Activity By Instance' panel, each line in the scrolling display represents a single LAMINA object in the application. The columns of the tables denote, respectively:

- the expected service time of the object, that is, the product of its average task execution time and the number of messages in its task stream. This is an indication of the degree to which this object is a bottleneck. The text lines are periodically sorted so that the objects that have the highest expected service time bubble to the top of the display. Objects forming potential bottlenecks are thereby evident.

- the number of messages on the object's task stream.

ACTIVITY BY INSTANCE				ACTIVITY BY CLASS			
Service/Q	*Avg*	*(Runs)*	*Delay Site*	*Service/Q*	*Avg*	*(Runs)*	*Instances*
1.3/11	0.115 (54)	1.445	(7 5) *EMITTER-OBSERVATION 12.0	0.2/ 0.6	0.298 (135)		15 (CLUSTER-STATUS . CLUSTER-REPOR
1.2/ 4	0.305 (18)	2.302	(7 8) *EMITTER-FIX 5 (7 8) 16902	0.1/ 1.0	0.137 (29)		3 (CLUSTER-TIMER . TIME)
1.0/ 4	0.239 (24)	0.727	(7 4) *CLUSTER-STATUS 3 (7 4) 13	0.1/ 1.0	0.104 (39)		3 (CLUSTER-TIMER . MATCH)
0.9/ 6	0.153 (11)	0.215	(4 2) *CLUSTER-TIMER 5.0 (4 2) 2	0.1/ 0.2	0.320 (305)		20 (EMITTER-FIX . REPORT)
0.8/ 3	0.250 (25)	0.306	(7 5) *CLUSTER-STATUS 3 (7 5) 13	0.0/ 0.6	0.081 (662)		20 (EMITTER-OBSERVATION . UPDATE-O
0.7/ 3	0.246 (26)	0.230	(7 8) *CLUSTER-STATUS 3 (7 8) 13	0.0/ 0.2	0.201 (312)		20 (EMITTER-OBSERVATION . REPORT)
0.5/ 2	0.259 (26)	0.313	(7 7) *CLUSTER-STATUS 2 (7 7) 13	0.0/ 0.1	0.223 (171)		10 (CLUSTER-STATUS . MATCH)
0.4/ 3	0.118 (62)	0.159	(7 1) *EMITTER-OBSERVATION 4.0 (	0.0/ 0.0	0.588 (1)		1 (ELINT 0)
0.3/ 1	0.260 (28)	0.299	(7 6) *CLUSTER-STATUS 0 (7 6) 13	0.0/ 0.0	0.063 (1)		1 (ELINT 0 0)
0.2/ 1	0.234 (35)	0.227	(4 2) *CLUSTER-STATUS 2 (4 2) 72	0.0/ 0.0	0.201 (3)		1 (CLUSTER-MANAGER . 2CONTINUATIO
0.1/ 1	0.116 (29)	0.110	(5 3) *EMITTER-OBSERVATION 0.2 (	0.0/ 0.0	0.242 (3)		3 (CLUSTER-TIMER . SET-CLUSTER-MA
0.0/ 0	0.141 (17)	1.180	(7 6) *EMITTER-STATUS 1.0 (7 6)	0.0/ 0.0	0.169 (3)		3 (CLUSTER-TIMER . SET-CLUSTER-PL

Figure 15.7
Activity Tables

- the average task execution time for the object, that is, the average time it has taken to process a message up to this point in the simulation.

- the number of messages that have been processed by the object, an indication of its relative activity.

- the delay experienced by the most recent message that was executed (as a task) by the object. (More precisely, the panel reflects the situation when it was last refreshed.) This delay is the interval from the generation of the message by the sending object at some remote site to the actual execution of the task by this object at its site. It represents the overhead involved in getting the task accomplished, and, as such, includes the latency in getting the message delivered as well as the scheduling delay before the task corresponding to the message is executed, which may include multiple schedulings of the process corresponding to the object.

- the site at which the object is located. This can be used to discover if the object is bottlenecking because of load imbalance, and this is apparent if the most backed-up objects are colocated.

- a printed representation of the object, showing in particular its class.

The 'Activity By Class' panel presents this information aggregated by the class of object and type of message, as shown in the rightmost column of the display. This information can be used to see the distribution of work due to the application design. An inappropriate distribution may indicate the application needs to be reorganized; the display provides guidance about where this effort should be concentrated.

15.4.0.5 Cumulative Latencies The 'Cumulative Latencies' panel in figure 15.8 is an example of a simple 'line plot' presentation. It displays a snapshot of the same message delays described above, but as experienced by the most recent messages received and processed by each of the extant application objects (shown along the bottom axis). There

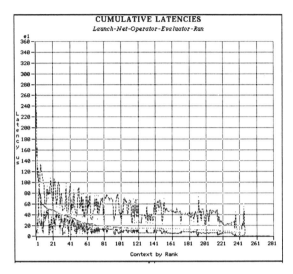

Figure 15.8
Cumulative Latencies

are five curves, incrementally showing the latency experienced by the message at the source operator, being routed in the network, waiting for service at the target operator, being serviced by the target operator, waiting for execution at the target evaluator, and, finally, being executed as the task that consumes the message. The curves are sorted by the sum of the first four delays above, which represents the overhead in getting the requested task accomplished at the targeted object.

15.4.0.6   A Complete Instrument   The panels described above have been collected into the CARE 'Observer' instrument shown in figure 15.9. Additionally, the instrument provides an 'annotation' panel reflecting system parameters and other data, so that experimental parameters are evident.

The instrument thereby provides a unified view of system operation that correlates the activity of hardware abstractions, that is multiprocessor subsystems, with application abstractions, that is, LAMINA objects.

15.5   Building Instrumentation

We have indicated throughout this article how SIMPLE/CARE lets application programmers and system designers see the operation of an application in a system 'on-line': as it is executing code doing the work of the application. In this section, we will describe the instrumentation architecture in greater detail.

15.5.0.1   Probes   Probes capture the data necessary to drive panels. Probes, like components, are represented by objects in SIMPLE. A probe instance is attached to a single component instance in the simulated system.

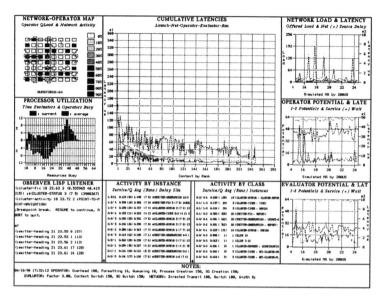

Figure 15.9
CARE 'Observer' Instrument

A probe is informed of all simulation events (signifying changes to component state) associated with its host component. The mechanism for this is straightforward: all components inherit functionality that passes on each simulation event handled by the component to trigger each of the probes attached to it. Triggering simply involves calling a standard method (namely, :trigger) on each of the probes.

Probes may examine the event that triggered them, query the state of their host (or some other) component, manipulate their own state (thus, probes can be history-sensitive), and, finally, forward computed data to attached panels.

Probe data is provided to clients as a property list that tags each value with an identifying keyword symbol. This is encapsulated with a 'probed object' for which the data is being reported and a number representing the 'current' simulated time. The probed object can be an arbitrary data structure; it may be the attached component or one related to it (for example, the component enclosing it), a data structure manipulated by the component (for example, a 'process' structure in an evaluator), or perhaps an application data structure (for example, a LAMINA object).

Figure 15.10 shows the definition of a CARE probe class that measures and reports the number of runnable processes queued on an evaluator. Since processes arriving from the local operator (via the packet-in port) increment the load, and since transitions in the evaluator's status reflect whether the evaluator is currently busy or idle, the :trigger code first checks to see if the triggering event is one of these two kinds (via the predicates state-event? and port-event?). If the event is found to be relevant, the probe computes the total queue load and passes it on to its downstream panels, via the inherited :select method.

The probe data property list in this example has a single entry (for the :busy key);

```
(DEFPROBE evaluator-queue-probe  () ; no mixins
  ;; instance variables: cache attached evaluator slots
  ((Input-Queue (PROBE-SLOT Evaluator-Queue))  ; process queue
   (Packet-In  (PROBE-SLOT Packet-In)) ; port
   (Site (PROBE-SLOT* Superior Superior))) ; enclosing site
  (:documentation "Reports process queue lengths")
  (:component-type evaluator) ; type specifier
  (:TRIGGER (tag value now)   ; event trigger and parameters
    (when (or (STATE-EVENT? status)      ; status change?
              (PORT-EVENT? packet-in))  ; process arrival?
      (send self :SELECT       ; [protocol] inform attached panels
        Site                   ; probed object = site component
        '(:busy ,(+ (queue-length Input-Queue) ; probe data plist
                    (case (PROBE-STATE Status)
                      ((ready stalled) 0) (t 1))))
          (simulated-microsecond-time now))))) ; probe time, scaled
```

Figure 15.10
Example Probe Definition

in general, it will provide a number of related properties. For example, an evaluator probe that monitors task executions reports, among other data, a process context for the LAMINA object, the stream it consumed a message from, its site, the method that it executed, and the timestamps on the packet that started the task. The example probe also identifies the data as being for the evaluator's enclosing site component, and it scales the reported time from (dimensionless) event time units to microseconds.

15.5.0.2 Panels Panels bring together the data analysis and presentation aspects of SIMPLE's instrumentation system. They take the data supplied by individual probes and successively transform and correlate this to produce the quantities that drive their particular style of display.

These transformation are conceptually accomplished through manipulations on 'records' that are maintained in two data structures by the panel. One set of records, the *state records*, is stored as a table indexed by the probed object reported by the probes driving the panel. Each record in this set stores information derived from the probe data passed in for that probed object. The second set of records, the *display records*, is organized along panel-specific dimensions (typically as a list) to satisfy display goals; each record in this set stores the quantities that need to be displayed along the various 'axes' of the panel. This set may thus contain records indexed by time, histogram bin, probed object, and so forth.

The actions taken by a panel are then to:

- update the relevant records corresponding to the probe data passed as parameters to the :update call. This involves extracting quantities from the probe data property list, computing transformed values based on this and the retained data stored in the records, and storing results back into the appropriate records.

- analyze the set of display records periodically, that is, reorganize them based on display objectives, such as sorting on display record fields.

- display the results of these periodic analyses in the display style of the panel, that is, transform display record quantities into graphics actions on the screen.

Panel classes are defined by subclassing the appropriate presentation (or panel) class and defining default values for the various attributes exported by the presentation (or panel) superclass. The attributes that customize a presentation are those that affect the panel's graphical appearance, such as legends, scales, axes labels and the like, as well as those that achieve its functional objectives: declarations of the types of probes required, and *transformation expressions*: arbitrary code expressions in an augmented Lisp syntax that specify the transformations between the information provided by the probes and that saved and displayed by the panel. Other attributes control the computing resources used by the panel; these are parameters such as sampling intervals, refresh periods, and history depths. Many of these parameters may also be customized dynamically through standard menus.

The transformation expressions provided for a panel are processed when a new panel is created. They are parsed and compiled at that time into code bodies that will maintain the record sets discussed above. The code bodies are then called at runtime by the underlying methods of the presentation.

```
(DEFPANEL evaluator-queue-history-panel
         (SCROLLING-LINE-PLOT-PRESENTATION) ; inheritance
  ;; attributes that are initialized once
  ((Name      "EVALUATOR QUEUE HISTORY")
   (Legend    "Total Evaluator Queue Lengths")
   (Sampling-Interval 200)     ; 1 sample kept per 200us
   (Time-Scale-Factor 0.001)   ; us [from probes] to ms [display]
   (Scroll-Range      10)      ; 10ms 'window' of time displayed
   (Probes            '((:queue-probe evaluator-queue-probe)))
   (Left-Axis-Form    '(:queue-probe :busy save-sum)) ; sum queue lengths
   (Bottom-Axis-Form  '(:simulator :time)) ; reported probe times
   (Plot-Update-Form  '(send self :update-time (:simulator :time))))
  ;; attributes that are reset between simulation runs
  ((Left-Axis  (axis :label "Evaluator Queue Sum" :range (range 0.0 nil)))
   (Bottom-Axis (axis :label (format nil "MS by ~DUS" Sampling-Interval)
                      :range Scroll-Range))))
```

Figure 15.11
Example Panel Definition

Figure 15.11 defines a strip chart that plots the recent history of total evaluator queue lengths in the system over time, thus providing a view of the available application concurrency.

The probes attribute defines the types of probes that the panel needs—in this case, evaluator-queue-probes of figure 15.10. When a panel of this type is created, the simulation system attaches probes of the desired types to all components of the type specified in the probe definition (in this case, evaluators) in the system design under study. The specification pairs a keyword symbol—the probe key—with a particular kind of probe; the keyword is then used to denote the data supplied by a probe of that type within the transformation expressions.[6]

The left-axis-form describes how the data provided by a probe is to be plotted along the left axis. Within such a transformation expression, the general form for denoting the keyed data values supplied by a probe is as a list composed of the relevant probe key and the relevant data key, such as (:queue-probe :busy). These value expressions can be combined with others as required (through built-in or user-defined functions) to compute derived values. For example, one definition of 'load' on a resource in CARE is through the formula $1 - (1/1 + Q)$, where Q denotes the total lengths of all the queues that need to be serviced by that resource. Its corresponding transformation expression might be

```
(- 1.0 (/ 1.0 (1+ (:queue-probe :busy))))
```

The optional save-sum modifier in the probe value expression for the left axis introduces a summation transformation, which requires that the overall sum be decremented by the previous :busy value reported for the probed object and then be incremented by the new reported value. Were the modifier absent, the relevant display record would simply reflect the value reported by the last probe; instead, it now stores the running total of the latest reported values per probed object. SIMPLE has a library of such procedures to aggregate and classify data for display; new procedures may also be defined.

The update-form specification organizes display lists along the dimension of simulated time, corresponding to the bottom axis of the display. In general, this needs to be specified only when mapping time; otherwise, the default presentation-specific behavior is sufficient, and nothing need be specified in the panel definition.

This panel does not need the analysis feature that most panels provide as an option. SIMPLE's basic analysis operation allows sorting display lists by arbitrary predicates applied to arbitrary record fields. This is expressed through an 'analysis form' declaration such as

```
(sort-arrays (list (list #'> (:latency-probe (+ :launch :network)))))
```

which specifies that display records are sorted in decreasing order of the sum of the 'launch' and 'network' delays reported by a 'latency' probe (presumably monitoring communication latencies). The list-of-lists format of the specification allows for progressively finer sorts on items that are equivalent with respect to a coarser sort predicate.

---

[6]This scheme allows the panel to distinguish or combine data from different types of probes. Furthermore, keeping probes isolated from the expressions in this way allows different probes to be 'plugged in' to the panel by simply specifying a different binding list. The resolution from probe type to probe key is automatically performed by the simulation system.

15.6   A Case Study

In this section, as an example of our experience with the tools documented above, we describe a performance study of a concurrent object-based application that was implemented in LAMINA, and we show how the underlying instrumentation system helped us understand and improve upon its performance. The study is reported upon more fully in [18].

Our example application, called ELINT, is a soft real-time system for interpreting preprocessed, passively-acquired radar emissions from aircraft [8, 27]. ELINT correlates the emissions observed by multiple, mobile detection sites into the individual radar emitters producing those emissions. It tracks the emitters and then groups them into clusters that are tracking together. Finally, it hypothesizes the types and number of platforms (aircraft) in the clusters and infers their activity.

The inputs to ELINT are time-ordered streams of preprocessed observations from the detection sites. Each observation contains an indication of the current data timeslice, an identifier for the detected radar emitter, and information regarding its current signal characteristics such as quality, operating mode and line of bearing. The outputs of ELINT are real-time reports on the tracks, constituent platforms, and activities of the clusters in the monitored airspace. These reports may be used, for example, to maintain a 'situation board' describing the status of the airspace.

15.6.1   Application Objects

ELINT exhibits a number of characteristics that are of interest when considering ways of organizing it as a parallel system.

- The system processes continuous, errorful, real-time input data.

- The input data describes relatively independent and persistent activities. Aircraft are independent entities (radar emitters somewhat less so), and they tend to be detected for long intervals, relative to the data period.

- The overall problem has an irregular, dynamic and data-dependent structure. Aircraft come and go over time, and their numbers, types, movements and intentions vary.

- Problem solution proceeds largely by 'abstracting' the input data. Detected emissions are correlated into radar emitters that are further tracked and consolidated into aircraft.

This suggests that any parallel decomposition scheme would do well to exploit the potentially large amount of data parallelism inherent in the problem as multiple, loosely-coupled activities are monitored. Pipelining is also indicated in the data-driven abstraction process. Lastly, the persistence of activities makes an object-oriented representation attractive because it localizes the data-driven state changes and generates concurrent processes (i.e., objects) only as needed. This allows the cost of establishing a concurrent process to be amortized over the lifetime of the activity it models.

15.6.1.1   Pipeline Flow   ELINT 's basic processing flow is data-driven. Every data timeslice, new observations are input into the system and either correlated with known emitters or used to create new emitters. The data contained in the observations are used to update the status and course history of the emitters. Any unclustered emitters with sufficient track data are matched against known clusters, and, failing that, formed into new clusters. Finally, data from the emitters are used to update the track, activity and platform history of their clusters.

The system is naturally organized as parallel, data-driven object pipelines in LAMINA , as shown in figure 15.12.

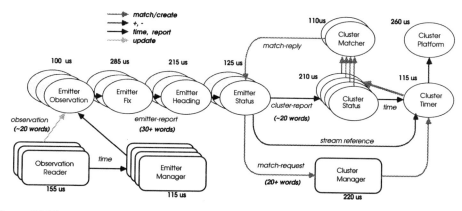

Figure 15.12
ELINT organization, with average task and message granularities

Observation-readers form the input interface of the system to the data collection sites. They read in time-tagged **observation** structures representing observed emissions, and pass these on to the **emitter-observations** for the identified emitters. If the emission represents a new emitter they instead pass it to the **emitter-manager** responsible, which creates a new one (if necessary) and so informs the readers.

Emitter-observations buffer the **observations** until the end of the current data timeslice is detected. Thereafter, they compute confidence and status information about the represented emitter and form an **emitter-report** structure that they pass down the pipeline. Successive pipeline stages compute and attach track (i.e., a location fix and a heading) information to this report.

Emitter-status objects link their respective emitters to an appropriate cluster, and, once clustered, propagate their reports to the cluster. Each group of **cluster-status** objects implements a distributed database of the track and activity history of a cluster; this is used both to report on the cluster periodically and to match against the tracks of new emitters that attempt to cluster. Finally, whenever an emitter is added to or removed from a cluster, the associated **cluster platform** object adjusts its hypothesis on the platforms forming the cluster.

15.6.1.2   Replication   Replication is a useful means of relieving congestion. When feasible, it allows for wider pipelines and increased throughput. Early experience with

instrumentation indicated that the observation-readers were obvious candidates for replication, since the rest of the system was often starved for data.

Instrumentation also pointed up a bottleneck that results when multiple constituent
emitters supply reports to a cluster every timeslice. Congestion was evident as growing
message queues for objects storing cluster track histories, and the resulting monotonically
increasing latencies at their evaluator resources as the pending messages awaited service.
This led to the replication of cluster-status objects to partition a cluster's history by data
time. Note, incidentally, that the benefit of replication here is two-fold: besides reducing
congestion, the grain size of the match performed at each object during clustering is also
reduced.

Finally, emitter-managers are also replicated to scale with the size of the system; a
simple modulo operation on an emitter's (integer) identifier is used to break dependencies
while maintaining creation consistency; this allows for more concurrent emitter creation.

15.6.1.3 Clustering An emitter that has been tracked for a sufficient period of time
must either match an existing cluster or be formed into a new one. This computation
is organized as a distributed loop as shown in figure 15.12. During each iteration of
the loop, the emitter attempts to match against those clusters that have been created
since the last iteration, and the loop terminates when it successfully matches an existing
cluster or causes a new one to be created.

An emitter-status object that needs to cluster sends the cluster-manager a match-request
structure containing the recent track history of the emitter and a counter of the number
of clusters that it has already (unsuccessfully) matched against. The latter maintains a
private list of all extant clusters; it multicasts the request to the cluster-timers of those
clusters that have not been matched against, first incrementing the counter to reflect the
total number of clusters. If, however, the counter shows that matches against all clusters
have failed, it creates and initializes a new cluster for the emitter, for which the match
always succeeds.

A cluster-timer defers the request until it is coincident in time, a decision that is based
upon the reports supplied by its constituent emitters. Thereupon it multicasts the request
to its cluster-status objects, specifying a selected cluster-matcher as the intermediate client
of the match to diffuse the fan-in load. The cluster-matcher collects the partial results of
the match and then sends a summary of the results to the original emitter-status client.
The latter awaits either a successful reply from one cluster or unsuccessful replies from all
the clusters that it attempted to match against during this iteration, and thus determines
whether to terminate or continue the distributed loop.

The multi-level fan-out and fan-in trees allow for significant throughput in the match
process. An emitter can concurrently match against multiple clusters, and each cluster
can concurrently service multiple matches as well as perform each individual match in
parallel. The major potential bottleneck in this scheme is the cluster-manager; instrumentation has shown this not to be so in practice.

15.6.1.4 Object Allocation ELINT uses only 'static' allocation of objects to processing sites. Multiple allocators, the managers, independently make the allocation decisions
at object creation time. The implementation reported here used no dynamic migration
of objects to balance load.

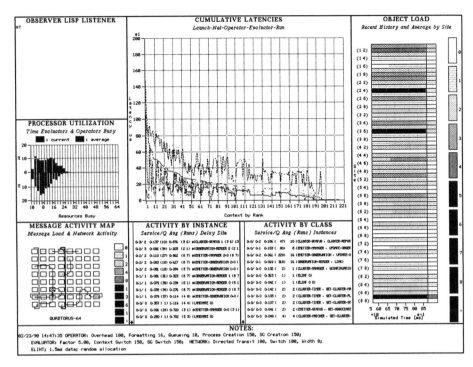

Figure 15.13
Load Balance

Random allocation performed well when the number of objects was far greater than the number of processing sites, but resulted in imbalances, often significant, with sparser distributions. A typical situation is depicted in figure 15.13, which provides an instrumented view of ELINT executing on a 64-site torus with random object allocation.

The 'Object Load' panel at the far right uses gray shades to map the number of objects at each site over time. The darker bands at the sites labeled (2 4), (3 6) and (8 7) indicate that these sites are more heavily loaded; in particular, site (8 7) has 6 objects. Conversely, a number of other sites have no objects on them, as indicated by the clear bands. As we shall see in section 15.6.2, this imbalance impacts the performance of the application by limiting the throughput of the system.

A better allocation scheme partitioned the processing sites among the object classes during initialization and allocated objects randomly within each block at runtime. The partition was based on the measured relative activity of the classes, using information such as that shown by the 'Activity' panels in figure 15.7. This strategy reserved resources for the expected critical path and reduced both the load variance over the processing grid as well as the interference between pipeline stages.

15.6.2   Application Performance

We analyzed the outputs of ELINT executions to determine the quantitative performance
of the system. Every report that is output by ELINT (e.g., an emitter fix) is pertinent
to a particular data timeslice, since it is based on new observations that were (or were
not) provided for that timeslice. Each timeslice represents one 'tick' of an external clock
(corresponding to the scan time of the detection sites) and thus also signifies the real
time at which the data for that cycle was available to the system. Thus we defined the
latency of a report to be the elapsed time from the start of the relevant timeslice to the
time that the report was generated by the system.

Averaging the latencies for certain classes of reports (e.g., emitter fixes) on a timeslice-
by-timeslice basis gave us a means of testing whether the system could process the data
at the rate at which it was provided—average latencies that increased over time meant
that it could not. Thus, the *sustainable data rate* for a given scenario and processor
population was the fastest rate (i.e., smallest timeslice duration) at which data could be
supplied to the system such that the latencies of these key inferences did not increase
over time.

The inferences we chose to look at were those which were indicative of the 'normal'
processing duties of the system, namely, emitter and cluster track computations. These
latencies were also a good choice from a pragmatic standpoint because they were sufficiently frequent for trends to be analysed programmatically without the problems induced
by sparse data. We also used scenarios that contained a stable population of emitters
and clusters so as to minimize the variations in observed latencies that could otherwise
be caused by the sudden variations in system load.

We measured *speedup* for a particular scenario by comparing the sustainable data
rate for various processor populations with that for a single processor. The scenario
reported upon here lasted forty timeslices and consisted of twenty emitters that formed
four clusters. The results are shown in figure 15.14.

With one object per site, ELINT could sustain a data rate of 400 microseconds per
timeslice, a speedup of eighty over the serial case. The grain sizes of ELINT tasks and
messages that are shown in figure 15.12 provide us with the explanation for this.

In particular, emitter-observations have an average task granularity of 100 microseconds, and they each typically receive and process three messages per timeslice before
initiating further pipeline activity. These are two :update messages providing an observation from each of the detection sites in the scenario and a :report message signifying
the end of the current timeslice. This creates a 'hard' performance limit of 300–400
microseconds per data timeslice, which is approached in this case. Note that the limit
is the maximum throughput of a single pipeline; it is independent of the 'width' of the
scenario, i.e., the number of pipelines. Conversely, speedup is proportional to the number
of pipelines that can operate in parallel, which is twenty in this case. The eighty-fold
overall gain is realized because each individual pipeline gives an additional factor of four.

As the load on the sites increases with smaller processor populations, the contention for
site resources degrades performance, even with balanced loads, because pipelines must
now run slower. A poor load balance additionally reduces performance, because pipelines
can only go as fast as their slowest stage—the sustainable data rate of the system is now

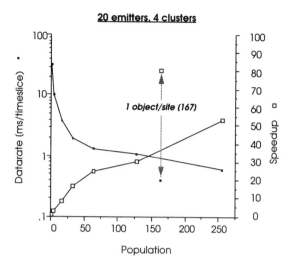

Figure 15.14
Speedup and Data Rate

limited by the throughput of the most heavily loaded site.

Load variance across the sites accounts for sub-unitary speedup[7]. Non-ideal load distributions occur as a consequence of any realistic allocation scheme. Independent allocators, necessary to alleviate bottlenecks, cannot easily share a consistent view of the global load because of the distributed nature of CARE. Thus, for example, in the 64 site case, 6 managers used the class-based scheme to allocate 80 dynamic emitter objects over a pool of 25 sites. The best distribution here would have been one where 3–4 objects resided on each site; in actuality, two sites hosted 5 objects each, which limited the throughput of the system to 1.3 milliseconds per data timeslice. However, as noted earlier, a purely random allocation scheme often resulted in more inter-site variance than this.

Figure 15.15 shows a similar situation (using a more recent, revised CARE model) with the same number of managers allocating over a pool of 31 sites. The system is being driven at a data rate of 800 microseconds per timeslice.

Site (5 4) is hosting 5 emitter-class objects, with one emitter-observation showing a queue of 27 messages. As shown in table 15.1, we can in fact directly use the information in figure 15.15 to estimate the sustainable data rate for this particular execution at 1.2 milliseconds:

Secondary factors affecting performance are:

• Dynamic object creation latencies are fixed costs (on the order of milliseconds) that become more dominant with higher data rates. Work that is deferred until creation is accomplished costs relatively more in terms of latency. This work blocks pipelines and then ties up system resources in attempting to flush the backlog and catch up

---
[7]Unitary speedup is defined as linear speedup with a slope of 1.

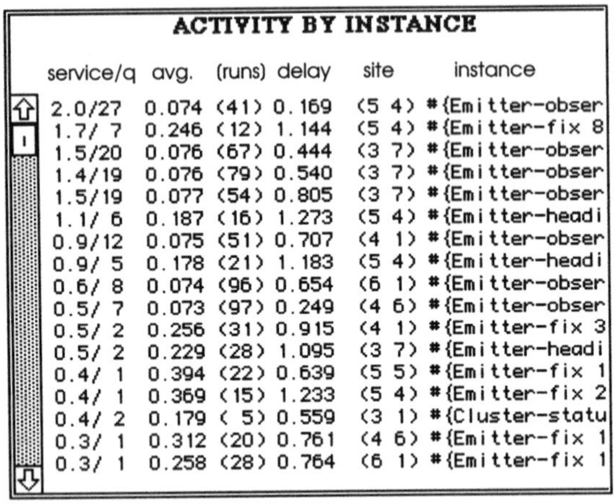

```
                    ACTIVITY BY INSTANCE

        service/q  avg.  (runs) delay   site     instance

   ⬆    2.0/27   0.074  (41)  0.169   (5 4)  #{Emitter-obser
   I    1.7/ 7   0.246  (12)  1.144   (5 4)  #{Emitter-fix 8
        1.5/20   0.076  (67)  0.444   (3 7)  #{Emitter-obser
        1.4/19   0.076  (79)  0.540   (3 7)  #{Emitter-obser
        1.5/19   0.077  (54)  0.805   (3 7)  #{Emitter-obser
        1.1/ 6   0.187  (16)  1.273   (5 4)  #{Emitter-headi
        0.9/12   0.075  (51)  0.707   (4 1)  #{Emitter-obser
        0.9/ 5   0.178  (21)  1.183   (5 4)  #{Emitter-headi
        0.6/ 8   0.074  (96)  0.654   (6 1)  #{Emitter-obser
        0.5/ 7   0.073  (97)  0.249   (4 6)  #{Emitter-obser
        0.5/ 2   0.256  (31)  0.915   (4 1)  #{Emitter-fix 3
        0.5/ 2   0.229  (28)  1.095   (3 7)  #{Emitter-headi
        0.4/ 1   0.394  (22)  0.639   (5 5)  #{Emitter-fix 1
        0.4/ 1   0.369  (15)  1.233   (5 4)  #{Emitter-fix 2
        0.4/ 2   0.179  ( 5)  0.559   (3 1)  #{Cluster-statu
        0.3/ 1   0.312  (20)  0.761   (4 6)  #{Emitter-fix 1
   ⬇    0.3/ 1   0.258  (28)  0.764   (6 1)  #{Emitter-fix 1
```

Figure 15.15
Induced Pipeline Imbalance

Object	Average (μs)	Frequency	Total (μs)
emitter-observation	74	3	222
emitter-fix	246	1	246
emitter-heading	187	1	187
emitter-heading	178	1	178
emitter-fix	369	1	369
Sustainable data rate			**1202**

Table 15.1
Estimated Sustainable Data Rate at (5 4)

with upstream producers.

- The relative sizes of the processing pools allocated to various classes are set without prior knowledge of the scenario. The partition attempts to cover a range of possible scenarios and is thus not optimal with respect to any particular one.

- Similarly, the degree of replication of various objects is not scenario-specific, but is rather precomputed based on expectations of 'typical' situations and available processing resources. Replicas and their processing sites may be under- or over-utilized for any given scenario.

- Finally, ELINT 's pipeline stages are only approximately balanced. As shown in figure 15.12, task granularities range from 100–300 microseconds (with varying frequencies) and messages are typically 20–30 words in length. Also, secondary message paths feed back into the pipes, for example, during fusion. Both these factors reduce overall efficiency.

15.7 Summary and Conclusions

In this article, we have described LAMINA, a concurrent object based programming language and CARE, an ensemble machine architecture for the support of LAMINA. Through architectural simulation, we were able to understand—and improve upon—the performance of ELINT, a soft real-time application written in LAMINA. System monitoring was the critical tool in allowing us to do so. We found the feedback provided by the instrumentation in our simulator essential in refining the design of ELINT to break bottlenecks, to balance pipelines, and to evaluate load balancing schemes to achieve increased performance. Our approach to instrumentation and simulation directly exploited a consistent model of system and application activity—based upon messages. By dealing only with the critical operations performed on messages, both by LAMINA objects and by the resources that made up the underlying multiprocessor system, we were able to efficiently simulate and monitor a relatively complex application.

We offer the following conclusions drawn from measurements of ELINT's operation as portrayed by these facilities:

- LAMINA's programming model of objects organized as pipelines effectively exploited the data and pipeline parallelism inherent in ELINT. Instrumentation allowed us to measure the granularity of pipeline stages and monitor the backlog at each stage, leading to more balanced implementations.

- Our implementation of ELINT in LAMINA achieved a speedup of eighty in the absence of contention between objects for processing resources, thus approaching the limits imposed by the measured task and message-handling granularities. Since speedup depends on the number of pipelines that can operate in parallel, twenty in our experiments, we expect performance to scale with with larger problems.

- Load balance was an important factor in the performance of ELINT, where the primary concern was throughput—an overloaded site limited the throughput of the entire system. Our class-based object allocation scheme often performed better than random allocation, but still limited ELINT to a speedup of fifty-three with 256 processing sites.

- Finally, our application ran on a simulated architecture for a high-performance implementation of streams, supporting the low-latency delivery of data values to where they are needed and the efficient scheduling of consumers of the values. The measurements of communication and synchronization overheads available to us from the instrumentation facility support the hypothesis that this capability, along with our cut-through network using adaptive routing, was adequate for the communication and computation grain size that characterized ELINT.

Acknowledgements

Many hands and minds have contributed to the development of SIMPLE/CARE and LAMINA. We are particularly indebted to Greg Byrd, Max Hailperin, Russ Nakano, and James Rice, all of whom contributed significantly to both the design and the implementation of the simulation system. Harold Brown provided valuable guidance throughout the course of this work.

We would also like to thank the members of the Advanced Architectures Project for providing a stimulating research environment, and the staff of the Symbolic Systems Resources Group of the Knowledge Systems Laboratory for providing excellent support of our computing environment. Special thanks to Ed Feigenbaum for his work in support of the Knowledge Systems Laboratory and the Advanced Architectures Project.

References

[1] G. A. Agha. An overview of Actor languages. *SIGPLAN Notices*, 21(10):58–67, October 1986.

[2] Harold Brown, Christopher Tong, and Gordon Foyster. Palladio: An exploratory environment for circuit design. *Computer*, 16(12):41–58, December 1983.

[3] Gregory T. Byrd, Russell Nakano, and Bruce A. Delagi. A dynamic, cut-through communications protocol with multicast. Technical Report STAN-CS-87-1128, Department of Computer Science, Stanford University, September 1987.

[4] Gregory T. Byrd, Nakul P. Saraiya, and Bruce A. Delagi. Multicast communication in multiprocessor systems. Technical Report KSL-88-81, Knowledge Systems Laboratory, Stanford University, December 1988. Also in *1989 International Conference on Parallel Processing*.

[5] William J. Dally. Wire-efficient VLSI multiprocessor communications networks. In *Advanced Research in VLSI: Proceedings of the 1987 Stanford Conference*, pages 391–415. The MIT Press, 1987.

[6] Bruce A. Delagi, Nakul P. Saraiya, and Gregory T. Byrd. LAMINA: CARE applications interface. In *3rd International Supercomputing Conference*. Information Sciences Institute, 1988.

[7] Bruce A. Delagi, Nakul P. Saraiya, Sayuri Nishimura, and Gregory T. Byrd. An instrumented architectural simulation system. In *Artificial Intelligence and Simulation: The Diversity of Applications*. The Society for Computer Simulation International, 1988.

[8] John R. Delaney. Multi-system report integration using blackboards. In Lee S. Baumann, editor, *Proceedings of Expert Systems Workshop*, pages 179–184. DARPA, Science Applications International Corporation, April 1986.

[9] Gordon Foyster. HELIOS user's manual. HPP Report HPP 84-34, Heuristic Programming Project, Stanford University, August 1984.

[10]   Daniel P. Friedman and David S. Wise. An indeterminate constructor for applicative programming. In *7th Annual Symposium on Principles of Programming Languages*, pages 245–250, 1980.

[11]   Robert H. Halstead Jr. Multilisp: A language for concurrent symbolic computation. *ACM Transactions on Programming Languages and Systems*, 7(4), October 1985.

[12]   P. Kermani and L. Kleinrock. Virtual cut-through: A new computer communication switching technique. *Computer Networks*, 3:267, 1979.

[13]   Henry Lieberman. Thinking about lots of things at once without getting confused: Parallelism in Act 1. AI Memo No. 626, MIT AI Laboratory, 1980.

[14]   Russell Nakano, Masafumi Minami, and John Delaney. Experiments with a knowledge-based system on a multiprocessor. In *3rd International Supercomputing Conference*. Information Sciences Institute, 1988.

[15]   Richard E. Nance. The time and state relationships in simulation modelling. *CACM*, 24(4):173–179, 1981.

[16]   Alan Noble and Chris Rogers. AIRTRAC Path Association: Development of a knowledge-based system for a multiprocessor. Technical Report KSL-88-44, Knowledge Systems Laboratory, Stanford University, 1988.

[17]   James P. Rice. The Elint application on Poligon: The architecture and performance of a concurrent blackboard system. Technical Report KSL-88-69, Knowledge Systems Laboratory, Stanford University, 1988.

[18]   Nakul P. Saraiya, Bruce A. Delagi, and Sayuri Nishimura. Design and performance evaluation of a parallel report integration system. Technical Report KSL-89-16, Knowledge Systems Laboratory, Stanford University, 1989.

[19]   Nakul P. Saraiya, Bruce A. Delagi, and Sayuri Nishimura. SIMPLE/CARE: An instrumented simulator for multiprocessor architectures. Technical Report KSL-90-66, Knowledge Systems Laboratory, Stanford University, September 1990.

[20]   Robert W. Scheifler and Jim Gettys. The X window system. *ACM Transactions on Graphics*, 5(2):79–109, April 1986.

[21]   Charles L. Seitz. Experiments with VLSI ensemble machines. Technical Report 5102, Department of Computer Science, California Institute of Technology, 1983.

[22]   Ehud Shapiro. Concurrent Prolog: A progress report. *Computer*, 18:44–58, August 1986.

[23]   Narinder Singh. Corona: A language for describing designs. HPP Report HPP 84-37, Stanford University, Department of Computer Science, September 1984.

[24]   Guy L. Steele Jr. LAMBDA: The ultimate declarative. AI Memo No. 379, MIT AI Laboratory, November 1976.

[25]   Guy L. Steele Jr. *Common Lisp: The Language*. Digital Press, 1984.

[26]   Daniel Weinreb and David Moon. Flavors: Message-passing in the Lisp Machine. AI Memo No. 602, MIT AI Laboratory, 1980.

[27]   Mark Williams, Harold Brown, and Terry Barnes. TRICERO design description. Technical Report ESL-NS539, ESL, Inc., May 1984.

Contributors

Gul Agha is Director of the Open Systems Laboratory at the University of Illinois at Urbana-Champaign. His research interests include models, languages, and tools for parallel computing and open distributed systems. In 1990 he was named Naval Young Investigator by the Office of Naval Research. He received an MS and PhD in Computer and Communication Science, and an MA in Psychology, all from the University of Michigan, Ann Arbor and a BS in an interdisciplinary program from the California Institute of Technology.

Address: Department of Computer Science, University of Illinois, Urbana, IL 61801.
Email: agha@cs.uiuc.edu

Jean-Marc Andreoli received his engineering degree from Ecole Centrale de Paris in 1985. After a few years at the IBM European production center in Montpellier (France), he joined the MAS-LOCO (Multi-Agent System/Logic, Object and COncurrency) project at the European Computer Industry Research Center (ECRC). He received his "Thèse d'informatique" (PhD in Computer Science) from the University of Paris VI in 1990. His research interests include analysis and design of concurrent multiagent systems, coordination languages, Logic and Object-Oriented programming languages and systems.

Address: E.C.R.C. GmbH, Arabellastr. 17, 81925 Munich Germany.
Email: jeanmarc@ecrc.de

Roy Campbell received his BS in Mathematics from the University of Sussex (England) and MS and PhD degrees in Computer Science from the University of Newcastle-upon-Tyne (England). He is currently the co-principal investigator of the NSF funded Tapestry Project investigating parallel processing and leads the design and construction of CHOICES. In addition, he is Director of the Illinois Software Engineering Program.

Address: Department of Computer Science, University of Illinois, Urbana, IL 61801.
Email: roy@cs.uiuc.edu

Mani Chandy received his PhD in 1969 from MIT. He has worked at Honeywell and IBM. He was Professor and Chair at the University of Texas at Austin, and is now Professor at the California Institute of Technology. He was given the A.A. Michelson Award for his contributions to computer performance analysis and he was a Sherman Fairchild Distinguished Scholar.

Address: Computer Science Department, California Institute of Technology 256-80, Pasadena, California 91125.
Email: mani@vlsi.caltech.edu

Andrew A. Chien received his BS degree in Electrical Engineering at the Massachusetts Institute of Technology in 1984. He also received his MS and PhD degrees in Computer Science at M.I.T. in 1987 and 1990 respectively. He is currently Assistant Professor in the Department of Computer Science at the University of Illinois, where he holds a joint appointment with the Department of Electrical and Computer Engineering. His research interests involve the interaction of architecture, system software, compilers, and programming languages in high-performance parallel systems and he has authored numerous research papers in those areas. He is author of *Concurrent Aggregates: Supporting*

Modularity in Massively Parallel Programs MIT Press, 1993.

Address: Department of Computer Science, University of Illinois, Urbana, IL 61801.
Email: achien@cs.uiuc.edu

Paolo Ciancarini is Associate Professor of Computer Science at the University of
Bologna. He received his PhD in Informatics from the University of Pisa in 1988, and
held a position of Research Associate at that university from 1988 to 1992. His research
interests include: parallel and distributed programming languages and systems, object-
oriented and logic programming languages, programming environments design, formal
methods in software engineering, and computer chess. In 1990-91 he was visiting scientist at the Yale University. He is author of over 25 papers and two books.

Address: Dept. of Mathematics, University of Bologna, Piazza di Porta S.Donato 5,
40127 Bologna Italy.
Email: cianca@dm.unibo.it

William J. Dally received the BS degree in Electrical Engineering from Virginia Polytechnic Institute, the MS degree in Electrical Engineering from Stanford University, and
the PhD degree in Computer Science from Caltech. He has worked at Bell Telephone
Laboratories where he contributed to the design of the BELLMAC32 microprocessor.
Later as a consultant to Bell Laboratories, he helped design the MARS hardware ac-
celerator. He was Research Assistant and then a Research Fellow at Caltech where he
designed the MOSSIM Simulation Engine and the Torus Routing Chip. He is currently
Associate Professor of Computer Science at the Massachusetts Institute of Technology
where he directs a research group that is building the J-Machine, a fine-grain concurrent
computer. His research interests include concurrent computing, computer architecture,
computer aided design, and VLSI design.

Address: Massachusetts Institute of Technology, Artificial Intelligence Laboratory and,
Laboratory for Computer Science, Cambridge, Massachusetts 02139.
Email: billd@ai.mit.edu

Andrew Davison received the BS degree in computing from the University of Manch-
ester Institute of Science and Technology (UMIST), England in 1983, and the MS in
computer science from Lehigh University, Pennsylvania, USA in 1985. In 1989, he received the PhD degree from the Imperial College, London, England, on the topic of
concurrent object oriented logic programming. He is currently Lecturer in the Computer
Science Department at the University of Melbourne, Australia. His research interests
include object oriented and logic programming extensions, concurrency, and logic grammar formalisms. He is the editor of the Association of Logic Programming newsletter.

Address: Department of Computer Science, University of Melbourne, Parkville, Victoria
3052, Australia.
Email: ad@cs.mu.oz.au

Bruce Delagi is one of the architects of the PDP-11 and designer of the 11/45. He
works at SUN Microsystems and is a consulting professor at Stanford University.

Address: Knowledge Systems Lab, Computer Science Department, Stanford University, Stanford, CA 94304.
Email: Bruce.Delagi@eng.sun.com

Svend Frølund is a doctoral candidate and Research Assistant at the Open Systems Laboratory, University of Illinois at Urbana-Champaign. His technical interests include infra-structures and languages for sharing and coordination in concurrent object-oriented systems. He received a Cand. Scient. (MS) degree in computer science from Århus University in Denmark. In 1990 he was awarded a research fellowship from the Natural Science Faculty of Århus University.

Address: Department of Computer Science, University of Illinois, Urbana, IL 61801.
Email: frolund@cs.uiuc.edu.

Steven Goering is Assistant Professor at the Department of Computer Information Systems, Trinity College, Deerfield, Illinois. He worked for CAS Medical Systems, New Haven, Connecticut from 1990-92. He obtained his BS from Bethel College, Kansas and MS and PhD from the Department of Computer Science, University of Illinois, Urbana-Champaign. His research interests include programming languages and concurrent programming.

Address: Computer Information Systems, Trinity College, Deerfield, Illinois.
Email: goering@trinity.edu

Seif Haridi received the PhD degree in computer science from the Royal Institute of Technology, Stockholm, Sweden, in 1981. Since 1985, he is the manager of the Logic Programming and Parallel Systems Laboratory of the Swedish Institute of Computer Science. He is Adjunct Professor at the Royal Institute of Technology and at Uppsala University. Before his current position, he was a visiting researcher at IBM Thomas J. Watson Research Center from 1984 to 1985. Prof. Haridi has been an active researcher in logic programming languages, parallel execution models, and computer architectures for many years.

Address: Swedish Institute of Computer Science, Sweden.
Email: seif@sics.se.

Waldemar Horwat received Bachelor's degrees in mathematics and electrical engineering from MIT in 1988, a Master's degree in computer science at MIT in 1989, and is currently working on a PhD degree in computer science at MIT. Waldemar has been with the J-Machine project since 1986 and is currently using it to investigate parallel data structure abstractions. His research interests include parallel programming, programming languages, compilers, operating systems, and secure communications. He is a Putnam fellow, gold medal winner at the 1985 International Mathematical Olympiad, and an ONR fellow. He has published several commercial Macintosh and PC products and is the Proceedings Chairman for the 1991, 1992, and 1993 Macintosh Technical Conferences.

Address: Artificial Intelligence Laboratory, Laboratory for Computer Science, Massachusetts Institute of Technology, Cambridge, Massachusetts 02139.
Email: waldemar@acm.org, waldemar@ai.mit.edu

Wenwey Hseush is a PhD candidate at Columbia University. His research interests include transaction processing, object-oriented programming languages/systems, parallel debugging and distributed computing. He is one of the principle designers of the MeldC object-oriented programming language, which has been used in several courses at Columbia University and released for external licensing. He received his MS from Columbia University in 1986 and his BS from National Taiwan University in 1981. He worked as a research staff member at Columbia University from 1986 to 1988.

Address: Columbia University, Department of Computer Science, New York, NY 10027.
Email: hseush@cs.columbia.edu

Nayeem Islam received his BSE in EECS from Princeton University in 1986 with High Honors, an MS in Computer Science from Stanford University in 1987 and is currently pursuing a PhD in Computer Science at the University of Illinois Urbana-Champaign. From 1987 to 1990 he was at Sun Microsystems and was one of the developers of Open-Windows. He has been associated with the Choices operating systems project since September 1990. His interests are in parallel and distributed operating systems and object-oriented programming. He is the recipient of an IBM Graduate Fellowship for 1992-93 and 1993-94.

Address: Department of Computer Science, University of Illinois, Urbana, IL 61801.
Email: nislam@cs.uiuc.edu

Sverker Janson received the MS degree in computer science from the University of Uppsala, Sweden, in 1988. Since 1989, he has been in the Logic Programming and Parallel Systems Laboratory of the Swedish Institute of Computer Science, where he is currently the manager of the Concurrent Constraint Programming group. He is interested in the design and implementation of high-level programming languages.

Address: Swedish Institute of Computer Science, Sweden.
Email: sverker@sics.se.

Gail E. Kaiser is an Associate Professor of Computer Science and Director of the Programming Systems Laboratory at Columbia University. She was selected as an NSF Presidential Young Investigator in Software Engineering in 1988. Prof. Kaiser has published over 80 papers in a range of areas, including software development environments, software process, extended transaction models, object-oriented languages and databases, and parallel and distributed systems. Prof. Kaiser is an associate editor of the ACM Transactions on Software Engineering and Methodology, and serves on numerous program committees for conferences. She received her PhD and MS from CMU and her ScB from MIT. She is a member of ACM and a senior member of IEEE.

Address: Columbia University, Department of Computer Science, New York, NY 10027.
Email: kaiser@cs.columbia.edu

Simon Kaplan is Associate Professor in the Department of Computer Science, University of Illinois at Urbana-Champaign. He obtained his BSc and PhD in Computer Science from University of Cape Town. His research interests include visual languages, collaborative computing, distributed programming environments and program systhesis.

Address: Department of Computer Science, University of Illinois, Urbana, IL 61801.
Email: kaplan@cs.uiuc.edu.

Carl Kesselman is Senior Research Fellow at the California Institute of Technology, Pasadena, California. He obtained his BS in Electrical Engineering and BA in Computer Science from the State University of New York at Buffalo. He obtained MS in Electrical Engineering and PhD in Computer Science from University of Southern California at Los Angeles. He is a member of Eta Kappa Nu and Tau Beta Pi.

Address: Computer Science Department, California Institute of Technology 256-80, Pasadena, California 91125.
Email: carl@vlsi.caltech.edu

WooYoung Kim is a doctoral candidate in the Open Systems Laboratory, University of Illinois at Urbana-Champaign. His research interests include the design of high level actor-based languages, compilation and optimization techniques for distributed memory machines, and the development of run-time support for actor languages. He was awarded a Fellowship by the Korean Ministry of Education in 1990. He received his BS Magna Cum Laude in 1987, and his MS in 1989, both in Computer Engineering from Seoul National University, Korea.

Address: Department of Computer Science, University of Illinois, Urbana, IL 61801.
Email: wooyoung@cs.uiuc.edu

Joseph Loyall received his PhD from the University of Illinois in 1991. He is currently a member of the technical staff at TASC (The Analytic Sciences Corporation) in Reading, Massachusetts, where he conducts research in software development environments, software verification, and software reengineering. He is a member of IEEE CS and ACM.

Address: TASC, 55 Walkers Brook Drive, Reading, Massachussets 01867.
Email: loyall@cs.uiuc.edu.

Satoshi Matsuoka received the BS, MS, and PhD degrees from Dept. of Information Science, the University of Tokyo. He is currently a Research Faculty at the same department. His current research interests are implementation and theory of Object-Oriented/Parallel/Reflective programming languages and systems, constraint languages, and graphical user interface software. He has been serving as a Secretary for SIGPRG (Programming) of the Information Processing Society of Japan (IPSJ) since 1991. He has also become the Secretary of the ACM Japan Chapter in June, 1993.

Address: Department of Information Science, The University of Tokyo.
Email: matsu@is.s.u-tokyo.ac.jp

José Meseguer received the Licentiate and PhD degrees in Mathematics from the University of Zaragoza, Spain, in 1972 and 1975, respectively. After holding teaching and research positions at the universities of Zaragoza and Santiago, Spain, UCLA, IBM T.J. Watson Research Center, and the University of California at Berkeley, he joined SRI International's Computer Science Laboratory in 1980, where he is currently a principal scientist leading the Declarative Languages and Architecture Group. Since 1984 he has also been a senior researcher at Stanford University's Center for the Study of Language and Information. He has done research on the semantics, design, and implementation of functional, logic and object-oriented programming languages, models of concurrent computation, massively parallel architecture and parallel programming, algebraic semantics, order-sorted algebra, abstract data types, higher order type theory, computer security, formal methods, and logical frameworks. Dr. Meseguer is an editor of the journal *Mathematical Structures in Computer Science*.

Address: Computer Science Laboratory, SRI International, 333 Ravenswood Avenue, Menlo Park, CA 94025, USA.
Email: meseguer@csl.sri.com

Johan Montelius received the MS degree in computer science from the University of Uppsala, Sweden, in 1989. Since 1990, he has been in the Logic Programming and Parallel Systems Laboratory of the Swedish Institute of Computer Science, where he is currently a member of the Concurrent Constraint Programming group. He is interested in parallel execution models of high-level programming languages.

Address: Swedish Institute of Computer Science, Sweden.
Email: jm@sics.se.

Oscar Nierstrasz is currently Maitre d'Enseignement et de Recherche (Assistant Professor) at the Centre Universitaire d'Informatique (CUI) of the University of Geneva, Switzerland. He completed his MSc in 1981 and his PhD in 1984 at the University of Toronto, in the area of Office Information Systems. Since then he has worked at the Institute of Computer Science in Crete and at the CUI, in the area of object-oriented programming languages and systems, particularly in the design of Hybrid, an experimental concurrent OOPL implemented at CUI during 1987-88. He is currently interested in computational models for concurrent object-oriented languages and systems, and in high-level programming tools to support reusability and evolution of open applications.

Address: University of Geneva, Switzerland.
Email: oscar@cui.unige.ch

Sayuri Nishimura received the MS degree in Chemistry from the University of Tokyo, Tokyo, Japan, in 1980, and the MS degree in Computer Science from the University of Minnesota, Minneapolis, MN, in 1984. She worked at the Knowledge Systems Laboratory, Stanford University, from 1985–1989, where she developed the instrumentation for the simulation system used by the Advanced Architectures Project. She is currently a Scientist at Lucid, Inc, Menlo Park, CA. Her professional interests include software development environments and tools for performance analysis.

Address: Lucid, Inc., 707 Laurel Street, Menlo Park, CA 94025.
Email: sayuri@lucid.com

Rajendra Panwar is a doctoral candidate and Research Assistant at the Open Systems Laboratory, University of Illinois at Urbana-Champaign. His research interests include concurrent object-oriented systems for efficient parallel and distributed computation. He received an MS from the Department of Computer Science and Automation, Indian Institute of Science, Bangalore, India and a BE degree in Electronics and Communication Engineering from Nagpur University, India.

Address: Department of Computer Science, University of Illinois, Urbana, IL 61801.
Email: panwar@cs.uiuc.edu.

Remo Pareschi received his Laurea degree from University of Bologna in 1982 and his Master's degree from University of Texas at Austin in 1984. He gained his PhD in 1988 with the Department of Artificial Intelligence of the University of Edinburgh. During the years 1987-88 he was a research associate at the Department of Computer and Information Sciences of the University of Pennsylvania, where he was active in the areas of computational logic and programming paradigms for artificial intelligence. At the end of 1988 he joined the European Computer Industry Research Center (ECRC), where he is project leader in the MAS LOCO (Multi-agent Systems/Logic, Objects and Concurrency) project. He is the author of numerous articles on the theory and applications computational logic and on the design and implementation of object-oriented coordination languages. He has served in the program committees of major conferences of logic programming and of object-oriented programming, such as ILPS and ECOOP, and is program co-chair for ECOOP'94.

Address: E.C.R.C. GmbH, Arabellastr. 17, 81925 Munich Germany.
Email: remo@ecrc.de

Anna Patterson is a doctoral candidate and Research Assistant in the Open Systems Laboratory at the University of Illinois at Urbana-Champaign. Her research interests include proof techniques, automated proof techniques, hierarchical specification languages, and model checking for open distributed computing. She received a BS in Computer Science and a BS in Electrical Engineering from Washington University in 1987, where she became a member of Eta Kappa Nu and held a Langsdorf-Woodward Fellowship.

Address: Department of Computer Science, University of Illinois, Urbana, IL 61801.
Email: annap@cs.uiuc.edu.

Steven S. Popovich is a doctoral candidate in the Programming Systems Laboratory of the Computer Science department at Columbia University. His research interests are in software development environments, software process and object-based concurrent systems. He is being supported by a graduate research fellowship from AT&T in his thesis work on rule-based process servers for software development environments. He received his MS from Columbia and his BS from CMU.

Address: Columbia University, Department of Computer Science, New York, NY 10027.
Email: popovich@cs.columbia.edu

Nakul Saraiya received the BS degree in computer engineering from Syracuse University, Syracuse, NY, in 1983, and the MS degree in computer science from Stanford

University, Stanford, CA, in 1986. He worked on the Advanced Architectures Project at the Knowledge Systems Laboratory, Stanford University, from 1986–1991. He is currently a member of the technical staff at Sun Microsystems, Mountain View, CA. His professional interests include parallel computing and tools for performance analysis.

Address: SunSoft, Inc., 2550 Garcia Ave., Mountain View, CA 94043.
Email: saraiya@eng.sun.com

Daniel Sturman is a doctoral candidate in the Open Systems Laboratory at the University of Illinois at Urbana-Champaign where he is a member of the Open System Laboratory. His research interests include the development of fault-tolerant distributed systems and computer security. He received a BS with distinction from Cornell University in 1991. He is a member of Tau Beta Pi.

Address: Department of Computer Science, University of Illinois, Urbana, IL 61801.
Email: sturman@cs.uiuc.edu.

Brian K. Totty received the BS degree in 1988 from the Massachusetts Institute of Technology, the MS degree in Computer Science in 1992 from the University of Illinois, Urbana-Champaign, and is nearing completion of the PhD degree in Computer Science from the University of Illinois. He was awarded an undergraduate Computer Systems Thesis Prize in 1988, a DARPA/NASA Assistantship in Parallel Processing in 1990 and 1991, and an IBM Graduate Fellowship in 1992. His interests are in the area of parallel processing, with an emphasis on software support for efficient program design and execution.

Address: Department of Computer Science, University of Illinois, Urbana, IL 61801.
Email: totty@cs.uiuc.edu

Peter Wegner is Professor of Computer Science at Brown University. His research interests include programming languages and software engineering. He was educated at London and Cambridge Universities, and taught at Cornell, Penn State, and the London School of Economics before going to Brown. He published the first book on Ada in 1980 and has since contributed to object-oriented programming in the area of type theory, concurrency, and language design issues. He is a member of the IEEE Computer Society and ACM.

Address: Brown University, Providence, RI, 02912.
Email: pw@cs.brown.edu

Shyhtsun F. Wu received the BS degree in Information Science from Tunghai University, Taichung, Republic of China, in 1985, and the MS degree in computer science from Columbia University, NY, in 1989. He is currently a doctoral candidate in the Computer Science Department, Columbia University, NY, where he has held a IBM Graduate Fellowship since 1991. His research interests include real-time systems, network management, and object-oriented systems. He is a student member of ACM and IEEE.

Address: Columbia University, Department of Computer Science, New York, NY 10027.
Email: wu@cs.columbia.edu

Akinori Yonezawa is Professor of Computer Science at the University of Tokyo, the main designer of the ABCL/1 object-oriented concurrent language, and author and editor of several books, including *Object-Oriented Concurrent Programming* (MIT Press, 1987) and *ABCL: An Object-Oriented Concurrent System* (MIT Press, 1990). His research interests are in parallel computation models, programming languages, and natural-language processing. He was Program Chair for the 1990 ACM Conference on Object-Oriented Programming, Systems, and Applications and had been a member of the editorial board of IEEE Computer Magazine from 1988 to 1992, and currently he is a member of the editorial board of IEEE Parallel and Distributed Technology. He received a PhD and MS in computer science from the Massachussets Institute of Technology in 1977, and a BE from the University of Tokyo in 1970. He is a member of IEEE, ACM and Sigma Xi.

Address: Department of Information Science, The University of Tokyo, Faculty of Science, Hongo bunkyo-ku, Tokyo, 113, Japan.
Email: yonezawa@is.s.u-tokyo.ac.jp

Name Index

Subject Index